The Final Act

AMERICA IN THE WORLD

SERIES EDITORS
SVEN BECKERT AND JEREMI SURI

The Final Act

The Helsinki Accords and the
Transformation of the Cold War

Michael Cotey Morgan

PRINCETON UNIVERSITY PRESS

PRINCETON AND OXFORD

Published by Princeton University Press
41 William Street, Princeton, New Jersey 08540
6 Oxford Street, Woodstock, Oxfordshire OX20 1TR

press.princeton.edu

Library of Congress Cataloging-in-Publication Data

Names: Morgan, Michael Cotey, author.
Title: The final act : the Helsinki Accords and the transformation
of the Cold War / Michael Cotey Morgan.
Description: Princeton : Princeton University Press, 2018. | Series: America in the world |
Includes bibliographical references and index.
Identifiers: LCCN 2017023099 | ISBN 9780691176062 (hardcover : alk. paper)
Subjects: LCSH: Conference on Security and Cooperation in Europe (1972–1975 :
Helsinki, Finland). Final Act. | Cold War—History.
Classification: LCC D849 .M695 2018 | DDC 341.4/8—dc23
LC record available at https://lccn.loc.gov/2017023099

British Library Cataloging-in-Publication Data is available

Editorial: Eric Crahan and Pamela Weidman
Production Editorial: Natalie Baan
Text and Jacket/Cover Design: Jessica Massabrook
Jacket photograph: Leonid Brezhnev and Gerald Ford.
ITAR-TASS Photo Agency / Alamy Stock Photo
Production: Jacqueline Poirier
Publicity: James Schneider
Copyeditor: Lynn Worth

This book has been composed in Sabon Next LT Pro

Printed on acid-free paper. ∞

Printed in the United States of America

10 9 8 7 6 5 4 3 2 1

For my mother, and in memory of
my father & grandmother

CONTENTS

ACKNOWLEDGMENTS

IN WRITING this book, I've accumulated a list of debts longer than the Helsinki Final Act itself. Several institutions and fellowships supported my research. I thank the Social Sciences and Humanities Research Council of Canada, the Miller Center of Public Affairs at the University of Virginia, the Smith Richardson Foundation, Yale's MacMillan Center, the Fox International Fellowships, the Crozier Fellowships, and International Security Studies for their generosity.

None of this work would have been possible without the assistance of archivists, librarians, and scholars on both sides of the Atlantic. In particular, I would like to recognize Michael Hussey, David Langbart, John Powers, and James Siekmeier in College Park; Svetlana Savranskaya and Mary Curry in Washington; Geir Gundersen in Ann Arbor; Micheline Robert in Ottawa; Olivier Rodilla and Grégoire Eldin in Paris; Nicholas Roche in Brussels; Johannes von Boeselager in Berlin; and Mikhail Prozumenshchikov in Moscow. The indefatigable staff of UNC's Davis Library, especially Kirill Tolpygo and Joanneke Elliott, fielded an unreasonable number of requests for books and microfilms without batting an eye. Mark Kramer alerted me to a collection of documents at RGANI in Moscow, and Joseph Torigian and Markian Dobczansky obtained copies for me.

Several CSCE veterans shared their recollections with me, both on and off the record. I am grateful to John Campbell, Richard Davy, the late Thomas Delworth, Brian Fall, John Maresca, and Gabriel Warren for giving me a sense of what life was like in Helsinki and Geneva.

I benefited from presenting portions of my research in conference papers and talks at ETH Zurich, Harvard, Ohio State, UC Berkeley, the Wilson Center, Cambridge, the Triangle Institute for Security Studies, and UNC's Center for Slavic, Eurasian, and East European Studies. I thank Andreas Wenger, Christian Nuenlist, Anna Locher, Daniel Sargent, Andrew Preston, Fredrik Logevall, Martin Klimke, Christian Ostermann, David Reynolds, Kristina Spohr, Peter Feaver, and Donald Raleigh for these invitations and for their helpful criticism.

It has been a pleasure to work with the team at Princeton University Press. My editor, Eric Crahan, has believed in this book since our first conversation about it, and, together with Natalie Baan, guided it to publication with wisdom and aplomb. Lynn Worth's copyediting rescued me from numerous errors. Jeremi Suri's enthusiasm for this project never flagged, and his guidance improved the manuscript at a critical stage. I must also thank Princeton's two anonymous reviewers for their feedback.

Friends and colleagues sustained me with good cheer, incisive suggestions, and lots of red ink. Richard Gowan, Peter MacLeod, Joshua Rovner, Andy Scott, and Helen Veit expanded my thinking about history and politics and provided welcome comic relief. Marco Duranti, Charles Edel, Sulmaan Khan, Ben Madley, Aaron O'Connell, and Michael Shenkman commented on large portions of the manuscript. In many conversations over the years, Daniel Sargent has spurred me to think more boldly about the history of the 1970s. He read the whole thing—twice—and his advice sharpened my argument and saved me from all manner of pitfalls. Petri Hakkarainen, Douglas Selvage, Sarah Snyder, and Takeshi Yamamoto, all of them experts on the history of the CSCE, shared their work and their ideas. Donald Raleigh pointed me toward several valuable sources on Leonid Brezhnev's life and career. Kazimierz Bem helped with the translation of Polish documents. Veronica Kitchen gave me a place to stay in Berlin, as did Marco Duranti in Florence.

It has been my good fortune to be affiliated with several wonderful institutions while writing this book. For their support and encouragement in ways large and small, I thank Fitz Brundage, Lloyd Kramer, Klaus Larres, Richard Kohn, and Joseph Glatthaar at UNC; Derek Allen at the University of Toronto; John Maurer and the strategy and policy team at the US Naval War College; and Pascal Delisle and Maurice Vaïsse at Sciences Po. Since my undergraduate days at the University of Toronto, Robert Bothwell has been an extraordinary mentor. It was he who first made me think that I might be cut out to be a historian. I cannot begin to list—let alone repay—everything that Bob has done for me in the years that I have known him.

This book started as a doctoral dissertation at Yale. I am much obliged to many people in the history department and at International Security Studies, especially Ted Bromund, Ann Carter-Drier, Susan Hennigan, Marcy Kaufman, Jeff Mankoff, Kathleen Murphy, the late Florence Thomas, and Monica Ward. I learned a great deal about the historian's craft from Laura Engelstein, Seth Fein, and Beverly Gage. Jay Winter helped me to think in new ways about the history of human rights and shared his time and ideas with unstinting generosity. Paul Kennedy encouraged me to see the big concepts that lay beyond the diplomatic minutiae and invited me on hawk-watching rambles even though I couldn't tell a turkey vulture from a golden eagle. My greatest intellectual debt is to John Lewis Gaddis, who whipped flabby drafts into shape and pushed me to be more ambitious, more elegant, more rigorous, and more creative. In his scholarship and his teaching, John sets the standard that I aspire to reach. I am profoundly grateful to him.

No words can describe what I owe my family. My wife, Molly Worthen, amazes, inspires, and makes me laugh me every day. Her unwavering love, which surpasses the power of human telling, gives me confidence and keeps me going. Our daughter, Winifred, puts the stresses of academic life in perspective and reminds me what really matters. This book is dedicated to my mother, Barbara Morgan, and to the memories of my father and my grandmother, Kenneth Morgan and Mildred Lewis. My grandmother taught me to love history and to be curious about the world. My parents taught me the importance of education and hard work. They provided unquestioning support in every way. I hope that these pages reward some small part of the faith they have always shown in me.

ABBREVIATIONS

AAD	Central Foreign Policy Files, Access to Archival Databases
AAPD	*Akten zur Auswärtigen Politik der Bundesrepublik Deutschland*
AEU	Archives of the European Union, Florence, Italy
AMAE	Archives du Ministère des Affaires Étrangères, La Courneuve, France
AN	Archives Nationales, Pierrefitte-sur-Seine, France
CWIHP	Cold War International History Project
DBPO	*Documents on British Policy Overseas*
FBIS	*Foreign Broadcast Information Service Daily Reports*
FCO	Foreign and Commonwealth Office, London, UK
FRUS	*Foreign Relations of the United States*
GRFL	Gerald R. Ford Presidential Library, Ann Arbor, MI
LAC	Library and Archives Canada, Ottawa, Canada
Memcon	Memorandum of Conversation
MfAA	Ministerium für Auswärtige Angelegenheiten der DDR
NARA	National Archives and Records Administration, College Park, MD
NATOA	NATO Archives, Brussels, Belgium
NYT	*The New York Times*
PAAA	Politisches Archiv des Auswärtigen Amts, Berlin, Germany
PCC	Political Consultative Committee of the Warsaw Pact
PDD	*Polskie Dokumenty Dyplomatyczne*
PHP	Parallel History Project
RGANI	Rossiĭskiĭ Gosudarstvennyĭ Arkhiv Noveĭsheĭ Istorii, Moscow, Russia
RMNL	Richard M. Nixon Presidential Library, Yorba Linda, CA
SAPMO	Stiftung Archiv der Parteien und Massenorganisationen der DDR im Bundesarchiv, Berlin, Germany
UKNA	National Archives, Kew, London, UK
YMA	Manuscripts and Archives, Sterling Memorial Library, Yale University, New Haven, CT

The Final Act

Introduction

TO THE HELSINKI STATION

At 2:30 p.m. on July 29, 1975, Leonid Brezhnev stepped off a train onto the platform of Helsinki's central station. Sixteen gleaming green cars, pulled by two red engines, had brought the Soviet leader and a clutch of senior officials on an overnight journey from Moscow to the concluding session of the Conference on Security and Cooperation in Europe (CSCE). Under a hot sun, Finland's long-serving president, Urho Kekkonen, stood waiting to receive them. Brezhnev embraced his host in a bear hug. As patrolmen kept watch on the station roof and a police helicopter buzzed overhead, the two men walked down the platform surrounded by advisors and body-guards. Outside the station, Brezhnev greeted a delegation of young Finnish communists sporting red scarves and bearing bouquets of gladioli. After waving to the crowd, he sped off in a black limousine bound for the Soviet embassy, where a grand apartment had been renovated for his three-day visit, decorated with paintings from Moscow's Tretyakov Gallery.[1]

The CSCE had originally been a Soviet idea, and Brezhnev had staked his reputation on its success. He had suffered a stroke a few months earlier and his personal physician worried that this trip would overtax his health, but he refused to be deterred. He insisted on taking his place alongside the thirty-four other leaders from Europe and North America who were gathering for this "star-studded summit spectacular," as one journalist described it.[2] After three days of speeches and scores of bilateral meetings, they would sign the CSCE's capstone agreement: the Helsinki Final Act. The 22,000-word text covered nearly every facet of international life, including the nature of states' borders, military security, the relationship between sovereignty and human rights, trade and economic cooperation, and the circulation of people and information. Commenting on the inscrutability of its prose, a diplomat said, "You are not supposed to understand it. Neither do we, and, what's more, we meant it that way."[3] Nonetheless, the agreement was a masterpiece of "diplomatic engineering," one observer wrote. "The silences and circumlocutions are often as significant as the clearer statements. Were it a modern novel by someone like Nabokov its labyrinths would be explored with delight by literary critics."[4]

The Final Act had consumed almost three years of constant work. At the preparatory talks in Helsinki from 1972 to 1973, then at the CSCE's formal negotiations in Geneva from 1973 to 1975, hundreds of diplomats produced almost ten million pages of drafts, declarations, proposals, and counterproposals during meetings that stretched on for thousands of hours.[5] The conference lasted so long that it acquired a life of its own. The delegates—almost all of them men—ate and drank together, danced at nightclubs, organized basketball tournaments, composed mournful poetry, and drafted satirical reports to pass the time. Some of them fell in love with the interpreters and conference staff, leading to several marriages and uncounted extramarital affairs.[6] "It wasn't so much a conference but a way of life," one diplomat told a reporter. "I felt at times as if I had boarded a ship that had gone adrift or that I was in a time warp."[7]

The Helsinki summit capped the most ambitious undertaking of an era of ambitious diplomacy. Over the preceding years, the world's leading powers had launched negotiations across a wide range of subjects, including nuclear arms control, conventional disarmament, the international monetary system, tariffs, the global oil market, and the Law of the Sea. By the summer of 1975, some of these efforts had borne fruit, some had failed, and some continued to grind away. Nothing symbolized the improvement in superpower relations better than the joint Apollo-Soyuz space flight that July, when an American astronaut and Soviet cosmonaut shook hands in orbit.[8]

Nevertheless, those who doubted the possibility of East-West reconciliation could find ample evidence to justify their pessimism. After the fall of Portugal's dictatorship in 1974, Western observers worried that communists might seize power both in Lisbon and in the country's newly independent African colonies. When Angola descended into civil war in 1975, the Americans and Soviets sent aid to opposing factions in an attempt to sway the outcome. The same year, North Vietnamese forces captured Saigon, sweeping away the 1973 Paris Peace Accords and the vestiges of American influence in the country. Meanwhile, surging unemployment, inflation, and energy prices shook the self-confidence of the Western economies, which had fallen into their worst slump since the Great Depression. These developments blighted the sunniest prognoses about global politics, but from the vantage point of the Finnish capital, they could not detract from the magnitude of the CSCE's achievement.

The scale and scope of the conference had no precedent in the Cold War. Participants and observers reached for historical analogies to make sense of its concluding summit. The world had seen nothing like it since the funeral of King Edward VII in 1910, one journalist remarked, when "nine reigning monarchs, five heirs apparent, seven queens, one archduke and 39 other royal highnesses, an American ex-President," and hundreds of other dignitaries gathered in London. Sixty-five years later, the panoply in Helsinki included eight presidents, eighteen prime ministers, six communist party leaders, two dozen foreign ministers, an Orthodox archbishop, and an archbishop of the Catholic Church.[9] King Edward's obsequies had marked the end of a long era of peace, but many of those at the CSCE hoped that their meeting would "begin, and not conclude, a relatively golden age."[10]

The participants were so numerous that the Finnish government had to dispense with the honor guard that traditionally welcomed visiting heads of state. Even this abbreviated diplomatic protocol required Kekkonen to spend nearly twelve hours greeting the visitors. Because the Soviets were the only delegation to come by train, the president needed a helicopter to dash from the airport to the station and back again in time to receive United Nations Secretary General Kurt Waldheim. The tight logistics sometimes required the mighty to make way for the humble. American president Gerald Ford, aboard Air Force One, had to circle the city for a quarter-hour to give Luxembourg's tiny delegation time to disembark.[11]

The Finns spared no effort for their moment in the global spotlight. Five thousand soldiers and police officers patrolled the city, some of whom had been brought in from the distant reaches of the country because Helsinki's municipal force could not cope on its own. Along the route from the airport to the city center, camouflaged troops with fixed bayonets manned tanks and armored personnel carriers. Antiaircraft batteries and fighter jets kept a lookout for hostile aircraft.[12] The city's main thoroughfare, Mannerheimintie, was closed to traffic, and some streetcars were rerouted for security reasons.[13] "As part of a general campaign to present Helsinki in a proper light," a reporter noted, the local "drunks . . . have been carted off the central streets and taken to the suburbs to dry out."[14] A few shops put portraits of the visiting statesmen in their windows, and the Stockmann department store offered commemorative T-shirts for sale. The clothes had been made in China, whose government bitterly denounced the conference as a super-power conspiracy to dominate Europe, but the CSCE initials had been added in Finland. "I hope China doesn't find out what we do to their shirts because I don't think they would be very happy," a store clerk said.[15]

The conference staff carried an enormous administrative burden. They prepared 5,500 color-coded badges, each bearing a Polaroid portrait, for delegates, journalists, and security personnel. They recruited more than 200 linguists to provide simultaneous interpretation in the CSCE's six official languages. For the 1,200 journalists covering the event, they assembled hundreds of ashtrays, mountains of copy paper, and scores of typewriters (with both Roman and Cyrillic keyboards), and installed 120 new telegraph lines to carry reports to the outside world.[16] Because hotel rooms were in short supply, the Finnish Travel Bureau transformed a local Red Cross blood transfusion center into temporary accommodations. Two ocean liners docked in Helsinki harbor to provide additional beds, one reserved for the exclusive use of Soviet personnel.[17]

At the center of the action stood Finlandia Hall, the modernist concert hall and conference center that was hosting the summit. Sitting in a park on Töölö Bay, the white-marble building had opened three and a half years previously. Bomb-sniffing dogs padded along its corridors, checking every light fixture and every piece of furniture, and a chain-link fence around the perimeter held curious passersby at bay. Locals who wanted to witness the proceedings had to watch them on television.[18]

The Finns expected the event to go down in history as a latter-day Paris Peace Conference or Congress of Vienna, not least because it was the first pan-European summit since the end of the Napoleonic Wars.[19] Others were not so sure. The summit "will bear about as much resemblance to the Congress of Vienna as a chamber of commerce luncheon to a costume ball," one journalist wrote.[20] The congress had been "a much better show" than this summit, another said. The negotiations in Vienna featured dancing, drinking, and all manner of diplomatic and romantic intrigue. By contrast, "no one will be waltzing in Helsinki, at least in public. They will be waiting for handouts, or storming buffet tables, or looking forward to a comfortable hotel room at their next destination."[21]

The skeptics were only half right. The Congress of Vienna had remade Europe and built a new international order on the wreckage of a generation of warfare. The statesmen in the Austrian capital redrew borders, shifted millions of people from the sovereignty of one ruler to that of another, approved the restoration of the French monarchy, and established a multilateral congress system to preserve great power comity. Perhaps because the CSCE did nothing so dramatic—and lacked Vienna's aristocratic glamor—few people in 1975 appreciated its full significance. However, the ensuing years would demonstrate that the Final Act was just as consequential for Europe's international system as the handiwork of Viscount Castlereagh and Prince Metternich had been more than a century and a half earlier.

I

This book is an international history of the Final Act. It addresses three main questions: Why was the CSCE created in the first place? Why did the Final Act take the shape that it did? And how did it influence the Cold War? Any historian who grapples with this subject faces several difficulties. The first is the sheer number of countries involved, each with its own ambitions and anxieties. Some of the thirty-five participants influenced the conference more than others, but no one dominated it, and although the negotiations often pitted the Eastern allies against their Western counterparts, neither group was monolithic. The arguments within each bloc could be as consequential as those between them, to say nothing of the arguments within each government. Besides, thirteen of the delegations belonged to neither alliance. In some cases they tried to mediate between East and West, while in others they pursued their own independent goals.

Because so many diplomats crowded the negotiations, and because their deliberations lasted so long, the conference left an enormous paper trail. The archives of the participating governments house tens of thousands of documents on the subject, written in nearly two dozen languages. Even if one discounted the challenge of reading this sprawling corpus, there would remain the task of reconstructing and interpreting the course of the negotiations, which officials variously described as "Talmudic," "Kantian," and "scholastic" in their complexity.[22] In recent years, historians have begun to assemble pieces of the puzzle. The new wave of scholarship has produced detailed studies of the CSCE, most of which examine the contributions of individual states or trace particular themes.[23] This book takes a different approach. Instead of focusing on one country or one side, it examines the conference in the round. Only by looking at the CSCE through the eyes of all of its leading participants, and setting it in its wider international context, can one grasp how the Final Act came into existence.

A number of myths have clung to the agreement since 1975. Some accounts of the Final Act present it as a quid pro quo, in which the West agreed to ratify the continent's postwar frontiers and accept the USSR's domination of its Eastern European neighbors in exchange for Soviet concessions on human rights.[24] In truth, on the question of Europe's frontiers and the status of Eastern Europe, the Western allies gave nothing away. Far from satisfying Brezhnev's hope of freezing the political and territorial status quo, the agreement made clear that borders could change, as could alliances, and it repudiated the Brezhnev Doctrine. The result was not a balanced tradeoff between the USSR's goals and those of its Western peers. On every significant point, the West prevailed. To be sure, the Final Act stood little chance of remaking the Soviet bloc in the short term, but the Western negotiators did not expect immediate results. Instead, they believed that they were sowing the seeds for long-term change by eroding the Soviet bloc's conceptual footings. For this reason, the agreement constituted a "monumental act of weakness" for the USSR, as KGB officer Nikolai Leonov later wrote.[25]

Assessments of the Final Act's significance also tend to stress its provisions on human rights, sometimes to the exclusion of its other contents.[26]

To suggest that respect for human rights stood at the heart of the agreement says both too much and too little. It says too much because, unlike the United Nations' Universal Declaration of Human Rights, the Final Act did not emphasize human rights in their entirety. Although it endorsed the general notion of universal rights, it remained silent about the rights to work, education, and leisure, among others. Instead, it focused on a particular subset of liberties that Western governments held dear, especially the freedom to travel, freedom of information, and freedom of the press. The NATO allies championed these ideas because they reflected core liberal democratic values and because they threatened the mechanisms on which the communist governments relied to control their societies.

This story illuminates the politics of human rights in a decisive period. It demonstrates that the rights revolution of the 1960s and 1970s was driven not just by grassroots mobilization, but by high politics too. Although activists performed a critical function in returning human rights to the top of the international agenda, Western diplomats also made a vital contribution to this process at an early stage—and well before Jimmy Carter entered the White House. For the officials who took the lead in this drama, human rights provided a weapon for fighting the Cold War, not an escape from it. At the CSCE, they stressed those rights that served their purposes, and they always understood them as part of a larger design to put pressure on the Soviets and reaffirm the moral superiority of liberal democracy. Besides, in trying to lower the barriers between states, these freedoms had as much to do with the logic of globalization and European integration as with the concepts that had shaped the Universal Declaration three decades earlier. In this way, the CSCE truncated the meaning of human rights, focusing on those negative liberties that helped the Western cause and marginalizing the rest.[27]

Treating the Final Act simply as an agreement about human rights, however, ignores its full significance. In response to the upheaval of the 1960s, the CSCE's participants wanted to open new avenues for cooperation and to articulate a code of conduct that they could all accept, East and West alike. However, communist and liberal democratic views on these subjects diverged dramatically, and although leaders on both sides genuinely wanted peace, they defined it in different ways. The result was a fight over the constitutive principles of international order and legitimacy: these were the real stakes at the CSCE. The Final Act therefore represented something far more ambitious than a declaration on human rights. Beneath its tangles of clauses and thickets of commas lay a sweeping vision of how governments should relate to each other and to their citizens in East and West alike.

The CSCE promulgated a common concept of legitimacy for all of Europe. By pledging to uphold the same standards and follow the same rules, regardless of their system of government, the Final Act's signatories laid the groundwork for a new international order on the continent, much as their predecessors had done at Westphalia in 1648, Utrecht in 1713, Vienna in 1815, and Paris in 1919. Even when superpower tensions returned to dangerous heights in the years after 1975, the agreement remained a touchstone in both East and West. Politicians and average citizens drew inspiration from its provisions, which accelerated the unraveling of the Soviet empire. The terms on which the Cold War ended came directly from its pages. Although it took more than a decade to make its full effects felt, the Final Act served the same purpose as the agreements negotiated at the grand diplomatic conferences of the past, and it influenced the direction of European affairs just as decisively. It deserves to be recognized as their Cold War-era successor.[28]

II

Historians have described the Cold War as a conflict between rival superpowers, rival ideologies, and rival empires. It was also a conflict between rival international orders and rival concepts of legitimacy. By contrast with earlier apocalyptic wars, the Second World War ended without a peace conference to put the broken state system back together. Because the victorious powers could not agree on a single set of rules to govern the postwar world, two parallel international orders took shape after 1945. In the East, the Soviet Union built an order on the principles of ideological conformity, deference to Moscow, and political and economic centralization. In the West, an American-led order emerged, based on the principles of pluralism, compromise, and openness in both politics and economics. The rift between the two orders fueled the Cold War and ensured that the conflict would endure until they were knit back together.

After bringing the world to the brink of destruction in the 1950s and early 1960s, the two orders reached an uneasy equilibrium. Premised on the theory of mutually assured destruction, it averted catastrophe but fell short of genuine peace. As the danger of war receded, however, the principles of legitimacy on which the orders relied came under attack. In the East, the familiar claims about Western revanchism—which the Soviet government used to justify domestic repression and claim its citizens' loyalty—wore thin. The Sino-Soviet split threatened the USSR's political and ideological primacy, as did the growing assertiveness of Eastern European leaders. Intellectuals and young people lost faith in Marxist-Leninist ideals and expressed their discontent in daring new ways. Economic growth rates sagged, and the gap between Eastern and Western living standards widened.

To the West, NATO's relevance seemed to fade along with the threat of war. On both sides of the Atlantic, calls to cut military spending grew louder, and students rebelled against a status quo that they found suffocating. In Western Europe, officials and citizens alike questioned Washington's leadership, especially in light of the Vietnam War. As the postwar economic boom fizzled out, the United States clashed with its European and Japanese partners over tariffs, subsidies, and monetary policy. The long postwar era came an end, but no one could tell what would follow it. As British analyst Alastair Buchan pointed out, "The problems created by the continued existence of two quite antithetical conceptions of domestic and world order . . . have not in any sense been solved."[29]

Leaders in both blocs grasped these dangers, but they responded in different ways. The Soviets and Americans developed conservative strategies that aimed to stabilize the Cold War. In Moscow, Brezhnev and his foreign minister, Andrei Gromyko, pursued agreements with the West to ratify Europe's postwar status quo and increase the USSR's access to foreign capital and technology. By replacing the exhausted ideals of communism with the new ideals of peace and prosperity, they reasoned, the Soviet government could reclaim its citizens' loyalty. In Washington, President Richard Nixon and national security advisor Henry Kissinger cut America's military commitments to alleviate the political and fiscal costs of international leadership. Meanwhile, they reestablished relations with Beijing to expand the United States' room for maneuver, and encouraged the USSR to behave like a satisfied, rather than a revisionist, power.

By contrast, Western Europe's leading statesmen pursued transformative strategies that sought to overcome the Cold War, not to entrench it. French President Georges Pompidou wanted to expand contacts between governments and individuals on either side of the Iron Curtain, while simultaneously loosening the ties that bound each alliance. Eventually, he hoped, this process of interpenetration would foster common values across the ideological divide, pull down the political and intellectual obstacles that separated East and West, and sweep away the communist order. In West Germany, Chancellor Willy Brandt reversed his country's longstanding refusal to recognize either the territorial results of the Second World War or its East German neighbor. By setting aside the diplomatic grievances that had pitted Bonn against Moscow and its allies, he reasoned, Ostpolitik would help states and citizens understand each other better, which in turn would alleviate the Cold War's human costs and enrich both sides. Over the long term, the process would reunify both Germany and the continent and establish a durable peace.

The interplay of these conservative and transformative strategies defined the process commonly known as détente. In responding to the crises that beset them, détente's protagonists did not simply want to reduce the danger of war or to quell internal unrest. More broadly, they sought new principles of legitimacy on which to rebuild both domestic and international

order. Their immediate goals overlapped enough to produce a series of diplomatic achievements, including the US-Soviet Interim Agreement on nuclear weapons, West Germany's treaties with its eastern neighbors, and the
four-power deal on Berlin. Because the leaders' worldviews and long-term
objectives diverged, however, they pursued different concepts of order and
interpreted these agreements in different ways.[30]

The creation of the CSCE epitomized détente's ambitions and tensions.
In the mid-1960s, the Warsaw Pact called on the Western allies to participate in negotiations on European security. Brezhnev and his colleagues
wanted a multilateral agreement to recognize the continent's post-1945 political and territorial status quo and, by extension, to secure the USSR's
reputation as a champion of peace and affirm its status as the equal of any
capitalist state. At a time when Marxist-Leninism had lost its vitality and
the command economy struggled to meet citizens' basic needs, a high-
profile conference along these lines would throw the communist system a
"life preserver" by renewing its popular appeal, as one official in Moscow
put it. To press their case, the Soviets sought to exploit the crisis of legitimacy unfolding in the capitalist world. They wagered that Western politicians would find themselves unable to resist a campaign that combined
diplomatic pressure and grassroots activism in the name of peace.[31]

The Western allies initially rebuffed the Warsaw Pact's appeals. In their
view, the Soviets simply wanted to foreclose the possibility of German reunification and expand their influence across the continent. They also
feared that a conference would further erode public support for NATO by
giving citizens the false impression that the Cold War's major problems
had been solved. But the Soviets refused to drop the idea, and Western officials eventually changed their minds. If the allies rejected the conference,
they reasoned, citizens might conclude that their governments did not take
peace seriously, and that NATO posed a greater threat to international stability than the Warsaw Pact. Besides, the 1967 Harmel Report had committed the alliance to negotiating with the Eastern powers. Unless Western officials pursued every diplomatic opening, including the conference idea,
they would make a mockery of this bid to renew NATO's purpose.

Having decided to participate in the conference, the Western allies devised a plan to turn it to their advantage. Through a series of contentious
discussions, the allies crafted a set of proposals that encapsulated their priorities. They announced that they would participate in a conference, but
only on condition that other East-West negotiations—especially on the status of Germany and Berlin—reached successful conclusions first. They also
insisted on expanding the conference agenda beyond the Soviets' narrow
conception of security. It had to include items designed to undermine the
Brezhnev Doctrine, communist restrictions on travel and emigration, and
strict censorship, among other things. In this way, the Western allies sought

to exploit the crisis of the Eastern order, claim the moral high ground in the Cold War, and advance the transformative strategy of détente.

This drawn-out process illustrated the political culture of each alliance and its understanding of international order. The Warsaw Pact operated on the principle of centralized control, with the USSR setting the direction and expecting its allies to follow. Some of the Eastern Europeans made their mark by pursuing their own goals, but Moscow's heavy-handed methods prevented them from stepping too far out of line. In persuading the West to participate in the conference, the Soviets relied on persistence rather than finesse, lobbying officials and appealing to public opinion until they finally got the answer they wanted. By contrast, NATO's messy, decentralized deliberations made up in creativity what they lacked in efficiency. Although the Nixon administration regarded the conference as a meaningless—perhaps even dangerous—exercise, it deferred to the Western Europeans' enthusiasm. Whereas the arguments within the Warsaw Pact stifled new ideas, those within NATO fostered them. In the process, the allies reworked a communist concept to suit liberal democratic purposes. The West transformed the conference from an exercise in damage control into a tool for waging cold war by other means.

III

In launching the CSCE, all of the participating states took a gamble. The conference offered the first chance in decades to reexamine "the legitimate design of the international system for all of Europe," as one observer put it, but no one could foresee its outcome. If it succeeded, it might resolve the crises that gripped East and West. If it failed, however, it could wreck détente and plunge the continent into a new era of confrontation. When the participants first assembled in 1972, they agreed to work by strict consensus, which meant that no one could impose his views on the others. The traditional measures of power, whether military, economic, or demographic, did not determine a state's influence at the bargaining table. Neither the Soviets nor the Americans dominated the proceedings, and a number of smaller countries—Eastern, Western, and neutral—enjoyed disproportionate clout, thanks to a combination of diplomatic savvy, stubbornness, and a willingness to take risks.[32]

At the conference, the Soviets championed an idea of peace in which security demanded impermeability. The more robust the barriers between states, they reasoned, the safer governments would be. They therefore urged the West to recognize Europe's frontiers as eternal and immutable, and they argued for a categorical understanding of sovereignty that empowered states to treat their citizens as they pleased (with the proviso that socialist states could forfeit their claims to sovereignty if they backslid into counter-revolution). By seeking better access to foreign markets for their exports while preserving the system of centralized planning, they tried to reap the rewards of globalization without succumbing to its liberalizing pressures. They wanted to protect their closed societies, keeping their own citizens in and dangerous ideas out. In short, they sought to bring the Soviet order into closer but strictly controlled contact with the rest of Europe, while maintaining the essential differences between East and West.

According to the Western concept of peace, by contrast, security required openness. As barriers between states fell, so would mutual suspicion and the danger of war. People, ideas, and goods ought to circulate more freely across borders. In line with the principle of self-determination, states had the right to redraw their frontiers peacefully and to choose their allies. They enjoyed the prerogatives of sovereignty, but were likewise constrained by the imperatives of human rights. One standard of conduct ought to govern the whole continent, with no distinction between communist and non-communist countries. This approach assumed that the creation of a single European order would gradually reunify East and West, and that, as the two systems came into closer contact, liberal democracy's inherent superiority would lead to its eventual triumph. In the first half of the twentieth century, most Western governments had feared the spread of Bolshevik ideas. Now, despite their ongoing domestic challenges, they welcomed the prospect of a head-to-head competition, while Soviet leaders feared it.

On nearly every issue, the Eastern and Western demands stood in opposition to each other. Because they shared so little common ground, the negotiators could not simply split their differences. Although the Soviets hoped to make rapid progress, the conference became a war of attrition. The Eastern representatives tried to flatter, persuade, and bully their challengers into accepting their proposals and endeavored to turn the Western allies against each other. Soviet leaders appealed to their Western counterparts, especially senior figures in the Nixon and Ford administrations, to rein in their demands. For their part, the Western delegations calculated that if the Kremlin wanted a successful outcome, it would agree to pay a high price for it. Sooner or later, the Soviets would lose their nerve and agree to make major concessions. For this approach to work, however, the allies had to outlast their interlocutors and stay united. To resolve their many disagreements—about what to demand, when to push, and when to conciliate—they consulted incessantly. The neutral and nonaligned states played a key role throughout, serving as go-betweens and working out solutions that both sides could accept.

As the Final Act took shape, its three main sections—dubbed "baskets" by the negotiators—hewed more closely to the West's goals than to those of the East. In the first basket, which focused on international security, the diplomats crafted a "Declaration on Principles Guiding Relations between Participating States." Its ten points included elements of both the Eastern and Western visions of international order, but it dashed the Soviets' hopes of entrenching Europe's territorial and political status quo. Although it endorsed the continent's existing borders, it did not recognize them as permanent. Instead, it affirmed that states could redraw them peacefully. By asserting that the principles of self-determination and nonintervention in domestic affairs applied to all states, regardless of their social systems, and that each state had the freedom to change its alliances, the Declaration invalidated the Brezhnev Doctrine. By proclaiming that respect for individual human rights constituted a core principle of international security, it pointed toward an expansive understanding of peace, in which the way that states treated their own citizens mattered as much as how they treated their neighbors. This emphasis on human rights also implied that certain universal values superseded the prerogatives of individual states, and that no state enjoyed unqualified sovereignty.

The other sections of the Final Act were shot through with the Western principles of openness and transparency. In the second basket, which dealt with economic, scientific, and environmental cooperation, the Soviets wanted the West to commit, at least in principle, to granting them most favored nation (MFN) status. The Western allies refused, largely because the Soviets rejected their demands to relax state management of international trade. Nonetheless, the participants agreed to publish more economic information, to expand contacts between enterprises, and to improve working conditions for foreign businessmen. More dramatically, the third basket, which concerned humanitarian cooperation, gave concrete form to Western ideas about freer movement. Participants had to expand international travel, promote the reunification of divided families, increase the circulation of foreign books, newspapers, and films, and improve journalists' working conditions. Finally, a set of military confidence-building measures (CBMs) required each government to provide advance notification of troop maneuvers and to invite foreign observers to watch them. According to the measures' Western originators, dispelling military secrecy would promote mutual understanding and mitigate the risk of conflict.

Although the Final Act endorsed a more open, flexible, and humane approach to international affairs, it left important questions unresolved. To attack the Brezhnev Doctrine, the Western allies emphasized that the principles of nonintervention and sovereign equality applied across Europe. But the USSR and its allies could cite these same principles to rebuff unwelcome demands on freer movement. In addition, the Soviets insisted on a number of stipulations that, in their view, would protect them from Western pressure to change their domestic systems. As a result of their efforts, the preamble to Basket III stipulated that humanitarian cooperation had to "take place in full respect for" the principles enumerated in the first basket, including nonintervention. The principle of sovereign equality recognized each state's right to "determine its laws and regulations." And the third basket's text on human contacts declared that its measures—on international travel and family reunification, among other things—could only be enacted "under mutually acceptable conditions." The resulting ambiguities about the relationship between the Final Act's promises and each state's sovereign authority set the stage for future disputes about how to implement the agreement.[33]

From a certain perspective, it is puzzling that the CSCE's results bore so little resemblance to the USSR's goals. After all, the Soviets recognized the dangers inherent in the West's objectives, they fielded an experienced and shrewd delegation, and the rule of consensus equipped them to reject any proposal they deemed unwelcome. But they also made tactical errors that allowed the Western allies to press their case. Soviet leaders were so determined to bring the CSCE to a successful conclusion that they imposed artificial time constraints on their own delegation, which found itself compelled to make major concessions to get a deal. They underestimated the strength of Western solidarity and overestimated their own ability to tamp down the West's most ambitious demands. Despite Brezhnev and Gromyko's entreaties, and despite his own skepticism of the CSCE, Henry Kissinger refused to provoke an intra-NATO rupture over the conference. He intervened in the negotiations on several occasions, but his efforts did more to advance Western European goals than those of the USSR.

The Eastern allies also suffered from strategic problems. They failed to develop an offensive concept of cooperation that served communist interests in the same way that openness and freer movement served liberal democratic ones. Instead of confronting Western demands in these areas with demands of their own, they played defense. They took refuge in linguistic ambiguities and hoped that oblique references to state sovereignty would blunt the impact of the concessions they made. Even more surprising, a number of Soviet officials sympathized with the Western allies' proposals. Although they remained committed communists, they believed that their country needed to open itself to the world. For this reason, they did not resist the West's demands as strenuously as they might have, and may even have welcomed the CSCE as an opportunity to push the Soviet system in the direction of reform.

The negotiations demonstrated the contradictions of Brezhnev's strategy. In trying to renew the Soviet order's claim to legitimacy, the general secretary invited challenges to that legitimacy. Unable to avoid the concessions that the Western allies demanded, he and his colleagues hoped to have it both ways. They planned to claim simultaneously that the Final Act was a sacred document that imposed solemn obligations, and that their governments' sovereign rights allowed them to violate it at will. They intended to publicize it as a victory for communism, but counted on their citizens to ignore the sections that the authorities found inconvenient. They demanded that foreign governments treat some provisions—such as the inviolability of frontiers—as meaningful, but expected them to accept others— such as the peaceful change of frontiers and freer movement—as dead letters.

In these ways, the CSCE illustrated the dilemmas of statecraft in the 1970s. Power came in many forms, not all of them commensurable. By any military criterion, for example, the USSR had never been so strong, and Brezhnev assumed that the recent expansion of the Soviet nuclear arsenal would give the country the upper hand at the negotiating table. But conventional forces and ballistic missiles could not make the country secure in the absence of legitimacy, nor did they translate directly into diplomatic influence. In Helsinki and Geneva, Soviet delegates often found themselves bereft of the leverage necessary to achieve their objectives. The Western allies used this dynamic to their advantage. The ability to shape the rules of the international game constituted a source of power in its own right— harder to measure than economic output or the size of an armored division, but no less important. The Final Act was only a nonbinding declaration, not a treaty. It had no army standing behind it, and no authority under international law. Yet by rewriting the principles of legitimacy, by articulating a particular definition of peace, and by establishing a single international order in Europe, it held out the possibility of transforming the Cold War.

IV

After the Helsinki summit, the struggle to craft the Final Act was replaced by a new struggle to interpret and implement it. Leaders and diplomats on both sides of the Iron Curtain claimed that the agreement vindicated their principles and reflected their goals. Nonetheless, it was the Kremlin's narrative of the CSCE that gained popular currency in East and West alike. Most Western onlookers read the agreement as an endorsement of Moscow's objectives, and they argued that the United States and its allies had capitulated to Brezhnev's demands. In the Soviet bloc, even those dissidents who mistrusted official pronouncements took the same view.

As the months passed, however, these doubters reconsidered the Final Act. Soviet and Eastern European intellectuals concluded that its provisions offered useful tools for challenging state control. Thousands of average Eastern Europeans cited the agreement when they applied for exit visas. Across the region, activists called on party leaders to respect fundamental human rights. In the West, politicians and campaigners started looking for ways to pressure the Eastern governments to live up to the promises they had made in Helsinki. During the original negotiations, the Western Europeans had charged ahead while the Americans had hung back. By the end of the decade, however, the Americans had been converted to their allies' transformational logic. A cross-border network took shape, connecting Western officials and civil society groups with activists in the East.

With the Americans in the lead, the Western allies used the CSCE's follow-up meetings to try to enforce the Final Act. At these conferences, held in Belgrade from 1977 to 1978 and Madrid from 1980 to 1983, they raised the cases of dozens of political prisoners and demanded that the Soviets and their allies honor the principles of freer movement and greater openness. These tactics outraged Brezhnev and his colleagues, who objected to what they regarded as interference in their domestic affairs. At the conferences, Soviet and Eastern European diplomats tried to redirect the conversation toward their ongoing peace campaign and proposals for disarmament, but had limited success. Because of this impasse, which reprised familiar arguments from Helsinki and Geneva, the meeting in Belgrade ended without substantive agreement. Exacerbated by the resurgence of international tensions and the violence in Afghanistan and Poland, the meeting in Madrid nearly collapsed entirely.

Nonetheless, the CSCE survived. At the nadir of East-West relations, the Soviets could have withdrawn from the conference to shield themselves from Western criticism, but they did not. Even as the two sides suspended arms control negotiations and engaged in bitter recriminations, the CSCE remained a vital channel of communication. By this point, the Soviet government had tied itself so closely to the Final Act that it could not afford to repudiate it without damaging its own legitimacy. During the Solidarity crisis in Poland, the USSR declined to act on the Brezhnev Doctrine and insisted that the government in Warsaw reestablish order on its own. Moreover, at the Madrid meeting, the Soviets and their allies agreed to expand the CSCE's guarantees of freer movement and individual rights.

The challenge of enforcing the Final Act changed dramatically in 1985 when Mikhail Gorbachev took office in Moscow. The new general secretary reexamined the USSR's longstanding concept of peace and concluded that cooperation in the name of universal values and shared interests had to replace the old dogmas of class conflict. States could only be secure if they understood each other, which in turn required the circulation of people and ideas across borders. This new commitment to openness, transparency, and interdependence echoed the Final Act's core principles. Instead of resisting his country's obligations under the CSCE, Gorbachev looked for ways to fulfill them. Soviet policy at home and abroad changed accordingly. The government released imprisoned dissidents, relaxed censorship, and consented to on-site military inspections. At the Vienna follow-up meeting, which ran from 1986 to 1989, the USSR's new flexibility yielded an agreement that outstripped anything negotiated in Belgrade or Madrid. In turn, Gorbachev cited its provisions to rebuff his domestic critics' complaints and justify further reforms.

The revolutions of 1989 demonstrated how profoundly the Final Act had reshaped international affairs in Europe. In Poland, the agreement had inspired Solidarity's organizers at the beginning of the decade. Now, it served as a reference point during the union's negotiations with the government, which paved the way for free elections. Hungarian leaders embraced the principle of freer movement in opening their borders to East German refugees who wanted to flee to the Federal Republic. The East German government honored the Final Act's provisions on the rights of foreign journalists, which in turn enabled West German correspondents to bring news and images of watershed protests to the rest of the world. Meanwhile, Gorbachev disclaimed the Brezhnev Doctrine on the grounds that self-determination and nonintervention trumped the logic of proletarian internationalism. The USSR left its Eastern European allies to make their own decisions.

After the Berlin Wall fell, the Final Act provided the blueprint for the peace settlement that ended the Cold War. In the talks on the future of Germany, it guided leaders on all sides. West German Chancellor Helmut Kohl invoked the principle of the peaceful change of frontiers to justify his plans for reunification. In making the case that the newly reunited country should be allowed to join NATO, the West Germans and Americans cited the agreement's stipulation that all countries had the authority to choose their own allies. The CSCE also figured prominently in Gorbachev's own designs for the future of Europe, although these differed from those of his Western interlocutors. Eventually, however, he accepted Bonn and Washington's arguments, endorsed German reunification, and consented to withdraw Soviet forces from German territory.

In November 1990, the second summit meeting in CSCE history set forth the principles that would govern the new Europe. The Paris Charter, signed in the French capital, recapitulated the Final Act's core ideas. It extolled the virtues of interdependence and freer movement, and committed its signatories to respect their citizens' fundamental rights and to promote greater transparency in military, economic, and cultural affairs. Compared to the original negotiations in Helsinki and Geneva, the drafting of the charter had moved rapidly, especially because the participants now shared similar assumptions about international politics. The Western concepts of legitimacy and peace, as embodied in the Final Act, had gained credence across the continent.

The signing of the Final Act was a watershed in the Cold War. In his memoirs, Anatoly Kovalev, who headed the Soviet delegation in Geneva, argued that the reunification of Europe represented "the victory of détente" and, especially, the victory of the Final Act.[34] The history of the CSCE bears out his point. It makes clear that détente was not an ephemeral phenomenon, but had transformative consequences. It also offers a powerful example of what diplomacy can achieve. The leaders who embarked on the CSCE turned the crises of the 1960s into an opportunity to reimagine East-West relations. In turn, the negotiators in Helsinki and Geneva articulated a new vision for Europe on the basis of shared values, common interests, and a unified international order. Their work, simultaneously epic and abstruse, did not create a perfect peace, but it hastened the end of the superpower conflict and laid the foundations for the post–Cold War world.

Chapter 1

CRISES OF LEGITIMACY

DURING THE 1960s, the post–World War II era drew to a close, but no single moment signaled its end. Many of the patterns that had defined international affairs since 1945 began to crack up, and the familiar elements of the high Cold War faded. The growing sophistication of nuclear weapons stabilized Soviet-American relations and forced the superpowers to recognize their shared interest in avoiding conflict. The bonds that held the Eastern and Western alliances together began to loosen, and some members of the Warsaw Pact and NATO demanded greater freedom of action. At home, citizens lost faith in their governments. Young people questioned longstanding political and social conventions. The economic systems that had operated since the war began to sputter, sowing doubts about the long-term viability of both capitalism and communism.

Contemporary observers saw that the world stood on the verge of a new age, but they could not discern its shape. "Events have drawn us beyond the postwar world into a perplexing period of transition whose rules we have not yet learned and whose rivalries we do not yet understand," an American commentator wrote in 1964. "The waters we are entering are uncharted and perhaps treacherous, and we are not likely to steer safely through them unless we have the courage to question the old assumptions which once seemed eternal and have now become so threadbare."[1] A French analyst echoed these sentiments a few years later: "It is almost impossible to escape the impression that we are entering a new period of international relations—and almost as difficult to agree on where we go from here," he wrote. "Our feeling of change is based on our witnessing the decay of the old, rather than on any concrete fears or hopes about the emergence of the new."[2] Some went so far as to claim that the conflict between the superpowers had ended. "The cold war is dead, in the popular view on this side of the Atlantic," the *Washington Post* reported from Bonn. Even those who disputed this suggestion acknowledged that the tectonic plates of international politics were shifting.[3]

These changes affected different countries in different ways, but no one, on either side of the Iron Curtain, could escape them. They affected the United States and the USSR alike, and Western Europe and Eastern Europe equally. Despite their political, economic, and social differences, a common thread connected them. In the 1960s, the two worlds of the Cold War—the American and the Soviet, the West and the East—fell into crises of legitimacy.

The crises fractured the rival international orders that had emerged at the end of the Second World War. The defeat of Germany and Japan in 1945 raised numerous questions about the shape of the postwar world: How should the vanquished powers be treated? What would be the fate of the lands liberated from occupation? How could war be prevented in the future? Starting from substantially different assumptions about the meaning of peace, democracy, and justice, the Soviets and Americans answered these questions in dramatically different ways. Unlike the allies who defeated France in 1815 and created a new international order at the Congress of Vienna, or the allies who defeated Germany in 1918 and established a new model for peacemaking in Paris, the victors of 1945 could not agree on common principles to guide the postwar world. Beyond respect for state sovereignty, which provided the foundation for the United Nations, no amount of diplomatic effort could reconcile incompatible Soviet and Western concepts. As a consequence, the world fragmented into two parallel societies of states.[4]

The Pax Americana and Pax Sovietica, which coalesced in the late 1940s, operated according to different standards of legitimacy. Legitimacy has two faces. One looks inward, at a state's domestic order, and defines the acceptable types of government and economic order. A government that enjoys popular legitimacy makes certain promises to its citizens to secure their consent to its rule. The other form of legitimacy looks outward. It provides, in Philip Bobbitt's phrase, a "constitution for the society of states" and stipulates how governments must behave internationally. The more that states exercise self-restraint and abide by these rules, the easier it is to maintain international peace.[5]

Because the nature of a regime influences how it treats its neighbors, these two kinds of legitimacy are interdependent. As a consequence, a stable peace settlement requires states to agree on common standards of domestic and international legitimacy. These standards do not prevent conflict, but provide the tools for keeping it contained. When a revisionist power questions the fundamental principles of legitimacy, disputes can spin out of control and spark cataclysmic wars that destroy order itself.[6]

The international order that the United States built after the Second World War extended from Japan to Western Europe. At its center stood the institutions of the Atlantic world, especially NATO, the European

Economic Community, the International Monetary Fund, and the General Agreement on Tariffs and Trade. In politics, its members adhered to liberal democratic values. In economics, they blended the free market with the principles of social democracy, and they promoted free trade and economic integration. In foreign affairs, they balanced the imperative of containing communism with respect for states' autonomy. With citizens and allies alike, they accommodated diverse political views and worked to reconcile competing interests.[7]

Under the pressure of the Cold War, the American government sometimes departed from its liberal democratic principles. It covertly intervened in the Italian election of 1948, for example. Countries that stood outside the American-led order, especially in Asia, Africa, and Latin America, suffered repeated interventions at the hands of Western powers in the name of containing communism, with bloody results. Nonetheless, at least from the perspective of leaders in Washington, London, and Paris, these cases remained exceptions to the rules of the Western order.[8]

The Soviet-led order crystallized in Eastern Europe. Its architects defined security in terms of territory and ideological affinity, redrawing the region's borders and installing new communist governments. Following the logic of Stalinism, they assumed that conflict between capitalist and communist states was inevitable because the capitalists intended "to combat Socialism and democracy, and to support reactionary and anti-democratic pro-fascist regimes and movements everywhere," as Andrei Zhdanov put it in 1947. Because of this threat, the Soviets demanded that their allies defer to their policies and interests.[9]

Working with local communists, the Soviets remade Eastern Europe in their image. Central planners organized industry and agriculture according to the Soviet model and refused to join the economic institutions of the Western order. They promised citizens that social justice and material plenty awaited them once the project of building a communist society had been achieved. In the meantime, that project demanded patience and self-sacrifice. Soviet and Eastern European leaders justified their rule by claiming the mantle of antifascism and anti-imperialism. To defend their rule against these threats from abroad and the danger of counterrevolution at home, communist leaders prioritized military over civilian spending and imposed tight controls on citizens' lives, restricting what they could read, what they could say, and where they could live.[10]

In the first two decades of the postwar period, the two international orders did not operate perfectly. The United States and its allies quarreled over military strategy and economic affairs. The 1956 Suez crisis caused a rift between the Americans on the one hand and the British and French on the other. In the Soviet bloc, even loyal allies sometimes chafed at ideological strictures and complained that Moscow provided too little economic assistance. Material privation and political repression prompted several domestic uprisings, which communist leaders put down by force. After Joseph Stalin's death, the USSR intervened in East Germany and Hungary to prevent the overthrow of communist rule, at considerable cost in human life. These episodes raised questions about the best means to preserve communism without resorting to Stalinist methods, but Soviet and Eastern European leaders nonetheless had faith that they could perfect their system, and millions of citizens continued to believe in the ideals of Marx and Lenin.

By the 1960s, however, the established ways of doing things had become unsustainable in both the American and Soviet orders. Governments were losing their citizens' support. The superpowers' relationships with their allies threatened to unravel. One scholar summed up the problem: "What is at stake is how both domestic politics and the international order are to be organized."[11] The status quo in the Pax Americana and Pax Sovietica could not endure.

I

During the high Cold War, the superpowers came to rely on nuclear weapons as the foundation of their security. In a series of confrontations, they stepped repeatedly to the brink of nuclear destruction. In the late 1950s and early 1960s, Soviet leader Nikita Khrushchev provoked crises over Berlin and Cuba by trying to overturn the political and strategic status quo. In a bid to force the Americans, British, and French to abandon Berlin, he threatened to give the East Germans control of the checkpoints into the city's Western zones. To defend Cuba's communist government against American attack, he deployed nuclear missiles to the island. In both instances, he wagered that only dramatic action could redress the imbalance between the superpowers and preserve the regimes in East Berlin and Havana. He expected that the United States would back down instead of risking a war that could annihilate everyone involved. These gambles tested nerves on all sides and nearly led to disaster. If a tank commander at Checkpoint Charlie or a naval officer in the Caribbean Sea had acted rashly, the results could have been catastrophic.[12]

After 1962, the superpowers reached a makeshift equilibrium. The Cold War stabilized. The same weapons that had threatened to destroy both sides now steadied their relationship. "In Europe, the feeling of insecurity which, at an earlier stage, came first from the fear of aggression and then from the fear of accidental war, has disappeared," French analyst Pierre Hassner observed. "A balance has been established."[13] Leaders in Washington and

Moscow recognized that the dangers of recklessness outweighed any possible rewards. On the basis of this military reality, they reached an understanding in Europe. The Western powers acquiesced in the newly built Berlin Wall, which prevented any more East Germans from fleeing westward. The Soviets tolerated the continued presence of American, British, and French troops in the city and in West Germany. The 1963 Limited Test Ban Treaty, which tacitly aimed to prevent nuclear proliferation, ensured that the Federal Republic would not acquire the ultimate weapon. However imperfect, this combination of political accommodation and strategic deadlock blunted the Cold War's existential dangers.[14] "Whereas fifteen years ago many believed the threat to be real and immediate it [has] now apparently diminished to the point where virtually no one in Europe, [or] in the United States, believe[s] in a Soviet attack," French President Charles de Gaulle told the American ambassador to Paris in 1964.[15]

The superpowers welcomed the respite from repeated crises. Yet life in the nuclear shadow exacted a steep psychological price from their citizens. British Prime Minister Winston Churchill told the House of Commons that the world had "reached a stage in this story where safety will be the sturdy child of terror and survival the twin brother of annihilation." Mutually assured destruction made life more predictable and imposed unrelenting anxiety. Security entailed vulnerability.[16]

Nuclear stability overturned traditional ideas about the relationship between military power and political influence. According to the logic of deterrence, the balance of terror guaranteed peace because each side understood that it could not hope to win a nuclear war. But as stability increased, the threats on which it depended lost credibility. Some observers doubted that the United States would retaliate with a full-scale nuclear strike if the Soviet Union attacked Western Europe with conventional forces. Nor could either superpower use its arsenal to bully its adversary. "[N]obody would believe a bluff that involved the threat of national suicide," American writer Ronald Steel argued. This did not mean that nuclear weapons had lost their value. Rather, they ushered in a new kind of superpower competition in which diplomacy and negotiation took precedence over brinksmanship and intimidation.[17]

The superpowers realized that their fates were now intertwined. Shortly after the Cuban crisis, Khrushchev acknowledged that the Cold War adversaries stood on common ground. "Of course I was scared. It would have been insane not to be scared. I was frightened about what could happen to my country—or your country or all the other countries that would be devastated by a nuclear war," he said. "One of the problems in the world today is that not enough people are sufficiently frightened by the danger of nuclear war."[18] American president John F. Kennedy likewise acknowledged the ironies of deterrence and the realities of interdependence. The United

States and the Soviet Union "have a mutually deep interest in a just and genuine peace and in halting the arms race," he told a university audience in June 1963. "For, in the final analysis, our most basic common link is that we all inhabit this small planet. We all breathe the same air. We all cherish our children's future. And we are all mortal."[19]

Interdependence blurred the line between Soviet and American interests. Security now transcended national boundaries and eluded strictly military calculations. But turning stability into peace required more than a balance of forces. It was necessary "to broaden our conception of security, in the realization that our security in the broadest sense of the word is interlocked with that of our adversary," Sovietologist Marshall Shulman argued.[20] Because neither the United States nor the USSR would benefit from war or unrestrained military spending, American and Soviet leaders committed themselves to arms control.[21]

They also looked for new ways to strengthen their relationship. Although they continued to jockey for military and geopolitical advantage, especially in the global south, the superpowers now sought to understand each other, cooperate across the Iron Curtain, and reach agreement on the rules that would govern their relations and their conduct in the world. Regular meetings between officials and closer contacts between average citizens would also help to establish "an easier pattern of human relations" between East and West, an eminent group of Western European analysts argued. But numerous obstacles stood in the way. Closer cooperation—and ultimately a durable peace settlement—required "radical changes in the present structure of greater Europe."[22]

Here lay another paradox of nuclear stability. As soon as the status quo had stabilized, it needed to be revised. The immediate danger of war faded, but public support for familiar Cold War patterns did too. Popular demands for a resolution to the conflict grew apace.[23] As the military situation became more rigid, the diplomatic situation became more flexible but also more urgent. "Precisely because we no longer fear war, we should start thinking about peace," Pierre Hassner concluded. "[W]e cannot afford not to start thinking about a new security system."[24] A window of opportunity had opened. It was now possible—and necessary—to address the problems that had created the Cold War in the first place.

II

As superpower relations stabilized, the Eastern and Western alliances fractured. Among the members of NATO, preserving allied unity no longer seemed so urgent. "On both sides of the Atlantic, there is a murmuring discontent with the prevailing philosophy of the Cold War, although no consensus has emerged as to what should take its place," Marshall Shulman noted. "This discontent is often part of the unarticulated background of policy differences within the Western alliance."[25]

Mutually assured destruction undermined the military assumptions on which NATO operated. In the early years of the alliance, the Western Europeans had played an important role as "forward-defense allies," hosting bases for the bombers that formed the backbone of the American nuclear deterrent. In the event of hostilities, they would also provide a buffer against a communist invasion. The development of intercontinental ballistic missiles (ICBMs), which enabled the superpowers to strike each other directly, reduced the allies' military importance. The missiles also raised uncomfortable questions about the logic of extended deterrence. By the mid-1960s, few officials in Paris or Bonn expected the American government to defend Western Europe as if it were its own territory. Because of the threat of Soviet retaliation, Washington would not "risk New York to save Paris."[26]

The American government's shift from the strategy of massive retaliation to flexible response magnified these fears. The British and French worried that the new approach, which put more emphasis on conventional forces, would reduce the value of their independent nuclear deterrents and place their cities at greater risk. If war did come, flexible response would turn "Europe into both the theater and victim of operations," French intellectual Raymond Aron argued.[27] As American and Soviet interests converged, American and Western European interests drifted apart.

These developments threatened the cohesion of the alliance. If the Western Europeans lost faith in Washington's willingness to defend them in all circumstances, they might take steps to fend for themselves, which in turn would only exacerbate the trans-Atlantic rift.[28] The American decision to redeploy troops from Europe to Vietnam in the latter half of the 1960s seemed to confirm the Western Europeans' fears.[29] Surveying these problems, American columnist Walter Lippmann reached a gloomy conclusion. NATO "is no longer a genuine military investment but an expensive and deteriorating ruin," he wrote. "It is like a mansion, once the pride of the neighborhood, from which the tenants have moved away, for which no new tenants can be found."[30]

Despite their anxieties, the Western Europeans understood that nuclear stability had opened new opportunities. The specter of Soviet armored divisions crashing across their borders began to recede. "NATO is sold as a kind of Noah's Ark, but no one in it expects any rain," American political scientist David Calleo wrote.[31] The allies reasoned that they could now pursue their own interests in ways that previously might have been unwise. "The sense of danger—'the ties of common funk,' as it used to be called—has certainly deserted the Western alliance to a considerable extent," British diplomat Gladwyn Jebb observed in 1966. By making Washington's allies less essential to American security, he noted, nuclear stalemate gave them "more freedom of action."[32]

This new freedom took several forms. Some of the allies began to criticize American hegemony in Europe. They argued that Washington exercised too much control over common policy and enjoyed so much influence that it threatened to erase an independent Western European identity. To restore the trans-Atlantic balance, they demanded a greater voice in NATO councils.[33] Others hoped that Western European integration would bolster their international clout. They wanted the European Communities, which had integrated their members' economies so successfully, to coordinate foreign policy as well. By speaking with a single voice in international affairs, the Western Europeans might exert greater control over their common destiny and counterbalance American preeminence within NATO. Perhaps they could even transform themselves into a new great power to rival the United States and the USSR. In the early postwar period, the Atlantic idea and the European idea had worked in harmony. Now, in some respects, they stood in tension.[34]

France posed the greatest threat to the Atlantic idea. In 1958, Charles de Gaulle argued that NATO "no longer corresponds to the necessary conditions of security as far as the whole of the free world is concerned." He proposed that the United States, Britain, and France establish a triumvirate to "take joint decisions on political questions affecting world security" and "put into effect strategic plans of action, notably with regard to the employment of nuclear weapons."[35] He wanted to revive French influence within the Western alliance—and international affairs more broadly—even if it meant antagonizing the United States.

When the other powers rejected the scheme, de Gaulle began to pull France out of the alliance's military command, starting with the country's Mediterranean fleet. In January 1963, he vetoed Britain's application to join the European Economic Community (EEC), rejected American plans for a multilateral nuclear force, and signed a treaty with West Germany that provided for close political and military cooperation between the two countries. The three decisions, which provoked an uproar, converged on the same goal: to reduce the influence of the United States (and Britain, which de Gaulle regarded as an American proxy) and build up Western Europe as an independent center of power, in which France would play a dominant role.[36]

Three years later, de Gaulle withdrew French forces entirely from NATO's command and evicted American and Canadian troops from French soil. France had "to determine its own direction," he told a press conference. It could not do so within "a defense organization in which it finds itself subordinate."[37] Having reclaimed its freedom of action, the country would now work to reconcile East and West and position itself as the privileged interlocutor of both superpowers, as de Gaulle's June 1966 visit to Moscow illustrated. In this view, NATO was not merely a relic but an obstacle to solving the problems of the Cold War.[38]

These moves angered France's allies. In 1963, President Kennedy speculated that de Gaulle might try to strike "a deal with the Russians, break up NATO, and push the US out of Europe."[39] Belgian foreign minister Paul-Henri Spaak called de Gaulle's policy "an attack on the Atlantic Alliance and the European Community."[40] The removal of French forces from the integrated command made life easier in certain respects, not least by eliminating the obstructionism that had bedeviled allied military planners for so long. Yet it also posed new problems for defending Western Europe and struck at the heart of NATO's raison d'être.[41] "Either war takes place in Europe and we're destroyed, or it's an exchange involving massive retaliation, and that's a matter for America and the Soviet Union," de Gaulle said. "So what's the alliance for?"[42]

By challenging American leadership and suggesting that the Western Europeans had to take responsibility for their own interests, the French president attacked the alliance's legitimacy.[43] Still, the United States responded with restraint, both to demonstrate its respect for French sovereignty and to avoid giving credence to de Gaulle's accusations of American domination. Instead of allowing France to weaken the alliance, the United States would work to "bind the Atlantic nations closer together," President Lyndon Johnson decided.[44]

Since its inception, NATO had operated according to more or less egalitarian principles. The United States encouraged European integration and the development of independent bases of power on the continent.[45] It exercised self-restraint and showed itself willing to compromise. When the Western Europeans challenged America's original strategic blueprint for NATO, or when Danes and Norwegians refused to allow foreign military bases or nuclear weapons on their territory, the Americans accepted their reservations as the price of allied unity. This "open hegemony" persuaded the Western Europeans that they, too, could benefit from an American-led order.[46]

The alliance respected dissenting points of view and welcomed ideas from all corners, in much the same way that its members' domestic political systems encouraged debate and negotiation as routine features of doing business in a liberal democracy.[47] To be sure, the United States claimed special prerogatives, especially in nuclear matters, and it sometimes imposed its will when its allies' actions threatened core interests, as in the Suez crisis. For their part, the allies occasionally objected that the United States only informed them of decisions that had already been made instead of engaging in genuine consultations. But American coercion was the exception.

After Suez, the allies had renewed their commitment to robust political cooperation, but the travails of the 1960s suggested that these principles were fraying.[48]

The roots of the crisis ran deeper than the challenge from France. "The conditions that originally inspired the alliance—a menacing Russia, an invulnerable America, a helpless Europe—have been overtaken by events," Ronald Steel concluded in 1967. "Having achieved so much of what it initially set out to do, NATO is in danger of foundering now that its virtues no longer seem so necessary. In this sense it has become the victim of its own success."[49] Western Europe now seemed to be secure from Soviet attack, but this newfound safety—and the nuclear balance on which it rested—gave the allies good reason to carve out greater roles for themselves. Moreover, by the mid-1960s the Western Europeans had recovered their economic strength and could now act in ways that had been inconceivable when the North Atlantic Treaty was signed in 1949. As NATO's twentieth anniversary loomed—the earliest date at which an ally could quit the alliance—there were good reasons to think that the system that had worked well for so long might be coming apart.

III

To the east, fault lines also opened in the Warsaw Pact. De-Stalinization raised awkward questions about ideological orthodoxy and sowed doubt about Soviet leadership in the international communist movement. Several Eastern European leaders came to resent the Kremlin's willingness to sacrifice their interests in pursuit of its own. Despite the power imbalance within the Warsaw Pact, they made their views heard and sought to exert greater influence on Soviet foreign policy. Meanwhile, at home, they appealed to nationalist sentiments to shore up their own legitimacy. By pushing back against Soviet supremacy, they threatened the underlying rules of the Soviet international order.

The Eastern Europeans challenged Moscow's power in a variety of ways. During the Berlin crisis, the East German government pursued its own goals over Soviet objections. Although Khrushchev had precipitated the standoff, he asked German Democratic Republic (GDR) leader Walter Ulbricht to act cautiously and follow his lead. Ulbricht refused. He resolved to follow East German priorities—especially its desire for international recognition—regardless of Khrushchev's preferences. He therefore demanded that the USSR provide the political and economic assistance that the GDR deserved and called for a tougher attitude toward the West. By any military or economic measure, East Germany hardly had the stature to issue orders to Moscow. But in light of the country's existing economic problems, the Soviets feared that a westward exodus of East German citizens might precipitate the collapse of communist rule and discredit the principles governing the whole Soviet bloc. For this reason, Ulbricht knew, Khrushchev had little choice but to support him. The East German leader turned weakness into strength.[50]

The Poles also concluded that they had to stand up for their own interests. In their view, the Warsaw Pact's military structures violated the "independence and sovereignty" of the Eastern Europeans but preserved total freedom of action for the USSR.[51] In the late 1950s, therefore, they proposed to reduce the power of the alliance's supreme commander and suggested that the position rotate among the allies instead of going to a Soviet officer by default. They also called for a new military front under Polish leadership and demanded that Soviet troops in Poland be made subject to Polish law.[52] The incumbent supreme commander, Soviet marshal Ivan Konev, ridiculed the egalitarian assumptions inherent in these ideas. "What do you imagine? That we would make some kind of NATO here?" he asked.[53] Although the Soviets made a few concessions, they still expected the countries under their protection to defer to their judgment.[54]

Khrushchev's risk-taking also prompted Polish leaders to act. They worried that Polish security would suffer if the Soviet leader reached an agreement with Bonn about the status of Germany without demanding West German recognition of Poland's western border. Worse, the prospect that Moscow might acquiesce in NATO's creation of a multilateral nuclear force, which could put nuclear weapons in West German hands, horrified Władysław Gomułka. He grew obsessed with preventing a nuclearized *Bundeswehr*.[55]

On its own initiative, the Polish government proposed in 1963 to freeze nuclear arsenals in central Europe. In meetings with Warsaw Pact leaders, Gomułka tried to steer Soviet policy in a more favorable direction.[56] "It is clear that both Poland as a country and our party are not the main creative force for the foreign policy of the socialist camp, and it is unthinkable that when we do have reservations to the policy of the Soviet Union, we would express them openly ... because the enemy would immediately detect it and exploit it," Gomułka told the Polish Central Committee the following year. Nonetheless, on subjects "in which our party, our government, our country, [are] deeply and directly interested, we demand, have the right to demand, and always will demand that these matters be discussed with us and approved."[57] Communist rule had erased neither Polish nationalism nor the country's long history of anti-Russian sentiment. Gomułka understood that challenging Soviet dictates and defending Polish interests would burnish his nationalist credentials, raise his personal standing, and shore up popular support for the communist party.[58]

The Romanians pushed this logic as far as it could go without provoking a violent response from Moscow. Gheorghe Gheorghiu-Dej and his successor, Nicolae Ceauşescu, chafed at the USSR's attempts to dictate to its allies. Like the Poles, they appealed to nationalist sentiment to strengthen their own grip on power. In 1962, the Soviets proposed a "socialist division of labor" in Eastern Europe, which would let the most advanced countries concentrate on manufacturing, consign the others to agriculture and natural resource extraction, and thereby reap the advantages of specialization. The East Germans and Czechoslovaks endorsed the plan because it guaranteed export markets for their industrial equipment. The Romanians rebelled. "Why should we send our corn to Poland? So Poland can fatten its pigs and buy machinery from the West?" Romanian premier Ion Maurer asked. "We can sell the corn directly and buy the machinery we need ourselves."[59]

Gheorghiu-Dej feared that the USSR's economic scheme would condemn Romania to economic oblivion. In his vision, socialism and industrialism went hand in hand. If Romania focused on agriculture, it would remain dependent on its neighbors. He therefore insisted that all economic cooperation be conducted on the basis of full respect for states' sovereign equality, which would allow Romania to pursue its own policies and develop its economy as it saw fit. Instead of cooperating with its socialist neighbors, it expanded its commercial ties with the capitalist world. The episode provoked a crisis between Bucharest and Moscow that dragged on for years.[60]

The challenge from Bucharest went well beyond economics. Like de Gaulle, Gheorghiu-Dej and Ceauşescu concluded that their country's interests often stood at odds with those of its superpower patron. They evicted the KGB officers who advised the Romanian security services and launched a campaign to root out "Soviet agent networks."[61] Foreign minister Corneliu Mănescu told American secretary of state Dean Rusk that Romania would abandon the USSR and remain neutral in the event of another nuclear standoff.[62]

In 1964, Romanian leaders articulated the new doctrine of "national communism." No matter what the Soviets wanted, Romania would pursue its own interests. "It is up to every Marxist-Leninist party, it is a sovereign right of each socialist state, to elaborate, choose or change the forms and methods of socialist construction," the Romanian communist party declared. "There does not and cannot exist a 'parent' party and a 'son-party,' parties that are 'superior' and parties that are 'subordinate,' but there exists the great family of communist and workers' parties, which have equal rights."[63] These assertions amounted to a declaration of independence from Soviet suzerainty and implied that Romania's superpower patron posed as great a threat to its sovereignty as did the capitalist states. Romania would remain a member of the Warsaw Pact, but it would make its own decisions on foreign and domestic policy, even when doing so put it at odds with its allies.[64]

This pattern of defiance culminated at the January 1965 gathering of Warsaw Pact leaders. Khrushchev's Politburo colleagues had deposed him three months prior, but the change of leadership did little to placate the allies who demanded more influence and more respect from Moscow. The meeting of the Political Consultative Committee (PCC) quickly turned contentious. For the first time in years, the leaders engaged in a real debate. The Poles criticized the Soviets for not consulting them on major decisions. The East Germans proposed a new council of foreign ministers, which would meet regularly and give the allies more input. The Romanians accused Moscow of violating their sovereignty by pursuing a nuclear nonproliferation treaty with the West. The conversation also revealed deep disagreements about the function of the Warsaw Pact. Gomułka and Ulbricht regarded the alliance as a vehicle for exerting control over Soviet policy and therefore wanted to strengthen its institutions, while Gheorghiu-Dej believed that Romanian freedom of action required a weaker alliance.[65]

The dispute put the new Soviet leaders in a quandary. How could they reassert Moscow's preeminent role in the bloc without provoking an even greater backlash? How could they reunify the alliance without imposing their will? At a PCC meeting the following year, one of Soviet foreign minister Andrei Gromyko's aides summed up the problem. "It used to be very easy: the [USSR] proposed something, and the other socialist countries adopted it without discussions," he noted. "Now it is no longer that simple. Every [country] has its own opinions."[66]

The USSR's most powerful ally also rebelled against its leadership. Since the birth of the Sino-Soviet alliance in 1950, numerous irritants—some with deep historical roots, others of more recent vintage—had complicated relations between Moscow and Beijing. During the Korean War, the Chinese relied on Soviet money and weapons, but Mao Zedong thought that the Soviets should have been even more generous. He resented their demands for payment, and concluded that Stalin put Soviet interests ahead of proletarian internationalism.[67] In 1956, when Khrushchev denounced his predecessor, he indirectly threatened Mao himself, who had modeled many of his policies on those of the late Soviet leader. Mao's indifference to the danger of nuclear war alarmed Khrushchev, who reneged on an earlier promise to supply Beijing with an atomic bomb.[68] At the end of the decade, when clashes broke out along the Sino-Indian frontier, Khrushchev outraged the Chinese by steering a middle course between the belligerents instead of supporting his ostensible allies.[69]

The rift threatened both the USSR's security and its stature in the communist world. In 1964, Mao complained about the history of Russian expansion at China's expense, implying that he might seek to reclaim parts of

Siberia by force. Khrushchev responded by likening the great helmsman to Adolf Hitler. The Red Army redeployed troops to the border between the two countries. Instead of guaranteeing Soviet security in East Asia, relations with China now endangered it.[70]

Some of Moscow's European allies drew inspiration from Beijing's example. By cultivating ties to China, Romania tried to exploit the Sino-Soviet split for its advantage. At the January 1965 PCC meeting, Gheorghiu-Dej repeated China's arguments against nuclear nonproliferation, hoping to demonstrate his independence from Moscow, earn Mao's gratitude, and gain more room for maneuver by playing one power against the other. The other leaders savaged this approach, but Ceaușescu continued it once he took power.[71] The Albanians sided even more firmly with the Chinese. Enver Hoxha embraced Maoism, criticized Soviet revisionism, and forced the USSR out of its naval base on the Adriatic. Moscow tried to whip its smallest ally back into line. It cut off economic aid, withdrew its advisors, and banished the Albanians from Warsaw Pact meetings. They refused to change course.[72]

In Western Europe, the Italian Communist Party (PCI) responded to the Sino-Soviet split (and the fracturing of the Western alliance) by embracing "polycentrism." Leader Palmiro Togliatti defended the autonomy of each national party and argued that communists had to adapt their ideology to suit local conditions. Shortly before he died in 1964, he criticized Moscow's policy toward China. He also called on Soviet bloc leaders to acknowledge their countries' problems and debate them in the open, and to end restrictions on citizens' personal freedoms. If communists wanted to exploit the growing crisis of the Western alliance, they had to change the way they operated, Togliatti insisted. Moscow had to stop acting as the sole guardian of communist orthodoxy.[73]

To be sure, polycentrism and nationalism had their limits. The Chinese might dispute Moscow's interpretation of Marxism-Leninism and precipitate a military confrontation, but the Eastern Europeans could not go that far. As the Hungarian Revolution and Prague Spring demonstrated, Moscow could react violently if an ally abandoned the Warsaw Pact or violated the precepts of communist governance. Still, the Eastern Europeans could contest Soviet foreign policy, push back when Moscow's interests clashed with their own, and seek their own paths to communism. The Romanians, for instance, refused to participate in the invasion of Czechoslovakia. Ceaușescu worried that if Moscow could violate Czechoslovak sovereignty with impunity, Romania might well be next. But rather than making him more pliable, this threat strengthened his resolve to pursue an independent foreign policy. The USSR's decisive action in 1968 preserved orthodoxy in Prague but widened the Warsaw Pact's fault lines.[74]

Soviet leaders faced a dilemma as they surveyed their fractured alliances. In the late 1940s, the rift with Yugoslavia had not threatened the USSR's preeminence or endangered its security. The challenges of the 1960s posed a more serious problem. Bowing to centrifugal pressures would undermine the hierarchical principles on which the Soviet international order had been built. But reasserting Soviet leadership might provoke a further backlash and make matters worse.[75] "Communism has now come to embrace so wide a spectrum of requirements and compulsions on the part of the respective parties and régimes that any determined attempt to re-impose unity on the movement would merely cause it to break violently apart at one point or another," American diplomat George Kennan wrote in 1964.[76] The Soviets somehow had to rebuild that unity with the support of their allies, not in defiance of them. To preserve the Soviet order, they had to change it.

IV

As the crises of the two alliances unfolded, new domestic problems afflicted leaders on both sides of the Atlantic. Ordinary people grew weary of the burdens that the Cold War had imposed for so long, and old certainties about their relationship with the state lost their power. In earlier decades, citizens had been expected to serve the state and make sacrifices for the greater good. In the 1960s, they increasingly expected the state to serve them. Practices that had previously been tolerated now elicited fierce criticism, and governments that had previously enjoyed popular support now attracted scorn.

After the end of the Second World War, most Western European governments poured unprecedented resources into new domestic programs. They aimed to educate their citizens, prevent economic distress, and provide quality medical care, all at public expense. Two developments enabled this boom in state spending. First, rapid economic growth yielded higher tax revenues. Second, the American security guarantee allowed Western Europeans to shrink the warfare state and expand the welfare state. As a share of national budgets, military spending fell and social spending rose. As new social programs blossomed, support for defense spending withered.

Social attitudes changed too. Citizens lost their earlier reverence for martial virtues. A career as an officer no longer carried the social cachet that it had fifty years before. Conscription persisted but many governments increased deferments, relaxed discipline, and allowed young men to do their mandatory service in schools and hospitals instead of barracks and parade grounds. For generations, the military had occupied a privileged place in public life—but no more.[77]

When fears of communist aggression stood at their apex in the 1950s, Western governments could justify military spending as a matter of national survival. As the danger of war receded, however, these arguments lost their force. Besides, the Sino-Soviet split dispelled the illusion of a globe-spanning communist monolith. Western citizens worried less about a hypothetical Soviet invasion and more about the realities of poverty, crime, disease, and pollution.[78] American leaders criticized the allies' "lack of zeal for defense" and lobbied them to increase their spending, but with little success.[79] If one ally cut back, they worried, others might follow suit.[80]

Similar budgetary pressures complicated American politics. Some commentators warned of resurgent isolationism in the United States.[81] "The serious nature of the problem we face in maintaining support for NATO must be conveyed to the allies," President Johnson told the National Security Council in 1966. "They must understand that the demands on us to meet home front needs are serious. . . . Expenditures for the poor in the U.S. have increased tremendously since the Kennedy administration. We are now very near a debt limit."[82] The following year, facing calls to maintain social spending in the teeth of a recession, West Germany cut its defense budget by more than 10 percent. In response, US Senate majority leader Mike Mansfield renewed his popular proposal to reduce the American troop presence in Europe.[83] As politicians and citizens turned inward, they weakened the political and military foundations of the Western order.

The popular backlash against the Vietnam War accelerated these trends. Antiwar protestors connected the injustice of the violence in Indochina to the ongoing problems in Western society. They demanded radical change. "We are convinced that the only way to stop this and future wars is to organize a domestic social movement which challenges the very legitimacy of our foreign policy," declared the left-wing American group Students for a Democratic Society in 1965. "[T]his movement must also fight to end racism, to end the paternalism of our welfare system, to guarantee decent incomes for all, and to supplant the authoritarian control of our universities with a community of scholars."[84] By 1968, growing numbers of citizens believed that the war had become unwinnable.[85] As part of the broader reaction against the status quo, protestors denounced military practices that had not previously attracted criticism. Napalm, for instance, had received little public scrutiny during the Korean War, when American forces used it extensively. In Vietnam, thanks to more intense press coverage and photographs depicting its effects on soldiers and civilians alike, it became a focal point for public outrage.[86]

Antiwar sentiment gripped Western Europe, too. In London, street demonstrations attracted tens of thousands of people in 1967 and 1968. Some turned violent.[87] In West Germany, protestors likened the American war effort to the Holocaust and exhorted their fellow citizens to "take up the struggle against the oppressors in our own country."[88] In the Netherlands, demonstrators denounced Lyndon Johnson as a war criminal and murderer.[89] Young people in Denmark had grown so disillusioned with the Cold War status quo that politicians began contemplating a referendum on withdrawing from NATO.[90]

Outrage at the war undermined support for the whole liberal democratic order. "There has been a spectacular decline in respect for United States foreign policy," Walter Lippmann reported in 1965.[91] Nearly two-thirds of French citizens said they had lost "confidence in the wisdom of US leadership."[92] Philosopher Herbert Marcuse wrote that he saw "in America today the historic heir to fascism."[93] Protestors denounced the mainstream political parties and called for both the revival of genuine democracy and "the immediate overthrow of social structures," West German philosopher Jürgen Habermas said in 1967.[94] Back in Washington, the Johnson administration worried that the Western Europeans' loss of confidence would spill over into the United States. "We are fast approaching a day of reckoning," the president told the National Security Council.[95]

The antiwar movement drew strength from the broader revolt of young people against institutions and tradition. As they came of age in the 1960s, the generation born after the Second World War questioned the domestic and international structures that their parents and grandparents had built. In previous generations, social fault lines had separated the educated from the uneducated. Now, as universities expanded to accommodate unprecedented numbers of students from a wide range of backgrounds, a new cleavage opened up, dividing the young from their elders, whose political commitments they mistrusted.[96] To the rising generation, the traditional concerns of the left and right seemed like vestiges of a bygone age, sociologist Daniel Bell argued. "[T]he old passions are spent" and the old ideologies "exhausted," he wrote. "The young intellectual is unhappy because the 'middle way' is for the middle-aged, not for him; it is without passion and is deadening."[97]

Student activists rejected the legitimacy of the political system, but they disagreed about what should replace it. "The once-solid core of American life—the cement of loyalty that people tender to institutions, certifying that the current order is going to last and deserves to—this loyalty, in select sectors, was decomposing," recalled former activist Todd Gitlin. "[T]he bureaucrats and generals and fathers had rested their legitimacy on a single 'American way,' so that when the rationales of the Pentagon and the University of California could no longer be taken for granted, the habit of doubt and defiance threatened to unravel the whole fabric."[98] Young Western Europeans, who had no memory of World War II, followed the same trajectory. They questioned "the conventional wisdom of the previous generation, embodied in such phrases as 'Atlantic community,' 'the iron curtain,' 'the containment of Germany,'" wrote Alastair Buchan. The geopolitical realities underpinning these concepts had not changed, but the rising tide of skepticism and rebellion meant that Western European politicians "will no longer be able to take popular acceptance of such concepts for granted."[99]

The violence that afflicted many Western countries in 1968 demonstrated the power of this rebellion. After the riots and demonstrations in Washington, West Berlin, and Paris, some observers concluded that the status quo's defenders and antagonists could no longer communicate. The rising generation started from different assumptions than did their parents and grandparents, and they used different language. Neither side understood the other.[100] The protestors demanded "a perpetual change of society, produced by revolutionary actions at each stage," French student leader Daniel Cohn-Bendit declared in 1968. He refused to play by the rules of mainstream politics or articulate a set of objectives. "[W]e must avoid building an organization immediately, or defining a program; that would inevitably paralyze us," he said. The goal was revolution itself.[101]

Statesmen wondered how to contain the "international sickness" that had infected their citizens, as West German chancellor Kurt Georg Kiesinger put it.[102] The sickness ran deeper than the outbursts in the streets, however. Restoring calm to the Latin Quarter or Charlottenburg would not cure it. Because the protestors attacked the legitimacy of liberal democracy itself, the arguments of liberal democratic politicians would not soothe them. Besides, when the authorities used force to clear the streets, they seemed to corroborate the rebels' arguments about the inherent violence of the established order.[103]

The events of 1968 produced few immediate political changes. In several countries, the images of young people attacking police and of rioters burning buildings provoked a backlash. Conservatives won large victories in the 1968 and 1969 presidential elections in the United States and France, for example. But after the students returned to their classrooms and the workers to their factories, the popular feelings of anxiety and uncertainty persisted, as did the sense that established political structures could not cope with the challenges of modern society. Citizens had lost faith in government, and their leaders had lost the ability "to articulate national goals [or] to develop a sense of national direction," American political scientist Zbigniew Brzezinski argued.[104] The bonds that held the Western alliance together had already weakened. Now the ties that held each Western society together were fraying too.[105]

V

Rifts opened up within communist societies as well. In 1956, Nikita Khrushchev's enumeration of Stalin's crimes exhilarated citizens across the Soviet bloc. For the first time, people could speak frankly about the realities of life in communist society. "Everybody is arguing—and moreover, absolutely everyone is beginning to think," one student said.[106] Khrushchev's honesty created a hunger for intellectual and artistic freedom. Soviet citizens began the painful process of coming to terms with their Stalinist past.[107]

Instead of reinvigorating the regime's popular legitimacy, this new openness undermined it. Khrushchev personally approved the publication of Aleksandr Solzhenitsyn's unsparing account of the gulag, *One Day in the Life of Ivan Denisovich*. The work electrified its readers. "Everything, everything, and everything, what and how you describe in your novella—everything, everything is authentic, everything is truthful to the utmost and is also rendered in a simple, human way," a former camp prisoner wrote to the author.[108] Ilya Ehrenburg's memoir *People, Years, Life* made a similar impression. Its portraits of long-suppressed writers and painters introduced readers to an unknown world of literature and art and set off heated arguments about guilt and complicity during the purges. "Your book is great and thrilling," wrote one of Ehrenburg's young readers. "It offers much to those of my age and to me, who have received a one-sided education, because it opens our eyes."[109]

Soviet leaders had long staked their claim to rule, in part, on tradition. As Lenin's heirs, they were the custodians of the revolution. The Communist Party had modernized the country, built a new socioeconomic system, and transformed the Soviet Union into a superpower. For the regime's defenders, this triumphant record secured its legitimacy. Khrushchev's Thaw threatened this principle by raising questions about the justice of Stalin's policies—and, by extension, about the policies of Stalin's heirs. It cast shadows over the whole Soviet record since 1917. "Can we still use the works of Stalin, and will they still be published?" one party member asked. "If Stalin created a dictatorship and many comrades died as a result of it, then how do we, as communists, explain this to non-party members?" asked another.[110] By shattering the party's claim to ideological infallibility, Khrushchev also endangered its claim to rule. If Soviet leaders had erred so egregiously during the terror, they could easily err again. If Stalin had been wrong, his successors might be wrong too.[111]

The tensions inherent in de-Stalinization pulled Khrushchev in opposite directions. He wanted to repudiate the Stalinist legacy and to lay claim to the tradition of communist rule. He wanted to encourage greater openness and to maintain the party's control over society. He wanted to reform the system and to preserve its essential characteristics. These contradictions provoked disagreements over ideological orthodoxy and communist unity across the Soviet bloc, inspiring political turmoil in Poland and revolution in Hungary. Khrushchev's violent response to these events suggested that a double standard applied within the Soviet bloc, with one set of rules for the USSR and another for its allies.[112] At home, Khrushchev zigzagged between repression and toleration. After endorsing such works as *Ivan Denisovich* and Aleksandr Tvardovsky's satirical poem "Tyorkin in the Other World," he suddenly cracked down, fulminating against leading Soviet writers and artists in off-the-cuff harangues. These moves bewildered hardliners and reformers alike. They muddied the Kremlin's position rather than clarifying it and damaged the legitimacy that Khrushchev hoped to rebuild.[113]

The Sino-Soviet split caused its own set of ideological problems. In Mao's view, Khrushchev had committed heresy. "The so-called de-Stalinization thus is simply de-Marxification, it is revisionism," Mao said.[114] He rejected the Thaw—and its implied criticism of the People's Republic of China's ideological foundations—as an act of "great power chauvinism."[115] The Chinese also denounced Moscow's commitment to "peaceful coexistence" with the West as a betrayal of the anticapitalist struggle.[116] By claiming Lenin and Stalin's mantle, Mao attempted to establish himself as the communist world's ideological arbiter and fount of orthodoxy.[117]

Conversely, Khrushchev criticized Mao for misunderstanding Marxism-Leninism and forsaking communist solidarity. This "Buddha who gets his theory out of his nose" ignored "any interests other than his own," Khrushchev said.[118] Nonetheless, he believed that China and the USSR still had to collaborate in the struggle against capitalism. No substantive differences divided Moscow and Beijing, he insisted, but Mao refused to reconcile.[119] "When I look at Mao Zedong," Khrushchev told the Central Committee in 1960, "I just see Stalin, an exact copy."[120]

The Thaw ended when Leonid Brezhnev ousted Khrushchev in 1964, but the quarrel with Beijing festered. Despite some attempts to find common ground, Brezhnev concluded that the Chinese had become ideological adversaries. The Chinese Communist Party was "moving further away from the principles of scientific socialism," he told a Central Committee plenum in 1966. Its ideology "has nothing to do with Marxism-Leninism, with proletarian internationalism," he said. By embracing "great power nationalist views," Mao had become "anti-Leninist."[121]

The consequences of Moscow and Beijing's falling out stretched beyond geopolitics. If all workers shared the same interests and stood on the same side of history, the two leading proletarian states ought to collaborate. If Marxism-Leninism offered scientific insight into politics and economics, the two most powerful communist states ought to agree on its basic precepts. The Sino-Soviet rift therefore damaged the ideological underpinnings of the Soviet international order. By extension, it damaged the legitimacy of the order itself.[122]

While the Soviets grappled with Beijing's hard line, they faced a different set of ideological challenges in Eastern Europe. Hungary's "goulash communism" loosened the state's control over society, allowed greater intellectual and cultural diversity, and tried to modernize the economy, all in an effort to win popular acceptance for the regime.[123] The Romanians welcomed capital investment from the West. Yugoslavia decentralized economic decision-making and introduced some elements of private enterprise under the rubric of "market socialism."[124] The Italian Communist Party pondered the benefits of cooperating with other parties in a Popular Front. From the Soviet perspective, these approaches blurred the line between pragmatism and ideological incoherence. "Heresy is now everywhere, which means that there is no longer any orthodoxy," one observer wrote in 1966.[125]

Brezhnev and his colleagues tried to rebuild communist unity while attacking their ideological opponents. The Soviet press continued to propound orthodox Marxism-Leninism and emphasized the Soviet Communist Party's role as its chief interpreter. Precisely because capitalists hoped that communist unity would splinter, defending "the purity of Marxism-Leninsm" had taken on special urgency, theoretician Fedor Konstantinov wrote in *Pravda*. He lashed out at left-wing and right-wing extremists within the communist movement, denouncing both Maoism, which was "a malicious parody of Marxism and a gross distortion of it," and the "non-Leninist interpretation of Marxism ... [that has] become the vogue among present-day revisionists." In this context, all true communists had a duty to resist "those who advocate opportunism instead of revolutionary principles" and who prefer a "mishmash of scraps and borrowings from bourgeois theories instead of clarity and definitiveness."[126] These attempts to re-establish doctrinal harmony floundered. An international gathering of communist parties in Moscow, for example, had to be postponed repeatedly. When it finally convened in May 1969, many countries stayed away, while some of those who did attend dissented openly from the Soviet line—hardly the demonstration of proletarian solidarity that the Kremlin had hoped for.[127]

Meanwhile, falling tensions with the West complicated the logic of Soviet foreign policy. The USSR had long justified its military presence in Eastern Europe and leading role in the Warsaw Pact on the grounds that American imperialism and West German revanchism threatened the security of the communist bloc.[128] This argument lost credibility as the 1960s wore on, particularly after the United States signed the nuclear test ban and nonproliferation treaties and the West German chancellor began calling for closer relations across the Iron Curtain.[129]

Soviet theoreticians grappled awkwardly with these developments. Now that the Kremlin had recognized that the Soviet Union and United States had common interests—not least in avoiding nuclear war—it could no longer insist on the old hierarchical model for organizing the socialist bloc, nor could it argue that conflict between the two social systems was inevitable. By removing the primary justification for keeping the Red Army in Eastern Europe, the Kremlin also encouraged the revival of nationalist sentiment, which usually manifested itself as resentment of Soviet highhand-edness. For Eastern European leaders, nationalism provided a welcome tool for rallying popular support. Soviet leaders still fulminated about imperialism, but they needed new ways to legitimize their power in the region.[130]

By holding fast to orthodoxy, Soviet ideology lost its vitality. The responsibility for new ideological pronouncements lay with career party officials, who operated by committee and preferred consensus to innovation. The process rewarded conformism and stifled intellectual creativity. One observer noted that the USSR had not produced a first-rate Marxist philosopher since the revolution, while innovative thinkers in Eastern Europe, such as György Lukács and Leszek Kołakowski, were marginalized or purged. Soviet theoreticians strained to answer basic questions about their country's difficulties. Why, for instance, had the socialist economies not yet overtaken those of the West? If socialism was supposed to foster greater intellectual creativity, why did Western technology still lead the world? Rather than tackling these problems, the party repeated familiar slogans. Its rhetoric remained revolutionary, but its substance turned conservative. The old messianic claims might still have inspired the Marxist-Leninist true believers, but they bored average citizens. In this context, the party found it all the more difficult to justify its monopoly on power or persuade anyone that it had a monopoly on the truth.[131]

Many intellectuals lost faith in the system. In the early years of the Thaw, some hoped to return to a purer version of Marxism-Leninism, free from the taint of Stalinism. The party might have harnessed their idealism, but Khrushchev's anti-intellectual crackdowns persuaded many of them that the system was irredeemable. "No more illusions and dreams of a better future. We are governed by the enemies of culture," novelist Boris Strugatsky said.[132]

By the mid-1960s, a small number began to challenge the authorities in public. They acted on the assumption that communism's rhetoric was sincere and demanded that the regime follow its own laws. In December 1965, following the arrest of writers Andrei Sinyavsky and Yuli Daniel, a group of 200 protesters gathered in central Moscow. They brandished signs urging the government to "Respect the Soviet Constitution," which explicitly protected free expression and free assembly. When KGB officers broke up the gathering, they drew international attention to the yawning gulf between the official commitment to individual freedom and the everyday reality of state control.[133] This pattern repeated itself in Poland, where reform-minded communists demanded that the party live up to its own emancipatory principles. They wanted to improve the system, not destroy it, but the police arrested them anyway.[134]

Students likewise grew disillusioned with the official ideology and culture. Their search for novel forms of self-expression found an outlet in literature. Young people formed new literary groups, often under official auspices. Budding poets rejected traditional socialist virtues by describing themselves as individualists. Literary discussions often took on political overtones. When a professor tried to impose order on an unruly session at Moscow State University, the students in the lecture hall screamed, "You are suppressing us, we have a right to state our position."[135]

Young writers and artists had a way of finding one another—and they found sympathetic audiences as well. The most notable group met in Moscow's Mayakovsky Square, where poets read transgressive works to hundreds of listeners who crowded around the statue of avant-garde writer Vladimir Mayakovsky. "Today I don't believe anything," declared one poem of this era. "Everything is propaganda. The whole world is propaganda." At first, the authorities tolerated the meetings. Eventually, however, they lost patience, banned them, and steered participants back toward state-sanctioned (and monitored) groups.[136] Yet the problem persisted. Like the United States, the USSR faced "an internal problem of a skeptical generation of young intellectuals" who questioned old assumptions about domestic politics and international affairs, an American political scientist wrote in 1967. For them, the familiar arguments about the superiority of socialism and menace of capitalism "appear[ed] to be troublesome legacies rather than pertinent aspects of the present."[137]

The patterns repeated themselves in Eastern Europe. In Poland, the banning of a play and expulsion of two students from Warsaw University sparked nationwide protests involving tens of thousands of people. The demonstrators presented an impeccably Marxist critique of the regime and demanded the abolition of censorship and respect for the freedoms guaranteed by the Polish constitution.[138] "We believed ourselves to be Communists," one of the student leaders, Adam Michnik, declared the following year. "We believed that the duty of a Communist is to combat every evil, every instance of lawlessness, every wrong and injustice he encounters in his country."[139] The government responded with force, arresting tens of thousands of people and purging the universities of nonconformists. In search of a scapegoat, the authorities launched an anti-Semitic propaganda campaign, which prompted most of Poland's tiny Jewish population to flee the country.[140]

East German intellectuals accused their government of betraying its own principles. Chemist Robert Havemann argued that the GDR's official ideology was "neither dialectic nor materialistic." So long as the state suppressed public debate, communism would remain elusive. Writer Stefan Heym echoed these complaints. In his view, the governments of Eastern Europe stifled honest criticism. "It was as if you wanted to take a photograph and someone held a threateningly raised finger directly before the lens of your camera," he wrote in 1966. "[Y]ou must tell him to take his finger away if you want a picture instead of a shadow."[141]

In Czechoslovakia, students and intellectuals publicly demanded freedom of expression and respect for "real public opinion."[142] Party leader Alexander Dubček stood with the reformers. His government abolished censorship and liberalized the economy even as it vowed to continue fighting "the forces of imperialist reaction."[143] Like the activists in Poland, Dubček remained a sincere communist. He hoped that the Prague Spring would revive the party's popular support and enable it to rule by consent rather than coercion.[144] The reforms failed to satisfy a number of prominent intellectuals, who insisted that the party remained mired in outmoded ideas. The party had long since squandered whatever goodwill it once enjoyed, declared writer Ludvík Vaculík, whose manifesto "Two Thousand Words" became the most prominent document of the Prague Spring. Vaculík remained sympathetic to Marxism, but advocated replacing monopoly rule with democratic pluralism.[145]

As they observed these events with growing alarm, Soviet leaders feared for the stability not just of Eastern Europe but the USSR itself. They craved popular support, but worried that reform would invite chaos. The members of the Politburo soon concluded that the Prague Spring did not represent a sincere attempt to improve socialism, but a counterrevolutionary coup orchestrated by socialism's enemies. Worse, the contagion threatened to spread to the Soviet Union itself.[146]

Soviet students were especially susceptible to infection. Many of them kept up with the news from Prague and had begun "contemplating the possibility of replicating the Czechoslovak experience in our own country," the KGB reported. Young people were embracing "false slogans about the 'liberalization' of socialism, which are being promoted by counterrevolutionaries."[147] One student wondered whether similar reforms were possible in the USSR. "I would personally participate," he said. The KGB also warned that Soviet youth were now taking their cues—in fashion, music, and sex—from their Western contemporaries. Brezhnev and his colleagues concluded that they had to take dramatic action to rescue Czechoslovak socialism from the forces of imperialism and to protect Soviet society.[148]

When the Red Army invaded Czechoslovakia in August 1968, it trampled whatever communist idealism remained in the Soviet bloc. Those romantics who had hoped to bring the USSR back to its Leninist roots concluded that they could never achieve any such thing. Some joined the dissident movement. Others turned away from politics and retreated into private life.[149] In Eastern Europe, reform-minded party members who had hoped to work within the system and reconcile Marxist values with pluralist, democratic politics concluded that communism could no longer be improved. The only alternative was to overthrow it. Communists in Western Europe broke with Moscow, too.[150] By ousting Dubček, the Soviets set strict limits on ideological experimentation among their allies. But this success came at a terrible price. It permanently alienated those citizens whom the Kremlin most needed to win over. It suggested that the communist world lacked the self-confidence to compete with rival ideas. It fueled nationalist resentment of Soviet influence. It demonstrated conclusively that the Soviet order ultimately rested on the threat of military force, not popular support. And it purchased short-term stability at the price of undermining long-term legitimacy.[151]

VI

These upheavals coincided with growing economic problems in both the East and West. The postwar years had brought unprecedented prosperity to the United States and Western Europe. The industrialized economies grew three times more quickly than they had before the war. In the twenty-five years after 1945, their output tripled. The era's economic openness fostered this growth, as did the new institutions that Western leaders built. The Bretton Woods monetary system, International Monetary Fund, and General Agreement on Tariffs and Trade kept exchange rates stable and encouraged international commerce. These successes vindicated the hopes of wartime planners. The Atlantic Charter, which Franklin D. Roosevelt and Winston Churchill issued in 1941, emphasized that economic openness reinforced political openness, and economic success reinforced political stability.[152] "[P]rosperous neighbors are the best neighbors," one of Bretton Woods's architects, Harry Dexter White, wrote during the war.[153]

The pace of growth in Western Europe and Japan outstripped that in the United States because they had started so much further behind. Access to American technology and capital and a boom in international trade also gave them a powerful boost. Consequently, the gap between the United States and its partners shrank rapidly. Between 1945 and 1960, the American share of the industrialized world's economic output fell from 56 to 43 percent, while Western Europe's rose from 35 to 44 percent and Japan's from 4 to 10 percent.[154] In this prosperous era, economic growth buoyed the legitimacy of every Western government. This dynamic also implied that if growth faltered, that legitimacy would come under threat too.[155]

From the inception of the Western economic order, the United States stood at its center. It safeguarded the monetary stability on which the whole system relied and provided constant demand for its partners' exports. Just as the participants shared common political and security goals, they also assumed that their economic interests were aligned. Rejecting the isolationism of the interwar years, they agreed that common rules and joint action on trade and monetary matters would advance those interests.[156]

In the early postwar years, the Western Europeans and Japanese relied heavily on their American patrons. But as their economies grew, so too did their self-confidence. By the mid-1960s, they no longer stood in the position of supplicants. Now they resolved to deal with the United States—in economic terms, at least—on an equal footing, and they expected the Americans to recognize them as equals. They felt capable of standing up for their interests, even if this sparked conflict with Washington. In turn, Washington came to regard the Western Europeans and Japanese as economic competitors, even if they remained political allies. The era of American economic hegemony had ended.[157]

The Western Europeans' resentment of American influence grew along with their wealth. They feared that US multinationals had established such a commanding position in vital industries—especially computers, chemicals, and automobiles—that their own firms would never be able to compete. Large flows of American capital investment fueled Western European industry but also raised fears about foreign control. If these trends continued, some commentators warned, the region would become "an economic satellite fated to produce American-designed products in American-owned factories on American licenses."[158] The rewards available in technologically intense, cutting-edge fields would all flow to the United States, consigning Europe to dependency. The continent's leaders therefore faced a choice. They could turn Europe into "the home of an autonomous civilization," or they could let "it become an annex of the United States," warned French journalist Jean-Jacques Servan-Schreiber in his 1967 bestseller *The American Challenge*.[159]

Trans-Atlantic economic relations turned stormy. True, the early postwar years had not been entirely placid. In the mid-1960s, however, the EEC grew more assertive as it surpassed the United States as the world's largest trade area. During the Kennedy Round of General Agreement on Tariffs and Trade (GATT) negotiations, when the EEC negotiated on behalf of its members for the first time, it clashed repeatedly with its American counterparts over tariffs and subsidies. The two sides eventually overcame their differences and, together with the British and Japanese, agreed to substantial tariff cuts. Nonetheless, the experience made clear that the interests of Western Europe no longer aligned perfectly with those of the United States.[160] "Today, we are seeing a resurgence of mercantilism, whereby governments meet domestic economic demands with conscious policies of manipulation, passing the costs of these policies as much as possible onto other countries," American trade negotiator Harald Malmgren warned.[161] Politicians across the West felt pressure from their constituents to save domestic firms—and jobs—from foreign competition, and the EEC regarded tariffs as a tool for building cohesion among its members. Although the Kennedy Round succeeded, trans-Atlantic economic friction continued, exacerbating the strains on the Western order.

Bretton Woods also began to show its age. The American commitment to monetary stability went hand in hand with its commitment to Western security. Peace allowed trade to flourish. In turn, economic growth helped to pay the costs of keeping the peace. But the large American military presence in Europe strained the monetary system by skewing Washington's balance of payments. In the mid-1960s, the added costs of President Johnson's Great Society social programs and the Vietnam War made the payments deficit even worse. For years, the American government had financed its international commitments by borrowing, with the result that dollars accumulated in foreign banks. As economist Robert Triffin pointed out, this dynamic made the Bretton Woods system inherently unstable. If foreign dollar balances continued to grow, sooner or later their holders would wonder whether the US government held sufficient reserves to convert them to gold at the official rate of $35 per ounce. If they lost confidence in Fort Knox, foreigners might rush to cash in their dollars before the gold ran out. A bank run along these lines would destroy the international monetary system.[162]

Policymakers on both sides of the Atlantic played for time and tried to keep Bretton Woods working. Central banks agreed to refrain from exchanging their currency holdings for gold, at least temporarily. To prop up the British pound and avert a devaluation that might hurt the dollar in turn, the New York Federal Reserve Bank extended billions in credits to the Bank of England. The British government was forced to devalue anyway. To help the dollar directly, the Western countries agreed to sell gold out of their own reserves, but this gold pool eventually collapsed. A new artificial currency—known as Special Drawing Rights—aimed to relieve the pressure on the dollar, but it failed to yield the anticipated benefits. At home, the Kennedy and Johnson administrations taxed foreign investments, tightened capital controls, and stopped exchanging private dollar holdings for gold.[163]

These measures only addressed the symptoms, not the disease itself. The underlying problem was structural. Politicians worried that voters would regard a currency devaluation as a sign of weakness. They hesitated to raise interest rates or cut spending because doing so might crimp growth rates and raise unemployment, and thereby violate the implicit postwar social contract. Because the system could not force countries that enjoyed trade surpluses to revalue their currencies, Bretton Woods had difficulty adapting to an evolving international economy. It lurched from crisis to crisis.

These monetary crises imposed political costs. French leaders resented the privileges that Bretton Woods bestowed on the United States. Because the dollar had become central banks' de facto reserve currency, Washington controlled liquidity for the whole system. French economist Jacques Rueff criticized the dollar's special status and argued for returning to a pure gold standard, which would put every country on an even footing and prevent the Americans from exporting inflation to Europe. Drawing on Rueff's analysis, de Gaulle threatened to exchange France's large dollar holdings for gold, which could force Washington to devalue.[164]

Monetary troubles also plagued American relations with West Germany. Under pressure from the Kennedy administration, in 1961 the Adenauer government agreed to make offset payments to cover the costs of stationing troops in the country. However, Konrad Adenauer's successor, Ludwig Erhard, balked at formalizing the arrangement. When the West German economy fell into a slump in 1966, he refused to cut social spending. Rather than running a deficit, he slashed defense spending and the offset payments. In response, US Secretary of Defense Robert McNamara threatened to withdraw American forces, eliciting howls of protest from Bonn. But when Washington pressed the West Germans to raise their defense spending, they answered that the receding Soviet threat made a larger Bundeswehr unnecessary. Outraged by what he regarded as free riding, Dean Rusk accused the West Germans of hypocrisy. Meanwhile, in the context of their own offset payments fight with Bonn, the British announced that they would shrink the size of their Army of the Rhine.[165]

The three countries eventually reached a compromise that preserved the offset payments, but the damage had been done. The crisis brought down Erhard's government and exacted a toll on trans-Atlantic relations, demonstrating that monetary questions had strategic implications. These disputes suggested that, until the underlying problems with Bretton Woods were resolved, the allies would continue to quarrel, with unpredictable consequences for Western security.

By the end of the decade, the postwar boom sputtered out as opportunities for extensive growth expired. The backlog of technology that had raised productivity so sharply in the 1940s and 1950s had been exhausted. The pools of labor—especially former agricultural workers and the unemployed—that had fueled industrial growth had been tapped out. In 1968 and 1969, major strikes broke out and wages rose. Because labor productivity did not rise commensurately, however, corporate profits—and, by extension, investment—fell. Inflation crept upwards. Governments tried to control prices, but failed. On both sides of the Atlantic, leaders appeared incapable of resolving their persistent trade and monetary disputes or of spurring the innovation necessary to raise growth rates. Battered by these headwinds, the economic golden age slouched toward its end.[166]

VII

The Soviet and Eastern European economies bounced back from the Second World War with astonishing speed. In the USSR, output in 1945 stood almost 20 percent lower than before the hostilities. Eastern Europe suffered even greater declines: 40 percent in Hungary, for instance, and 50 percent in Poland.[167] By 1950, however, national incomes had returned to prewar levels in every country in the Soviet sphere except East Germany. Annual growth rates soared. Although the bloc's economies still trailed far behind the West, they were quickly gaining ground. Communist leaders expected that, as living standards rose, prosperous workers would come to support the party of workers. As the Soviet bloc economies caught up with and overtook those of the West, communism would prove its superiority to capitalism. The regimes would entrench their popular legitimacy and earn their citizens' unshakeable loyalty.[168]

The bloc's economies operated according to similar principles. When the communists took control in Eastern Europe in the late 1940s, they emulated the Soviets by banning private enterprise, nationalizing factories, closing stock markets, and collectivizing agriculture. Central planners, not market forces, set prices. Five-year plans established production targets. Coal and steel production reached record highs. Industrialization pulled many workers away from their farms and into factories. The transfer of labor accelerated the growth of industrial output, as did technology developed by American and Western European firms before the war. In some cases, growth rates surpassed 10 percent. Under the state's near-total control, economic activity flourished.[169]

These impressive results masked underlying problems. Factories operated with obsolete equipment. They wasted resources, burning far more fuel and using far more steel than their Western counterparts to produce the same goods. Central planners channeled vast sums of capital into heavy industry while starving consumer goods, housing, and agriculture. As the pool of rural labor shrank, industrial growth rates sagged. When the backlog of off-the-shelf technology ran out, enterprises struggled to develop their own innovations. Because they could not go bankrupt, they had little incentive to cut costs or invest in research and development. Marxist principles made it difficult to reward efficient workers with higher pay, while punishing laggards made little difference to their output. Managers who found better ways of doing things received higher production quotas, not bonuses.[170] Officials boasted that the postwar economic expansion demonstrated the superiority of the communist model. In reality, much of the growth reflected one-time boons that central planners could neither sustain nor reproduce. The potential for extensive growth had been exhausted.[171]

International trade offered few benefits. The Council for Mutual Economic Assistance (Comecon) coordinated the USSR's hub-and-spoke system of bilateral trade with its Eastern European allies. The Soviets shipped raw materials and petroleum at artificially low prices to the more advanced countries—Czechoslovakia, East Germany, Hungary, and Poland—and received manufactures of dubious quality in return. The Romanians and Bulgarians paid for Soviet goods with food and raw materials, but chafed at the pressure to forgo industrial specialization for Soviet benefit.[172] The more advanced Eastern European economies fared little better. Pursuing Stalinism and self-sufficiency, each industrialized along similar lines, making it difficult to exploit economies of scale or competitive advantage. Trade served little purpose because their products were largely interchangeable. Even sympathetic observers mocked the flow of goods within the bloc as an "exchange of inefficiencies."[173] Leaders hoped that Comecon would rival the European Economic Community, but it fell far short. Rather than creating a single integrated market, it simply coordinated national plans.[174]

The structural weakness of the communist economies became obvious in the 1960s. Growth rates tumbled. Between 1953 and 1960, Soviet gross domestic product per capita grew by 3.9 percent per year on average, but only 3.0 percent between 1960 and 1964.[175] The same trends prevailed across Eastern Europe, with no sign of improvement.[176] Citizens suffered privations because the governments scrimped on agriculture in order to accumulate capital. Food shortages became commonplace. The USSR made huge investments in scientific research—especially in military equipment and space exploration—but it offered few spillover benefits for other sectors, not least because innovations were often kept classified. Factories could not produce manufactures of sufficient quality to compete with Western goods on international markets. Consumer goods made for the domestic market were typically shoddy. In low-tech industries, such as automobile manufacturing, the USSR often had to rely on foreign know-how and technology. In cutting-edge fields, such as electronics, the USSR lagged even further behind the West.[177]

Soviet leaders searched for solutions. Khrushchev launched a huge effort to build more housing. He poured resources into agriculture and consumer products. For the first time, many families moved into apartments of their own and bought goods that had previously been out of reach. The results, nevertheless, fell short of Khrushchev's promises. In 1962, increases in food prices sparked protests across the USSR. At Novocherkassk, soldiers turned their machine guns on angry demonstrators.[178] Unable to cope with the ongoing agricultural crisis, Moscow swallowed its pride and imported grain from the West to satisfy domestic demand.[179] Khrushchev's successors fared little better. Premier Aleksei Kosygin unveiled a new package of economic reforms in 1965, but they made little difference—partly because of their internal contradictions, partly because many bureaucrats had an interest in preserving the status quo. Growth rates continued to slide, and shortages got worse.[180]

Eastern European leaders confronted a similar dilemma. They understood that economic stagnation could jeopardize their rule. Stalinist austerity triggered the 1953 revolt in East Germany.[181] Three years later, discontent over wages and food prices brought tens of thousands of Poles into the

streets, eventually toppling party leader Edward Ochab.[182] In Czechoslovakia, output actually fell in 1963, undermining the theory that a centrally
planned economy could not suffer a recession.[183]

Leaders grasped that the policies offering the greatest chance of reviving
their economies, such as decentralizing control and rewarding efficiency,
conflicted with Marxism-Leninism. Attempts at reform varied from country to country, but the disappointment did not. In 1956, Polish central planners gave state enterprises greater autonomy, but growth rates continued to
fall despite substantial industrial investment, and the planners reasserted
control a few years later. In East Germany, producers gained a greater share
of profits, to little avail. Even Hungary's daring reforms, notably the 1968
New Economic Mechanism, failed to hit their target. The iron-fisted response to the radical experiments of the Prague Spring demonstrated that
the USSR would not tolerate economic policies that challenged the fundamental assumptions of the socialist state.[184]

The best hope for the communist economies lay in moving from extensive to intensive growth. By the 1960s, the old formula—putting more resources to work—had worn out. Planners could no longer throw capital at
a factory and expect production to rise in response. Intensive growth, by
contrast, promised to boost output by improving efficiency and worker
productivity. Soviet bloc officials understood the nature of the problem,
and the stakes. "In the economic competition with imperialism, our victory
will ultimately depend on increasing labor productivity, together with improvements in science, technology, and manufacturing," a meeting of Comecon leaders concluded in 1969.[185]

The challenge of transitioning from extensive to intensive growth was
not unique to the planned economies. The United States and Western Europe encountered the same problem at roughly the same time. But by contrast with the West, the socialist world had never prioritized efficiency or
innovation except in a handful of sectors, such as aerospace and military
technology. Its enterprises tended to maximize production instead. For
them, intensive growth remained an unrealized ambition.[186]

Pinning the blame on counterrevolutionaries, saboteurs, kulaks, and
other internal enemies might have persuaded citizens in the 1930s or 1940s.
By the 1960s, however, the old excuses had worn thin, as had the official
exhortations to be patient and sacrifice for the sake of building communism. Thanks to Western radio and television broadcasts and contact with
Western travelers, Soviet and Eastern European citizens became more aware
of what life on the other side of the Cold War divide had to offer. They understood how far their living standards fell short. Unless the Soviet bloc's
leaders could revive their economies and raise growth rates above those
of the capitalist economies, communism might never regain its popular
legitimacy.[187]

VIII

"This is a moment of slack water in the tide of European affairs, of uncertainty and of frustration," Alastair Buchan wrote in 1969. "The clarity that the Cold War imposed upon relations between the countries of the developed world, in particular the sense of solidarity within each of the two main alliances, has become blurred; the assumption of a natural community of interest between the nations of the Atlantic world has been weakened, and so has an equivalent sense of identity between Eastern Europe and the Soviet Union."[188] In retrospect, it is easy to dismiss Buchan's assumption that the Cold War had ended. But his diagnosis of the structural changes afoot in both East and West stands the test of time. Compared to the 1950s, superpower tensions had fallen and the risk of war had diminished, but geopolitical problems had not become any more tractable. They merely changed shape.

Instead of settling into quiescence, the Eastern and Western international orders each slid into crisis. These crises did not emerge between the two orders, but within them. They did not represent passing dangers that resulted from foolish provocations, but grew out of contradictions inherent in the organizing principles of the orders themselves. As the claims to legitimacy that each order depended upon weakened, leaders on both sides of the Iron Curtain needed to reconsider their relations with their allies and the state's relationship to the citizen. The structures of the postwar world were passing away, forcing governments in the East and West to build new ones in their place. No one could predict what shape they would take.

Chapter 2

THE CLASS OF 1969

IN 1969, quiet returned to the streets of Paris, Berlin, Prague, and Washington. The barricades had been torn down, the tear gas had dissipated, and the tanks had rolled away. In Western Europe, most of the students who had waved banners and thrown rocks at police went back to class. A few, clinging to dreams of revolution, veered toward terrorism, hoping that bombings and kidnappings might succeed where mass demonstrations had failed. In the United States, the antiwar movement continued and racial tensions persisted, exacerbated by growing worries of economic dislocation. In Czechoslovakia, Soviet-backed "normalization" smothered the immediate prospects for reform but did not quench the youthful desire for greater freedom. In East and West alike, the storm had passed, but equilibrium had not yet returned. The underlying crises of domestic and international legitimacy persisted.

As if on cue, a new class of Cold War leaders assumed power that year. Elections in the United States, France, and West Germany brought Richard Nixon, Georges Pompidou, and Willy Brandt to power. In Moscow, Leonid Brezhnev established his preeminence within the Soviet leadership. Despite their differences, they all understood that the usual ways of doing things no longer sufficed. They had to challenge old Cold War habits and develop new policies. Solving the crises of legitimacy required new strategies.

The similarities between their strategies provided the foundation for détente. All four leaders wanted to step away from the East-West conflicts of the past and find more predictable ways of relating to each other. Like the radical *soixante-huitards*, they rejected the policies and assumptions of the high Cold War. But unlike the radicals, they sought stability, not revolution. They wanted to complete the work that had been left unfinished at the end of the Second World War and forge a lasting peace. This task in turn required them to establish common principles that would knit the two parallel international orders back together and repair the rift in the fabric of geopolitics that had persisted since 1945.

The differences in their strategies and worldviews ensured that the course of détente would not run smooth. Brezhnev and Nixon wanted to reduce the burden on their national resources, stabilize the international system, normalize superpower relations, and make the coexistence of the Eastern and Western systems bearable. Pompidou and Brandt likewise valued stability. But they did not simply want to make the Cold War less volatile. They wanted to overcome it. In their view, stability would allow human and economic contacts between East and West to flourish. Over the longer term, these contacts would punch progressively larger holes in the Iron Curtain, eventually undermining the communist regimes and ending the continent's ideological division. On the basis of their shared assumptions and immediate objectives, the four leaders could work together and reach international agreements. But even if they signed the same declarations, they would not always understand them in the same way or expect them to yield the same results.

I

In July 1968, Leonid Brezhnev surveyed the domestic and international scene in a memorandum for his Politburo colleagues. "It is impossible not to see that the course of events both in international life, and in the life of our country, puts forward new, complex problems that demand serious changes and major decisions from us," Brezhnev wrote. The recent growth of the Soviet economy concealed "serious problems that are already beginning to make themselves felt," especially inefficiencies in production, the poor use of capital, and "scientific and technological backwardness." Social problems, including intellectual dissent and the political indifference of young people, demanded "serious study." In foreign policy, because the government did not explain its goals clearly enough to the public, even party members were asking difficult questions. Within the Warsaw Pact, Brezhnev worried about allied leaders' subjectivist mood and "the ups and downs of the struggle for leadership in one party or other," especially in Czechoslovakia, where the Prague Spring remained in full flower. Finally, NATO "continued to pose a threat to the security of the Soviet Union," and "the danger of West German militarism and revanchism" persisted. In these circumstances, he concluded, "[W]e really need peace and the reduction of tensions, because this would create more favorable conditions for internal development and give us time to win in the struggle against imperialism."[1]

The following month, Brezhnev took dramatic action to solve one of the problems that he had enumerated. His decision to crush the Prague Spring solidified his control over Soviet foreign policy and confirmed his place atop the Kremlin hierarchy. After orchestrating the 1964 ouster of Nikita Khrushchev, Brezhnev had taken the post of general secretary and formed a triumvirate along with Aleksei Kosygin and Nikolai Podgorny. Now he stood first among equals, though he would never acquire absolute power. By necessity and temperament, he governed by building consensus among his Politburo colleagues.[2]

Brezhnev's ascent demonstrated the value of bureaucratic skill, loyalty, and luck in the Soviet system. Born into a family of steelworkers, he moved quickly through the party's ranks, thanks in part to Stalin's purges. As senior officials lost their positions, younger apparatchiks—the *vydvizhentsy* ("promoted ones")—rose to replace them.[3] Like many members of his cohort, Brezhnev enthusiastically supported communism but paid more attention to practical problems than to Marxist theory. "It was almost impossible to persuade Leonid Ilyich to read an interesting, relevant book of any kind," his longtime aide Andrei Aleksandrov-Agentov recalled. "In 21 years of working with him I never once saw him on his own initiative pick up a volume of Lenin's works, to say nothing of Marx or Engels."[4] Politburo member Aleksandr Shelepin later recalled that "over the course of numerous conversations with him, I became convinced that he was not familiar with Lenin's fundamental works."[5]

This is not to say that Brezhnev lacked ideas. By the time he became general secretary, he had developed strong convictions about foreign affairs. These had their roots in his service in the Second World War, when he marched with the Red Army from the Caucasus all the way to Berlin. Like Stalin, he concluded that the country's disproportionate suffering entitled it to certain privileges in Eastern Europe. The imperatives of security required the USSR to push its frontiers westward and to create a cordon of friendly governments that would block future German aggression. Brezhnev understood that the regime's safety depended on its ability to defend the war's political and territorial results.[6]

The war also inspired a profound commitment to peace. Lenin, Stalin, and Khrushchev had failed to establish lasting peace in Europe, but Brezhnev vowed to succeed. On one occasion, while working with his advisors at his dacha, he delivered an extemporaneous monologue on the history of human conflict, with the Second World War as its centerpiece. "We at the front dreamed of the day when the cannonades would subside and it would be possible to go to Paris, to climb the Eiffel Tower, and to announce, in a way that would be audible everywhere, that it was all over, over forever!" he said. "It is necessary to write clearly about this. And not only to write it and say it, but to do it." The Soviet Union had "to give Europe the peace and tranquility that it had earned by suffering."[7] Whenever he returned to Moscow, Soviet ambassador to Washington Anatoly Dobrynin asked Brezhnev for instructions. "What instructions do you need?—you know better than I how to deal with the Americans," Brezhnev told him. "Let there be peace; that's the main thing."[8] In this regard, Brezhnev resembled Isaiah Berlin's hedgehog, motivated by a single great conviction that would establish his claim to greatness.

Diplomacy alone could not build peace. Military power was necessary too. Khrushchev had dealt with the United States from a position of strategic inferiority, but Brezhnev refused to repeat his predecessor's mistake. Instead of taking reckless gambles, he would change the correlation of forces in the USSR's favor and negotiate patiently from a position of strength. The approach would give the USSR new diplomatic options and fend off hardline domestic critics who doubted the value of cooperating with the West.[9]

At Brezhnev's direction, the Soviet Union undertook a major nuclear buildup. By the end of the 1960s, it had nearly eliminated the twenty-to-one edge in ICBMs that the Americans had enjoyed in 1962. Meanwhile, the Red Army expanded to five million soldiers. Between 1965 and 1970, military spending grew by 40 percent, accounting for a quarter of the gross national product. Brezhnev expected the USSR's weight in international councils to grow commensurately. "The higher our defensive capacity, the greater our fighting power, the more serene we can be, the more confidently we can guarantee peace to our people and to other peoples, the more they will take into account our every word," he told a Leningrad audience in 1965.[10]

Drawing on the country's burgeoning military power, Brezhnev developed a grand strategy to solve the crisis that had befallen it. The strategy consisted of several interlocking pieces, each of which reinforced the others. They formed a coherent whole, a "single line that had been deeply thought out by Brezhnev and his closest colleagues," Aleksandrov-Agentov observed. Internationally, the strategy aimed to guarantee the Soviet Union's security, confirm its preeminent position in the society of states, and reassert its leading role within the international communist movement. Domestically, it endeavored to reinvigorate the Soviet economy, raise living standards, and boost the regime's popular support.[11]

The pursuit of peace was the key concept that tied all of the components together. Earlier generations of Soviet leaders had built political support by emphasizing the hostility of the outside world. They presented the USSR as a bulwark against the threat of imperialist and revanchist aggression. As the Cold War stabilized during the 1960s, however, these claims wore thin. Now Brezhnev would construct a new claim to legitimacy and renew citizens' faith in communism by championing the cause of peace. By negotiating agreements with allies and adversaries alike, the USSR would reduce the burdens of the Cold War and gain access to the capital and technology necessary for economic growth. These diplomatic achievements would affirm the country's international legitimacy and give it the tools to revive its domestic legitimacy. The USSR would present itself not primarily as a revolutionary power, but as the architect of international stability and the main force for peace in the world.[12]

To flesh out and implement his ideas, Brezhnev relied on a number of collaborators. None was more important than foreign minister Andrei Gromyko, who shared Brezhnev's worldview and handled the detailed diplomatic work that his approach to détente required. The general secretary also recruited an inner circle of advisors from the ranks of the party, foreign ministry, and academe. These figures—including Aleksandrov-Agentov, Anatoly Chernyaev, Anatoly Kovalev, and Georgy Arbatov—met regularly at Brezhnev's dacha to discuss policy. They also wrote the major speeches in which Brezhnev laid out his plans, especially his address to the 1969 Moscow conference of international communist parties and his report to the 24th Congress of the Soviet Communist Party in 1971. The Party Congress empowered Brezhnev by endorsing his strategy, the centerpiece of which was known as the "Peace Program." It also constrained him. After winning support for his lofty ambitions, he had to follow through.[13]

Ideological innovation bought time to put the strategy into action. At the Party Congress, Brezhnev announced that the USSR had made the transition to the era of "developed socialism."[14] The concept turned a setback into an advance. Khrushchev had promised that the USSR would surpass Western production levels and achieve full-scale communism—the highest stage of Marxist-Leninist development, characterized by high living standards—by 1980. In the early 1970s, however, it was clear that the USSR could not meet this timetable. Developed socialism—a stage of historical development in its own right—offered a way out. Creating the illusion of progress gave Soviet leaders some breathing room to get the country back on track. It affirmed that the USSR remained the leading state in the socialist world and that all other socialist states had to continue following its example. It also invited trouble. By measuring the USSR's progress according to Western levels of consumption, it put the onus on the government to raise living standards, satisfy citizens' consumerist expectations, and match the capitalist pace of development.[15]

Achieving these goals required new economic policies. Instead of reforming domestic institutions, which would entail ideological and political risks, Brezhnev looked abroad.[16] To start, the USSR would coordinate its production more closely with its Eastern European partners. "The possibilities of the socialist division of labor are not yet being fully used," Brezhnev told the Party Congress.[17] This policy had provoked a Romanian backlash in the 1960s, but he believed that it offered political as well as economic advantages. A reinvigorated Comecon would demonstrate that the socialist states could build transnational institutions to match the European Economic Community. Besides, unless the USSR could demonstrate to its allies the benefits of cooperation, Brezhnev warned the Politburo, "they will inevitably reach out to the West," with dangerous consequences for the cohesion of the Warsaw Pact.[18]

Yet Brezhnev wanted the USSR itself to reach out to the West. The resources of the capitalist world could help solve the economic problems of socialism. The USSR would import food and consumer goods to make up for domestic shortfalls. It would raise sluggish productivity rates and foster innovation by tapping foreign capital and advanced technology.[19] It would catch up with the West by spending more on education and research and expanding "mutually advantageous economic, trade, scientific and technical and cultural ties" with all Western countries, including the United States. These efforts would build on the successes of the 1960s, when the Soviets had signed several important economic agreements with Western European countries. The USSR could not afford to lose this competition, Brezhnev told the Politburo, because "we are talking about the factors that in 15 to 20 years will determine the face of the world."[20]

To counteract the centrifugal forces that had strained the Warsaw Pact during the 1960s and fortify it against the temptations of the West, the USSR would tighten the bonds of the bloc. In his 1969 speech, Brezhnev emphasized the importance of "strengthening of the unity of the Communist movement."[21] The Warsaw Pact would be the main vehicle for these efforts. A package of new intra-bloc treaties would ratify the principles of the Brezhnev Doctrine and reassert Soviet primacy. New pact-wide bodies would coordinate allied military policy, give the Soviets more control over their allies' forces, and expand their ability to deal with the threat from Beijing. Regular meetings of allied officials would help Moscow control the Eastern Europeans' dealings with the West and prevent future Prague Springs. A stronger Warsaw Pact would keep the allies on the path of orthodoxy and establish new mechanisms for Soviet influence beyond the threat of force.[22]

In parallel with these efforts, the Soviet Union had to reach a new understanding with its Western adversaries. "Our principled line with respect to the capitalist countries, including the USA, is consistently and fully to practice the principles of peaceful coexistence, to develop mutually advantageous ties, and to co-operate, with states prepared to do so, in strengthening peace, making our relations with them as stable as possible," Brezhnev told the 1971 Congress.[23] Now that the Soviet nuclear arsenal had caught up to that of the United States, he wanted to sign arms control agreements to reduce the danger of war and redirect "colossal resources to constructive purposes."[24] Addressing the Party Congress, Andrei Gromyko said that "[t]here is no question of any significance which can be decided without the Soviet

Union, or in opposition to her."[25] Cooperating with the United States would affirm the truth of this claim.

These efforts had to include Europe, where the task of peacemaking had been left incomplete in 1945. The time had come to finish the job. "It goes without saying that the solution to this problem requires constant initiatives on our part," Brezhnev told the Politburo.[26] The USSR would work to forge a comprehensive peace settlement and solve the problems that had repeatedly brought the continent to the brink of war. An international agreement to affirm "the stability of borders" in Europe would provide the foundation for a new security system and bestow international legitimacy on the communist governments that had taken power in the late 1940s. Reducing tensions with the West would also allow the USSR to devote more resources to the struggle with China. Brezhnev would use diplomacy, backed by military strength, to establish lasting peace across the ideological divide.[27]

The memory of the Second World War influenced every aspect of Brezhnev's plans. During his time as general secretary, he built a cult to the country's wartime sacrifices. New symbols and monuments, such as Moscow's tomb of the unknown soldier, gave the Soviet state a "new founding myth" to complement that of the October Revolution.[28] Brezhnev regularly invoked the war to justify his foreign policy. "For us," he told Czechoslovak leader Alexander Dubček, "the results of the Second World War are inviolable, and we will defend them even at the cost of risking a new war."[29] Following the same logic, the Peace Program sought "the final recognition of the territorial changes that took place in Europe as a result of the Second World War," Brezhnev told the Party Congress. It would protect the gains for which the Soviet people had paid such a high price.[30]

For all its talk of international cooperation, the Peace Program did not require the USSR to abandon its ideological commitments. According to the Leninist concept of peaceful coexistence, capitalist and communist states could forswear state-on-state war and cooperate. Brezhnev himself, unlike other senior officials, genuinely believed that capitalists and communists could make peace with each other. This did not mean, however, that the ideological struggle would end. The USSR was committed to peace, but no one should "confuse our persistence and consistency in this question with pacifism, with 'nonresistance to evil'—to the evil that the imperialist aggressors are inflicting on the peoples," Brezhnev said in 1970. "A genuine love of peace in our age presupposes resolute opposition to the aggressive claims of imperialism." According to Marxist-Leninist theory, peace and communist revolution complemented each other, because capitalism itself was the ultimate cause of warfare. Brezhnev could therefore proclaim that the fight against imperialism would continue until socialism had won its inevitable worldwide victory.[31]

To an orthodox communist, this logic was entirely consistent. To Western liberal democrats, however, it contradicted itself. From their perspective, the spread of communism threatened international peace and stability. Aiding foreign revolutionaries could constitute an act of aggression analogous to invading a sovereign state. Despite Brezhnev's sincere commitment to peace, his understanding of the concept meant that East-West rapprochement could only go so far. Over the longer term, the gap between the Leninist and liberal democratic ideas of peace would complicate the USSR's approach to détente. In the short term, however, the prospects for Brezhnev's strategy shone brightly, especially because the other members of the class of 1969 shared some of his central goals.

II

Against a background of war and domestic unrest, Richard Nixon took office as president of the United States in January 1969. "We are caught in war, wanting peace. We are torn by division, wanting unity," he said in his inaugural address. He pledged to set the country on a new course. "We are entering an era of negotiation," he declared. The United States would defend its interests through diplomacy instead of war, seeking not "victory over any other people, but the peace that comes 'with healing in its wings.'"[32] The pledge left some listeners unconvinced. Along the parade route, protestors threw bottles at Nixon's motorcade.[33]

The optimism that had characterized the early 1960s now seemed like the relic of a bygone age. Observers wondered whether the United States was doomed to lose its dominant global position, and how it would cope with the fallout. The conflict in Vietnam had undermined the credibility of American military power and continued to fuel domestic strife. The expansion of Soviet nuclear and conventional forces gave the USSR unprecedented global reach. The rising economic strength and growing assertiveness of Western Europe and Japan strained America's alliances. In Asia and Africa, many newly independent states demanded respect for the interests of the global South, while others tumbled into civil war. Nixon recognized that the international system had entered a new era. "The postwar period in international relations has ended," Nixon declared in his first foreign policy report to Congress. Now that the bipolar structure of the past had broken down, the United States could only solve its problems by "realiz[ing] the creative possibilities of a pluralistic world."[34]

If any American politician was equipped for the challenge, it was Nixon. During a hardscrabble youth, he achieved academic success through sheer hard work. Wartime service with the US Navy in the Pacific persuaded him that national security and international stability required a vigorous

foreign policy even in peacetime. Fierce anticommunist rhetoric fueled his
meteoric political rise in the late 1940s. As Dwight Eisenhower's vice president, Nixon developed his foreign policy credentials. He toured Latin
America—where he narrowly escaped from a mob of stone-throwing Ven-
ezuelans—and went head-to-head with Khrushchev in an impromptu televised debate in Moscow. Even after the 1960 presidential election—the first
defeat of his career—he continued traveling abroad to maintain his profile
as a statesman and keep in touch with foreign leaders. By the time he finally
entered the White House, he had acquired more foreign policy experience
than any new president in decades.[35]

Once in office, Nixon made foreign affairs his top priority. "I've always
thought this country could run itself domestically without a president," he
told journalist Theodore White in 1967. "You need a president for foreign
policy."[36] To help with this task, he appointed Henry Kissinger, a German-
Jewish Harvard professor, as his national security advisor.[37] Compared to
Nixon, Kissinger took a less idealistic and more ambiguous view of American power. He believed that a truly great statesman could transcend the
status quo and the limits of his country's power by dint of willpower and
creativity. But as a historian of nineteenth-century diplomacy, he also argued that international order depended on the balance of power. The
United States could not afford to moralize about its adversaries' domestic
policies. It had to focus, instead, on maintaining peace, which required
dealing with the other great powers as they were, not as it wished them to
be. Kissinger sometimes wondered whether democratic states damaged
their own interests by demanding that foreign policy be both transparent
and virtuous. In his view, the United States had to conduct secret diplomacy
and collaborate with unsavory governments in order to preserve the geopolitical equilibrium.[38]

Notwithstanding the differences in their views, Nixon and Kissinger
agreed about the main tasks of American foreign policy. They proceeded
from the conviction that the country had to stay engaged with the world.
Like his predecessor Woodrow Wilson, whom he admired, Nixon believed
that Americans' superior virtue bestowed a responsibility to preserve international order.[39] At home, the backlash against Vietnam had engendered
isolationist sentiments that threatened this responsibility. Abroad, the communist threat had evolved but remained undiminished, as did the need to
contain Soviet power.[40] After the domestic turmoil of the late 1960s, Nixon
wondered "whether America has the national character and moral stamina
to see us through this long and difficult struggle."[41] Likewise, Kissinger criticized American leaders' habitual passivity in the face of crisis. "[O]ur policies have lacked vitality and . . . public discussion has focused on symptoms,
not causes," he wrote.[42] If the country's willpower and self-discipline collapsed, so too would its international influence. Even if peace endured in

these circumstances, "it would be the kind of peace that suffocated freedom in Czechoslovakia," Nixon said.[43]

Piecemeal responses would not suffice. "The crises which form the headlines of the day are symptoms of deep-seated structural problems," Kissinger concluded.[44] The American government could not merely treat those symptoms. It needed an integrated strategy to revive the country's influence in a rapidly changing international system. At a minimum, Nixon argued, the United States would have to withdraw from Vietnam without compromising its credibility as a superpower, preserve transatlantic cohesion despite the growing strains on the Western alliance, and persuade Soviet and Chinese leaders to follow the "basic rules of international civility."[45] In the long term, the United States might still hope to defeat the USSR. In the short term, however, it had to cooperate with the Soviets to stabilize the international system and carve out some room to maneuver.

To this end, Nixon and Kissinger devised a two-pronged strategy. Each of its components buttressed the other. Superpower détente would ease tensions and thereby reduce the need for containment. Meanwhile, the Nixon Doctrine, which the president announced at a 1969 press conference in Guam, would lighten the burden of fighting communism worldwide. According to its tenets, the United States would continue to honor its commitments to its Asian allies after the Vietnam War ended. If any country vital to American security were threatened with nuclear attack, the US government would not shrink from using its own nuclear arsenal to defend it. In all other cases, however, including a communist insurgency, Washington would send only weapons and economic assistance. Each country would have to supply the soldiers for its own defense. "America cannot—and will not—conceive all the plans, design all the programs, execute all the decisions and undertake all the defense of the free world," declared the Nixon administration's first foreign policy report to Congress. "We will help where it makes a real difference and is considered in our interest." The Nixon administration implemented this principle in Indochina, where it gradually shifted the burden of defending South Vietnam to the South Vietnamese themselves.[46]

Retrenchment offered an attractive alternative to the Vietnam War's political and economic costs. Cutting the Pentagon's budget may have been more palatable than slashing domestic spending, but it carried risks. Nixon and Kissinger, who drew a strong correlation between credibility and security, worried that America's allies might conclude that the superpower had shirked its international commitments. The realignment of great power politics provided a way out. Pentagon planners had assumed that the United States might have to fight two major wars simultaneously—one in Europe, one in Asia—plus a smaller regional conflict. By the late 1960s, however, the Sino-Soviet split made this so-called 2½ war model seem obsolete. The Nixon administration concluded that it could shift to a 1½ war model without endangering American security. It reaped huge savings—some five billion dollars—at little strategic cost.[47]

The second element of Nixon and Kissinger's strategy—superpower détente—started from the conviction that the United States should set ideological questions aside in dealing with Moscow. The USSR was a great power like any other, and the United States should treat it like one. Ideological differences should not affect a state's legitimacy, nor should its domestic system or the way it treated its citizens. "[W]e have to deal in the first instance with Soviet foreign and not with its domestic policy," Kissinger wrote. Only the USSR's international behavior mattered: how it treated its neighbors, whether it lived up to its promises, and whether it abided by the generally accepted code of conduct. If the two countries focused on their shared interests, they could make deals that benefited them both. This approach broke with the ideological hostility of the high Cold War and regarded the Eisenhower's administration's moralizing about rollback, for example, as obsolete. Instead of trying to defeat each other, the superpowers should learn to live together. By respecting each other's interests, they could find common ground, contain the danger of nuclear destruction, and reduce the costs of global power.[48]

On the basis of these principles, Nixon and Kissinger pursued two major goals. First, in light of the USSR's rapid military buildup, they wanted to end the arms race. Doing so would stabilize international politics and relieve a major source of pressure on American resources. Second, over the longer term, they wanted to persuade the Soviets to accept the international status quo and abandon their commitment to spreading revolution. In this respect, their nonideological approach to international affairs was both a method and a goal. They assumed that, if they treated the USSR as a satisfied—rather than a revisionist—great power, the USSR would behave like one. The costs of containment would fall.[49]

Success required secret diplomacy. Because the strategy broke with long-standing habits of American foreign policy, Nixon and Kissinger decided that they could not leave its implementation to career officials. Working through the State Department would give the custodians of the conventional wisdom too many chances to interfere. Consigning Secretary of State William P. Rogers to deal with issues of secondary importance, the White House asserted direct control over the most critical files. Kissinger set up a backchannel to the Kremlin through Anatoly Dobrynin, who relayed messages between Nixon and the Politburo. Working through the backchannel, the Nixon administration aimed to spin a web of mutually advantageous agreements.[50]

To prevent Moscow from focusing on issues of particular Soviet interest while neglecting American goals on separate questions, the system of linkage would connect otherwise unrelated diplomatic problems by means of rewards and punishments. In this way, Nixon and Kissinger hoped to exploit their relationship with the Soviets to advance their other foreign policy goals. In particular, they expected the Kremlin to use its influence in Hanoi (which turned out to be more modest than they assumed) to speed the American withdrawal from Vietnam.[51]

Exploiting the rift between Moscow and Beijing would also encourage the Soviets to moderate their behavior. Before becoming president, Nixon developed a plan to reestablish diplomatic relations with China, which had been cut off since Mao took power in 1949. "We simply cannot afford to leave China forever outside the family of nations, there to nurture its fantasies, cherish its hates and threaten its neighbors," Nixon wrote in 1967.[52] Rapprochement between the two countries would lower tensions in Asia and beyond and reduce the demands on American power. Kissinger told reporters that "we cannot imagine a stable, international peace in which a country of 750 million people is kept in isolation."[53]

The opening to China would establish a system of triangular diplomacy—linking Washington, Moscow, and Beijing—in which the United States held the balance. In mid-1971, after the announcement of Nixon's forthcoming trip to Beijing, Kissinger emphasized that the opening to China was not "directed against any third country." Nixon reassured Soviet leaders that his dealings with Mao "change[d] nothing" in Soviet-American relations. These disavowals did not alter the underlying logic of triangular diplomacy. So long as the United States maintained closer relations with the USSR and China than those powers had with each other, it would gain leverage over both. In this way, Nixon and Kissinger could seize the initiative and reclaim America's ability to set the international agenda.[54]

Average citizens hardly featured in Nixon and Kissinger's conception of international affairs. The two men focused on the balance of power above all, and believed that only the leaders of the major powers could meaningfully affect the course of events. As the concept of *détente* gained public currency in the West in the early 1970s, what had originally been a generic term denoting the reduction of tensions between two countries became synonymous with Nixon and Kissinger's particular strategy. When that strategy fell into disrepute a few years later, not least because it ignored humanitarian questions, détente itself became a dirty word in the American political lexicon.[55]

In response to the crises of the 1960s, Nixon and Kissinger formulated a strategy that was simultaneously bold and restrained. Sensitive to the limits of American power, it pared down the country's international commitments. It distinguished essential interests from extraneous distractions. It looked for creative ways to preserve American influence in a world that was rapidly becoming multipolar. It aimed to reduce the risks of war, especially nuclear war. Yet Nixon and Kissinger aspired neither to eliminate the Soviet-American competition or to end the antagonism between the super-powers' political systems. Rather, they worked to manage the rivalry and make relations between the two countries more predictable. They did not seek victory in the Cold War, but stability.[56]

III

Shortly after midnight on April 28, 1969, French president Charles de Gaulle issued a statement from Colombey-les-Deux-Églises, the village where he often sought refuge from political storms. "I am ceasing my duties as President of the Republic," he said. "This decision takes effect at noon today." The previous day, a national referendum had rejected his proposal to decentralize the system of government. After the protests and strikes that had shaken the French establishment the previous year, de Gaulle wanted a vote of public confidence to restore his political standing. When the voters rebuffed him, he concluded that he had to resign.[57]

De Gaulle's departure created a power vacuum in French politics. If any-one personified postwar France, *le grand Charles* did. Hero of the country's liberation from German occupation, its savior during the Algerian crisis, and the architect of its Fifth Republic, his influence extended into every corner of government and society. To his supporters, he embodied the best of the country's spirit. To his critics, he symbolized a sclerotic order that defended entrenched interests and stifled free expression. The students and workers who took to the streets in 1968 demanded liberation from the liberator. They wanted a "new society" free from the "hierarchical military and Napoleonic organization of the state." Although de Gaulle initially de-fied the radicals, the scope of the unrest shook his self-confidence. His party's resounding victory in the June 1968 legislative elections did not restore it.[58]

The day that de Gaulle resigned, Georges Pompidou announced his can-didacy to succeed him. Pompidou had worked with de Gaulle for a quarter-century and served as his prime minister for six years. In his 1969 presiden-tial campaign, he presented himself as the general's heir. His artful slogan—"Change within continuity"—appealed to both de Gaulle's parti-sans and those eager for reform. In the runoff vote, he defeated interim president Alain Poher by a wide margin. As de Gaulle's successor, he had to reestablish the legitimacy of the French state and demonstrate that the Fifth Republic could survive in the absence of its founder.[59]

By comparison with the leading French politicians of his generation, Pompidou travelled an unusual path to power. After a rural upbringing, he amassed a distinguished academic record and embarked on a career teaching literature. He fought the Germans in 1940, but unlike the future barons of Gaullism, he declined to join the resistance or the Free French Forces. After the liberation, he changed the trajectory of his life by going to work for de Gaulle. As his career progressed, he alternated between government and the banking house Rothschild Frères. His six years as de Gaulle's prime minister coincided with the height of the postwar economic boom known as *les trente glorieuses*. In 1968, he oversaw the government's negotiations with organized labor that helped to bring the nationwide protests to a peaceful conclusion. Yet his time in office ended bitterly. Pompidou's commitment to classical liberalism clashed with de Gaulle's statism, and the president demanded his resignation after the 1968 elections. The two men never reconciled.[60]

Cast into the political wilderness, Pompidou sat down to write. The result was *The Gordian Knot*, a book that encapsulated his worldview. By analyzing the crisis of the French state, Pompidou articulated his own political philosophy. He grasped that Western society was suffering a crisis of legitimacy: "Our civilization is at stake," he told the National Assembly in May 1968. "The challenge is to recreate a lifestyle accepted by everyone, to reconcile order and liberty, spirit and conviction, civilization and personality, material progress and the meaning of effort, free competition and justice, individualism and solidarity."[61] Governments could deal with the complexities of modernity in one of two ways, he argued: they could redouble their commitment to liberal democracy and the free market, or they could take refuge in a fascist or communist dictatorship. "We have arrived at an extreme point where it will be necessary—let us not doubt it—to stop speculating and recreate a social order. Someone will cut the Gordian knot," Pompidou wrote. "The question is to know whether it will be by imposing a democratic discipline that guarantees our liberties, or whether some strong, helmeted man will draw his sword like Alexander."[62]

The problems of the late 1960s did not shake Pompidou's faith in the strengths of liberal democracy and capitalism. Only capitalism could satisfy citizens' material needs, and every political leader had a duty to encourage economic growth. A few years later, as president, he told a journalist that his "first priority is to make France a strong, economically prosperous country, [because] this prosperity is the precondition for our national independence and all social progress."[63]

Prosperity alone did not suffice, however. The upheavals of 1968 did not grow out of material deprivation, Pompidou argued, but from deeper problems. Because modern society failed to satisfy its citizens' spiritual needs, it allowed nihilism to take root, especially among young people. Western governments had to rebuild the moral order of society by protecting the dignity and liberty of the individual citizen. To emphasize the point, he quoted Baudelaire, another Frenchman who wrestled with the challenges of modernity: "There cannot be real, that is to say moral, progress except in the individual and through the individual himself."[64]

The other essential element of Pompidou's worldview was his Gaullism, a school of politics that eludes easy description. It offers no grand theories about the way the world works. Rather, it blends populism, nationalism, and conservatism with the ultimate aim of reclaiming French grandeur.[65] One might call it realism with French characteristics, or a Gallic analogue to American exceptionalism. As president, de Gaulle wanted to pursue French interests without worrying about ideological shibboleths. His approach challenged the received wisdom of the Cold War and aimed to transcend it. "If there is a voice that can be heard, an action that can be effective in establishing an order to replace the Cold War," de Gaulle said, "they are *par excellence* the voice and the action of France."[66]

Like Nixon, de Gaulle regarded the USSR as a normal great power, not a pariah. The common interests of the leading states superseded their philosophical differences. "A multipolar world of nation-states [would be] more balanced, and therefore more stable, than a bipolar world," de Gaulle concluded.[67] If the international system operated as a concert of great powers—including France—it could avoid existential crises and allow states to deal with each other in a businesslike fashion. Two slogans—"détente, entente, and cooperation" and Europe "from the Atlantic to the Urals"—summarized his pan-European ambitions. He wanted to collaborate with the Americans, West Germans, and Soviets. He also wanted to keep them in check, so as to maximize French influence.[68]

Pompidou remained a Gaullist even after falling out with the general. He shared his predecessor's convictions about French greatness and independence. Where de Gaulle was forceful and dramatic, however, Pompidou was restrained and thoughtful.[69] In 1970, an interviewer asked him if there was such a thing as Pompidolism. "If it's a question of [having] a set of political ideas, I'll say yes," he replied. "If it's a question of a doctrine that will be imposed like Gaullism, I'll say no."[70] He rejected grand plans in favor of incremental solutions and preferred to negotiate instead of acting unilaterally. "Nothing is accomplished except over the long term, nothing is won except by patience," he declared in 1972. "[E]verything can be lost by disorder."[71]

Perhaps for these reasons, Pompidou's views on international affairs diverged from his predecessor's. Whereas de Gaulle aspired to recreate an idealized nineteenth-century order, in which France exercised global influence, Pompidou looked to the future and focused on his country's place in Europe. He believed in the Atlantic alliance and in containing the Soviet Union, but also hoped to mediate between the United States and Europe, and between the West and the USSR. Ultimately, the West should not seek to crush the Soviet system, but to coax it into adopting Western values through a long process of rapprochement. Over time, he hoped, this approach would cement France's influence, increase its economic growth, strengthen international peace, and overcome the division of Europe.[72]

After moving into the Elysée, Pompidou developed a strategy to implement this vision. First, Western European states had to cooperate politically, not just economically, because France relied on European integration as a vehicle for its own ambitions. "France cannot protect and increase its role in the world except by uniting with the other European nations," Pompidou insisted. "It cannot realize its destiny except in a strong Europe."[73] At the same time, much like de Gaulle, Pompidou rejected supranational integration. Paris had no business transferring its sovereignty to Brussels, but should use Brussels to maximize its own influence. He broke with de Gaulle, however, by endorsing British membership in the EEC as a means to keep up the momentum of intergovernmental cooperation and counterbalance West Germany's growing economic strength. The community's members would continue working together as equals—with France in the lead.[74]

Pompidou never doubted that his country's destiny lay with the West. "France is a Western country. This [is] true historically and in sentiment," Pompidou told Nixon in 1971. "She [is] determined to remain a friend and ally of the U.S."[75] Because the American presence in Europe underwrote French security, he did not seek to dissolve the Atlantic alliance. Nonetheless, he sometimes questioned American motives, and understood that French and American interests did not always coincide. In particular, he feared that the warming of superpower relations would give rise to a US-Soviet condominium in Europe and trample French autonomy. Defending French interests within the Atlantic alliance required a delicate balancing act.[76]

If Pompidou realized his vision, France would become the fulcrum on which East-West relations pivoted. Even as he worked to maintain good relations with Washington, he also reached out to Moscow. Given the military balance in Europe, and France's proximity to the Soviet bloc, "only two policies were possible," Pompidou reasoned. "Either she hid behind a wall or [France and the USSR] tried to understand one another."[77] For both security and economic reasons, he preferred the latter course. Because France would gain more by working with the Soviets than by trying to isolate them, it had to come to terms with the postwar map of Europe.

In 1966, when de Gaulle visited Moscow, he and Brezhnev issued a declaration on international peace. They affirmed the principles of independence and noninterference in domestic affairs and called for the normalization of relations among all European states.[78] Although the declaration carried no legal weight and left the status of Berlin unresolved, it implicitly recognized the continent's postwar status quo and opened the door to closer Franco-Soviet cooperation. Pompidou wanted to take advantage of the new economic opportunities that the relationship afforded. "The USSR has enormous development needs because of its size, its population, its undeveloped natural resources, its lag in consumer goods production," Pompidou told reporters. By satisfying them, French industry could profit handsomely.[79]

Like Nixon and Brezhnev, Pompidou sought to stabilize the international system. But unlike them, he regarded stability as a means, not an end. He did not want to freeze the two blocs, but to loosen their bonds and eventually undermine communism itself. Pompidou did not doubt NATO's importance, but he also believed that the alliance presented an obstacle to overcoming the Cold War. It fueled Soviet suspicions and gave the Kremlin an excuse to impose its will on Eastern Europe. If France challenged the Cold War's traditional bloc-to-bloc dynamics and encouraged the Western allies to deal one-on-one with their Eastern counterparts, it could usher in a more fluid international system. This approach might weaken NATO, but it could also encourage the Soviet Union to tolerate more freedom of action among its allies and constrain its ability to strong-arm them. As the Poles, Hungarians, and others pursued their own national interests and asserted their independence from Moscow, ideological diversity would take root. Eventually the division of Europe would break down along with the Cold War itself.[80]

This strategy emphasized evolution over revolution. Although it would take many years to show results, Pompidou had confidence that it would eventually succeed because the socialist system was inherently unsustainable. "The Marxist economy is clearly losing the competition with the Western economies," Pompidou wrote in *The Gordian Knot*. The command economies owed their limited success to a combination of individual talent and state compulsion, not the superiority of their system. Sooner or later, the Soviets would have to decide whether to cleave to economic orthodoxy and keep losing ground to the West, or to reform their system to encourage growth. They could have a healthy economy or a communist one, but not both.[81]

Closer contacts between East and West would bring the day of reckoning closer. The more the two systems dealt with each other, the harder it would be to deny the superiority of liberal democracy, whose ideas and practices would slowly seep into Soviet and Eastern European society. De Gaulle imagined "dismantl[ing] the Iron Curtain piece by piece."[82] Pompidou referred to this process as "interpenetration." As the Soviets grew more comfortable with the West and yielded to its attractions, and members of the two camps cooperated with each other, the Cold War would fade and France would regain its historic influence over the destiny of the continent. "The problem is to know which side will let itself be corrupted by the other, and I have faith in liberty," he told Willy Brandt. "In the end, it is always more attractive and more penetrating than totalitarianism."[83] The Soviets might crack down on their citizens, "but there will come a time when they will have to liberalize."[84] Pompidou expressed a similar idea to Nixon in more graphic terms: "The more contacts we have with the East, the more liberty will become contagious. Bismarck said of France in 1870: 'We gave them the republic like syphilis.' I believe that liberty is also a contagious disease that spreads through constant and repeated contact."[85]

Expanding East-West contacts required Moscow's consent, so Pompidou appealed to the USSR's own priorities. "All countries must meet with each other and speak freely," he told Gromyko in 1970. "Though interpenetration, we will contribute to European security."[86] This process would encourage the Soviets to see themselves as Europeans who shared common values and a common commitment to peace with the West. "If we are resolved to develop economic, technical, cultural, and human exchanges," Pompidou said on his first presidential visit to Moscow, "we will respond to the desire of peoples to achieve progressively an interpenetration that will give birth to a true European feeling."[87] Pompidou understood that forcing the pace of change could prompt a Soviet backlash. For this reason, it was essential to assuage Soviet anxieties about the political and territorial status quo first. But for Pompidou, stability was not an end in itself. Rather, it was the prerequisite for his strategy's ultimate objective—the transformation of Europe.

IV

By a slim majority, a rancorous West German Bundestag elected Willy Brandt as chancellor in October 1969. No Social Democrat had held the office since the Weimar era.[88] The ouster of the Christian Democrats, who had governed since the establishment of the Federal Republic, foretold a major shift in the country's relations with the rest of the world. In his first legislative speech as chancellor, Brandt promised to transform West German foreign policy. He would tackle the problems that had torn Europe asunder and build a more stable and more humane continent. "This government acts on the assumption that the questions that arose for the German people out of the Second World War and out of the national betrayal by the Hitler regime can only conclusively be answered in a European peace order," he said. "Only peace makes our world safe; only on the basis of security can peace spread."[89]

Brandt aimed not just to prevent war, but to overcome the Cold War. So long as East and West disagreed about the basic principles of domestic and international legitimacy, the conflict would continue. His concept of a

European peace order provided the solution. As it emerged naturally "from an agreed renunciation of force by way of a guaranteed and balanced European security system, with the participation of both world powers," it would establish "rules for the coexistence of both parts" of the continent, he wrote in 1968.[90] Besides the nonuse of force, this common standard of conduct might include nonintervention in states' domestic affairs, "freedom of transit, and the free exchange of information." A collective security system would "result from agreements related to the alliances which, to begin with, would continue to exist" and would guarantee the security of all states.[91] Despite this talk of coexistence, however, the establishment of shared principles of legitimacy—including Western freedoms—would ensure the eventual triumph of the liberal democratic order over its communist rival in Europe.

These aspirations reflected the blend of idealism and pragmatism that Brandt had developed over the course of a tumultuous life. Born to a working-class single mother, he discovered journalism and left-wing politics as an adolescent. His early articles for a local newspaper grappled with the economic strife and political polarization of the late Weimar Republic. When Hitler came to power, he fled to Oslo and established himself as a leader of the expatriate resistance movement. The long experience of exile persuaded him that democratic societies had to build political and military bulwarks against extremists of all stripes. A trip to Barcelona during the Spanish Civil War left him with an abiding distrust of the Soviet Union. As the Second World War engulfed his homeland, he developed a vision for postwar Europe based on respect for human rights, international law, and economic cooperation.[92]

The early Cold War refined Brandt's convictions. As an aide to West Berlin's socialist mayor, he visited Britain, France, and the United States during the Berlin Blockade to drum up support for the beleaguered city. His anticommunism, support for rearmament, and Atlanticism put him at odds with Social Democratic leaders, who questioned Washington's motives. In Brandt's analysis, however, democracy could not survive without military power. West Berlin's foreign defenders guaranteed its freedom.[93] In 1957, as mayor of West Berlin in his own right, he again toured Europe and North America while Nikita Khrushchev threatened to strangle the city. He exhorted the Western powers not to concede one inch.[94] The construction of the Berlin Wall bought a measure of stability at a terrible price. The division of the city distressed Brandt, and he seethed at the Western allies' limp response. The Americans were "neither all-powerful nor all-willing," he concluded. On the most important questions, West Germany could not count on their support. It had to look out for its own interests.[95]

Much of Brandt's subsequent thinking grew out of this insight. "In August 1961 a curtain was drawn aside to reveal an empty stage," Brandt later wrote. "To put it more bluntly, we lost certain illusions that had outlived the hopes underlying them."[96] Brandt grasped the human costs of geopolitical division. Families that had been separated could not reunite. East Germans who tried to escape often died at the hands of border guards. Because West Berliners could not change these realities, they had to "learn to live with the wall." They also had to work around it. "We must think—patiently and thoroughly—how we can make it transparent," Brandt argued. "It will not be removed but it must be made superfluous in a wider context." Defying West German political orthodoxy, he resolved to work with communist officials to improve daily life. In 1963, he took the first step in this direction by striking a deal with the East Berlin authorities. The Pass Agreement enabled hundreds of thousands of West Berliners to visit their relatives on the other side of the wall at Christmas.[97]

Three years later, Brandt became foreign minister in Christian Democratic chancellor Kurt Georg Kiesinger's Grand Coalition government. In his new position, he met with Andrei Gromyko at the United Nations, exchanged messages with Eastern European governments, and opened relations with Romania. Kiesinger welcomed these improvements, but worried that going any further would impede the prospects for reunification, antagonize NATO, and alienate conservative voters. These risks did not deter Brandt. After the 1969 election, he forged a precarious coalition with the Free Democrats and became chancellor.[98]

Brandt seized the opportunity to take West Germany in a new direction. No government ought to endorse the continent's tense status quo as a long-term solution to the problems of the Cold War, he reasoned. The division of Germany—to cite only the most obvious problem—was a moral obscenity. It imposed a terrible cost on ordinary people and ignored the German nation's right to self-determination. Besides, it made no economic sense. "The scientific-technical, the economic, and the political potential of the individual states is governed today by direct interdependence," Brandt noted. "The viability of states in the future will depend more and more strongly on their participation in and their contribution to technological progress."[99] If states hoped to prosper, they could not afford to cut themselves off from their neighbors.

More ominously, so long as the rift between East and West persisted, the risk of war would never entirely disappear. "Power blocs that have been formed against one another and are more or less solidly constructed cannot last very long in a narrow space without lapsing into the dreadful danger of a conflict," Brandt wrote.[100] Since 1945, Europe was fortunate to have avoided another war, but in the absence of fundamental change, its luck would eventually run out. In the past, some states might have accepted this uncertainty, but the advent of nuclear weapons made it unthinkable. "Anyone carrying on a foreign policy as a function of military strategy remains a captive of the vicious cycle of atomic armament," Brandt argued. "War is no longer an alternative to peace."[101]

Because twenty years of West German foreign policy had not solved these problems, Brandt reexamined the assumptions that had long guided Bonn's relations with the East. Foremost among these was the Hallstein Doctrine, which decreed that only the Federal Republic could claim to represent the whole German nation. Because East Germany's very existence stood in the way of reunification, Bonn resolved to sever ties with any government that recognized it. Trapped in diplomatic seclusion, the socialist state would eventually wither away—or so went the theory. Konrad Adenauer's government broke off relations with Yugoslavia and Cuba in 1957 after Tito exchanged envoys with East Berlin, and later did the same with Cuba. Adenauer implicitly acknowledged the doctrine's limits when he opened diplomatic relations with the USSR in 1955, but nonetheless succeeded in confining the GDR to a corner of international society, where it enjoyed relations only with other socialist states. Fearing for their state's legitimacy, East German leaders structured their foreign policy around the pursuit of international recognition, something that most other governments took for granted.[102]

Brandt developed a strategy to come to terms with Europe's political and territorial realities. His 1968 book, *A Peace Policy for Europe*, laid out its main components. He proposed to work with the East Germans and their Soviet patrons. He would recognize the results of the Second World War, including the continent's frontiers, so as to draw a conclusive line under the conflict. "The war has been over for a long time, but the peace cannot be won unless Europe is created and the account for Hitler's war settled," he wrote. "This account is still outstanding."[103] But recognizing East Germany did not mean that Bonn had to treat it like any other state. The GDR and FRG were "not foreign to each other," he argued.[104]

This new approach, which became known as *Ostpolitik*, turned the Hallstein Doctrine upside down. It accepted reality in order to transcend it. "The main goal of Soviet policy in Europe is the legalization of the status quo," Egon Bahr, Brandt's most trusted advisor, wrote in 1969, but "the main goal of our policy is overcoming the status quo."[105] As the first step in this direction, Brandt declared, West Germany would renounce force as a tool of foreign policy and would sign agreements to this effect with the Soviets and their allies. Granting the Eastern Europeans the recognition they had long sought would lower military tensions and put to rest the accusations of fascism and revanchism that featured so prominently in communist propaganda. Once Bonn had normalized relations with its eastern neighbors, it could establish strong connections "in all areas of interstate relations," "building a bridge between East and West" and creating "a compatible Europe that will work together in as friendly a way as possible." As these links multiplied, the FRG's prosperity and openness would pull its neighbors westward.[106] The Cold War would end and a reunited Europe would enjoy "peace in the fullest sense of the world," Brandt told the Bundestag.[107] Bahr captured this logic in the phrase *Wandel durch Annäherung*: change through rapprochement.[108]

Rapprochement made ethical and strategic sense. Brandt felt a deep responsibility to help his fellow Germans, and he understood the political benefits of doing so. "There is no point in policies which do not aim to make people's lives easier," he said. "What is good for the people in a divided country is good for the nation too."[109] He and Bahr applied the Pass Agreement's logic on a larger scale. By increasing human contacts not just between the two halves of a city but between the two halves of the country, they wagered, they could eventually knit Germany back together. Contrary to those who argued that the only way to bring down the East German regime was to isolate it, engagement was essential. This principle took on special importance in light of the GDR's attacks on the idea of a united Germany. Its 1967 citizenship law, for instance, eliminated the single German citizenship that both East and West had recognized since the war and established a uniquely East German citizenship in its stead.[110] It therefore made sense to defend the rights of all Germans, regardless of where they lived. Doing so would assert the essential unity of the nation.

Permeability, Brandt and Bahr's core strategic idea, resembled Pompidou's notion of interpenetration. By building barriers against the free movement of people, information, and goods, communist governments demonstrated their weakness, not their strength. Contrary to the official East German explanation, the Berlin Wall did not keep Western provocateurs out but Eastern workers in. More contacts between people and more access to Western consumer goods would hasten the regime's collapse and bring reunification closer. To critics who argued that economic engagement bolstered the communist regime's hold on power, Brandt and Bahr could reply that it also left the East dependent on the West, which in turn gave democratic governments bargaining power and discouraged the socialists from doing anything that might jeopardize relations.[111]

The strategy operated on two levels. It began with diplomacy and treaty-making, but Brandt and Bahr understood that they also had to show results that benefited individual citizens. The Cold War had divided countries and families alike. The geopolitical and human rifts reinforced each other. Consequently, progress at the lowest level—defending individual rights, increasing travel, and reuniting families—could yield benefits at the highest. Small changes would also build trust and persuade the socialist states that closer ties posed no threat to their security. The agreement to allow West Berlin families to visit relatives on the other side of the wall exemplified

Brandt and Bahr's "policy of small steps." It might have seemed mundane, but it offered concrete benefits and built momentum for further progress. Changing the lives of citizens, they hoped, could change the destinies of states.[112]

West Germany could not bring peace to Europe single-handedly. Breaking through the Iron Curtain required Eastern consent. Bonn also needed the support of its allies, to whom it would remain committed as it reached out to the East. "The Atlantic Alliance and the close relationship to the USA must continue to remain the basis of our policy," Bahr wrote. He and Brandt saw no trade-off between East and West and reassured their allies that they would not abandon them for the sake of better relations with Moscow.[113] "Our national interest does not allow standing between East and West," Brandt told the Bundestag. "[O]ur country needs cooperation and harmonization with the West and understanding with the East."[114] The two halves of the nation and the two halves of the continent had to reunite simultaneously, which made NATO's support all the more important.[115]

Transforming West German foreign policy required domestic political support. Given his slim margin in the Bundestag, Brandt had to preempt critics—especially the vocal lobby of former Silesians and East Prussians who had been evicted from their ancestral homes at the end of the war—who might accuse him of abandoning Germany's historic possessions and consigning the nation to permanent division. Many Christian Democrats interpreted Brandt's boldness as naïveté. In their view, he planned to give too much away and would get nothing in return. The former finance minister, Franz Josef Strauss, denounced Brandt's "humble, whining attitude" toward the Soviet bloc. "I am not of the opinion," he said, "that in order to be everybody's darling you have to be everybody's asshole."[116]

The barb highlighted the risks of Brandt's strategy. In the long term, it promised to change the political and territorial status quo for the better, and perhaps even rescue Europe from the Cold War. But to do so, it first had to confirm the status quo. The Soviets and their allies would make gains immediately. The benefits for the West would only come later, if ever. Besides, the notion that closer connections between states and people could eventually redraw the map of the continent ultimately rested on little more than faith. The communist regimes would certainly resist any changes to their system. If Ostpolitik solidified their grip on power, it could entrench the division of Europe instead of overcoming it.

V

When Brandt and his counterparts took office, they set about restructuring international politics. The changes they sought were all the more significant because their ambitions, at least in the short term, were so similar. All four men questioned the logic that had given rise to the Cold War. By reexamining these earlier assumptions, they found new ways to cooperate—and to stabilize the international system.

Their strategies attempted to solve the crises that they had inherited and correct their predecessors' mistakes. Khrushchev had gambled from a position of weakness, provoking nuclear crises in the hope of improving the USSR's geopolitical fortunes. Brezhnev, by contrast, harbored romantic visions of peace, not revolution. He built up the Soviet Union's nuclear arsenal to provide the foundation for a grand diplomatic offensive. In Washington, Nixon and Kissinger rejected the assumptions that had sucked the United States into Vietnam. Instead of combating communism wherever it appeared, they looked for ways to live with it. They reasoned that American security would benefit from treating the USSR and China as great powers with traditional interests rather than as implacable adversaries.

In Bonn, Willy Brandt wanted to reunify his country no less than Adenauer had, but reasoned that he could only achieve this goal by overturning the old taboos on cooperating with the Soviet bloc. By mitigating the costs of the East-West divide, West Germany could become a force for reconciliation in the Cold War rather than a source of conflict. In a certain sense, Pompidou represented an exception to this trend. He shared many of de Gaulle's principles, but the general's foreign policy itself emerged in reaction to the Cold War system of the 1940s and '50s. Pompidou, like his predecessor, repudiated the idea that ideological rifts had to translate into geopolitical ones.

For all of the similarities between the four leaders' short-term goals, their long-term ambitions diverged radically. Brezhnev and Nixon wanted to stabilize the Cold War and reduce its burdens. In their view, détente ought to make the Cold War tolerable for its two leading states. By taking a respite from the superpower competition, they could rebuild their states' legitimacy and reassert their leadership. They did not seek a final triumph. Averting destruction would be enough. One version of the Cold War—the superpower struggle that carried with it the constant threat of nuclear destruction—would come to an end. But another version—the perpetuation of two incompatible systems—would take its place, although on a firmer footing than before.

By contrast, Pompidou and Brandt did not seek stability for its own sake but as a means to a higher goal. Accepting the territorial status quo would reassure Soviet leaders and provide the foundation for political changes, albeit over the long term. France would carve out a more independent role for itself and replace the pattern of bloc-to-bloc confrontation with cooperation among individual states. Increased contact between Eastern and Western Europe would open up the Soviet bloc's closed societies, give them greater freedom of action, and sow the seeds for liberal democracy. Brandt's strategy, which focused as much on the lives of individual citizens as relations between governments, was similarly transformative.

The differences between the Nixon-Brezhnev and Pompidou-Brandt strategies emerged not just from ideology and geopolitics, but also from different understandings of peace. All four leaders understood that their predecessors in 1945 had left the work of peacemaking unfinished. For Nixon, peace meant stabilizing the relationship between the two orders but allowing the underlying ideological conflict to continue. Stability would ensure that the United States could continue competing over the long run. More importantly, it would prevent the competition from tipping over into nuclear war.

For Brezhnev, peace meant ending state-on-state war, especially in Europe, where the most destructive wars of the previous four hundred years had begun. Diplomatic agreements to recognize the territorial and political status quo would eliminate the threat of future conflict and reinvigorate the Soviet system. But this would be a peace without victory. Brezhnev's strategy implicitly acknowledged the USSR's economic dependence on the West. Socialism would not defeat capitalism, but feed off of it. Nonetheless, Brezhnev's concept still allowed the Kremlin to support revolutionary movements abroad. It therefore contained the seeds of future conflict, even as Brezhnev pursued the agreements that he hoped would bring conflict to an end.

Pompidou and Brandt shared a more robust idea of peace. In their view, peace was not just a matter of avoiding war. It required shared values, mutual understanding, and cooperation between states and individuals. A peace that preserved the division of Europe would be no peace at all, so their strategies aimed to overcome that division. They did not want to make the Cold War tolerable but to make it obsolete. If peace required shared values, however, it also required the overthrow of the Soviet order—not suddenly and violently, but gradually and quietly. Only a reunified Europe could enjoy real peace.

The class of 1969 pursued competing strategies of détente. One aimed to stabilize the international system, the other to transform it. The struggle between them animated the diplomacy of the early 1970s, nowhere more acutely than in the creation of the Helsinki Final Act.

Chapter 3

CREATING THE CSCE

THE LEADERS of the class of 1969 wasted no time putting their strategies into action. Nixon and Kissinger sought to withdraw from Vietnam, establish ties to China, and set superpower relations on a new footing. Brandt rushed to improve West Germany's relations with its eastern neighbors. Pompidou worked to expand Franco-Soviet cooperation. And Brezhnev launched a diplomatic campaign to strengthen the Warsaw Pact and improve relations with the Western powers. But he nurtured an even grander ambition. He wanted to convene a grand multilateral conference to put a capstone on détente's bilateral agreements, freeze the division of Europe, and complete his Peace Program. After years of effort, he got his wish. In 1972, the Western allies and Europe's neutrals agreed to open preparatory talks in Helsinki to establish the Conference on Security and Cooperation in Europe (CSCE).

The conference should not have happened for many reasons. The Soviet government had first floated an idea for a similar undertaking in 1954, but for years Western leaders refused to take part. In 1969, when they finally began to consider the possibility, many Western governments—especially the Nixon administration—regarded it with skepticism. After lengthy deliberations, the NATO allies established a series of preconditions that had to be satisfied before they would participate. They also demanded an agenda whose scope far exceeded what the Soviets had in mind and whose key ideas stood at odds with Brezhnev's goals. Any one of these factors might have derailed the conference and relegated it to the footnotes of Cold War history.

Yet the conference did come into being. The North Americans and Western Europeans agreed to take part. Their preconditions were met. The Soviets and Eastern Europeans consented to expand the agenda beyond their initial proposals. These developments owed something to chance. If the Bundestag had turned against Brandt, for example, Ostpolitik would have collapsed and the prospects for a conference along with it. However, the genesis of the CSCE also owed a great deal to the crises of legitimacy of the 1960s. In agitating for the conference, the Soviets and their allies tried to take advantage of the upheaval that was shaking the West. They appealed to public opinion to persuade Western leaders that they could not reject the proposal without damaging their own domestic standing and NATO's fragile legitimacy.

The Soviets succeeded. After fifteen years of batting away the idea of a European security conference, the Western allies concluded that they could not afford to say no. In turn, they looked for ways to exploit the crisis underway in the East. They insisted on discussing subjects that targeted the most sensitive areas of communist governance and called the legitimacy of the Soviet order into question. Eager to hold the conference, and confident that they could defend themselves against this challenge, the Soviets and their allies accepted the Western demands. In this respect, the West also succeeded. It would use the conference to fight the Cold War by other means.

Three sets of parallel negotiations created the CSCE: one within each of the two alliances, conducted behind closed doors, and one between NATO and the Warsaw Pact, conducted in both private meetings and a series of public communiqués and countercommuniqués. The different cultures of the two alliances—and their relative strengths and weaknesses—shaped this painstaking work. The Warsaw Pact's approach demonstrated its resolution and determination, but also its intellectual rigidity and discomfort with freewheeling argument. During NATO's deliberations, the allies often disagreed with each other. Western unity remained a slippery goal. However, unlike the USSR, the United States did not seek to impose its judgments on its allies. The Nixon administration questioned the value of a pan-European conference, but let its allies take the lead rather than trying to bend them to its will. The inefficiency of this process made room for creativity and generated new ideas. The allies transformed a proposal designed to benefit the Soviet bloc into one that served Western interests.

I

In April 1965, a few months after assuming the post of general secretary, Leonid Brezhnev called for a grand conference on European security. He warned that the unfinished business of 1945, especially the ongoing disputes over the continent's postwar frontiers, posed a serious threat to peace. "No direct war danger is visible here today," he told a crowd in Warsaw, "but it would be unforgivably shortsighted not to notice that plenty of inflammable material is accumulating in this part of the world."[1] A pan-European conference would sweep it away. By recognizing these frontiers—and the regimes within them—it would "completely remove the vestiges of World War II" and put the continent on a more secure footing, Brezhnev told the Soviet Communist Party's 23rd Congress in 1966. Every country in Europe stood to benefit, he argued.[2]

The conference would also offer collateral benefits to the Soviet bloc. By reducing the risk of war, it would eliminate the need for the rival military alliances and undermine NATO. It would prevent West Germany from acquiring nuclear weapons. And it would boost the socialist economies by "creat[ing] the conditions for broad and mutually beneficial cooperation in Europe between countries with different social systems," he told a Central Committee Plenum.[3] The conference would cure the Cold War's ills.

In making these proposals, Brezhnev latched onto an old idea. More than a decade earlier, Soviet foreign minister Vyacheslav Molotov had presented a European peace plan that shocked his Western counterparts. At the 1954 Council of Foreign Ministers meeting in Berlin, he argued that the great powers should replace the fragile division of the continent with a system in which all European states—East and West alike—collaborated to protect each other. "Instead of an arrangement whereby some European states are placed in opposition to others," he said, "there should be established an all-European system of collective security."[4] By creating a single set of rules for all of Europe, the scheme would reunify Germany and lay the groundwork for a comprehensive peace settlement.[5]

The Western foreign ministers rejected Molotov's plan on the spot. British foreign secretary Anthony Eden denounced it as a "Monroe doctrine for Europe" that would marginalize the United States and pave the way for Soviet hegemony.[6] American secretary of state John Foster Dulles agreed. "The last Soviet project for what Mr. Molotov called 'European security' was so preposterous that when he read it laughter rippled around the Western sides of the table," he told a radio audience.[7] With the two sides unable to find common ground, the Berlin conference sputtered out.[8]

The Soviets persevered. At the 1955 Geneva Summit, premier Nikolai Bulganin gave his American, British, and French counterparts a draft treaty that included the main elements of Molotov's plan. Defense minister Georgy Zhukov tried to persuade his old comrade, American president Dwight Eisenhower, that Europe needed a collective security system. The Western allies remained unconvinced.[9]

A decade later, Brezhnev revived Molotov's proposal but did not share his purpose. Molotov called for new security structures because he wanted to tear down those of his adversaries. He envisioned replacing NATO with a Europe-wide security system, which would abort Western plans for a European Defense Community and evict American forces from the continent. The USSR would gain new opportunities to interfere in Western European affairs. Germany would reunify as a neutral state, or even join the communist fold. In these respects, Molotov's plan attacked the pillars of the Western order.[10]

Brezhnev's ambitions were more modest. To be sure, he talked about dissolving NATO and peeling the Western Europeans away from the United States, but these were goals for the long term. More immediately, Brezhnev wanted to sharpen the lines that separated East and West, whereas Molotov wanted to blur them. Brezhnev agreed with Molotov and other Soviet leaders that the Federal Republic of Germany's commitment to reunification posed an ongoing threat to peace. But instead of gambling on reunifying Germany as a neutral state, he wanted to affirm the division of the country. If the FRG—and every other European state—recognized the postwar frontiers as permanent and confirmed the division of the continent, the risk of war would decline and the governments of the Soviet bloc would gain an international stamp of legitimacy. This was the logic behind his appeal for a security conference.[11]

The proposal aimed to put NATO in a difficult position. Brezhnev emphasized that the USSR remained sincerely committed to peace. If NATO turned him down, he could pin the blame for Cold War tensions on Western policy and argue that it preferred reckless schemes—such as the multilateral nuclear force (MLF), still in the planning stages—to the hard work of reconciliation. In this way, Brezhnev would arm NATO's domestic critics and accelerate "the growth of contradictions" within the alliance, an East German foreign ministry report argued. Whether the Western allies embraced the security conference or rejected it, the USSR stood to gain.[12]

The conference would also expand the USSR's influence over its European allies. By contrast with NATO, the Warsaw Pact lacked a standing body to coordinate foreign policy. Its leaders only met sporadically. It had no unified military command. Its secretariat had minimal capabilities. The Soviets therefore launched an initiative to reform it, hoping that more robust structures would provide new mechanisms to keep their allies in line. The security conference provided a perfect excuse to put these ideas into action. The Kremlin would work out its policies in advance and then, in the name of closer consultations, present them to the allies for their endorsement.[13]

The allies saw matters differently. The Romanians complained that the Soviets refused to treat them as equals and routinely ignored their preferences. At Warsaw Pact meetings, Nicolae Ceaușescu and other Romanian officials engaged in "sharp polemical exchanges" with their allies and criticized the documents that the Soviets expected them to rubber-stamp.[14] In 1967, Ceaușescu defied his allies and unilaterally established diplomatic relations with Bonn, hoping to develop lucrative ties to the capitalist world. The move infuriated the Soviets and other Eastern Europeans, as did Ceaușescu's demand that they take a more conciliatory attitude to the

West.[15] In turn, the Soviet attempts to strengthen the Warsaw Pact outraged the Romanians, who refused to put their national forces under the command of a Russian general. From the vantage point of Bucharest, a weaker alliance was a better alliance.[16]

The Polish government had similar anxieties but reached different conclusions. Its leaders had long fretted about their country's postwar frontiers, which encompassed lands that had historically belonged to Germany but that the FRG refused to relinquish officially. This ambiguity raised questions about the communist regime's security and legitimacy.[17] With some justification, they worried that the Soviets would ignore these concerns in pursuing a deal with the West Germans. The specter of a "new Rapallo"—a reincarnation of the 1922 treaty that repaired relations between the USSR and the Weimar Republic at the expense of their neighbors—haunted party chief Władysław Gomułka and foreign minister Adam Rapacki.[18]

They decided to take matters into their own hands. Even before Brezhnev resurrected Molotov's idea, the Poles called for a meeting of all European states to discuss collective security, affirm "the present frontiers of Germany," including the Oder-Neisse Line, and strike a deal on nuclear disarmament. Until the Federal Republic recognized Poland's borders, accepted East Germany's existence, and renounced nuclear weapons, Gomułka insisted in 1965, no Warsaw Pact country should upgrade its relations with Bonn.[19]

Events justified Gomułka and Rapacki's fears. A 1967 Soviet draft for a renunciation-of-force agreement with the FRG cast doubt on Poland's sovereignty and implied that the country's western frontier remained open to debate.[20] After Romania established relations with Bonn, Gomułka worried that other Eastern European states, who did not share Poland's territorial quarrels with West Germany, would follow suit. "The Warsaw Pact is dissolving," he warned Brezhnev.[21] The only solution was to strengthen the alliance. In a more consultative organization, Gomułka reasoned, Poland could exert more influence over Soviet policy and prevent the other allies from betraying its core interests.

To this end, the Polish government endorsed Brezhnev's reform project. Rapacki called for new decision-making bodies within the Warsaw Pact, including a forum for regular discussions among foreign ministers, which would ensure "systematic and frequent consultations among member countries."[22] And in 1967, a meeting of allied foreign ministers endorsed Gomułka's "Warsaw Package," the three criteria—on borders, the GDR, and nuclear weapons—that the FRG had to fulfill before any Eastern European state could establish relations with Bonn.[23]

East Germany's concerns echoed Poland's. Walter Ulbricht and his colleagues wanted Western states—especially the Federal Republic—to recognize the GDR and its borders under international law. As long as Bonn refused to do so, Europe would live under the threat of nuclear war.[24] Like the

Poles, the East Germans worried that Moscow would abandon them if it served Soviet interests to do so. They therefore refused to let the Kremlin dictate Warsaw Pact policy, and considered taking unilateral action on the subjects that mattered most to them. According to a Foreign Ministry report, the GDR might consult its allies, but not "in such a way that the partner could infer that we would make our proposals subject to their approval." The East Germans needed no one's consent to act.[25] In 1966, they published an appeal of their own on European security.[26]

The Poles and East Germans hoped that a conference would achieve similar results. By putting Europe's postwar frontiers at the top of its agenda, the undertaking would prevent the USSR and the other allies from dodging the question or cutting bilateral deals with Bonn. By placing every state on an equal footing, it would affirm the Eastern Europeans' capacity to act independently of the USSR.[27] Simply by participating in the multilateral forum, the GDR would gain de facto recognition as a sovereign state and undermine the FRG's claim to speak on behalf of all of Germany. In this way, the conference would contribute to "strengthening the international position of the GDR, the increase of its authority and its equal participation in peaceful European cooperation," the East German foreign ministry predicted.[28] It would also yield economic benefits. Ideally, it would loosen Western restrictions on trade and foster East-West partnerships.[29] Poland and East Germany could not gain total independence in foreign policy, but they might carve out more room for maneuver.[30]

The Romanians also wanted a conference to affirm their sovereignty and expand their economic ties to the West.[31] At a 1966 Warsaw Pact meeting, Romanian foreign minister Corneliu Mănescu objected to a Soviet draft declaration on peace in Europe that the other allies had already approved. He presented a draft of his own. It borrowed some of the Soviets' formulations, but refused to criticize West Germany or demand that Western governments recognize the continent's frontiers as immutable. Every state had to respect its neighbors' sovereignty and refrain from interfering in their internal affairs, it insisted, implicitly warning the USSR to stay out of Romanian domestic politics. Finally, it called on Western leaders to begin talks on European security immediately and without prerequisites. Like the Soviets, Poles, and East Germans, the Romanians wanted to convene a security conference, but they did not share their allies' goals.[32]

The tension between these competing approaches came to a head a few weeks later. When the Warsaw Pact's leaders gathered in Bucharest, they wasted no time before attacking each other. Gomułka called a Romanian proposal frivolous. Ceaușescu alleged in turn that the Poles had "capitulat[ed] to American imperialism," and denounced the Soviets for trying to impose their preferences on the allies. At first, Brezhnev tried to mediate the dispute, but he soon lost patience and accused Ceauşescu of threatening him.[33] The quarrel thwarted his plan to strengthen the alliance's military structures. In the absence of unanimous consent, Brezhnev had to back down.[34]

When the conversation turned to European security, however, the Romanians had to give ground. Brezhnev tried to reconcile Gomułka and Ulbricht's approach with Ceauşescu's, and brokered a deal to issue a joint declaration.[35] By giving something to each side, the text suffered from internal tensions. On the one hand, it denounced "the militarist and revanchist forces of West Germany," criticized "the American ruling circles" for trying "to impose their will on their allies in Western Europe," demanded that the United States withdraw its forces from the continent, and promised to "crush any aggression" against "the inviolability of the existing frontiers" in Europe. On the other, it invited Western governments to participate in a conference on European security and proposed expanding economic, scientific, and cultural collaboration between East and West.[36] The 1967 meeting of European communist parties in Karlovy Vary, Czechoslovakia produced a document in the same vein.[37]

These declarations attracted international attention but lacked coherence. Born of awkward compromises between the allies' competing positions, they simultaneously castigated the West and appealed for its cooperation. A litany of other demands—on Vietnam, Germany, and nuclear weapons—overshadowed the conference proposal. Some of the Warsaw Pact allies wanted to hold the conference as soon as possible, whereas others wanted to delay it until their demands regarding Germany were satisfied. In the absence of conceptual clarity and political unity, the conference idea went nowhere.

II

In March 1969, Brezhnev launched a new effort to breathe life into the security conference. On ten days' notice, he convened a meeting of the Warsaw Pact's Political Consultative Committee in Budapest.[38] The session had originally been scheduled for the previous autumn, but the Romanians delayed it by objecting to a new set of proposals for military reform.[39] Now, after invading Czechoslovakia and demonstrating how tough he could be, Brezhnev felt empowered to take a more conciliatory line and give détente a fresh impetus. The recent elections of presidents Richard Nixon in the United States and Gustav Heinemann in West Germany suggested that the Western powers might be open to repairing their relations with the USSR. Meanwhile, the growing threat that China posed to Soviet security redoubled the Kremlin's determination to improve its position in Europe. Days before the Budapest meeting opened, Chinese soldiers attacked Soviet troops along the Ussuri River in eastern Siberia, inflicting dozens of casualties. Brezhnev arrived in the Hungarian capital determined to rally his allies. He wanted to issue a new call for a security conference.[40]

The meeting nearly collapsed in acrimony. As in Bucharest three years earlier, Brezhnev stood in the crossfire of contending views. Gomułka and Ulbricht had not changed their minds. They insisted that Western governments had to recognize the territorial status quo before any conference could meet and demanded a "very sharply worded" declaration to this effect.[41] By contrast, Ceauşescu wanted a moderate declaration that laid down no prerequisites and appealed to Western sensibilities. The night before the meeting officially opened, Brezhnev walked from room to room in Budapest's Grand Hotel, visiting each delegation in turn. He denounced Gomułka and Ulbricht for obstructing détente, and he railed at Ceauşescu for following his own whims at the expense of allied solidarity.[42] "You are as bad as that bastard Hoxha!" he reportedly said. The Albanian leader had left the Warsaw Pact because he refused to toe the Soviet line on China. Now, Brezhnev feared, Ceauşescu might follow suit.[43]

The last-ditch negotiations paid off when Ceauşescu cut a deal with Brezhnev. The Soviets abandoned their draft declaration denouncing Beijing. In exchange, the Romanians dropped their demand for a statement criticizing the invasion of Czechoslovakia. The two men then joined forces to squeeze the Poles and East Germans, who gave way at the last possible moment.[44] When the PCC officially opened, the Warsaw Pact leaders unanimously issued a new proposal for a European conference. "One of the basic preconditions for safeguarding the security of Europe is the inviolability of the existing European frontiers," it declared. "A practical step toward strengthening European security would be a meeting in the immediate future between representatives of all the European States concerned in order to establish by mutual agreement the procedure for convening the Conference and to determine the items on its agenda."[45]

The Budapest appeal was a watershed. It eschewed the vitriol of the Bucharest declaration in favor of a more moderate approach. Contrary to the East Germans' and Poles' original demands, it did not fulminate against American imperialism or excoriate West German revanchism. It laid down no preconditions for the conference. Brezhnev and Ceauşescu continued to disagree on fundamental questions, but their flexible approach had prevailed over Gomułka and Ulbricht's hard line.[46] European security still required that all states recognize the continent's frontiers, but the appeal implied that this might be the *result* of the conference rather than its prerequisite.[47]

After the meeting, the allies congratulated each other on a job well done, but disagreements persisted.[48] The Poles and East Germans feared that the

Soviets had abandoned them. Polish foreign minister Stefan Jędrychowski warned that some socialist states wanted to restrict the conference to discussing "non-controversial topics that have only marginal importance for solving key problems in Europe."[49] Walter Ulbricht told Brezhnev that entrenching the political and territorial status quo had to remain the allies' first priority.[50] An East German diplomat elaborated on this argument. "The recognition of current borders, as they have developed since the end of the Second World War, and the territorial integrity of all states of our continent is a fundamental problem of achieving and ensuring European security," he wrote. "Even today the non-recognition of current borders, especially the borders between the two German states and Poland's western border on the Oder and Neisse, is a permanent menace to peace and security in Europe."[51] If the conference did not solve this problem, it hardly deserved the Warsaw Pact's support.

Through the summer of 1969, some of the Eastern Europeans grumbled that the Soviets had not thought the conference through. They "have no detailed ideas and plans in matters of either substance or organizational structure, or if they do, they have not yet shared them with us," a report from the Hungarian foreign ministry complained. Rather than fleshing out the agenda and developing a plan of attack, Moscow preferred to focus on "the idea and preparation of the conference" for their own sake.[52] "The countries of the Warsaw Pact must make their proposals concrete" if they hoped to persuade the Western allies to participate, Hungary's deputy foreign minister insisted.[53] Polish officials criticized the Soviets for dragging their feet. Unless the allies stepped up the pace of "practical work on implementation of the idea of the Budapest Appeal," Western governments might hijack the conference for their own purposes.[54]

These criticisms got it half right. The Soviets did not want a conference for its own sake. Foreign minister Andrei Gromyko did argue, however, that the conference should only discuss "political issues of a general nature." He proposed two subjects for the agenda: an agreement to renounce the use of force, and measures to expand economic, scientific, and technological cooperation. The nonuse of force declaration offered fewer assurances than an ironclad treaty on borders but would still "contribute to the consolidation of the existing situation on the European continent," he argued. If the Warsaw Pact demanded anything more ambitious, he warned, it might alienate the Western powers and abort the conference before it got underway.[55]

In September and October, Soviet deputy foreign minister Vladimir Semenov travelled across Eastern Europe to solicit the allies' support. The scope of the conference had to be modest, he told his Polish counterpart. The Warsaw Pact should seek "de facto recognition of the status quo" and improve the atmosphere of East-West relations, but no more.[56] It certainly could not repeat Molotov's demand for a collective security system,

Semenov argued in Budapest. That "would practically turn the security conference into a peace conference, making it impossible to hold it," he said, "for the Western countries would not be willing to discuss such issues." If the first conference succeeded, the Warsaw Pact could always propose holding subsequent meetings, each more ambitious than the last. For the moment, however, trying to do too much risked "choking the infant in its cradle."[57] He made a similar case in East Berlin.[58]

The Soviets' caution divided their allies. The Poles conceded that demanding too much would "make the convocation of a European conference impossible." Nonetheless, they complained that Moscow's pessimistic approach "overlook[ed] the basic questions of European security."[59] They pushed back by drafting an ambitious proposal for a security treaty and asking the allies to endorse it.[60] It required signatories to renounce the use of force against all states, recognize Europe's existing frontiers, treat an attack on any state as an attack on all, eliminate barriers to economic cooperation, and work toward complete disarmament.[61] By contrast, the East Germans sided with the Kremlin. State secretary Günther Kohrt and Soviet deputy foreign minister Leonid Ilyichev agreed that the Poles' lofty demands would alienate the West and "endanger the rapid convening of a European security conference."[62] East German officials wanted all states to recognize the sanctity of their borders eventually, but they acknowledged that it would take time to achieve this goal. In the meantime, a declaration on the nonuse of force would be a step in the right direction.[63]

The Soviets prevailed upon the Poles to drop their objections. In October 1969, the allied foreign ministers endorsed a minimalist agenda for the security conference. Echoing Gromyko's proposal, the Prague Declaration included only two items: renouncing the use of force and expanding international cooperation.[64] The allies agreed on "the fundamental issues," the Hungarian foreign ministry reported.[65] But the façade of unity concealed lingering dissatisfaction. Under pressure from Moscow, the Poles abandoned their demand to discuss frontier recognition and collective security at the conference. In exchange, the Soviets added a clause to the draft declaration on the nonuse of force that they would present at the conference. The new version required signatories to "recognize and unconditionally observe the territorial integrity of all European states within their existing borders."[66] Jędrychowski accepted this compromise but emphasized that it was the "minimum that we can agree with."[67] A few weeks later, the Poles complained to the Soviets that the declaration was "too general and cautious."[68] By contrast, the other allies—especially the Romanians—expressed their approval. Deputy foreign minister George Macovescu told the Soviet chargé d'affaires in Bucharest that the Warsaw Pact should "continue to act in this direction" and bring the Western states to the negotiating table.[69]

The Soviets adopted a more moderate vision for the security conference and bullied their allies into supporting it. This unity came at a price. Instead of increasing allied cohesion, the Budapest and Prague meetings redoubled the Romanians' and Poles' determination to act independently. Ceaușescu decided to use the conference to advance the cause of Romanian autonomy, regardless of what the USSR wanted. In Warsaw, Gomułka concluded that he could not count on the USSR to respect Poland's interests or support its bid to win recognition of the Oder-Neisse Line. Circumventing the Soviets, he offered to negotiate an agreement regarding Germany's borders directly with the Federal Republic. Willy Brandt signaled his interest, and talks began the following year.[70] Moscow resorted to heavy-handed tactics to produce an even-handed declaration, but instead of combating the centrifugal tendencies in the alliance, it exacerbated them.

III

After their exertions within the Warsaw Pact, the Soviets had to persuade the Western powers to come to the table. Despite the problems with their own allies, they believed that they would succeed because the underlying trends in international affairs were moving in their favor. A "general crisis" had gripped the capitalist world, Brezhnev told the Central Committee. "The deepest contradictions lurking in the depths" of Western society had come to the surface in 1968. The Vietnam War had shaken the Western Europeans' trust in American leadership. They increasingly resented NATO and, over time, would want expand their ties to the socialist bloc.[71] Meanwhile, optimists within the Warsaw Pact believed that their alliance was gaining strength. "The tendency toward closer union and integration has clearly been achieved and the common ground for action on fundamental political questions has grown," an East German foreign ministry report concluded.[72] Sooner or later, the United States and its allies would find themselves powerless to resist the communist proposals for a conference.

To take advantage of the crisis afflicting the West, the Soviets counted on mobilizing Western public opinion. Grassroots organizations, backed by Moscow, agitated for a security conference. The International Committee for Security and Cooperation in Europe (ICSCE) and World Council for Peace distributed pamphlets and organized conferences attended by communists, left-wing activists, and pacifists from both sides of the Iron Curtain.[73] The ICSCE's first meeting, held in Vienna in late 1969, called on Western leaders to act. "Europeans can and must demand that their parliaments and governments . . . take measures for the solution of the problems of security and cooperation on our continent," its communiqué said.[74]

This public relations effort assumed that energized voters could compel reluctant governments to agree to a conference. It aimed to put politicians "on the spot." If they refused to participate, domestic critics would accuse them of not taking the threat of war seriously.[75] "[O]ur efforts will generate sympathy in European public opinion" because citizens were tired of the Cold War, Hungarian deputy foreign minister Frigyes Puja told his Soviet bloc counterparts.[76] NATO could not reject the conference "without a loss of face."[77] These efforts echoed Vyacheslav Molotov's logic fifteen years before. In 1954, Molotov had assured his Kremlin colleagues that the Western powers "will have exposed themselves once again as the organizers of a military bloc against other states" if they refused his proposal. Once again, communist leaders hoped to use democratic means to serve undemocratic purposes.[78]

To complement this pressure from below, a diplomatic campaign put pressure on the West from above. The Politburo equipped Soviet ambassadors with a straightforward argument: dozens of international conferences had been held around the world since 1945, but the fundamental problems of European security remained unresolved. Even though "their lack of resolution carries a particularly serious threat to peace . . . during this time there has not taken place any conference, not a single meeting, in which representatives of the governments of all European countries participated." The conference had to affirm the nonuse of force, but because the Budapest appeal imposed no preconditions, each state was welcome to propose its own ideas for the agenda.[79] In Washington, Soviet ambassador Anatoly Dobrynin told Kissinger that "the highest level of the Politburo" wanted the conference to happen.[80] In Moscow, Gromyko assured the British ambassador that the USSR and its allies "were not following their own narrow interests" but acting for the benefit of all Europeans.[81] Polish and East German envoys made a similar case to their hosts.[82] Only the Romanians followed a different script, hinting that a conference might weaken Soviet hegemony as it strengthened European security.[83]

Finally, the Soviets tried to win over the neutral European governments. If they backed the conference, no one could argue that it was a socialist ploy. But the Austrians rebuffed Moscow's overtures.[84] In Helsinki, Finnish leaders also hesitated. When Soviet ambassador Anatoly Kovalev asked President Urho Kekkonen to speak out in favor of a conference, Kekkonen doubted that Western governments would agree to participate. He worried that endorsing the Warsaw Pact's proposal would make Finland seem like "the Soviet Union's errand boy."[85] Getting involved in an East-West argument would also violate the foundational principle of Finnish neutrality.[86]

However, Kekkonen also saw the danger of rejecting the Soviet proposal. If the USSR had lost patience with independent action in its sphere of influence, as the invasion of Czechoslovakia seemed to demonstrate, Finland would suffer the consequences. Besides, Moscow had been leaning heavily on Kekkonen for several years to extend full recognition to the GDR. He refused on the grounds that doing so would contradict Finland's scrupulous neutrality on the German question, according to which it maintained diplomatic relations with both German states at the consular level only. In a future crisis, however, the Soviets might refuse to accept Finland's excuses—or its neutrality—and send the Red Army across the border.[87]

In these crosscurrents, Kekkonen perceived an opportunity. He decided to do as Kovalev asked, but with a twist. Finland would not just declare its support for a conference, but offer to host the negotiations. Kekkonen's policy of "active neutrality" had brought US-Soviet arms control negotiations to Helsinki in 1969 and inspired Finland's successful pursuit of a seat on the UN Security Council in 1969–70.[88] Organizing the conference would complement these efforts, safeguard Finland's even-handed position on Germany, and forestall future pressure from Moscow. The USSR could hardly invade a neutral neighbor while simultaneously proclaiming its commitment to peace at a major international conference.[89] In this respect, Kekkonen's calculations resembled Ceaușescu's. Supporting the conference presented an opportunity to defend national autonomy. "This is going to be good," he noted in his diary.[90]

On May 5, 1969, Finnish diplomats delivered an aide-mémoire to every state in Europe, the United States, and Canada. "Finland is willing to act as the host for the security conference," it said. The country was well positioned to serve in this role because it maintained "good relations with all the countries which are concerned with European security and [an] impartial attitude toward the most vital problem of European security, the German question." No state ought to impose any preconditions—whether recognition of postwar frontiers or anything else—to convening the conference.[91]

The move satisfied the Soviets. The USSR "appreciates the initiative shown by the Government of Finland and is ready to provide all possible assistance to its implementation," Kovalev told Kekkonen.[92] Following up on their invitation, the Finns appointed a roving ambassador to build support for the conference and solicit new ideas. Over the course of fifty trips to European and North American capitals, Ralph Enckell became a familiar figure in many foreign ministries.[93]

Despite these efforts, the Finns did not expect that the conference would actually take place. By seizing the initiative, they hoped to fend off Soviet pressure and maintain their neutrality. They agreed to keep Moscow informed as their plans evolved, but this did not signify that they had become Soviet puppets—precisely the opposite.[94] Kekkonen's overriding goal was to protect Finland's freedom of action. "We weren't fools. In May 1969, we didn't think that the Finnish government's circular would lead to a conference. At best we would be able to organize some kind of diplomatic tea party in Helsinki," diplomat Keijo Korhonen later wrote. "A lush tree grew out of a mustard seed. But future historians shouldn't think that we intended to plant a tree. It simply grew."[95]

IV

Western leaders had to decide how to respond. In 1954, the Americans, British, and French had rejected Molotov's gambit in Berlin. When Brezhnev picked up the security conference idea a decade later, their views did not change. The succession of Warsaw Pact declarations and appeals repeated the familiar themes of communist propaganda and blamed Europe's unresolved problems on the West. With the exception of the Danes, who wanted to see where the Bucharest Declaration might lead, the allies squashed the idea. "It was dangerous to raise false hopes in this area," Secretary of State Dean Rusk argued.[96] Britain's representative to the North Atlantic Council warned that Moscow hoped to undermine NATO by exploiting Western voters' waning support for the alliance.[97] The next year, after the Karlovy Vary declaration, American, British, and West German diplomats agreed that a conference could "only have negative consequences." They had no desire to participate in a "propaganda circus."[98]

They remained skeptical even when the Warsaw Pact moderated its demands. The Budapest appeal "stinks to high heaven of propaganda," French foreign minister Michel Debré told American Secretary of State William Rogers in 1969. "An analysis of the facts shows that such a conference could not currently yield a useful result."[99] Rogers agreed, as did Henry Kissinger, who warned Nixon about the "dangers of holding grandiose conferences."[100] In London, Foreign Office officials concluded that the Warsaw Pact remained wedded to demands that the West could not accept.[101] Kurt Georg Kiesinger and senior West German diplomats also distrusted the Soviets' motives.[102] Across the alliance, caution prevailed.[103]

The allies feared that the conference would erode support for NATO at home. If Western governments sat down with the Soviets to discuss peace in Europe, citizens might assume that every East-West problem had been solved, even if the conference yielded meager results. This false sense of security—or "euphoria," as many officials called it—would embolden NATO's critics. In turn, allied governments would find it harder to maintain adequate military spending. "The recent Warsaw Pact appeal ... is adversely affecting our Allies' determination to maintain defense contributions," Rogers explained to Nixon in April 1969. "Euphoria, as a complement to the prospect of East-West negotiations, is threatening."[104] Many Western European officials felt the same way. Dutch diplomats argued that a conference might blind voters to the continued danger that the USSR posed.[105] At a time when Soviet military spending was rising, euphoria could do serious damage.[106]

Public calls for defense cuts demonstrated that NATO's crisis of domestic legitimacy had not abated. In 1969, Canadian prime minister Pierre Trudeau reduced the country's forces stationed in Europe by half.[107] By itself, this decision did not jeopardize Western security. But leaders on both sides of the Atlantic worried that it foretold worse things to come, especially since a growing chorus of voices in the US Congress demanded similarly drastic measures.[108] In this era, more than half of Americans thought their government spent too much money on defense. A majority of Britons believed that the USSR was friendly toward the West and that there was little danger of nuclear war. A majority of West Germans told pollsters that the Soviets posed no threat. In Belgium, 83 percent of those surveyed thought that war was unlikely. The figures were only slightly lower in France, the Netherlands, and Italy.[109] No matter what politicians thought about the alliance, this climate of opinion made it difficult to maintain an effective military deterrent.[110]

The Budapest appeal tested the allies' pledge to reduce East-West tensions. After Charles de Gaulle abandoned NATO's integrated military command in 1966, Belgian foreign minister Pierre Harmel concluded that the alliance had to articulate a new raison d'être. The North Atlantic Treaty authorized members to withdraw as soon as 1969. If France or any other member decided that the alliance had outlived its purpose and left, the alliance's twentieth anniversary would give cause for mourning, not celebration. The allies instructed Harmel to "identify the tasks which lie before [them], in order to strengthen the Alliance as a factor for a durable peace."[111] The mandate required him to consider whether NATO should commit itself to promoting détente and whether it should strengthen the ties that bound its members, for instance by improving the mechanisms for intra-allied consultations.[112]

Completed in 1967, the Harmel Report reconciled NATO's military responsibilities with its diplomatic aspirations. It refused to choose between those allies who wanted to focus on traditional security questions and those who wanted new avenues for cooperation with the Soviet bloc.[113] Defense and détente were not "contradictory but complementary," it concluded. NATO ought to pursue both.[114] This ambivalence prepared the alliance for any future climate. If East-West relations took a turn for the worse, NATO could stand firm in its familiar military role. If relations with the Soviets improved, it could coordinate Western policy. Embracing détente would keep the alliance relevant in the eyes of voters who believed that the Soviet threat was receding. Whatever happened, the alliance could renew its claim to legitimacy.[115] This new approach had a downside, however. Now that the allies had committed themselves to détente, they had to respond to the Warsaw Pact's overtures.

In 1969, in response to these pressures, the allies changed their minds about the security conference. After spurning the idea for fifteen years, they decided that the costs of saying no outweighed the dangers of saying yes. If they snubbed the Warsaw Pact's unusually moderate overtures, Western citizens might conclude that their leaders were not serious about peace. Georges Pompidou made the point bluntly. "We cannot reject [the conference] without being considered villains," he said.[116] Some officials worried in particular about the attitudes of young people. NATO would need their support in the future, but they will "lose all sympathy for [the alliance] if we cannot give it a dynamic and positive role," British foreign secretary Michael Stewart argued.[117]

For similar reasons, the West German, Canadian, Dutch, Belgian, Danish, and Norwegian governments felt compelled to seize every opportunity to improve East-West relations. If they failed to do so, they might provoke an outcry that would further damage NATO's standing and help opposition politicians who questioned the very idea of the alliance.[118] Regardless of the Budapest appeal's merits, and whatever one's doubts about the Kremlin's motives, appearances mattered as much as substance. "This is a field for a propaganda battle and it will not be enough for our policy to be right," wrote the Foreign Office's deputy undersecretary, Sir Thomas Brimelow. "It must look right as well."[119] The allies felt compelled to take a risk.

Despite these anxieties, average citizens paid little heed to the conference idea. No demonstrators took to the streets to demand that NATO participate.[120] The two alliances fought a "long-range artillery duel via public declarations," Henry Kissinger's adviser Helmut Sonnenfeldt observed, but Western journalists barely covered it.[121] The few articles that did appear emphasized the risks that any conference would entail.[122] "We find it difficult from here to assess [the] real extent of pressures" on Western governments, the US mission to NATO reported in October 1969. "To some extent, ministers may be anticipating public opinion rather than reacting to it."[123] Nonetheless, given the very real decline in support for the alliance, most Western governments erred on the side of caution.

Because the allies felt compelled to participate in a security conference, they resolved to mitigate its risks. They would tamp down any signs of euphoria by reminding citizens that the conference offered no quick solutions and that the Soviet threat remained real. "[W]e must urge public opinion in our countries to be patient and to ward off all excessively high hopes for a rapid détente," the British and West Germans agreed.[124] Addressing the deep-seated causes of the Cold War required careful preparation and hard work on specific problems. "We should never leave doubt that we sincerely want to make progress, where progress can be made. But we should not settle for the illusion of progress," American undersecretary of state Elliot Richardson told his NATO counterparts. "A crucial distinction must be drawn between a grand Conference on European security and a series of negotiations on concrete issues. This distinction must also be conveyed to Allied public opinion."[125] The high-flying rhetoric that the Warsaw Pact favored would not suffice. For the security conference to succeed, it had to yield precise commitments.

V

The Western allies decided to put their own stamp on the conference. The negotiations did not have to serve the USSR's purposes or endorse the status quo. "We can say for certain that the Soviets want the conference with the goal of reinforcing their hegemony" in Eastern Europe, officials at the Quai d'Orsay noted. "But are the Russians the masters of what the conference will be?" Instead of accepting Moscow's agenda, the allies developed their own. They would use the Soviet idea to advance Western interests.[126]

Even the skeptics acquiesced. In Washington, Nixon and Kissinger believed that the net result of negotiations with the Warsaw Pact "might well be frustration and western disunity, both of which would tend to set back prospects for an eventual resolution of European issues."[127] Helmut Sonnenfeldt groused about an excess of enthusiasm for the conference in certain corners of the State Department.[128] But compared to the war in Vietnam, the opening to China, and nuclear arms control, Kissinger regarded the conference as a trivial undertaking unlikely to affect core American interests. Despite its reservations, the Nixon administration followed its allies' lead in the name of NATO solidarity. The "US would not try to veto the holding of such a conference if the Europeans desired it," Kissinger told the West German ambassador in Washington.[129]

Over the course of 1969, the allies developed their plan of attack.[130] They established a series of preconditions that had to be satisfied before any conference could begin. The first of these concerned the division of Germany and the status of West Berlin. Willy Brandt and his advisor Egon Bahr welcomed the conference proposal because it would help them to pursue Ostpolitik. "We have to try to use it as an instrument for asserting our interests," Bahr argued. "Above all, we should use the conference idea as a lever to compel the GDR to agree to a rapprochement of both German states."[131] In December, the allied foreign ministers agreed to follow the Federal Republic's lead. They would refuse to participate in a conference until West

Germany had normalized relations with the USSR, Poland, and East Germany, and until the four occupying powers in Berlin had reached an agreement to regulate access to the city.[132]

The Soviets complained that the West was procrastinating. "We are convinced that, if guided by the interests of the convocation and success of the pan-European conference, the imposition of any preconditions cannot be justified," the Soviet Ministry of Foreign Affairs argued. "It would be wrong to connect in a single bundle, for example, the negotiations between the FRG and some of the socialist countries with the efforts of states in convening the pan-European conference. Following this logic, one could also, with equal justification, make these negotiations contingent on the success of the conference." From Moscow's vantage point, the conference ought to take place right away, unencumbered by the fate of any other negotiations. Since the Soviets were the ones proposing the conference, however, they had little leverage on this point.[133]

The allies stood firm. They insisted that they only wanted to make the conference viable. Arguments about Germany and Berlin would sidetrack it unless deals on those questions were negotiated beforehand. "If one were to say now that the German question should be solved at [a conference], that would be equivalent to torpedoing the conference," Egon Bahr told Gromyko.[134] Besides, negotiations could not begin until the West agreed to participate. "If you want to go by yourself to your wedding, you risk not getting very much satisfaction from it," Willy Brandt told the Soviets.[135]

The North Americans also had to participate in the conference on an equal footing with every other state. The Warsaw Pact's public statements had not specified whether the conference should be open to the United States and Canada. The Bucharest declaration and Prague communiqué called for an "all-European conference." The Budapest appeal proposed "a general European conference" that would "meet the interests of all European states."[136] The ambiguity of these formulations did not escape the Western allies, nor did the Soviets' regular polemics against the American military presence on the continent. In response, officials in Washington and Ottawa insisted, with their allies' support, that no conference on the future of Europe could take place without them. "Full Canadian and United States participation from the outset was indispensable and was not a matter for discussion with the East," NATO Secretary General Manlio Brosio said.[137]

Soviet diplomats tried to dodge the question. Anatoly Dobrynin told Elliot Richardson that the USSR would not object "if all European states believe that US participation is necessary or desirable."[138] The Soviet ambassador in Ottawa said that it was premature to raise the matter.[139] In Moscow, however, Soviet leaders had already decided to give way. They understood that the Western powers would never agree to a conference unless the

North Americans had a seat at the table. In exchange, they wanted East Germany to participate alongside the Federal Republic. In this way, the conference would win de facto recognition for the GDR and yield "a major political success for the socialist community," Andrei Gromyko argued.[140] Besides, if the Warsaw Pact demonstrated that it was willing to compromise, it might persuade the West "to take a definitively positive position" on the conference.[141] The USSR's allies endorsed this logic.[142] In January 1970, Gromyko told American ambassador Jacob Beam that it was clear that the United States and Canada could participate provided that both German states did too.[143] By the middle of the year, NATO had settled the question to its satisfaction.[144]

After laying out their preconditions, the allies had to decide what they wanted the conference to discuss. They agreed that the Warsaw Pact's goal of entrenching Europe's territorial and political status quo was unacceptable. In the spring of 1969, they undertook a brainstorming exercise to compile a list of subjects that might serve Western interests.[145] NATO should "do its utmost to reach some positive and even bold conclusions," Brosio said. There was "no reason why the Alliance should not present its proposed solutions, even though they might not be popular with the other side." Rather than trying to minimize the Warsaw Pact's gains, the allies agreed to take the offensive.[146]

To make a meaningful difference to European security, the conference had to tackle the conceptual problems that underlay the Cold War. "For the Russians, European security means upholding and guaranteeing the status quo in that part of Europe which they control," Sir Thomas Brimelow wrote. "Our concept of security is that no state in Europe should be exposed to the risk of pressure or armed intervention from any other."[147] The Soviets wanted the conference to issue a brief declaration on the nonuse of force, which would affirm the status quo and bolster communist legitimacy. Instead, the allies should propose that the conference negotiate a comprehensive "code of good conduct" that took aim at the principles of the Soviet order, French foreign minister Maurice Schumann argued.[148]

First and foremost, the allies targeted the Brezhnev Doctrine. As Schumann envisioned it, the code of conduct would enumerate all of the "basic principles which should govern international relations," including respect for territorial integrity, noninterference in domestic affairs, the sovereign equality of all states, and the right to neutrality. William Rogers urged the allies "to challenge explicitly the notion that intervention by one state in the affairs of another—whether they are in the same or different social systems—is an admissible principle of international law."[149] In this way, the West could undermine the Brezhnev Doctrine and, by extension, the USSR's hierarchical concept of order in Eastern Europe. If the Soviets staked their legitimacy on an international agreement that forbade such an invasion, they might think twice before violating a neighbor's sovereignty again.[150]

Affirming states' inherent equality would also expand the Eastern Europeans' freedom of action. Simply assembling all of the European states around the same table could grant "greater freedom of speech to the countries of the East," Pompidou told Brandt.[151] No matter how much the USSR tried, it would find it impossible "to impose all the rigid unity it might like" on its allies during the give-and-take of a conference, Canadian ambassador Robert Ford predicted from Moscow.[152] Besides, if the conference affirmed the principles of nonintervention and sovereign equality, it might embolden East German, Czechoslovak, and Romanian leaders to distance themselves from the USSR.[153] Some Eastern European diplomats quietly endorsed this analysis. According to Brandt, officials in Warsaw and Budapest hoped that the conference would give them "more room for maneuver" within the Warsaw Pact.[154]

These freedoms ought to extend to the Soviet bloc's citizens too. In April 1969, the American ambassador in Moscow told Aleksei Kosygin that the United States intended to promote the "free flow of information and ideas between our two peoples" and "to remove existing barriers to the free flow of information," such as Moscow's jamming of Voice of America broadcasts.[155] French officials conveyed the same message a few months later. The conference had to discuss "the protection of human rights, [and] the free circulation of people, ideas, and information."[156]

These proposals were limited in scope but carefully targeted. They assumed that making the Iron Curtain more permeable would mitigate the human costs of the Cold War. Divided families would reunite. Travelers would cross borders more easily. Average citizens would read newspapers and watch films that had previously been out of reach. In these small ways, the conference would "make people's lives easier," as Brandt put it.[157] These humanitarian aspirations also offered hard-edged benefits. American officials noted that emphasizing freer movement would focus "the attention of Western public opinion upon the closed nature of the Soviet regime" and remind citizens of the justice of the Western cause. It might also embarrass the Soviets into implementing some liberal reforms.[158] Loosening the restrictions the communist regimes depended on to maintain social control could weaken the regimes themselves. Although de Gaulle had been skeptical of the conference, he saw the potential of this approach early on. As trade and travel expanded between East and West, "the less the communist bloc will be communist," he told Kurt Georg Kiesinger.[159] In line with Brandt's and Pompidou's strategies of détente, the Western allies agreed that the security conference could transform the European status quo by promoting basic human freedoms.[160]

The conference would put both alliances to the test. It would lay bare their ideas of security and subject them to public scrutiny. It would also strain their political cohesion and offer every participant ample opportunity to express its views. "Given the cosmopolitan makeup of the conference, and the necessarily very broad agenda, intra-alliance (NATO or Warsaw Pact) cohesion will be difficult at times to maintain," the State Department predicted. In any such trial, however, the Western allies would have the advantage, since they regularly disagreed with each other: "[O]ur allies are partners, not satellites, and we are more experienced in alliance diplomacy." The Warsaw Pact, however, operated according to different principles. It could ill tolerate this kind of pluralism.[161]

VI

As the Western allies refined their goals, they grappled with a difficult question: Did a conference on European security have to discuss disarmament? Some Western leaders insisted that it could not ignore the continent's military balance. A declaration of principles would suffice "as a side dish, but was too small as a main course," Pierre Harmel told Hungarian foreign minister János Péter.[162] In 1968, when NATO's foreign ministers responded to the Warsaw Pact's Bucharest declaration, they called for talks on cutting troop levels in Europe, an idea that they soon dubbed "mutual and balanced force reductions," or MBFR.[163] Kissinger regarded MBFR as "the only real issue" worthy of a conference, which would otherwise be "a meaningless psychological exercise."[164] Because nuclear arms control remained the preserve of the few nuclear powers, a conference that included dozens of states would have to focus on conventional forces.[165]

Even at this early stage, however, MBFR suffered from a conceptual flaw. The Warsaw Pact's conventional forces outnumbered NATO's by a wide margin. In 1970, for instance, the Warsaw Pact had 1.3 million men and 19,000 tanks stationed in Central and Eastern Europe, compared to NATO's 1.1 million men and 7,600 tanks. The Warsaw Pact's advantage grew even wider when accounting for mobilization rates and geography. If war broke out, the Soviets would need less than a month to double their forces in Central Europe. By contrast, it would take many weeks to deploy NATO's reinforcements—which were predominantly American—across the Atlantic. The allies had an interest in reducing the size of the Red Army, but their numerical inferiority made it hard to see how they could reach a deal that both sides could accept.[166]

If NATO and the Warsaw Pact followed a symmetrical approach and reduced their forces by the same proportion—say 10 or 15 percent—Western security would suffer. As NATO's forces shrank, the Warsaw Pact's manpower advantage would grow more significant. In this case, NATO's strategy of flexible response would become untenable. The alliance would have to revert to massive retaliation, a British analysis concluded. But this approach "would be unattractive politically and would lack credibility" because it relied on the threat of nuclear annihilation.[167]

On the other hand, an asymmetrical approach—cutting the Warsaw Pact's forces by a higher percentage than NATO's, or cutting different types of weapons—would improve Western security, but the Soviets had no incentive to accept it. Some of the Western allies looked for creative solutions, to little avail. When the West Germans proposed exchanging NATO's tactical nuclear weapons for the Warsaw Pact's tanks and soldiers, the idea attracted few supporters.[168] A NATO working group developed a list of principles to guide deliberations, but the allies continued to squabble about what they wanted to accomplish.[169] "Almost every model for reductions that would be negotiable with the Soviets would damage the Western military position," Kissinger told Nixon.[170]

To complicate matters further, the French opposed MBFR outright. If the negotiations succeeded, Pompidou warned Brandt, they would weaken NATO and encourage the Americans to withdraw from the continent. Western Europe would lie at the USSR's mercy.[171] Even if the negotiations failed, they would damage Western interests. By pitting one alliance against the other, the talks would induce the communist states to close ranks. If NATO hoped to weaken the Warsaw Pact, encourage the Eastern Europeans to act independently, and foster interpenetration, this "bloc-to-bloc" approach made little sense.[172] "One must constantly remember the noxious character of the bloc policy," he told Brosio in November 1969. "It represents a defeat of the policy that we want to see prevail in Europe." No Gaullist could endorse a plan that would allow the two superpowers to elbow the smaller states aside and, by virtue of their military superiority, dominate the negotiations. "This would erase Europe," Pompidou said.[173]

At least one influential diplomat at the Quai d'Orsay thought that Pompidou's squeamishness "did not make sense." Given the military situation on the continent, he argued, any attempt at disarmament had to involve the two alliances. Avoiding a bloc-to-bloc approach would be impossible. However, this remained a minority view in Paris. At every opportunity, the French government opposed the MBFR talks and dissociated itself from NATO's proposals on the subject.[174]

The other allies pressed forward. Although the British government worried about MBFR's consequences for Western security, it supported the idea in order to persuade its citizens that it was working toward détente.[175] Others insisted that a security conference had to deal with "real security issues," as the US mission to NATO put it. Putting MBFR on the agenda would test whether the Soviets wanted to engage in a propaganda battle or negotiate seriously.[176] The West Germans acknowledged that the asymmetrical approach stood little chance of success, but decided that NATO had to take "a clear step forward" in pursuit of Brandt's European peace order.[177] Without disarmament, Egon Bahr said, détente would remain elusive.[178] Moreover, because Soviet forces enforced communist orthodoxy in Eastern Europe, reducing their numbers might open new possibilities for reform and undermine the military foundation on which Moscow's international order rested.[179]

American domestic politics also weighed heavily in the allies' calculations. For a decade, Montana senator Mike Mansfield had proposed to slash the American military presence in Europe. The allies ought to shoulder more of the burden of their own defense, he argued. In May 1971, as antiwar sentiment and economic pressures fueled public demands to cut defense spending and bring troops home, Mansfield put forward a measure to cut US forces on the continent by 50 percent. He garnered considerable support and stood a good chance of succeeding.[180]

Officials in the Nixon administration feared that NATO would collapse if the Mansfield amendment passed. As they scrambled to fight back, they seized on MBFR. The disarmament talks would sap Mansfield's support by demonstrating that the executive branch already had the matter in hand. The White House could also argue that Congress would destroy America's bargaining position if it backed Mansfield. "The subject is essentially a holding action to avoid Congressional action that would unilaterally reduce our military presence in Europe," Nixon told British prime minister Edward Heath.[181] Most of the Western Europeans supported MBFR for the same reason. Negotiating with the Warsaw Pact was "necessary to keep the Americans here," Brandt told Pompidou.[182]

This plan could only work if the Soviets agreed to participate, but they showed little interest. The Strategic Arms Limitation Talks (SALT), which had opened in Helsinki in 1969, were making satisfactory progress, and it made little sense to launch another set of military negotiations before these had concluded. Besides, adding such a controversial subject to the security conference agenda could mire it in fruitless arguments. NATO wanted MBFR negotiations solely "for propaganda purposes" and "as an excuse for delaying the convening" of the security conference, Soviet officials concluded.[183] The Politburo agreed that "advancing this issue now would only complicate the preparation of the European Conference and undermine the prospects for its fruitful work."[184] The Warsaw Pact might agree to discuss conventional disarmament alongside other unpleasant subjects, such as cultural cooperation, in a follow-up meeting after the security conference, but not at the conference itself. For the moment, MBFR had no place on the agenda.[185]

Just when the US Senate stood on the verge of endorsing Mansfield's proposal, Brezhnev delivered a surprise. In a May 1971 speech in Tbilisi, he said that the USSR welcomed conventional disarmament negotiations. Just as one cannot predict how a wine will taste by looking at the bottle, he argued, it is impossible to predict what a set of negotiations will produce before they start. "All that is necessary is to muster the resolve to taste the proposals that interest you, which, in diplomatic language, means to enter into negotiations," he said.[186]

Although Brezhnev's motives were unclear, the Nixon administration greeted this reversal of Soviet policy with relief. It represented "a windfall in terms of the debate in this country over the Mansfield Amendment," Kissinger told the president.[187] Helmut Sonnenfeldt speculated that the Soviet leader had changed course in order to demonstrate just how seriously he took his Peace Program, which the 24th Party Congress had endorsed the previous month.[188] Whatever Brezhnev's reasons, Mansfield's support in the Senate evaporated. When his proposal came to a vote a few days later, it failed 36 to 61.[189] Despite this success, Nixon understood that more work remained necessary to rebuild popular support for the country's international commitments. MBFR had to remain on the agenda. "We have to press forward," he said. "We have to give [the] American people hope."[190]

After dodging one problem, NATO faced another. The allies struggled to establish a common policy on MBFR and debated how it should relate to the security conference.[191] Most accepted that it would be unwise to try to negotiate a disarmament agreement at the conference itself, where dozens of states would want their say. Nonetheless, if the conference could not discuss MBFR itself, it should at least establish the principles that would guide the MBFR talks. Ignoring one of the central questions of European security would make a mockery of the conference, the Italians and Belgians insisted.[192] This argument appealed to NATO's smaller powers, who regarded the conference as a rare opportunity to make themselves heard on military affairs.[193]

By contrast, the Americans wanted to separate the conference and MBFR. Secretary of Defense Melvin Laird warned Nixon that handling both subjects together would "greatly complicate our problems" and "make a serious negotiation improbable."[194] Even setting aside these concerns, the smaller states and the neutrals had no business discussing military problems in which they had little stake.[195] "[I]t makes no sense to have large numbers of European governments involved in MBFR negotiations that only affect a few countries," Sonnenfeldt argued.[196] Nixon agreed. The relationship between MBFR and the security conference should be minimal, he decided.[197]

In the hope of sounding out Soviet views, the Western allies appointed Manlio Brosio as their "MBFR explorer," with a mandate to travel to Moscow and lay the groundwork for the disarmament talks.[198] Brosio had just stepped down as NATO secretary general, but the Soviets refused to receive him.[199] Dealing with someone claiming to represent the whole alliance would give the talks an unwelcome "bloc-to-bloc" character, they argued. Individual states ought to assert their own interests. This fidelity to national autonomy might have surprised the USSR's Eastern European allies. Nonetheless, the Brosio mission was "stillborn," as deputy foreign minister Anatoly Kovalev put it.[200]

In a curious twist, Soviet and American views on the subject had converged. Echoing the Nixon administration's own position, Gromyko told Rogers that MBFR ought to be handled in a separate set of negotiations so as "not to burden the main conference with too many items." The smaller allies took a different view, but stood little chance of changing the superpowers' minds.[201]

If the two negotiations were going to proceed separately, which one should start first? Kissinger dismissed the question as "another one of those talmudic topics."[202] It nevertheless had important consequences. Some members of the Nixon administration preferred to begin with MBFR, on the grounds that it "dealt with a real security concern," whereas the security conference "would be most likely to deal in atmospherics."[203] Britain's Conservative foreign secretary, Alec Douglas-Home, disagreed. He proposed that the security conference should establish a special body to handle MBFR. Because the French would participate fully in the security conference, they would find it difficult to escape from any new forum that the conference created. Despite their qualms about bloc-to-bloc negotiations, this approach would draw them into the force reduction talks.[204]

Douglas-Home also hoped for damage control. "One way to reduce the inherent risks in [the MBFR talks] might be to channel them into some permanent machinery developed by a conference," he suggested.[205] This view resonated in the State Department. Connecting the force reduction negotiations to the security conference would bring it greater publicity, soothing American public opinion and placating those allies—especially the West Germans—who wanted a clear link between the two. On the other hand, postponing MBFR until after the conference carried considerable dangers. For one thing, the Soviet desire for a successful conference would only give NATO leverage at the force reduction talks if the two ran in parallel. If the security conference were held first, as Douglas-Home suggested, the Western allies would lose this advantage and find it even more difficult to negotiate an acceptable MBFR deal.[206]

Secret diplomacy ended the debate. In keeping with Nixon's insistence that the United States assert "ball control on MBFR," Kissinger performed the role that Brosio could not.[207] Without consulting the allies, he offered the Soviets a bargain. "How about if side by side with preparations for a

European Security Conference we begin discussions on reductions, directed at basic principles?" he asked Brezhnev during an April 1972 visit to Moscow. "In general, that would be a very good thing," the Soviet leader replied.[208]

The following month, Nixon and Brezhnev endorsed this arrangement at their summit meeting. The two sets of negotiations would unfurl in parallel, but, at Brezhnev's insistence, neither would depend on the other's success.[209] Among the Western allies, the news of the arrangement aroused concerns about backchannel collusion between the superpowers, and it disappointed those who had wanted the security conference to handle MBFR. Nonetheless, because they had proven unable to forge a common position of their own on MBFR, they could not resist the superpowers' deal.[210] Disarmament would not appear on the conference's agenda.[211]

VII

The preconditions that NATO established in 1969 and 1970 meant that the fate of the security conference depended on the big picture of détente. Unless the efforts to establish a modus vivendi in Germany succeeded, the conference might not take place. But the relationship between détente and the conference ran both ways. The West's conditional agreement to participate in a conference also shaped its negotiations with the East between 1970 and 1972.

Willy Brandt drew strength from the prerequisites that NATO had laid down. Because the Western allies had declared that they would not participate in a security conference until the Federal Republic had reached an accommodation with its neighbors to the east, the Soviets had an incentive to strike a bargain with Bonn. Brandt understood, however, that this leverage would only last for so long. As the conference gathered momentum, the Western allies would come under increasing pressure to participate, regardless of how much progress Ostpolitik had made. The Federal Republic had no time to lose.[212]

In January 1970, Egon Bahr traveled to Moscow to open negotiations on a nonaggression treaty. He faced a tangle of political and linguistic questions that echoed the arguments over the security conference. He and his interlocutors debated whether Europe's borders—including the Oder-Neisse Line and the frontier between East Germany and West Germany—were "immutable" or "inviolable." The Soviets insisted on the first adjective because it implied permanence. For the same reason, Bahr ruled it out. The Federal Republic's constitutional commitment to reunification forbade him from recognizing the continent's frontiers as eternal. Gromyko eventually settled for "inviolable." He also demanded a declaration of support for the security conference. Bahr agreed, on the condition that the agenda include more than just security, and that the North Americans be invited to participate.[213]

After four months of talks, Bahr summarized the preliminary agreement that he and Gromyko had reached. The so-called Bahr Paper included the compromises on borders and the security conference alongside a declaration of respect for states' territorial integrity and a commitment to expand economic, scientific, technical, and cultural relations. On this basis, Gromyko and West German foreign minister Walter Scheel finalized the Moscow Treaty, which Brandt signed at the Kremlin in August.[214] A similar agreement with Poland quickly followed. In December 1970, the Warsaw Treaty recognized the Oder-Neisse Line as Poland's western frontier. It too declared that the border was inviolable, not immutable.[215]

Each side presented the Eastern Treaties as the starting point for a new European order. Brandt argued that, by ending the legal fiction that Germany still existed within its 1937 frontiers, the Moscow Treaty simply recognized reality. "With this treaty nothing is lost that had not long since been gambled away," he told his countrymen in a televised address from Moscow.[216] In Poland, he offered a vivid gesture of penance for the National Socialists' crimes. After laying a wreath at the Warsaw Ghetto memorial, he dropped to his knees on the wet stone steps. The *Kniefall* demonstrated more eloquently than any speech that the Federal Republic had accepted responsibility for its past.[217]

Having recognized Germany's history, Brandt now hoped to move beyond it. The Letter on German Unity, which a West German diplomat delivered to the Soviet government shortly before the Moscow Treaty was signed, affirmed that Bonn remained committed to reunification.[218] Similarly, Brandt promised economic aid to Warsaw in the hope of securing exit visas for Poland's ethnic Germans. In 1970, when he met East German premier Willi Stoph, he emphasized that détente required a human dimension. Their two countries had to expand human ties, not just diplomatic ones.[219]

For Brezhnev, the Moscow Treaty also drew a line under the past and vindicated his approach to détente. It reflected "our policy of eliminating the vestiges of the Second World War in Europe, of consolidating the outcome of the Soviet people's heroic struggle in the Great Patriotic War and the gains of the anti-fascist liberation struggle of the peoples of Europe," he said.[220] Now that the USSR and Federal Republic had recognized Europe's frontiers in a bilateral agreement, it was time for the security conference to do the same thing on a multilateral basis. Far from making the conference redundant, the Moscow Treaty had cleared the way for it. These efforts would demonstrate "that the world socialist system is the chief bulwark of peace and international security in our epoch," Brezhnev argued.[221]

The Soviets championed this concept of legitimacy in negotiations with other Western powers. In drafting declarations on international conduct, they emphasized principles that affirmed their understanding of peace. France provided a crucial test case. In advance of Georges Pompidou's October 1970 visit to the USSR, the Soviet ministry of foreign affairs proposed that the two countries sign a treaty of friendship and nonaggression along the lines of the Moscow Treaty.[222] The French refused, not least because Pompidou did not want to be seen trailing in Brandt's wake.[223] Nonetheless, they agreed to issue two documents, to which Brezhnev attached great importance: a protocol requiring the two sides to consult in the event of an international crisis, and a declaration affirming their commitment to détente.[224] When the Soviet leader visited France a year later—his first voyage west of Berlin, and an attempt to establish his credentials as a statesman—he and Pompidou signed a document enumerating the rules of Franco-Soviet cooperation, which Gromyko had personally negotiated.[225] At Soviet insistence, the inviolability of frontiers stood at the top of the list, ahead of noninterference in internal affairs and the nonuse of force.[226]

From Paris's vantage point, these principles mattered less than the substance of bilateral relations, especially the expansion of trade. The declaration "contain[ed] hardly anything new," a senior French diplomat confided to his diary.[227] From Moscow's perspective, however, it represented a major achievement.[228] On a trip to Warsaw in December 1971, Brezhnev held up the Franco-Soviet principles as the conceptual framework for the new order that he wanted to build. "In our view, all the states and peoples of Europe would only gain if similar principles became the generally recognized norm of international life," he said.[229]

Although the Soviets issued similar statements with Canada and Turkey, their overriding goal was an agreement with the United States.[230] In preparing for the 1972 Moscow Summit, Dobrynin asked Kissinger whether the Nixon administration would consider issuing a declaration modeled on the one that Brezhnev and Pompidou had endorsed a few months earlier. Kissinger did not rule it out, and when Dobrynin asked him to write a first draft, he agreed.[231]

Negotiations continued during Kissinger's secret visit to Moscow to complete the summit preparations. Brezhnev gave him a heavily revised declaration based on the original American version. At Kissinger's request, Sonnenfeldt sat down with Soviet diplomat Georgy Kornienko to finalize a version that both sides could accept.[232] At the end of May, in a solemn ceremony at the Kremlin, Nixon and Brezhnev signed the Basic Principles Agreement. They promised to respect state sovereignty, recognize each other as equals, not interfere in each other's domestic affairs, not seek advantage at the other's expense, and conduct "their mutual relations on the basis of peaceful coexistence."[233]

The Soviet and American attitudes to the agreement diverged sharply. The Soviet Ministry of Foreign Affairs had worked intensively on successive drafts. Officials wanted the United States to endorse the principle of peaceful coexistence and, by implication, Brezhnev's Peace Program.[234] Brezhnev's foreign policy advisor, Andrei Aleksandrov-Agentov, and Kornienko both called it a statement of fundamental importance.[235] In Brezhnev's assessment, the Basic Principles Agreement was the Moscow Summit's most important document, surpassing even the SALT nuclear arms control deal, which had taken almost three years to negotiate. It provided the "foundation of a new era in relations between the USSR and the USA," he told Nixon. In a speech to the Central Committee, he presented the text in a slightly different light. The USSR was taking advantage of the United States' economic and social crisis to advance "the consolidation of peace in the world," he said.[236] Brezhnev and other Soviet leaders also believed that it served an important domestic purpose: it raised their prestige and, like SALT, demonstrated to their citizens that the leading Western power had finally recognized the Soviet Union as its equal.[237]

By contrast, the Nixon administration treated the document as a sop to the Soviets. The president understood that it offered a chance to establish a "single standard" for the conduct of both countries. He wanted to push back against the Soviet conceit that different principles governed relations between communist countries. "We can't have this crap in effect that they can support liberation in the non-Communist world but that ... the Brezhnev Doctrine must apply in their world," he told Kissinger in advance of the latter's secret visit to Moscow.[238] Nonetheless, Kissinger invested little effort in the agreement's preparation and kept it a secret from the State Department, lest its experts interfere.[239] In Moscow, Sonnenfeldt rushed through the final negotiations with Kornienko because he did not want to miss Kissinger's discussion with Gromyko on the Middle East.[240]

After the declaration had been drafted, Nixon showed a lack of interest that belied his earlier comments. He did not examine the text, which included an elementary error about the status of Berlin and the extraordinary endorsement of the Leninist principle of peaceful coexistence. Rather, he worried about how to present it to William Rogers, who had not even been informed of its existence before the summit began.[241] Addressing journalists in Moscow, Kissinger described the principles as a modest achievement. "[T]his document indicates an aspiration and an attitude, and if either the aspiration or the attitude changes, then, of course, as sovereign countries, either side can change its course," he said.[242]

From the perspective of both the Nixon administration and the American press, the SALT agreement was the centerpiece of the Moscow Summit. Before the arms control talks got underway in 1969, Nixon wondered whether they would enhance American security and questioned why the

Soviets wanted them so eagerly.[243] Nevertheless, he understood the urgency of freezing the arms race and halting the Soviet nuclear buildup. SALT offered domestic dividends too, since it would show American voters that the administration took arms control seriously.[244] After more than two years of slow-moving negotiations in Helsinki, Nixon and Kissinger hurriedly worked out the final details with their Soviet counterparts at the Moscow Summit. The administration presented the deal, which capped intercontinental and submarine-launched ballistic missile numbers, as a major victory.[245]

These bilateral agreements might have been welcome, but they could not clear the path to the security conference by themselves. The Bundestag still had to ratify the Eastern Treaties. The two Germanies had to reach an accommodation. And the four occupying powers had to conclude their negotiations over the status of Berlin, which had opened in March 1970. When they laid down these prerequisites, the Western allies intended to make the most of the leverage that the security conference idea offered. After the Eastern Treaties were signed, however, some officials concluded that the West had exhausted its leverage. Others proposed to soften the prerequisites and open the conference sooner.

Eager for progress, the Soviets turned up the diplomatic pressure. In Bonn, ambassador Semyon Tsarapkin demanded that Walter Scheel make good on the agreement in the Bahr Paper to convene a security conference.[246] The paper swept away any objections to a security conference that the Federal Republic might raise, officials at the East German foreign ministry reasoned.[247] Soviet and Eastern European diplomats told their Western counterparts that the conference could not afford to wait for an agreement on Berlin or any other question. Insisting on prerequisites was "not only wrong, but also harmful to the cause of peace in Europe," the Soviet foreign ministry argued.[248]

The ensuing debate divided the Western alliance. Even within certain governments, opinions diverged. Brandt and Bahr no longer wanted to use the prospect of a security conference to extract concessions on other matters from the Soviets and East Germans.[249] Pompidou agreed. He worried that persisting with hardline demands might alienate the Soviets, and argued that NATO ought to abandon its prerequisites, including on Berlin. Otherwise, "we risk being the laughingstocks and finding ourselves isolated," he warned. "We must therefore be more positive even while trying to obtain certain advantages from the Russians before the conference is held."[250]

The West German and French foreign ministers saw the matter differently. Scheel insisted on maintaining the Berlin prerequisite.[251] Schumann did likewise, though he called on the allies to drop their insistence on a deal between the FRG and GDR.[252] "Concentrating on one demand would induce the Soviet Union to give way on the Berlin question," he told West Germany's ambassador in Paris.[253] In any case, a four-power agreement on Berlin could not happen if the two Germanies remained at odds. In this sense, the Berlin prerequisite implied progress in other areas too.[254]

American and British officials took a similarly tough stance. "As long as the Berlin problem had not been settled, no useful purpose could be served by a Conference on European Security," the American ambassador to NATO argued.[255] The USSR had refused to compromise thus far in the Berlin talks. If NATO backed off its preconditions, the Soviets would conclude that Western resolve was breaking and dig in their heels on the three issues that mattered to the West: *Zuordnung* (the connection between the FRG and West Berlin), *Zugang* (access to West Berlin), and *Zutritt* (West Berliners' right to enter East Berlin and the GDR).[256] Most of the other allies concurred.[257]

A compromise ended the dispute. The Americans, British, and other allies who had wanted to stand firm gave way. William Rogers and Alec Douglas-Home conceded that, on a question that involved the fate of Germany, they had to defer to Bonn and abandon all prerequisites other than a Berlin agreement. At the same time, however, they rejected Schumann's calls to water down this last demand "to avoid the risk of giving the Soviets an excuse for jeopardizing negotiations" on the city.[258] Further, the Nixon administration made clear that it would not agree to open any talks on European security until after the 1972 presidential election.[259] In June 1971, NATO's foreign ministers announced from Lisbon that they would agree to participate in a security conference once the negotiations on Berlin's status concluded. Until the talks produced an agreement, however, Brandt would not put the Moscow Treaty before the Bundestag for ratification.[260]

This pressure induced the Soviets to soften their position on the divided city. In September, the occupying powers reached a compromise. They accepted the GDR's de facto control over East Berlin, affirmed that West Berlin remained independent of the FRG, eased travel between West Berlin and the Federal Republic, and expanded West Berliners' access to East Berlin. These principles set Berlin on a stable footing for the first time since the Cold War began, but they would not enter into force until the foreign ministers signed the text of the agreement and the FRG and GDR reached a transit accord of their own.[261] After another round of heated debate and despite Soviet lobbying to begin the security conference immediately, the Western allies agreed that it had to wait until after these steps. In turn, the Soviets declared that they would not sign the final protocol on Berlin until the Bundestag ratified the Moscow Treaty.[262]

These webs of contingencies meant that, by the spring of 1972, the fate not just of Ostpolitik but of détente itself depended on the will of the West

German parliament. "The Ostpolitik is like an enormous chandelier. Over Europe there dangles a glittering cluster of interconnected agreements and treaties and understandings, all perilously suspended from a single link at the top. This link is ratification of the Moscow and Warsaw treaties of 1970," British journalist Neal Ascherson observed. "If this link snaps, the chandelier of provisional détente, which depends upon the positive Bundestag vote in order to come into force, will collapse on the statesmen below." The Berlin agreement would crumble along with the Eastern Treaties, the ongoing negotiations between East and West Germany would grind to a halt, Soviet-American relations would unravel, and the prospects of a security conference would evaporate.[263]

After fending off legal challenges and surviving a no-confidence motion by the thinnest of margins, Brandt prevailed. Over fierce opposition from the Christian Democrats, the Bundestag ratified the Eastern Treaties in May. A relieved Brezhnev hailed the result as a major victory, not least because his Peace Program and strategy of détente had hung in the balance.[264] He and other communist leaders concluded that they had forced the Western revanchists to come to terms with the geopolitical realities born of the Second World War. Now they had to keep up the fight and win another victory at the security conference.[265] The following month, the four powers signed the Final Protocol to bring the Berlin deal into effect.[266] Meanwhile, NATO's foreign ministers convened in Bonn. They agreed not to delay any further. They declared themselves ready to launch a security conference, now officially known as the Conference on Security and Cooperation in Europe.[267]

The creation of the CSCE illustrated the interdependence of circumstance, strategy, and fortune. Leonid Brezhnev championed the conference as a way to implement his grand strategy. He hoped that it would address the crises that the Soviet Union faced in the late 1960s and take advantage of the West's own crises. Although some of his Eastern European counterparts disagreed with his approach, the Warsaw Pact came together and waged a sustained campaign to persuade the Western powers to participate. The United States and its allies finally agreed to take part, both because they believed they had no alternative and because they counted on using the conference to advance their own strategic goals. The CSCE grew out this nexus of domestic pressures and international debates, political leadership and structural weakness. In 1972, however, one vote in the legislature of one state could have swept away the years of effort. The process was simultaneously robust and fragile. It demonstrated the creative possibilities of diplomacy and its limits.

It also highlighted the political cultures of the rival alliances. In the Warsaw Pact, the Soviets expected their allies to defer to their judgment and subordinate their interests to Moscow's. When some of the Eastern Europeans tried to seize the initiative and turn the conference to their own purposes, the Soviets sometimes had to compromise. However, the Soviets ultimately controlled the process. They set the Warsaw Pact's priorities and determined how to respond to the West. This pattern demonstrated the virtues and vices of the Soviet order. When the Western powers rejected the Warsaw Pact's initial overtures, Soviet diplomats refused to be dissuaded and slowly wore down NATO's resistance. This approach allowed little room for discussion or adaptation. It succeeded through determination and repetition, but suppressed genuine debate. Over the years that the Soviets and their allies discussed the security conference proposal, they contemplated only a narrow range of options, spawned few new ideas, and responded to Western counterproposals with difficulty.

The Western deliberations about the conference brought the Atlantic alliance's strengths and weaknesses to the surface. In long-winded and messy discussions over several years, NATO's members presented their own ideas about how to respond to the Warsaw Pact's indefatigable campaign. Because the Nixon administration saw little value in a conference, it allowed the more enthusiastic Western Europeans and Canadians to take the lead. Whatever this decentralized approach lacked in efficiency, it made up in creativity. In the mid-1960s, Canadian diplomat John Holmes extolled the benefits of "heresy from lesser voices" within NATO. The experience of creating the CSCE bore out his argument that the allies could "achieve more for the common good if we resist a policy of automatic alignment" with American preferences.[268]

If the White House had imposed its preferences on the allies, NATO would have treated the CSCE merely as a concession to the Soviets. The conference would have done little to advance Western interests. Instead, the allies devised ways to expand the Soviets' preferred agenda and transform the conference. NATO's approach illustrated the organizational principles of the Western order itself, drawing strength from decentralized control and freewheeling debate. The creativity of the two alliances varied in direct proportion to their democracy, yielding new possibilities for the West and dangerous consequences for the East.

Chapter 4

THE MEANING OF SECURITY

IN LATE November 1972, diplomats from across Europe and North America gathered on the campus of the Helsinki University of Technology, a few miles outside the Finnish capital, for the CSCE's Multilateral Preparatory Talks (MPT). They had "very little idea of what awaited them," the head of the British delegation later wrote.[1] No one knew how long the negotiations would last or what results they would produce. In its size and scope, the undertaking had few precedents in modern diplomacy. "We were beginning a new adventure, something completely new," an Italian participant recalled many years later.[2]

To host the talks, the Finnish government had commandeered the university's student union, known as Dipoli, which one witness described as a "modern and rather complicated structure conceived as a series of interconnected caves."[3] At the opening ceremonies, the thirty-four delegations took their seats in a converted lecture hall around a large hexagonal table. With the exception of Albania, which regarded the enterprise as a superpower conspiracy, and Monaco, which would join later, every country in Europe was represented, as were the United States and Canada.[4] They sat in French alphabetical order, with the West Germans and East Germans—*Allemagne, République Fédérale d'* and *Allemande, République Démocratique*—next to one another. Bonn had insisted on this sleight of hand, despite Soviet and East German protests, to emphasize the unity of the German nation.[5] That evening, Finnish president Urho Kekkonen hosted a dinner to welcome the participants. "The expectations of the peoples of Europe are focused upon your work," he said. "We hope that as a result of this we can really relieve ourselves of the burden of the past and start a new era."[6]

The MPT's purpose was to draft an agenda and rules of procedure for the full CSCE, which would meet at an unspecified future date. The rules, which the delegates formulated in their first month of work, exchanged efficiency for goodwill. From beginning to end, the CSCE operated on the basis of consensus. Granting every state a veto over every decision increased the risk that the proceedings would end up stalemated, but it also protected participants from unpalatable results and gave the resulting agreement a political weight that it would not have enjoyed if decisions had been taken by majority vote. No country could say that its voice had not been heard.[7]

The participants dramatically raised the cost and complexity of the proceedings by designating six official languages. Besides English, French, and Russian, they included Italian and Spanish to placate Rome and Madrid. The most important of all was German, the only language spoken on both sides of the Iron Curtain. Had it been excluded, the West Germans would have spoken French and the East Germans Russian, which would have emphasized the division of the country and the continent. The proliferation of tongues required participants to keep track of multiple versions of the texts they were negotiating. Either by accident or design, a phrase drafted in one language might acquire new shades of meaning when translated into another.[8]

In a series of dueling communiques over the preceding years, the Warsaw Pact and NATO had put forward suggestions about what the CSCE ought to discuss. To impose coherence on these ideas, the MPT sorted them into three categories, which—at the suggestion of the Swiss ambassador—became known as "baskets," by analogy with a "housewife.... separat[ing] laundry of different colors." The first basket, which focused on security, had as its centerpiece a declaration on the principles governing relations between states. The second dealt with economic, scientific, technological, and environmental cooperation. Humanitarian cooperation, especially the freer movement of people and information, was the subject of the third. The MPT also added a fourth basket, which would address ways to continue the CSCE's work after the end of the conference. At the end of the preparatory talks, the agenda and rules of procedure were codified in a document titled the "Final Recommendations," popularly called the Blue Book, after the color of its cover.[9]

The CSCE's work unfolded in several stages. After the MPT concluded in June 1973, the foreign ministers of the participating countries gathered in Helsinki for Stage I, where they gave speeches, adopted the Blue Book, and set the CSCE itself in motion. But the Finnish city lacked the facilities to host an event of the CSCE's size, and most Western diplomats found it inconveniently remote from their own capitals. In September 1973, therefore, Stage II moved to Geneva, where the Swiss hosts had booked the newly opened Centre International de Conférences Genève (CICG) to house the proceedings. The Coordinating Committee, composed of the heads of all the delegations, set the schedule and oversaw the work of the whole conference, while a series of committees and subcommittees handled the substance of the individual baskets.[10]

When the second stage got underway, few expected it to last very long, but the Western delegates refused to be rushed or to agree to a timetable. Delegations on both sides dug in and resolved to outlast their adversaries, testing the cohesion and patience of both blocs. Whereas Western diplomats undertook a process of intense consultations—especially in Helsinki, Geneva, and Brussels—to hammer out positions they could all support, the Soviets generally expected their allies to follow their lead and endorse positions that had been worked out in Moscow. The process strained both alliances and sparked heated debates about the value of the CSCE within many of the participating governments.

Political leaders relied on the professional diplomats to handle the painstaking work of the conference. The professionals enjoyed considerable latitude to make decisions, but when they hit a roadblock, the politicians often had to intervene—whether overtly or covertly—to find a way forward. Some of these leaders, especially Leonid Brezhnev and Andrei Gromyko, paid close attention to the negotiations and wanted them to succeed at almost any cost. Others, such as Henry Kissinger, held the conference in much lower esteem but played a crucial role in its outcome nonetheless.[11]

Because the talks in Geneva dragged on longer than anyone, including the Swiss, had anticipated, the delegates had to decamp from the CICG to make room for another international gathering that had reserved the building. Most preferred the new premises in the International Labor Organization's splendid former headquarters on the shores of Lake Geneva to the CICG's brutalist surroundings. When the participants finally completed their work in July 1975, they cleared the way for the third and final stage, held back in Helsinki, where the leaders of the thirty-five countries signed the Final Act.[12]

Throughout the negotiations, the Soviets concentrated their efforts—and their hopes—on Basket I, where their concepts of security and peace clashed with those of the West. Taking their cue from Brezhnev's Peace Program, which remained the touchstone of the USSR's foreign policy, they wanted the declaration of principles to freeze Europe's borders and ban states from making any claims against the territory of their neighbors. In their view, the greater the barriers to territorial and political change, the longer peace would last.

The Western allies rebuffed the Soviets' ideas. They wanted the declaration to define the ways in which the territorial and political status quo could evolve. States ought to be able to change their borders, their systems of government, and their alliances. Their traditional prerogatives, especially the doctrine of sovereignty, had to be balanced against the universal imperatives of human rights. When the CSCE's participants began drafting the declaration of principles, they reexamined the fundamental rules of the international system. Their work would determine whether a Soviet or a Western concept of legitimacy would prevail in Europe.[13]

I

The preparatory talks opened in an atmosphere of optimism and unease. The achievements of the previous few years, especially the Moscow Treaty and SALT agreement, suggested that diplomacy could transform East-West relations for the better. Two weeks before the talks began at Dipoli, the FRG and GDR concluded negotiations on their Basic Treaty, in which each recognized the other's authority.[14] But if the risk of war in Europe seemed to be ebbing, the threat of violence remained real. Earlier that year, Croatian nationalists had bombed a Yugoslav Airlines flight en route from Stockholm to Belgrade, and Palestinian terrorists had massacred Israeli athletes at the Munich Olympics. Fearing a similar attack at the MPT, the Finnish authorities put stringent security measures in place to protect the participants.[15]

During the three years that elapsed between the opening of the MPT and the conclusion of the CSCE, a series of dramatic events rattled the international scene. In 1973, the Yom Kippur War threatened to draw the superpowers into a direct confrontation in the Middle East. The ensuing oil crisis exposed the industrialized world's geopolitical and economic vulnerability. In 1974, the Carnation Revolution toppled Portugal's authoritarian regime, raising fears of a communist takeover. Turkish forces invaded Cyprus a few months later, partitioning a sovereign state and triggering the collapse of Greece's military dictatorship. The same year, four of the leading Western states underwent sudden changes in leadership: Britain's Conservative prime minister, Ted Heath, lost a general election to Labour's Harold Wilson; Georges Pompidou succumbed to cancer; an espionage scandal forced Willy Brandt from office; and Richard Nixon resigned in disgrace. In 1975, a three-sided civil war broke out in Angola, and North Vietnamese forces overran South Vietnam.[16]

These shocks hardly affected the CSCE. Some Western representatives argued that the USSR's support for Israel's Arab antagonists violated the principles of détente. The Greek delegates protested that Turkey had "deprived the conference of its credibility" by committing an act of aggression against a fellow participant. Some of the Eastern allies, who were frustrated at the CSCE's glacial pace, contemplated using the invasion of Cyprus as a pretext to adjourn. But Soviet leaders refused to endanger the negotiations, and Western governments saw no reason to change course. When the new leaders in Washington, London, Paris, and Bonn took office, they adjusted tactics here and there, but did not change their countries' fundamental attitudes toward the CSCE. A few Western officials feared that the conference might "isolate itself from reality," but most regarded the drama in the Middle East, Asia, and Africa as a useful distraction. By drawing attention away from Helsinki and Geneva, it insulated the allies from the vagaries of public opinion and empowered them to press their demands.[17]

Few Western journalists paid much attention to the CSCE. Because the negotiations took place behind closed doors, reporters in Helsinki and Geneva had to rely on official briefings and off-the-record conversations. Although they wrote the occasional article on the proceedings, by late 1973 the *Economist* noted that people had "almost forgotten" the conference.[18] Newspapers and magazines in the Soviet bloc gave it more coverage. Adhering to official media plans, they presented the conference in a positive light and criticized Western governments for demanding too much.[19]

Out of the media spotlight, the diplomats in Helsinki and Geneva created a culture of their own. They numbered more than four hundred and relied on the work of hundreds more—secretaries, interpreters, drivers, security personnel, and perhaps a few spies—to keep the conference running. The members of this tribe got to know one another over countless lunches at fine restaurants and buffet suppers at their embassies and missions. During the breaks between the formal sessions, they continued their conversations in informal drafting groups, over coffee in the hallways, and by telephone. After hours, they caroused in bars and nightclubs, relaxed at sauna parties, and lamented their host cities' dearth of cultural attractions.[20]

Through many months and thousands of meetings, they came to respect and even like one another. Each side learned that its adversaries were "human beings like us, with whom we could joke around or be serious, talk about important things, [and] have open discussions," Swiss diplomat Édouard Brunner later recalled. This "plausible simulacrum of friendship" across the ideological divide, as one British delegate described it, may have blunted the political conflicts that animated the negotiations, but it could not eliminate them. The participants still questioned each other's motives, accused each other of stonewalling, and lost their tempers.[21]

The Soviets fielded the largest of all the delegations. Three ambassadors led their team at the preparatory talks, a sign of how seriously the Kremlin took the enterprise. Valerian Zorin had represented the USSR on the UN Security Council during the Cuban Missile Crisis. At the MPT, Western delegates referred to him as "the poisoned dwarf" because of his abrasive style. Perhaps for this reason, he did not take part in the Geneva talks, where Anatoly Kovalev took charge of the hundred-strong Soviet team. The chain-smoking, poetry-writing deputy foreign minister had helped to craft Brezhnev's Peace Program and had a hand in almost every component of the General Secretary's détente strategy, including his summits with Brandt, Pompidou, and Nixon.[22]

Kovalev's two deputies in Geneva, both of ambassadorial rank, were almost as accomplished. Western diplomats regarded Lev Mendelevich, a protegé of Gromyko, as "professional, shrewd and sophisticated," and "a wily old fox" who delighted in haranguing his counterparts. Yuri Dubinin, who had spent many years in Paris, combined worldly sophistication with unyielding dogmatism. He loved "the good things of life" and dressed in the latest Western fashions, but his "negotiating posture was always inflexible and the mailed fist was never far beneath the table." He alternated between trying to charm his negotiating partners and bludgeoning them with rudeness and contempt. The three men epitomized the *mezhdunarodniki*, the educated, cosmopolitan, and pragmatic cohort of Soviet diplomats who hoped that cooperation with the West could improve the communist system. By contrast, their Eastern European counterparts gained a reputation for charmless dogmatism, albeit with a few exceptions. East Germany's Siegfried Bock demonstrated an "irrepressible intelligence and sophistication of manner" that impressed Western diplomats. Similarly, Romania's Valentin Lipatti earned Western admiration by regularly challenging Soviet views and staking out an independent position. His efforts notwithstanding, the Soviets dominated the Eastern side of the negotiations, and their allies usually followed their lead.[23]

No country played an equivalent role on the Western side, though the British, French, and West Germans all figured prominently. Some Western diplomats had already acquired substantial experience dealing with East-West problems, but none boasted the credentials of Zorin or Kovalev. The British government, for example, assigned junior personnel to the negotiations to send a message: it did not regard the CSCE as a priority and would be prepared to walk away if the Soviets refused to compromise. The same was true of most other Western delegations. Their representatives, many of whom were in their late 20s and early 30s and ranked no higher than first secretary, regularly faced down Soviet interlocutors who stood several rungs above them on the diplomatic ladder and were at least a decade older. For these Western diplomats, the CSCE represented both danger and opportunity. If their inexperience led them to make a mistake, they might suffer perilous consequences. If they distinguished themselves, however, the conference could accelerate their careers.[24]

The leading figures of the Western delegations ranged widely in character. France's Jacques Andréani concealed a sharp sense of humor and a love of contemporary art behind his outward gruffness and professorial demeanor. West German ambassador Guido Brunner combined a passionate commitment to European integration with a lively interest in topics from science to soccer. Britain's Toby Hildyard had repeatedly distinguished himself by acts of physical courage, first as a Second World War pilot, and later as a hostage negotiator in the hideouts of Uruguayan guerrillas. The first head of the American delegation, George Vest, combined a down-to-earth manner with intellectual sophistication. At one moment, he compared the conference to a "team of mules" who refused to pull in the same direction. At another, he quoted Juvenal's *Satires* to puncture a display of Soviet bombast. While some of his counterparts in Geneva set themselves up in grand villas, he contented himself with a one-room apartment.[25]

Several of the neutral delegations played a vigorous part. On many questions the Swiss, Austrians, Swedes, and Finns sympathized with their Western colleagues and used their independent status to broker compromises that favored them. Other neutrals sent delegations so small that they struggled to keep up. Malta assigned only one diplomat to the preparatory talks. Liechtenstein fielded one prince and two counts, who made their views known but were nevertheless "generally incapable of suppressing the echoes of musical comedy which followed them about," a British diplomat reported.[26]

No matter its size, every delegation had to cope with the mixture of tedium and exhilaration that characterized life at the CSCE. Tracking and reporting the latest developments devoured uncounted hours of labor. "We ourselves were appalled by the stream of telegraphic reports" sent back to London, and "[we] pitied our readers," British diplomat George Walden wrote at the end of the preparatory talks. The West German delegation in Geneva wrote more than a thousand dispatches home.[27] The Quai d'Orsay's secretary-general pleaded with the French delegation to stanch the flood of its cable traffic to rein in costs.[28]

Despite the workload, the high stakes kept participants alert. "It was the hunt; the chase," one later recalled. "For the first time we were able to discuss issues openly with the Warsaw Pact countries, issues which they always tried to keep off the table." Another likened the process to a "pitched battle." If it was a battle, however, it could not be decided in an afternoon. "We have to proceed carefully across a broad front rather than registering agreements where possible and working on the principle of the coral reef rather than the prefabricated house," wrote Crispin Tickell, who coordinated Britain's CSCE efforts from London.[29] The participants had to strike a balance between pushing forward to keep the negotiations moving and hanging back lest they appear too eager to reach an agreement.

Their tactics varied with their personalities. Sometimes the Soviets tried to flatter their negotiating partners. Albert Sherer, who led the US delegation in 1974–75, noted that Kovalev urged him to support the USSR's proposals in order to preserve their countries' "special relationship." In other cases, the Soviets attempted to bully their counterparts into submission, whether by issuing threats, grabbing the microphone out of turn, or—in the case of Dubinin—flying into "a rage of belittling and insulting language." Whenever possible, they tried to negotiate one-on-one with Western delegations to break the allies' united front and turn them against one another. They also played language games, producing Russian translations of English or French texts that conveyed a slightly different—and more advantageous—meaning.[30] The strengths and weaknesses of the Soviet approach were those of the Soviet political system as a whole. The delegation's "clarity of purpose, persistence and stamina" were counterbalanced by its "remarkable rigidity and unresponsiveness . . . its insensitivity, inability to delegate and poor sense of proportion," a British diplomat observed.[31]

As the negotiations unfolded, the Soviet government kept up its efforts to seduce Western public opinion. It mobilized front groups and organized conferences, such as the Assembly of Representatives of Public Opinion, the World Congress of Peace Forces, and the European Youth Security Conference. By supporting "all social movements," the communists could bring the CSCE to a successful conclusion, Boris Ponomarev, the head of the Central Committee's international department, told the East Germans. If the socialist states could disseminate their ideas and persuade Western citizens to embrace their conception of European security, Western governments would eventually have to give way at the negotiating table.[32]

The Western delegates approached their task differently. They reminded the Soviets that the conference would make no progress unless it produced specific commitments on freer movement and other areas of vital interest.[33] The allies also worked hard to remain united. When the French negotiated a deal with the Soviets in secret and presented the fait accompli to their allies, the gambit backfired, eliciting accusations of deceit and bad faith. The Americans, by contrast, kept a low profile. George Vest consistently supported the Western Europeans, but rather than pressing his case in the heat of argument, he perched himself on one of the backless leather benches in the conference center lobby and let other ambassadors approach him with questions or proposals. "If you just sit there, and are prepared to listen to people, people will come and talk to you," he said.[34]

Before the negotiations began, few anticipated that they would last more than a few months. When the Italian delegation arrived in Geneva in September 1973, for example, it expected to be home by the end of the year. Its members neglected to pack any cold weather clothes and shivered through their first Swiss winter. Once the diplomats grasped the difficulty of the task ahead, some delegations took pains to signal that they were prepared for the long haul. Because most Western diplomats had come without their families, Anatoly Kovalev asked Brezhnev to allow the members of the Soviet team, including the translators, to move their wives to Geneva. Brezhnev agreed. The Finnish ambassador brought his children—and his horse—with him. British diplomats reported these developments with a pang of envy, and complained to their penny-pinching authorities that they could not operate as if the negotiations were a short-term assignment. They appealed for similar permission and larger living allowances.[35]

The passage of time weighed on everyone. Soviet officials from the Politburo on down complained that the Western delegations were dragging their feet. During the preparatory talks, when Western diplomats insisted on drafting a detailed agenda for the conference, the Soviets accused them of trying to delay the negotiations.[36] During the Geneva negotiations, Brezhnev sent personal appeals to Western leaders urging them to intervene with their delegations to speed up the pace of work.[37] "I'm sick and tired of endless delays in bringing the Conference to a close," he told Kissinger in 1974.[38] He had worked hard to make the CSCE a reality and wanted it to succeed. The sooner the negotiations ended, the fewer unwelcome demands the Soviets would face. In the meantime, they played their own delaying game, trying to hold up progress on the West's favorite subjects.[39]

This pressure created openings—and hazards—for Western officials. The Soviets gave "the impression of ill-restrained eagerness to move swiftly," a member of the British delegation reported. By contrast, the Western Europeans wanted to let the conference "proceed on its own rhythm," without a fixed timetable. Sooner or later, they reasoned, the Soviets would give ground to bring the CSCE to a conclusion.[40] But Western diplomats also worried that, as the months passed, they would find it increasingly difficult to speak with one voice. Their political leaders might succumb to Brezhnev's cajoling, public opinion might grow restive, or a member of the alliance might cut a separate deal with Moscow in pursuit of unilateral advantage. In mid-1974, some Western delegations almost lost their nerve. If the CSCE did not conclude that summer, they worried, it would lose all forward momentum. Western solidarity would crumble in a storm of mutual recrimination, and the Soviets would sweep the field.[41] Because both sides regarded time as a tool and a threat, the CSCE became a war of attrition. Participants tried to gain advantage by outlasting their adversaries and grinding down their resolve.

II

Most of the arguments in Helsinki and Geneva unfolded along East-West lines. However, the delegates also had to contend with other conflicts that were less visible, pitting allies—and even members of the same government—against one another. In the Nixon administration, for instance, a number of senior officials had opposed the conference for years. Henry Kissinger had criticized the Budapest appeal in 1969, and his disdain for the CSCE only grew stronger with time. On various occasions, he called it a "meaningless psychological exercise," a "never-never land," and "totally frivolous," and joked that the substance was either too boring or too esoteric to understand.[42]

Some of the Western Europeans also questioned the CSCE's value, albeit with less vehemence. A group of "recalcitrants" in the Foreign Office opposed the negotiations "even to the verge of sabotage," a British diplomat recalled.[43] Ted Heath worried that the Soviets would use the conference to "undermin[e] the cohesion of the West by inducing a false sense of security." Even Pompidou and Brandt, whose concepts of détente had strongly influenced NATO's approach to the conference, began to lose patience as the talks crawled along. Egon Bahr speculated that the CSCE might produce nothing more than "high flown sentiments."[44]

This skepticism complicated Western efforts, but it never grew strong enough to derail the conference. Most of the diplomats on the scene resolved to keep going regardless of the opposition they faced in their own capitals. In Bonn, officials at the Auswärtiges Amt remained convinced that the conference could serve West Germany's concept of détente.[45] At the Foreign Office, Crispin Tickell understood the skeptics' concerns, but insisted that the Western allies could turn the conference to their advantage so long as they remained patient and stuck together.[46] Roger Seydoux, the French ambassador in Moscow, insisted on pushing the Soviets as hard as possible on intellectual freedom and the freer movement of people. "We should not be afraid to proclaim our ideals," he wrote.[47] Although Kissinger wanted to give in to Soviet demands without a fight, Secretary of State William Rogers and other State Department officials resisted this pressure, which allowed the American delegation to hold firm.[48]

The task of forging a unified Western position on the CSCE's wide range of subjects also caused considerable friction among the allies. They disagreed about the substance of the conference and how to coordinate their views. Before the negotiations, NATO had provided the main forum for these discussions. When the preparatory talks opened, however, the French objected to regular meetings of allied delegations, lest the Americans dominate the proceedings and lest the Soviets respond by imposing "bloc discipline on their East European allies."[49] Officials at the Quai d'Orsay preferred to work through the European Community. The CSCE offered the perfect opportunity to test the EC's new mechanisms for coordinating its members' foreign policies.

These mechanisms had been several years in the making. In December 1969, as the latest step toward political integration, EC leaders agreed to harmonize their foreign policies. The following year, a committee under the leadership of Belgian diplomat Étienne Davignon concluded that Western Europe had to "express itself with a single voice" and "discharge the imperative world duties entailed by its greater cohesion and increasing role."[50] Twice a year, the EC's foreign ministers would meet to discuss issues of common concern, and a political committee (also known as the Davignon Committee) of senior diplomats would take up particular subjects in the interim. In 1971, it decided to tackle the CSCE and the Middle East. Over the years that followed, and especially after the UK joined the EC in 1973, the mechanisms of European political cooperation—the political committee, its CSCE subcommittee, and its ad hoc group, which focused on the CSCE's economic issues—became important forums for harmonizing Western policy.[51]

The new bodies sowed conflict in the Atlantic community. The Davignon Committee's mandate overlapped with that of NATO's North Atlantic Council, raising questions about who should do what. The Americans preferred to work solely through NATO. The French argued that the members of the European Community should first work out a common line and then present it at NATO for the allies' endorsement. With fewer members, the EC committees could reach consensus more efficiently than NATO's larger forums, but the West Germans worried that the tangled lines of responsibility would cause confusion and disunity at the CSCE. The costs of establishing a strict relationship between the two sets of institutions would exceed the benefits, the British concluded. In the absence of an obvious solution, however, the argument remained unresolved.[52]

Throughout the negotiations, the Western governments collaborated through both NATO and EC channels. This worked better in practice than in theory. The tensions over which mechanism ought to take precedence never faded, and the cumbersome approach frustrated participants. Nonetheless, the extended process of multilateral consultations stress-tested ideas and ensured that the West's negotiating positions were robust enough to withstand Eastern counterattacks. The guidelines established by the EC political committee seldom clashed with those of the Atlantic alliance. On some questions, NATO endorsed positions that the EC had already worked out. On others, the main work took place under NATO's auspices. In Helsinki and Geneva, the Western delegates convened regular—often daily— meetings of the NATO and EC caucuses. Albert Sherer noted in his diary that these discussions occasionally descended into bickering and neglected substantive matters in favor of trivialities, but most of the time the Western delegations managed to work out positions they could all accept.[53]

The Eastern allies faced a similar set of challenges. At the highest reaches of the Soviet government, the CSCE enjoyed strong support. In November 1972, Brezhnev told the Central Committee secretariat that the opening of the preparatory talks was "a great victory" for the USSR. "We should always have this issue at the center of our attention. . . . In the struggle for peace we are the masterminds and organizers of this policy in Europe."[54] Gromyko likewise worked hard to bring the negotiations to fruition. "At the conference, one milestone after another is being conquered in favor of our policy, in favor of peace," he said at the Central Committee's April 1975 plenum. Within the foreign ministry and party apparat, reform-minded officials also supported the conference, albeit for different reasons. Kovalev, Mendelevich, and others hoped that more openness to the West would reinvigorate the Soviet system and save it from the hardliners' orthodoxy.[55]

A number of influential figures dissented from this enthusiasm. These "people of the Cold War," as Kovalev called them, regarded the conference as a threat to the Soviet system. Politburo members Mikhail Suslov and Boris Ponomarev argued that it would damage the country's security and undermine orthodoxy. The USSR stood to gain nothing from the negotiations, which were "turning against us," Ponomarev warned in 1973. Some members of the Soviet delegation in Geneva voiced similar concerns. Dubinin took a much harder line on Western demands than either Kovalev or Mendelevich. In Geneva, he argued openly with Mendelevich and sometimes even ignored Kovalev's instructions, which he regarded as too conciliatory. The CSCE fueled similar arguments in every Warsaw Pact capital, pitting reform-minded officials against their conservative rivals.[56]

The Soviets also had to wrangle their allies into line. The socialist states had stood together in fighting to create the CSCE, Brezhnev said, so they had to stand together at the negotiations too. "This historical achievement demonstrates the tremendous importance of coordinating our foreign policy efforts," he told Eastern European leaders in 1972. To establish a "common platform" for the negotiations, the Soviets sent draft proposals to their allies for every item on the CSCE agenda and expected their support. The Bulgarians, Czechoslovaks, and Hungarians asked few questions. By the time the negotiations opened, the Poles and East Germans also felt more comfortable with the USSR's priorities. Although their views continued to differ from Moscow's in some respects, the Warsaw Treaty and Basic Treaty had given them more confidence about their place in the world. They no longer felt the need to assert themselves so strongly against their superpower patron.[57]

The Romanians, however, stuck to their independent line. During the first working session of the preparatory talks, they rejected a proposal—to which the participants had agreed beforehand—to give the Finns, who were already chairing the talks, the deputy chairmanship too. The Romanians insisted that the position should rotate so as to emphasize the equality of all participants. They also argued that the rules of procedure should stipulate that the participants acted as "independent and sovereign states under conditions of full equality," without regard for the military blocs. On most issues at the conference, Romania's views did not differ much from those of its allies, but it provoked these scuffles to make clear that it "retained its freedom" to speak for itself, foreign minister George Macovescu told Kovalev. An irritated Gromyko denounced Bucharest's attempt to "move away from the agreed course of the Warsaw Pact countries." Even the Poles lectured Ceauşescu on the importance of allied solidarity. Nonetheless, the Soviets recognized that putting too much pressure on Romania would only "confirm Bucharest's warnings against the danger of major-power domination," one observer noted.[58]

The crosscurrents of bureaucratic and alliance politics shaped the work of every delegation. In deciding what to demand, what to reject, when to stand firm, and when to back down, participants had to weigh their instructions, their allies' preferences, and their own assessments of what was feasible. The complexity of this task afforded them significant latitude. The delegates received orders from their authorities at home, but because it was nearly impossible to steer—or even understand—the negotiations from a distance, these typically established only broad guidelines. The participants "had a merciful lack of interference from above," Cripsin Tickell recalled. As a result, they often made crucial decisions on the spot.[59]

The Soviet government exerted firm control over its representatives, but they still enjoyed considerable room for maneuver. Kovalev cultivated good relations with many of the Kremlin's top figures, especially Gromyko and KGB chief Yuri Andropov, and kept them apprised of the latest developments. On the CSCE's most sensitive issues, Brezhnev, Gromkyo, and Andropov set policy themselves and insisted that Kovalev seek their approval before making any concessions. Nonetheless, when the delegation's instructions—which, by Soviet standards, were quite broad—conflicted with a decision that Kovalev believed was necessary, he could persuade Gromyko to change them.[60] Sometimes heated disputes broke out when hardliners in Moscow objected to the direction of the talks. In these cases, the Soviet delegation's negotiations with its authorities back home were even more important than the negotiations with its interlocutors in Geneva. In the end, Kovalev usually got his way.[61]

Although Western political leaders retained ultimate authority, the professional diplomats—especially those on the scene in Helsinki and Geneva—made most of the important decisions. Several delegations wrote their own instructions. At the end of a week in Geneva, Andréani would send a summary of events to the Quai d'Orsay and request guidance on what to do next. He would then return to Paris and reply to his own message on Monday morning, in part because none of his superiors could follow the CSCE's intricacies. The British adopted a similar procedure.[62] The American delegates kept in regular touch with Washington by telegram and telephone, but did not receive written orders. Because the highest levels of the Nixon administration were either indifferent or hostile to the conference, the State Department officials who supported it worried that issuing formal instructions would invite White House interference. So long as the delegation did not attract Kissinger's ire or provoke a rupture with the Soviets, it could operate with considerable autonomy. "It was the most fun I've ever had," George Vest later said.[63]

III

The success of Soviet diplomacy in the early 1970s fueled Brezhnev's ambitions for the CSCE. The Eastern Treaties, the declaration on Franco-Soviet cooperation, and the Basic Principles Agreement had vindicated his approach to détente. Far from making the security conference redundant, they offered a prototype for it to emulate. Because Brandt, Pompidou, and Nixon had already endorsed the inviolability of Europe's frontiers, the nonuse of force, and nonintervention in internal affairs, the Soviets and their allies expected the CSCE to reaffirm them without too much difficulty.[64] "By declaring these important principles as the basis of the relations among states in Europe, the all-European conference will take a decision of great historical importance," the Warsaw Pact's leaders said in January 1972. "This will constitute the beginning of joint fruitful work capable of making Europe really peaceful."[65]

Since 1969, the Eastern allies had raised their expectations for the conference. At the time of the Budapest appeal, they wagered that Western leaders would refuse to recognize the continent's frontiers as permanent. They therefore proposed that the CSCE issue only a declaration on the nonuse of force.[66] Once West Germany ratified the Eastern Treaties, however, the Soviets decided to go further. "The chief political result of the all-European conference, I repeat, must be to entrench in international law on a multilateral basis ... the inviolability of the present frontiers of the European states," Leonid Brezhnev told his Warsaw Pact counterparts in July 1972. From his perspective, the correlation of forces was continuing to change in the USSR's favor, and his grand strategy was paying off. It only made sense to demand more from the CSCE.[67]

Brezhnev's expectations were not unlimited. Since the 1950s, some Soviet and Eastern European officials had argued that a security conference should try to make NATO and the Warsaw Pact redundant. The USSR's premier foreign policy think tank, the Institute of World Economy and International Relations, concluded that the CSCE would strengthen the centrifugal forces within the Western alliance in the short term. Over the longer term, if it established the conditions for pan-European security, it might replace the two alliances.[68] Brezhnev dismissed these ambitions: "We are realists and understand that in all likelihood the political-military alliances in Europe will not be dissolved," he told his allies. "The imperialist powers are unwilling to do so and will not be in the foreseeable future. Thus, we must give thought to how we can strengthen security in Europe even with the military blocs surviving for some time to come." In the meantime, the socialist states should concentrate on building a "perfect" Warsaw Pact.[69]

These constraints made it all the more important to secure a legally binding treaty on Europe's frontiers. Such an agreement would do far more than just affirm the territorial status quo. It would also recognize "the achievements of socialism" and affirm that the socialist states were full members of the international system, the Warsaw Pact's deputy foreign ministers concluded.[70] More importantly, Brezhnev argued, it would stand as "a symbol for the end of the Cold War," "preserv[e] the results of the postwar world," and establish "the conditions for a solid peace on the continent."[71] The Second World War had ended without a peace treaty, but now the CSCE would furnish a substitute.[72] Even before the negotiations had ended, Warsaw Pact leaders rejoiced that "the postwar period in Europe is over."[73] From the vantage point of Moscow, Warsaw, and Prague, a new era was dawning in European politics. The continent would soon finish exorcising the ghosts of the past.

Brezhnev presented his hopes for the CSCE in grandiose historical and moral terms. The conference "would be a great historic event whose meaning, the nobility and the value of the humanitarian ideal, would be without comparison," he told Pompidou. "There have been many wars, many victors and vanquished, friendships and diverse blocs, but such an event would be unprecedented and we are standing on its threshold." At the 1972 Moscow Summit, he reminded Nixon that "the Russian people and the other peoples of the Soviet Union have suffered quite enough from wars that have originated on European soil. We do not want this to be repeated anew.... That is the objective of our Europe policy." He did not offer this reasoning merely for Western consumption. "The lives of twenty million Soviet people and millions of lives of other European peoples, whom you represent, were not sacrificed in order to start a war again," he told Warsaw Pact leaders. "We need peace, peace, and again peace." As the culmination of Brezhnev's Peace Program, the CSCE turned the cult of the Great Patriotic War into political action.[74]

By making peace in Europe permanent, the conference would also put the capstone on Brezhnev's grand strategy to rebuild the legitimacy of the Soviet system. A successful CSCE "will have not just a general political impact, but we will also win powerful allies in the form of the peoples," Brezhnev told East German party chief Erich Honecker. If it failed, however, the consequences would be dire. "Without it, no socialist or communist construction is thinkable," he warned. "We would lose prestige and influence." At the Central Committee, Anatoly Chernyaev grasped the strategy's underlying logic. "No one believes in our 'revolutionary example' anymore. But by our nature as a great power, we have to preserve our ideological character—both for the outside world and for the communists," he wrote in his diary. "Therefore, we have to have a universalist mission. Peace—this is our mission."[75] The imperative of making good on the claim that socialism meant peace put enormous pressure on Soviet negotiators at the conference. They had to bring Brezhnev's ambitions—especially on the inviolability of frontiers—to fruition.[76]

The Romanians challenged the USSR's plans. The status of their frontiers had never been in doubt, but they did worry about the danger of a Red Army invasion. They wanted the conference to affirm their country's sovereignty and equality with the USSR and protect it against a repeat of Czechoslovakia's fate in 1968. Consequently, the Soviet decision to prioritize the inviolability of frontiers over the nonuse of force caused dismay in Bucharest. George Macovescu told Kovalev that the Soviet government should have consulted its allies before expanding the goals that the Warsaw Pact had endorsed in 1969. Kovalev rejected this reasoning. Since 1969, Soviet agreements with West Germany, France, and the United States had all affirmed the nonuse of force. Doing the same at the CSCE would waste the opportunity that the conference presented, Kovalev argued. It is doubtful that he persuaded his challenger, because the Romanians did not hesitate to inform the West about the dispute. On an issue of supreme importance, the Soviets could not count on allied solidarity.[77]

In the USSR's earliest days, its ideology put it at odds with the established international order. Its revolutionary commitment to spread communism threatened all of the great powers. In some of his rhetoric, Brezhnev suggested that the CSCE would reinvigorate this old mission. "[A]ll actions we are now taking will result in the ultimate victory of our ideology," he told Bulgarian leader Todor Zhivkov.[78] But this claim stood at odds with his defensive strategy for the conference. By trying to ratify the status quo and articulate an international code of conduct that all states could accept, Brezhnev abandoned revolutionary élan in favor of membership in the club of satisfied powers. Indeed, party hardliners accused him of violating the tenets of Marxism-Leninism. His unrelenting commitment to peace "fundamentally contradicts the Marxist position that as long as capitalism exists, war is inevitable," Boris Ponomarev complained. Anatoly Chernyaev, who hoped to reform the Soviet system from within, replied that peace did not have to wait for socialism's global triumph. This view echoed Brezhnev's own interpretation of peaceful coexistence between the two ideological systems. Nevertheless, the tension in the general secretary's strategy persisted.[79]

In pursuing the CSCE, Brezhnev resurrected a nineteenth-century concept of order. In the 1820s and 1830s, Russia had played an integral part in the Concert of Europe. It took an active role in European politics, with the goal not of overturning the established order but of protecting it from revolutionary upheaval. Similarly, Brezhnev conceived the CSCE as a means to lock down the status quo on the continent. He liked to portray himself as Lenin's heir, but in this respect he owed more to Tsar Alexander I, whose messianic understanding of his role as Europe's peacemaker had done so much to shape the Congress of Vienna more than 150 years earlier.[80]

IV

The West repudiated the concepts that the Soviets wanted the CSCE to endorse. Whereas the Warsaw Pact hoped to freeze the postwar status quo, the Western allies prioritized change. They wanted the declaration of principles to affirm that borders could be redrawn. Instead of affirming the supremacy of the state, they proposed a qualified notion of sovereignty that balanced the prerogatives of governments with those of individuals. Brezhnev hoped that the declaration would reinvigorate the Soviet order. The Western allies saw the declaration as a tool to destroy it.

By 1972, all of the allies had accepted—de facto if not de jure—the territorial status quo. When Dobrynin told Kissinger that the USSR wanted the CSCE to recognize the continent's frontiers, Kissinger replied, "No one is challenging the existing frontiers."[81] This did not mean, however, that the West would accept those frontiers as permanent, or give the Soviets the declaration that they wanted with nothing in return. "A formal public multilateral act acknowledging these frontiers would meet important Soviet objectives without any corresponding advantage to the West," the State Department's bureau of European affairs reasoned. Besides, the Eastern Treaties had only established an interim modus vivendi, and the Letter on German Unity had stipulated Bonn's commitment to achieving "a state of peace in Europe in which the German nation will recover its unity in free self-determination." A definitive settlement of the continent's frontiers still lay in the future.[82]

In the Western view, inviolability did not entail permanence. The West Germans maintained that the CSCE could not declare the continent's frontiers to be immutable. It could not forbid the pursuit of reunification or imply that the German question had been resolved. And it could not produce "a surrogate for a German peace treaty," which would destabilize West Berlin, whose autonomy depended on the legal fiction that the war had not yet ended. The other allies, who shared Bonn's concerns about the future of Germany, agreed.[83] They also wanted to prevent a backlash from Baltic émigrés, especially in North America, who would protest any international declaration that endorsed Soviet control of their homelands. In addition, the EC's members insisted that freezing the continent's borders was antithetical to the project of European integration. To preserve the hypothetical possibility of creating a United States of Europe, the CSCE had to recognize that borders could change.[84]

The allies planned to challenge the Warsaw Pact's designs in two ways. First, any statement on frontiers had to be embedded within the principle forbidding the use of force. Linking the two would imply that inviolability only prevented states from redrawing borders by military means. Going a step further, the declaration had to affirm that frontiers could be changed peacefully. If the allies got their way, the CSCE would turn immutability on its head. Contrary to the Warsaw Pact's designs, it would establish the peaceful change of frontiers as a core principle of international security. Instead of ratifying Europe's territorial status quo, the conference would specify how to revise it.[85]

The Western allies also took aim at the political status quo in the Soviet bloc. They reasoned that the USSR's thinking about the rules of international behavior contradicted itself. On the one hand, it championed international law and the United Nations Charter. On the other, it espoused a concept of limited sovereignty that violated international law. The Soviets reconciled these claims by suggesting that one set of rules governed relations between socialist states and another applied to relations between socialist and nonsocialist states. At the CSCE, the West intended to expose the flaws in this logic. The Soviets would have to "to make [an] uncomfortable choice," as the French put it: either accept a declaration that repudiated the Brezhnev Doctrine and recognized the sovereign equality of all states, or expose themselves as hypocrites for upholding a double standard.[86]

Over the course of 1971 and 1972, the allies devised several lines of attack on the Brezhnev Doctrine. The simplest approach would use the CSCE's code of conduct to reaffirm existing international agreements. The UN Declarations on Friendly Relations and on the Strengthening of International Security, which the General Assembly had promulgated in 1970, forbade states from using force against their neighbors, as did the UN Charter itself.[87] The code could also include statements on sovereignty, nonintervention in states' internal affairs, and the right of each state to choose its own political system. As the Canadian mission to NATO put it, the "internal social, political, and economic policies of sovereign states must not only be respected, but orderly changes or developments in these policies must not be interfered with from outside."[88]

These principles did not go far enough, however, because the Soviets could endorse all of them without admitting that they contradicted the Brezhnev Doctrine. In 1968, when Brezhnev explained why the Red Army had invaded Czechoslovakia, he insisted that "the socialist states stand for strict respect for the sovereignty of all countries." Far from violating Czechoslovakia's sovereignty, the USSR had helped the country fend off counterrevolution and had vindicated its right to self-determination. When

Moscow and Prague signed a friendship treaty in 1970, they renewed their commitment to state sovereignty. However, they also affirmed that the duties of proletarian internationalism superseded it, and pledged to take all "necessary measures to protect the socialist achievements of the people."[89] In order to undermine the Brezhnev Doctrine, therefore, the Western allies had to do more than articulate rules that the Soviets already claimed to honor.

They found two ways to escape this quandary. At a minimum, the CSCE had to specify that the same principles of international conduct applied to every country, regardless of its political system. The French suggested quoting the "Litvinov Doctrine" back to the Soviets. In a 1933 speech to the League of Nations, Soviet foreign minister Maksim Litvinov had insisted that no excuse could justify the use of force against any other country, not even "the internal situation of any state . . . [or] the establishment or maintenance in any state of a particular political, economic, or social regime." The same logic that Litvinov hoped would delegitimize foreign intervention against the USSR could now delegitimize Soviet intervention in Eastern Europe.[90] In addition, Western diplomats would demand a statement affirming every state's right to join or leave an alliance. "Membership in an alliance should not serve as an excuse for one or more members to restrict the exercise of sovereignty of the others," a report of the North Atlantic Council concluded. Just as the peaceful change of frontiers aimed to overcome Europe's territorial divide, here the allies aimed to overcome its political divide.[91]

Admittedly, no piece of paper could compel the Soviets to change their behavior. In the best case scenario, however, the declaration might embolden the USSR's allies to assert their independence. If the West "pressed hard on the doctrine of limited sovereignty," Canadian ambassador Robert Ford wrote from Moscow, "the Eastern European countries would have a fair chance of achieving something short of Finnish status."[92] Even if they remained under Moscow's thumb and the Soviets flouted the CSCE's principles, the declaration could help Western governments regain the moral high ground. "Public opinion needs to be reminded on occasion which of the two sides bears blame for Europe's insecurity," Elliot Richardson argued. After signing a CSCE declaration that rejected the Brezhnev Doctrine, the Soviets could never justify invading an ally again. If they did march back into Czechoslovakia or Hungary, their hypocrisy would help NATO to rally public support. No matter how the Soviets acted, a clear standard for measuring their conduct would serve Western interests.[93]

Finally, the Western allies wanted the CSCE to establish human rights as a core principle of international security. The French first suggested raising human rights in 1969, but for the next two years, NATO focused its attention on other subjects, particularly the Brezhnev Doctrine and freer move-

ment. In late 1971, however, the West Germans and Americans proposed
that the code of good conduct list respect for universal rights as a free-
standing principle, alongside the nonuse of force and nonintervention in
states' domestic affairs.[94] The other allies endorsed the idea. If the CSCE
aimed to strengthen European security, it had to recognize that human
rights constituted an integral principle of international order. The Soviets
had to understand that unless they began to demonstrate "strict respect"
for their citizens' rights, "the atmosphere of confidence which was the
basis of genuine détente could not develop," West Germany's ambassador
to NATO said.[95]

This emphasis on human rights came from a variety of sources. A number of allies cited the UN Charter and Universal Declaration of Human
Rights to explain their interest in the subject. For the members of the EC,
human rights had been entwined with the project of integration since at
least the Brussels Treaty in 1948. In 1970, the Davignon Report declared
that a "united Europe must be founded upon the common heritage of respect for the liberty and the rights of men." In 1973 and 1974, the EC and
NATO went even further, issuing declarations that presented human rights
as a central component of Western identity. If the USSR wanted to unite
the continent under a single code of conduct—if it wanted to become fully
European—it had to subscribe to these values.[96]

More profound than any of these considerations, however, were the intellectual, cultural, social, and technological changes that put human rights at
the center of the Western ethical imagination in the 1970s. After a brief ef-
florescence in the 1940s, human rights faded from prominence, attracting
little attention beyond the arid debates of the United Nations. Three decades later, however, it returned to the forefront of popular consciousness.
Decolonization and the American civil rights movement removed the
stains that had made the Americans, British, and French wary of discussing
the subject in earlier years. New transportation and communications technology gave the suffering of distant strangers—whether in Vietnam, Biafra,
or Bangladesh—unprecedented immediacy. A fresh willingness to confront
the crimes of Nazi Germany and Vichy France generated a new moral vo-
cabulary with the Holocaust at its center. The explosion of transnational
civil society created hundreds of new nongovernmental organizations.
Many of them dedicated themselves to human rights, none more prominently than Amnesty International, founded in 1961. A "global human conscience is for the first time beginning to manifest itself," one scholar observed in 1970.[97]

A new concept of peace emerged from the confluence of these factors. In
the Soviet interpretation, peace depended on states' external conduct and
required only the absence of international aggression. When Brezhnev discussed the horrors of the Second World War, he emphasized that Germany

had violated its neighbors' sovereignty and invaded their territory. From this reading of history, it followed that the Peace Program and CSCE should sanctify borders and prohibit states from using force against each other. By contrast, the draft declaration of principles that the British circulated at the North Atlantic Council in 1972 said that peace required the "full observance" of human rights. Some civil society groups made a similar argument. The CSCE had to "preserve intact the link that exists and must exist between security and liberty," jurist and Nobel laureate René Cassin insisted in a letter to Western governments. "[O]nly the pairing of security and liberty can enable the construction of fruitful and lasting cooperation." These claims presupposed a broad understanding of peace. It was not enough for states to refrain from attacking their neighbors. Governments also had to treat their citizens with respect.[98]

From this perspective, international stability depended as much on states' domestic conduct as on their foreign policy. The security of the individual mattered as much as the security of the state. States could therefore claim a prerogative, perhaps even a duty, to monitor how foreign governments behaved within their own frontiers. By framing human rights as a core principle of international security, the Western allies issued a rejoinder to Brezhnev's Peace Program and the organizing principles of the general secretary's foreign policy. They also gambled that they could channel citizens' growing discomfort with state power, which affected the West as much as the East, against the Soviet system. They would insist that communist officials pay closer attention to what philosopher Isaiah Berlin in 1972 called the "specific wishes and hopes and fears and goals of individual human beings," and thereby coax the Soviet government to bring its domestic practices into line with Western norms.[99]

The Western vision of international security suffered from internal tensions. For one thing, championing human rights when dictatorships ruled Greece and Portugal created a certain awkwardness.[100] More fundamentally, the Western concept of human rights raised questions about the meaning of state sovereignty. In this respect, it had something in common with the Brezhnev Doctrine. Both assumed that foreign governments could justifiably take an interest in a regime's internal character, that certain obligations transcended state sovereignty, and that international action was sometimes necessary to enforce those obligations. Of course, the Brezhnev Doctrine applied only to socialist states, whereas human rights held true everywhere, at least in principle. And whereas the Soviets promised to uphold socialist rule by force when necessary, the Western allies anticipated defending human rights by political—not military—means. Nonetheless, the Eastern and Western concepts both placed limits on state sovereignty.

The allies had to find a way to reconcile their objectives. They needed a concept of sovereignty that would be robust enough to forbid the USSR from invading its allies but flexible enough to justify pressuring communist governments to change their domestic ways. In a sympathetic reading, they wanted to ban military action in the name of ideology, which threatened peace, but authorize diplomatic action in the name of morality, which strengthened it. In an unsympathetic interpretation, however, they wanted to prohibit for the East what was acceptable for the West. The allies were walking a conceptual tightrope. At the CSCE, they had to find their balance.

V

The preparatory talks in Helsinki made clear that there was no middle ground between the Eastern and Western positions on Europe's frontiers. Borders could not be both immutable and subject to change. Soon after the talks began, the Soviets proposed to list the inviolability of frontiers as the first principle in the code of good conduct. They circulated a draft declaration that required signatories to respect states' territorial integrity unconditionally, regard "any attempt of encroaching upon the inviolability of existing borders . . . as an act of aggression," and incorporate these principles into domestic law.[101] If the CSCE adopted this language, the Soviets could claim that the conference had produced a peace settlement for the Second World War. Moscow's expansive definition of aggression treated "any claim or proposal for even peaceful change" as a threat to the status quo and "therefore [a] threat to peace," a Canadian official wrote. A British diplomat put it succinctly: It was "pie in a Soviet-dominated sky."[102]

With the West Germans in the lead, the Western allies protested that the Soviet proposal went further than the Moscow Treaty or any of the USSR's other bilateral agreements with Western countries. It would jeopardize the equilibrium that had been so delicately achieved on the German question. Neither the UN Charter nor the Declaration on Friendly Relations listed the inviolability of frontiers as a core principle of international affairs. There was no reason for the CSCE to break with this tradition. At most, the Western allies said, the declaration might include inviolability as a subsidiary point under the nonuse of force.[103]

The West wanted to make clear that the CSCE prohibited only the redrawing of borders by aggression and avoid any suggestion that the conference had produced a peace treaty. Lev Mendelevich, the lead Soviet negotiator on the declaration, rejected this idea. The supremacy of inviolability was "the central principle that arose from Europe's historical experience," he said. "It was the question of war or peace. It was unacceptable to degrade this principle." Meeting in Moscow, the Warsaw Pact's deputy foreign ministers agreed that, on this point, they could give no ground.[104]

The talks hit an impasse. To break it, the Swiss proposed a trade-off. They put forward a ten-point declaration that featured inviolability as a free-standing principle, immediately following the nonuse of force. It also listed human rights and self-determination as independent principles—something to which the Russians had previously objected on the grounds that they were not fundamental to security—and declared that the principles would apply to all states, regardless of their political systems. The Western allies decided that they could accept this compromise. Finally, Mendelevich announced that the USSR could too.[105]

The deal allowed some room for interpretation. The Russian and German versions of the list of principles used the language of the Moscow Treaty, translating inviolability as *nerushimost'* and *Unverletzlichkeit*. From the West German perspective, the words only forbade attempts to change frontiers by military means. "This term does not stand opposed to the possibility of peaceful border changes," the West German foreign ministry concluded. But to the leaders of the Warsaw Pact, it connoted permanence. At the January 1972 meeting in Prague, for instance, Polish leader Edward Gierek denounced the suggestion that the Moscow and Warsaw Treaties implied "only a renunciation of force." They constituted promises not to change Europe's frontiers by any means, he insisted. When the preparatory talks concluded in June 1973, both sides declared themselves satisfied with the result.[106]

When Stage II opened in Geneva three months later, charged with turning the bullet-point list of principles into a full declaration, the two sides resumed the fight. Aside from a few cosmetic changes, the Soviets stuck to their position. The Western allies demanded a clear affirmation that frontiers could be changed peacefully. They maintained that the statement on inviolability represented only "a territorial concretization of the ban on resorting to violence," as a French official put it. Because the stakes for the future of Germany were so high, and because whatever text the CSCE produced would be subjected to intense public scrutiny, they could not allow any room for ambiguity.[107]

The Soviets and their allies refused to discuss peaceful change or to link inviolability to the nonuse of force. Gromyko accused the West Germans, French, and Americans of "contradict[ing] the often-stated, solemn, high-level declarations" they had signed over the previous few years. He urged Kissinger to pressure the Western Europeans to drop their "unacceptable and, indeed, absurd" demands. Communist officials insisted that the CSCE had to learn the lessons of the 1930s, implying that Bonn's commitment to peaceful reunification amounted to aggression against its neighbors. The Czechoslovaks said that their man in the street has "the right to know that the frontiers of his country [are] secure and that history would not repeat itself." In a letter approved by the Politburo, Brezhnev made a similar case to Nixon, Brandt, Pompidou, and Heath. "Obviously some people would like to weaken—in a roundabout way—the basic principle of European security and to leave a loophole for the revanchist forces," he wrote. "Of course, this cannot be allowed. It is not difficult to visualize where it could lead to." In Geneva, the diplomats searched in vain for common ground. Speaking to a Soviet journalist about the deadlock, Kovalev quoted a popular Russian song. "The river is moving and not moving," he said.[108]

The Nixon administration tried to play both sides. Kissinger refused to let the conference damage superpower relations, but he also understood the importance of trans-Atlantic solidarity, especially in light of the Year of Europe debacle a few months before. Meeting with Brezhnev in Moscow, he said that the fight over inviolability was "not primarily an American issue," and promised to lean on the Western Europeans to find "a reasonable solution." When West Germany's new foreign minister visited San Clemente in July 1974, however, Nixon applied no such pressure. The president reassured Hans-Dietrich Genscher that he was on his side. "Our Russian friends cannot take the position that they can simply draw a line down the middle of Europe, on one side of which nothing can change but the other side of which is a happy hunting ground for them," Nixon said. "We should not at this point in history ratify the Iron Curtain, as the Soviets want us to do." Meanwhile, in Geneva, the State Department's career diplomats looked for a compromise.[109]

At the beginning of April, the negotiators made a breakthrough. They worked out a deal on inviolability, defining the concept in military terms. In the English version, the participants agreed to treat "as inviolable all one another's frontiers as well as the frontiers of all States in Europe and therefore they will refrain now and in the future from assaulting these frontiers." From the West's perspective, the principle merely entailed a promise not to attack one's neighbors.[110] The Russian version was more ambiguous. The word used for "assaulting" came from the verb *posyagat'*, meaning "to infringe" or "to intrude." The Soviets claimed that the text virtually declared frontiers to be immutable. Nevertheless, it fell short of the Soviets' initial hopes. Kovalev was "clearly under highest level pressure to get [a] clear text agreed before Easter break," the American delegation reported. He "settled for less than [he] could have gotten" in order to resolve the matter for Brezhnev, who had been keeping daily track of the negotiations.[111]

The participants also settled the debate on peaceful change. For several months, the Soviets had hinted that they might be able to swallow a text on the subject. So long as the principle of inviolability stood alone "with crystal purity and clarity," as Brezhnev put it, the USSR could be flexible on peaceful change. The general secretary told Kissinger that he might accept "something like voluntary change in frontiers by the consent of the states concerned."[112] In Geneva, the West Germans surprised their allies by dropping their demand that the statement on the peaceful change of frontiers be attached to the principle of inviolability. Eventually the delegates worked out an acceptable text, but could not agree where to place it. A Spanish diplomat solved the problem. Secretly acting at the Soviets' behest, he proposed to register the text on a separate piece of paper now, and decide where to insert it in the declaration later.[113]

The deal nearly fell apart at the last minute. When word of the compromise reached Berlin, it set off a fierce argument at the highest level of the East German government. Politburo member and foreign policy expert Hermann Axen rushed to see Erich Honecker. He urged Honecker to intervene with the Soviets to block the deal, which threatened the GDR's very existence by admitting the possibility of German reunification. "You must call Comrade Brezhnev immediately!" Axen said. Honecker refused. He did not want to risk wrecking or even delaying the negotiations. Under orders from Berlin, the head of the East German delegation in Geneva, Siegfried Bock, acted against his better judgment and accepted the peaceful change clause.[114]

Meanwhile, the West Germans suffered their own crisis of confidence. Two days before the Easter recess, Bonn instructed its delegation in Geneva to demand more favorable language on inviolability. Privately, Guido Brunner said that his superiors feared the compromise deal would expose them to attack by Ostpolitik's conservative critics. The sudden change infuriated Eastern and Western delegations alike. Kovalev found himself in a bind. His superiors were impatient for progress, but he had no time to consult Moscow before the talks adjourned. Unable to contain his frustration, he approached the head of the West German delegation and said, "Now we're going to punch you in the face—politically." Unless the West Germans withdrew their objections, he warned, the Soviet delegation would publicly declare that Bonn's position violated the spirit of the Moscow Treaty and Ostpolitik. Meanwhile, Brunner tried to persuade his foreign ministry to relent. Only hours before the recess, officials in Bonn gave way. Late on the night of April 5, Brunner accepted the compromise as it stood.[115]

VI

Just when it seemed that one of the toughest problems on the CSCE's agenda had been solved, the West Germans snatched discord from the jaws of agreement. After the delegates in Geneva finalized the statement on peaceful change, Bonn insisted on rewriting it. The registered text said that "the participating states consider that their frontiers can be changed only in accordance with international law, through peaceful means and by agreement." According to the West Germans, the reference to international law suggested that states lacked an inherent right to change their borders peacefully, and implied that additional conditions had to be met beyond peaceful means and agreement. Officials in Bonn feared that the Soviets would use this loophole to declare that frontiers had been frozen after all. To avert this danger, the West Germans proposed to remove the word "only" and add a comma before the phrase "in accordance with international law." These revisions would make clear that only two conditions had to be met: the frontiers had be redrawn peacefully, and with the consent of the countries involved. They would also prevent the Soviets from arguing that international law imposed a third, unspecified set of conditions.[116]

This reversal of policy on a point of excruciating subtlety aggravated allies and adversaries alike. "I can't understand why this is so important," Kissinger told Genscher in June 1974. "I will be surprised if there are ten human beings who remain to understand the document 30 minutes after it is signed." Nonetheless, Genscher refused to budge. Having taken over as foreign minister the previous month, after the Günter Guillaume spy scandal brought down Brandt's government, he wanted to prove that he could stand up to the Soviets and East Germans and deny the Christian Democratic opposition any chance to criticize his handling of policy. At few other times in the history of diplomacy could statesmen have argued that the fate of a continent might turn on the placement of a comma.[117]

West Germany's allies reluctantly supported its new demands, but the Soviets refused to reopen a text that had been finalized. Besides, they argued, borders could only be changed as an exception to the rules of international law, not as a core principle. To break the stalemate, the West Germans quietly enlisted Henry Kissinger's help. He agreed to raise the matter directly with Brezhnev and Gromyko. At the June 1974 Moscow Summit and on several occasions thereafter, he put forward Bonn's preferred formula, and the American delegation in Geneva did the same. The Soviets demurred. "The purpose obviously is to try to weaken the principle of inviolability," Gromyko said. Brezhnev complained that the proposed text suggests that the "most important purpose of international law is to change frontiers."[118]

Perhaps in an attempt to confuse the Western allies, the Soviets advanced several counterproposals of their own. Each differed subtly from the others, but all resembled the text that had already been registered. Kissinger did not conceal his exasperation. "This is childish," he told a State Department staff meeting. In conversation with French president Valéry Giscard d'Estaing, he insisted that "[n]o frontier will change on the basis of a sentence in a document." The whole matter was "absurd." He urged the West Germans to take up the problem directly with Moscow, but they protested that only the United States had enough influence to work out a satisfactory agreement. Meanwhile, progress in Geneva remained at a standstill.

"The conference is bathing, like the city, in the fog," Kovalev complained, insisting that the Soviets could make no more concessions on frontiers.[119]

Finally, Kissinger relented. In February 1975, he raised the matter again with Gromyko. The Soviet foreign minister now agreed to consider Kissinger's formula. After further refinement, the two sides settled on the new text and proposed to insert it in the principle on the sovereign equality of states. After the West Germans endorsed it, the Americans formally presented it in Geneva. The agreement, negotiated in secret, took many diplomats by surprise. On March 17, almost a year after the original compromise, the participants finalized the new text on peaceful change. According to this version, they acknowledged that "their frontiers can be changed, in accordance with international law, by peaceful means and by agreement." Bonn had won the battle of the comma.[120]

One further obstacle remained. Because of the tension between inviolability and peaceful change, the Western allies wanted to clarify "the unity of the principles and their inter-relationship," as the EC's foreign ministers put it. The French proposed adding a statement that principles had "equal value" and that "each of them must be interpreted in the context of the others." By implication, the texts on the nonuse of force and peaceful change would constrain the principle of inviolability.[121]

The Soviets spurned this idea. In a memorandum to the Politburo, Gromyko said that the French proposal aimed "to limit the independent significance of the principle of inviolability [and] to put it at the mercy of the effectiveness of the other principles." In conversation with Kissinger, he made the point more bluntly. "Equal validity is nonsense," he said, because some of the principles were more important than others. If anything, the principles should apply "equally strictly," which (in the Soviet view) would prevent any constraints on the rule of inviolability. Here again, Kissinger tried to broker a deal even as he professed that the nuances of the dispute remained "a mystery to me." In parallel with the American efforts, the French also looked for an acceptable compromise. Finally, they devised a text that the Soviets could accept. It affirmed that all of the principles were "of primary significance" and would be "equally and unreservedly applied" and "interpreted taking into account the others."[122]

Both sides claimed victory. "This will make clear that we keep the German question open, as laid down in the Letter on German Unity," Genscher told a television interviewer. The Soviets and their allies did not mind that the West had largely achieved its goals in the fight over equal validity, or that the declaration provided for peaceful change. What really mattered, the Polish foreign ministry concluded, was that CSCE had confirmed the division of Germany and all of Europe's postwar frontiers by establishing the inviolability of frontiers as a distinct principle "of fundamental importance." The socialist states should take pride in its "clear and precise wording."[123]

This interpretation put an optimistic gloss on a defeat. No matter how clearly the principle of inviolability was worded, the statements on peaceful change and the interdependence of the principles made it impossible to claim that Europe's frontiers were permanent. Some East German officials grasped the magnitude of what had happened. Accepting the peaceful change of frontiers was "an utterly fundamental concession" to the interests of West Germany, Siegfried Bock later wrote. On this point, the USSR betrayed its ally's core interests, just as it did by dropping its proposal to ban states from making peaceful claims on their neighbors' territory.[124] Historians commonly describe the Helsinki Final Act as a quid pro quo: the West ratified the continent's borders and, in exchange, the Soviets agreed to certain provisions on human rights.[125] This shorthand misrepresents the agreement. Instead of cementing the status quo, the Final Act established the rules for revising it.

VII

In crafting the CSCE's territorial bargain, participants wrestled with the meaning of borders. In crafting its political bargain, they wrestled with the meaning of sovereignty. According to one classic definition, sovereignty is "the idea that there is a final and absolute political authority in the political community . . . and no final and absolute authority exists elsewhere."[126] Following this principle, sovereign states have the categorical right to determine what may and may not take place within their borders, and to prevent outside actors from interfering in their domestic affairs. The realities of statecraft rarely live up to this abstract standard, however, whether because governments voluntarily relinquish their sovereignty in certain areas or lack the wherewithal to exercise it in others. As the second wave of globalization gathered momentum in the 1960s and 1970s, states struggled to reconcile their traditional prerogatives with the unprecedented flows of capital, goods, and information that crossed their frontiers.[127]

As the diplomats in Helsinki and Geneva pondered these questions, they had to balance their own competing priorities. On the one hand, the Warsaw Pact states wanted to protect the Brezhnev Doctrine and its concept of limited sovereignty. On the other, they refused to let foreigners scrutinize their internal affairs. Similarly, the Western allies wanted to undermine the Brezhnev Doctrine by reaffirming the primacy of sovereignty and nonintervention. Yet they also wanted to limit state sovereignty by declaring human rights a core principle of international security.

The Soviets and their allies insisted that the declaration of principles should only govern relations between East and West. If the Western allies tried "to make the principles of relations between the socialist countries a central question at the conference," they would fail, Hungarian foreign minister Frigyes Puja warned. The socialist states agreed to uphold the principle of proletarian internationalism and to resist any attempt to interfere in their relations with each other. Because a special set of rules governed relations within the socialist community, the CSCE should not declare that the code of conduct applied equally to all states. Among the Eastern Europeans, only Romania, which regarded proletarian internationalism as an excuse to violate its sovereignty, dissented from this consensus.[128]

At the preparatory talks, the Italians presented a draft of the principles on behalf of the Western allies. Although Europe was divided into different social systems, they declared, the principles should apply to all states, no matter their regime. In response, the Soviets demanded that the principles acknowledge existing treaties between participating states, which would empower them to argue that the Warsaw Pact's bilateral friendship treaties—and, by extension, proletarian internationalism—trumped anything in the code of conduct. They also proposed that the declaration should apply "irrespective of the differences" in social systems, which suggested that it only guided relations between the two blocs, not within them. The quarrel struck at the heart of the CSCE's purpose. The Western allies wanted the conference to establish a set of rules to unite Europe under a single concept of international legitimacy. The Soviets, by contrast, would only go halfway. They wanted to bring peace to the whole continent, but insisted on sharpening the distinction between its socialist and capitalist zones, not blurring it.[129]

Nonetheless, the Soviets' desire for progress outweighed their attachment to their bargaining position. Thanks to a compromise orchestrated by Sweden's Hans Blix, they gave way on two crucial points. They agreed that the principles would apply "irrespective of [the participants'] political, social, or economic systems," and would govern relations among all states "equally and unreservedly." A report from the State Department noted that these provisions in the Blue Book "implicitly reject[ed] any Soviet doctrine of limited sovereignty." On this basis, the Western allies hoped that the CSCE would do away with the Brezhnev Doctrine once and for all.[130]

After making these concessions, the Soviets tried to claw them back. At the Stage I opening ceremonies in Helsinki, Andrei Gromyko dismissed the idea that the same rules applied on both sides of the Iron Curtain. There existed a "visible boundary between the two social worlds," he said. By implication, the socialist countries did not have to abide by the same standards as the West, either in the way they dealt with other states or in the way they treated their own citizens.[131] At Stage II in Geneva, the Soviets refused to repeat the sentences from the Blue Book in the declaration of principles, and they insisted that the doctrine of nonintervention required states to respect "the political, economic, and social foundations" of their neighbors. They went so far as to argue that a "lack of respect for [a political] system could be interpreted as intervention." By this sweeping definition, the West could not criticize the socialist states' policies without violating their sovereignty.[132]

Rather than meeting the Soviets halfway, the Western allies expanded their demands. France put forward a draft declaration of principles that forbade infringing a state's independence and recognized each state's right to choose its own political system and to join—or not join—an alliance. Western diplomats argued that these claims emerged naturally from the principles that the Soviets themselves supported, including sovereign equality, nonintervention, and self-determination. Walter Scheel expressed optimism that the declaration would force the USSR to change its ways. "All actions will be measured against the CSCE," he told Kissinger. "[T]his could have an influence on the Brezhnev Doctrine."[133]

In June 1974, the neutral countries stepped forward with a "package deal" that aimed to satisfy everyone. It proposed that the first principle of the declaration—on sovereign equality—require participants to "respect each other's right to choose" their own political systems. To balance this provision, it also required states to respect each other's "laws and regulations." After heated debate, all thirty-five delegations in Geneva endorsed the deal. Meanwhile, in their haste to conclude the negotiations, the Soviets accepted other Western demands. The principles would govern relations among all states and affirm every state's right to determine its own foreign policy, including its membership in an alliance. One set of rules would unite Europe. By delegitimizing the Brezhnev Doctrine, these provisions dealt a blow to the Warsaw Pact's hopes of entrenching the status quo.[134]

Now the Western allies had to prevent the CSCE from endorsing limited sovereignty by the back door. Since NATO's earliest consultations on the security conference, the Americans, British, and French had worried that a declaration affirming Europe's frontiers might foreclose the occupying powers' rights in West Berlin. Unless the text were drafted carefully, it could jeopardize the enclave's existence as a democratic polity independent of East Germany and nullify the 1971 quadripartite agreement. The Final Act had to make allowance for the occupying powers' prerogatives, or else the results would be catastrophic, Jacques Andréani said. To complicate matters further, any statement on the subject had to be phrased in oblique language, because referring explicitly to either Germany or Berlin could imply that the FRG and GDR lacked full sovereignty.[135]

The Western allies struggled to harmonize these goals with their attack on the Brezhnev Doctrine. An early proposal declared that the Final Act "cannot and will not affect [the signatories'] rights, obligations or responsibilities nor the treaties, agreements or arrangements in conformity with international law which reflect them, previously entered into by those States or which concern them."[136] This language would allow the Soviets to insist that they had a responsibility to defend socialism, in keeping with the Soviet-Czechoslovak friendship treaty. To underscore the point, Gromyko told French foreign minister Jean Sauvagnargues that it was difficult to interpret the meaning of the phrase "in the light of the very different character of existing obligations . . . between socialist countries and other countries." This comment brought the difficulty of the problem home to Western officials. The preservation of quadripartite rights in Berlin stood in direct conflict with the rejection of limited sovereignty, British diplomat Brian Fall concluded.[137]

In early 1975, the Americans, British, French, and West Germans resorted to a more ambiguous formulation. The Final Act "cannot and will not affect [the signatories'] rights, obligations or responsibilities, nor the treaties, agreements or arrangements in conformity with international law which reflect them, previously entered into by those States or which concern them," it said.[138] The Soviets, who had no interest in destabilizing the situation in Berlin, accepted it. But several NATO allies—particularly the Dutch, Italians, and Canadians—objected on the grounds that the new wording created a loophole that the Brezhnev Doctrine could squeeze through. The Romanians protested for the same reason, and because they rejected the notion that one state had any right to give "approval to treaties about other people." Even the Swiss complained, calling the proposal "bad in law" and "bad politically."[139]

The standoff persisted until the last days of the conference. In July, the recalcitrants accepted a shorter formulation that the Swiss devised. It removed the term "responsibilities" and dropped the clause about international law. Instead of solving the problem, it dodged it. Nonetheless, the Final Act still required participants to follow the same rules in their relations with all states. The principles that applied between East and West, including respect for sovereignty and nonintervention, also applied within the Warsaw Pact.[140]

VIII

Although the USSR initially refused to discuss human rights at the CSCE, the concept had deep roots in Soviet political life, albeit with a different meaning than in the West. Under Joseph Stalin, rights meant nothing in practice. Nonetheless, his 1936 constitution promulgated a series of rights that all citizens enjoyed, if only in theory. They included the rights to employment and to health care and freedoms of speech and of assembly. During the early years of the Cold War, Soviet officials used the rhetoric of human rights to criticize Western imperialism and racism, and Khrushchev tried to fulfill long-promised rights to education and to a pension. By the Brezhnev era, the notion—if not the reality—of socialist human rights had become an important component of political discourse in the USSR. In 1973, one theoretician boasted that the Soviet system offered its citizens "real guarantees for the broadest possible rights and freedoms."[141]

This track record demonstrated that the Soviet government had no trouble subscribing to human rights in word while ignoring them in deed. The USSR participated in the drafting of the United Nations Covenants on Civil-Political and Economic-Social Rights, and then signed them in 1968. A few years later, when Anatoly Kovalev told Gromyko that the USSR had not yet ratified the covenants, the foreign minister demanded to know who was responsible for the oversight and soon corrected it. In 1973, the Soviet government ratified both covenants—before the United States, Britain, or France had done the same. Kovalev believed that the move strengthened the USSR's bargaining position at the CSCE by giving it the standing to negotiate a suitable agreement on human rights rather than simply stonewalling. At the preparatory talks, this logic informed the Soviets' decision to accept the Swiss compromise that added both human rights and the inviolability of frontiers to the declaration of principles.[142]

The question for Stage II was not whether the CSCE would discuss human rights, but how. The Eastern allies had no qualms about the subject, Hermann Axen later recalled, but they opposed anything more than a cursory reference to it. Because the USSR had already ratified the UN Covenants and other international agreements, and the "Soviet legislative system and constitution were well equipped to give concrete form to the principle of human rights," Lev Mendelevich argued, a comprehensive statement was unnecessary. Besides, trying to enumerate a detailed list of rights would bog the negotiations down in "ideological quarrels." If the declaration had to mention human rights, it ought to do so in the most general terms and make clear that every state still retained supreme authority over its own territory. The East Germans believed that, because human rights was the eighth item in the declaration, the principles that came before it—especially sovereign equality and nonintervention—took precedence. The declaration could not turn human rights into a matter of international concern, or grant individuals standing under international law, because these matters fell within states' internal competence.[143]

In Geneva and elsewhere, the USSR denied that human rights had anything to do with international security. "We have no reason to shun a serious discussion of human rights" because socialism has done more to protect those rights than capitalism, Brezhnev told the World Congress of

Peace Forces in 1973. Nevertheless, the Western campaign to defend human rights endangered peace because it "serves only one purpose: to cover up attempts at interference in the internal affairs of the socialist states." Far from threatening human rights, he said, state sovereignty offered a "reliable guarantee" of them. Even Western governments accepted that human rights could not trump the need for domestic and international security, Soviet bloc officials argued. "If peace reigns, then you can speak about humanitarian concerns as much as you like; but if you have war, everything is chaos and ends in a heap of ruins. That was our basic position," East German diplomat Peter Steglich later recalled. From the communist vantage point, the supreme human right was the right to peace.[144]

This approach to human rights misconstrued the concept, the Western allies insisted. Respect for fundamental rights "constitutes one of the essential bases for cooperation" among states, as the Davignon Committee put it. Consequently, states could not make arguments from sovereignty to justify curtailing citizens' rights. To the contrary, the concept of sovereignty now had to accommodate human rights' universal scope. In Geneva, Western diplomats made this case in a variety of ways. Only respect for human rights could "create a state of 'positive peace.' Mere absence of conflict was not enough," the American delegation argued. "Other states had the right to express concern if human rights were not being respected in another state. That did not constitute intervention." Because human rights "were an expression of civilization," the Italians said, the CSCE should help states "achieve greater benefit from their common heritage." Some of the neutrals, especially the Swedes and Finns, echoed these arguments.[145]

Despite this self-assurance, the Western allies—like their Eastern interlocutors—wanted to avoid a philosophical wrangle. Debating the finer points of human rights at the CSCE would "be likely to embarrass us without gaining anything from the East," Brian Fall noted. It would allow the Soviets to enumerate the ways in which the West fell short of the socialist notion of human rights, and to boast about their own superiority for ratifying the UN Covenants ahead of the major Western powers. Even if the delegates agreed to draft a list of specific rights, it would be so "watered down in negotiation" that it "would be regarded as unsatisfactory [by] our human rights experts." In any case, the West did not require an elaborate statement on human rights in the declaration of principles. Western negotiators only wanted a brief text that emphasized civil-political rights and provided an anchor for their demands on freer movement in Basket III.[146]

After more than fifty negotiating sessions, the delegates finalized the principle on human rights in in November 1974. The Western allies demanded explicit guarantees for "freedom of thought" and "personal freedom." At first, the Soviets resisted, but they eventually gave way. The final text required states to "respect human rights and fundamental freedoms, including the freedom of thought, conscience, religion or belief" and to "recognize the universal significance of human rights and fundamental freedoms, respect for which is an essential factor for ... peace, justice and well-being." The signatories also acknowledged that the individual citizen had a right "to know and act upon his rights and duties." In this way, the Final Act struck a delicate—but ambiguous—balance between these commitments and the principles of sovereign equality and nonintervention. These required states to "respect each other's sovereign equality and individuality as well as all the rights inherent in and encompassed by its sovereignty," including each state's ability to determine its own laws and to "refrain from any intervention ... in the internal or external affairs falling within [another state's] domestic jurisdiction." For the same reason, the Soviets insisted that the Final Act invoke the UN Covenants, which, in their view, subordinated the claims of human rights to each state's sovereign prerogatives.[147]

The compromise fulfilled the West's goals and assuaged the East's concerns. From the West's perspective, its concepts of peace and human rights had won out, and it had acquired a way to press the Soviets to change their domestic conduct. Moreover, the Soviets and their allies had given away more than they wanted. In retrospect, Hermann Axen lamented that they had failed to "seize the initiative, but relinquished it to others." Because the Final Act affirmed the Western interpretation of human rights, over the years that followed it "divert[ed] us from the most important problems— peace and security." Nonetheless, at the time they regarded the final text as "balanced and sustainable," as a Polish report put it. In the final analysis, they believed, the principles of sovereignty and nonintervention would protect their vital interests.[148]

IX

In negotiating the declaration of principles, the diplomats in Helsinki and Geneva reexamined the foundations of the international system. They grappled with the meaning of borders, sovereignty, and human rights, and tabled drafts and counterdrafts in an effort to produce an agreement that they could all support. Because they shied away from philosophical discussions of the concepts in the declaration, they had to distill their conflicting ideas and worldviews into the texts that they put forward. The presence of a word here or absence of a comma there could mean the difference between a principle that favored the Soviet vision of Europe's future and one that favored its Western European rival. In arguing about linguistic nuances, the participants fought a proxy war over the rules of international legitimacy.

The fights in Basket I did not pit a moral view of international politics against an amoral one. Rather, two different moralities—and two concepts of peace—clashed at the CSCE. By trying to make the division of Europe permanent, the Soviets were not just defending their own interests or the interests of communism. They were also trying to prevent a great power war, which they regarded as the highest moral imperative for statesmen living in the shadow of thermonuclear weapons. Although Kissinger did not share Brezhnev's enthusiasm for the negotiations, he did agree with this proposition. "As long as we remain powerful, we will use our influence to promote freedom, as we always have," he said in 1973. "But in the nuclear age we are obliged to recognize that the issue of war and peace also involves human lives and that the attainment of peace is a profound moral concern." If recognizing Europe's territorial and political status quo reduced the danger of conflict, one could hardly object to it.[149]

Yet the Western Europeans did object. They did not want to fight a war any more than the Soviets or the Nixon administration did, but they did want to change the status quo. Instead of locking down Europe's frontiers, the declaration of principles had to allow them to evolve over time. These rules had to apply to the continent as a whole, and define how all of its states—regardless of their system of government—related to each other. The concept of peace had to expand beyond mere respect for state sovereignty. Emphasizing human rights as a fundamental principle of international relations implied that the security of the individual mattered as much as the security of the state. Whereas Brezhnev and Kissinger worried about the danger of nuclear war, the Western Europeans seemed to take nuclear stability for granted. Indeed, in the absence of that stability they could not have thought about transcending the status quo. In a curious way, the threat of annihilation made it possible to talk about human rights.

The CSCE exemplified the challenges of diplomacy in this era. The career diplomats did most of the work, but intervention at the highest level sometimes proved necessary to solve the problems that bedeviled the experts. When the talks in Geneva stalled over peaceful change, for instance, Kissinger and Gromyko stepped in to craft a formula that they and the West Germans could accept. But in turn they relied on the career diplomats, who understood the nuances of the negotiations and carefully assembled the declaration from hundreds of proposals and counterproposals. Similarly, the Eastern and Western allies defined the terms of the debate, but they depended on the neutral states to broker compromises on the most sensitive questions. This interdependence—between the professionals and their political masters, and between the East, West, and neutrals— meant that no one person or country could control the CSCE's direction. The conference was a complex system whose results could not have been predicted at the outset.[150]

In its territorial and political bargains, the declaration of principles balanced Eastern and Western demands. It affirmed the inviolability of Europe's frontiers, but specified the conditions in which they could change. It endorsed state sovereignty and nonintervention, but required all states to adhere to universal principles. This balance did not serve Eastern and Western goals equally. The Warsaw Pact states defended all-or-nothing propositions that admitted no uncertainty. Frontiers were either permanent or they were not. State sovereignty was either absolute or it was not. The declaration either applied to all states or only between East and West. As a consequence, because the rules allowed for peaceful change, endorsed human rights, and governed the whole of Europe, the USSR and its allies lost the fight.

The declaration vindicated the Western concepts of legitimacy and security. It gave the Soviets their stand-alone principle of inviolability, but they could only claim it as a victory by taking it out of context and trusting that others would do the same. For West Germany, the agreement went further than the Moscow Treaty, which had not explicitly provided for peaceful change. For Western Cold Warriors, it refuted the Brezhnev Doctrine. For partisans of the liberal concept of human rights, it represented an advance on the UN Charter, which had subordinated human rights to the imperatives of sovereignty and nonintervention.

The West had succeeded on each of these points, but vital questions remained unresolved. How could the Federal Republic use the declaration to advance the cause of German unification when every communist government in Europe opposed the idea? If the USSR decided to invade one of its allies, could the declaration restrain it? If human rights now constrained state sovereignty, how could governments enforce respect for those rights in foreign countries? Despite these uncertainties, however, it was clear that the declaration pointed in the direction of change, not stability.

The USSR's defeat was not preordained, but resulted from tactical and conceptual mistakes. Its representatives in Geneva lacked leverage in Basket I because they acted as *demandeurs*. Nonetheless, Brezhnev wanted to end the conference as soon as possible and bring his Peace Program to a successful conclusion. He urged Western leaders to make concessions and demanded that the Soviet delegation produce results. This impatience put Kovalev in an impossible position. So long as the Western allies remained united, it almost guaranteed that he would have to give way sooner or later. The Soviets gave up so much in pursuit of their goal that they compromised the goal itself.

To be fair, Western diplomats worried that if the negotiations dragged on indefinitely or broke down altogether, public opinion and the press would blame them for squandering a chance to improve East-West relations. Indeed, the Soviets had exploited this fear of public disapproval to bring the

CSCE into being in the first place, and they expected the same pressures to exert themselves during the negotiations in Helsinki and Geneva. But once the conference got underway, Western citizens and journalists took little notice of the negotiations, removing one of the few tools at Moscow's disposal. As a consequence, the Western delegations managed to stand together and outlast the Soviets, who eventually accepted painful concessions in order to get a deal.[151]

Soviet leaders made erroneous assumptions about how the CSCE would unfold. They expected it to move as quickly as their bilateral negotiations with the West Germans, French, and Americans at the beginning of the decade. The Basic Principles agreement had come together easily, and Kissinger had granted the Soviets most of what they had sought. Brezhnev and Gromyko anticipated that the Americans would prove equally pliable in Helsinki and Geneva. When events took a different course and stymied these expectations, the USSR's negotiating strategy ran aground.[152]

The contradictions at the heart of Brezhnev's détente strategy caused the most serious problems of all. The general secretary hoped to revive the legitimacy of the Soviet system by persuading the Western powers to sign on to his concept of peace. In a certain sense, he put the fate of the leading communist power in the hands of its capitalist rivals. This gamble might have succeeded if Brezhnev's vision of Europe had been congruent with that of the West. But because the West's goals stood opposed to his on every important point, the Soviets had to compromise their most important objectives.

In the USSR's earliest days, Lenin and his colleagues refused to cooperate with the other great powers and cared little for their approval. A half-century later, however, the USSR had transformed from a revisionist into a satisfied power and counted on negotiating with like-minded states. When the Soviets confronted Western governments that advanced revisionist demands of their own, they could not adapt. Instead of reconsidering their goals, they pressed forward. Brezhnev boasted that his efforts to expand the USSR's nuclear arsenal had changed the correlation of forces in his country's favor, and he expected it to yield political results. The CSCE demonstrated the limits of this approach. The USSR's vast military power could not compel the West to endorse its concept of legitimacy or recognize Europe's borders as permanent. As a consequence, the prize that Brezhnev had sought for so long slipped through his fingers.

Chapter 5

A DECLARATION OF INTERDEPENDENCE?

THE CSCE unfolded against the backdrop of global economic tumult. The early 1970s witnessed the end of the Bretton Woods monetary system that had stabilized the Western economies for more than two decades. In 1970, world oil prices began to rise. Three years later, in the aftermath of the Yom Kippur War, they spiked. In most Western countries, the end of cheap energy sent gross domestic product and growth rates tumbling. Over the course of the decade, unemployment jumped and inflation accelerated. The developed economies began to undergo a structural transformation, tilting away from heavy industry and manufacturing and toward services and post-industrial production. Prevailing economic theory could not explain what was happening, and governments' usual Keynesian remedies had lost their effectiveness. While the CSCE's participants argued in Helsinki and Geneva, Western academics and officials searched for new ideas and policies to replace those that had failed.[1]

In the socialist world, the challenges were less dramatic but no less difficult. Growth rates were slipping and the economies were falling further and further behind the West in the race to develop new technology. Some officials argued that reforming the mechanisms of central planning and cooperating more with the West would raise productivity rates and strengthen popular support for the system. Hardliners rejected these ideas, insisting that if the socialist world came to rely too heavily on the capitalist world and abandoned ideological orthodoxy, it would undermine its own reason for being. Leonid Brezhnev and other communist leaders wanted to have it both ways, seeking the benefits of Western markets, capital, and technology while preserving the communist system.

The East needed the West more than the West needed the East. Western governments saw advantages in greater economic cooperation. They hoped to export more goods to the Soviet bloc and gain access to new sources of fossil fuels and other raw materials. But they also understood that the solution to their economic woes lay primarily within the capitalist world. By contrast, the USSR and most of its allies counted on doing business with the West in order to reinvigorate socialism. These dynamics had two important consequences for the CSCE's second basket. The Eastern delegations entered the negotiations without having reconciled their own conflicting impulses. They had not decided exactly what they wanted, nor what they would pay to get it. Meanwhile, Western diplomats agreed to approach the conference with open minds. If their counterparts agreed to make meaningful economic concessions, they would do business with them. Everyone had to understand, however, that the Eastern countries were the demandeurs and therefore had to give more away.

Compared to the rest of the Final Act, the negotiations in Basket II offered modest results. Nonetheless, they shed important light on détente's underlying economic dilemmas and therefore deserve close attention in their own right. The CSCE made clear that, if the socialist states wanted to reap the benefits of Western trade and technology, they had to open their economies and compromise on the core principles of central planning. Forced to choose between competing priorities, Eastern European leaders refused to bear the costs that interdependence would impose. Although they conceded a handful of principles that served Western interests, they got little of what they wanted in return. The outcome represented the victory of the communists' political fears over their economic aspirations and reflected the tensions inherent in Brezhnev's economic strategy.

I

As the CSCE got underway, the performance of the Eastern economies offered some grounds for optimism. Soviet citizens enjoyed a higher quality of life than they had a decade previously. In 1960, 60 percent of people lived in shared apartments. By the early 1970s, massive investments in housing construction had cut that figure in half. Consumption of meat, fish, vegetables, and fruit was rising. Average wages increased by 50 percent over the same period, giving families more disposable income to spend on a growing range of consumer goods, including clothes, furniture, and appliances. Most homes had a television set, a radio, and a washing machine, and nearly half had a refrigerator. Similar trends were visible elsewhere in Eastern Europe, particularly East Germany and Hungary.[2]

The USSR's economic ties to the West were also expanding. During the 1960s, the development of vast oil and gas reserves in Siberia transformed the Soviet Union from an oil importer into an exporter. Especially after the price of oil quadrupled in 1973–74, the earnings swelled the state's coffers and provided the vast majority of its hard currency revenue, which the Soviet government relied on to purchase badly needed capital and technology from the West.[3] In 1964, Britain extended $278 million in credit to buy industrial equipment. Another $332 million came from France. Three years later, with Italian government financing, Fiat began building a $367 million factory on the Volga River to manufacture private cars for Soviet citizens.[4] In 1969, the industrial conglomerate Thyssen agreed to build two factories—one in West Germany, one in the USSR—to manufacture the steel pipes necessary for transporting Siberian natural gas to European export markets.[5] The Soviets and Eastern Europeans signed a number of other trade, research, and industrial agreements and established joint commissions with Western governments to promote bilateral trade. By 1973, these initiatives numbered in the hundreds and accounted for a significant proportion of the command economies' exports to the West.[6]

This growth in East-West cooperation seemed to vindicate contemporary theories of economic convergence. Since the 1950s, Western scholars had speculated that the industrial societies on either side of the Iron Curtain would seek to cooperate with each other because they shared certain interests and characteristics that transcended the ideological divide. Eventually, they would overcome their differences and converge on a common political and economic model. Some exponents of this idea argued that Eastern and Western societies would evolve toward a new system that combined the best of both worlds. Others insisted that the structural weaknesses of the Soviet system would force it to abandon the communist model and embrace Western principles outright. The more the two sides did business with each other, the faster this process would take place. "As the collectivist economies falter beneath the burden of excessive regimentation and the liberal economies brace themselves for the onslaught of social disorder, freer interaction between them, and the experience of one to the other, become steadily more relevant," Franco-American lawyer Samuel Pisar argued in 1970. "Far from moving apart, capitalism and communism are actually creeping toward convergence."[7]

Soviet scholars repudiated this theory. In their view, Pisar and his ilk failed to appreciate the essential qualities that distinguished the USSR from the West. Academician Pyotr Fedoseev dismissed convergence as a fantasy based on the mistaken claim "that revolutionary theory has allegedly 'become obsolete.'" The USSR would continue to develop according to socialist principles. It had no need to become more like the West.[8] Convergence attracted more interest in Eastern European capitals. A Polish foreign ministry report predicted that the alignment of Eastern and Western economic interests would reduce international tensions over time. However, the study's authors stopped short of concluding that this process would change communist society itself.[9]

Despite this optimism in communism's resilience, several trends told a more ominous story. Growth rates had fallen during the 1960s and kept falling in the 1970s. Even in a period when the American economy faced serious difficulties, the Soviet Union never came close to matching its rate of expansion. Year after year, Soviet agricultural and industrial output rose less than expected. Labor productivity stalled. Consumers faced widespread shortages of everyday goods, from salami to rubber boots.[10] In 1972, the USSR purchased hundreds of millions of dollars of American grain to meet domestic shortfalls.[11] In Hungary, labor shortages hampered economic activity. In Czechoslovakia, production costs grew more rapidly than productivity.[12] Although the oil shock brought a windfall to the USSR, it damaged the countries of Eastern Europe, which now had to export more goods to purchase the same quantity of oil from their ally.[13]

The most dramatic illustration of the communist bloc's economic problems came in December 1970. When the Polish government raised food prices by 40 percent, it provoked a huge uprising. Thousands took to the streets of Gdańsk and other cities shouting, "We want bread! We want truth!" The army killed hundreds of protestors in an effort to restore order. When the government turned to its Soviet ally for help, the Kremlin ignored its request. The authorities eventually regained control of the situation, but the unrest forced Władysław Gomułka and other top officials from office. Although the state retained its monopoly on the use of force, the episode demonstrated that, in economic affairs, its power remained limited.[14]

To compound these difficulties, the communist economies could not innovate as quickly as those in the West. In the early 1970s, Soviet analysts argued that the world was undergoing a "scientific-technological revolution," with profound consequences for the future of both Eastern and Western economies. In such fields as communications, transport, computing, weaponry, energy production, and consumer goods, the West had taken the lead. "This is where the decisive battle will be fought. It is the field of decisive importance for the destiny of socialism," Secretary Pyotr Demichev of the Soviet Central Committee told East German leaders in 1970. The Western countries were "trying to turn [their] temporary advantage into an absolute win. That is why they claim the future does not belong to socialism."[15]

Communist officials struggled to develop solutions that were adequate to the task. The "most decisive and important condition for the victory of socialism" in this contest was to raise "the general interest of the people in the mastery of the scientific-technical revolution," Demichev insisted. Other officials proposed signing long-term agreements with Western countries to import the latest technology and thereby invigorate the Soviet economy.[16] The Poles took a similar view, but they also recognized that cooperation across the Cold War divide threatened communist solidarity. As East-West ties proliferated, the Polish foreign ministry warned, Eastern European governments would increasingly look to the capitalist world, rather than the USSR, as a source of economic development. These "centrifugal tendencies" could have dangerous consequences for communism's long-term viability.[17]

These dynamics created an asymmetry in economic relations. Trade across the Iron Curtain grew rapidly in the late 1960s. A number of Western firms, especially in West Germany, wanted greater access to Eastern markets, where the appetite for advanced machinery and technology was strong. Under pressure from these companies, and hoping to create new jobs for their workers, some Western countries defected from the Coordinating Committee for Multilateral Export Controls (Cocom), the US-led embargo on the sale of strategically sensitive goods to the Soviet bloc.[18] Despite this growth, however, commerce with the East represented only a marginal share of the West's foreign trade in the early 1970s, accounting for less than four percent of the exports of NATO's European members.[19] To give one example, Britain exported more than twice as much to Denmark as it did to the USSR, even though the USSR had fifty times Denmark's population. With the exception of grain sales, exports to the USSR and its allies mattered even less to American and Canadian producers. By contrast, one quarter of all Soviet imports came from the capitalist world, mostly in the form of advanced industrial equipment. In Eastern Europe, the figures were even higher. This imbalance meant any change in commercial flows would reverberate more strongly in Moscow and Warsaw than in Washington and Paris.[20]

Brezhnev and his Eastern European colleagues found themselves caught between the competing demands of ideological dogma, economic exigency, and popular legitimacy. If they wanted to avoid Gomułka's fate, living standards had to improve, which in turn required higher rates of growth. By the early 1970s, East German officials had stopped talking about overtaking the West German economy. Instead, they told citizens that "socialism means permanently rising living and cultural standards," but even this more modest goal required greater economic prosperity. In theory, they might increase productivity by decentralizing planning and allowing local managers to make more decisions. In order to build some slack in the system and provide these managers with the necessary reserves of material and equipment, capital investment would have to fall. But if officials wanted to boost consumption and raise living standards, capital investment would have to rise. The imperatives of technological innovation and intensive growth complicated matters further. Setting aside funds for research and development would further strain a limited pool of resources and divert capital away from consumption, with no guarantee of a payoff. Communist leaders faced no easy choices.[21]

Some experts advocated reforming the Soviet economy. They faced an uphill battle that echoed the nineteenth-century Westernizers' struggle against their Slavophile adversaries. In 1972 and 1973, a number of economists called for new measures to help the USSR catch up in technological innovation. Nikolai Shmelev, for example, proposed to end the government monopoly on international trade, import even more goods from abroad, and adopt world market prices. In the socialist economies, he argued, no "objective developmental factors ... require[d] autarky." Kosygin rebuked the economists for even putting these ideas forward, and hardliners insisted that the USSR had to remain "an independent economic unit." Freer international trade would disrupt the system of centralized planning, which required state control over all imports and exports and stable input and output figures. Foreign direct investment would undermine the principle of state ownership. Relying on imports from the capitalist world would compromise national security. Instead of running experiments with unpredictable consequences, the defenders of the status quo preferred to look for solutions within the existing economic paradigm.[22]

Some Eastern European leaders believed that Western loans offered a way out of their dilemma. In 1970, Walter Ulbricht decided that East Germany could borrow from Western banks to purchase cutting-edge manufacturing equipment. Using this new technology, East German factories could produce high-quality goods for export. In turn, the state would use the additional revenue to repay the initial loans. In Poland, Gomułka's successor Edward Gierek reached a similar conclusion. In theory, this plan could raise productivity and unlock the intensive growth that the communist economies so badly needed. But it assumed that East Germany and Poland would in fact be able to make products that could compete on Western markets. Despite the risks involved, the two countries pushed ahead. Consumption and economic output grew, but so too did foreign indebtedness, which swelled to unprecedented levels. When the new products that rolled off the assembly line failed to find many foreign buyers, it became clear that the gamble had gone wrong. Officials kept hoping that the picture would eventually improve. In the meantime, their economic fate depended on Western forbearance.[23]

For his part, Brezhnev hoped to strike a balance between openness and self-reliance. On the one hand, he believed that the Western economies posed a threat to socialism. "The situation on the front of the anti-imperialist struggle is in large part determined by the course of the economic competition between socialism and capitalism," he told the 1969 Moscow Conference of Communist Parties. That struggle had to culminate in the "total annihilation of the rule of the capitalists and the triumph of socialism."[24] On the other hand, he insisted that the USSR had to work with the West in order to realize its economic potential. "Our plans are by no means plans with an eye to autarky. We are not following a policy of isolating our country from the outer world," he told West German television in

1973.[25] Keen observers within the Soviet government grasped that Brezhnev's hopes for economic engagement stood in tension with his commitment to ideological stability. If the USSR opened itself to international trade and foreign investment, it could hardly expect the "conscious part of society" to continue believing in the "dry dogmas" of communist orthodoxy, Anatoly Chernyaev noted in his diary.[26] The CSCE forced Soviet officials to confront this dilemma head-on.

II

Economic cooperation had been part of the USSR's vision for the CSCE from the beginning. The Warsaw Pact's 1966 Bucharest declaration included a proposal to increase East-West trade. Commercial, scientific, and technical cooperation across the Iron Curtain could furnish "a material base for European security and for the strengthening of peace throughout the world," it said.[27] Three years later, the Budapest appeal argued that a security conference would "clear the way for the development of cooperation among all European countries irrespective of their social systems," especially in energy production, transport, and environmental protection.[28] These proposals offered an alternative vision of continental integration to that of the European Economic Community and suggested that states did not need to share the same ideology to benefit from working together.

For many years, the Soviets had been seeking wider access to Western markets. At the United Nations' Economic Commission for Europe (ECE) in the 1950s, they argued that Western countries ought to lower their barriers to Soviet goods and extend Most Favored Nation (MFN) treatment to the USSR. They made little progress.[29] Brezhnev did score an important success, however, in bilateral negotiations with the United States. "If you do extend MFN to us, it will be profitable for us but the growth will be reciprocal in trade and so forth," he told Kissinger in September 1972. "It will not entail losses for the United States. The situation now is no trade. Since there is no MFN, no growth is possible." The following month, after the Soviet government agreed to repay its wartime lend-lease debts, the Nixon administration pledged to extend MFN status to the USSR, subject to Congressional approval. Brezhnev had high hopes for the deal. At a Central Committee Plenum, he predicted that it would raise Soviet exports by as much as 50 percent, bring the latest industrial equipment to the USSR, and expand scientific and technological cooperation.[30]

The Soviets wanted to build on this success at the CSCE. The Institute of World Economy and International Relations proposed that the conference should establish a "Council for the Coordination of Cooperation," which would promote trade between the EEC and Comecon.[31] Above all,

Brezhnev wanted the West to stop treating the Soviet bloc as an economic threat. "During the conference itself, it must be made clear that it is essential to establish equality of rights in economic relations, to accord each other MFN status, to abolish discrimination, and to establish it as a principle of relations between European states," he told his colleagues at the 1972 meeting of Warsaw Pact leaders in Prague.[32] The political attractions of MFN status went beyond its putative economic benefits. It would signal that the Western countries had given up on their decades-old efforts to quarantine the socialist economies and demonstrate that they now accepted them as equals. From this angle, the USSR's economic plans for the CSCE reinforced its political objectives.[33]

The East-West projects of the 1960s also offered a model for the CSCE to emulate. Brezhnev urged Eastern European leaders to work with the capitalist countries to address their own economic difficulties. "The questions of economic and scientific-technical connections on an all-European scale are of no small interest to the socialist countries and we must prepare to discuss them at the conference so as to achieve maximum benefit for ourselves," he said.[34] Soviet trade minister Nikolai Patolichev made a similar case. He proposed that Eastern and Western governments collaborate to build new oil and gas pipelines, and develop new techniques in manufacturing, engineering, and chemistry.[35] Other Soviet officials returned to these themes as the negotiations got underway.[36]

Some of the Eastern Europeans regarded the CSCE's economic prospects with even more enthusiasm. In 1970, a gathering of Warsaw Pact economists agreed that the security conference could yield concrete improvements in freer trade, joint industrial projects, and scientific-technological cooperation. Some of the participants called for specific initiatives that did not feature in the Soviet proposals. The Hungarians suggested merging the Eastern and Western electricity grids to reduce energy shortages. The Poles, who for years had urged their allies to engage more deeply with noncommunist economies, criticized the Soviets for lacking ambition. Having resolved to make the most of the CSCE, they wanted the conference to establish a European investment bank and produce a treaty on economic cooperation. Officials in Budapest and Warsaw returned to these ideas in the years that followed. The development of economic cooperation "would be the most important function arising from the political results of the conference," a meeting of Polish ambassadors concluded in 1973.[37]

This optimism sprang from economic necessity. Because the Eastern European economies were smaller than the USSR's and lacked its natural resources, they relied more heavily on international trade to meet their needs. The Hungarian and Polish governments in particular wanted new connections with the West in order to reduce their reliance on Moscow and create opportunities outside the international socialist division of labor. In 1967,

Poland had joined GATT and, under the terms of its membership, it had to increase its imports from the West by 7 percent annually, which it could only do by earning more hard currency or borrowing more heavily. To complicate matters further, the European Economic Community's tariffs on food imports hampered Polish agricultural exports.[38] In this tenuous situation, Polish and Hungarian leaders imagined that the CSCE could expand their access to Western markets, technology, and capital without endangering their centralized control over the domestic economy. They wanted to open themselves to the parts of the global economy that they liked while shutting the door on those—like domestic liberalization and foreign direct investment—that they did not.[39]

By contrast, the East Germans worried about the risks of exposing the socialist economies to the global market. "Bourgeois ideologues consider intersystemic economic cooperation to be the core of the ideological-political struggle against socialism," observed an East German foreign ministry report in October 1970. Western officials prioritized economic cooperation "because they expect that it will produce a 'new political situation,' which will favor the realization of imperialist anti-socialist goals."[40] Another report warned that the West would propose joint projects at the CSCE to gain "influence over the internal development of socialist states."[41] Rather than strengthening the members of the Warsaw Pact, economic cooperation would leave them exposed. The East Germans therefore rejected the Polish and Hungarian initiatives and urged their allies to approach the subject with caution.[42] An agreement on scientific-technological collaboration would only be acceptable if it recognized the supreme principles of state sovereignty and noninterference and avoided binding obligations. It "can only have a general political character for the time being," the East German foreign ministry concluded. Instead of putting their faith in cooperation with the West, the socialist states ought to focus on helping each other.[43]

The Soviets steered a middle course between their allies' opposing views. When they drafted their proposed agenda for the CSCE, they emphasized MFN treatment, industrial cooperation, and scientific-technological cooperation.[44] But they also rebuffed the Poles' proposal for a European treaty on economic cooperation and concrete ideas for industrial cooperation.[45] They told their allies not to "expect much from the conference in the area of economic cooperation." Instead, the Warsaw Pact should only aim to "create a favorable atmosphere for the development of cooperation through bilateral channels."[46] In economic affairs, the CSCE could lay down broad principles, but it had to avoid specific commitments.

This caution reflected the USSR's hierarchy of priorities for the CSCE. They wanted the conference to focus on security issues, to which they ascribed the utmost importance. "We must not fail to see that the most important thing in the work of the security conference remains the adoption of a major political document," Brezhnev told Warsaw Pact leaders in 1972. Economic questions would have to wait until after "the threat of war is eliminated," as *Pravda* put it the following year.[47] Besides, for every economic proposal that the Soviets made at the CSCE, the West would probably demand something in return. The Warsaw Pact could minimize its vulnerability to Western pressure at the negotiating table by minimizing its ambitions.[48]

Some Soviet officials also worried that economic cooperation would do political damage. Like the East Germans, they anticipated that the lure of prosperity might pull the Eastern Europeans out of Moscow's orbit and toward the West. Western governments would use cooperation agreements "to penetrate into the socialist countries' economic life," Soviet deputy foreign minister Nikolai Rodionov warned his Warsaw Pact counterparts.[49] If the socialist states developed close economic relationships across the Iron Curtain, Soviet officials argued, the Eastern Europeans might become "dependent on the capitalist countries."[50]

Despite these anxieties, the Soviets saw some opportunities to take the offensive. In particular, they hoped to exploit the growing economic conflicts among Western countries. "The European capitalist states, and especially the countries of the Common Market, have gained significantly in economic strength and increased their political influence within NATO," Brezhnev told his allied counterparts in Prague in 1972. No longer were the Western Europeans "vassals" who had to defer to an American "overlord." Consequently, "we can also increase our influence on the Western European countries through economic relations and thus reduce American influence, even if we cannot eliminate it completely."[51] Above all, the Soviets hoped to stymie the process of Western European integration and prevent the EEC's emergence as an international power to rival the Soviet bloc. The Eastern Europeans shared this goal. Because Western Europe was "much more attractive to our societies than the culturally foreign United States or Japan," a Polish official reasoned, the stronger it grew, the greater the pull it would exert on the loyalties of the Soviet bloc's citizens. Besides, the Eastern Europeans wanted access to Western European markets, and reasoned that a weaker EEC would increase their odds of success.[52]

The CSCE forced the Soviets and their allies to ponder fundamental questions about the relationship between commerce, peace, and the competition between capitalism and socialism. Despite several years of discussions, they could not reach a consensus. Some argued that the benefits of cooperating with the West offered the lifeline that the socialist economies desperately needed. Others regarded it as a trap. Some suggested that trade and security reinforced one another. Others thought that they stood at odds. The intractability of these questions pointed to a deeper ambivalence in the socialist countries' attitude toward the Western world. Brezhnev and his colleagues simultaneously believed that socialism had to defeat capitalism and that it needed capitalism. These contending impulses were not necessarily irreconcilable, but the Eastern allies could not untangle them to everyone's satisfaction. On economic matters, they entered the negotiations without a coherent strategy.

III

While these debates swirled within the Warsaw Pact, the Western allies tried to establish a common policy. They wrestled with their own set of philosophical questions about cooperating with their ideological adversaries. Above all, they debated whether more commerce across the Iron Curtain would serve Western interests. Many conservatives argued that trade would only strengthen the USSR and extend its lease on life. In this view, the Western powers ought not to aid communism while simultaneously trying to contain it. Throughout the Cold War, as superpower tensions waxed and waned, so too did opposition to trade with the Soviet bloc. During the crises over Berlin and Cuba, for instance, the US Congress tightened the restrictions on doing business with Moscow. In 1964, the Johnson administration granted commercial loans to Hungary and Romania, but political opposition prevented the program from expanding to other communist countries. At the grassroots level, conservative activists periodically boycotted goods imported from Eastern Europe and picketed American firms doing business in the Soviet bloc. "We cannot feed and fight communism at the same time," as one popular slogan put it.[53]

In the early 1970s, however, the balance of American and Western European opinion shifted in favor of East-West trade. Optimists argued that it would pull the socialist countries toward the West and coax them to liberalize. The memorable German expression for this approach was *Wandel durch Handel*—change through trade.[54] It echoed the theory of convergence and Georges Pompidou's notion of interpenetration, which envisaged that economic cooperation would yield political changes in the East. If this prospect made some communist leaders nervous, the West had all the more reason to pursue it.[55] Many American diplomats shared this view. A "greater flow of trade between East and West might ... have some internal liberalizing effect, especially on the smaller Warsaw Pact states, and would reduce somewhat their economic dependence upon the Soviet Union," the US mission to NATO argued. Although "these beneficial political side-effects of expanded trade would be gradual in nature and limited in scope," they would be steps in the right direction.[56]

The promise of increased trade could also serve other objectives. When Richard Nixon and Henry Kissinger decided to offer MFN status and trade credits to the USSR, they hoped to induce Soviet leaders to exercise self-restraint on political and military questions. Secretary of Defense Melvin Laird objected that this policy would free up Soviet resources that could then be put to military use. In Nixon and Kissinger's judgment, however, the geopolitical utility of helping the USSR in this way outweighed Laird's cavils. Nor did they ignore the policy's domestic benefits. "Increased economic interchange with the Communist world can both strengthen the fabric of international peace and provide tangible benefits to American workers and consumers," argued Nixon's 1973 international economic report to Congress.[57]

Western officials disagreed about whether they could make progress on any of these matters at the CSCE. The conference was "not a suitable forum for the negotiation of any detailed agreements on East/West economic and technical cooperation," argued Milton Kovner, the counselor for economic affairs at the US mission to NATO. Even in the best of circumstances, multilateral trade negotiations exhausted their participants, and the conference could not easily accommodate the technical discussions necessary to reach a trade deal. Besides, the Economic Commission for Europe was already working on the problem, and European Economic Community rules restricted its members' ability to reach new commercial agreements without the participation of the European Commission.[58] At the same time, however, officials at the commission thought the CSCE could provide a fruitful alternative to existing international bodies. Since the Economic Commission for Europe remained paralyzed and the USSR had not joined GATT, the conference might "unblock the situation and foster a discussion of the whole collection of problems determining the evolution of East-West commerce."[59]

The most important of those problems remained the structure of the Soviet bloc's economies. Few Soviet goods could compete against high-quality products in Western markets, whether or not they enjoyed MFN treatment. Despite its vast industrial base, the USSR exported more canned crab meat than machinery to the West. Hard currency remained in short supply and largely depended on the sale of raw materials, especially timber and oil.[60] If an enterprise wanted to purchase a product from abroad, it had to channel its request through the government agency responsible for all foreign trade. But state planners would only import goods that domestic enterprise could not supply. Once shortfalls in domestic production became apparent—usually at the last minute—it was too late for Western firms to meet the demand.[61]

Although the West's Cocom rules and import quotas did restrict the flow of some goods, the biggest barriers to trade stood on the Soviet bloc's side. "While acknowledging that US and allied restrictions are considered by the East as discriminatory, the planning and foreign trade systems of [Warsaw] Pact countries implicitly or de facto impose more onerous restrictions and difficulties to the expansion of East-West economic cooperation," Kovner told his allied counterparts in 1972.[62] If the Soviets tried to score a propaganda victory by blaming the West for restricting trade, the allies had to respond clearly and bluntly. The fault lay in the nature of the command economies.[63]

Specific policies exacerbated these structural problems. Soviet and Eastern European governments published few economic statistics and treated even basic information as a state secret. Consequently, Western firms could not easily gauge the socialist economies' health or evaluate their commercial prospects there. Even if they wanted to do business in the Soviet bloc, regulations made it difficult for them to set up offices or work directly with enterprises. Having to work through central government agencies added layers of complexity to straightforward transactions.[64]

Notwithstanding these obstacles, most of the allies wanted to adopt a "forthcoming posture" on economic questions at the conference.[65] "A careful subject-by-subject examination ... would open up new prospects for East/West trade," a NATO report predicted.[66] In particular, Western officials hoped to establish principles that would benefit Western firms and expand their access to communist markets. Joint projects to tap Soviet raw materials could also help satisfy Western demand, especially for oil and gas. In these respects, the CSCE would test whether the Warsaw Pact was willing to integrate itself into the global economic system.[67]

Western officials also recognized that economic agreements could advance their broader political goals. "Increased Soviet interdependence with the rest of the world might also help reduce ideological differences," a Foreign Office study concluded.[68] A senior French official took an even more aggressive approach. The allies should use the CSCE to increase East-West trade, and thereby "give an impetus to the liberalization of the Eastern system as a whole," he reasoned.[69] The Soviets also had to prove that they were willing to change their practices across the whole spectrum of East-West relations, and not simply concentrate on the questions that they found most congenial. "Détente must affect all areas of East/West relations," a British diplomat argued. If the Soviets wanted economic succor from the West, they would have to open up their economies in return. Greater freedoms in business might eventually translate into greater freedoms in Soviet society more generally.[70]

For these reasons, the Western allies agreed to explore the possibilities for economic cooperation at the CSCE, but the Soviets would have to play the supplicant. "The net advantage ... from a general expansion of exchanges would accrue to the Warsaw Pact states," the State Department concluded. If they wanted an agreement, they would have to make it worth the West's while.[71] The Western Europeans agreed. Moscow stood to gain by liberalizing its economic policies, and ought to do so unilaterally. At the CSCE, therefore, the Soviets would have to come up with terms to entice their interlocutors, perhaps by making concessions on security and freer movement in exchange for progress in Basket II.[72]

Some Western Europeans also wanted the CSCE to bolster the European Community's international standing. They insisted that the Soviets and their allies should officially recognize the EEC and allow members of the European Commission to participate directly in the negotiations. The French, who had long been wary of giving the EEC too much independent authority, quashed this idea. The CSCE was a forum for states alone, they argued.[73] Nevertheless, they agreed that the West had to refute Soviet complaints of unfair discrimination against Comecon exports and block any Soviet attempt to interfere with the EEC's future development. Moreover, the CSCE had to respect the EEC's jurisdiction and avoid any commitments that infringed on its competence. In particular, the Common Commercial Policy—due to come into effect at the beginning of 1973—required all EEC members to levy the same tariffs on imports from a given country. For all of these reasons, the community's nine members had to remain united at the bargaining table and had to coordinate their positions with the commission.[74]

On the basis of these considerations, Western diplomats formulated two specific goals. The first was reciprocity. The West might reduce tariffs on imports from Eastern Europe. It made no sense, however, to demand that the Eastern Europeans reduce their tariffs in return, because it was government regulations—not tariffs—that impeded Western exports to the socialist bloc. The Soviet government "buys everything and sells everything for what are clearly reasons of its own. For that reason, what it buys, what it sells, who it buys from, who it sells to, and what it pays can obviously be subjective decisions, not market decisions," American secretary of commerce Peter Peterson said at a 1972 press conference. "And therefore there is potential for discrimination, whether that is the intent or not."[75] Reciprocity implied equivalent but not necessarily identical concessions, all with a view to "protect[ing] the principle of mutual advantage," as a European Commission report put it. If the Soviets wanted lower Western tariffs, they would have to respond with alternative measures that would have a similar effect, perhaps by relaxing centralized controls over foreign trade.[76]

The West also hoped to open up the communist economies in other ways. Better working conditions for foreign businessmen and firms in the Soviet bloc, including the ability to open offices, would remove some of the logistical obstacles to trade. The communist authorities should publish more economic statistics and make it easier to deal directly with state-owned enterprises. They should allow businessmen to work together freely and without government mediation. They should grant Western firms direct access to consumers. Some Western officials even wanted to see Western firms establish manufacturing operations in Eastern Europe.[77]

Openness in scientific research had to accompany economic openness. The Western Europeans wanted to foster contacts between scientists not in the hope of making new discoveries, but as a way to punch another hole in the Iron Curtain. "Although any symmetrical increase in access to each other's knowledge in this field would, generally speaking, probably be more beneficial per se to the East than to the Allies, we also stand to gain from such exchanges," concluded a State Department study. The West had an "interest both in promoting the position and influencing the attitudes of scientific elites in the Soviet Union [and] in lessening Eastern European dependence on the Soviet Union."[78] On this point, Western goals for the second basket overlapped with its ambitions regarding the freer movement of people and information. It also echoed the ideas of prominent Soviet dissidents, especially the eminent physicist Andrei Sakharov, who argued that economic and scientific openness would benefit the Soviet economy, increase mutual understanding, and reduce the risk of war.[79]

Success on any of these points would increase the permeability of the socialist economies and make it easier for goods to flow across the continent. It would erode some of the barriers that divided the East from the West, and represent another step toward unifying Europe under a single set of economic principles. But because reciprocity and economic openness implied major changes in the way that the socialist economies operated, Western diplomats did not expect the Soviets to accept them. But even raising these questions at the CSCE might spark some small improvements.[80] In the absence of structural reform, however, the Soviet bloc would remain on the periphery of the international economy. If the USSR and its allies hoped to increase their access to foreign goods and technology, the burden of action lay with them. It was not a matter of lowering barriers between the socialist and capitalist world, but of lowering barriers within the socialist world itself.[81]

IV

The preparatory talks in Helsinki laid bare the differences between the Eastern and Western approaches. In theory, every delegation spoke only on its own behalf. In practice, however, the discussion of economics and trade turned into a bilateral fight pitting the Soviets against the Belgians. Each put forth a draft that encapsulated its allies' priorities for Basket II. The Soviets proposed measures to expand scientific and technological cooperation and called for pan-European projects in energy production, transportation, and the extraction of raw materials. But above all they emphasized the need for "general rules" on international trade, including MFN treatment. Their call for nondiscrimination represented a thinly veiled attack on the EEC's import rules and implied that East-West commerce would only increase if the Western Europeans changed their practices. The Soviet draft aimed to reinforce the legitimacy of the socialist economic system and secure Western assent to principles that might prove useful in bilateral negotiations after the CSCE.[82]

The Belgians offered a different diagnosis. They insisted that East-West trade could only expand "under conditions of reciprocity and mutual benefit," with everything that implied for changing the communist economic system. Beyond this general principle, however, they focused on concrete measures. They called for better working conditions for foreign businessmen, easier access to economic data, and harmonized procedures for resolving commercial disputes.[83] Western diplomats acknowledged that agreements in these areas might be unenforceable, but establishing a standard by which to measure Soviet conduct could prove useful nonetheless. If the communists failed to follow through, the West could use their violations as propaganda fodder or as leverage in subsequent negotiations.[84]

To bridge their differences of opinion, the delegates relied on ambiguity and equivocation. The agenda for Basket II slowly came into shape, featuring "laborious formulas which were not always easy to interpret without difficulty or ambiguity," Italian diplomat Luigi Ferraris later wrote.[85] In Helsinki, the Western allies agreed to discuss MFN status and the Soviets' general principles at Stage II in Geneva. In turn, the Soviets and their allies grudgingly accepted the West's proposals on economic openness. The Blue Book balanced the Soviet insistence on respecting "the diversity of economic and social systems" with the Western principle of "reciprocity of advantages and obligations."[86] Surveying the results of the preparatory talks, a State Department report noted that the West had achieved its goals "without acceding to the Soviet preference for sweeping language on general trade principles." At the same time, however, a French diplomat warned that the West would have to work hard to prevent the discussion of tariffs from serving Soviet goals.[87]

When the full CSCE negotiations opened in Geneva, the Eastern allies reprised their old arguments. They made an aggressive bid to put MFN status at the center of Basket II, hoping "thereby to gain trade policy advantages from the Americans over tariffs and from the Europeans over quantitative restrictions without making any commitment to effective reciprocity," a British diplomat observed.[88] Privately the Soviets explained to the Poles that they "attach[ed] great importance to the MFN issue." They wanted the West to make an "unconditional" commitment to the principle in order to set "a precedent in multilateral economic relations between East and West." If anything, the Poles felt even more strongly about this question than their allies, and complained that the Soviet proposals were too abstract. In their view, the CSCE ought to take concrete steps to eliminate all barriers to East-West trade and secure MFN treatment from the West.[89]

These demands elicited little enthusiasm among the Western Europeans. The French perceived that the USSR wanted MFN status to apply not just to tariffs, but to nontariff barriers too. If the Soviets managed to impose this "broad interpretation" of MFN, warned Anthony Elliott, the head of the British delegation, they could use it to attack the EEC's quotas on imports from the Soviet bloc.[90] Western European officials regarded these restrictions as essential to the survival of their manufacturing industries. Because central planners—not market forces—set prices in the socialist economies, the Eastern Europeans could export such products as steel at arbitrarily low prices. Eliminating quantitative restrictions would invite the Soviets and their allies to dump their goods in Western Europe. "The question of MFN treatment is clearly the principal one for the Soviet Bloc," the head of the Foreign and Commonwealth Office's trade relations department noted, "but it is one on which the West can give away nothing of substance at the CSCE." In any case, unless the Soviets accepted the principle of reciprocity, there could be no deal.[91]

The Americans had even less room for maneuver than their allies. Congress refused to ratify Nixon's pledge to grant MFN status to the USSR. When the matter came before the Senate, Democratic senator Henry "Scoop" Jackson proposed a measure to restrict MFN status to countries that allowed their citizens to emigrate freely, which would exclude the communist states. Jackson took particular interest in the plight of the "refuse-niks," Soviet Jews whom the communist authorities had barred from moving to Israel or the West. He criticized the Nixon administration for working too closely with Soviet leaders and regarded the MFN debate as an opportunity to put pressure on the White House and the Kremlin simultaneously. The core idea of the Jackson-Vanik Amendment, as it came to be known, was that nondemocratic regimes had to allow the free movement of people if they wanted to enjoy the free movement of goods. They could not open themselves piecemeal to the world. Openness was indivisible.[92]

Nixon and Kissinger fumed at this Congressional interference in their conduct of foreign policy. They believed that they could do more for Soviet Jews by lobbying the Soviets behind the scenes than by bludgeoning them in public. More importantly, they feared that Jackson's agitation could wreck their project of putting superpower relations on a more stable footing. When Brezhnev and Gromyko complained about this meddling in their domestic politics, Nixon and Kissinger sympathized. "We have a common enemy—Senator Jackson," Kissinger told the Soviet foreign minister. "These people want to change Soviet society totally," he said at another meeting. "This is not our policy ... I don't know what the outcome will be, but I can assure you that we won't change our policy."[93] In October 1974, Kissinger tried to persuade Jackson to drop his campaign in exchange for a Soviet promise to grant 60,000 exit visas. At a press conference, Jackson boasted about his victory. An infuriated Brezhnev told Kissinger that the USSR had always acted in "good faith to fulfill our obligations" but that the United States was now reneging on its promises. Despite Kissinger's exhortations, Jackson moved ahead with his amendment. When Congress passed it in December 1974, the Soviet-American trade deal fell apart.[94]

In Geneva, the Soviets pressed ahead. They told American diplomats that "their attitude toward détente in general and especially [the] CSCE has not changed."[95] Perhaps they wagered that if the CSCE established MFN treatment as a fundamental principle, they might be able to resurrect their agreement with the United States. In conversation with West German foreign minister Hans-Dietrich Genscher, Gromyko argued that extending MFN status to the USSR would benefit everyone. Behind the scenes in Geneva, however, the Soviets warned their allies to lower their expectations. Several Eastern European diplomats passed this news along to their Western counterparts. They "did not expect to get MFN."[96] If substantive progress was out of reach, the Soviets would settle for "some form of cosmetic wording" that they could present as a success and use to justify any concessions that they might have to make.[97] For tactical reasons, however, they insisted on keeping the MFN question open as long as possible. Once it became clear that everyone wanted to bring the conference to an end, the Soviets would orchestrate a final grand bargain to drop their MFN demands in exchange for Western concessions elsewhere. For months, therefore, the Soviets resisted Western proposals for a statement on reciprocity, arguing that the differences in the two economic systems posed no obstacles to trade.[98]

Whatever the Soviets' motives, Jackson's success in Washington tied the hands of the American delegation in Geneva. Some Western representatives at the conference recognized the constraints on their American colleagues and offered their support. "Any indication that we regarded MFN treatment as something which states have some sort of obligation to extend would be likely to embarrass the Americans," a British diplomat noted. No matter how long the Soviets persisted with their demands, the Americans refused to make any commitments on MFN status. The Western allies stood firm alongside them.[99]

This stalemate prevailed until almost the last moment. In July 1975, the Swiss stepped forward with several finely calibrated compromises. These aimed to solve, among other problems, the East-West standoff over whether to share trade obligations on an "equitable" or a "balanced" basis. The abstruse terms of debate did not prevent delegates from engaging in "rather bad-tempered discussions and attempts by both sides to manipulate the Swiss formula to their own advantage," the British delegation reported. The Swedes attempted to break the logjam by presenting two new texts on reciprocity, but the Soviets refused to accept either one.[100]

Late on July 15, the Soviets invited the French diplomat responsible for the second basket to drop by their mission for a drink. They kept him up all night negotiating. Eventually, he agreed to drop the connection between MFN and reciprocity on which the Western delegations had long insisted. He left the Soviet mission at dawn, returned to his residence, and fell asleep before passing word of the compromise to Gérard André, the head of the French delegation. Meanwhile, the Western European ambassadors developed a proposal of their own on the same subject. At the formal negotiating session that afternoon, the Soviets presented the compromise that they had worked out during the night. The hung-over French diplomat voiced his support and tried to persuade the other Western Europeans and the Americans to join him. Surprised and angry that no one had consulted them, they rejected the deal.[101]

Despite the fiasco, the participants knew that they had to try again. This time, the Americans dealt with the Soviets. After a day of frantic discussions, they agreed on a text so anodyne as to be nearly meaningless. The participants recognized "the beneficial effects which can result for the development of trade from the application of most favored nation treatment" and pledged to cooperate "on the basis of equality and mutual satisfaction of the partners, and of reciprocity permitting, as a whole, an equitable distribution of advantages and obligations of comparable scale."[102]

Two years of negotiations had yielded no grand declarations on international trade. The final agreement only faintly resembled the Soviets' initial demands and would offer thin sustenance in future trade negotiations. Similarly, the statement on reciprocity gave the West little ammunition with which to attack the Soviet bloc's structural barriers to trade. The results could not have disappointed the Western allies much. Despite their own serious economic difficulties, they did not count on solving them by means of East-West cooperation. They had entered the talks determined to put the burden of compromise on the communist states. If the USSR wanted to reach a significant agreement, it had to make concessions accordingly. Contrary to Western expectations, however, the Soviets did not place much emphasis on these matters when the negotiations got underway. To be sure, they stuck to their MFN and nondiscrimination demands throughout the negotiations, but they refused to beg. Their priorities lay elsewhere.[103]

V

The negotiations over economic openness avoided explicit ideological arguments. Nonetheless, they illustrated the difficulty of reconciling Eastern and Western assumptions about the relationships among the state, the economy, and international peace. Beginning at the preparatory talks, the Western delegations called for bold measures to improve the flow of commercial information and make it easier for foreign firms to operate in the Soviet bloc and cooperate with communist enterprises. They emphasized that these proposals sprang from the same source as their demands on freedom of movement in Basket III. In both cases, reducing the barriers to cooperation and mutual understanding would strengthen European security.[104]

The Eastern allies reacted with deep suspicion. They concluded that the West was not trying to expand economic cooperation, but to undermine the socialist system. The United States and its allies wanted to "erod[e] the sovereignty of the socialist states," East German ambassador Siegfried Bock reported. The Soviets and Eastern Europeans had to resist this attempt to enable the "expansion of monopolies" into the socialist community, Czechoslovak foreign minister Bohuslav Chňoupek insisted. Polish officials shared his views.[105] The Warsaw Pact allies wanted to cooperate with the West, but only in ways that did not threaten state control over the economy or give their adversaries the ability to "interfer[e] in the internal affairs of the socialist states."[106] As Brezhnev warned Honecker, "Ideology comes with the automobiles."[107]

In Helsinki and Geneva, the Warsaw Pact representatives dug in their heels. The Soviets resisted what they regarded as an "uncontrolled expansion of information and contacts."[108] The Bulgarians made "pretty crude arguments" against the Western European proposals, British officials reported. They "characteriz[ed] a free flow of information as virtual commercial espionage and increased contacts as a mini brain-drain."[109] Communist diplomats objected to any discussion of publishing their balance of payments figures, presumably for fear that the data would reveal the weakness of the socialist economies.[110] When Western delegations proposed to improve working conditions for foreign businessmen, their Eastern peers refused on the grounds that such a measure "touches on their sovereignty."[111] The Soviets suggested that they might accept a few Western desiderata if the West moderated its demands in the other baskets. The offer was rejected. "The concessions we are asking from the East [in Basket II] are in their own interests," the British delegation argued. "If they do not wish to make them, we will certainly not pay them to do so."[112]

Controversy did not dog every element of the second basket. A declaration on expanding scientific and technological cooperation came together with relative ease. The participants agreed to foster cross-border research in agriculture, energy production, and computer systems. In keeping with the era's surge of interest in environmentalism, they also committed themselves to fighting pollution. Undertakings such as these built on existing East-West initiatives, such as the global effort to eradicate smallpox and the joint

Apollo-Soyuz space mission that launched in July 1975. Crucially, from the Soviet perspective, they would take place under government auspices or through state institutions. They did not threaten centralized control of the economy, did not infringe on the communist understanding of sovereignty, and would not provide the Western states with the tools to interfere in the Soviet bloc's internal affairs. At the same time, however, they stopped well short of granting the USSR or its allies access to Western technology and capital. In these areas, the Final Act promised to benefit the Soviet bloc's universities more than its factories.[113]

The participants also made modest progress on some controversial points. The Soviets surprised the Western allies by assenting to several demands on economic openness, perhaps in the hope of eliciting concessions on MFN treatment. The Final Act thus required states to "improve conditions for the expansion of contacts between representatives of official bodies, of the different organizations, enterprises, firms and banks concerned with foreign trade, in particular, where useful, between sellers and users of products and services." To improve the working conditions of foreign businessmen, the signatories promised to judge "as favorably as possible requests for the establishment of permanent representation and of offices for this purpose." In the name of expanding the flow of economic statistics, they agreed "to improve the quality and increase the quantity and supply of economic and relevant administrative information." These measures "should be of practical use for us," especially in future bilateral negotiations with the East, West German ambassador Klaus Blech reported to Bonn.[114]

By no means did these clauses compel the Soviets or their allies to change their behavior. The preamble to Basket II affirmed that its provisions would be implemented with "full respect" for the principles in the first basket, including state sovereignty, which would protect the socialist governments against any unwelcome Western demands. Nonetheless, they had recognized the importance of greater economic transparency.[115] The Final Act's emphasis on economic openness suggested that the agreement incorporated not just the principles of détente but those of globalization too. It remained to be seen, however, whether the USSR and its allies would take any steps to integrate themselves into the global marketplace.

VI

Both Eastern and Western diplomats regarded the second basket's results as meager. In the British assessment, the battle over trade, MFN treatment, and reciprocity had ended in a draw. The East Germans noted that the socialist countries had failed to affirm the principle of nondiscrimination against their exports. On matters of economic cooperation and openness, however, they had ensured that "everything must be designed in the light of domestic law," which would protect the socialist system against outside interference. These results must have disappointed the Poles, whose economic ambitions for the CSCE had outstripped those of their allies. Nonetheless, they looked on the bright side. The Final Act would benefit Polish scientists, and it created new opportunities for industrial cooperation.[116]

The Soviets achieved little in Basket II because they concentrated their efforts elsewhere. From Brezhnev's perspective, the declaration of principles in Basket I—especially the inviolability of frontiers—took priority over everything else. Even if he hoped to make progress on the MFN question, he declined to spend diplomatic capital on issues of secondary importance. In retrospect, considering the USSR's material needs in the early 1970s, these priorities seem upside down. The country's economic woes posed far greater risks to its long-term strength than did the status of Eastern Europe's borders, which the Western powers had all accepted either de jure or de facto. Besides, economic cooperation had featured in the Warsaw Pact's security conference proposals since the mid-1960s. For these reasons, Western diplomats expected the Soviet delegation to make the second basket a priority. In the event, however, it did not.[117]

This outcome reflected the tensions inherent in Brezhnev's grand strategy. He and his Politburo colleagues had wagered that they could preserve the command economy by drawing on the West but without being drawn into the Western system. They wanted to cooperate with the capitalists, but feared the consequences of doing so. Substantial results in Basket II, such as a commitment to eliminate trade barriers or a detailed agreement on access to Western technology, would have required the Soviets to give the West much of what it demanded on reciprocity and openness. Acceding to such principles would have pulled the socialist economies closer to the West and elicited demands to reform the system of central planning—precisely the outcome that Brezhnev wished to avoid. Even if the USSR could ignore these pressures, some of the other Eastern Europeans, especially the Poles and Hungarians, might have found the temptations of the West too strong to resist.

As a result, the Soviets and their allies made lofty demands without offering much in return. This approach brought some success in dealing with the Nixon administration, which dangled economic carrots in exchange for Soviet geopolitical moderation and did not seek to change the socialist system. It also worked bilaterally with individual Western European governments, which tendered credits and industrial cooperation schemes. But it did not work at the CSCE, which examined the principles that undergirded economic détente rather than negotiating a detailed trade agreement. The conference exposed the difficulties of reconciling the globalizing marketplace with the precepts of central planning. The USSR could uphold orthodoxy and preserve its existing system, or it could pursue the advantages of the Western system, with all the risks that it entailed. It could not do both.[118]

The early 1970s tested the Western economies too. Despite their best efforts, they could not rescue Bretton Woods. When the system of fixed exchange rates collapsed, officials worried that currency fluctuations would damage competitiveness and cramp international trade. Unemployment rose along with energy prices and inflation. Innovation and productivity growth slumped, further impeding the transition to intensive growth. Despite these dislocations, Western leaders sought solutions within the bounds of their own economic system. Cooperation with the Soviet bloc did not feature prominently in their plans. The mixed results of their experiments forced them to reexamine the norms of Keynesian economics, but they did not have to wrestle with the same contradictions that Brezhnev and other communist leaders faced.[119]

At the end of the decade, China radically changed its economic policy. Mao's successor, Deng Xiaoping, believed that his country could embrace certain elements of a market economy without abandoning its communist ideology. Starting in Guangdong and Fujian, he gradually replaced Maoist austerity and egalitarianism with production incentives and decentralization. China left autarky behind and began to embrace the global economy instead. Deng's reforms did not follow a straight path. Periods of innovation alternated with crackdowns. Under careful state supervision, however, China opened itself to the world.[120]

In light of Deng's success, why did Brezhnev not attempt similar reforms in the USSR? If anyone in the Soviet hierarchy had the bureaucratic know-how to implement a radical change in policy, it was Brezhnev. But he remained wedded to the status quo. He aimed to preserve the Soviet system, not to transform it. Moreover, even if he had wanted to chart a new economic course, he could not have done so alone. Thousands of party officials and state managers had a stake in the existing system and the ability to impede any changes ordered by the Kremlin. In the mid-1960s, they had hamstrung Kosygin's comparatively mild reforms, and would certainly have resisted an even more daring program.[121] Deng could take advantage of the instability that followed Mao's death and the Cultural Revolution, but no period of Soviet history enjoyed more political stability than the 1970s. For better and for worse, Brezhnev lacked a window of opportunity to implement major changes.[122]

Above all, the Soviet economy did not appear to need radical transformation in the mid-1970s. The economy continued to grow, albeit by smaller increments each year. Improvements were necessary, but no immediate crisis loomed. Besides, revenues from oil exports—and the sale of weapons to Arab petrostates—allowed leaders to buy Western technology and raise living standards for consumers, for instance by subsidizing food prices. So long as the price of oil remained high, this process could continue. In Basket II and elsewhere, Brezhnev saw no need to make painful choices.[123]

The Final Act did not establish bold new principles to hasten the convergence of the capitalist and communist systems. The shortcomings of Basket II made clear that Eastern and Western economic concepts remained worlds apart. Outside the CSCE, however, the Soviets and their allies increasingly relied on their economic ties to the West, whether by selling oil, borrowing money, or importing technology. In these transactions, they operated according to market principles. As a result, they would find it increasingly difficult to disentangle themselves from the logic of capitalism even as they fought to preserve communism at home.

Chapter 6

THE CLOSED SOCIETY AND ITS ENEMIES

IN THE early 1970s, the societies of the Soviet bloc were not sealed off from the outside world. Each year, tens of thousands of people traveled across the Iron Curtain. In the USSR and Eastern Europe, libraries collected Western books and periodicals, cinemas screened Western films, and theaters staged Western plays. Across the region, citizens could tune in to Western radio broadcasts. In some places, especially East Germany and Czechoslovakia, they could watch Western television. The black market brought the latest Western fashions and cassette tapes of rock music to young people. According to a 1970 study, citizens in both East and West believed that national frontiers were declining in importance, and they anticipated that people and goods would flow ever more freely between countries in the years to come.[1]

In nearly every area of life, however, the governments of the bloc tightly controlled—or attempted to control—these points of contact between East and West. Although Russians visited Eastern Europe by the hundreds of thousands every year, only small numbers of trusted party members could travel to the West, and then only on carefully regimented group tours. Even the comparatively liberal governments of Eastern Europe, such as Poland and Hungary, denied five out of six applications to visit the West and made it difficult for citizens to obtain hard currency. Western tourists and journalists in the Soviet bloc could only visit preapproved destinations, and the secret police monitored their contact with locals and sometimes confiscated the journalists' notes and tapes. Libraries kept most Western publications in closed reading rooms—known in East Germany as *Giftschränke*, or "poison cupboards"—that could only be accessed with special permission. Newsstands sold no Western newspapers or magazines. Bookshops generally carried only those Western books deemed politically inoffensive or that depicted capitalism in an unflattering light, often in bowdlerized editions. Cinemas tended to show Western movies that met the same criteria. Powerful antennas jammed many Western radio stations.

Across the region, the authorities were caught between their citizens' hunger for Western culture and the imperative of protecting their societies from ideological pollution.[2]

Western governments wanted to use the CSCE to loosen these constraints and open up the governments and societies of the Soviet bloc. Their demands in Basket III for the freer movement of people and information reflected both humanitarian aspirations and Cold War imperatives. They aimed to lower the physical and intellectual barriers between the two halves of the continent, make the Iron Curtain more permeable, and expose socialist societies to liberal democratic influence. By making it easier to read foreign books and travel abroad, for example, the conference could improve the lives of average people in the Soviet bloc—but it could also erode the repressive policies on which the communist regimes depended for their survival. The allies complemented these efforts with a set of proposals for military confidence-building measures (CBMs). By opening routine training exercises to foreign observers and announcing them in advance, they hoped to reduce mutual suspicions and make it harder for states to intimidate their neighbors with shows of force. Optimists argued that freer movement and CBMs would provide a new foundation for peace, in which transparency and cooperation replaced repression and secrecy.

The Soviets and their allies struggled to respond to this Western offensive. Conceptually, they failed to develop proposals that might turn freer movement to their advantage. Tactically, they found it difficult to resist the West because they needed the West's consent to their own demands on frontiers and the declaration of principles. They tried to escape from this dilemma in a number of ways. They stalled the negotiations, hectored Western diplomats, and appealed to the Nixon and Ford administrations for help in persuading the unyielding Western Europeans to back down.

Eventually, however, the Soviets and Eastern Europeans gave way. On both freer movement and CBMs, they conceded the West's most significant demands. In exchange, however, they extracted a preamble to the third basket that obliquely recognized the principles of sovereignty and noninterference, and a clause that CBMs were strictly voluntary. Brezhnev, Gromyko, and their Eastern European colleagues reassured themselves that these stipulations empowered them to implement the Final Act as they saw fit—and to ignore any provisions that threatened state security. They could not deny, however, that the agreement affirmed the Western concept of peace and the virtues of openness. It represented a major victory for the Western allies, and for those in the Soviet bloc—including both dissidents and reform-minded officials—who hoped that the CSCE would usher in a freer and more humane society.

I

Western governments had long regarded freer movement—of people, ideas, and goods—as a hallmark of an open society and a crucial component of international order. In the nineteenth century, the concept helped to justify American expansion. At the 1919 Paris Peace Conference, the American delegation insisted that "civilization depends upon open communication among nations."[3] In 1955, the American, British, and French foreign ministers pressed the Soviets to eliminate "barriers to free communications and trade" and to establish freer contacts between East and West.[4] A few years later, they used similar language to defend travel between the two halves of Berlin.[5] Even the Catholic Church embraced the idea. In the 1963 encyclical *Pacem in Terris*, Pope John XXIII described freedom of movement as an essential human right, echoing the Universal Declaration of Human Rights, which affirmed citizens' rights to emigrate and "to seek, receive and impart information and ideas through any media and regardless of frontiers."[6] Of course, Western governments limited free movement in some ways—not least by imposing controls on immigration—but they generally regarded the concept as both politically expedient and morally necessary.

During the mid-1960s, American officials theorized that freer movement might mitigate superpower tensions. If East and West understood each other better and average people could communicate across the Iron Curtain, the Cold War itself might be transcended. In 1966, Lyndon Johnson proposed a campaign of "bridge building" and called for "a shift from the narrow concept of coexistence to the broader vision of peaceful engagement" with the Soviet bloc.[7] Although the president eschewed the older and more confrontational language of "rollback," he hoped that his new approach, which resembled Willy Brandt's concept of change through rapprochement, would weaken Soviet power and "help the nations of Eastern Europe move toward independence."[8]

In pursuit of political freedom and mutual understanding, dissidents in the Soviet bloc endeavored to build bridges of their own. In collaboration with foreign journalists, they exploited gaps in the apparatus of state control to communicate across borders. Their work informed the Western public about daily life under communism and gave the bloc's citizens alternatives to the party-controlled media. Drawing on interviews with émigrés and foreign travelers and intelligence supplied by sympathizers working within the communist governments, Radio Free Europe (RFE) and Radio Liberty (RL) disseminated news and commentary about events in Eastern Europe and the USSR. Based in Munich but funded by the CIA, they also broadcast dissidents' essays and novels, bringing them to a wider audience than they could have reached through underground networks alone. Despite attempts to jam their signals, RFE and RL reached about one-third of all adults living in Soviet cities and half of all adults in Eastern Europe. Other Western outlets, especially the BBC, Deutsche Welle, and Voice of America, also broadcast to the Soviet bloc and reached similarly large audiences.[9]

These efforts brought some dissidents to worldwide attention. In 1968, the Moscow correspondent of the Dutch newspaper *Het Parool* obtained a samizdat copy of Andrei Sakharov's *Reflections on Progress, Co-existence, and Intellectual Freedom*, a manifesto for opening the USSR to new ideas. One Saturday, Karel van het Reve dictated the text over the telephone to his editor in Amsterdam. "Whoever of the Soviet censors was listening in on my call apparently did not know enough Dutch to understand what I was doing," he later recalled.[10] Within a year, eighteen million copies of the essay had been published worldwide. In 1970, an American reporter filmed an interview with the writer Andrei Amalrik, who predicted that the Soviet system would soon collapse. The reporter smuggled the tape back to the United States, where it aired on national television.[11]

Nongovernmental organizations reinforced these informational networks. The members of the Moscow Human Rights Committee kept in regular contact with the New York–based International League for Human Rights, which in turn lobbied Western governments on the committee's behalf. The two groups exchanged reports by mail, telephone, and the occasional face-to-face meeting in Moscow, giving the committee a crucial source of information and support.[12] In 1969, a group of British and Dutch writers—including van het Reve—established the Alexander Herzen Foundation with a mandate to publish dissident literature. One of its founders, Peter Reddaway, also translated the first issues of the *Chronicle of Current Events*, a samizdat record of Soviet human rights abuses. Amnesty International took over from him a few years later.[13] In 1972, some British writers and academics started the *Index on Censorship*, which featured dissidents' writings alongside stories on state repression in the Soviet bloc and beyond. "Information, facts, truth, knowledge, [and] communication are the enemies of tyrants," its editor declared.[14]

The Western allies put these ideas at the heart of their CSCE strategy. At the simplest level, they wanted to improve the lives of average citizens and help the two halves of Europe understand each other better. The goal was to create "a better life for people," as Ted Heath told Willy Brandt.[15] West German officials sought to build on the success of Ostpolitik and provide "human relief" to anyone affected by the division of the continent.[16] Western officials also believed that the circulation of ideas and people would strengthen international peace. "A genuine order of peace and cooperation in Europe will depend ultimately upon normalization of human contacts," George Vest wrote in 1972. "More open relations and closer ties ... are the indispensable elements of progress toward mutual knowledge and understanding throughout the continent and toward the resolution of common problems."[17] If the Soviets challenged this claim, Western diplomats should reply that "there can be no genuine détente or security in Europe so long as there is no real understanding in one part of the continent of the values, attitudes, beliefs, culture and way of life of people in the other," a British official wrote. Peace could only take hold if East and West cooperated in "progressively demolishing the barriers" that separated them.[18]

Demolishing these barriers might eventually help to demolish the whole Soviet system. If citizens in the East could read, write, and speak more freely, travel more widely, and engage with Western ideas, communist leaders would find it increasingly difficult to sustain their rule. Even small gains would serve as "acid that would eventually eat away" at the structures of Soviet power, argued Georges Pompidou's advisor Gabriel Robin.[19] State Department officials, who played a central role in developing the concept of freer movement, agreed. By generating pressure for liberal reforms within the Soviet bloc, the wider circulation of people and ideas would help to "overcome the unnatural division" of the continent.[20] Once the USSR's defenses were lowered, Western ideas would proliferate organically. "Reducing barriers within Europe," a British diplomat argued, would help "to spread the contagion of liberty ... [and] introduce another germ of freedom into the East."[21] In any contest of ideas, a Quai d'Orsay official noted, the West enjoyed an inherent advantage because its open societies were "superior to the communist world in being better able to tolerate diversity" of opinion.[22]

The West stood to gain even if the Soviets rejected freer movement. Some of the Eastern Europeans might defy Moscow and seek to expand their cultural ties across the Iron Curtain. In that case, the West could exploit the disagreement to weaken socialist unity.[23] If the Soviets and their allies stood together, however, the debate at the CSCE would focus "the attention of Western public opinion upon the closed nature of the Soviet regime," the US delegation to NATO argued. Because NATO's proposals appealed to "the popular imagination," George Walden predicted, they would elicit sympathy for the victims of the Soviet system and make clear that the Eastern governments bore primary responsibility for the Cold War's human costs. By drawing this sharp contrast between the two camps, NATO could claim the moral high ground and renew Western voters' support for the alliance.[24]

Once the allies agreed to pursue freer movement in principle, they had to define what it meant in practice. Intense deliberations under NATO's auspices yielded a wide range of ideas. Some were new and some built on older efforts, such as the cultural exchange programs that France launched with the USSR in the 1960s. Readers in Eastern Europe ought to have access to more Western books and newspapers. The Soviet authorities should cease jamming Western radio broadcasts. Eastern and Western television stations ought to broadcast each other's shows, and create a linked discussion program that would air simultaneously across Europe. Grandparents in the East should be allowed to join their families in the West. Citizens of all ages should travel across the Cold War divide. Western journalists should be able to move freely in the Soviet Union and contact whichever sources they chose. These proposals gave concrete form to the abstractions of freer movement, and they defined the concept in a way that played to the strengths of the West's open societies.[25]

The allies developed arguments to rebut the likeliest objections to these ideas. If the Soviets insisted on their sole prerogative to control everything and everyone that crossed their borders, Western diplomats could argue that freer movement epitomized the spirit of détente. To improve relations between governments, relations between societies had to improve too, and people had to get to know each other. If the Soviets denied that freer movement constituted a fit topic for negotiation, Western diplomats could argue that international opinion had long "recognize[d] that these matters are of concern to all states and are therefore legitimate subjects of international discussion," as the Universal Declaration of Human Rights and UN Covenants attested. Agreements on the freer movement of people and information no more impinged on states' sovereignty than did agreements on international trade and the freer movement of goods.[26]

Freer movement did not elicit universal support in Western capitals. Senior members of the Nixon administration regarded the idea with particular skepticism. The president believed that the Western Europeans—and the denizens of the State Department—were deluding themselves about the significance of an agreement on the subject. "What the hell comes out of [the conference]? Hope?" Nixon asked Kissinger in 1971. "Nothing but a conference," Kissinger replied. "Well, we can have a lot of nice little truisms about travel," Nixon said. Two years later, Kissinger told Luxembourg's foreign minister that discussing freer movement at the CSCE "would lead to nothing."[27] Helmut Sonnenfeldt argued that freer movement could even backfire on the West. "These measures would seek to destabilize what had just been stabilized," he told Kissinger.[28]

Some of the Western Europeans who had high hopes for freer movement also worried about antagonizing Moscow. The French and the West Germans warned that NATO should rein in its demands, lest the Soviets refuse to discuss the subject or pull out of the negotiations entirely. The allies had to approach the CSCE in "a spirit of compromise and pragmatism," which meant starting with anodyne proposals, argued Roger Seydoux, the French ambassador in Moscow. After winning the communists' support for cultural exchanges, for example, the West could make headway on more difficult questions, such as emigration and radio jamming.[29] Using this logic, the French convinced the allies to change the title of their proposals from the "Freer movement of people, ideas, and information" to the less inflammatory "Contact between peoples."[30]

NATO's maximalists dismissed these concerns. If the allies ratcheted up their demands over the course of the conference, they would only anger the Soviets. Instead, the British, Dutch, and Canadians argued that the West should stake out an ambitious position first, and then work toward a compromise. "It is tactically wrong to do [the Warsaw Pact's] negotiating" on its behalf, commented one Canadian official.[31] Because the Soviets were the supplicants at the CSCE, the Western allies had "little to lose by playing as hard as [they] can for considerable concessions from the East," a British diplomat reasoned. At the State Department, William Rogers broke with Nixon and Kissinger by urging the allies to "engage in controversy where necessary on issues which the Soviets will want either to avoid or to gloss over."[32] By the time that the preparatory talks opened in Helsinki, however, these intra-NATO arguments about negotiating tactics remained unresolved. So long as they continued to rage, they threatened allied solidarity.[33]

II

Long before the negotiations began, Soviet and Eastern European leaders grasped the dangers of freer movement. At the very least, the West hoped to "divert attention from the most basic issues of European security to 'problems' such as the 'free exchange of opinion' [and] 'freedom of movement,'" Brezhnev argued.[34] More seriously, freer movement represented an attempt at "ideological subversion" by "influencing the consciousness of the societies of the socialist countries," he told Edward Gierek.[35] Gierek and other Eastern European leaders shared this assessment. Unless the Warsaw Pact blocked Western demands, the conference would become a "a pulpit for attacks against the socialist countries . . . [and] a means of broad ideological penetration into our countries," Todor Zhivkov warned. Nicolae Ceauşescu, who disagreed with his allies about many aspects of the CSCE, sided with them on this subject.[36]

In contrast to these views, some Soviet bloc officials believed that their societies might benefit from wider access to Western ideas. Many of the USSR's *mezhdunarodniki* had been profoundly shaped by reading American books on international politics, by studying at Western universities, and by serving in Western capitals. One diplomat who had been posted to London recalled that he and his colleagues devoured books that were banned at home, including samizdat. "Hardly anybody withstood the temptation of tasting the forbidden fruit," he said. Thanks to experiences of this sort, these officials set aside old dogmas about the outside world. They had no desire to overthrow socialism, but they concluded that their country could learn from capitalist societies and ways of thinking. They remained a distinct minority within their own governments, but their positions in their foreign ministries gave them an opportunity to act on their views.[37]

Nonetheless, the Soviet bloc's leaders agreed that they either had to resist the West's demands or face dire consequences. The spread of bourgeois ideas and exposure to Western allures would erode citizens' loyalty and might inspire another Prague Spring. Over time, "more people from one side would identify themselves with people from the other side," an East German report predicted. Sooner or later, they would lose faith in communism itself. According to Soviet diplomat Nikolai Polianski, "Contact with the material and spiritual wealth of Western countries—the abundance of goods and free information—would immediately reveal to the Soviet citizen his material and spiritual poverty." The USSR and its allies could not afford to take this risk.[38] For years, they had grappled with Western attempts to spread hostile ideas. They complained about Radio Free Europe and Radio Liberty's "unlawful interference" in their internal affairs and used a variety of means—including jamming and espionage—to frustrate the stations' "sabotage campaigns" and "psychological warfare." These efforts consumed huge sums of money, but succeeded only in part. The broadcasts still reached millions of listeners.[39] The Red Army newspaper *Krasnaya Zvezda* warned that Western governments might eventually develop the technology to beam television programs directly into Soviet homes from satellites in orbit, which would lead to the "uncontrolled brainwashing" of viewers.[40]

Soviet leaders regarded their domestic critics as tools of these Western campaigns. The dissidents' ideas were "planted by our adversary" in an attempt to "weaken socialist society," KGB chief Yuri Andropov argued.[41] After Aleksandr Solzhenitsyn won the Nobel Prize for literature in 1970, the KGB subjected the writer to special scrutiny. Agents insisted that he "willingly [took] the part of 'leader' of anti-Soviet elements at the West's dictation, and [tried] to instigate openly antisocial actions against our country." Because the writer and his kind threatened the stability of the Soviet system, the authorities had to respond.[42]

The crackdown took a number of forms. New laws made it a crime to meet with foreigners to spread "false" or "slanderous" information about the USSR, or to use the telephone system "for purposes contrary to State interests and public order."[43] In some cases, the KGB simply issued warnings, but it did not hesitate to arrest Andrei Amalrik or other prominent dissidents. To prevent the news of Amalrik's trial from spreading abroad, it was held in Sverdlovsk, a city far from Moscow that foreigners could not visit. Nonetheless, the word got out, prompting domestic and international appeals for his release. Unmoved, the court sentenced him to three years.[44] Other dissidents, including *Chronicle of Current Events* editor Natalya Gorbanevskaya, were confined to psychiatric hospitals and forcibly drugged under the pretense that they were mentally ill. Gorbanevskaya's collaborators temporarily kept the *Chronicle* going, but in early 1972 the authorities shut it down, putting hundreds of people in prison. For the moment, it seemed that the dissident movement had been broken.[45]

Developing a strategy to thwart the West's demands on freer movement proved more difficult. To Warsaw Pact leaders, NATO's proposals stood at odds with the spirit of the CSCE. They threatened to divert the conference from its original purpose and sought to exploit it in order to damage the interests of socialism. Brezhnev took the danger seriously, but he refused to be deterred. "We should go into this embrace, but we should not forget where we are going," he told Gierek. "We must outwit the devil, and not let the devil outwit us."[46] Some Soviet bloc officials proposed to take the offensive. The socialist states should advance their own ideas on freer movement and establish "an edge in the battle for the minds of men," Soviet and Polish diplomats agreed. An aggressive concept of cultural cooperation would encourage "the penetration of our ideology in the West" and build public support for the communist vision of Europe, the Warsaw Pact's deputy foreign ministers concluded.[47] Other than calling for an end to Western radio broadcasts, however, the Soviets and Eastern Europeans struggled to articulate concrete proposals that might turn freer movement to their advantage.

By default, they fell back on a defensive strategy. First, they tried to keep freer movement off the CSCE's agenda. In 1972, the Soviet ambassador in London told Foreign Secretary Alec Douglas-Home that gradual improvements might be possible in time, but raising the subject immediately "would not be useful." For the moment, the conference ought to focus exclusively on the problems of European security and leave cooperation and freer movement for some future meeting. Taking a blunter approach, the Bulgarians and Hungarians urged their allies to refuse to discuss the matter at all.[48] In the hope of watering down Western proposals, the USSR's proposed conference agenda lumped cultural cooperation—the Warsaw Pact's anemic answer to freer movement—in with economic cooperation under a single heading.[49]

If the Eastern allies could not stop the CSCE from discussing freer movement, however, they could still limit its scope. Since the mid-1960s, Soviet cultural exchanges with the West had operated under tight government control. To prevent the contamination of Soviet society by unwelcome ideas, only state-run organizations—not individual citizens—could take part, while in the West, the Soviet participants touted the superiority of the socialist system and worked to spread Marxist-Leninist ideology. Using this model at the CSCE would empower the socialist governments to keep a tight grip on all cross-border exchanges, and it would prevent Western states from threatening their internal security or making room for spontaneous contacts between individuals.[50] In all cases, the Warsaw Pact would "strive for strict respect for the principles of sovereignty [and] non-interference in domestic affairs," Brezhnev said.[51] So long as the conference reaffirmed these principles, the Soviet bloc would stay safe. The West could put forward as many proposals as it liked but sovereignty and the power of the state would eviscerate them all.

III

From the outset of the preparatory talks in Helsinki, East and West clashed vociferously over freer movement. The Western representatives pushed hard to place the subject on the CSCE's agenda. "We seek a more open world—open to closer cooperation and to great contacts among people, as well as to a free interchange of ideas and information," George Vest said at the opening session. The French, Dutch, Canadians, and others made a similar case, insisting that the CSCE had to make détente meaningful to average citizens, not just to heads of state.[52]

The Soviets and Eastern Europeans rejected these claims. In their view, contacts between people had nothing to do with détente and had no bearing on international peace. "Wars did not break out because of a lack of contact between the Schmidt and Kowalski families," Poland's deputy foreign minister told the West Germans. Peace had to come first. It would produce mutual understanding, not the other way around.[53] Besides, freer movement violated state sovereignty, the Eastern allies alleged. When Alec Douglas-Home suggested that relations between Eastern and Western Europe should resemble relations within Western Europe, with a "real intermingling of people at all levels," Andrei Gromyko reacted with horror. The Soviet Union "would not accept a lesson from anyone on how to conduct [its] internal affairs," he said. "Internal law and order was not just small change which could be handed over in the marketplace."[54] No agreement could be reached in the absence of categorical respect for the sovereignty of each state, the East German Politburo insisted. Domestic laws always superseded international agreements.[55] At most, the conference might discuss "cultural cooperation" alongside economic and scientific cooperation in what later became the second basket. Freer movement was out of the question.[56]

The Western allies persisted nonetheless. When they threatened to block progress on the inviolability of frontiers unless the CSCE discussed freer movement, Soviet officials concluded that they could not keep stonewall-ing. It was "tactically advantageous" to grant the Western demand, Gromyko told the Politburo in December 1972, but "it goes without saying that this does not in any way prevent us from continuing strongly to oppose any at-tempt by the capitalist countries to impose on us the 'freedom' of spreading hostile propaganda and ideology."[57] The same month, Brezhnev declared that the USSR welcomed contacts between peoples and the exchange of ideas, but only insofar as they fostered peace and showed due respect for state sovereignty.[58]

In Helsinki, the Soviets adjusted their position accordingly. They agreed to consider cultural exchange, tourism, and contacts between young peo-ple, and to create a separate agenda item—Basket III—for these questions. At the same time, however, they stipulated that transnational contacts had to be conducted through state organizations, and had to serve the purpose of strengthening peace.[59] In no circumstances would the USSR tolerate "the dissemination of anti-culture—pornography, racism, fascism, the cult of violence, hostility among peoples and false slanderous propaganda," am-bassador Viktor Maltsev said. Basket III required a preamble that recog-nized the principle of noninterference in domestic affairs and subordi-nated international cooperation to "the sovereignty, laws, and customs of each state," Valerian Zorin insisted. (The Western allies denied that nonin-terference, which restricted all manner of peaceful activities, such as radio broadcasting, constituted a legitimate principle of international affairs. They preferred to speak of nonintervention, which forbade only military incursions into the territory of another state.) Until the text of the pream-ble had been finalized, the Soviets said, they would not discuss the sub-stance of Basket III.[60]

After a fierce debate about how to respond, the Western allies suggested a compromise. Rather than invoking sovereignty or nonintervention by name, the preamble to Basket III should refer to the whole declaration of principles from Basket I. Under apparent pressure from Moscow to make progress, Zorin dropped his earlier insistence on noninterference.[61] In the first week of June, a deal took shape. Any agreement on freer movement would be "based on full respect" for the declaration of principles, which included human rights alongside sovereignty and nonintervention. This formulation gave neither side a clear victory. It provided both the means of justifying freer movement and the means of restricting it.[62]

Similar controversies raged over the substance of Basket III. With the Danes and Canadians in the lead, the Western allies made a series of bold proposals. They demanded the "greater freedom of movement and ex-change of persons" and "the wider flow of information," and called for con-crete agreements on family reunification, travel, access to foreign books and magazines, the freer circulation of films, radio, and television broadcasts, and improved working conditions for journalists.[63] These ideas met immediate resistance. The USSR refused to be blackmailed into "purchas[ing] peace ... at the expense of changes in its internal arrangements," Lev Mendelevich said. At most, it might agree to expand cultural and educational exchanges under state control.[64] Facing constant Western pressure to expand the agenda, however, the Soviets and their allies eventually dropped most of their objections in order to bring the preparatory talks to a close.[65]

The Blue Book did not give the West everything that it wanted, but it came close. Although the allies had to drop the reference to the freer exchange of ideas, the text declared that Basket III would "facilitate freer movement and contacts" between people and "facilitate the freer and wider dissemination of information of all kinds." It also included specific items on family reunification; marriage between citizens of different states; access to oral, printed, filmed, and broadcast information; and journalists' working conditions. These "amazing concession[s]" by the Warsaw Pact surprised Western negotiators, British delegate Brian Fall later recalled. The result far exceeded expectations, especially considering that the Soviets had initially refused to discuss freer movement at all. "We have, through perseverance and patience, gained more ... than could have been thought possible last November when the talks opened," a Canadian report on the preparatory talks concluded.[66]

The Soviets and their allies refused to concede defeat. "The West failed to push through their subversive proposals," a Polish official insisted. The East Germans counted on using the preamble to block Western ambitions in Geneva.[67] At the foreign ministers' gathering that officially launched the CSCE in June 1973, Andrei Gromyko warned that the USSR intended to refight every battle from the preparatory talks. At Stage II it would demand an unequivocal statement that sovereignty and noninterference trumped the provisions of Basket III.[68] A West German official observed that the USSR seemed determined to "raise fundamental barriers" between East and West. The West would have to fight hard to resist this effort and to pull down those barriers that already existed.[69] From Moscow, British ambassador Sir John Killick warned that NATO had to match the Warsaw Pact's stubbornness if it hoped to succeed. "We must be prepared to go over every inch of all this ground again," he wrote, "if necessary with endless repetition."[70]

When the full negotiations opened in Geneva, the Soviets reprised their familiar arguments. Addressing the World Congress of Peace Forces in November 1973, Leonid Brezhnev attacked the West's "hypocritical" campaign to change "the internal systems of the socialist countries." The USSR and its allies would "defend the system their hands have created against any infringements," he vowed, and would not "change their protective laws any more than bourgeois states will do the same where their laws contradict

Soviet notions of justice and democracy."[71] On this basis, the Soviet and Eastern European negotiators demanded that the Basket III preamble refer explicitly to sovereignty, nonintervention, and respect for states' laws and customs. They promised to show greater flexibility on the substance of freer movement if the West endorsed these "rules of the game" first.[72]

Brezhnev and Gromyko pressed their case at the highest levels. In January 1974, the general secretary wrote to Nixon, Pompidou, Brandt, and Heath. The USSR supported cultural cooperation, he explained, but "if someone wants to use cultural and other exchanges for unfriendly purposes then we have but one reply: no."[73] Gromyko told Kissinger that his government only wanted to reaffirm the existing rules of international conduct. "It all boils down to whether there will be an opening of the door or whether the principle of noninterference will be left intact," he said. "This is after all the basis of all our post-war agreements, including the charter of the United Nations." Western demands in Basket III, by contrast, endangered the CSCE and cast doubt on the postwar world's foundational assumptions.[74]

As if to underscore their refusal to be cowed, Soviet leaders ordered a crackdown on the dissident movement. In mid-1973, *Pravda* denounced Aleksandr Solzhenitsyn and Andrei Sakharov as "internal spiritual emigrants, alien to the socialist system and to the whole life of the Soviet people," and criticized Western governments for treating them as "fighters for human rights."[75] Andropov told the Politburo that the Western allies planned to use Solzhenitsyn's case to press their demands at the CSCE. After Solzhenitsyn's masterpiece, *The Gulag Archipelago*, was published in Paris that December, Soviet leaders resolved to act. Anatoly Kovalev warned Andropov that putting the writer on trial might derail the CSCE. Gromyko voiced similar concerns. When the Politburo decided to expel Solzhenitsyn from the country instead of jailing him, however, Brezhnev predicted that "the effect will not be great." On February 13, 1974, Solzhenitsyn was stripped of his Soviet citizenship and put on a plane to Frankfurt.[76]

Brezhnev was right. A Polish diplomat was spotted at the conference center with a copy of *The Gulag Archipelago*, but otherwise the negotiators in Geneva hardly discussed the writer. "Like most other manifestations of [the] real world, [the] Solzhenitsyn affair has had little immediate effect on the CSCE," the Canadian delegation reported. This is not to say that Western diplomats were indifferent to Solzhenitsyn's fate. Had the Soviet government imprisoned or executed him, they might have felt compelled to take dramatic action. Because he was exiled, however, they saw no reason to change course. His punishment only confirmed what they already knew about the Soviet system and illustrated why their demands in Basket III mattered so much. As the negotiations over the basket's substance and preamble ground to a halt, they stood their ground.[77]

Despite the Western delegations' resolve, Nixon and Kissinger sympathized with the Kremlin's plight. No agreement reached at the CSCE could change the nature of the Soviet regime, Kissinger reasoned. "I don't believe that a bunch of revolutionaries who manage to cling to power for fifty years are going to be euchred out of it by the sort of people we have got negotiating at the European Security Conference through an oversight," he told a State Department staff meeting.[78] Because the United States had no vital interests at stake in the negotiations, it ought to give the Soviets what they wanted. "We can't be sons-of-bitches everywhere," he said. "We have to show the Russians they are getting something out of détente," or else the whole structure of superpower relations could collapse.[79]

When Kissinger offered to work with the Soviets to defang the Western Europeans' demands and solve the preamble problem, Gromyko accepted. With the Politburo's approval, he ordered Yuli Vorontsov in Washington to handle the matter.[80] Although Gromyko informed Kovalev of the back-channel démarche, Kissinger kept the American delegation—and America's allies—in the dark. In April 1974, after secret talks in Washington and Moscow, the two sides agreed on a formula that satisfied the USSR's concerns.[81] The Basket III preamble would cite the declaration of principles from Basket I and, in turn, the principle on nonintervention would affirm each state's right to determine its "own legislative and regulatory system." The formula gave the USSR more explicit protection than the text that had been reached at the preparatory talks. Gromyko asked Kissinger to remind the Western Europeans that his government would tolerate no interference in its domestic affairs. "We sometimes think that some circles underestimate the strength of our position," he said. "[T]hey should remember the strength of the diamond because that is how tough we feel on this issue."[82]

Now that the superpowers had reached a consensus, they had to win over the Western Europeans. Gromyko suggested that the Soviet and American delegations jointly present the compromise at the CSCE, but Kissinger refused. Such a move would alienate the Western allies, who had long suspected that the White House was collaborating with the Kremlin to undercut NATO's position.[83] Willy Brandt, for example, told Kissinger that he feared Nixon would reach "an understanding with Brezhnev before coming to an understanding with the allies."[84] Kissinger and Gromyko therefore decided that a neutral party, preferably Finland, should introduce their proposal without divulging its origins. Under pressure from Moscow, Urho Kekkonen agreed to do so. At the beginning of June, as part of the "package deal" that cleared the roadblock in Basket I, the Finnish delegation in Geneva put forward a text that differed only slightly from the US-Soviet bargain.[85]

Finland's initiative did not impress the Western Europeans. A few months previously, they had made a significant concession to Soviet demands by agreeing to draft the preamble and substance of Basket III simultaneously, rather than negotiating the substance first.[86] Since then, however, the lack of progress had frustrated them. In this context, the Finnish proposal seemed like yet another attempt to "turn the flank of our Basket III defenses," a British diplomat remarked. Several of the allies suspected that Moscow had put the Finns up to it, and rumors circulated that the Americans had also been involved.[87] The head of the American delegation, Albert Sherer, tried to persuade the Western Europeans to set aside their "caution and skepticism," but received "very little support," he noted in his diary.[88]

In the hope of clearing the impasse, the Finns tried again, this time with Swiss and Austrian help. Their new proposal removed all references to national laws from the text of Basket III. Instead of recognizing each state's "legislative and regulatory system," it acknowledged its "laws and regulations," a slightly weaker formulation, and placed this stipulation in the principle on sovereign equality rather than nonintervention. Finally, it required participants to fulfil their obligations under international law, which implicitly included respect for human rights. These changes blunted the Soviet attempt to "cut the bottom out of that third basket," as Gromyko had so often put it. A state's domestic rules could not absolve it of its international responsibilities.[89]

At first, Gromyko insisted on standing by the original US-Soviet compromise and demanded more robust protections for Soviet domestic policies. At a June meeting in Moscow, he urged Nixon and Kissinger to press their allies harder on this point.[90] Nonetheless, the Western Europeans refused to budge, and after several weeks, Gromyko gave in. In Geneva, Anatoly Kovalev and his Eastern European counterparts accepted the neutrals' proposal, believing that it reflected their essential objectives. On July 26, the day before the summer recess and ten months into Stage II, the negotiators unanimously adopted the new compromise.[91]

IV

The agreement on the preamble did nothing to resolve the standoff over the substance of Basket III. Since the beginning of the Geneva negotiations, the Western allies had demanded specific commitments on every point listed in the Blue Book. They called for the unimpeded dissemination of books and newspapers; an end to radio jamming; fewer restraints on the work of foreign correspondents; and the removal of all measures that prevented citizens from leaving their own country.[92] In each case, they sought "to establish obligations of a normative character that will apply generally and in all circumstances" to the CSCE's participants, a French official wrote.[93]

By mid-summer 1974, the negotiators had agreed on only a few uncontentious items. They had drafted texts on state-to-state collaboration on cultural projects and knowledge of foreign cultural works, but the most controversial issues remained untouched.[94] The Soviets and Eastern Europeans responded to every proposal by trying "to whittle away at the Western texts and to water them down until they become virtually meaningless," the British complained. For the moment, Western diplomats stood firm, but they worried about how long they could remain united. If their resolve cracked, the Soviets might escape meaningful obligations.[95]

Western officials understood that their citizens would hold them accountable for the CSCE's results. Few newspapers were paying much attention to the negotiations, Crispin Tickell noted, but public opinion, "from left to right, supports the substance of the Western case" in Basket III. During the preparatory talks, a group of Soviet Jews called on the allies to demand an end to Soviet restrictions on emigration.[96] In 1973 and again in 1974, a number of celebrated writers—including Raymond Aron, Eugène Ionesco, Günter Grass, Graham Greene, and Arthur Miller—publicly chastised Western governments for squandering their considerable leverage to expand intellectual freedom and "the free flow of knowledge" in Eastern Europe. These figures enjoyed enough prestige that their criticism could sting Western leaders. If the allies settled for meager results in Basket III, they might provoke a domestic backlash.[97]

In Geneva, the Western delegations used this scrutiny as a negotiating tool. They emphasized that, because their citizens expected concrete results, they could not go home empty-handed. To underscore this point, the British delegation cited the 1974 writers' appeal, which elicited an angry response from the Soviets. French and Danish officials made the same case to their Polish counterparts.[98] Even if the Western allies despaired of achieving their most ambitious goals in Basket III, they had to stay on the attack and wring as much as possible from their Eastern counterparts. If the negotiations bore little fruit, at least Western citizens would see who bore the primary responsibility for the failure. "We must squeeze the Russian lemon very hard to demonstrate to public opinion how little juice there is in détente à la Russe," George Walden insisted.[99]

In the hope of blunting these demands and burnishing their public image, the Soviets tried to show that they too valued freer movement. On the eve of Stage II, the Politburo decided to stop jamming the BBC, Deutsche Welle, and Voice of America (but not Radio Liberty), and contemplated relaxing the restrictions that prevented foreign journalists from venturing beyond Moscow without a special permit. Brezhnev also ordered Soviet officials to devise new proposals to make the USSR seem forthcoming at the CSCE without "shock[ing] our ideological principles." In a televised speech, he said that the Soviet Union even stood to gain from the third basket. Expanded contacts—between states, if not between individuals—would "serve well to spread the truth about socialism" and win converts to the cause, he said.[100] Some of the Eastern Europeans tried a similar approach. Basket III presented "no serious obstacles for us," Polish foreign minister Stefan Olszowski told Kissinger.[101]

The Soviets and their allies attempted to make a virtue of necessity. At a meeting of Brezhnev's advisors, Anatoly Kovalev argued that the USSR could not hold out indefinitely in Basket III. Unless it granted some Western demands, the CSCE might fail.[102] Yuri Andropov shared this assessment. When the KGB officer attached to the Soviet delegation denounced Kovalev's spinelessness, Andropov replaced him with Sergei Kondrashev, who had previously run operations in East Berlin. "With your experience in counterintelligence you understand our problems and you know the limits," Andropov told him. "We must make progress in human rights—we are doomed if we don't." Andropov was no liberal, but he understood that the CSCE could put pressure on the Central Committee's hardliners and help reformers create a domestic system that could survive without relying on Stalinist practices. When Kondrashev arrived in Geneva in mid-1974 with Andropov's instructions to seek a compromise agreement, he immediately acquired considerable influence. In the Soviet delegation, bitter arguments pitted him and Kovalev against Yuri Dubinin, who nominally led the Soviet efforts in Basket III and took a harder line than his colleagues. These disagreements echoed the ongoing battle in Moscow between Brezhnev's allies and their anti-détente opponents.[103]

For the time being, however, the Soviets refused to yield. Although they worried that the continued stalemate would damage the CSCE, their proposals merely reproduced the Blue Book's vague language. They suggested expanding cultural cooperation and "broadening ... the exchange of information," but offered no details on either subject.[104] Meanwhile, they rejected virtually every Western proposal. They insisted that some issues could only be discussed bilaterally, not at the CSCE. They protested attempts to interfere with their domestic affairs. They groused about Western radio stations, demanded that governments take responsibility for all broadcasts from their territory, and refused to countenance spontaneous contacts between individuals. In every case, they resolved to "eliminate the negative impact" of the West's "anti-socialist goals," as Czechoslovak officials put it.[105]

Because the Western delegations kept pressing their unreasonable demands, the Soviets again tried to circumvent them. Brezhnev complained to Nixon—and to the new Western European leaders Valéry Giscard d'Estaing, Helmut Schmidt, and Harold Wilson—that the conference was "being bogged down in trivia."[106] The Dutch delegation's bold demands on cultural exchange particularly irritated him. "What kind of proposal is it if they want to arrogate to themselves the right to open theaters in the Soviet Union without any control by the Soviet administration?" he asked Kissinger in March 1974. "It's just wrong to have ideas like that."[107] If the impasse in Basket III wrecked the negotiations, the general secretary warned, "there will be, instead of security, insecurity." The Western Europeans had to stop trying to interfere in the USSR's internal affairs, or else the high Cold War would return, along with all the dangers of superpower conflict.[108]

Kissinger tried to reassure Brezhnev and endeavored to rein in the Western Europeans' enthusiasm for the "meaningless" third basket. He dismissed the notion that freer movement threatened the USSR's stability. "I don't think the Soviet system will be changed by the opening of a Dutch cabaret in Moscow," he told Brezhnev.[109] Because the Western Europeans' "pet schemes" would go nowhere, the allies ought to reassess their approach, he told Hans-Dietrich Genscher. They would only stand a chance of negotiating an acceptable compromise if they drew up a definitive list of their minimum requirements and shared it with the East, instead of persisting with their seemingly unlimited array of demands.[110] At a NATO meeting in Ottawa, Kissinger rebuked the assembled foreign ministers for provoking the Soviets. Borrowing one of Brezhnev's arguments, he warned that if the conference collapsed in a stalemate, it might irreparably damage East-West relations.[111]

Kissinger's review exercise elicited a barrage of allied criticism. Some Western officials saw value in privately examining their Basket III goals, but most decided that the risks outweighed the benefits.[112] In London, Crispin Tickell warned that any list would almost certainly leak to the Soviets. In that case, Kissinger's proposal would result in "first the abandonment of all requirements not included in the list; and secondly failure to achieve even our minimum requirements (as the Russians would certainly regard these as the starting rather than the ending point for subsequent negotiation)."[113] The other allies likewise insisted on standing firm.[114] "[W]e ought to be more difficult, not to be giving in," argued Dutch foreign minister Max van der Stoel.[115] When Sherer, operating on instructions from Washington, tried to persuade the Western Europeans to drop their objections, his "unreasonable and imprudent" proposal met with a "bitter and resentful" response.[116] The American effort was "astonishingly tactless," a British diplomat in Geneva fumed. It disregarded Western European views and demonstrated "no understanding at all of the character of the CSCE."[117]

By early autumn, Kissinger's review exercise was dead. His advisors grumbled that the Western Europeans refused to cooperate, but they could not bring them around. The more that the United States pressed them to act, "the more their suspicions are aroused," assistant secretary of state Arthur Hartman noted.[118] Kissinger's defeat galvanized Western resolve.[119] No allied official expected the CSCE to change the communist system immediately, but the conference had the power to legitimize certain principles, as the Soviets themselves understood. A robust third basket would create "a *locus standi* for those, both within the socialist countries and outside them, who are trying to promote a more normal flow" of information and ideas into and out of the Soviet bloc, argued Britain's ambassador in Moscow, Sir Terence Garvey. After the CSCE, the communist authorities would find it increasingly difficult to persuade their citizens to accept heavy-handed restrictions on their freedoms. Over time, the combination of internal and external pressure could open up the bloc's governments and societies.[120]

In the second half of 1974, Kissinger changed his mind about Basket III. Détente's critics in the United States were growing more vocal and gaining political support, as the passage of the Jackson-Vanik amendment at the end of the year attested.[121] The following spring, as South Vietnamese forces crumbled in the face of a fresh North Vietnamese offensive, the backlash gathered strength. Some prominent Republicans, including former California governor Ronald Reagan and Nixon's Secretary of Defense Melvin Laird, criticized the Ford administration for being soft on the USSR.[122] Meanwhile, the American Jewish Committee urged a tougher stance at the CSCE, as did the *Washington Post* and *New York Times*.[123] Although Kissinger still questioned the value of the conference, he decided that the tide of domestic opinion forced the administration to change course. "No more concessions to the Soviet Union," Kissinger told Ford. "If they want a conference, let them concede."[124] Beginning in late 1974, the US delegation in Geneva received instructions to support the Western Europeans more vigorously on freer movement.[125]

The Soviets and their allies reluctantly gave way. Boris Ponomarev protested that Western governments were "blackmail[ing] us and abus[ing] our honest desire for good results" to satisfy their demands on freer movement. The East German Politburo similarly objected to attempts to "interfer[e] in the internal affairs of states."[126] Nonetheless, the Eastern allies started to show unprecedented flexibility on nearly every subject in the third basket, accepting some proposals that they had dismissed only a few months before. By the end of 1974, the delegates had finalized texts on family reunification, the marriage of citizens to foreign nationals, and the circulation of written information. In nearly every case, the results reflected Western demands. "The promise of Western achievement contained in the Helsinki Final Recommendations is being realized," Canadian ambassador Thomas Delworth reported.[127]

By early 1975, only a few sticking points remained. The Soviets continued to rebuff Western proposals on travel, radio and television broadcasts, journalists' working conditions, and the opening of foreign reading rooms. Brezhnev reassured his fellow Warsaw Pact leaders that "the excessive and obnoxious demands of some Western countries have been repelled," but his assessment proved premature.[128] In Geneva, Anatoly Kovalev found himself caught between competing demands. His superiors in Moscow expected him to make rapid progress, but insisted that he concede as little as possible.[129] In search of a solution, the Soviets tried to persuade their Western peers to set a firm date for the high-level meeting that would formally conclude the CSCE. They hoped that, as the date approached, they could "force a showdown" and compel the West "to sacrifice essential objectives" to meet the deadline, British ambassador Toby Hildyard wrote. When the Western delegates rejected the gambit, an ill-tempered Kovalev began to run out of options.[130]

The turning point came in the middle of May. After heated deliberations, the Western allies presented a "global package" of demands, explaining that they would withdraw the offer unless every item on the list were accepted.[131] Under pressure to wrap up the negotiations, the Soviets grumbled but did not reject the ultimatum. Kovalev concluded that the USSR could hold out no longer. He understood that the decision might harm his career, but saw no alternative to accepting the West's demands. His wife told him that it was his duty to do so. When he explained his reasoning to the Soviet delegation, Dubinin and Kondrashev objected, so Kovalev sent his recommendations to Moscow in his own name, rather than in the name of the whole delegation. Within hours, he received the authorization to proceed.[132] Dropping the pretense that he would wait as long as necessary to get a satisfactory deal, Kovalev told a few Western ambassadors that his government had resolved to "make a great effort to finish the conference," and urged them to move as quickly as possible.[133]

Eschewing the formal negotiating sessions in order to save time, a small group of Soviet and Western diplomats began to work out the final text of Basket III, sidelining both the Eastern Europeans and the neutrals. Kovalev, Dubinin, and Kondrashev sat at one end of a hallway in the ILO building, their Western counterparts sat at the other, and British diplomat Michael Alexander shuttled the offers and counteroffers back and forth. The Soviets bowed to nearly every Western proposal. When the Eastern Europeans read what their Soviet colleagues had negotiated on their behalf, they could not disguise their astonishment.[134] The GDR's Siegfried Bock fumed that the Soviets could not appreciate that the freer movement of information posed an intolerable threat to East Germany, whose citizens were already bombarded by West German television and radio broadcasts. Among the USSR's allies, however, he stood alone. Despite his reservations, he soon relented because he refused to be held solely responsible for thwarting the CSCE.[135]

The highest levels of the Soviet government approved all of the concessions. Brezhnev and Gromyko accepted them because they wanted to bring the CSCE to an end. They also believed that the preamble to Basket III gave the USSR "multiple safeguards of its interests," in Kovalev's phrase. It would protect the Soviets and their allies against unwelcome outside interference and empower them to implement the basket's provisions as they saw fit.[136] A number of senior Soviet officials had also concluded that the USSR's longstanding restrictions on information and travel had become unsustainable. The country had to shake up its "stuffy atmosphere" and open itself to the outside world, as Kovalev put it in his memoirs.[137] Even Andropov, who publicly denounced Western attempts at "ideological sabotage," shared this view. He worried that Soviet society would not be prepared to handle greater freedoms for at least another decade, but believed that it had little choice but to accept them. When Kovalev asked him to approve concessions to Western demands, he agreed. "The USSR can no longer be governed as in Stalin's time," he told Kondrashev.[138]

The final text of Basket III reflected some of the West's most ambitious goals. The signatories agreed to make it easier for citizens to travel internationally and—when their family members already lived abroad—to emigrate. They pledged to disseminate foreign newspapers, magazines, books, and films more widely. They endorsed international radio broadcasts. They undertook to grant foreign journalists multiple-entry visas, to remove restrictions on their travel within their host countries, and to make it easier for them to send their reports and recordings home. And they promised to encourage direct contacts between artists, performers, and others in the field of culture. None of these measures heralded a revolution in East-West relations. None would change the relationship between the citizen and the state in the Soviet bloc overnight. Taken together, however, they offered a vision of greater intellectual openness, greater individual autonomy, and greater international transparency.[139]

V

A commitment to openness likewise animated the West's proposals on military affairs. In 1972, when the Americans and Soviets decided to keep disarmament off the CSCE agenda and conduct MBFR negotiations separately, the Western allies accepted the arrangement. Nonetheless, they argued that the security conference—if it hoped to be worthy of the name—still had to discuss the military balance in Europe. They took up a proposal for "confidence-building measures" (CBMs), which had emerged from NATO's 1969 brainstorming exercise. Sometimes called "stabilizing measures" or "collateral constraints," CBMs would require participants to give each other advance notification of military exercises and movements, and to invite foreign officers to observe those exercises. They proposed to make the East's defense efforts more visible to the West, and vice versa.[140]

The measures' main purpose was political, not military. By clarifying the purpose of troop maneuvers, they would "reduc[e] ambiguities about military activities" and prevent routine exercises—whose intent might otherwise be opaque—from being interpreted as preparations for an invasion. Each side would gain insight into the other's capabilities, officers from opposing sides would come to understand each other, and governments that might otherwise worry about their neighbors' intentions would be reassured. In this way, CBMs would help avert the "outbreak of war through surprise or error," Crispin Tickell explained to a group of Soviet officials in 1972. They would also establish a precedent for pan-European restraints on conventional military activities. NATO's proposal would not instantly transform the military situation in Europe, but it might reduce mistrust over time. In the most optimistic interpretation, CBMs might even pioneer a new concept of security in which openness took the place of secrecy. They had much in common with the West's ideas of freer movement in the third basket, but one could also trace their intellectual lineage to American President Dwight Eisenhower's 1955 Open Skies idea.[141]

In a roundabout way, CBMs also promised to strengthen the Western alliance and make life more difficult for the Soviets. Because army maneuvers often served a diplomatic purpose, such as sending a warning or demonstrating resolve, Western officials wanted to constrain the USSR from pressuring other states—especially its own allies—in this way. In this respect, CBMs would complement the Western attempt to subvert the Brezhnev Doctrine. They would also test the sincerity of Moscow's vociferous commitment to arms control. If the Soviets rejected the measures, Western voters would see that the Soviet bloc remained untrustworthy and that security in Europe still depended on the balance of military power. Each of these points would bolster public support for NATO and relieve the pressure to cut defense spending.[142]

The Soviets responded ambivalently. At a meeting of Warsaw Pact leaders in January 1972, Brezhnev raised the possibility of discussing "military détente" at the CSCE. Because the rival alliances did not yet trust each other enough to take ambitious steps toward disarmament, he suggested that they begin with more modest measures that resembled the West's CBM ideas, including restrictions on military exercises near national frontiers. At the same time, however, he and other Soviet officials worried that discussing military problems at the CSCE would distract participants from their top priority, the declaration on the inviolability of borders. Moreover, hardliners in the Central Committee questioned the wisdom of attempting to build trust with the imperialists, and members of the general staff feared that exposing the country's military secrets would compromise its security. In any case, the conference itself "was the biggest confidence-building measure imaginable," Soviet diplomat E. F. Rogov told the British, so it made little sense to overburden its agenda with contentious military issues. Soviet envoys repeated this argument in other Western capitals.[143]

Although most of the Eastern Europeans endorsed the Soviets' logic, the Romanians greeted the CBM idea enthusiastically. Above all, they hoped to blunt Moscow's ability to intimidate its allies with demonstrations of military force. They also proposed that the CSCE negotiate an agreement on withdrawing all foreign troops from Europe, including Soviet forces stationed in Eastern Europe. If the conference wanted to make a real difference to European security, it had to take bold measures, Romanian foreign minister George Macovescu told Kovalev. Kovalev responded that the USSR would welcome the withdrawal of American and Canadian forces from Europe, but said nothing about the Red Army. If the Romanians thought that the conference could make rapid progress on the subject, however, they were "naïve." The Soviets thus faced the double challenge of resisting Western pressure for CBMs and tamping down their own ally's enthusiasm.[144]

During the preparatory talks, the Eastern allies initially refused to consider CBMs. In order to keep the negotiations moving and to preserve their professed commitment to disarmament, however, they soon reconsidered their position. The USSR might agree to add some limited measures to the conference agenda if the Western powers insisted, Andrei Gromyko told the Politburo.[145] By early 1973, the Soviets were showing greater flexibility in Helsinki. They offered to discuss the exchange of observers and the advance notification of military maneuvers, so long as participation remained strictly voluntary. They also stipulated that states should notify only their immediate neighbors, not every CSCE participant, and exchange observers by invitation only, not as a matter of course. On the basis of these concessions, the delegates in Helsinki agreed to tackle maneuvers and military observers at the CSCE, and—contrary to Romanian protests—reaffirmed their original decision to confine disarmament talks to the MBFR negotiations.[146]

The question of movements proved more vexing. In Helsinki, many of the Western allies insisted that governments should notify each other when their troops traveled from place to place. This measure would encompass a much wider range of activities than military exercises alone, and would provide a much clearer picture of each country's forces. The Soviets rejected it. Red Army units moved around Russia so frequently that it would create an intolerable bureaucratic burden, they argued. Besides, the USSR had already made a major concession in agreeing to discuss CBMs at all, Soviet diplomat Yuli Vorontsov told assistant secretary of state Walt Stoessel. Now it was the West's turn to show some flexibility.[147]

Once again, Kissinger took the Soviets' side. "Our allies are getting totally obnoxious," he told Stoessel. The United States had no need for Soviet reports on military movements, he argued, because American reconnaissance satellites could already detect the redeployment of large units around the country. Discussing the subject at the CSCE would also cause unnecessary complications by encroaching on MBFR's remit. For all of these reasons, Kissinger told Dobrynin, the American government would work with the USSR to limit CBMs to the notification of maneuvers and the exchange of observers.[148]

Under instructions from Washington, George Vest initially supported Western demands on movements at the MPT. When the Soviets demurred—as agreed in advance—he told the Western Europeans that the time had come to seek a compromise. The ensuing standoff pitted the American and Soviet delegations, who wanted to set movements aside, against the Dutch and Romanians, who refused to drop them. Eventually, the participants dodged the problem by agreeing on a watered-down formula that called for "study[ing] the question of prior notification of major military movements" at the CSCE. With the exception of the Dutch, who regarded the Blue Book's language on CBMs as insufficient, most of the participants left Helsinki satisfied that they had achieved their main goals. As with the other subjects on the CSCE's agenda, however, the real fights still lay ahead.[149]

When the participants assembled in Geneva for Stage II, they debated whether CBMs would strengthen international security or damage it. Prior notification would "greatly reduce the opportunities for misunderstanding and suspicion," the British delegation argued, and thereby reduce the risk of war. Nevertheless, some senior Soviet bloc officials refused to see CBMs as anything other than a Western ruse. In Moscow, defense minister Andrei Grechko insisted that informing Western governments of army maneuvers in the Soviet heartland would compromise national security. "They will know everything about us," he told the Politburo. At a cocktail party in Geneva, Lev Mendelevich accused the West of proposing CBMs for "intelligence rather than confidence-building objectives." He hinted that China might also take advantage of the measures to threaten the USSR. Revealing the Red Army's activities "would enable certain other states to exploit weaknesses in the Soviet deployment of troops," he told a British diplomat. Some Polish officials reached similar conclusions.[150]

The participants also quarreled over the scope of the confidence building measures. Any deal on the notification of maneuvers had to address a number of technical details: How far in advance should participants give notice? How many soldiers had to be involved for an exercise to require notification? Should exercises anywhere in Europe—and anywhere in the USSR—be included, or only those in a limited area? On each of these points, the Soviets and their allies complained that Western proposals went too far. They prescribed too much advance notice, required notification for absurdly small groups of soldiers, and encompassed too much Soviet territory.

The USSR would never acquiesce in these "completely unacceptable" demands, Gromyko told Max van der Stoel. Nor would it or its allies agree to the notification of troop movements.[151]

Soviet leaders appealed for American help to chip away at NATO's position. By contrast with the USSR's military establishment, Brezhnev and Gromyko insisted that they could accept CBMs in principle, not least because American reconnaissance satellites could track Red Army forces with or without Soviet consent. But the Western proposals in Geneva were "nothing short of ridiculous," Gromyko told Kissinger. These "humiliating demands," as Brezhnev called them, required too much information, expected the USSR to cooperate in revealing its own military secrets, and imposed an impossible administrative burden. The country would not give three months' advance notice of every maneuver, nor would it reveal its activities across the whole of European Russia. "When questions regarding our territory to the Urals are raised, then European security is not really the subject," Brezhnev said. Besides, sending out notifications every time a Soviet division participated in maneuvers or moved from one place to another would generate mountains of paper but do nothing for security. Unless the Western Europeans backed down, the discussion of CBMs would raise tensions, not lower them, he warned.[152]

Moscow's initiative provoked another fight among the Western allies. "The trouble is that you have a bunch of bureaucrats in Geneva who are trying to impress each other with their toughness," Kissinger told Gromyko. He proposed to end "this sterile debate" by working out a backchannel deal and presenting it in Geneva as a fait accompli.[153] Over the months that followed, the American government pressured its allies to relax their demands, arguing that CBMs held only minor importance and should not obstruct a final agreement. It also proposed to drop the notification of movements lest the CSCE encroach on the ongoing MBFR negotiations. The Western Europeans rejected this logic. A meaningless agreement on CBMs would mar the credibility of the whole conference, the West Germans insisted. The British refused to abandon the notification of movements prematurely because it could serve as a bargaining chip later in the negotiations.[154]

As this trans-Atlantic dispute smoldered, the talks remained deadlocked through most of 1974. The delegates reached an agreement on the exchange of observers—the least controversial of all the measures—but they disagreed about everything else. Early the following year, however, the Western allies stopped insisting on the notification of movements. In response to hints from Kovalev and Mendelevich, they also agreed to state explicitly that all CBMs would be strictly voluntary. The Romanians objected strenuously, preferring language that implied a stronger commitment, but they persuaded no one. Although the voluntary principle reassured the Soviets, it hardly affected the substance of the agreement, since no Western diplomat expected Moscow to undertake legal obligations in this area.[155]

In turn, the Soviets relented on the notification of maneuvers. For months, Kovalev and Mendelevich had faithfully carried out Moscow's instructions in Geneva, but they believed those instructions were too restrictive. They therefore lobbied the Soviet Ministry of Defense, which had taken an uncompromising position on CBMs, to show more flexibility. Because the Soviet delegation had not been authorized to make any concessions on the notification of maneuvers, it had "no cartridges in [its] bandoliers," Kovalev told Grechko. "Would you send soldiers into battle without ammunition?" He suggested that the USSR had the opportunity to strike an advantageous bargain. If it agreed to notify Western governments of exercises held in a strip of territory along its western frontier, they would inform the USSR of exercises held anywhere in their own countries. Finally, Grechko consented, as did Brezhnev and the Politburo. They granted the Soviet delegation considerable latitude to negotiate an agreement on maneuver notification.[156]

After months of haggling, the two sides began to close on a deal. The Soviets, who had previously offered to inform only neighboring states of military exercises, now agreed to notify every participant. Their proposal included maneuvers conducted in a 50-kilometer strip of territory from their western border, but then they raised that figure to 100 kilometers. The Western delegations reciprocated. Instead of demanding the notification of maneuvers anywhere in Soviet Russia, they called for notification in the territory stretching 500 kilometers from the USSR's western border. The two sides also moderated their proposals on the size of units involved and the days of advance notice required.[157]

Impatient to accelerate the process, Kissinger agreed to settle the parameters directly with Gromyko. During the first half of 1975, the talks unfolded between the two men face-to-face, via the backchannel, and between Kovalev and Sherer in Geneva. In June 1975, they converged on 18 days' advance notice for exercises involving at least 30,000 men anywhere in Europe, including a 250-kilometer band of Soviet territory.[158] When Sherer informed the Western Europeans, most expressed outrage that the Americans had undercut them. Hans-Dietrich Genscher, for example, protested that the Soviets would go further—particularly on the depth of the notification zone—if only they were pushed harder. He was right. The Politburo had authorized the Soviet delegation to offer more generous terms if required, but Kovalev did not have to retreat to his final fallback position. Working at a feverish pace, the neutrals brokered a deal that was slightly tougher than the US-Soviet bargain but less demanding than what the Politburo had approved. The participants agreed to 21 days, 25,000 men, and 250 kilometers.[159]

The exact parameters mattered less than the underlying principles. A NATO report emphasized that CBMs had little military value, did nothing to curtail military activities, and added nothing to military intelligence. Politically speaking, however, they represented a major victory for the West—and a significant innovation in international security. The measures would lower "the huge barriers of secrecy within which the Russians, and above all the Soviet State, have always operated," Toby Hildyard pointed out. By requiring every participant to make its military activities more transparent, they would ease mutual suspicion and reduce the danger of a war triggered by misperception or miscalculation. They rejected the notion that stability depended on the military equilibrium of opposing armies. Instead, they affirmed that security in Europe had become a collective enterprise, in which Eastern and Western states operated as partners, not rivals. In time, if CBMs succeeded, the logic of openness and mutual understanding might replace the logic of secrecy and the balance of power.[160]

VI

As the diplomats in Geneva drafted the Final Act's three baskets, they also had to tackle crucial questions about the status of the agreement and how to implement it. Should the agreement be binding under international law? Should the participants continue their work after the Final Act had been drafted? How should the agreement be signed, and with how much fanfare? From one angle, these were simply matters of form and organization. From a different perspective, however, they were matters of substance, because they carried enormous consequences for the CSCE's ultimate significance.

To answer these questions, the participants relied on conjecture. They had to make judgments about whether the negotiations were moving in their favor, and whether they were likely to achieve their objectives in Helsinki and Geneva. They also had to predict how citizens in the East and West would receive the Final Act, and how the agreement might shape international affairs—whether to their own benefit, or that of their adversaries. Their positions evolved as the negotiations unfolded, but even as the Final Act took shape their views were not entirely consistent. In some respects, the Soviets and Eastern Europeans hailed the agreement as a victory for their cause. In others, however, they worried about its consequences and tried to limit them. The same held true in the West. This pattern illustrated the uncertainty inherent in trying to foresee the consequences of an enterprise as complex as the CSCE, and the inescapable importance of good judgment in the conduct of statecraft.

The Western allies never wanted the CSCE to produce a legally binding treaty. Although their reasons varied, they agreed that a treaty would cause serious problems but offer few compensating benefits. For fear of provoking a domestic backlash or damaging the cause of reunification, the West Germans refused to countenance anything that might imply that the German Question had been definitively settled.[161] The Nixon and Ford administrations reasoned that a treaty—and the inevitably fractious process of Senate ratification—would encourage the delusion that Europe's problems had all been solved and feed fresh demands for troop withdrawals.[162] To ensure that a treaty did not contradict existing domestic legislation, the Western allies would have to insert caveats and exceptions. These in turn would help the Soviets escape from meaningful commitments, British diplomats argued.[163] In any event, Europe's fundamental problems were political, not legal. If participants sincerely wanted to solve them, they only had to make political commitments and follow through.[164]

When the USSR and its allies launched their campaign for the security conference in the 1960s, they took the opposite view. In the wake of the Budapest appeal, the Soviet foreign ministry argued that conference's final agreement "should be as binding as possible" under international law so as to maximize its impact. The Poles and East Germans, who wanted the conference to ratify their frontiers, shared this objective. Likewise, the Romanians, who feared Soviet coercion, hoped that a binding agreement might protect them in a dispute with their more powerful neighbor.[165] As détente gathered strength in the early 1970s, Moscow's ambitions grew apace. The CSCE's participants should do more than sign a treaty, the Soviets argued: they should incorporate its results into their domestic legislation. "We should not be content with a resolution of no binding force, which would have purely propaganda value," Gromyko told the British ambassador in Moscow.[166]

Once the negotiations started, however, this enthusiasm evaporated. In his memoirs, Kovalev suggests that Soviet leaders reevaluated their position because they feared that the Bundestag and the US Senate would balk at ratifying a treaty, but the success of the Moscow and SALT treaties casts doubt on this reasoning. Western progress in Basket III offers a more likely explanation. Giving its provisions the force of international law would increase foreign criticism of the USSR's domestic practices and cause unnecessary complications for the government's efforts to preserve order. Whatever the reason, by 1974 the USSR and its allies had come around to the Western point of view. The diplomats in Geneva agreed that the CSCE's results would only be politically binding.[167] For this reason, they called the fruit of their work the "Final Act." The term, borrowed from the Congress of Vienna, suggested a major diplomatic agreement but lacked a treaty's legal implications.[168]

The participants also had to decide whether to continue their discussions after the Final Act had been drafted. In 1969, Gromyko told the Politburo that the security conference should establish a new, permanent organization dedicated to peace in Europe. This body would implement the CSCE's decisions, organize subsequent meetings, and provide a forum for discussing mutual problems. The USSR could use this platform to defend the Peace Program and champion disarmament.[169] Some Western officials entertained a similar idea, though their goals differed from Gromyko's. Canadian diplomats suggested that a standing commission on European security would pressure the Soviets to follow through on the Final Act. If they reneged, Western governments could use the commission to agitate against Soviet policy and persuade their own citizens that Moscow bore the blame for prolonging the Cold War. The British and French picked up this idea. By subjecting participants' behavior to international scrutiny, the commission might deter the USSR from bullying its allies, and further constrain the Brezhnev Doctrine. "I wonder if to a certain extent this wouldn't be a way to make acts of force and brutality more difficult," Pompidou told Brandt.[170]

This initial surge of interest eventually gave way to skepticism. In Eastern and Western capitals alike, officials concluded that a permanent body presented unacceptable risks. The Americans feared that their citizens might regard a new institution as a substitute for NATO and lose interest in sustaining the alliance. Pompidou's enthusiasm notwithstanding, French diplomats worried about giving the USSR a tool for interfering in Western European affairs. If the European Community tried to develop a common defense policy, for instance, the Soviets could use the body to mobilize public opinion against the endeavor.[171] In much the same way, Eastern officials concluded that a permanent organization would expose them to intolerable pressure. Western governments might use it to press unacceptable demands on "so-called humanitarian issues," as a Polish report put it. In Helsinki and Geneva, the Soviets found themselves "cornered, on the defensive, and perpetually insulted," and had little desire to repeat this experience indefinitely, a Romanian diplomat confided to a British colleague.[172] This symmetry of Eastern and Western anxieties suggested that the CSCE's long-term consequences remained unclear. Each side hoped that this ambitious diplomatic experiment would advance its goals, but also strove to contain its dangers.

Despite these concerns, none of the participants wanted to let the CSCE fizzle out. By late 1973, the Western allies had decided that, instead of establishing a new organization with a headquarters and secretariat, the CSCE's participants should simply organize ad hoc meetings to monitor compliance with the Final Act. This follow-up mechanism would provide the benefits of a permanent institution but mitigate the risks. If the process turned sour, the West could simply put off the next meeting. If it worked, however, it would help the West "keep Soviet noses to the abrasive grindstone" of living up to their promises, as Tom Delworth put it.[173] The Soviets also decided that periodic meetings would keep multilateral détente alive, but shield them from the most unpleasant aspects of a permanent body.[174] East and West had reached the same conclusion, but expected different results. In early 1975, the delegations in Geneva agreed to hold the first follow-up meeting in Belgrade in 1977, on the assumption that the two-year interval would provide enough time to assess how well each country was implementing the Final Act.[175]

Because the Final Act entailed only a political commitment, not a legal one, much of its force would depend on how it was unveiled to the world. On this point, as on many others, ceremony and symbolism had real consequences. Even before the preparatory talks, the Soviets argued that the CSCE should culminate in a grand summit meeting—known as Stage III—where all thirty-five leaders would sign the agreement before the eyes of the world. By establishing shared principles of legitimacy and demonstrating that the Western powers accepted the USSR and its allies as their equals, the meeting would put a capstone on Brezhnev's Peace Program, strengthen the general secretary's position at home, and cement his legacy. The statesmen who brought the CSCE to fruition "deserve attention and will go down in history," Brezhnev told Erich Honecker, no doubt with himself in mind.[176]

The USSR's desire for a summit gave the Western delegations leverage. They told the Soviets that the format of the CSCE's concluding meeting depended on the negotiations' results. Only an outstanding agreement could justify a summit. Anything less would be signed by the countries' foreign ministers, which Brezhnev would almost certainly regard as a failure. The decision about the level of Stage III was the West's "last trump card," a Canadian diplomat wrote. To maximize the pressure on the USSR, "this card [must] not be played prematurely by any of the allies."[177]

Many of the allies worried that someone would break ranks. British and Italian officials speculated that the Americans might unilaterally agree to a summit meeting, regardless of where matters stood in Geneva, in order to curry Soviet favor on other matters. The Americans and Canadians entertained similar concerns about Giscard, who seemed to crave international attention more than Pompidou had.[178] Throughout 1974, Western officials scrutinized the communiqués of US-Soviet and Franco-Soviet meetings for signs of betrayal, and despaired that the slow pace in Geneva would never produce an agreement worthy of a summit. Nonetheless, their united front held. Nixon, Ford, and Giscard all told the Soviets that they would participate in a CSCE summit, but only if the negotiations' results proved satisfactory. By spring 1975, nearly all the Western allies had accepted the summit in principle, but they refused to fix its date until all the major issues at Stage II had been solved.[179]

In early summer, as the diplomats in Geneva surmounted the last obstacles, they wondered if the end was in sight. If all went well, Stage III might convene as early as June or July. Suddenly, a problem emerged from an unexpected direction and threatened the CSCE's fragile optimism. The Maltese, acting on orders from Prime Minister Dom Mintoff, declared that they would refuse to accept any final agreement unless the conference endorsed their proposals for the Final Act's declaration on Mediterranean security. In particular, Mintoff called for a new federation of European and Arab states as a counterweight to the superpowers and demanded that all naval fleets be withdrawn from the Mediterranean. Since the negotiations began, most of the participants had regarded the declaration as a distraction from the real work of drafting the three baskets. Now, however, it occupied the center of their attention. By issuing this last-minute ultimatum, Malta took the conference hostage.[180]

Neither the proposal nor the tactics were new, but they flummoxed everyone. In the closing days of the preparatory talks, Mintoff had used a similar gambit. He coerced the other participants into inviting representatives from the Mediterranean's littoral states to address the conference about their security concerns.[181] In July 1975, the familiar feelings of irritation at Mintoff boiled over into anger.[182] Finland's ambassador nearly came to blows with his Maltese counterpart. Kovalev vowed to go Malta and dismantle the island stone by stone. Kissinger joked about assassinating "Mintoff the Terrible." More seriously, Gromyko proposed to circumvent the problem by abolishing the requirement that all decisions be taken by consensus, but the other delegations balked at changing the CSCE's rules. With quiet support from the Italians and French, who had originally championed the Mediterranean declaration, Mintoff ignored his counterparts' curses and refused to take their calls. Desperate to end the negotiations, the other delegations accepted a clause about reducing their armed forces in the Mediterranean. A banner headline in the *Malta News* rejoiced: "Europe bows to Mintoff."[183]

Although the prime minister's opponents saw his antics as an infuriating side-show, the episode said something important about why the CSCE mattered. Had the participants ignored Mintoff and proceeded to the summit without him, as Gromyko recommended, they would have sent a clear message about the hierarchy of power: some states mattered, but others did not. No one could deny the military, economic, and demographic differences between the participants, especially since Malta had fewer people than many European cities. Since the CSCE's inception, however, its influence depended in part on its universality. It proposed to establish certain principles that all states—large and small, powerful and weak—had accepted, and by which they would all be bound. Scrapping the rule of consensus would have undermined the CSCE's implicit claim that international affairs in Europe were governed as much by rules—and the concept of legitimacy that emerged from those rules—as by power. Mintoff grasped this logic and exploited it to the hilt.

With the Maltese contretemps behind them, and after satisfying some last-minute Turkish demands on CBMs, the diplomats in Geneva adopted the Final Act in the early hours of July 19. "In an atmosphere of rather artificial bonhomie and general exhaustion," the negotiations came to a sudden end, with none of "the gestures of friendship or the plethora of congratulatory speeches which we had all expected," Toby Hildyard reported. The CSCE's concluding summit would open on July 30, giving the leaders of the participating states only a few days to decide whether to travel to Helsinki to sign the Final Act.[184]

In many capitals, the question prompted little debate. The negotiations had ended successfully, and there was no time for second thoughts. In a few places, however, influential figures railed against the Final Act. Western critics argued that the agreement endorsed Soviet tyranny and permanently divided Europe. Groups representing Americans of Central and Eastern European descent expressed their "disappointment" to Gerald Ford and compared his prospective trip to Helsinki to Franklin D. Roosevelt's alleged betrayal of Eastern Europe at Yalta.[185] In a rare show of unanimity, the *New York Times* and *Wall Street Journal* both urged the president not to go.[186] Ronald Reagan, who was preparing to contest the Republican presidential nomination the following year, said, "I am against it, and I think all Americans should be against it."[187] In the West German Bundestag, the opposition parties demanded that Helmut Schmidt stay home. Christian Social Union leader Franz Josef Strauss denounced the Final Act as a latter-day Munich Agreement. "You have cleared the way for the implementation of the Soviet Union's imperial strategic goals," he said.[188]

These criticisms failed to dissuade Ford. In the months since assuming the presidency, he had expressed no strong views on the CSCE and generally deferred to Kissinger's judgment. Ford reassured himself—and his critics—that the Final Act entailed no legal commitments, recognized neither the Soviet annexation of the Baltic states nor Soviet influence in Eastern Europe, and required the United States to change none of its practices. Besides, it might help Moscow's allies reassert their independence. "Why did the East Europeans want CSCE? To keep the Soviet Union off their backs," he told Kissinger. If the agreement threatened no American interests, there was no reason not to sign it.[189]

West German leaders made a more optimistic case. The Final Act did nothing to foreclose the possibility of German reunification, Hans-Dietrich Genscher told the Bundestag, nor did it entrench Soviet power. But by affirming the possibility of territorial change and holding out the prospect of better lives for millions of Europeans, however, the agreement reflected "our ideals and our image of man as a free individual." Helmut Schmidt echoed these arguments. After decades of confrontation, the CSCE had established a common set of principles that bridged the Cold War divide for the first time. These principles did not guarantee progress, but progress would be impossible without them. For West Germany, the alternative was not a better deal, but isolation. On the strength of these claims—and the governing coalition's majority—the Bundestag easily defeated the opposition motion.[190]

In the East, the Final Act's critics voiced their concerns behind closed doors, but their arguments mirrored those heard in the West. Conservatives in Moscow insisted that the Soviet delegation had given away too much in exchange for too little. Because the Western powers had long since recognized Europe's postwar borders and the GDR's existence de facto, the USSR had gained nothing of value from the negotiations. On the other hand, the CSCE gave the West new opportunities to meddle in the country's internal affairs. The Final Act's provisions on human contacts and the freer movement of information contradicted the core principles of communist ideology, argued the Politburo's chief ideologue, Mikhail Suslov. He lashed out at the head of the Soviet delegation for accepting them. "For the sake of the pan-European conference's success, Kovalev is ready to conclude an anti-Comintern Pact," he said. Other members of the Central Committee, including Sergei Trapeznikov, Pyotr Demichev, and Boris Ponomarev, shared Suslov's antagonism to these Western values and his low opinion of the CSCE.[191]

Whatever the hardliners' reservations, they stood little chance of dissuading Brezhnev or Gromyko. The two men understood the West's intentions in Basket III, but concluded that nothing in the Final Act could force the Kremlin to alter its policies. By affirming the principle of sovereignty, the agreement empowered the Soviet government to ignore whatever provisions it found unhelpful. "We are masters in our own house," Gromyko told the Politburo. Nixon and Kissinger had also offered their personal assurances that the United States would not try to change the Soviet system or embarrass its leaders.[192]

Besides, the general secretary regarded the Final Act as both a political and a personal victory. Only a few years before, the Berlin crisis had brought Europe to the brink of war, he told Edward Gierek, but now the CSCE had put peace on a secure footing. The summit also promised to elevate Brezhnev to the pantheon of great statesmen. "If Helsinki is held, then I can die," he told a senior diplomat. The influence of reformist officials—including Kovalev, Mendelevich, and Chernyaev—reinforced his commitment. Their motives differed from his, but they too believed in the conference's historic potential. If the Final Act could coax the USSR to abandon "Suslov's ideological orthodoxy [and] the 'besieged fortress' philosophy," as diplomat Yuri Kashlev put it, it might give rise to a more humane, democratic, and sustainable kind of socialism.[193]

When the Final Act came before the Politburo in late July, Suslov did not attend the meeting. In a brief presentation, Kovalev emphasized that the Soviet delegation had fended off the West's most extreme demands, and it had made fewer concessions than the Politburo had authorized. More importantly, the Final Act had brought Brezhnev's Peace Program to its culmination. The general secretary took up this theme in his own remarks, describing the agreement as the final confirmation of the Second World War's results and a decisive step toward lasting peace. Brezhnev's colleagues followed suit. They congratulated him on his success and approved his trip to Helsinki. Even if they harbored reservations, they could hardly have overruled a general secretary who had invested years of effort in the CSCE and insisted on pressing ahead.[194]

The same considerations influenced the decisions of Moscow's allies. At a meeting of the East German Politburo in July 1975, for example, Stasi chief Erich Mielke and like-minded conservatives raised concerns about foreign interference, but Erich Honecker rebuffed them. He did not dare break with Moscow, nor would he miss the chance to attend the summit as the equal of Brezhnev, Ford, and Schmidt. The conference had once seemed so unlikely, but now had acquired almost unstoppable momentum. None of its participants dared to stand in its way and none wanted to be left out.[195]

VII

In agreeing to sign the Final Act at the highest level, each of the thirty-five participating governments took a calculated risk. Each wagered that the agreement would serve its interests and that its own interpretation of the text would prevail. Although the diplomats had reached consensus in Geneva, a gulf still yawned between the Eastern and Western concepts of security and peace. The negotiations on freer movement and confidence-building measures vividly illustrated these disagreements. According to the Western Europeans and their supporters in the State Department, peace demanded transparency and openness. Information and people had to flow freely across borders, mutual understanding had to grow, and states had to learn to trust each other. Enmeshing governments and citizens alike in webs of cultural, intellectual, and human ties would make it easier to preempt crises and settle disputes.

This logic embodied core Western values. In negotiating the Basket III and CBM texts, the Western Europeans projected the tenets of liberal democracy and European integration onto the continent as a whole, and elevated the dynamics of globalization—especially faster travel, easier communication, and wider transnational networks connecting private citizens—into a moral virtue. Their motives were both idealistic and self-serving. They wanted to improve the lives of average people whose families had been divided and horizons truncated by the Cold War, but they also hoped to weaken communism's hold on power. The CSCE allowed them to be good Europeans, good humanitarians, and good Cold Warriors all at once.

The Soviets and their allies rejected these ideas. In their view, international peace required stronger frontiers, not weaker ones. Exposing socialist governments to counterrevolution and hostile propaganda—by relaxing controls on information and travel, and by encouraging the spread of transnational networks—would exacerbate tensions instead of fostering understanding. In much the same way, senior officers assumed that revealing military secrets would make countries more vulnerable and, by extension, make war more likely. Peace could only prevail if every government felt secure against both foreign and domestic threats. Orthodox communists made universalist claims about the inevitable worldwide victory of their ideology, but they championed particularism at the CSCE. Each country had its own laws and customs that neighboring governments had to accept. Each had to show respect for its neighbors' sovereignty, not try to impose its allegedly transcendent values.

The clash between these two approaches to peace echoed the clash between the conservative and transformational strategies of détente. On both Basket III and CBMs, the Nixon and Ford administrations worked with the Kremlin to advance their shared vision and undermine that of the Western Europeans. The mixed results of these efforts demonstrated the limits of superpower influence. Eventually, the Ford administration reversed course, not because the president or his secretary of state had suddenly embraced the Western Europeans' logic, but because they worried about the growing backlash against détente in the United States. Domestic politics also shaped the Western Europeans' emphasis on humanitarian questions, since they wanted to give their citizens concrete evidence of détente's benefits.

The final texts on Basket III and CBMs hewed much closer to Western European goals than Soviet ones. They upheld the claims that security required openness and that transparency should trump secrecy. These principles were grounded in a liberal democratic understanding of human rights, but they also reflected Western assumptions about globalization, integration, and interdependence. Moreover, the Western allies crafted their demands to support their concepts of peace and legitimacy, and to attack the practices on which the communist regimes relied to preserve order. In Basket III, they did not argue for human rights in the abstract, but for a narrow set of concrete measures. They used the CSCE to define humanitarianism in a way that suited their interests and would advance their cause. To suggest that Basket III was synonymous with human rights misrepresents both its provisions and the strategy that shaped them.

The result gave the West a major victory. One British assessment judged that the allies' success in the third basket was so great that it would have "seemed inconceivable" just a few years earlier.[196] In retrospect, KGB officer Nikolai Leonov lamented that "the international community imposed its ideas about democracy on the Soviet Union, forcing it to take up a game for which it was not prepared."[197] Yet the CSCE operated by consensus, and the West had no power to compel the USSR to accept its ideas. The Soviets granted Western demands not because of force majeure, but because their delegation in Geneva occupied an untenable position, caught between Moscow's demands for progress on the one hand and Western tenacity and unity on the other. Besides, some reform-minded officials believed that the communist status quo had to change, and that the country had to open itself—in a carefully controlled way—to the world. The third basket reflected their ideas, too.[198]

When Soviet leaders authorized their delegation to accept the West's demands, they believed that they could mitigate the risks involved. During the negotiations, they secured multiple provisions that emphasized the voluntary nature of their obligations regarding freer movement and CBMs. They ensured that the Final Act would neither shackle its signatories under international law, nor create a permanent organization that might subject them to unrelenting scrutiny. They put their faith in the supremacy of sovereignty and believed that they alone would decide which of the Final Act's provisions to implement.[199]

This rationale entailed considerable dangers. Despite Polish and East German exhortations, the Eastern allies had not developed an offensive concept of cooperation or a suitable negotiating strategy. They could, for example, have countered Western calls for free emigration by demanding free immigration, which the Western allies could never have accepted and would have forced them to back down. Instead, they played defense. Perhaps for fear of delaying the negotiations even further, they "content[ed] themselves with inserting safeguards rather than attempting to recast [the] whole exercise in [the] spirit and terminology of state control," Delworth observed.[200]

The result was a lopsided agreement. The third basket required dramatic changes in the domestic practices of the USSR and its allies, but imposed few countervailing obligations on Western governments. Although Soviet ideas and propaganda had circulated freely in the West for decades, they had never won over a majority of Western citizens. In countries such as France, whatever allure communism had once enjoyed was waning by the mid-1970s, as epitomized by the anti-Marxist *Nouveau Philosophes*.[201] By contrast, the appetite for Western culture in the East showed no signs of fading. To take but one example, a book that catalogued the decadence of bourgeois life became a surprise hit in the USSR, as readers clamored for a glimpse of the latest in foreign books, films, and art. In this context, the Final Act's provisions on freer movement promised only to sharpen the intellectual and cultural competition between East and West.[202]

Soviet and Eastern European officials assumed that absolute state sovereignty would protect them from foreign ideas and pressure. In one sense, they were right. No matter what the Final Act said, they could still censor publications, monitor citizens' communications, arrest dissidents, and limit emigration. The East Germans, for instance, "clung to the belief that domestic legislation was the Alpha and Omega," ambassador Siegfried Bock wrote. The Stasi's leaders also reasoned that they could combat the negative consequences of East-West contacts by expanding the ranks of the secret police and tightening its control over society.[203] In another sense, however, communist leaders stood on shaky ground. Even if the USSR and its allies enjoyed absolute sovereignty in theory, they did not in practice. Despite their most strenuous efforts, they could not control what ideas crossed their borders or circulated within them, and new technology only made the problem worse. "With all the innovations in the domain of information transmission," Andropov told Kondrashev, "the frontiers of this country will never be watertight again."[204]

Sovereignty was not—and had never been—merely a matter of force or control. It also required legitimacy, and the CSCE stood at the heart of Brezhnev's strategy for rebuilding the USSR's domestic and international claims to that vital asset. If the Final Act were to serve this purpose, the USSR could not undermine it by routinely flouting it. This tension helps to explain why the Soviets and their allies fought so hard in the Basket III and CBM negotiations, and why they worried so much about what was, after all, an unenforceable piece of paper. When Nixon hinted to Brezhnev that the Final Act, whatever it said, could not change the Soviet system, Brezhnev replied, "That is true, but there are some things that concern matters of principle and are not minor matters." Gromyko made the same point to Kissinger. The USSR had to take the Basket III negotiations seriously because "we don't want to be in violation of an agreement we have made," he said. Soviet diplomats in Geneva likewise told their Western counterparts that their government would find it difficult to renege on the text.[205]

The Final Act caught the Soviets in a paradox. They needed it but also recognized that it might pose a threat. They had built convoluted safeguards into the text—including the references to national laws and regulations, the Basket III preamble, and the voluntary nature of CBMs—and they ensured that the text would only bind them politically, which some officials believed would protect them from dangerous repercussions.[206] Yet the Soviet strategy counted on using the Final Act to earn the trust of foreign politicians and the allegiance of average citizens, who were unlikely to read the text with an eye for these subtleties or give credence to legalistic arguments that the USSR did not have to make good on its promises. Brezhnev and Gromyko wanted to hold the Final Act up as a great victory and reap the benefits of the Helsinki summit, but also hoped that no one would take the more dangerous sections of the agreement seriously.

This dilemma illustrated a crucial contradiction in Soviet strategy. Brezhnev and his supporters struggled to reconcile the demands of internal stability with the pressures for greater openness. They wanted to secure a more prominent place for the USSR in the international system, not retreat from it. They sought the benefits of globalization without the costs, and craved Western approval while hoping to ward off the scrutiny that it entailed. In domestic affairs, Brezhnev wanted to preserve the Soviet domestic system without resorting to Stalin's methods for exerting control. He claimed the awkward middle ground between openness and repression, trying to engage with the outside world without putting communism at risk. The response to the summit meeting and the CSCE's follow-up mechanism would test how well the USSR could strike this balance.

Chapter 7

THE PENS OF AUGUST

The CSCE's concluding summit opened at noon on July 30 in Finlandia Hall. Some delegations arrived in style. The Soviet motorcade provided "a show all of its own: tires screeching, doors banging . . . a helicopter whirring overhead," reported the *Helsingin Sanomat*, the capital's leading newspaper.[1] Brezhnev stepped out of "a limousine so large that it almost sagged in the middle, and surrounded by 11 car-loads of KGB men, all expert leapers-out." The white suit and shoes of Yugoslavia's Josip Tito likewise caught the attention of the assembled journalists. Others took a lower-key approach. Eschewing a limousine, British Prime Minister Harold Wilson walked the short distance from his hotel. Gerald Ford and Henry Kissinger also appeared on foot. "It isn't the common touch," a Finnish official explained. The Americans' Lincoln limousine was too wide for Finlandia Hall's narrow driveway, forcing the president and secretary of state to disembark in the street and walk through the grounds.[2]

Inside the cavernous hall, hundreds of diplomats and journalists settled in for the opening session. The scene resembled "a giant Gilbert and Sullivan extravaganza where Prime Ministers and Presidents are two a penny, and everyone you meet is sure to be somebody," a British journalist reported.[3] From the front row, Ford greeted other leaders with a handshake. Farther back, Brezhnev "hamm[ed] it up, shook his fist good-naturedly at someone across the room, and then broke into a grin and shook his finger."[4] The leaders of the two German states sat across the aisle from each other. Helmut Schmidt chatted with Ford, walked past his East German counterpart, Erich Honecker, and took his seat. Then, thinking better of it, he turned around to say hello. It was the first time the two men met.[5]

Urho Kekkonen called the meeting to order. "This is a day of joy and hope for Europe," the Finnish president said. "[A] new era in our mutual relations is dawning and . . . we have set out on a journey through détente to stability and enduring peace."[6] He had every reason to celebrate the

CSCE's success, not least because the summit meeting gave Finland—and its leader—a rare moment in the international spotlight. Gossip in Helsinki speculated that Kekkonen might receive the Nobel Peace Prize for his role in organizing the event.[7] After some remarks from the guest of honor, United Nations Secretary General Kurt Waldheim, it was time for the leaders' speeches. To pack thirty-five into the summit's three days, the organizers set a 20-minute time limit and counted on the smaller states to take even less.[8] Each speaker described the Final Act in ways that reflected his country's priorities, emphasizing its advantageous elements, ignoring its ambiguities, and downplaying the concessions that had been necessary to get a deal. The kaleidoscopic result—by turns celebratory, circumspect, hopeful, and hard-edged—suggested that the CSCE's heated arguments would not end in Helsinki.

The Western leaders emphasized openness, the primacy of the individual, and personal contacts unmediated by governments. "Détente means little if it is not reflected in the daily lives of our peoples," said British Prime Minister Harold Wilson, who spoke first. "There is no reason why in 1975 Europeans should not be allowed to marry whom they want, hear and read what they want, travel abroad when and where they want, meet whom they want. To deny that proposition is a sign not of strength but of weakness."[9] These values were not mere frills, but the building blocks of stability. Before the summit, Gerald Ford had insisted on re-writing the "diplomatic gobbledygook" that the State Department had drafted for him in order to emphasize the Final Act's humanitarian elements more strongly. Now, addressing his fellow leaders, he insisted that the participants had to follow through on all of their commitments. "Peace is not a piece of paper," he said, but rather "a process requiring mutual restraint and practical arrangements." The line earned him more applause than any other speaker at the summit.[10]

Several of the neutral states also took a robust view of individual freedoms, just as they had during the negotiations. Austrian chancellor Bruno Kreisky trumpeted the superiority of liberal democracy over its rivals.[11] The principle of nonintervention could not shield countries from scrutiny of their domestic practices, insisted Swedish prime minister Olof Palme. "The respect for human rights has been accepted as a norm of equal rank with other principles of international relations," he said. "Frank criticism must also be allowed to make itself heard in the face of phenomena such as the oppression of dissidents, torture and racial discrimination."[12]

Global politics were changing in profound ways, the speakers emphasized. New values were coming to the forefront, countries and peoples were growing closer together, and the barriers between states were falling. The Final Act embodied these dynamics. Détente demanded "an ever-increasing deepening of contacts and co-operation between States, as well as between individuals," said Danish prime minister Anker Jørgensen.[13] Countries could no longer disentangle themselves from each other's affairs, nor could they seal themselves off from events elsewhere, Ford insisted. "I am here because I believe, and my countrymen believe, in the interdependence of Europe and North America—indeed in the interdependence of the entire family of man," he said.[14]

The Soviets and their allies also hailed the Final Act, but for starkly different reasons. A visibly tired Brezhnev slurred his way through his speech, but his message came through clearly. "The outcome of the prolonged negotiations is such that there are neither victors nor vanquished, neither winners nor losers. It has been a victory of reason. Everyone has won," he said. "It has been a gain for all who cherish peace and security on our planet." Much of the speech had been drafted by Anatoly Kovalev, whose even-handed approach emphasized every element of the Final Act, including its humanitarian provisions.[15]

Still, the general secretary seemed to be discussing a completely different document from his Western counterparts. In his presentation, the Final Act affirmed the supremacy of state sovereignty, not the sanctity of the individual. "[N]o-one should try to dictate to other peoples on the basis of foreign policy considerations of one kind or another the manner in which they ought to manage their internal affairs," he said.[16] In place of individual human rights, he described a universal "right to peace."[17] The Western statesmen had welcomed the freer flow of information, but Brezhnev argued that it posed a threat. "It is no secret that information media can serve the purposes of peace and confidence; they can also spread throughout the world the poison of discord between countries and peoples."[18] States therefore had to stay on their guard—and exercise the prerogatives of sovereignty—to protect their borders and keep this poison out.

The Eastern Europeans took a similar approach. They welcomed international cooperation, but only insofar as it respected the communist system and served their definition of peace. "Opened doors are a symbol of trust and hospitality," said Bulgarian leader Todor Zhivkov. "Our doors will be open to all people with open hearts, with good and honest intentions, who observe the laws, traditions and customs of their hosts."[19] The CSCE's real achievement was to affirm the Second World War's results. It has created "a peaceful order in Europe . . . based on the universal acceptance of the sovereign rights and interests of all States of our continent," said Polish leader Edward Gierek. The Final Act was "a Magna Carta of European peace."[20]

Nevertheless, some of the Eastern European leaders suggested that the agreement affirmed their own independence from the Soviet Union. In the past, peace had rested on shaky ground, Gierek said, because "it had been based upon fragile foundations of spheres of influence and upon domination of some countries over others."[21] Now the Final Act acknowledged that each state could stand on its own and make its own decisions. Romanian leader Nicolae Ceauşescu emphasized the supreme importance of state sovereignty and equality. To ensure that no one mistook his meaning, he declared that the "goal of our work ought to be the building up of a united Europe based on independent nations, and peaceful co-operation among all States on an equal footing, irrespective of their social system or size," he said. In its majesty, the Final Act forbade the Soviet Union and Western states alike from interfering in Romania's internal affairs.[22]

After three days of speeches, receptions, and dinners, the last word went to God, "or at least one of his representatives," as one report put it.[23] On August 1, the Vatican's Archbishop Agostino Casaroli offered a benediction and called upon "the help and protection of God to assist the efforts of all men of good will gathered here."[24] The leaders then assembled on stage, taking their seats at a long table adorned only with thirty-five pens. They sat in the customary French alphabetical order, with Schmidt (*Allemagne, République Fédérale d'*) at one end and Tito (*Yougoslavie*) at the other.

Now the summit reached its climax. The conference's executive secretary stepped forward with a copy of the Final Act bound in green leather. The doors to the hall swung open and the press rushed to the foot of the stage to record the solemn ceremony. As dozens of flashbulbs popped, the leaders chatted quietly. For seventeen minutes, the volume moved from one signatory to the next, with a fresh page for each. Italian prime minister Aldo Moro signed his name and added "President of the European Economic Community" to indicate that he was signing in the EEC's name as well as Italy's. When the Final Act reached Leonid Brezhnev, he wagged his finger, as if to say that he had changed his mind about the agreement. The conference staff suffered a moment of panic, but then the general secretary picked up his pen and affixed his signature. When the document reached the end of the line, the hall burst into applause.[25] "The Final Act which we have adopted today constitutes a serious attempt to lay foundations on which we and the coming generations can build a world better than the one we live in," Kekkonen said. "This was achieved by following the advice of an ancient Finnish proverb: 'Know your own stand and give the others their due.'"[26]

The conference staff whisked the signed copy of the Final Act away to its permanent home in a vault beneath the state archives. In the lobby, the leaders raised glasses of champagne to toast their success and then filed out of the building alongside the journalists, bodyguards, and staff. On the streets of the city, small groups of onlookers watched the limousines head for the airport. That evening, a number of diplomats gathered for dinner. They had spent almost three years working toward this day and now contemplated the fruits of their labor:

"Well, they signed it," said one.

"And now it will be buried and forgotten," said another.

"No," replied a third, "you are wrong. We have started something."[27]

I

What exactly had the CSCE started? In the weeks before the summit and over the months that followed, the participants tried to answer that question. The Soviets celebrated what they regarded as a diplomatic triumph. The Final Act was "unprecedented in history," concluded a memorandum to the Politburo. The agreement "ushered in a new phase of détente," confirmed the results of the Second World War, and rejected "the futility and harmfulness of power politics and the 'Cold War.'"[28] In Berlin, Hermann Axen said that the CSCE had solved all of the problems that a postwar peace treaty would have addressed. The Polish report on the summit declared that the Final Act expressed Soviet ideas, not Western ones. The agreement was "a great achievement for the peaceful policies of the socialist community," especially Brezhnev's Peace Program.[29] It gave concrete meaning to détente and established the Leninist principle of peaceful coexistence as the guiding rule of international affairs. The international balance of power was changing in favor of socialism, and "the reactionary, revanchist, and most militant circles" of the capitalist world were losing ground. A "new chapter in the struggle for peace and security" had begun.[30]

The Soviet and Eastern European press recapitulated these themes in front-page stories. No one could miss the CSCE's "epochal significance," said one Soviet commentator.[31] "Remember this day," *Pravda* admonished its readers. It "will be spoken and written about for many years, it will go down in history as the most important milestone on the path to lasting peace in Europe."[32] In East Germany, *Neues Deutschland* called the summit "one of the most significant state forums in European history."[33] European peace now rested on a firm foundation, said Poland's *Trybuna Ludu*.[34] In Czechoslovakia, *Rudé Právo* published a poem marking the occasion.[35] Hungarian, Bulgarian, and Romanian newspapers praised the CSCE in similar terms.[36] The long quest for peace in Europe, which had begun with the Enlightenment, had reached its culmination. In Leonid Brezhnev, Diderot and Kant had found their rightful heir, *Pravda* declared. The Final Act's critics, who refused to recognize this success, resembled the Chekhovian pessimist who insisted on wearing galoshes and carrying an umbrella in the blazing sun.[37]

Soviet newspapers did their utmost to fulfill the prediction that the Final Act "will become the property of many millions of people." *Pravda* and *Izvestiia*, whose combined circulation approached twenty million, carried the full text of the agreement. The move made good on the Final Act's stipulation that signatories publish the agreement, and, together with Brezhnev's signature in Helsinki, gave the text the strongest possible official endorsement.[38] The issue of *Neues Deutschland* that carried the full text of the Final Act—some 1.6 million copies—sold out, for the first time in the newspaper's history.[39] *Rudé Právo* also published the agreement in its entirety, but newspapers in the rest of Eastern Europe countries stopped short of doing so.[40] They printed summaries of the Final Act instead, emphasizing the aspects of the agreement that suited their governments' goals and glossing over the rest.[41] When these governments did publish the Final Act in full, they tried to shape readers' interpretations. The Hungarians, for instance, bound the text in a volume with Kadar's summit speech and the transcript of a television interview that he gave upon his return from Helsinki, which spun the agreement to suit his purposes.[42]

Western reactions to the Final Act diverged sharply. Official assessments ranged from the cautious to the enthusiastic. Although the summit marked "an important step in the process of stabilizing Europe," it was "neither a turning point nor a coronation of détente," the West German foreign ministry noted.[43] The British, Canadians, and Americans were more sanguine. Western ideas had prevailed at the CSCE, argued British foreign secretary Jim Callaghan. NATO had scored "an undoubted success." Canadian ambassador Tom Delworth commented that the Final Act itself was "a distinctly Western-type text" and offered the Soviets "pretty meagre grounds for satisfaction."[44] Even Henry Kissinger, who had held the CSCE in contempt for years, admitted that "intellectually the Conference has been dominated by the West. If a man from the moon were to walk into [Finlandia] Hall, he would think it was a Western conference."[45] The summit revealed "the total bankruptcy of the Communist system," he said.[46]

A close reading of the text demonstrated the extent of the Western victory. Far from consecrating the European status quo, Basket I recognized that frontiers could change. The statements on nonintervention, self-determination, and human rights all reflected Western values. Because these principles applied to all states, no matter their form of government, the Final Act repudiated the Brezhnev Doctrine. The confidence-building measures introduced unprecedented obligations that might establish a new basis for international security. In Basket III, the agreement empowered "people in the East as well as in the West in Europe to communicate, to re-establish family relationships," Gerald Ford told reporters. Canada's secretary of state for external affairs argued that the text imposed "a clear moral and political commitment" on its signatories, and established that multilateral consultations could negotiate agreements on human rights and other sensitive topics without violating state sovereignty.[47]

Regardless, the Final Act's ultimate significance would depend on how governments implemented it. "No complete assessment can be reached before years have passed," wrote British ambassador Anthony Elliott. Only time would tell if the Soviets intended to fulfill the promises they had made. But thanks to the follow-up process, the West would have the opportunity to hold them accountable. These meetings would pressure them to live up to their word—and shame them publicly if they did not.[48]

In the Western press, a few writers suggested that the West had gained more from the CSCE than it had given away. The Final Act would compel the communists to adopt "a whole new outlook toward the rights and problems of people," wrote Don Cook of the *Los Angeles Times*.[49] In the *Guardian*, Jonathan Steele suggested that the agreement would "end the cold war, by creating a new climate of respect between States in Europe, by sanctifying the enormous surge in economic cooperation which has developed in the last three years, and by providing for some marginal improvements in human contacts between East and West."[50] *Die Zeit* suggested that, over the long run, the CSCE might improve the lot of the Eastern bloc's citizens.[51]

These arguments failed to persuade the majority of Western commentators, who savaged the Final Act. "Never had a conference lasted so long and brought together so many diplomats to produce so paltry a result," wrote Raymond Aron in *Le Figaro*. "It takes much optimism or naïveté to believe that promises, some specific and insignificant, the others vague, will change the practices of Moscow's bureaucracy toward foreigners or Soviet citizens."[52] The editor of *Le Monde* agreed.[53] *Die Welt* called it "the biggest hoax in postwar history" and likened it to the Yalta agreement.[54] Margaret Thatcher, Britain's Conservative leader, derided the CSCE—and détente more generally—as a dangerous illusion in the face of rising Soviet military spending.[55] Aleksandr Solzhenitsyn called the Final Act "an amicable agreement of diplomatic shovels [that] will bury and pack down corpses still breathing in a common grave." The agreement amounted to "a lot of nonsense" and an "exercise in semantics," American diplomat George Kennan concluded. In the poem "Proverbs of Détente," historian Robert Conquest declared that "the road to Helsinki is paved with good intentions."[56]

By insisting that the Final Act represented a victory for socialism and demonstrated the USSR's growing strength, these critics unwittingly repeated the official Soviet line. The prevailing public antipathy to the CSCE reflected the rise in anti-détente sentiment in the United States, a skepticism of the power of ideas, and perhaps the broader pessimism of an era marked by political disillusion and economic malaise. Besides, Western leaders had failed to explain the CSCE to their citizens while the negotiations were underway and did little to champion the Final Act once it had been completed. Some may have worried that presenting it as a Western success would antagonize the USSR. Others were haunted by the familiar specters of euphoria and "wishful fantasies," as former American diplomat George Ball put it. If the Soviet claim that "peace has broken out and the era of confrontation is over" gained credence, public demands to cut defense spending might rise. In the Ford administration, some officials doubted the agreement's significance and refused to trumpet one of détente's achievements when détente was becoming a dirty word.[57]

The Chinese got in on the act, too, arguing that the Soviets had outmaneuvered the West. The Final Act would not change the map of Europe but might nonetheless "deceive the European peoples" into thinking that the USSR's intentions were wholly peaceful, said Deng Xiaoping.[58] The CSCE would not create security in Europe, warned China's ambassador in London, but only "the illusion of security."[59] The agreement might just be "scraps of paper," to quote the *People's Daily*, but it concealed Moscow's limitless ambitions.[60]

These conflicts suggested that the pageantry in Helsinki left the underlying disagreements over the Final Act unresolved. Every participant understood that more battles over sovereignty, security, and individual rights still lay ahead.

II

In December 1975, Andrei Gromyko exhorted the Warsaw Pact's foreign ministers to "take the offensive." If they wanted their interpretation of the Final Act to prevail, they would have to fight for it over the long term. The agreement had reduced the danger of war and created a "broad platform for peace and security," Gromyko said, but it had also accelerated the ideological competition between capitalism and communism. His colleagues agreed that they had to act decisively—and coordinate their efforts—if they hoped to prevail.[61]

Propaganda figured prominently in their efforts. Domestically, the communist states had to persuade their citizens that they had won a great victory for the cause of peace, and that the capitalist states had recognized them as their equals.[62] In Moscow, the Politburo prescribed "mass political work among the working people" to promote the Final Act, rebut "the fictions of bourgeois propaganda about the alleged reluctance or unwillingness of the Soviet side to adhere to the letter and spirit" of the agreement, and "clearly and convincingly show the advantages of socialist democracy and the Soviet way of life."[63] The Poles boasted that their domestic practices already "exceed[ed] the standards provided in the Final Act."[64] They incorporated the Final Act into the school curriculum, teaching pupils that the communist status quo now enjoyed full international recognition, and that any attempts—whether domestic or foreign—to change it were, by definition, illegitimate.[65] Hungary planned a press campaign to explain the Final Act to its citizens, with similar goals. The Final Act had strengthened the communist governments' international legitimacy, and it would do the same for their domestic legitimacy.[66]

Abroad, they had to win over Western citizens and refute misinformation. The capitalist states' governments planned "large-scale political and diplomatic activities to distort the decisions taken in Helsinki," East Germany's foreign minister noted, so the Warsaw Pact had to make clear that the Final Act's real purpose had little to do with humanitarian cooperation. The agreement had made Europe's frontiers permanent and established lasting peace on the basis of sovereignty and noninterference.[67] If Western voters believed that the Soviet bloc stood for peace, they would compel their governments to accept the international status quo and the Soviet interpretation of the Final Act along with it.[68] Polish leaders highlighted the "importance of the deepening struggle to win public opinion" as a central front in the fight over the Final Act.[69]

To this end, the Kremlin planned to mobilize international groups—including communist fronts such as the Brussels International Committee for European Security and Cooperation and the International Association of Democratic Lawyers—to promote the Soviet interpretation of the Final Act and demonstrate that Soviet citizens already enjoyed ample protections of their rights.[70] It also considered founding an English-language daily newspaper for Western readers, as an answer to the *International Herald Tribune*.[71] Since the Final Act prescribed wider cultural and educational exchanges, these programs ought to serve ideological purposes. Citizens who travelled to the West would have to carry out "specific propaganda assignments" while abroad. In turn, when Western groups visited the USSR, the citizens they met had to "give a decisive rebuff to the various kinds of fabrications of bourgeois propaganda" and explain that the country was faithfully implementing the Final Act.[72] If these campaigns succeeded, the Czechoslovak government concluded, they would "broaden the material base of détente, thus making it permanent and irreversible."[73]

To prevent the Western states from claiming the moral high ground, the Soviets and their allies would publicize the capitalists' transgressions. The Kremlin enjoined the KGB to undertake "special operations overseas aimed at exposing violations [of the Final Act] by the Western powers." Soviet agents would organize popular campaigns in Western Europe and North America criticizing these governments for abusing their citizens' civil rights and endorsing racial and religious discrimination.[74] Polish officials planned to attack Western hypocrisy in Basket III. The capitalist states criticized Poland for denying exit visas to its citizens and impeding family reunification, but they routinely denied Eastern European citizens entry and restricted their ability to work.[75] To emphasize that human rights were "uncomfortable for the West," Poland ratified the UN Human Rights Covenants, which nearly every state in the Soviet bloc had already done, but most members of NATO had not.[76]

Western governments could not be allowed to turn the Final Act against the communist regimes. The Soviet and Eastern European press had to explain the crimes of the so-called dissidents and the real meaning of human rights. Books and magazines that promoted capitalist and "anti-Soviet" values had to be kept out. The Soviets would reprise their demands from Geneva that Western governments take responsibility for the information published and broadcast within their borders, and that they stop funding the "subversive radio stations" that broadcast counterrevolutionary slander, especially Radio Liberty and Radio Free Europe.[77] To defend themselves against the Western abuse of Basket III, the communist governments should "insist consistently on compliance with the agreed superiority of the adopted principles of relations between states, including the principles of sovereignty and noninterference," argued the Polish Ministry of Foreign Affairs.[78] Anatoly Chernyaev summarized the attitude of Soviet leaders: "We are not about to change our rules because of Helsinki, and we had never planned to."[79]

The challenge was to fulfil the Final Act's promises without compromising domestic security.[80] Although the Soviets continued to insist on the cardinal importance of sovereignty, they began to change their practices in line with the agreement and loosened restrictions on the movement of people and information. The Kremlin agreed to import leading Western newspapers, with the catch that they would be sold only at tourist hotels, not newsstands. It granted foreign journalists multiple-entry visas and abolished their need for a permit to travel more than 40 kilometers beyond Moscow. It lowered exit visa fees for Soviet citizens and began to process their applications more quickly.[81] It followed through on confidence-building measures, notifying Western governments of some military maneuvers and inviting foreign officers to observe them.[82] Other Warsaw Pact states did likewise.[83]

The Kremlin's grandest ambition was to use the Final Act to reconfigure international politics far beyond Europe. By citing the decalogue in every treaty with a non-European state, it aspired to "universalize" the agreement's declaration of principles. By touting their interpretation of the Final Act at the UN and championing the "right to peace," the Soviets hoped to win new friends for the USSR, stymie the efforts of their Western and Chinese rivals, and shift the understanding of international legitimacy in their favor. Invoking noninterference in Africa and Asia, for example, could block Western involvement in those regions. At the same time, the principle of peaceful coexistence would authorize the spread of communism and Soviet influence. Brezhnev and his colleagues saw no contradiction in these aspirations, but the case of Angola suggested that the matter was more complicated than they admitted. The general secretary initially rejected a proposal to intervene in the country's civil war on the grounds that the Final

Act forbade such adventures. His advisor Andrei Aleksandrov-Agentov pushed back, however, insisting on the USSR's internationalist duty to help its comrades. Rather than standing firm, Brezhnev simply gave in.[84]

Meanwhile, the Western allies developed their own plans of attack that mirrored those of the East. They aimed to dispel the misinformation many journalists (and the Soviets themselves) had spread about the Final Act, and guard against both excessive pessimism and optimism. Citizens had to understand that the CSCE had "not set the present frontiers of Europe in concrete; nor ratified the Soviet hold on Eastern Europe," the British Foreign Office argued.[85] Far from being defeated on humanitarian questions, the West had achieved more than anyone had expected before the negotiations, when the Soviets had refused to discuss the subject. That said, the agreement represented only a step in the right direction, not a definitive solution to the Cold War's problems. "The final document does not signal the achievement of détente," concluded a memorandum to the Canadian cabinet, "but rather establishes a solid and realistic basis for future steps in the process of furthering détente."[86] A NATO report called for a renewed commitment to the military defense of Western Europe in the face of ongoing Soviet challenges, which in turn made it necessary to rally public support for the Final Act and for the alliance itself.[87]

The Ford administration regarded this publicity effort with ambivalence. "I have no hesitancy speaking up for CSCE and the whole thing," the president said, but he mustered only vague arguments in its favor.[88] Instead of promoting the Final Act's merits in public, Kissinger preferred to grouse about its critics in private. "The complaints we are seeing show the moral collapse of the academic community," he said. "They are bitching now about the borders we did nothing to change when we had a nuclear monopoly."[89] Those who attacked the Ford administration for consigning Eastern Europe to Soviet domination were cowards peddling "total unmitigated nonsense" who "would pee in their pants the minute a real first-class crisis started," he told Israeli Prime Minister Yitzhak Rabin.[90] In a series of speeches in 1975 and 1976, Kissinger tried to educate voters about the moral logic of American foreign policy, which prioritized peace with the USSR over all other considerations. Although he did not mention the Final Act, he implicitly rebuffed both those who criticized the agreement as a giveaway to Moscow and those who hoped it would provide a platform for humanitarian activism.[91] By refusing to tackle the Final Act's opponents head-on, however, the administration allowed the public's negative perception of the agreement to fester.

The White House's skepticism threatened to inhibit Western efforts to monitor Soviet compliance. The West German foreign ministry argued that the NATO allies had to share information about the communist states' domestic practices and put them on the defensive.[92] The American ambassador in Moscow agreed. The US had to make clear "that we regard CSCE obligations as real guideposts to future contacts between peoples" and "use our own media to emphasize the content of these obligations."[93] But the State Department devoted few resources to the task, and some officials in Washington even resisted it.[94] The Western allies pushed ahead regardless. In the months following the Helsinki summit, they agreed to collaborate in scrutinizing Warsaw Pact behavior and compiled a report on East-West flows of people and information.[95] The members of the European Community followed suit.[96]

The most extensive monitoring efforts would mean little, however, if they did not produce concrete results. The West had "to create verifiable reality out of chances, offers, representations, and promises," wrote a West German official.[97] The Soviets had to live up to the new standard of conduct that the decalogue established. They also had to follow through on confidence-building measures and the dissemination of economic information, but humanitarian questions loomed largest of all. Détente would mean nothing if the daily lives of people across the continent did not improve, argued a British diplomat.[98]

If Moscow invoked the Final Act's "escape clauses"—its references to sovereignty, nonintervention, and domestic legislation—to justify inaction, the Western allies had to respond forcefully. Because the Final Act "predominantly contains texts that generally reflect our liberal order," the West Germans emphasized, the West could criticize the USSR if it refused to change its practices.[99] "We must not be afraid to speak out" and hold the communist states accountable, British officials urged. The decalogue now provided "an authoritative point of reference in the future conduct of relations between states in Europe." If Moscow tried to invoke the Brezhnev Doctrine, for example, or continued to abuse its citizens' rights, the West could point to the declaration of principles to demonstrate the illegitimacy of Soviet conduct. To reinforce these standards of conduct, the Western allies should "refer to [the decalogue] extensively in future bilateral documents"—just as the Warsaw Pact states intended to do.[100] The Soviets could not easily repudiate the agreement because they had boasted so much about its success. If the West pushed them hard, especially at the Belgrade follow-up meeting, they would have no way to escape without destroying the CSCE itself.[101]

No amount of cajoling or public exhortation could guarantee compliance, however. In a diplomatic process based on consensus, there was no room for compulsion. The East counted on its ability to win over public opinion, the West on its powers of persuasion and, failing that, public humiliation. The struggle to negotiate the Final Act had ended. A new struggle—over the meaning of the Final Act in practice—had taken its place.

III

When the Final Act appeared in 1975, Soviet citizens generally greeted it with skepticism. Although the Communist Party touted it as a victory for peace and socialism, few expected it to change daily life.[102] One prominent dissident found the agreement "too boring" to read.[103] Others drew dimmer conclusions. "The Helsinki Agreement evoked a certain pessimism," Lithuanian scholar Tomas Venclova later said, "since it seemed that it would only confirm the European status quo, and that the humanitarian articles would be, even under the best circumstances, no more than good intentions."[104] Vladimir Bukovsky, a Soviet dissident, offered a more scathing assessment. "It wasn't the first time that the West's 'friendly relations' with the Soviet Union had been built on our bones. The most repulsive thing of all was that the West tried to justify itself with all sorts of intricate doctrines and theories," he wrote. "Just as Soviet man created a countless multitude of self-justifications to facilitate his collusion with total violence, so the West too likes to soothe its conscience."[105]

Many Eastern Europeans took a similarly gloomy view. Those who read the official coverage may well have concluded that, by affirming the European status quo, the Final Act amounted to a new Yalta agreement. East Germans doubted that CSCE would make it easier for them to visit their families in the West.[106] Czechoslovak poet Egon Bondy called the Final Act a "disgusting pact" and a "negotiation of universal subjugation."[107] Few of his compatriots even knew about its humanitarian provisions because the official press had glossed over them.[108] "[W]e in the Polish opposition had some serious doubts about the Helsinki process," Bronisław Geremek recalled. "We initially thought it was another situation where the Russians were superior negotiators to the Western politicians, as expressed by Lenin when he said the West would 'produce the rope that would hang themselves.'"[109]

Before long, however, dissidents in the Soviet bloc began to recognize the Final Act's potential. A few saw it right away. In June 1975, a group of Latvians and Estonians implored the CSCE's participants to acknowledge that the USSR was violating their fundamental rights. On the first day of the Helsinki summit, political prisoners in a Soviet labor camp launched a hunger strike to protest their treatment.[110] Andrei Amalrik accused Soviet authorities of violating the Final Act by denying him permission to travel abroad. When they ordered him to leave Moscow, he refused on the grounds that it would separate him from his wife and thereby violate the principle of family reunification.[111]

In May 1976, several prominent dissidents established the Moscow Helsinki Group, with a mandate to monitor Soviet compliance with the Final Act. Andrei Sakharov, Anatoly Shcharansky, and Yuri Orlov cultivated contacts with foreign journalists who could seed stories in the Western press and smuggle the group's reports out of the country. Because Brezhnev had so prominently endorsed the Final Act and staked his—and his regime's—legitimacy on the agreement, they reasoned, the authorities would find it difficult to punish them for demanding its implementation. Nonetheless, they harbored no illusions about what lay in store. "To the success of our hopeless cause!" Orlov said in toasting the group's founding.[112]

Likeminded citizens in Eastern Europe also embraced the Final Act to put pressure on their governments. In late 1975, the Polish government proposed amending the constitution to affirm the Communist Party's "leading role" and the country's "unshakeable and fraternal bonds" with the USSR. Prominent intellectuals objected that the revisions contravened the Final Act by curtailing Poland's ability to choose its allies and subordinating individual rights to the party's prerogatives. The Catholic hierarchy declared that any constitutional amendment had to conform to the Final Act. Intellectuals and average citizens echoed these arguments in open letters and petitions to the authorities, who eventually abandoned some of the most contentious changes.[113]

The following year, when security forces attacked strikers who were protesting rising food prices, a number of intellectuals formed the Committee for the Defense of Workers. The group, known as KOR (its Polish acronym), aimed to defend those who had been punished for participating in the strikes, collect information about rights violations, and disseminate its findings.[114] As other groups formed in KOR's wake, an alliance coalesced between intellectuals, workers, and the church, based on a shared commitment to human rights, the Final Act, and the UN Covenants.[115] "An unceasing struggle for reform and evolution that seeks an expansion of civil liberties and human rights is the only course East European dissidents can take," one of the movement's founders, Adam Michnik, wrote in 1976. Having learned from the failures of the 1950s and 1960s, they sought "gradual and piecemeal change, not violent upheaval and forceful destruction of the existing system."[116]

Czechoslovak dissidents seized on the Final Act in much the same way. In September 1975, Jiří Hájek and Zdeněk Mlynář, former members of Dubček's government who had been ousted after the Prague Spring, declared that the CSCE had delegitimized the Warsaw Pact's 1968 invasion and barred Moscow from interfering in the country's affairs again. It also compelled the authorities to respect citizens' basic freedoms. Helsinki "represents a recognition of what is common to Europe, a recognition of European civilization and cultural values" that transcend the East-West divide, Mlynář said. All European states now had to respect these values, especially regarding individual rights, and change their laws and practices accordingly. Other intellectuals and activists publicly repeated these arguments.[117]

The persecution of an underground rock band inspired further action. In 1976, police arrested several members and friends of the Plastic People of the Universe, whose songs satirized communist propaganda and post-1968 conformism. In response, a group of writers and intellectuals drafted a public appeal. Charter 77 demanded respect for the human rights provisions of the Final Act and the UN Covenants, which the government had ratified after the Helsinki summit.[118] Its authors, who espoused a wide range of political views, did not learn the concept of human rights from the Final Act, but they took advantage of the agreement (and the ratification of the covenants) to pursue their longstanding goals.[119] They hoped that their manifesto's plodding, antipolemical style would let the facts speak for themselves and deflect accusations of anti-communist fervor.[120]

Spokesman Jan Patočka argued that the charter's values transcended politics and superseded sovereignty. "The concept of human rights is nothing other than the conviction that states, too, and all of society are placed under the supremacy of moral feeling; that they recognize something unconditioned, above them, something weighty and sacrosanct even for them; and that, by their own powers with which they create and secure legal norms, they intend to contribute to this goal," he wrote. So long as states ignored these supreme moral principles, détente would remain an illusion and the shadow of war would continue to loom across Europe.[121] From his hospital bed, where he lay dying after a harsh police interrogation, Patočka told *Die Zeit* that the "world is not split, but united in its assessment of certain kinds of behavior, that despotism is frowned upon by civilized people everywhere, and any defense of such practices is considered a lazy excuse."[122] Western states therefore had to put the Soviet bloc "in the dock at Belgrade" and use the CSCE to hold it to its promises. As word of the charter spread, it attracted hundreds of new signatures. The government estimated that two million people might have signed had they not feared the consequences.[123]

In East Germany, citizens began to take the promises of freer movement seriously. In the year following the Helsinki summit, exit visa applications spiked to 100,000, or roughly one percent of the country's population.[124] Many applications—not just in the GDR, but in Czechoslovakia, Poland, and Romania besides—cited the Final Act. At local party meetings, workers asked when they could join their fiancés in the West. In July 1975, activists smuggled a petition demanding respect for the Final Act into West Germany, where the press welcomed it. A year later, a Lutheran minister set himself on fire to protest religious persecution, and a group of Christians drafted a manifesto inspired by Charter 77.[125] The Final Act had connected "security and humanitarian concerns for the first time: the security of human life and human dignity," the East German *Kirschenbund* noted. "Without this security, there can be no enduring peace."[126]

These movements operated on the "as if" principle. They behaved as if their activities were perfectly legal and the official promises to respect human rights were sincere. Far from defying the state, they were helping it to implement its own policies. Since the state claimed authority over every sphere of life, they reasoned that they could resist simply by living their lives as if they enjoyed privacy and autonomy, and by refusing to make the everyday moral compromises necessary to avoid trouble from the authorities.[127] One of Charter 77's authors, Václav Havel, called this approach "living within the truth."[128] Another, Ladislav Hejdánek, said, "We had to find out whether we were supposed to live as liars."[129] These activists did not aim to overthrow communism, but to carve out space for individual action and individual dignity.

Cross-border networks connected them with supporters around the Soviet bloc. Shortly after the Moscow Helsinki Group formed, it received a visit from a Polish lawyer who had been inspired by the news. After returning to Warsaw, Zbigniew Romaszewski helped to establish KOR. The two groups continued to exchange information by telephone and the occasional personal visit.[130] Intrepid Polish and Czechoslovak activists met in the mountains straddling the border between their countries.[131] Hungarian intellectuals publicly defended the work of their Czechoslovak counterparts, and Romanian dissident Paul Goma offered his support to Charter 77's organizers.[132]

The activists also sought Western help. Polish groups appealed for the support of figures ranging from Italian Communist Enrico Berlinguer to British conservative Robert Conquest.[133] When the *Frankfurter Allgemeine Zeitung* published the text of Charter 77 the day after its authors' arrest, it elicited an outpouring of international support from across the political spectrum.[134] Writers and intellectuals such as Jean-Paul Sartre, Heinrich Böll, Günter Grass, Jürgen Habermas, and Arthur Miller—many of whom had lobbied Western governments during the CSCE—declared their support for Charter 77 and criticized the Czechoslovak government for violating its Helsinki promises.[135] Whereas dissident groups before 1975 tended to be constrained by national frontiers, the Final Act inspired the creation of networks that spread information and ideas across borders, in the spirit of the agreement itself.[136]

These emerging networks received a powerful boost from the other side of the Atlantic. Shortly after the Helsinki summit, a US congressional delegation visited the Soviet Union. When Republican Millicent Fenwick asked officials about their plans for implementing the Final Act, they replied that the agreement was not binding. Brezhnev told the delegation that further bilateral negotiations would be necessary to put it into practice. After speaking to several dissidents, many of whom expressed high hopes for the Final Act, Fenwick concluded that they needed Washington's support. On her return, she drafted legislation to create the Commission on Security and Cooperation in Europe, with a mandate to investigate and report on Soviet and Eastern European compliance with the Final Act.[137]

The Ford administration tried to block the commission. Fenwick wanted it to include members from both Congress and the executive branch, but Ford and Kissinger rejected the idea as legislative overreach.[138] In the context of growing congressional assertiveness and rising antidétente sentiment, however, their argument for preserving executive control of foreign policy fell flat. Large bipartisan majorities in both houses passed Fenwick's bill. As the presidential election loomed, Ford decided not to use his veto lest he anger Republicans who wanted a tougher line on the Soviet Union, or Eastern European émigré groups who supported the commission.[139]

The commission quickly got to work. Members traveled around the Soviet bloc to gather evidence, held public hearings in Washington, and published their findings.[140] Unsolicited reports from Eastern Europe began to arrive, along with the latest samizdat. The commission shared this information with other Western governments, nongovernmental organizations, and exiles. It raised the CSCE's profile in the United States just as the Final Act's critics on both sides of the Atlantic began to change their minds about the agreement.[141] By giving dissidents in Eastern Europe a megaphone for their views and shining a spotlight on their plight, it strengthened the nascent Helsinki network.[142]

The 1976 presidential election transformed the American government's attitude to the CSCE. Both Ronald Reagan, from the right, and Jimmy Carter, from the left, attacked Ford for conciliating the Soviets and presented the Final Act as an unconditional victory for Moscow. The revelation of the so-called Sonnenfeldt Doctrine, which accepted Soviet domination of Eastern Europe, seemed to undermine Ford's claims that he was getting tough with Brezhnev. Although Reagan lost the fight for the Republican nomination, he forced the president to accept a campaign plank on "Morality in Foreign Policy," which criticized the CSCE. In the general election campaign against Carter, Ford struggled to make the case that the Final Act had not helped the Soviets. During a televised debate, Ford fumbled a question on the subject. Instead of saying that the agreement had not ratified a Soviet sphere of influence, he insisted that "there is no Soviet domination of Eastern Europe." The gaffe may have cost him the election. To the end, he failed to articulate how the agreement advanced Western goals.[143]

Jimmy Carter made the Final Act a centerpiece of his new design for American foreign policy. His national security advisor, Zbigniew Brzezinski, had previously criticized Nixon and Kissinger for pursuing a "foreign policy based largely on maneuver among the more powerful nation-states" and "largely devoid of moral concerns."[144] At Brzezinski's urging, Carter dropped his earlier skepticism of the CSCE and now attacked Ford for wasting the opportunity to press the Soviets on humanitarian questions. In his inaugural address, the new president emphasized his commitment to human rights.[145] It only made sense, therefore, that his administration would closely monitor the Soviet bloc's adherence to Helsinki's principles.[146]

A week after the inauguration, the State Department criticized the Czechoslovak government. The persecution of Charter 77's signatories violated the Final Act, it argued.[147] Carter also paid close attention to relations with Poland and Hungary, not because they had the bloc's worst human rights records, but because they seemed the most susceptible to outside pressure.[148] A presidential directive formalized this "peaceful engagement" strategy, which would evaluate the domestic and international conduct of Soviet bloc governments and cultivate ties to dissidents as well as officials. As Poland sought Western loans to cope with a fresh economic crisis, the administration signaled that aid would be forthcoming only if the regime honored the Final Act.[149]

In response to the rising tide of domestic and international criticism, the Soviets and Eastern Europeans dug in their heels. Yuri Andropov may have believed that the Soviet system needed gradual reform, but he refused to endanger domestic order or tolerate public opposition. He warned the Politburo that hundreds of thousands of citizens were either trying to undermine the regime or would do so if they had the opportunity. The KGB chief's figures were almost certainly exaggerated, but the point was clear. The dissidents had to be locked up no matter what the West might say. Over the next few years, the authorities sent hundreds of people to prison, sentenced them to internal exile, or confined them in psychiatric hospitals on the grounds that criticizing real existing socialism could only be a symptom of mental illness.[150]

When the Norwegian Nobel Committee awarded the 1975 Peace Prize to Andrei Sakharov, the Kremlin treated the decision as proof of the scientist's treason. Brezhnev, who coveted the prize for himself, insisted that the committee was headed by "ardent anti-Soviet figures, pursuing their goal of undermining the socialist camp." By accepting the honor, Sakharov had revealed himself as a "Judas" who was willing to sell his country for "30 pieces of silver," the newspaper *Trud* declared. Because the authorities denied him permission to travel to Oslo, his wife Elena Bonner, who was already abroad for medical treatment, went in his stead. She read the lecture that he had prepared, which emphasized that "the defense of human rights [is] the only sure basis for genuine and lasting international cooperation." In making this point, Sakharov echoed the West's own arguments from Geneva about the nature of peace.[151]

Meanwhile, the authorities in Eastern Europe struggled to respond to the growing wave of activism. East German leaders worried about the rising demand for exit visas, especially the applications that cited the Final Act. They remembered of the exodus of skilled workers that had nearly destroyed the country's economy in the late 1950s and believed that they now faced a similar risk. At first, they responded by dramatically increasing the number of exit visas, on the assumption that this would rid the country of its most antisocial elements. Soon, however, they reversed themselves and, in the name of stability, ordered a crackdown on those who sought to leave. It was clear, however, that the authorities had not been prepared for the response that the Final Act elicited in East German society. They could not preserve order simply by replying on nostrums about sovereignty and noninterference.[152]

Although the Czechoslovak authorities had jailed Charter 77's ringleaders, they believed that they also had to win the intellectual contest against their critics. To this end, they published an "anticharter." Much like the Soviet campaign against Sakharov, this document depicted the Chartists as sell-outs who colluded with socialism's foreign enemies for personal gain. The state remained faithful to the Final Act's humanitarian values, it argued, but the Chartists violated the agreement by undermining Czechoslovak sovereignty. The authorities understood that the Final Act and the charter had raised doubts about the legitimacy of the communist system, and that the state had to fight back with ideas, not just prison terms.[153]

The Kremlin also stepped up the counteroffensive against its foreign critics. Brezhnev told Warsaw Pact leaders that they faced a "sharp ideological struggle concerning the substance and perspectives of the process of international détente."[154] If anyone was guilty of violating the Final Act, it was the West. Georgy Kornienko complained to American diplomat Jack Matlock that, contrary to the agreement, Western governments regularly rejected Soviet visa applicants, and Western radio broadcasts infringed Soviet sovereignty.[155] In Paris, the Soviet ambassador demanded that Giscard stop the French press from publishing "unfair and sensational" stories about Soviet violations of the Final Act. Nothing in the agreement authorized anti-Soviet agitation or required the USSR to welcome "subversive propaganda, material preaching violence or inciting national and racial hatred, and pornography," political scientist Georgy Arbatov wrote in *Izvestiia*. Other articles in the Soviet press condemned the "wild malice" of Western radio broadcasts, and the government successfully lobbied to strip Radio Free Europe of its accreditation to the 1976 Winter Olympics.[156]

By contrast, Soviet officials argued, the USSR was faithfully fulfilling the Final Act. It had improved working conditions for foreign journalists and allowed some Soviet citizens to join their family members abroad, Kornienko said. In any case, the Kremlin owed the West nothing in exchange for recognizing Europe's borders, which had been paid for with the blood of the USSR's twenty million war dead, Arbatov insisted. In the age of Watergate, Vietnam, and the Black Panthers, the US had no standing to lecture others about freedom and democracy. Similar arguments appeared elsewhere in the Soviet press, which returned to them regularly in the years that followed.[157]

Even as they defended their system against subversion, the Soviets continued to celebrate the Final Act. In February 1976, Brezhnev told the 25th Communist Party Congress that the agreement fulfilled the promise that he had made in announcing the Peace Program five years earlier. The triumphant event was the domestic counterpart to the Helsinki summit. It represented the "apotheosis" of Brezhnev's foreign policy, KGB officer Nikolai Leonov recalled. A few months later, special television programs and newspaper articles marked the Final Act's first anniversary, emphasizing that the agreement had strengthened the socialist system.[158] The new Soviet constitution, which Brezhnev promulgated in 1977, listed the Final Act's ten principles of international relations, which would guide the country's foreign policy. On a visit to France the same year, Brezhnev boasted that no other country in the world had incorporated these principles into its foundational document. (The constitution also stipulated that "the interests of the people" and "the aims of building communism" superseded the rights of the individual.)[159] Notwithstanding the barrage of foreign and domestic criticism, the Kremlin still relied on the Final Act as a indispensable tool for bolstering its legitimacy.

IV

The Soviets remained committed to the CSCE but wanted to change its tone. If the West tried to use the Belgrade follow-up meeting "as a complaints office for so-called humanitarian affairs," the Warsaw Pact would refuse. Instead, they would focus on strengthening détente, pressing NATO on disarmament, and expanding international cooperation in "a broader, positive sense."[160] To demonstrate their good faith, the Soviets allowed some leading dissidents to emigrate, and Polish officials amnestied several imprisoned members of KOR. At the same time, however, Andropov continued to fulminate against dissidents' lawlessness, and the Czechoslovak authorities put three Chartists on trial. If Western governments pushed their counterrevolutionary agenda too far, Soviet and Eastern European officials agreed, the communist states should cut the Belgrade conference short or withdraw from the CSCE entirely.[161]

Western governments wrestled with a similar dilemma. French and West German officials worried that antagonizing the Soviets and Eastern Europeans at Belgrade might exacerbate the domestic crackdown and reverse even the modest progress that the communist governments had made in implementing the Final Act. They therefore refused to meet with Andrei Amalrik, now living in exile. Helmut Schmidt demanded the removal of Radio Free Europe, which he called a "cold war relic," from West German soil.[162] In the United States, Secretary of State Cyrus Vance feared rupturing US-Soviet relations, as did some career diplomats.[163] By contrast, Brzezinski urged Carter to treat Belgrade as a "battlefield to wage ideological conflict," especially by emphasizing human rights violations in the Soviet bloc. He won the debate.[164] Shortly before the conference opened, the president appointed former Supreme Court Justice Arthur Goldberg to lead the US delegation. Quiet diplomacy had not persuaded the Kremlin to keep its humanitarian promises. Because the Soviets tied their domestic and international legitimacy to the Final Act, Goldberg concluded, vigorous public criticism might get better results.[165]

When the conference opened in October 1977, heated arguments flared between East and West, and within each bloc too. The Soviets wanted to focus on their new disarmament proposals, but Goldberg insisted on reviewing participants' track records first.[166] With little regard for diplomatic convention, he criticized Soviet bloc countries by name for violating the Final Act, quoted news reports about the treatment of dissidents, and publicly briefed journalists on the proceedings of the closed-door meetings.[167] Internal arguments about Goldberg's tactics roiled the unusually large American delegation, pitting its skeptical career diplomats against members of the Helsinki Commission, academics, and activists.[168] The Soviets, who suffered some criticism from their own allies for refusing to compromise, protested the interference in their domestic affairs and repeated the familiar argument that international security had nothing to do with human rights. "If these attacks continue, it will break up the conference," warned Yuli Vorontsov, the head of the Soviet delegation.[169] The British, French, and West German delegates initially quailed at Goldberg's blunt style, but eventually came around. Having concluded that Brezhnev remained too invested in the CSCE to abandon it, they rejected Vorontsov's bid to escape scrutiny by invoking nonintervention.[170]

The debates in Belgrade raised familiar conceptual problems. Did peace depend on respect for humanitarian principles? Did détente promote respect for human rights, or was respect for human rights a prerequisite for détente? What constituted intervention in another country's domestic affairs? Goldberg's tactics aggravated the inherent difficulty of reaching consensus on these questions. Because he refused to back down and because Vorontsov refused to endorse any text that mentioned human rights, the conference hit an impasse. Soviet leaders worried that continuing to pursue a substantive agreement in such circumstances would only force them to make unpleasant concessions. As a result, the conference ended with an anemic declaration in March 1978. The participants resolved to keep the CSCE alive and meet again in Madrid in 1980, but could not agree on anything further.[171]

In the aftermath, they weighed the results. "One can say that this conference is a one per cent success and a 99 per cent failure," the head of the Swiss delegation told the press.[172] The Eastern allies congratulated themselves for resisting the West's pressure on humanitarian questions. Nonetheless, Brezhnev expressed outrage at the Americans' conduct. "This campaign represents an attempt at an impudent interference in the internal affairs of the socialist countries," he said. "It was calculated to sow mistrust, and to impede mutual understanding between countries with opposing social systems." At the same time, however, he and other Soviet leaders had decided that the USSR could not afford to withdraw from the CSCE entirely. The Final Act and the follow-up process had become too important to Soviet foreign policy to be tossed aside. The Eastern allies would simply have to weather further Western pressure and seek ways to turn the negotiations to their advantage. Andropov privately suggested that the USSR might even make more concessions on human rights if the West responded to its overtures on disarmament.[173]

From the perspective of many Western capitals, however, the picture looked brighter. Belgrade expanded the East-West dialogue to include the "open discussion of matters which previously had, to a large extent, been diplomatic taboos," said West German State Secretary Günther van Well. By breaking "the silence barrier," the conference set an important precedent, concluded US Helsinki Commission chair Dante Fascell. The West had raised specific violations of the decalogue's principle on human rights and of the third basket, but the Soviets and their allies did not walk out. Belgrade had also provided a forum for disseminating reports from Eastern European activists, which Western radio stations in turn broadcast back into the Soviet bloc, bringing samizdat to new audiences.[174]

The fireworks in Belgrade galvanized Western public support for the CSCE. In 1975, most media outlets in the United States and Western Europe attacked the Final Act. By 1978, the tide had turned. Commentators increasingly regarded the CSCE as a boon to the West. It could not single-handedly enforce the rights of citizens in the Soviet bloc, but it offered useful tools.[175] The conference—and the crackdown on dissidents—also inspired private citizens to take action. With the support of the Ford Foundation, several writers and activists in New York founded Helsinki Watch, modeled on the Moscow Helsinki Group. The organization aimed to support activists in the Soviet bloc, build Western support for the CSCE, and lobby the Soviets and their allies to meet their humanitarian obligations.[176] In 1982, a group of Western European nongovernmental organizations collaborated with Helsinki Watch to establish the International Helsinki Federation for Human Rights in the hope of coordinating Western efforts.[177]

As this new wave of activism took shape, East-West relations continued to deteriorate. The superpowers' military spending rose rapidly. In 1976, the Soviets began deploying cutting-edge intermediate-range nuclear missiles in Eastern Europe, which threatened to tip the strategic balance in Moscow's favor. As NATO considered whether to respond in kind, leaders in both camps worried about the rising danger of thermonuclear war. The Red Army's invasion of Afghanistan and Moscow's support for revolutionary forces in Africa seemed to confirm Western Cold Warriors' darkest prophecies about Soviet adventurism.[178] Meanwhile, the communist governments intensified their campaigns against their domestic critics. To this point, fear of an international backlash had restrained the KGB. After the Belgrade conference, however, it decided to take tough measures. Yuri Orlov was sent to a prison camp. Anatoly Shcharansky was sentenced to forced labor. Andrei Sakharov was banished from Moscow to Gorky, a closed city. Cellist Mstislav Rostropovich and his wife, who had criticized the Soviet system for years, were stripped of their citizenship while on tour abroad. The jamming of Western radio stations resumed, and the authorities began to impede the work of Western journalists once more.[179]

Even at this nadir, the CSCE remained a vital reference point for governments and activists alike. In 1980–81, a series of strikes gripped Poland and gave birth to an independent trade union, Solidarity. The demonstrators demanded that the government abide by the Final Act and distribute copies of the agreement across the country.[180] "We knew the document well," recalled Bogdan Borusewicz, a Solidarity leader. "It is no coincidence that there are direct references to Helsinki among the strike's postulates." By signing the Final Act and endorsing its guarantees of individual rights, the communist governments conceded "that our nations [did] have the right to these freedoms."[181]

Soviet leaders observed these events with growing alarm, but felt constrained in their ability to respond. To be sure, they feared that the turmoil might topple the government in Warsaw and spill over Poland's frontiers. To protect the USSR, they halted tourist travel, stopped cultural exchanges, censored letters from Poland, embargoed Polish periodicals, and jammed Polish radio.[182] Brezhnev warned Polish leaders that the Red Army might intervene if they could not stabilize the situation themselves.[183] Behind closed doors, however, Soviet leaders concluded that the USSR could not bear the political or economic costs of invading Poland. Yuri Andropov, for example, argued that sending in troops would sweep away what remained of détente and destroy the CSCE, the premier achievement of the last decade of Soviet diplomacy. Even Mikhail Suslov accepted this argument. "We cannot subject our country to international condemnation yet again," he told his colleagues. In the circumstances, the Polish government had to fend for itself. The decision hollowed out the Brezhnev Doctrine.[184]

Despite the crisis in Poland, the CSCE's Madrid follow-up meeting opened as scheduled in November 1980. As Cold War tensions rose, it remained the only forum where East-West negotiations continued unimpeded. It also kept informal lines of communication open, as diplomats from the opposing sides often met for dinner and reported their conversa-

230 • Chapter 7

tions back to their governments.[185] The Spanish capital drew hundreds of activists and many civil society groups from across Europe and North America. Helsinki Watch briefed reporters about individual political prisoners and shared reports about the situation in the Soviet bloc with Western delegations. Those who could not travel to Madrid tried to influence the conference from afar. Incarcerated in a prison camp, for instance, Yuri Orlov launched a hunger strike to protest his treatment. "The whole point of the Helsinki Accords is mutual monitoring, not mutual evasion of difficult problems," Andrei Sakharov said in a public statement. Although the communist governments were reluctant to roll back all of the changes they had made to implement the Final Act, the new wave of domestic repression had the unintended consequence of drawing unprecedented international attention to the Helsinki process.[186]

The United States resumed its confrontational tactics from Belgrade but now enjoyed the Western Europeans' full support. American ambassador Max Kampelman consulted with them extensively before and during the negotiations to establish this common front. Because of the recent downturn in East-West relations, the French and West Germans set aside their earlier concerns about antagonizing Moscow, which further strengthened NATO unity.[187] The Western allies now demanded action from the Soviets, not just another declaration. In Belgrade, Goldberg had mentioned seven individual cases by name. In Madrid, Western diplomats raised more than 120. By contrast, when they tried to draw attention to the dissidents' plight at the United Nations, a representative from one of the communist states would object and call for a vote on a point of order. Outnumbered by the communists and their supporters from the global south, the Western governments would lose the vote and the matter would be dropped. At the CSCE, the principle of consensus—and the substance of the Final Act itself—allowed Goldberg, Kampelman, and their Western European counterparts to shine a spotlight on subjects that the USSR would have preferred to avoid.[188]

This approach put the Soviet government on trial in a "world court in continuous session," as Kampelman put it. Ostracizing Moscow for violating the norms of respectable international society, he reasoned, would stop it from using the CSCE to burnish its legitimacy. As the peace movement grew and demonstrators criticized plans to deploy new intermediate-range nuclear missiles in Western Europe, the allies could shore up Western public support for NATO by highlighting how the communist regimes had violated the Final Act. The Soviets could not claim they took peace seriously unless they respected all of its components, including human rights.[189] In Czechoslovakia, Jiří Hájek made a similar case. Because the Final Act's principles were indivisible, individual freedoms mattered just as much as military security. "The point is to ensure that all parties properly understand the interdependence of peaceful coexistence and the respect for human rights, freedoms and dignity," he said.[190] If the Soviets did not wish to revive the dangerous confrontations of the high Cold War, they had to modify their domestic behavior, not just their foreign policy.

The Soviets tried to change the subject. They hoped that the conference would repair their international reputation after the invasion of Afghanistan, and wanted it to launch a Conference on Disarmament in Europe. Because NATO's 1979 dual-track decision threatened to tilt the nuclear balance in Europe against the Eastern allies, they needed to regain the initiative. As the Euromissile debates raged and hundreds of thousands of protesters criticized the American military buildup, the Soviets counted on using the CSCE to rally Western public opinion against defense spending and pit the Americans against the Western Europeans. If this plan worked, the Eastern allies would gain the breathing room they needed to cut their own military budgets to a more sustainable level. If it failed and the Western buildup continued unabated, however, Moscow might lose the strategic parity that it valued so highly. When the conference opened, the Soviet representatives refused to discuss Basket III and declared that the USSR would not feel secure enough to implement the Final Act's humanitarian provisions unless the West took action on disarmament.[191] "The more détente prospers, the more Basket III prospers," said Sergei Kondrashev, now serving as deputy head of the Soviet delegation.[192]

These struggles, which reflected long-running disputes about the meaning of détente, established the contours of the negotiations. Bitter arguments consumed the delegates for months, until the neutrals helped to broker a compromise.[193] But the deal fell apart in December 1981, when the Polish government imposed martial law to deal with Solidarity. In response, the Western allies took an even harder line. The new American president, Ronald Reagan, who had previously criticized the Final Act, now embraced the agreement as a weapon for fighting the Cold War. He denounced the use of martial law as a "gross violation of the Helsinki pact" and called for sanctions against Moscow. In warning the Soviets not to invade, Helmut Schmidt, Hans-Dietrich Genscher, British foreign secretary Lord Carrington, and other Western European leaders invoked the Final Act's principle of nonintervention—and its implicit repudiation of the Brezhnev Doctrine. In Madrid, the Western allies also demanded that their Eastern counterparts recognize the right to form a trade union and the right to strike. If they refused, the Americans hinted, the meeting would end without an agreement.[194]

This pointed response belied the allies' own disagreements. The Reagan administration considered abandoning the negotiations entirely to punish the Soviets for the crisis in Poland. But the Western Europeans objected that a failure in Madrid might turn public opinion against the Euromissiles and ultimately endanger trans-Atlantic security. They also feared damaging their lucrative economic ties to the Eastern bloc. Besides, Hans-Dietrich Genscher told American Secretary of State Alexander Haig, the West had to keep the CSCE alive because it provided an essential tool for defending human rights and advocating for disarmament. Killing the conference would only help the Soviets by relieving the pressure on them. As so many times before at the CSCE, the West was playing a game of diplomatic chicken, daring the Soviets to abandon the conference but counting on them to stay at the negotiating table.[195]

After an eight-month recess to evaluate their options, the delegates reconvened in November 1982 and hunkered down in their familiar positions. Martial law persisted in Poland, and—as the nuclear freeze movement grew—so did Western officials' anxieties about public opinion. The Soviets still refused to end radio jamming, accept external human rights monitoring, or convene a special CSCE meeting on human contacts. Eventually, a Soviet-American side deal helped to break the impasse. On the margins of the conference, Kampelman and Kondrashev found a solution to the problem of the Siberian Seven, a group of Pentecostals who had sought refuge from religious persecution in the US embassy in Moscow. Once they were allowed to emigrate in July 1983, bilateral relations thawed slightly.[196]

The Spanish government took advantage of the opening to broker a compromise on the main agenda items. Against the better judgment of some of their allies, the Soviets accepted more stringent measures on humanitarian affairs and human contacts. The Madrid agreement recognized the right to form trade unions, gave more scope to religious freedom, removed restrictions on journalists, and approved future specialized meetings on human rights, culture, and human contacts. The East Germans strenuously opposed the provisions that prohibited discrimination against would-be emigrés and required the rapid adjudication of exit visa applications, but the Soviets overruled them. In exchange for these concessions, the Western allies announced they would participate in fresh negotiations on disarmament and confidence-building measures, which the Soviets now agreed to apply to all of European Russia.[197]

Yuri Andropov, who had succeeded Brezhnev in November 1982, praised Madrid's results. The socialist states were keeping up the fight to save détente from the Reagan administration's attempts to revive old tensions, he said. Western citizens would see that the USSR remained committed to peace even while the United States was agitating for war.[198] But if he hoped that the Madrid agreement would empower Western anti-nuclear activists, events disappointed him. The peace movement failed to dissuade NATO's leaders—or the Bundestag—from deploying American Pershing-II missiles in West Germany. In protest, the Kremlin pulled out of the Geneva arms control talks with the US. Nonetheless, it remained committed to the CSCE.

The Madrid agreement held up even after Soviet fighter jets shot down a Korean passenger airliner in September, the United States invaded Grenada in October, and NATO's Able Archer exercise raised nuclear tensions to their highest point in decades.[199]

V

The Soviets and their allies lost the fight over how to interpret the Final Act. In the aftermath of the Helsinki summit, they made a major effort to persuade their citizens that the agreement legitimized their regimes and testified to their growing strength. Most Western observers—and many in the Soviet bloc besides—accepted this interpretation. Those who did not see the Final Act as a pile of meaningless paper regarded it as an act of capitulation to Moscow. Within just a few years, however, this dynamic reversed itself. Communism's opponents in the USSR and Eastern Europe discerned that they could use the Final Act to agitate for greater openness. They rejected the notion that the agreement subordinated its humanitarian provisions and universal values to state sovereignty or domestic legislation. Regardless of its loopholes or its status under international law, a plain reading of the text demonstrated that the leaders of every communist country in Europe had promised to respect fundamental rights and to promote the freer movement of people and information.

Western politicians and activists came to share this view, leading them to the same optimistic conclusions that many Western diplomats had drawn in 1975. Former critics of the Final Act recanted their earlier opinions. In 1983, Ronald Reagan praised its "clear code of conduct," which every participant had to honor, and insisted that the tenor of US-Soviet relations depended on Moscow's respect for the agreement. The West could use these shared principles of order to serve its goals in the Cold War. By establishing the interdependence of human rights and international security, the CSCE would "erode the cruel divisions between East and West in Europe," Secretary of State George Shultz said. If the USSR wanted peace, it would have to stop being "afraid of its own people."[200]

In Belgrade and Madrid, the fight over the interpretation of the Final Act expanded into a larger contest over its implementation. Although the Western allies argued—often fiercely—about tactics, the disputes at the follow-up conferences did not drive them apart. Instead, they stuck together in a joint effort to defend the Final Act and oppose the abuse of individual rights in Eastern Europe. For their part, the Soviets and their allies resolved to stand firm, and they lashed out at their counterparts for interfering in their internal affairs. Eventually, however, after suffering fusillades of Western vituperation, they accepted proposals that they had previously rejected.

The Madrid agreement expanded on the Final Act's original provisions in significant ways.

At home, the Soviets and Eastern Europeans jailed, expelled, and bullied their opponents and tried to choke off civil society. In these policies, Western governments found little evidence of concrete progress on humanitarian questions. In some cases, however, communist leaders made painful decisions to honor their CSCE obligations even when they contradicted their fundamental concepts of domestic order. In 1984, for example, the number of applications to emigrate from East Germany surged, and the authorities approved nearly 50,000 of them. The communists had originally expected that state sovereignty would shield them from unwelcome obligations. Under intense domestic and international pressure, this plan did not work as well as they had anticipated.[201]

Despite the turmoil of the early 1980s and the polemics at the follow-up conferences, the USSR remained committed to the CSCE. The real mystery of this period is not why Cold War tensions returned but why the Soviets refused to walk away from a diplomatic process that seemed only to be causing them grief. Bureaucratic politics offer one reason. "Once the Central Committee determined a particular course of action it became very difficult to change it," Lev Mendelevich told a Swiss diplomat in the mid-1980s. "It was practically impossible to do otherwise."[202]

The USSR's original motives for the security conference point to a more profound answer. The Final Act was the centerpiece of Brezhnev's strategy to rebuild the USSR's domestic and international legitimacy. By signing the agreement in 1975, celebrating his success at the 1976 party congress, and incorporating its principles into his country's constitution in 1977, he tied his reputation and his legacy to the CSCE. Even as the Final Act became a tool for communism's internal and external adversaries, Brezhnev could not repudiate it without causing even greater damage to his own reputation and to the legitimacy of the Soviet system. Before the Helsinki summit, Anatoly Chernyaev foresaw this dilemma. If the CSCE turned against the USSR, he predicted that Brezhnev would refuse to abandon "something that is associated with his name worldwide." The general secretary reached the same conclusion, though he made his case in less personal terms. "[I]t is absolutely important to preserve the positive things that have been achieved over the years," he said in 1980. "No matter what our political enemies might say, the peaceful path delineated in Helsinki is of the greatest importance."[203]

Epilogue

REUNIFICATIONS

When the Soviet Politburo elected Mikhail Gorbachev to succeed Konstantin Chernenko in March 1985, the new general secretary faced no immediate crises. Europe's communist regimes remained remarkably stable despite international pressure and domestic problems. Their economies trudged along, wasting enormous quantities of resources and offering few returns on capital investment. Governments that had grown dependent on foreign credit and consumer goods plunged deeper into debt. Living standards fell further behind the West, and growth rates dropped. Yet there was no sign of impending collapse. Bureaucracies still functioned. Armies continued to train for combat. Citizens went about their day-to-day lives under the eye of the secret police.[1]

Nevertheless, Gorbachev believed that the system required urgent reform. He did not want to dismantle socialism, but to help it realize its potential by solving the problems that plagued it. He embraced new ideas and cleared the way for them by marginalizing the conservative skeptics who still populated the Kremlin. At home, he set about reinvigorating the economy and opening up political life. The "new political thinking" shaped his approach to international politics. Over time, he grew ever more confident and more radical, eventually coming to regard his policies in universalistic—even messianic—terms, as if he were creating a new world order.[2]

The Final Act exerted a powerful influence on Gorbachev's views, and on those of his advisors and supporters. The general secretary rejected old Soviet assumptions about the nature of international security, the inevitability of conflict between the capitalist and socialist worlds, the bonds between the USSR and its Warsaw Pact allies, and the relationship between the individual and the state. Instead, he made the case for common values and common interests that transcended the Cold War divide, and for a broad understanding of peace that integrated military and humanitarian considerations. After the decade-long fight over the meaning of the Final Act, Gorbachev adopted the Western interpretation of the document and put it into practice. Many of his most significant decisions bore the CSCE's imprint, and he cited the Final Act to justify his policies to his critics. Thanks in large part to the new direction of Soviet foreign policy, the follow-up conference in Vienna yielded significant results.

The revolutions that erupted in Eastern Europe in 1989—and the dramatic changes that they catalyzed—were also shaped by the Final Act. In these events, the first basket's principles of security played as significant a role as the third basket's humanitarian commitments. In some places, the opposition movements that helped to topple the communist governments, notably Solidarity in Poland and the Civic Forum in Czechoslovakia, drew inspiration from the agreement's vision of openness and individual freedom. In Hungary and East Germany, the authorities ignored many of their CSCE obligations, but they honored others. Even these modest openings gave activists and average citizens a vital chance to circumvent the states' usual methods of control. After the Berlin Wall fell, political leaders on all sides looked to the Final Act to guide the process of German reunification. Once it became clear that the Cold War itself was ending, they turned again to the CSCE to negotiate what amounted to a peace treaty for the decades-long conflict. In establishing Europe's post–Cold War contours, the 1990 Paris Charter closely followed the blueprint laid down in Helsinki. At the moment of its signature, the long struggle to negotiate a new concept of legitimacy and construct a new international order finally reached its culmination.

I

Despite his communist bona fides and his fidelity to the Soviet system, Mikhail Gorbachev's core commitments reflected Western values. In his younger days, he had taken advantage of the privilege afforded to the *nomenklatura* to read Western books and magazines. He had traveled more extensively in Western Europe and North America than any of his predecessors. As the Politburo's expert on agriculture, he looked to Western farms for new methods to apply at home. After assuming the top job, he surrounded himself with advisors who shared his willingness to reconsider old assumptions and turn heterodox ideas into action.[3]

Many of the reformers' ideas, especially in foreign policy, had taken root in the Brezhnev era. In the 1970s, a number of mid-career officials who later rose to prominence with Gorbachev reconsidered the Soviet approach to security. Aleksandr Yakovlev, Anatoly Chernyaev, Georgy Arbatov, and Georgi Shakhnazarov, among others, questioned the nostrums that Soviet strength required Western weakness, and that military superiority would solve all problems. In the thermonuclear age, East and West shared vital security interests despite their ideological differences. The demands of "common security" meant that "we cannot guarantee our own security at the expense of someone else's, but only on the basis of mutual interests," Arbatov wrote.[4] This approach had much in common with the logic of the Final Act, and with the ideas of Andrei Sakharov and other dissidents, who emphasized East-West interdependence and called for greater openness to reduce the threat of nuclear war. The Soviet authorities had punished Sakharov, but many of the figures who went on to serve Gorbachev sympathized with his views.[5]

Common security rejected the two-camps theory that had underpinned Soviet foreign policy since the 1940s. By contrast with the Stalinists who believed that class conflict inhered in the structure of world politics, Gorbachev and his advisors argued that all peoples and states shared the same fate.[6] "[H]uman values" took precedence "over the interests of a given class," Gorbachev declared in 1986.[7] His repudiation of Marxist-Leninist orthodoxy on this subject reflected his childhood experience of war and his revulsion at violence. Brezhnev had taken pride in achieving nuclear parity with the United States, but now Gorbachev warned of "nuclear suicide."[8] If only the communist and capitalist states could recognize how much they had in common, he reasoned, they could overcome their differences. He envisioned a "new world where class struggle, ideology, polarity and enmity are no longer determinate," Chernyaev wrote in his diary.[9]

If humanity shared common interests, it also had to share universal political principles. There could not be two sets of values, one for the bourgeoisie and another for the proletariat, but only a single creed that transcended the divisions between classes, countries, and blocs. "The very words 'human rights' are put in quotation marks and we speak of so-called human rights, as if our own revolution had nothing to do with human rights," Gorbachev said. Alluding to the Final Act, he emphasized that the USSR had to abandon this old approach and "view it more broadly, particularly with regard to such specific issues as reunification of families, [and] exit and entry visas."[10] In preparing to address the UN General Assembly in 1988, Gorbachev argued that "the rights of the peoples, their right of free choice, human rights" applied worldwide.[11]

Soviet security policy had to change accordingly. Brezhnev's old strategy, which emphasized military stability and the inviolability of borders as the foundations of peace, had become obsolete. In order to build "a comprehensive system of international security," the USSR had to come to terms with the reality of interdependence. It had to lower the barriers between states, instead of raising them, and needed to encourage closer human contacts across borders.[12] A new set of precepts now guided Soviet policy: the freedom of people to choose their own political systems, the renunciation of force, mutual respect between East and West, and nuclear abolition.[13] Gorbachev had abandoned Brezhnev's interpretation of the Final Act and adopted that of the West instead.

Gorbachev's views were not heterodox simply because he believed in universal principles. Marxism posits certain scientific laws that apply across countries and cultures. Rather, Gorbachev's approach was radical because he embraced fundamental Western values, though he did not recognize them as such. He warned the United States not to try to export "Western values" to Eastern Europe, and distinguished between them and "general human values." In practice, however, he himself brought liberal democratic principles to the USSR in the guise of universalism.[14]

At the center of Gorbachev's foreign policy stood the idea of the "Common European Home." Echoing de Gaulle's vision of a "Europe from the Atlantic to the Urals," it assumed that more united the countries of the continent than divided them. They therefore ought to collaborate in building a shared international order based on shared principles. Gorbachev first used the concept to make the case for nuclear disarmament in his 1984 speech to the British House of Commons. As time went on, the idea grew more expansive. Eventually it came to describe an entirely new international order based on universal values and—crucially—on the Final Act, whose common standard of conduct applied to the whole continent. States would enjoy complete self-determination, reduce their conventional and nuclear arsenals, reject the use of force, and forge a single pan-European economy. Only by rejecting the balance of power and by bringing East and West back together could the superpowers and their allies create genuine security in Europe.[15]

In the old contest between Westernizers and Slavophiles, the Westernizers had gained the upper hand. Because the USSR was a European country, it had to "make Europe and European politics our first priority," Gorbachev said in 1986.[16] The goal was to participate "in the common European process and form together with Europe a unified economic, legal, humanitarian, cultural and ecological space," foreign minister Eduard Shevardnadze declared.[17] No longer would the USSR seek security by building barriers between the two halves of Europe, or seek to drive a wedge between Western Europe and the United States. To the contrary, Gorbachev and his advisors maintained that the more the USSR and its allies collaborated with the West, the more secure they would become. The USSR would embrace international society and integrate itself politically, economically, and culturally with the West. In Chernyaev's words, the country would "return to Europe."[18]

The common European home reflected the principles of the Final Act. In both cases, a single set of values and the construction of a single, integrated international order replaced the old Cold War logic of division and ideological confrontation. In March 1986, Gorbachev told the 27th Party Congress that the time had come to build "a comprehensive system of international security" that recognized the interdependence of military and humanitarian concerns. According to Anatoly Kovalev, who helped to write the report, these ideas came directly from the CSCE.[19] Gorbachev himself explicitly acknowledged the Final Act's importance to his vision. "Both historically and politically [the common European home] is a direct continuation of those ideas that were included in the All-European Conference in its time. The Helsinki process was a great achievement; its potential is far from exhausted," he told his hosts on a 1988 visit to Warsaw. It was therefore necessary to push its ideas even further, "to rethink the entire situation in Europe from the standpoint of the new political thinking."[20]

Gorbachev reimagined the relationship between sovereignty, security, and universal values. The USSR and its allies had no intention of relinquishing their sovereign prerogatives, but they could no longer rely on them to deflect international scrutiny. Other principles had to take precedence. "Humanitarian problems, human rights—these are subjects of legal concern to the entire world community," he told Warsaw Pact leaders.[21] In a 1989 speech to the Council of Europe, he argued that Helsinki had set in motion an "immense effort of world significance" to reform international affairs "in the spirit of humanism, equality, and justice and by setting an example of democracy and social achievements." Likewise, the Final Act had established that military security and human rights could not be disentangled. "A world in which military arsenals would be cut but in which human rights would be violated cannot feel secure," he said. The time had come to "replace the traditional balance of forces with a balance of interests" and to create "one Europe—peaceful and democratic—a Europe that preserves all of its diversity and abides by common human ideals." The CSCE provided an ideal vehicle for this project.[22]

In rethinking the axioms of Soviet foreign policy, Gorbachev also sought to build a new foundation for the socialist commonwealth. Soviet influence in Eastern Europe had long depended on Moscow's willingness to use force against its allies and spend lavishly to support their economies. But "the use of force was naturally disgusting for Gorbachev," Chernyaev recalled.[23] In 1989, Gorbachev told the Politburo, "We have accepted that even in foreign policy force is to no avail. So especially internally—we cannot resort and will not resort to force."[24] Moreover, Moscow could no longer afford to subsidize Eastern Europe. As Comecon's hopes of economic integration and greater efficiencies evaporated, the Eastern Europeans were turning westward in search of the advanced technology that the USSR could not provide. Previous Soviet leaders had believed that the country's security depended on maintaining friendly governments and a strong military alliance in Eastern Europe, but Gorbachev saw things differently. The cost of holding onto Eastern Europe—in moral and material terms—now outstripped the benefits.[25]

In one sense, Gorbachev had drawn the same conclusion as Brezhnev and his colleagues when they decided they could not invade Poland at the height of the Solidarity crisis. They too had fretted about the USSR's international standing and material capabilities, and quietly set the Brezhnev Doctrine aside. But Gorbachev's reasoning contained a utopian element that theirs did not. The new world order that he envisioned—based on nonviolence, sovereign equality, and consent—would start in Eastern Europe. By reestablishing communism's legitimacy on these principles, the USSR's influence would become more sustainable and its interests more secure.[26]

This new attitude to Eastern Europe, combined with his own aversion to force, led Gorbachev to scrap the Brezhnev Doctrine once and for all. Respect for self-determination and nonintervention took its place. Scholars have debated when Gorbachev reached this decision, with some placing it as early as the moment he assumed office in March 1985.[27] By 1988 at the latest, however, he had made up his mind. "No one can impose anything on anyone," he told Yugoslav leader Lazar Mojsov. "The world is different now, each state strives to determine its fate independently, and we must take that into account. Of course, the major powers carry more responsibility than the smaller countries. But they must not crush the rights of others."[28] In conversation with West German chancellor Helmut Kohl the following summer, he acknowledged the growing clamor for reform in several Eastern European countries. "Everything is moving in the direction of a strengthening of democratic foundations. Every country is deciding on its own how to do it. It is their internal affair," he said. "I think that what I have just said makes it clear whether there is a 'Brezhnev Doctrine.'"[29]

II

These ideas transformed the Soviet bloc and its relationship to the West. In searching for new sources of legitimacy, Gorbachev introduced greater openness, transparency, and pluralism in foreign and domestic affairs alike. Instead of obstructing the CSCE, Gorbachev worked with the Western powers to invigorate it. Bringing Soviet policy into line with the Final Act had dramatic consequences for Europe and for the Cold War more broadly.

To put the new thinking into practice, Gorbachev assembled a team of likeminded reformers. He appointed Chernyaev, Yakovlev, and Shakhnazarov to influential positions. To shake up the Ministry of Foreign Affairs, he turned to Shevardnadze, whose lack of diplomatic experience made it easier to break with the rigid assumptions of Soviet foreign policy. Kovalev, whom Mikhail Suslov had blacklisted in 1976 for "liberalism and deviating from Party norms" in negotiating the Final Act, became Shevardnadze's top deputy and a key member of the general secretary's foreign policy team.[30]

In the months following Gorbachev's accession, Western leaders wondered whether he would make a real break with the past. At the CSCE's Ottawa conference on human rights in 1985, Soviet delegates reprised their familiar arguments. They insisted, for example, that the "right to life in peace" trumped all other rights. The claim implied that domestic liberalization could somehow lead to nuclear war, and that diplomats had no business discussing other countries' internal practices.[31] The Soviets also bitterly criticized Western governments for their own human rights failures, ranging from excessive unemployment to racial discrimination.[32]

The arguments about freedom of movement and civil society continued at the CSCE's Budapest Cultural Forum later that year. While communist delegates insisted that art had to serve the state's purposes, such as educating the public about the horrors of war, private apartments around the city hosted free-wheeling discussions between Hungarian intellectuals and visitors from the West. The contrast between the official conference and these unofficial symposia illustrated the persistent disconnect between the communist and liberal democratic notions of individual freedom.[33] To underscore the point, when the CSCE foreign ministers met in Helsinki to mark the Final Act's tenth anniversary, George Shultz told Shevardnadze that unless the USSR made progress in fulfilling its human rights promises, American-Soviet relations would not improve.[34]

The Soviets soon began to move in a new direction. The 27th Party Congress ratified Gorbachev's new thinking and gave him the political backing required to transform Soviet foreign policy.[35] Around the same time, Aleksandr Yakovlev urged the general secretary to expand the "democratization of public life" by loosening restrictions on information and expanding freedom of speech and freedom of travel. "We want everybody to have great civic responsibilities," he wrote, "but that is only possible if there are great civil rights."[36] Some Politburo members expressed concern that punishing Sakharov and other dissidents had damaged the USSR's international standing.[37] Gorbachev himself told the Politburo that "we need seriously to rethink" how to approach the problem of human rights. "Nobody in our country has done this in a serious way, either theoretically or by generalizing from experience," he said. By placing the party's interests ahead of individual liberty and demanding political conformism, the existing approach "only produces dissidents."[38]

Gorbachev took dramatic steps to demonstrate his commitment. His policy of glasnost scrapped some of the tactics the state had long used to suppress criticism. An independent civil society blossomed around informal discussion groups, which—consciously or not—took impetus from the

Final Act, and pressed the general secretary to implement even bolder re-forms.[39] In February 1986, Anatoly Shcharansky was set free and joined his wife in Israel. Several months later, the authorities sent Yuri Orlov to the United States.[40] After the 1986 Reykjavik summit, the Politburo agreed to let Sakharov return to Moscow. Hundreds of other political prisoners were likewise released, including all of those whose cases Shultz had personally raised with Shevardnadze.[41]

The government also began to make good on the Final Act's promises of openness, transparency, and freedom of movement. Shevardnadze chal-lenged the KGB's hardline views on these questions by ordering deputy foreign minister Anatoly Adamishin to rethink Soviet human rights diplo-macy.[42] When the CSCE's Bern meeting on human contacts ended in May without an agreement, Gorbachev concluded that building the common European home required unilateral action on humanitarian questions. Modest improvements in family reunification and travel policies followed. If citizens wanted to leave the USSR, he reasoned, why should the state force them to stay?[43]

Brezhnev had tried to strengthen the barriers that separated the Soviet bloc from the West, but now Gorbachev worked to lower them. "We shouldn't be afraid to allow free travel in both directions. Let our people find out that the world is large and diverse, and let foreigners discover that there is no 'Soviet threat,'" he told the Politburo in 1985. "We have to learn to debate, to listen, to be convincing. We shouldn't be afraid of any ques-tions; we have to teach people to argue, to carry on a dialogue."[44] When the KGB and conservative Communist Party members resisted this turn toward openness, Gorbachev sometimes cited the Final Act to justify reform. At another Politburo meeting, for instance, he argued that Basket III required the USSR to stop jamming Western radio broadcasts. No one objected.[45] Gorbachev had initially pursued glasnost and relaxed official censorship to rehabilitate the Communist Party in the eyes of Soviet intellectuals. But as time went on, he became convinced of the inherent virtues of openness. "There will be no concessions on the matter of glasnost, notwithstanding the accusation that we are 'stripping naked' in front of the world," he said. "It is our strength, not a weakness."[46]

The Kremlin's new direction encompassed more than humanitarian con-cerns. In March 1986, Shevardnadze told the Warsaw Pact's foreign minis-ters that the continent had to move "from the initial phase of détente to a more mature and permanent one," in which the Helsinki process would build the foundation for a new "reliable security system."[47] In November, he elaborated on this point in Vienna at the CSCE's third follow-up meeting. Security was "acquiring new dimensions," Shevardnadze said. It now in-cluded far more than just military affairs. States had to act across a wide range of subjects to create "a system of comprehensive security" that would "rule out the very possibility of war breaking out." The Final Act embodied the new ideal of security, he said.[48]

Military policy changed accordingly. In 1984, Gromyko had rejected a proposal at the Stockholm conference on confidence- and security-building measures to authorize on-site inspections of ground troops. The West was "trying to drill a peephole in our fence," he argued. Hans-Dietrich Genscher denied the accusation. "No, I'm not," he said. "I'm trying to get rid of the fence altogether."[49] Two years later, the chief of the Soviet General Staff, Marshal Sergei Akhromeev, reiterated Gromyko's criticism. He insisted that inviting Western inspectors into Soviet military installations would humiliate the Red Army and open the door to espionage. At a tense Politburo meeting, Gorbachev overruled him. He sent Akhromeev to Stockholm to announce the change in Soviet policy in person. The Soviets likewise accepted robust verification measures in the talks on conventional disarmament in Europe, which had grown out of the stalled Mutual and Balanced Force Reduction talks.[50]

The new spirit of transparency applied to nuclear weapons too. In January 1986, as part of a proposal for total nuclear disarmament, Gorbachev announced that the USSR would accept on-site inspections by American officials.[51] The Chernobyl accident in April underscored the need to stop fetishizing secrecy and to build trust with the West instead. The Intermediate-Range Nuclear Forces Treaty, signed in December 1987, likewise endorsed greater transparency through on-the-spot verification measures.[52] By opening the USSR's defenses to unprecedented international scrutiny, Gorbachev demonstrated his hopes for "transparency and candor" in military affairs. The extensive East-West cooperation in both the conventional and nuclear disarmament negotiations demonstrated just how drastically Soviet defense policy had changed.[53]

Neither this diplomatic progress nor Gorbachev's reforming zeal could save the USSR from its serious economic woes. In some ways, perestroika's attempts to improve the situation made matters worse. In 1986, a collapse in the price of oil slashed Soviet export earnings, and Gorbachev's anti-alcohol campaign reduced tax revenues by a similar amount, causing a huge budgetary shortfall. Because entrenched interests made it impossible to close the deficit by cutting subsidies, and the Politburo feared that raising prices would provoke a popular backlash, Gorbachev and his colleagues decided to print money instead. The decision induced major shortages in food and consumer goods. In tandem with these problems, massive new investments in industrial production led only to further waste, and agricultural reforms ran into a bureaucratic dead-end. In Eastern Europe, where several governments staggered under the burden of their foreign debts, the picture was bleaker still. As the economic crisis unfolded across the bloc, it left the Soviet government and its allies even more exposed to the demands of their Western counterparts.[54]

Against this backdrop, the CSCE's Vienna follow-up meeting put the USSR's new foreign policy commitments to the test. In his speech to the opening session in November 1986, Eduard Shevardnadze proposed to hold a conference on human contacts in Moscow, an idea that had originated with Kovalev. Doubting his sincerity, the Western diplomats kept up their attacks on Soviet and Eastern European human rights practices.[55] Although the Soviets initially resisted the Western demands for greater openness, their attitude evolved as the negotiations continued. As in Geneva, Belgrade, and Madrid, they met regularly with allied delegations, but now, instead of attempting to dictate policy to them, they expected the Eastern Europeans to come up with their own ideas. On matters of substance, too, the Soviet delegation broke with the past. In the name of reaching a deal with the West, it urged the decision-makers in Moscow to end radio jamming, stop imprisoning dissidents in psychiatric hospitals, and remove all barriers to emigration.[56]

When hardliners in the Central Committee tried to quash these ideas, Gorbachev circumvented them. He established a special committee, chaired by Yakovlev, to evaluate the Soviet delegation's recommendations, which were duly implemented with Shevardnadze's support. In Vienna, the Soviets announced that they would stop jamming all foreign radio broadcasts and cajoled their allies to follow suit. "The level of glasnost is now so high in the Soviet Union that we can afford to hear three more voices or 20 more languages," said Yuri Kashlev, the head of the delegation. In a bid to win support for the Moscow human rights conference, the Soviets invited the International Helsinki Federation to visit the country. Meanwhile, some Eastern European officials began speaking to Helsinki Watch representatives. By the end of 1988, the government had jettisoned the Marxist-Leninist interpretation of human rights in favor of a liberal democratic one, and affirmed that all citizens had a right to emigrate so long as they did not possess state secrets.[57]

The final agreement reached in Vienna in January 1989 went well beyond the texts negotiated in Belgrade and Madrid. It affirmed citizens' freedom to travel, empowered them to appeal administrative decisions (regarding exit visa applications, for example), required governments to tolerate Helsinki monitoring groups, and established a procedure for monitoring how well each state implemented its CSCE promises. In exchange, the Western allies agreed to participate in conventional disarmament negotiations, a new round of talks on confidence- and security-building measures, and the human rights conference in Moscow. On nearly every point, the agreement embodied the values of glasnost and the common European home. In turn, the document gave Gorbachev a new tool to override his critics and justify further domestic reforms.[58]

The USSR's more conservative allies tried to impede this turn to openness. Although most Eastern European leaders accepted the INF Treaty and backed the Moscow conference proposal, some worried that Gorbachev and Shevardnadze were going too far.[59] East German foreign minister Oskar Fischer insisted that Western governments were collaborating with the "internal opposition" across Eastern Europe. If the Soviets capitulated to this "especially extortionary" pressure on human rights, they would erode communist sovereignty, consecrate a "right to interfere" and a "right to complain" under the auspices of the CSCE, and eventually help the West to dismantle socialism by infecting the socialist states with bourgeois values. The Romanians, who made similar objections, declared that they would not treat any agreement in Vienna as binding. In light of Gorbachev's determination to press forward, however, these skeptics stood little chance of blocking the reorientation of Soviet foreign policy.[60]

Some allies wanted Moscow to move faster, even at the expense of communist solidarity. During a Soviet-American argument in Vienna over humanitarian measures, for instance, the Poles and the Hungarians took Washington's side.[61] "It is not always necessary to speak with a single voice" at the CSCE, because the conference transcended the blocs, Poland's foreign minister told his Warsaw Pact colleagues. States could no longer escape international scrutiny, added his Hungarian counterpart. "It is the inalienable right and obligation of the community of nations to monitor how states adhere to their commitments in the area of human rights and humanitarian issues, and to hold them accountable," he said. If the Eastern allies neglected this principle, they would damage their ties to the Western world and, by extension, their own stability. While the East Germans, Czechoslovaks, Bulgarians, and Romanians grumbled about state sovereignty, the Soviets sided with the Hungarians. In Moscow's view, the solidarity of the Warsaw Pact now mattered less than the USSR's commitment to openness and universal values.[62]

III

By 1989, the principles of the Final Act had profoundly shaped the imaginations of leaders in the Soviet bloc—and the revolutions that erupted that year proved it. In March, the Hungarian authorities decided to remove the surveillance systems that had protected their border with Austria. "We have outlived the need for it, and now it serves only for catching citizens of Romania and the GDR who try to illegally escape to the West," said the chairman of the Council of Ministers, Miklós Németh. Gorbachev did not object. "We have a strict regime on our borders, but we are also becoming more open," he replied. The logic of freer movement supplanted the old restrictions on emigration.[63]

That summer, the West German government paid the Hungarians one billion Deutschmarks to open their frontiers to East German refugees. Officials in Budapest decided that the principles of the Final Act trumped their agreement with the GDR on repatriating defectors. If East Germans wanted to leave Hungary, the Hungarian government would not stop them.[64] Citing the principle of self-determination, the Soviets declined to get involved, even as the number of citizens emigrating from the USSR grew exponentially. "This is an affair that concerns Hungary, the GDR, and the FRG," Shevardnadze said.[65] The exodus from the GDR spiraled into an existential crisis that soon toppled the regime.[66] The CSCE also helped to deter communist leaders from using force against the thousands of demonstrators who filled the streets of Eastern Europe over the summer and into the fall. The intense international scrutiny of their domestic policies, combined with their growing economic reliance on the West, forced communist officials to reconsider the calculus of domestic repression.[67]

Because the Cold War had split Europe in two, the conflict could only end by making the continent whole again. "[O]ur overall aim is to overcome the division of Europe and forge a unity based on Western values," the new American president, George H. W. Bush, told reporters in May 1989.[68] By this stage, Gorbachev had concluded that his country could survive only if it abandoned the logic of socialist legality and adopted the rule of law. That year, the CSCE's conference on humanitarian affairs gave the USSR a chance to demonstrate its commitment to this principle. Working with the French, West Germans, and Austrians, the Soviets agreed to create a common European "legal space" that connected the rule of law and respect for individual rights.[69]

At a CSCE meeting on economic cooperation several months later, the Soviets and Eastern Europeans repudiated central planning and agreed to build free market economies. The GDR's new defense minister—the first noncommunist to hold the position—told his Soviet counterpart that, in the name of European unity, they had to work with the West to build common security for the whole continent under the auspices of the CSCE.[70] The principles of the Final Act guided the communist governments as they dismantled their own systems.

The Final Act also played a central role in the process of German unification. Helmut Kohl and Hans-Dietrich Genscher placed the CSCE at the center of their policy toward the GDR. In particular, they demanded that East German leaders make good on the Final Act's promises, especially regarding human rights and self-determination.[71] At the Vienna conference, East German diplomats had accepted the principle that citizens had the right to leave their country, but the country's leaders had no intention of following through. Nevertheless, they worried that Bonn would withhold financial aid unless they honored it. In July 1989, for example, a senior official from the Federal Republic's Chancellery warned Erich Honecker that West German public opinion might lose patience with Ostpolitik if the GDR did not honor its CSCE promise to let its citizens emigrate.[72]

Although Honecker rebuffed this demand, his government implemented other elements of the Final Act, with fateful consequences. *Der Spiegel*'s East Berlin correspondent, Ulrich Schwarz, became a crucial conduit for dissidents in the GDR because the East German border authorities, in deference to the CSCE's provisions on journalists' working conditions, refrained from searching his luggage when he crossed back and forth. In October 1989, activists in Leipzig trusted him with their surreptitious video recording of the massive street demonstrations that engulfed the city. Schwarz hid the tape in his underwear and crossed into West Berlin. Within hours, the images of thousands of East German citizens defying their government were broadcast back into GDR on West German television, which gave a vital impetus to the demonstrators. This dynamic significantly increased the pressure on the communist authorities and made a major contribution to the chain of events that culminated in the opening of the Berlin Wall in November.[73]

After the wall fell, governments on both sides developed competing models for the process of unification. All of them treated the Final Act as a lodestar. By this point, Gorbachev had accepted that Germany would eventually unify. "[H]istory should decide" the country's fate, he told Bush, although he hoped that the process would play out gradually as the two blocs drew closer to one another within a pan-European security system under CSCE auspices.[74] Even as the pace of events accelerated beyond his control in late 1989 and 1990, he remained committed to the Helsinki process. He challenged Helmut Kohl's ten-point program, which he regarded as an ultimatum rather than a proposal. "How can we talk about 'building a new Europe' if you act this way?" he asked Genscher. "An all-European process is under way, we want to build a new Europe, a common European home. We need trust to do that." Despite this criticism, however, Gorbachev accepted that the principles of self-determination and the peaceful change of frontiers had opened the door to unification.[75]

Western leaders also relied on the CSCE to guide and legitimize their efforts. Kohl envisioned a "confederation" of East Germany and West Germany, within which the two states would gradually work toward unification. The CSCE would provide the overarching framework. "The future architecture of Germany must fit in the future pan-European architecture," his plan declared.[76] Events moved so quickly, however, that Kohl changed his mind. Unification could not wait. At the Malta summit in December

1989, Bush had told Gorbachev that the Final Act ruled out unification. Kohl immediately challenged this idea and changed the president's mind. The principle of the peaceful change of frontiers legitimized unification, the chancellor insisted. Bush conceded the point.[77]

In France, President François Mitterand developed his own ideas about Germany's future. He too anchored them in the CSCE. In a televised speech on New Year's Eve, he called for a pan-European confederation on the basis of the Final Act. It would unite the peoples of the continent in a shared commitment to peace, representative government, and freedom of information.[78] Although Bush worried that Mitterand's confederation would weaken NATO, the Helsinki process also featured prominently in his own administration's plans.[79] Secretary of State James Baker suggested that the CSCE could supervise the conduct of free elections in the Soviet bloc. Voting was "the ultimate human right, the right that secures all others," he said.[80] Even Margaret Thatcher, who doubted the wisdom of German unification, cited the Final Act to make her case. By recognizing Europe's frontiers, the agreement prevented East Germany and West Germany from erasing the border that separated them, she told Kohl. Her argument, which ignored the principle of peaceful change, proved unpersuasive. Nonetheless, it demonstrated that even those who opposed the reconfiguration of the continent regarded the Final Act as a constitution for international order in Europe.[81]

As the movement toward unification gathered steam, the Final Act shaped the debate about Germany's relationship to NATO. Gorbachev accepted that the GDR could no longer be saved, but he still refused to let a unified Germany join the Western alliance. The presence of Soviet troops in the GDR gave him considerable leverage on this point. As the Americans and West Germans pondered how to overcome his objections, Baker hit upon the solution. In May 1990, he and Genscher reminded Gorbachev that the Final Act stipulated that every country could choose its own alliances. Once Germany unified, therefore, it could leave the Warsaw Pact, join NATO, and station Western troops anywhere within its borders, no matter what Moscow might say.[82]

Gorbachev protested at first, but eventually told Bush and Kohl that he would accept this "Helsinki principle." In exchange for billions of Deutschmarks in economic aid, he agreed to withdraw all Soviet forces from German territory. In July, NATO's leaders agreed to bring the united country into the alliance. Their summit communique recognized the CSCE's importance to European security and declared that it ought to play a still greater role as "a forum for wider political dialogue in a more united Europe."[83]

The process of reunification prompted some leaders to ask whether it had finally become possible to sign the Second World War peace treaty that had eluded the belligerents in 1945. Margaret Thatcher called for treaty negotiations, not least because she remained uneasy with the notion that states as important as the FRG and GDR could change their frontiers at will. Poland's new freely elected government, which resented its exclusion from the two-plus-four talks, took the same position, as did Gorbachev, who wanted war reparations from the unified German government. Meanwhile, the French proposed a CSCE meeting to discuss Germany.[84]

These ideas went nowhere. Kohl feared that a peace conference would drag things out and cripple the united country with reparations. Instead, he and Bush decided to settle the terms for unification at the two-plus-four talks. Likewise, they concluded that negotiating any aspect of Germany's future at a CSCE meeting, with dozens of countries around the table, would guarantee deadlock.[85] Nonetheless, they agreed—as did the French and British—that the CSCE had to play a central role in the process. Using its framework would "help avoid Soviet isolation [and] help balance German dominance in Europe," Thatcher told Bush. Once the two-plus-four talks had concluded, the CSCE would endorse its results and put the stamp of multilateral legitimacy on Europe's new map. When the thirty-five foreign ministers met in New York at the beginning of October, they did exactly this. The next day, the two Germanies became one.[86]

IV

In November 1990, fifteen years after the Final Act was signed, the CSCE held another summit. The leaders, who now numbered thirty-four, assembled in Paris to assess Europe's transformation and take another step forward. Former dissidents, such as Václav Havel, the newly elected president of Czechoslovakia, sat down alongside veteran politicians, illustrating just how dramatically the continent had changed over the previous year. Although the meeting took place against the backdrop of a crisis in the Persian Gulf, the threat of famine and secession in the Soviet Union, and domestic political intrigue in Britain and France, there remained ample cause for celebration.[87]

The centerpiece of the meeting, dubbed the Paris Charter, reaffirmed the principles of the Final Act but went beyond them. The signatories declared their "steadfast commitment to democracy based on human rights and fundamental freedoms, prosperity through economic liberty and social justice, and equal security for all countries."[88] As the neutral states watched, the members of NATO and the Warsaw Pact also signed the Treaty on Conventional Forces in Europe (CFE). In the sweeping agreement, which the *Economist* described as "the largest scrap-metal deal in history," they promised to destroy thousands of tanks and artillery pieces. East-West parity replaced the

Soviet bloc's longstanding superiority, and the Warsaw Pact's members declared their alliance obsolete.[89] Four decades earlier, when the Soviets originally called for a European security conference to replace the alliance systems, they did not anticipate this outcome.

The leaders rejoiced at the historic significance of their achievement. "The cold war is over," George Bush said. "In signing the Charter of Paris we have closed a chapter of history."[90] Mikhail Gorbachev echoed his sentiments. "What a long way the world has come!" he said. For the first time in modern history, as François Mitterand noted, Europe's political order was being reconfigured in the absence of war or revolution.[91] In the 1960s and 1970s, many politicians and commentators had equated détente with the end of the Cold War. Their assessments had proved premature. Now, however, the conflict really had come to a close. A new era of international affairs was dawning.

The idea for the summit had originated in Moscow. In 1989, Gorbachev called for a meeting of CSCE leaders to work out a common vision for "the subsequent stages in the movement toward the European community of the twenty-first century."[92] He regarded the summit as "the pinnacle of his European policy," Anatoly Chernyaev recalled, and an essential step toward lasting peace.[93] Gorbachev also wanted to assert Soviet control over German unification and salvage the common European home, which would preserve both German states—and both political systems—under a shared standard of international legitimacy. The CSCE summit should also set the terms for the eventual dissolution of the two military blocs, he insisted. In this respect, his hopes for the CSCE resembled those of his predecessors in the Kremlin. But the situation in Europe was now unlike what Brezhnev had faced, and Gorbachev was far more open to Western ideas than his predecessor.[94]

The proposal elicited a range of responses in Western capitals. British and French officials declared themselves open to the idea, and the EC's foreign ministers endorsed it. Genscher suggested that the summit ought to reaffirm the Final Act's principles, but now make them legally binding.[95] The Americans reacted more skeptically. Some in Washington feared that planning a summit would only yield interminable abstract discussions. Besides, including so many states would needlessly complicate matters. Still, in the right circumstances, it could serve American interests, not least by exploiting—just as in the 1970s—the Soviet desire to bring it to fruition.[96]

The US agreed to take part, therefore, provided that three conditions were met. The summit had to take a major step forward on human rights. It could only convene after the CFE negotiations had concluded. Finally, it could not turn into a peace conference for Germany. The two-plus-four process had to settle the country's future first. The CSCE might "sanction the result of the unification process," James Baker said, "but it could not be a near-term practical mechanism for helping to shape it." If Gorbachev wanted the summit, therefore, he would have to abandon one of his goals for the meeting in the first place.[97] The Soviets reluctantly accepted these conditions, but retained their other lofty ambitions, especially now that the Warsaw Pact stood on the brink of collapse. "There is no more important or crucial cause for Soviet foreign policy currently than the creation, together with other states, of a new system of security in Europe" through the CSCE, Shevardnadze said in April 1990.[98]

Work on the Paris Charter began that summer in Vienna. By contrast with the struggle to draft the Final Act, the participants now started from common assumptions about domestic and international legitimacy. Everyone was in "broad agreement about the basic underlying concepts, both within national societies and among independent states," the head of the American delegation, John Maresca, later wrote.[99] The Final Act had established all of the crucial "underlying political values" the Eastern Europeans had embraced in the years since 1975. "[T]hey did not need to be renegotiated."[100] The participants aspired to create a "new Europe" rooted in "universal concepts of human rights, independence of states, and representative governments."[101]

Although the delegates wasted no time arguing about sovereignty or state control over citizens' lives, they did disagree about the future of the CSCE. The Poles and Czechoslovaks wanted to turn it into a full-fledged collective security organization. However, the Americans and the British wanted NATO to remain the continent's preeminent security structure. They therefore insisted on preserving the CSCE as a consultative political body. Because most of the delegations deferred to American leadership, Maresca assembled a finely balanced compromise that gave something to everyone. It modestly expanded the CSCE's existing structure and established a council of foreign ministers, a council of senior officials, a permanent secretariat, an office for conflict prevention, and an office for free elections. The other participants accepted the proposal unanimously.[102]

The Paris Charter amounted to a final peace settlement for the Cold War. "The era of confrontation and division of Europe has ended," it declared. "The power of the ideas of the Helsinki Final Act have opened a new era of democracy, peace and unity in Europe." Democracy meant free elections and respect for human rights. Peace meant a commitment to disarmament, as embodied in the CFE treaty. Unity meant the unification not only of Germany but of the whole continent. By establishing how states should relate to one another and how they should treat their own citizens, the charter emphasized the interdependence of international and domestic affairs. No longer could states resort to arguments about sovereignty and noninterference to shield themselves from outside scrutiny. They agreed that their internal character had become a proper subject for international debate.[103]

The Cold War had been a conflict between rival concepts of domestic and international legitimacy. Now, in place of that rivalry, the Paris Charter established a single common standard and a shared concept of legitimacy for both superpowers and their allies. Margaret Thatcher recognized the document's landmark importance when she called it "a new Magna Carta."[104] In a curious echo of Brezhnev's original ambition to universalize the principles of the Final Act, George Bush declared that "the principles that have given life to the CSCE, that have guided our success in Europe have no geographic limits. Our success here can be neither profound nor enduring if the rule of law is shamelessly disregarded elsewhere." The comment demonstrated both optimism and hubris. The values that the charter embodied might well have been universal, but no Asian, African, or Latin American governments had participated in the negotiations. If the president hoped to turn these principles of European order into the foundation for a new global order, more work would be needed.[105]

The charter's principles were not new. Rather, they came from the CSCE's founding document. The Final Act had embodied several key propositions: a single set of rules should apply across all of Europe; the continent's fate was tied to that of North America; international security depended on respect for human rights; states should lower the barriers that separated them (or erase them entirely, in the case of Germany); they should encourage the freer movement of people and information; and they should seek greater transparency—in military affairs, commerce, and culture—in the name of both stability and prosperity.

The charter endorsed all of these ideas. Its signatories pledged their fidelity to a list of fundamental rights and recognized liberal democracy and political pluralism as the only way to defend them. "Full respect for these precepts is the bedrock on which we will seek to construct the new Europe," it declared. It affirmed the September 1990 Moscow treaty on German unification and underscored the interdependence of Europe and North America. In economics, it embraced the values of the free market. In military affairs, it validated the confidence- and security-building measures agreed on earlier that year in Vienna, which envisioned still greater transparency, and it welcomed the CFE treaty, which aimed to demilitarize European security. The Paris Charter was briefer and less complex than the Final Act. Because the participants now shared many of the same assumptions about legitimacy and the meaning of peace, they no longer had to resort to calculated ambiguities and finely balanced compromises. They made forthright declarations and categorical promises instead. Nonetheless, the charter recognized its profound debt to the Final Act, which "lighted our way toward better relations for the past fifteen years" and "will guide us toward this ambitious future."[106]

Perhaps because the Paris Summit affirmed longstanding ideas rather than establishing a wholly new set of principles, many observers failed to grasp its importance. One American official called the meeting "anticlimactic," and noted that it "generated little real dialogue about the future of European security."[107] British journalists said that it offered "more spectacle than substance."[108] In retrospect, however, its significance is unmistakable. The Paris Charter, the CFE treaty, and the unification of Germany affirmed the Western concepts of legitimacy and peace. The CSCE's participants built a single international order to replace the two competing ones that had divided Europe for more than four decades. They brought the Cold War to an end and laid the foundations for the new world that would emerge out of it.

V

The Helsinki Final Act did not cause the end of the Cold War. The reasons why that long struggle finally drew to a close were too complex to be explained by a single factor or a single person. Nor was the collapse of communism in Europe inevitable. It is easy to imagine scenarios in which the division of Germany persisted, the Soviet Union survived, and Eastern Europe remained under the dictatorship of the proletariat. These regimes might not have prospered, but they could have remained stable.

Still, the Final Act helped to resolve the Cold War in two important ways. First, in response to the parallel crises of legitimacy that wracked East and West in the late 1960s, the CSCE laid the foundations of a new, integrated international order. It articulated a single set of principles that spanned the Iron Curtain, promising a vision of peace and security that both East and West could accept. At first, the two sides disagreed about the details of that vision, and they interpreted the agreement in different ways. Nonetheless, by signing the agreement they started the process of knitting their rival orders back together. In the years after 1975, the Final Act provided a beacon to officials and individual citizens on both sides. It animated debates at the CSCE's follow-up conferences, and inspired the creation of new organizations to monitor Soviet conduct. The agreement profoundly influenced Mikhail Gorbachev's approach to foreign policy and gave him and his supporters an essential tool for reforming the communist system. In these ways, it hastened the Cold War's end.

Second, the Final Act furnished the blueprint for the peace settlement that ended the Cold War. All of the leading players in the drama of 1989 and 1990 used its principles to guide—and to legitimize—their decisions. Although the agreement had been written fifteen years previously, it contained nearly all of the components of the new order that they created: the end of the Brezhnev Doctrine; German unification; states' ability to choose their own alliances; greater military transparency; respect for human rights; the interdependence of human rights and international security; the freer movement of people and ideas; and the economic integration of Europe according to free market principles. In negotiating the Final Act, the Soviets believed they were negotiating a definitive end to the Second World War, but it turned out that they were laying the foundations for the post–Cold War world instead. For all of these reasons, Helsinki deserves a place alongside Westphalia, Utrecht, Vienna, and Paris in the list of epoch-making diplomatic conferences.

None of the diplomats who did the hard work of negotiating the Final Act in Helsinki and Geneva anticipated the agreement's dramatic impact. "Turning points often pass unrecognized by contemporaries," Henry Kissinger said of the CSCE in 1999.[109] The archival record demonstrates that this observation held true not just for Kissinger himself, but for many of his Western colleagues too. One must not interpret the CSCE teleologically or assume that every development was foreseeable and every proposal led inescapably toward the ultimate result. At any number of points between 1972 and 1975 (or indeed 1954 and 1990), events might have veered off on a profoundly different course.

Even by these standards, however, the Western allies scored a decisive victory in 1975. They owed their success to a number of factors. Their diplomatic creativity turned the Warsaw Pact's initial proposals into a project that would serve their own interests. They expanded the CSCE's agenda to include questions that played to their strengths. They used Moscow's desire for a successful conference to extract important concessions. The diversity of views within the alliance yielded acrimonious but ultimately fruitful discussions about what to demand and how hard to push. To be sure, the process put considerable strain on the alliance, not least because the Western Europeans valued the CSCE more than the Nixon and Ford administrations did, and because NATO's consultative process overlapped with the European Community's. Nonetheless, by exercising patience and preserving a common front, the allies outlasted the Warsaw Pact at the negotiating table. After the Helsinki summit, they stood by their interpretation of the agreement and pressed the Soviets and their allies to live up to their promises. This was more a strategy of conversion than of containment.

The Eastern allies had strengths of their own, but they did not prove adequate to the task. The Warsaw Pact's consistency and solidarity exceeded the West's. But the allies' consistency shaded into inflexibility, and their solidarity inhibited creativity. The Soviets often expected that they could succeed simply by wearing down their peers, or by recruiting the United States to rein in Western European demands. In the late 1960s, the USSR's persistence cajoled the West into participating in the CSCE. After the talks opened, however, it lost its effectiveness. Within the Warsaw Pact, the Eastern Europeans sometimes disagreed with the Soviet position, but the culture of the alliance stifled the heated debates that had produced new ideas within NATO. Perhaps as a result, the Eastern allies struggled to respond to the West's offensive strategy, especially in the first and third baskets.

Nothing compelled the USSR to accept the West's demands. From the moment the CSCE started, however, Soviet leaders resolved to bring it to an end as quickly as possible. Given the success of their bilateral negotiations with West Germany, France, and the United States in the early 1970s, they may have assumed that drafting an agreement would require only a few months' work. More importantly, Brezhnev was reluctant to drag the negotiations out. As relations with China deteriorated, he resolved to stabilize the USSR's western flank. As the 25th Communist Party Congress approached in 1976, he wanted to demonstrate that his Peace Program had borne fruit. The Western allies exploited the USSR's haste to powerful effect. But it would be wrong to say that they simply imposed their views on the Soviets, because a number of influential Soviet officials recognized the need for greater openness and transparency along the lines that the West proposed. Anatoly Kovalev, who enjoyed considerable influence over the Soviet negotiating position, pressed his superiors in Moscow to approve concessions to Western demands. He recognized that a deal would be impossible otherwise, but he also hoped that the Final Act could help reform the USSR and humanize the socialist system.

The CSCE demonstrated the paradoxes of Soviet power in the 1970s. Although the USSR and its allies relied on their military forces and domestic security services to defend their borders and suppress internal threats, physical power did not easily translate into popular legitimacy. Brezhnev pursued the CSCE, and accepted its costs, as part of a strategy to shore up the Soviet order. This strategy, however, was divided against itself. By counting on the Western powers to endorse his concept of peace, Brezhnev allowed them to advance a concept of their own that attacked the foundations of the Soviet order instead of strengthening it. By seeking the rewards of commercial interdependence while refusing to compromise the tenets of central planning, he ensured that the CSCE offered few economic benefits. By making promises they did not intend to keep, especially in the third basket, the Warsaw Pact's leaders put the demands of international legitimacy at odds with the imperatives of domestic stability.

Throughout, Brezhnev and his colleagues trusted that sovereignty would protect them from the Final Act's more dangerous provisions. By the 1970s, however, the days of absolute sovereignty were gone—if they ever existed in the first place. As time went on, the USSR found itself increasingly exposed to external pressure but unable to counter the threat without destroying the structure on which it had premised its claims to domestic and international legitimacy. Caught between its internal contradictions, Brezhnev's strategy failed, even as the CSCE itself succeeded.

This success should not distract from the CSCE's shortcomings, or from the problems that it bequeathed to the post–Cold War order. In the Final Act, sovereignty stood in tension with international human rights standards, greater transparency, and freer movement, all of which constrained governments' control over what happened within their borders and what crossed them. The Paris Charter celebrated these universal obligations in the hope that they would create a more integrated, more interdependent, more humane, and more peaceful world. This reasoning was attractive but left fundamental questions unresolved. When should states respond to violations of these principles, for example, and how? Neither the Paris Charter nor any of the other agreements signed at the end of the Cold War addressed these dilemmas or explained how to reconcile supranational imperatives with sovereign prerogatives.

The crises of the 1990s—in the Balkans, Rwanda, and beyond—demonstrated that this abstract problem had real-world consequences. In some cases, the United States and its allies launched military operations to halt genocide and civil war and bring humanitarian relief to the suffering. In others, they declined to get involved and rebuffed suggestions that they had a duty to act. In the aftermath of the 1999 Kosovo War, when NATO bombed Serbian targets without the approval of the UN Security Council, an international panel of policy-makers and academics attempted to clarify the circumstances in which human rights might trump sovereignty. Yet even their careful analysis could not dispel the conceptual ambiguities at the heart of the matter. *The Responsibility to Protect* declared that sovereignty was contingent, not absolute, but this distinction made it no easier to decide how to act in a particular case, nor could it guarantee that all states would reach the same verdict.

A more serious problem concerned the reach of the Final Act and the Paris Charter. Because the Cold War had begun in Europe, it was fitting that these agreements established common principles that applied across the continent. The conflict's central problems—the division of Germany and of the continent—were European problems. By contributing to their resolution, and by ushering the USSR and its allies into the Western-led post–Cold War consensus, the CSCE helped bring the conflict to an end. By the 1970s, however, the Cold War had expanded far beyond Europe's confines into every corner of the world. A comprehensive post–Cold War settlement therefore demanded more than just a new international order for Europe and the north Atlantic, but the major non-Western powers remained outside the new European consensus. The Chinese, for instance, opposed the CSCE from the beginning and retained their own ideas about international order. During the 1990 Paris summit, Japanese officials complained that they had been excluded. "The first and second worlds have joined together but left us out," one said. "Aren't we a vital part of the first world?"[110] The process of peacemaking therefore remained incomplete. A truly global order failed to take shape.

After 1991, even the consensus in Europe began to crack. The Russian government that emerged out of the USSR initially bought into the post–Cold War settlement, building a workable liberal democratic and free-market system. As time went on, however, the system's skeptics in Moscow gained strength. Russian leaders concluded that their country had been stripped of its rightful place in the world and now demanded that it be restored. One influential Russian commentator argued that the terms on which the Cold War had ended amounted to "a kinder, gentler version of the Treaty of Versailles" with the defeated Soviet Union in the place of Weimar Germany. As the Kremlin questioned the principles that it had previously endorsed, this revisionist backlash put an end to hopes that global harmony would prevail after the fall of the USSR.[111]

Some politicians and commentators celebrate the Final Act as an unambiguous success for peace and liberal democracy and treat it as a model for solving other international problems. The CSCE worked so well in Europe, the logic goes, that a Helsinki process ought to be created for the Middle East, South Asia, or East Asia.[112] These appeals caricature the origins of the Final Act and misrepresent the ideas and efforts of the politicians and diplomats who brought it into being. The CSCE succeeded because all of its participants believed they would gain more from it than they would lose. To get a deal, the Soviets were willing to make major concessions on their initial objectives. In the absence of Brezhnev's self-imposed time pressure, his confidence in state sovereignty, and, above all, his determination to establish a new basis for the legitimacy of the Soviet system, the CSCE may well have foundered. The conflict between the conservative and transformative strategies of détente and the Eastern and Western concepts of international order may have gone unresolved. In the absence of these conditions, nothing guarantees that the model pioneered in Helsinki could work anywhere else.

The CSCE was a product of its era. It reflected that era's crises, anxieties, ambitions, and personalities. Contending notions of legitimacy collided at the negotiations in Helsinki and Geneva, each anchored in a particular understanding of security and sovereignty, a particular relationship between the citizen and the state, and a particular conception of peace. The negotiators' fundamental task was to knit the competing postwar international orders back together by developing a single set of principles to which both could subscribe. The principles that emerged reflected Western notions more than Eastern ones. After 1975, the East-West rivalry evolved from a competition over the basic rules of the international game to a struggle to enforce the rules laid down in Helsinki. Eventually, the Soviets embraced the Western interpretation of the Final Act, with transformative consequences.

The story of the Helsinki process demonstrates the interplay between ideas and action, and legitimacy and power. It shows how consequential, how contested, and how changeable are the fundamental concepts of diplomacy and of international order itself. No matter how influential, the principles of any peace agreement can only last as long as citizens believe them to be legitimate and governments abide by them. Because even the most carefully crafted settlements eventually become obsolete, international order requires constant maintenance and periodic reconstruction. The Final Act may have been a victory for Western principles, but in diplomacy, as in war, no result is ever final.[113]

NOTES

Introduction: To the Helsinki Station

1. David Spanier, "Heads of Government Gather in Helsinki," *The Times*, July 30, 1975, 1; Christopher Wren, "Helsinki Greets Visitors and Guards Them Well," *NYT*, July 30, 1975, 9; Hal Piper, "Helsinki Welcomes Summit Delegates," *Baltimore Sun*, July 30, 1975, A2; Jean-Claude Guillebaud, "Le train de M. Brejnev," *Le Monde*, July 31, 1975, 5; and Iurii Deriabin, *Legko li byt' poslom? Zapiski o zhizni i kar'ere diplomata* (Moscow: Ves' Mir, 2010) 206–208.

2. Evgenii Chazov, *Zdorov'e i vlast': Vospominaniia "kremlevskogo vracha"* (Moscow: Novosti, 1992) 129–132; "A Star-Studded Summit Spectacular," *Time*, Aug. 4, 1975, 20.

3. Victor Lusinchi, "The Document: Broth from 35 Cooks," *NYT*, July 30, 1975, 9; and Christopher Wren, "Behind the Scenes, Active Negotiations," *NYT*, July 31, 1975, 2. The full text of the Final Act is printed in James Mayall and Cornelia Navari, eds., *The End of the Post-War Era: Documents on Great Power Relations 1968–1975* (Cambridge: Cambridge UP, 1980) 293–344.

4. Richard Davy, "Why the Russians Will Have to Change their Habits at the Helsinki Summit," *The Times*, July 28, 1975, 12; and Flora Lewis, "Not a Treaty, but a Declaration of Intentions in Europe," *NYT*, July 27, 1975, E1.

5. Felix Kessler, "You Need Not be Big Nation to Take Part in a Big Summit," *Wall Street Journal*, July 25, 1975, 1.

6. Kessler, "You Need Not be Big Nation"; "Proposal by the Delegation of the Disunited Republic of Upper Ruritania," Dec. 32 [*sic*], 1973, AEU, BAC 28/1980/652-1973; "Lay of the Military Man or Confidence is Good for You," n.d. [July 1975], UKNA, FCO 41/1758; letter from M. A. Pakenham, Geneva, to BJP Fall, FCO, "CSCE: Basket III," July 26, 1974, *DBPO* III:II, Appendix II; Anatolii Kovalev, "Na beregakh Zhenevskogo ozera: Liricheskii reportazh," *Druzhba Narodov* 1978 (4): 113–123; author's interviews with Thomas Delworth, Ottawa, July 25, 2003, and John Campbell, by telephone, April 11, 2008. For a list of the delegates to the Geneva negotiations, see "Liste provisoire des participants," Sept. 20, 1973, UKNA, FCO 41/1322.

7. Kessler, "You Need Not be Big Nation."

8. Alastair Buchan, *The End of the Postwar Era: A New Balance of World Power* (London: Weidenfeld and Nicolson, 1974) 12–13.

9. Piper, "Helsinki Welcomes Summit Delegates." The CSCE was the first international conference in which the Vatican had participated since the Congress of Vienna. Peter Hebblethwaite, "The Vatican's Last Word at Helsinki," *The Times*, Aug. 9, 1975, 14; and "Liste provisoire des participants," July 28, 1975, GRFL, Ron Nessen Papers, Box 65.

10. Robert Keatley, "When East Meets West in Helsinki," *Wall Street Journal*, July 9, 1975, 10.

11. Piper, "Helsinki Welcomes Summit Delegates"; and Don Cook, "Europe Summit Long on VIP Security," *Los Angeles Times*, July 30, 1975, B6.

12. James O. Jackson, "Finnish Ring of Steel Guarding Summit Site," *Chicago Tribune*, July 29, 1975, 2; Piper, "Helsinki Welcomes Summit Delegates"; Wren, "Helsinki Greets Visitors and Guards Them Well"; Spanier, "Heads of Government Gather."

13. Don Cook, "Finnish-ing Touch Given Europe Talks," *Los Angeles Times*, July 29, 1975, 1; and Cook, "Europe Summit Long on VIP Security."

14. David Spanier, "Helsinki Moves Out its Drunks for Opening of Security Conference," *The Times*, July 30, 1975, 5; and Piper, "Helsinki Welcomes Summit Delegates."

15. Christopher Wren, "Curtain Falls Softly at Helsinki Parley," *NYT*, Aug. 2, 1975, 8; and "Shirts Chinese, Initials Finnish," *Washington Post*, Aug. 1, 1975, A21.

16. External Affairs Memorandum, "Linguistic Staff for the CSCE, III Stage, Helsinki," April 9, 1975, LAC, RG-25 Vol. 9054 File 20-4-CSCE Vol. 52; Cook, "Finnish-ing Touch Given Europe Talks"; Wren, "Curtain Falls Softly"; and Kaius Niemi, "When Andrei Gromyko Fell in My Lap," *Helsingin Sanomat* (International Edition) Aug. 2, 2005.

17. "Harbor is Soviet 'Water Bed' at Short-Winded Security Talks," *Baltimore Sun*, Aug. 1, 1975, A2; and Wren, "Curtain Falls Softly at Helsinki Parley."

18. Piper, "Helsinki Welcomes Summit Delegates"; and Cook, "Europe Summit Long on VIP Security."

19. David Spanier, "Heads of Government Gather"; "La grande embrassade de Genève," *Le Monde*, July 16, 1975, 1; and André Fontaine, "Les mots et les choses," *Le Monde*, July 29, 1975, 1, 3.

20. Cook, "Finnish-ing Touch Given Europe Talks." See also Jean-Claude Guillebaud, "La grand'messe de la technique," *Le Monde*, Aug. 2, 1975, 2.

21. "No Waltzing in Helsinki," *Baltimore Sun*, July 28, 1975, A8. In 1814, Metternich invited the Congress of Vienna's participants to a costume ball, at which he encouraged guests to don the traditional garb of the Austrian Empire's constituent nations. Brian Vick, *The Congress of Vienna: Power and Politics after Napoleon* (Cambridge, MA: Harvard UP, 2014) 46–47.

22. Kissinger-Gromyko Memcon, May 6, 1973, *FRUS 1969–1976*, Vol. 39, doc. 147; Ford-Brezhnev Memcon, Nov. 24, 1974, ibid., doc. 261; and George Walden, *Lucky George: Memoirs of an Anti-Politician* (London: Allen Lane, 1999) 149.

23. For examples of recent work on the CSCE, see Carla Meneguzzi Rostagni, ed. *The Helsinki Process: A Historical Reappraisal* (Padua: CEDAM, 2005); Elisabeth du Réau and Christine Manigand, eds., *Vers la réunification de l'Europe: Apports et limites du processus d'Helsinki de 1975 à nos jours* (Paris: L'Harmattan, 2005); Oliver Bange and Gottfried Niedhart, eds., *Helsinki 1975 and the Transformation of Europe* (New York: Berghahn, 2008); Andreas Wenger, Vojtech Mastny, and Christian Nuenlist, eds., *Origins of the European Security System: The Helsinki Process Revisited, 1965–75* (New York: Routledge, 2008); Thomas Fischer, *Neutral Power in the CSCE: The N+N States and the Making of the Helsinki Accords 1975* (Baden-Baden: Nomos, 2009); Petri Hakkarainen, *A State of Peace in Europe: West Germany and the CSCE, 1966–1975* (New York: Berghahn, 2011); Anja Hanisch, *Die DDR im KSZE-Prozess 1972–1985* (Munich: Oldenbourg, 2012); Nicolas Badalassi, *En finir avec la guerre froide: La France, l'Europe et le processus d'Helsinki, 1965–1975* (Rennes: Presses universitaires de Rennes, 2014); Matthias Peter, *Die Bundesrepublik im KSZE-Prozess 1975–1983: Die Umkehrung der Diplomatie* (Berlin: de Gruyter

Oldenbourg, 2015); and Aryo Makko, *Ambassadors of Realpolitik: Sweden, the CSCE and the Cold War* (New York: Berghahn, 2017).

24. For a list of examples, see Richard Davy, "Helsinki Myths: Setting the Record Straight on the Final Act of the CSCE, 1975," *Cold War History* 9:1 (Feb. 2009): 1–22. Two further instances are Flora Lewis, *Europe: A Tapestry of Nations* (New York: Simon and Schuster, 1987) 14–15; and Campbell Craig and Fredrik Logevall, *America's Cold War: The Politics of Insecurity* (Cambridge, MA: Harvard UP, 2009) 285.

25. Nikolaĭ Leonov, *Likholet'e* (Moscow: Mezhdunarodnye Otnosheniia, 1995) 163.

26. Two indispensable accounts of human rights in the CSCE are Daniel C. Thomas, *The Helsinki Effect: International Norms, Human Rights, and the Demise of Communism* (Princeton, NJ: Princeton UP, 2001); and Sarah B. Snyder, *Human Rights Activism and the End of the Cold War: A Transnational History of the Helsinki Network* (New York: Cambridge UP, 2011). Historians and journalists commonly describe the Final Act as the "Helsinki human rights accords" or "Helsinki agreement on human rights." See, for example, Warren I. Cohen, *Profiles in Humanity: The Battle for Peace, Freedom, Equality, and Human Rights* (Lanham, MD: Rowman and Littlefield, 2009) 30; Fred Coleman, *The Decline and Fall of the Soviet Empire: Forty Years That Shook The World, From Stalin to Yeltsin* (New York: St. Martin's, 1996) 104–105; John Prados, *How the Cold War Ended: Debating and Doing History* (Dulles, VA: Potomac, 2011) 1; Susan Strange, *States and Markets* (London: Bloomsbury, 2015) 236; Robert Conquest, *The Dragons of Expectation: Reality and Delusion in the Course of History* (New York: W. W. Norton, 2005) 61; Zinovy Zinik, "Obituary: Alexander Ginzburg," *The Guardian*, July 26, 2002, 26; Arnold Beichman, "Why I Miss the Cold War," *Wall Street Journal*, Oct. 28, 2003, A16; David Brooks, "The Education of Robert Gates," *NYT*, Sept. 19, 2007, A25; and Douglas Martin, "Helmut Sonnenfeldt Is Dead at 86," *NYT*, Nov. 22, 2012, B10.

27. The Western approach to human rights at the CSCE offers a counterpoint to Samuel Moyn, *The Last Utopia: Human Rights in History* (Cambridge, MA: Harvard UP, 2010); Barbara J. Keys, *Reclaiming American Virtue: The Human Rights Revolution of the 1970s* (Cambridge MA, Harvard UP, 2014); and Mark Philip Bradley, *The World Reimagined: Americans and Human Rights in the Twentieth Century* (New York: Cambridge UP, 2016).

28. On the significance of peace conferences in European history, see Philip Bobbitt, *The Shield of Achilles: War, Peace, and the Course of History* (New York: Knopf, 2002); Andreas Osiander, *The States System of Europe, 1640-1990: Peacemaking and the Conditions of International Stability* (New York: Oxford UP, 1994); and Williamson Murray and Jim Lacey, eds., *The Making of Peace: Rulers, States, and the Aftermath of War* (New York: Cambridge UP, 2009).

29. Buchan, *The End of the Postwar Era* 5.

30. In arguing that various strategies of détente emerged in response to the legitimacy crises of the 1960s, and that they aimed, above all, to construct new foundations for domestic and international legitimacy in the wake of those crises, this account diverges from Raymond Garthoff, *Détente and Confrontation: American-Soviet Relations from Nixon to Reagan*, rev. ed. (Washington, DC: Brookings, 1994); and Jeremi Suri, *Power and Protest: Global Revolution and the Rise of Détente* (Cambridge, MA: Harvard UP, 2003).

31. Jacques Andréani, *Le Piège: Helsinki et la chute du communisme* (Paris: Odile Jacob, 2005) 36; and Anatoliĭ Cherniaev, *Sovmestnyĭ iskhod: Dnevnik dvukh epokh, 1972–1991 gody* (Moscow: Rosspen, 2010) 128.

32. Seyom Brown, *New Forces in World Politics* (Washington, DC: Brookings, 1974) 92; and

K. J. Holsti, "Bargaining Theory and Diplomatic Reality: The CSCE Negotiations," *Review of International Studies* 8:3 (July 1982): 159–170.

33. See, for instance, a telegram from Fernand-Laurent, Geneva, to Quai d'Orsay, "CSCE: Contacts Humains," Dec. 3, 1974, AMAE, CSCE 1969–1975, Box 19; letter from Alexander, Geneva, to Young, FCO, "Human Contacts," Dec. 13, 1974, UKNA, FCO 28/2472; telegram from Delworth, Geneva, to External Affairs, "CSCE: General Assessment," Dec. 21, 1974, LAC, RG-25 Vol. 9054 File 20-4-CSCE Vol. 49; and "Notatka informacyjna o końcowych wynikach II fazy KBWE," July 24, 1975, *PDD 1975*, doc. 200.

34. Anatoliĭ Kovalev, *Iskusstvo vozmozhnogo: Vospominaniia* (Moscow: Novyĭ Khronograf, 2016) 445.

Chapter 1: Crises of Legitimacy

1. Ronald Steel, *The End of Alliance: America and the Future of Europe* (New York: Viking, 1964) 19.

2. Pierre Hassner, "Change and Security in Europe Part I: The Background," *Adelphi Papers* 8:45 (February 1968) 1.

3. Chalmers M. Roberts, "NATO: 'Give' or Give Up," *Washington Post*, June 5, 1966, E1. See also Paul Seabury, *The Rise and Decline of the Cold War* (New York: Basic Books, 1967) 130 and 148; Marshall D. Shulman, *Beyond the Cold War* (New Haven: Yale UP, 1966) 1; Kenneth N. Waltz, "The Politics of Peace," *International Studies Quarterly* 11:3 (September 1967) 199; and Hans J. Morgenthau, "Arguing about the Cold War," *Encounter* (May 1967) 40.

4. Melvyn P. Leffler, *For the Soul of Mankind: The United States, The Soviet Union, and the Cold War* (New York: Hill and Wang, 2007) chapter 1; Mark Mazower, *Governing the World: The History of an Idea* (New York: Penguin, 2012) chapters 7–8; David Reynolds, *Summits: Six Meetings that Shaped the Twentieth Century* (New York: Basic Books, 2007) chapter 3; David Engerman, "Ideology and the Origins of the Cold War, 1917–1962," *Cambridge History of the Cold War*, eds. Melvyn P. Leffler and Odd Arne Westad, Vol. 1 (New York: Cambridge UP, 2010) 20–43.

5. Bobbitt xxiii and 5–17. See also Osiander, 1–15.

6. On international legitimacy and the rules that constitute international orders, see Henry Kissinger, *A World Restored: Metternich, Castlereagh, and the Problems of Peace, 1812–1822* (Boston: Houghton Mifflin, 1957); Hedley Bull, *The Anarchical Society: A Study of Order in World Politics* (New York: Columbia UP, 1977); Robert Gilpin, *War and Change in World Politics* (New York: Cambridge UP, 1981); Mlada Bukovansky, *Legitimacy and Power Politics: The American and French Revolutions in International Political Culture* (Princeton, NJ: Princeton UP, 2002); Ian Clark, *Legitimacy in International Society* (New York: Oxford UP, 2005); Ian Clark, *International Legitimacy and World Society* (New York: Oxford UP, 2007); and Andrew Phillips, *War, Religion and Empire: The Transformation of International Orders* (New York: Cambridge UP, 2011).

7. G. John Ikenberry, *After Victory: Institutions, Strategic Restraint, and the Rebuilding of Order after Major Wars* (Princeton, NJ: Princeton UP, 2001) chapter 6; and Daniel J. Sargent, *A Superpower Transformed: The Remaking of American Foreign Relations in the 1970s* (New York: Oxford UP, 2015) chapter 1.

8. Michael H. Hunt, *The American Ascendancy: How the United States Gained and Wielded*

Global Dominance (Chapel Hill, NC: UNC Press, 2007) chapter 5; Tony Judt, *Postwar: A History of Europe since 1945* (New York: Penguin, 2005) chapters 4–5; and Odd Arne Westad, *The Global Cold War: Third World Interventions and the Making of Our Times* (New York: Cambridge UP, 2005) chapter 1.

9. Andrei Zhdanov, *The International Situation: Speech Delivered at the Informatory Conference of Representatives of a Number of Communist Parties Held in Poland in the Latter Part of September 1947* (Moscow: Foreign Languages Publishing House, 1947) 18.

10. Vladislav Zubok and Constantine Pleshakov, *Inside the Kremlin's Cold War: From Stalin to Khrushchev* (Cambridge, MA: Harvard UP, 1996) chapters 2–4; Anne Applebaum, *Iron Curtain: The Crushing of Eastern Europe, 1944–1956* (New York: Doubleday, 2012) especially chapter 9; Silvio Pons, *The Global Revolution: A History of International Communism 1917–1991*, trans. Allan Cameron (New York: Oxford UP, 2014) chapter 4; Archie Brown, *The Rise and Fall of Communism* (New York: HarperCollins, 2009) chapter 6; Judt chapter 6; and Westad chapter 2. On the relationship between ideology and legitimacy in Soviet foreign policy, see Margot Light, "Belief Systems and Soviet Foreign Policy," *Belief Systems and International Relations*, eds. Richard Little and Steve Smith (New York: Basil Blackwell, 1988) 109–126.

11. Stanley Hoffmann, "Restraints and Choices in American Foreign Policy," *Daedalus* 91:4 (Fall 1962) 671.

12. On the Berlin Crisis, see Aleksandr Fursenko and Timothy Naftali, *Khrushchev's Cold War: The Inside Story of an American Adversary* (New York: Norton, 2006) 185–213 and 409–423; Francis J. Gavin, *Nuclear Statecraft: History and Strategy in America's Atomic Age* (Ithaca, NY: Cornell UP, 2012) 57–74; and Andreas Wenger, *Living with Peril: Eisenhower, Kennedy, and Nuclear Weapons* (Lanham, MD: Rowman and Littlefield, 1997) 197–239. On Cuba, see Aleksandr Fursenko and Timothy Naftali, *"One Hell of a Gamble": Khrushchev, Castro, and Kennedy, 1958–1964* (New York: Norton, 1997).

13. Pierre Hassner, "Change and Security in Europe Part I: The Background," *Adelphi Papers* 8:45 (February 1968) 5.

14. Marc Trachtenberg, *A Constructed Peace: The Making of the European Settlement, 1945–1963* (Princeton, NJ: Princeton UP, 1999) 352–402.

15. Telegram from the embassy in France to the Department of State, Nov. 30, 1964, *FRUS 1964–1968*, Vol. 13, doc. 53.

16. Shulman 22; Hassner 5; and Winston Churchill in the House of Commons, HC Deb 1 March 1955 Vol. 537 c. 1899.

17. Ronald Steel, *Pax Americana* (New York: Viking, 1967) 40–41. See also Karl Birnbaum, "The Future of the Soviet and American International Systems," *Adelphi Papers* 10:66 (1970) 31; and Stanley Hoffmann, "Restraints and Choices in American Foreign Policy," *Daedalus* 91:4 (Fall 1962) 674.

18. Khrushchev quoted in Fursenko and Naftali, *Khrushchev's Cold War* 508.

19. John F. Kennedy, "Commencement Address at American University in Washington," June 10, 1963, *Public Papers of the Presidents: John F. Kennedy, 1963* (Washington, DC: USGPO, 1964) 462.

20. Shulman 93–94; and Steel 32.

21. Wenger, *Living with Peril* 308–312; and Steel 47.

22. Alastair Buchan and Philip Windsor, *Arms and Stability in Europe: A British-French-German Enquiry* (London: Chatto and Windus, 1963) 6–7.

23. David Calleo, *The Atlantic Fantasy: The US, NATO, and Europe* (Baltimore: Johns Hopkins Press, 1970) 5–6.

24. Hassner 5 and 7.

25. Shulman 1.

26. Brown, *New Forces in World Politics* 10–13; Buchan and Windsor 8; Steel 50.

27. Raymond Aron, *The Great Debate: Theories of Nuclear Strategy*, trans. Ernst Pawel (Garden City, NY: Doubleday, 1965) 168.

28. Calleo 78–81.

29. Lawrence S. Kaplan, *NATO Divided, NATO United: The Evolution of an Alliance* (Westport, CT: Praeger, 2004) 49–50.

30. Walter Lippmann, "NATO and Its Future," *Washington Post*, Dec. 15, 1966, A21.

31. Calleo 30.

32. Gladwyn Jebb, *Halfway to 1984* (New York: Columbia UP, 1966) 23 and 41–42; and Judt 255–256.

33. Steel 34 and 50.

34. Harold van B. Cleveland, *The Atlantic Idea and Its European Rivals* (New York: McGraw-Hill, 1966) xxix–xxxi and 124–149.

35. Memorandum from President de Gaulle to President Eisenhower, Sept. 17, 1958, *FRUS 1958–1960*, Vol. 7, Part 2 (Washington, DC: USGPO, 1993) doc. 45.

36. Maurice Vaïsse, *La Grandeur: politique étrangère du général de Gaulle, 1958–1969* (Paris: Fayard, 1998) 381–395; Frédéric Bozo, *Deux stratégies pour l'Europe: de Gaulle, les États-Unis et l'Alliance atlantique: 1958–1969* (Paris: Plon, 1998) 133–166; Jean Lacouture, *De Gaulle*, Vol. 3, *Le Souverain, 1959–1970* (Paris: Éditions du Seuil, 1986) 343–381; and Garret Joseph Martin, *General de Gaulle's Cold War: Challenging American Hegemony, 1963–1968* (New York: Berghahn, 2013) 104–110.

37. Charles de Gaulle, press conference, Feb. 21, 1966, *Discours et messages*, Vol. 5 (Paris: Plon, 1970) 18–19.

38. "Aide-Memoire from the French Government to the U.S. Government," March 11, 1966, *FRUS 1964–1968*, Vol. 8, doc. 142.

39. "Summary Record of NSC Executive Committee Meeting No. 38 (Part II)," Jan. 25, 1963, *FRUS 1961–1963*, Vol. 13 (Washington, DC: USGPO, 1994) doc. 169.

40. Paul-Henri Spaak, "Hold Fast," *Foreign Affairs* 41:4 (July 1963) 611.

41. Kaplan 32–34; and Calleo 33–34.

42. Quoted in Lacouture 376.

43. Andreas Wenger, "NATO's Transformation in the 1960s and the Ensuing Political Order in Europe," *Transforming NATO in the Cold War: Challenges beyond Deterrence in the 1960s*, eds. Andreas Wenger, Christian Nuenlist, and Anna Locher (New York: Routledge, 2007) 223–226.

44. "Memorandum from President Johnson to Secretary of State Rusk and Secretary of Defense McNamara," May 4, 1966, *FRUS 1964–1968*, Vol. 13, doc. 161; and Thomas Alan Schwartz, *Lyndon Johnson and Europe: In the Shadow of Vietnam* (Cambridge, MA: Harvard UP, 2003) 99–105.

45. Geir Lundestad, *"Empire" by Integration: The United States and European Integration, 1945–1997* (New York: Oxford UP, 1998) 40–82.

46. Kaplan, *NATO Divided* 6–8; Andrew M. Johnston, *Hegemony and Culture in the Origins of NATO Nuclear First Use, 1945–1955* (New York: Palgrave Macmillan, 2005) 77–80; Beatrice Heuser, "Alliance of Democracies and Nuclear Deterrence," *War Plans and Alliances in the*

Cold War: Threat Perceptions in the East and West, eds. Vojtech Mastny, Sven G. Holtsmark, and Andreas Wenger (London: Routledge, 2006) 198–199; and Kjell Inge Bjerga and Kjetil Skogrand, "Securing Small-State Interests: Norway in NATO," ibid., 226–228.

47. Ikenberry, 199–204; and John Lewis Gaddis, *We Now Know: Rethinking Cold War History* (New York: Oxford UP, 1997) 201.

48. Frédéric Bozo, "Defense versus Security? Reflections on the Past and Present of the 'Future Tasks' of the Alliance (1949–99)," *A History of NATO: The First Fifty Years*, Vol. 2, ed. Gustav Schmidt (Basingstoke: Palgrave, 2001) 69–70; and Martin A. Smith, *NATO in the First Decade after the Cold War* (Dordrecht: Kluwer, 2000) 14–15.

49. Steel 59–60.

50. Hope Harrison, *Driving the Soviets Up the Wall: Soviet-East German Relations, 1953–1961* (Princeton, NJ: Princeton UP, 2003) 139–223.

51. "Gen. Jan Drzewiecki's Critique of the Statute of the Unified Command," Nov. 3, 1956; and "Polish Memorandum on Reform of the Warsaw Pact," Jan. 10, 1957, Vojtech Mastny and Malcolm Byrne, eds., *A Cardboard Castle? The Inside History of the Warsaw Pact, 1955–1991* (Budapest: Central European University Press, 2005) docs. 4 and 5; and Mastny, "The Warsaw Pact as History," ibid. 7–8.

52. Mastny, "The Warsaw Pact as History" 8–10.

53. Konev quoted in Vojtech Mastny, "'We Are in a Bind': Polish and Czechoslovak Attempts at Reforming the Warsaw Pact, 1956–1969," *CWIHP Bulletin* 11 (Winter 1998) 232.

54. Piotr Wandycz, "Adam Rapacki and the Search for European Security," *The Diplomats 1939–1979*, eds. Gordon A. Craig and Francis L. Loewenheim (Princeton, NJ: Princeton UP, 1994) 295; and Mastny, "The Warsaw Pact as History" 9–10.

55. Letter from Gomułka to Khrushchev, Oct. 8, 1963, in Douglas Selvage, "The Warsaw Pact and Nuclear Nonproliferation, 1963–1965," CWIHP Working Paper No. 32 (Washington: Woodrow Wilson International Center for Scholars, 2001), doc. 2; and Wandycz 296.

56. Laurien Crump, *The Warsaw Pact Reconsidered: International Relations in Eastern Europe, 1955–1969* (New York: Routledge, 2015) 98–130.

57. Quoted in Selvage, "The Warsaw Pact and Nuclear Non-Proliferation" 12.

58. Anita Prazmowska, *Wladyslaw Gomulka: A Biography* (London: I. B. Tauris, 2016) 215–236; and Crump 40.

59. Quoted in Anatole Shub, *An Empire Loses Hope: The Return of Stalin's Ghost* (New York: W. W. Norton, 1970) 203–204.

60. Vladimir Tismaneanu, "Gheorghiu-Dej and the Romanian Workers' Party: From De-Sovietization to the Emergence of National Communism," CWIHP Working Paper No. 37 (Washington, DC: Woodrow Wilson International Center for Scholars, 2002) 44–50; and Shub 204–205.

61. Dennis Deletant and Mihail Ionescu, "Romania and the Warsaw Pact: 1955–1989," CWIHP Working Paper No. 43 (Washington, DC: Woodrow Wilson International Center for Scholars, 2004) 16–9; and Larry Watts, ed., "Divided Loyalties Within the Bloc: Romanian Objection to Soviet Informal Controls, 1963–1964," CWIHP e-Dossier 42, October 2013. Available at: https://www.wilsoncenter.org/publication/divided-loyalties-within-the-bloc-romanian-objection-to-soviet-informal-controls-1963.

62. Raymond L. Garthoff, "When and Why Romania Distanced Itself from the Warsaw Pact," *CWIHP Bulletin* 5 (1995) 111; and Larry Watts, ed., "Romania Security Policy and the

Cuban Missile Crisis," CWIHP e-Dossier 38, April 2013. Available at: https://www.wilson center.org/publication/romania-security-policy-and-the-cuban-missile-crisis.

63. *Statement on the Stand of the Rumanian Workers' Party Concerning the Problems of the World Communist and Working-Class Movement, Endorsed by the Enlarged Plenum of the CC of the RWP Held in April 1964* (Bucharest: Agerpres, 1964) 37 and 49–50.

64. Walter A. Kemp, *Nationalism and Communism in Eastern Europe and the Soviet Union: A Basic Contradiction?* (Basingstoke: Macmillan, 1999) 149–154.

65. "Minutes of Discussion at Political Consultative Committee Meeting in Warsaw," Jan. 20, 1965, *A Cardboard Castle?* doc. 30; and Crump 137–140.

66. Quoted in Crump 170.

67. Chen Jian, *Mao's China and the Cold War* (Chapel Hill, NC: UNC Press, 2001) 59–61.

68. Austin Jersild, *The Sino-Soviet Alliance: An International History* (Chapel Hill, NC: UNC Press, 2014) 144–149; and Lorenz M. Lüthi, *The Sino-Soviet Split: Cold War in the Communist World* (Princeton, NJ: Princeton UP, 2008) 148.

69. Lüthi, *The Sino-Soviet Split* 138–146.

70. Sergey Radchenko, *Two Suns in the Heavens: The Sino-Soviet Struggle for Supremacy, 1962–1967* (Palo Alto, CA: Stanford UP, 2009) 113–117.

71. "Gedächtnisprotokoll der Tagung des Politischen Beratenden Ausschusses der Teilnehmerstaaten des Warschauer Vertrages vom 19. und 20. Januar 1965 in Warschau," PAAA, Bestand MfAA, G-A 541; "Minutes of Discussion at Political Consultative Committee Meeting in Warsaw," Jan. 20, 1965, *A Cardboard Castle?* doc. 30; Vojtech Mastny, "Meeting of the PCC, Warsaw, Jan. 19–20 1965: Editorial Note," PHP; Csaba Békés, "The Warsaw Pact and the CSCE Process from 1965 to 1970," *The Making of Détente: Eastern and Western Europe in the Cold War, 1965–75,* eds. Wilfried Loth and Georges-Henri Soutou (New York: Routledge, 2008) 202; and Crump 170–182.

72. Crump 57–73; and Lüthi 201–205.

73. Maud Bracke, *Which Socialism, Whose Détente? West European Communism and the Czechoslovak Crisis, 1968* (Budapest: Central European UP, 2007) 63–67 and 106–107; "Text of Togliatti Memorandum on the Problems of World Communist Tactics," *NYT,* Sept. 5, 1964, 2.

74. Mihai Retegan, *In the Shadow of the Prague Spring: Romanian Foreign Policy and the Crisis in Czechoslovakia, 1968* (Iasi: Center for Romanian Studies, 2000); and Deletant and Ionescu 27–28.

75. Steel, *Pax Americana* 34–37; and Brown, *New Forces in World Politics* 65.

76. George F. Kennan, "Polycentrism and Western Policy," *Foreign Affairs* 42:2 (January 1964) 174.

77. James J. Sheehan, *Where Have All the Soldiers Gone? The Transformation of Modern Europe* (Boston: Houghton Mifflin, 2008) 172–180; Judt 360–373; and Michael Howard, *The Invention of Peace: Reflections on War and International Order* (New Haven, CT: Yale UP, 2001) 99–100. For historical statistics on military spending, see the data collected by the Stockholm International Peace Research Institute: http://www.sipri.org/databases.

78. Brown, *New Forces* 26 and 42–44.

79. US House of Representatives Committee on Foreign Affairs, *Report of the Subcommittee for Review of the Mutual Security Programs on Military Aid to Western Europe* (Washington, DC: USGPO, 1963) 5. See also Waverly Root, "US 'Concerned' Over NATO Costs," *Washington Post,* July 26, 1966, A12.

80. Rusk-Stewart Memcon, Jan. 27, 1966, *FRUS 1964–1968,* Vol. 13 (Washington, DC:

USGPO, 1995) doc. 126; and Memorandum from Bator to Johnson, "Your Meeting This Afternoon at 6:30 on German Offset and U.S. and UK Forces in Germany," Aug. 23, 1966, *FRUS 1964–1968*, Vol. 13, doc. 197.

81. Alastair Buchan, "Back to Isolationism—US Attention is Turning Inward," *Los Angeles Times*, Aug. 21, 1966, F1.

82. "Summary Notes of the 566th Meeting of the National Security Council," Dec. 13, 1966, *FRUS 1964–1968*, Vol. 13, doc. 226.

83. David Binder, "Kiesinger on the Spot," *NYT*, July 9, 1967, 133; David Binder, "West German Army Faces Broad Reorganization," *NYT*, July 12, 1967, 7; and Max Frankel, "Bonn Defense Cut is Worrying US," *NYT*, July 15, 1967, 3.

84. "An SDS Antiwar Leaflet: November 27, 1965," *The Sixties Papers: Documents of a Rebellious Decade*, eds. Judith Clavir Albert and Stewart Edward Albert (New York: Praeger, 1984) 226–227. See also Paul Potter, "Speech to the April 17, 1965 March on Washington," ibid. 218–225.

85. Mark Atwood Lawrence, *The Vietnam War: A Concise International History* (New York: Oxford UP, 2008) 125.

86. Robert M. Neer, *Napalm: An American Biography* (Cambridge, MA: Harvard UP, 2013) 91–148. I am grateful to Andrew Preston for suggesting this point.

87. Holger Nehring, "Great Britain," *1968 in Europe: A History of Protest and Activism, 1956–1977*, eds. Martin Klimke and Joachim Scharloth (New York: Palgrave Macmillan, 2008), 130–131.

88. Wilfried Mausbach, "Auschwitz and Vietnam: West German Protest against America's War during the 1960s," *America, the Vietnam War, and the World: Comparative and International Perspectives*, eds. Andreas W. Daum, Lloyd C. Gardner, and Wilfried Mausbach (New York: Cambridge UP, 2003) 279–298. Quotation from 207.

89. Rimko van der Maar, "'Johnson War Criminal!' Vietnam War Protests in the Netherlands," *Between Prague Spring and French May: Opposition and Revolt in Europe, 1960–1980*, eds. Martin Klimke, Jacco Pekelder, and Joachim Scharloth (New York: Berghahn, 2011) 103–115.

90. Jonathan Søborg Agger, "Striving for Détente: Denmark and NATO, 1966–67," *Transforming NATO in the Cold War* 196–197.

91. Lippmann quoted in Schwartz 84.

92. Public opinion survey quoted in Schwartz 93.

93. Ibid. 291.

94. Jürgen Habermas, *Toward a Rational Society: Student Protest, Science, and Politics*, trans. Jeremy J. Shapiro (Boston: Beacon Press, 1970) 18.

95. "Summary Notes of the 566th Meeting of the National Security Council," Dec. 13, 1966, *FRUS 1964–1968*, Vol. 8, doc. 226.

96. Judt 390–398.

97. Daniel Bell, *The End of Ideology: On the Exhaustion of Political Ideas in the Fifties* (New York: Free Press, 2000) 402 and 404. See also Suri, *Power and Protest* 94–96.

98. Todd Gitlin, *The Sixties: Years of Hope, Days of Rage* (New York: Bantam, 1987) 343–344.

99. Alastair Buchan, ed., *Europe's Future, Europe's Choices* (New York: Columbia UP, 1969) 2; and Maurice Isserman and Michael Kazin, *America Divided: The Civil War of the 1960s* (New York: Oxford UP, 1999) 167–168.

100. Zbigniew Brzezinski, *Between Two Ages: America's Role in the Technetronic Era* (New York: Viking, 1970) 17–18.

101. Daniel Cohn-Bendit Interview with Jean-Paul Sartre, May 20, 1968, in *The French Student Revolt: The Leaders Speak*, ed. Hervé Bourges, trans. B. R. Brewster (New York: Hill and Wang, 1968) 79. See also "The Amnesty of Blinded Eyes," in Andrew Feenberg and Jim Freedman, *When Poetry Ruled the Streets: The French May Events of 1968* (Albany, NY: SUNY Press, 2001) 81–86.

102. Kiesinger quoted in Suri, *Power and Protest* 178.

103. Ingrid Gilcher-Holtey, "May 1968 in France," *1968: The World Transformed*, eds. Carole Fink, Philipp Gassert, and Detlef Junker (New York: Cambridge UP, 1998) 261–262; Stuart J. Hilwig, "The Revolt against the Establishment," ibid. 321–349; and Harold Marcuse, "The Revival of Holocaust Awareness in West Germany, Israel, and the United States," ibid. 421–438.

104. Brzezinski 215.

105. Brzezinski 215–216; and Brown 20–21. See also Jürgen Habermas, *Legitimation Crisis*, trans. Thomas McCarthy (Boston: Beacon Press, 1975).

106. Quoted in Vladislav Zubok, *Zhivago's Children: The Last Soviet Intelligentsia* (Cambridge, MA: Harvard UP, 2009) 63.

107. Ibid. 79–87.

108. Alexander Solzhenitsyn, *One Day in the Life of Ivan Denisovich* (New York: Signet, 1998); and Denis Kozlov, *The Readers of* Novyi Mir: *Coming to Terms with the Stalinist Past* (Cambridge, MA: Harvard UP, 2013) 218.

109. Kozlov 173–204. Quotation from 180.

110. Jersild 111.

111. Agnes Heller, "Phases of Legitimation in Soviet-type Societies," *Political Legitimation in Communist States*, eds. T. H. Rigby and Ferenc Fehér (New York: St. Martin's Press, 1982) 57–59; Denis Kozlov, "Remembering and Explaining the Terror during the Thaw: Soviet Readers of Ehrenburg and Solzhenitsyn in the 1960s," *The Thaw: Soviet Society and Culture during the 1950s and 1960s*, eds. Denis Kozlov and Eleonory Gilburd (Toronto: University of Toronto Press, 2013) 216–218; Brown 46–47; and Brzezinski 128–129.

112. Applebaum 435–461.

113. Zubok, *Zhivago's Children* 193–225.

114. Lüthi, *The Sino-Soviet Split* 63.

115. Ibid. 50.

116. Ibid. 155–156.

117. Ibid. 163.

118. Quoted in William Taubman, *Khrushchev: The Man and His Era* (New York: W.W. Norton, 2003) 471.

119. Radchenko, *Two Suns in the Heavens* 69 and 88–91.

120. Lüthi, *The Sino-Soviet Split* 173.

121. Leonid Brezhnev, "Mezhdunarodnaya politika SSSR i bor'ba KPSS za splochennost' kommunisticheskogo dvizheniya," Plenum TsK KPSS, Dec. 12, 1966, RGANI, f.2 op.3 d.49 ll.25–26; Radchenko, *Two Suns in the Heavens* 131–138; and "Stenogram: Meeting of the Delegations of the Communist Party of the Soviet Union and the Chinese Communist Party, Moscow, 5–20 July 1963," *CWIHP Bulletin* 10 (March 1998) 175–182.

122. Sergey Radchenko, "The Sino-Soviet Split," *Cambridge History of the Cold War*, Vol. 2, eds. Melvyn P. Leffler and Odd Arne Westad (New York, Cambridge UP, 2010) 349; and Pons xix.

123. Joseph Rothschild and Nancy M. Wingfield, *Return to Diversity: A Political History of*

East Central Europe since World War II (New York: Oxford UP, 2008) 162–165; Joseph Held, "Hungary: Iron out of Wood," *Problems of Communism* (November–December 1966) 37–43.

124. Włodzimierz Brus, "1957 to 1965: In Search of Balanced Development" and "1966 to 1975: Normalization and Conflict," *The Economic History of Eastern Europe, 1919–1975*, ed. M. C. Kaser, Vol. 3 (Oxford: Oxford UP, 1986) 117–121 and 165–174.

125. Steel, *Pax Americana* 36.

126. F. Konstantinov, "Marxism-Leninism is a Unified International Doctrine," *Current Digest of the Soviet Press*, Vol. 20, No. 24 (July 3, 1968) 9–11.

127. Anatoliĭ Cherniaev, *Moia zhizn' i moë vremia* (Moscow: Mezhdunarodnye Otnosheniia, 1995) 268–71; Henry Kamm, "World Reds End Moscow Parley," *NYT*, June 18, 1969, 3; and Jeremy Friedman, *Shadow Cold War: The Sino-Soviet Competition for the Third World* (Chapel Hill, NC: UNC Press, 2015) 176–180.

128. See, for example, "Khrushchev on Berlin Question, Soviet-Polish Relations," *Current Digest of the Soviet Press*, Vol. 10, No. 45 (Dec. 17, 1958) 7–12.

129. "Le traité de Rome et le rassemblement de l'Europe occidentale. Entretien avec le Chancelier Adenauer," *Le Monde*, March 10, 1962. See also Hans-Peter Schwarz, *Adenauer. Der Staatsmann: 1952–1967* (Stuttgart: Deutsche Verlags-Anstalt, 1991) 843–844; and Trachtenberg 274–276.

130. Brown, *New Forces in World Politics* 24–25, 55–56, 62–63, 72–73, and 86–87; and William Zimmerman, *Soviet Perspectives on International Relations, 1956–1967* (Princeton, NJ: Princeton UP, 1969) 275–294.

131. Brzezinski, *Between Two Ages* 78–9, 138–39, and 152–154; Jebb 54; Hassner 8; and Richard Löwenthal, "Changing Soviet Policies and Interests," *Adelphi Papers* 10:66 (1970) 12.

132. Zubok, *Zhivago's Children* 161–225. Quotation from 222.

133. Peter Grose, "Noted Poet Detained in Moscow Protest," *NYT*, Dec. 18, 1965, 1; and Benjamin Nathans, "The Dictatorship of Reason: Aleksandr Vol'pin and the Idea of Rights under 'Developed Socialism,'" *Slavic Review* 66:4 (Winter 2007) 630–663.

134. Judt 432–447. Quotation from 447.

135. Juliane Fürst, *Stalin's Last Generation: Soviet Post-war Youth and the Emergence of Mature Socialism* (New York: Oxford UP, 2010) 355–357.

136. Vladimir Bukovsky, *To Build a Castle: My Life as a Dissenter* (New York: Viking, 1978) 143–165; A. Zr., "Poems Underground," *Harper's*, May 1961, 132–134; and Fürst 359–361.

137. Seabury 142–143.

138. Peter Raina, *Political Opposition in Poland* (London: Poets and Painters Press, 1978) 126 and 130–132.

139. Ibid. 186.

140. Irena Grudzinska Gross, "1968 in Poland: Spoiled Children, Marxists, and Jews," *Promises of 1968: Crisis, Illusion, and Utopia*, ed. Vladimir Tismaneanu (Budapest: Central European University Press, 2010) 43–53; and Tom Junes, *Student Politics in Communist Poland: Generations of Consent and Dissent* (Lanham, MD: Lexington Books, 2015) 103–129.

141. Stefan Heym, "The Boredom of Minsk," *Meanjin Quarterly* 25:2 (June 1966) 196–199; and Werner Volkmer, "East Germany: Dissenting Views during the Last Decade," *Opposition in Eastern Europe*, ed. Rudolf L. Tőkés (London: Macmillan, 1979) 124–125.

142. H. Gordon Skilling, *Czechoslovakia's Interrupted Revolution* (Princeton, NJ: Princeton UP, 1976) 196–203.

143. "The CPCz CC Action Program," April 1968, *The Prague Spring 1968: A National Security Archive Documents Reader*, ed. Jaromír Navrátil (Budapest: Central European University Press, 1998) 92–95.

144. Skilling, *Czechoslovakia's Interrupted Revolution* 183–224.

145. "The 'Two Thousand Words Manifesto,' " June 27, 1968, *The Prague Spring 1968* 177–78.

146. Shulman, *Beyond the Cold War* 71–72.

147. Quoted in Mark Kramer, "The Czechoslovak Crisis and the Brezhnev Doctrine," in *1968: The World Transformed*, eds. Fink et al., 143.

148. Quoted in Friedman 172.

149. Zubok, *Zhivago's Children* 293–334.

150. Bracke, *Which Socialism,Whose Détente?* 209–240.

151. Kramer, "The Czechoslovak Crisis and the Brezhnev Doctrine," 111; Kieran Williams, *The Prague Spring and Its Aftermath* (Cambridge: Cambridge UP, 1997) 112–113; Matthew J. Ouimet, *The Brezhnev Doctrine in Soviet Foreign Policy* (Chapel Hill, NC: UNC Press, 2003) 60–63; Brown, *New Forces in World Politics* 48–49; and Suri, *Power and Protest* 166.

152. Jeffry A. Frieden, *Global Capitalism: Its Fall and Rise in the Twentieth Century* (New York: W.W. Norton, 2006) 279; and Thomas W. Zeiler, *Free Trade, Free World: The Advent of GATT* (Chapel Hill, NC: UNC Press, 1999). The text of the Atlantic Charter is available at: http://avalon.law.yale.edu/wwii/atlantic.asp.

153. Quoted in Eric Helleiner, *Forgotten Foundations of Bretton Woods: International Development and the Making of the Postwar Order* (Ithaca, NY: Cornell UP, 2014) 103.

154. Frieden, *Global Capitalism* 278–283; Angus Maddison, *The World Economy: Historical Statistics* (Paris: Development Centre of the OECD, 2006) 429, 463, and 550; Barry Eichengreen, *The European Economy since 1945: Coordinated Capitalism and Beyond* (Princeton, NJ: Princeton UP, 2008) 23–31.

155. Sheehan, *Where Have All the Soldiers Gone?* 174.

156. Frieden, *Global Capitalism* 254–260; and Barry Eichengreen, *Globalizing Capital: A History of the International Monetary System* (Princeton, NJ: Princeton UP, 1996) 96–102.

157. Thomas W. Zeiler, *American Trade and Power in the 1960s* (New York: Columbia UP, 1992) chapter 6.

158. Steel, *Pax Americana* 63.

159. Jean-Jacques Servan-Schreiber, *Le Défi américain* (Paris: Denoël, 1967) 209.

160. Zeiler, *American Trade*, 244; and Schwartz 166.

161. Harald B. Malmgren, "Coming Trade Wars? (Neo-Mercantilism and Foreign Policy)," *Foreign Policy* 1 (Winter 1970–71) 120.

162. Eichengreen, *Globalizing Capital* 113–117; Robert M. Collins, "The Economic Crisis of 1968 and the Waning of the 'American Century,' " *American Historical Review*, 101:2 (April 1996); Schwartz 175; and Robert Triffin, *Gold and the Dollar Crisis: The Future of Convertibility*, Rev. ed. (New Haven, CT: Yale UP, 1961).

163. Sargent 30–33; Francis J. Gavin, *Gold, Dollars, and Power: The Politics of International Monetary Relations, 1958–1971* (Chapel Hill, NC: UNC Press, 2004) 117–118 and 166–173; Eichengreen, *Globalizing Capital* 117–129; Schwartz 188–205; and Calleo 84–98.

164. Gavin, *Gold, Dollars, and Power* 74–80; Martin, *General de Gaulle's Cold War* 39–42; Charles de Gaulle, press conference, Feb. 4, 1965, *Discours et messages*, Vol. 4 (Paris: Plon, 1970) 330–334.

165. Gavin, *Gold, Dollars, and Power* 64–67 and 135–164; Schwartz, *Lyndon Johnson and Europe* 115–133.

166. Eichengreen, *The European Economy* 216–224.

167. Ibid. 131; Alec Nove, *An Economic History of the USSR, 1917–1991*, 3rd ed. (New York: Penguin, 1992) 294–298; and Paul R. Gregory and Robert C. Stuart, *Soviet Economic Structure and Performance*, 4th ed. (New York: Harper and Row, 1990) 137–138.

168. Ibid. 139; Applebaum 236; Taubman 427–428; Seabury 134–135.

169. Mark Harrison, "Economic Growth and Slowdown," *Brezhnev Reconsidered*, eds. Edwin Bacon and Mark Sandle (New York: Palgrave Macmillan, 2002) 44–47; and Eichengreen, *The European Economy* 133–136 and 140.

170. Ibid. 154.

171. Ivan T. Berend, *An Economic History of Twentieth-Century Europe: Economic Regimes from Laissez-Faire to Globalization* (New York: Cambridge University Press, 2006) 175; Eichengreen, *The European Economy* 136–146.

172. Adam Zwass, *The Council for Mutual Economic Assistance: The Thorny Path from Political to Economic Integration* (Armonk, NY: ME Sharpe, 1989) 14–15; Roger Munting, *The Economic Development of the USSR* (London: Croon Helm, 1982) 196–197; Deletant and Ionescu 16–17; and Eichengreen, *The European Economy* 157.

173. Philip Hanson, *The Rise and Fall of the Soviet Economy: An Economic History of the USSR from 1945* (London: Pearson, 2003) 119–121.

174. Harrison, "Economic Growth and Slowdown" 50–52.

175. Hanson 243.

176. Eichengreen, *The European Economy* 146–152.

177. Timothy Garton Ash, *In Europe's Name: Germany and the Divided Continent* (New York: Vintage, 1993) 141; Brzezinski, *Between Two Ages* 156–157.

178. Taubman 516–523; and Samuel H. Baron, *Bloody Saturday in the Soviet Union: Novocherkassk, 1962* (Stanford, CA: Stanford UP, 2001).

179. Taubman 10–13 and 606–609.

180. Nove 378–393; and Harrison, "Economic Growth and Slowdown," 38–63.

181. Stephen Kotkin, *Uncivil Society: 1989 and the Implosion of the Communist Establishment* (New York: Modern Library, 2009) 46–47.

182. Mark Kramer, "The Soviet Union and the 1956 Crises in Hungary and Poland: Reassessments and New Findings," *Journal of Contemporary History* 33:2 (April 1998) 168–174.

183. Eichengreen, *The European Economy* 141.

184. Geoffrey Swain and Nigel Swain, *Eastern Europe since 1945*, 4th ed. (New York: Palgrave Macmillan, 2009) 142–171; and Brus, "1957 to 1965: In Search of Balanced Development" 71–138.

185. Gerhard Weiss, "Reshaiushchee napravlenie," *Pravda*, July 2, 1969, 4.

186. J. Wilczynski, *Socialist Economic Development and Reforms: From Extensive to Intensive Growth under Central Planning in the USSR, Eastern Europe and Yugoslavia* (London: Palgrave Macmillan, 1972) 39–46; Shulman 35–37; and Zbigniew M. Fallenbuchl, "Economic Questions," *Canada and the Conference on Security and Cooperation in Europe*, ed. Robert Spencer (Toronto: University of Toronto Centre for International Studies, 1984) 233.

187. Maria Markus, "Overt and Covert Modes of Legitimation in East European Societies," *Political Legitimation in Communist States*, eds. Rigby and Fehér 88–91; Henry Krisch, "Politi-

cal Legitimation in the German Democratic Republic," ibid. 112–118; Brzezinski, *Between Two Ages* 155; Eichengreen, *The European Economy* 150–162; and Judt 428–429.

188. Buchan, *Europe's Future, Europe's Choices* vii.

CHAPTER 2: THE CLASS OF 1969

1. Draft memorandum from Leonid Brezhnev to the Politburo, July 6, 1968, *General'nyĭ sekretar' L. I. Brezhnev 1964–1982*, ed. Sergeĭ Kudriashov (Moscow: Arkhiv Prezidenta Rossiĭskoĭ Federatsii, 2006) 70–80.

2. Dmitri Volkogonov, *Autopsy for an Empire: The Seven Leaders Who Built the Soviet Regime* (New York: Simon and Schuster, 1999) 253; Vladislav Zubok, *A Failed Empire: The Soviet Union in the Cold War from Stalin to Gorbachev* (Chapel Hill, NC: UNC Press, 2007) 204–209; and George W. Breslauer, *Khrushchev and Brezhnev as Leaders: Building Authority in Soviet Politics* (London: George Allen and Unwin, 1982) 167–168.

3. Edwin Bacon, "Reconsidering Brezhnev," *Brezhnev Reconsidered* 6; and Sheila Fitzpatrick, *The Cultural Front: Power and Culture in Revolutionary Russia* (Ithaca: Cornell UP, 1992) 12–13. On the vydvizhentsy, see Sheila Fitzpatrick, *Education and Social Mobility in the Soviet Union, 1921–1934* (Cambridge: Cambridge UP, 1979). On Brezhnev's youth and early career, see Luba Brezhneva, *The World I Left Behind: Pieces of a Past*, trans. Geoffrey Polk (New York: Random House, 1995) 1–39.

4. A. M. Aleksandrov-Agentov, *Ot Kollontaĭ do Gorbacheva: vospominaniia diplomata, sovetnika A.A. Gromyko, pomoshchnika L.I. Brezhneva, Iu.V. Andropova, K.U. Chernenko i M.S. Gorbacheva* (Moscow: Mezhdunarodnye Otnosheniia, 1994) 116.

5. Shelepin quoted in Bernard Féron and Michel Tatu, *Au Kremlin comme si vous y étiez: Khrouchtchev, Brejnev, Gorbatchev et les autres sous les feux de la Glasnost* (Paris: Le Monde, 1991) 147–148. Brezhnev kept a work log during his years in the Kremlin, but the laconic entries offer only a glimpse into the workings of his mind. See Leonid Brezhnev, *Rabochie i dnevnikovye zapisi: v 3-kh tomakh* (Moscow: IstLit, 2016).

6. Brezhneva 60–67 and 362; and Zubok, *A Failed Empire* 202.

7. Iuriĭ Dubinin, *Diplomaticheskaya byl': Zapiski posla vo Frantsii* (Moscow: Rosspen, 1997) 169–170.

8. Anatoly Dobrynin, *In Confidence: Moscow's Ambassador to Six Cold War Presidents* (New York: Times Books, 1995) 134–135.

9. Donald J. Raleigh, " 'Soviet' Man of Peace: Leonid Il'ich Brezhnev and His Diaries," *Kritika* 17:4 (Fall 2016) 842–845.

10. Mike Bowker, "Brezhnev and Superpower Relations," *Brezhnev Reconsidered* 91 and 95; Zubok, *A Failed Empire* 205; Vladislav Zubok, "The Soviet Union and Détente of the 1970s," *Cold War History* 8:4 (November 2008) 430; William Curti Wohlforth, *The Elusive Balance: Power and Perceptions during the Cold War* (Ithaca, NY: Cornell UP, 1993) 184–185; Robin Edmonds, *Soviet Foreign Policy: The Brezhnev Years* (New York: Oxford UP, 1983) 76; and Fursenko and Naftali, *Khrushchev's Cold War* 531–537. Quotation from transcript of Brezhnev's speech to a meeting of leaders of district party committees and major enterprises, Leningrad, July 12, 1965, in Kudriashov, ed., *General'nyĭ sekretar'* 48.

11. Aleksandrov-Agentov 206.

12. Zubok, "The Soviet Union and Détente of the 1970s" 432; and Shulman 38 and 45.

13. Cherniaev, *Moia zhizn'* 257–261; Kovalev, *Iskusstvo vozmozhnogo* 170–172 and 177–179; Raleigh 846; and "Report of the Central Committee of the Communist Party of the Soviet Union to the 24th Congress of the CPSU," *24th Congress of the Communist Party of the Soviet Union, March 30–April 9, 1971: Documents* (Moscow: Novosti, 1971), especially 8–39. In his memoirs, Kovalev claimed that he conceived the idea of the Peace Program. See Kovalev 170.

14. Mark Sandle, "Brezhnev and Developed Socialism: The Ideology of Zastoi?" *Brezhnev Reconsidered* 166.

15. Ibid. 175–185.

16. Harrison 57.

17. "Report of the Central Committee" 13.

18. Draft memorandum from Leonid Brezhnev to the Politburo, July 6, 1968. See also Randall W. Stone, *Satellites and Commissars: Strategy and Conflict in the Politics of Soviet-Bloc Trade* (Princeton, NJ: Princeton UP, 1996) 33–46.

19. Jeremi Suri, "The Promise and Failure of 'Developed Socialism': The Soviet 'Thaw' and the Crucible of the Prague Spring, 1964–1972," *Contemporary European History* 15:2 (2006) 138–140; and Breslauer 164–165 and 181–182.

20. Draft memorandum from Leonid Brezhnev to the Politburo, July 6, 1968. See also "For Strengthening the Solidarity of Communists, for a New Upswing in the Anti-Imperialist Struggle—Speech by Comrade L. I. Brezhnev," *Current Digest of the Soviet Press*, Vol. 21, No. 23 (July 2, 1969) 15; and Garton Ash 57.

21. "For Strengthening the Solidarity of Communists" 12.

22. "Report of the Central Committee" 10–12; and Ouimet 72–84.

23. "Report of the Central Committee" 35.

24. "For Strengthening the Solidarity of Communists" 17. See also Bowker 91; and Draft memorandum from Leonid Brezhnev to the Politburo, July 6, 1968.

25. Andrei Gromyko's address to the 24th Party Congress, quoted in Mike Bowker and Phil Williams, *Superpower Détente: A Reappraisal* (London: Sage, 1988) 38.

26. Draft memorandum from Leonid Brezhnev to the Politburo, July 6, 1968.

27. "For Strengthening the Solidarity of Communists" 16; Zubok, *A Failed Empire* 206 and 211; and Wohlforth 196–198.

28. Graeme Gill, *Symbols and Legitimacy in Soviet Politics* (New York: Cambridge UP, 2011) 198–200.

29. Zdeněk Mlynář, *Nightfrost in Prague: The End of Humane Socialism*, trans. Paul Wilson (New York: Karz Publishers, 1980) 241.

30. "Report of the Central Committee" 37.

31. "Speech by Comrade L.I. Brezhnev," *Current Digest of the Soviet Press*, Vol. 22, No. 25 (July 21, 1970) 11–12; "Report of the Central Committee" 28; Cherniaev, *Moia zhizn'* 292; and Paul Marantz, "Peaceful Coexistence: From Heresy to Orthodoxy," *The Dynamics of Soviet Politics*, ed. Paul Cocks, Robert V. Daniels, and Nancy Whittier Heer (Cambridge, MA: Harvard UP, 1976) 293–308.

32. Richard Nixon's Inaugural Address, Jan. 20, 1969, *Public Papers of the Presidents of the United States: Richard Nixon [PPP:RN], 1969*, 3–4.

33. Robert B. Semple, Jr., "Nixon, Sworn, Dedicates Office to Peace," *NYT*, Jan. 21, 1969, 1, 22; and Russell Baker, "Gloomy Day Casts a Pall Over Inauguration Mood," *NYT*, Jan. 21, 1969, 23.

34. Richard Nixon, "US Foreign Policy for the 1970s: A New Strategy for Peace," *PPP:RN*, *1970*, 116–190; George C. Herring, *America's Longest War: The United States and Vietnam, 1950–1975*, 3rd ed. (New York: McGraw-Hill, 1996) 211–218; Jussi M. Hanhimäki, "An Elusive Grand Design," *Nixon in the World: American Foreign Relations, 1969–1977*, eds. Fredrik Logevall and Andrew Preston (New York: Oxford UP, 2008) 28–29; and Henry A. Kissinger, *American Foreign Policy: Three Essays* (New York: W.W. Norton, 1969) 65–78.

35. On Nixon's youth and pre-presidential career, see Stephen E. Ambrose, *Nixon: The Education of a Politician, 1913–1962* (New York: Simon and Schuster, 1987); Garry Wills, *Nixon Agonistes: The Crisis of the Self-Made Man* (Boston: Houghton Mifflin, 2002); Jonathan Aitken, *Nixon: A Life* (London: Weidenfeld and Nicolson, 1993); Tom Wicker, *One of Us: Richard Nixon and the American Dream* (New York: Random House, 1995); Conrad Black, *The Invincible Quest: The Life of Richard Milhous Nixon* (Toronto: McClelland and Stewart, 2007); Robert Dallek, *Nixon and Kissinger: Partners in Power* (New York: Random House, 2007) chapter 1; and Athan G. Theoharis, *The Yalta Myths: An Issue in US Politics, 1945–1955* (Columbia, MO: University of Missouri Press, 1970) chapter 8. On Nixon's trip to Caracas and the kitchen debate, see Richard M. Nixon, *Six Crises* (Garden City, NY: Doubleday, 1962) 213–231 and 255–258.

36. Theodore H. White, *The Making of the President 1968* (New York: Atheneum, 1969) 147.

37. Ivo H. Daalder and I. M. Destler, *In the Shadow of the Oval Office: Profiles of the National Security Advisers and the Presidents They Served—from JFK to George W. Bush* (New York: Scribner, 2009) chapter 3.

38. Robert Litwak, *Détente and the Nixon Doctrine: American Foreign Policy and the Pursuit of Stability, 1969–1976* (New York: Cambridge UP, 1984) 58–63.

39. Nixon told a journalist that Wilson had been the "greatest President of this century. . . . You'll notice, too, that he was the best-educated." Wills 20. See also Richard Nixon, *RN: The Memoirs of Richard Nixon*, Vol. 1 (New York: Warner Books, 1979) 54. In his inaugural address Nixon alluded subtly to one of Wilson's best-known speeches by using the same phrase—"the peace that comes with healing in its wings"—that Wilson had quoted from the Book of Malachi. See Woodrow Wilson's "Address to the Senate," Jan. 22, 1917, in Mario R. DiNunzio, ed., *Woodrow Wilson: Essential Writings and Speeches of the Scholar-President* (New York: NYU Press, 2006) 391–397.

40. Richard Nixon, "Asia after Viet Nam," *Foreign Affairs* 46:1 (October 1967) 113–125.

41. "Address by Richard M. Nixon to the Bohemian Club," July 29, 1967, *FRUS 1969–1976*, Vol. 1 (Washington: USGPO, 2003) doc. 2.

42. Henry A. Kissinger, *The Necessity for Choice: Prospects of American Foreign Policy* (New York: Harper, 1961) 5–6.

43. Address by President Nixon, June 4, 1969, *PPP:RN, 1969*, 432–437.

44. Kissinger, *American Foreign Policy* 52.

45. "Address by Richard M. Nixon to the Bohemian Club"; and Nixon, "Asia after Viet Nam."

46. "Informal Remarks in Guam with Newsmen," July 25, 1969, *PPP: RN, 1969*, 548; Litwak 54; and "US Foreign Policy for the 1970s," 5.

47. Sargent 53–59; Litwak 123; and Wills 419–433.

48. Kissinger, *Necessity for Choice* 200.

49. Sargent 61–62.

50. Hanhimäki 34–38. For the US and Soviet accounts of the meeting that established

the backchannel, see Memorandum of Conversation (US) between Nixon, Kissinger, Malcolm Toon, and Dobrynin; and Memorandum of Conversation (USSR), Feb. 17, 1969, *Soviet-American Relations: The Détente Years, 1969–1972* (Washington, DC: USGPO, 2007), docs. 5 and 6.

51. Stanley Hoffmann, *Primacy or World Order: American Foreign Policy since the Cold War* (New York: McGraw-Hill, 1978) 46; and Garthoff, *Détente and Confrontation* 31–33. See also Helmut Sonnenfeldt, "Linkage: A Strategy for Tempering Soviet Antagonism," *NATO Review*, No. 1 (February 1979).

52. Nixon, "Asia After Viet Nam."

53. Editorial Note, *FRUS 1969–1976*, Vol. 1, doc. 93.

54. Ibid. doc. 98; Nixon quotation from Kissinger-Dobrynin Telcon, July 15, 1971, *Soviet-American Relations*, doc. 175. See also Editorial Note, *FRUS 1969–1976*, Vol. 1, doc. 14. For Dobrynin's reaction to the news, see "Telegram from Ambassador Dobrynin to the Soviet Foreign Ministry," July 17, 1971; and Kissinger-Dobrynin Memcon, July 17, 1971, *Soviet-American Relations* docs. 177 and 178. The best recent study of the opening to China is Margaret Mac-Millan, *Nixon in China: The Week that Changed the World* (Toronto: Viking, 2006).

55. Julian E. Zelizer, "Détente and Domestic Politics," *Diplomatic History* 33:4 (September 2009): 653–670.

56. "We seek peace as an end in itself," Nixon said before he took office. "They seek victory with peace being at this time a means toward that end . . . [and] until they give up their goal for world conquest it will be for them a peace of necessity and not of choice." "Address by Richard M. Nixon to the Bohemian Club."

57. Lacouture 723–758; and Frédéric Abadie and Jean-Pierre Corcelette, *Georges Pompidou: Le désir et le destin* (Paris: Balland, 2004) 234–240.

58. Suri, *Power and Protest* 190–194.

59. Serge Berstein and Jean-Pierre Rioux, *The Pompidou Years, 1969–1974*, trans. Christopher Woodall (New York: Cambridge UP, 2000) 5–16.

60. Pompidou admitted in his memoir that he had the opportunity to join the Resistance but passed it up. By his own account, he lacked the requisite "spirit of adventure" and, besides, had a wife and family to care for. Emmanuel Naquet, "Georges Pompidou dans les années 1930," *Un politique: Georges Pompidou*, eds. Jean-Paul Cointet et al. (Paris: Presses universitaires de France, 2001) 9–27; Eric Roussel, *Georges Pompidou* (Paris: Perrin, 2004) 253–56; and Abadie and Corcelette 11–40, 231–234, and 254–289.

61. Speech to the National Assembly on May 14, 1968, quoted in Georges Pompidou, *Le Noeud gordien* (Paris: Plon, 1974) 26.

62. Pompidou, *Le Noeud gordien* 205.

63. Letter from Georges Pompidou to Claude Bourdet, Feb. 2, 1972, *Georges Pompidou: Lettres, notes et portraits, 1928–1974*, eds. Alain Pompidou and Éric Roussel (Paris: Robert Laffont, 2012) 454. On Pompidou's first years in government, see René Brouillet, "La libéra-tion," and Olivier Guichard, "La traversée du désert," *Georges Pompidou hier et aujourd'hui: Témoignages*, ed. Pierre Messmer (Paris: Breet, 1990), 17–26 and 26–34; and Roussel 63–94. On Pompidou's career at Rothschild Frères, see Niall Ferguson, *The House of Rothschild*, Vol. 2 (New York: Penguin, 2000) 488.

64. Pompidou, *Le Noeud gordien* 26–29 and 176–194. Quotation from 193.

65. Stéphane Rials, *Idées politiques du président Georges Pompidou* (Paris: Presses universita-ires de France, 1977) 5; and Vaïsse, *La Grandeur* 22–58.

66. Quoted in Marie-Pierre Rey, "Georges Pompidou, l'Union soviétique et l'Europe," *Georges Pompidou et l'Europe* (Paris: Complexe, 1993) 143–144.

67. Maurice Vaïsse, "La Puissance ou l'influence?" *Histoire de la diplomatie française*, ed. Jean-Claude Allain et al. (Paris: Perrin, 2005) 864.

68. Georges-Henri Soutou, "The Linkage between European Integration and Détente: The Contrasting Approaches of de Gaulle and Pompidou, 1965 to 1974," *European Integration and the Cold War: Ostpolitik-Westpolitik*, ed. N. Piers Ludlow (New York: Routledge, 2007) 14–22.

69. Vaïsse, "La Puissance ou l'influence?" 867 and 898–899; and Rials 125.

70. Quoted in Roussel 332.

71. Speech on the occasion of the centennial of Sciences Po, Dec. 8, 1972, quoted in Rials 106.

72. Pompidou, *Le Noeud gordien* 171–75; Rials 125; Rey, "Georges Pompidou, l'Union Soviétique et l'Europe," 146–148; Soutou 12; and Vaïsse, "La Puissance ou l'influence?" 899.

73. Georges Pompidou, "Allocution radiotélévisée," April 11, 1972, *Entretiens et discours, 1968–1974*, Vol. 2 (Paris: Plon, 1975) 150–153.

74. Rials 133–137; Berstein and Rioux 11. See also Jean-René Bernard, "L'élargissement de la Communauté, vu de Paris," *Georges Pompidou et l'Europe* 237–252.

75. Nixon-Pompidou Memcon, Dec. 13, 1971, *FRUS, 1969–1976*, Vol. 41, doc. 158.

76. Soutou 23–25.

77. Nixon-Pompidou Memcon, Dec. 13, 1971.

78. For the text of the declaration, see "Text of Soviet-French Declaration on Intent to Cooperate for European Progress," *NYT*, July 1, 1966, 14.

79. Georges Pompidou, "Conférence de presse tenue à l'Elysée," Sept. 23, 1971, *Entretiens et discours*, Vol. 2, 163.

80. Pompidou's logic was not far-fetched. As early as 1966, Brezhnev fretted that France's independent attitude toward NATO might inspire Ceauşescu and other Eastern European leaders to challenge Soviet authority within the Warsaw Pact. See Mastny, "The Warsaw Pact as History" 32–33; Alain Peyrefitte, *C'était de Gaulle*, Vol. 2 (Paris: Fayard, 1997) 313–318.

81. Pompidou, *Le Noeud gordien* 111.

82. Charles de Gaulle, *Mémoires d'espoir, Tome 1: Le renouveau (1958–1962)* (Paris: Plon, 1970) 226.

83. Quoted in Rey, "Georges Pompidou, l'Union Soviétique et l'Europe," 147.

84. Pompidou-Brandt Memcon, Jan. 25, 1971, AN, 5 AG 2/1010; Rey, "Georges Pompidou, l'Union soviétique et l'Europe," 144; Vaïsse, "La Puissance ou l'influence?" 888; and Hervé Alphand, *L'Étonnement d'être: Journal (1939–1973)* (Paris: Fayard, 1977) 477.

85. Pompidou-Nixon Memcon, Feb. 24, 1970, AMAE, Secrétariat général—Entretiens et Messages—Vol. 40. For the US record of the conversation, see Pompidou-Nixon Memcon, Feb. 24, 1970, RMNL, NSC Files, Box 1023. Pompidou also used an epidemiological metaphor with Ted Heath: "We believe that rapprochement, exchanges, cooperation and contagion between the two worlds offer us chances to spread the virus of liberty, rather than us getting contaminated ourselves. It's a wager, but it is likely gradually to be won." Pompidou-Heath Memcon, March 19, 1972, AN, 5 AG 2/1014.

86. "Audience de Monsieur Gromyko," June 2, 1970, AMAE, Secrétariat général, Entretiens et Messages, Vol. 43.

87. Georges Pompidou, "Allocution prononcée lors du dîner offert au Kremlin au cours du voyage en URSS," Oct. 6, 1970, *Entretiens et discours*, Vol. 2, 175.

88. David Binder, *The Other German: Willy Brandt's Life and Times* (Washington, DC: New Republic, 1975) 259.

89. Willy Brandt, "Aus der Regierungserklärung des Bundeskanzlers, Brandt, vor dem Deutschen Bundestag," Oct. 28, 1969, *Berliner Ausgabe*, Vol. 6 (Bonn: J.H.W. Dietz, 2005) 236–246.

90. Willy Brandt, "German Policy toward the East," *Foreign Affairs* (April 1968) 486; and Willy Brandt, *A Peace Policy for Europe*, trans. Joel Carmichael (New York: Holt, Rinehart and Winston, 1969) 142.

91. Brandt, *A Peace Policy* 170–171.

92. Peter Merseburger, *Willy Brandt, 1913–1992: Visionär und Realist* (Stuttgart: Deutsche Verlags-Anstalt, 2002) 13–56. For an overview of Brandt's wartime ideas about the postwar world, see Willy Brandt, *In Exile: Essays, Reflections, and Letters 1933–1974*, trans. R. W. Last (London: Oswald Wolff, 1971) 19–54.

93. Barbara Marshall, *Willy Brandt: A Political Biography* (Basingstoke: Macmillan, 1997) 32.

94. Ibid. 35–36.

95. Garton Ash 60; and Willy Brandt, *My Life in Politics*, trans. Anthea Bell (London: Hamish Hamilton, 1992) 51–52.

96. Willy Brandt, *People and Politics: The Years 1960–1975*, trans. J. Maxwell Brownjohn (Boston: Little, Brown, 1978) 20.

97. Brandt quoted in Marshall 42.

98. Garton Ash 67–68; and Helga Haftendorn, *Coming of Age: German Foreign Policy since 1945* (Lanham, MD: Rowman and Littlefield, 2006) 161. See also Klaus Hildebrand, *Von Erhard zur Großen Koalition 1963–1969* (Stuttgart and Wiesbaden: Deutsche Verlags-Anstalt and FA Brockhaus, 1984) 301–352.

99. Brandt, *A Peace Policy* 70–71.

100. Ibid. 214.

101. Ibid. 27.

102. On the Hallstein Doctrine, see William Glenn Gray, *Germany's Cold War: The Global Campaign to Isolate East Germany, 1949–1969* (Chapel Hill: UNC Press, 2003) 81ff.; and Werner Kilian, *Die Hallstein-Doktrin: Der Diplomatische Krieg zwischen der BRD und der DDR 1955–1973* (Berlin: Duncker und Humblot, 2001).

103. Brandt, *A Peace Policy* 14.

104. Willy Brandt, "Aus der Regierungserklärung des Bundeskanzlers, Brandt, vor dem Deutschen Bundestag," Oct. 28, 1969.

105. "Aufzeichnung des Ministerialdirektors Bahr," Sept. 18, 1969, *AAPD 1969*, doc. 295.

106. Brandt, *A Peace Policy* 104, 116–118, and 156.

107. Brandt, "Aus der Regierungserklärung des Bundeskanzlers."

108. Garton Ash 65–67.

109. Brandt, *My Life in Politics* 54. In a speech at Harvard, Brandt acknowledged that helping the nation and helping individuals might be incompatible in some cases: "If the choice was unavoidable to bring human or national interests into harmony, we would have to place the human interests more in the foreground than the national," but his policy as chancellor presumed that they were in harmony. Binder 200.

110. Jan Palmowski, "Citizenship, Identity, and Community in the German Democratic Republic," *Citizenship and National Identity in Twentieth-Century Germany*, eds. Geoff Eley and Jan Palmowski (Stanford, CA: Stanford UP, 2008) 76–77.

111. Garton Ash 66; and M. E. Sarotte, *Dealing with the Devil: East Germany, Détente, and Ostpolitik, 1969–1973* (Chapel Hill: UNC Press, 2001) 16.

112. Garton Ash 129.

113. Garton Ash 68; and Marshall 68.

114. Brandt, "Aus der Regierungserklärung des Bundeskanzlers."

115. Brandt, *A Peace Policy* 98.

116. "Teutonische Ruhe," *Der Spiegel*, Jan. 12, 1970, 20.

CHAPTER 3: CREATING THE CSCE

1. "Brezhnev Speech at 8 April Warsaw Rally," *FBIS*, April 9, 1965, FF9.

2. "Text of Central Committee Report," *FBIS*, March 30, 1966, 28.

3. Brezhnev speech to Central Committee Plenum, Dec. 12, 1966, RGANI, f.2 op.3 d.49 l. 9.

4. "Speech by M. Molotov," Feb. 10, 1954, *Documents Relating to the Meeting of Foreign Ministers of France, the United Kingdom, the Soviet Union and the United States of America, Berlin* 110–111.

5. Geoffrey Roberts, "Moscow's Campaign against the Cold War, 1948–1955," *Visions of the End of the Cold War in Europe*, eds. Frédéric Bozo et al. (New York: Berghahn, 2012) 54.

6. "Speech by Mr. Eden," Feb. 10, 1954, *Documents Relating to the Meeting of Foreign Ministers of France, the United Kingdom, the Soviet Union and the United States of America, Berlin*, 116.

7. John Foster Dulles, "Report on Berlin," *Department of State Bulletin*, March 8, 1954, 344.

8. The most detailed account of the Berlin conference is Nikolaus Katzer, *"Eine Übung im kalten Krieg": die Berliner Aussenministerkonferenz von 1954* (Cologne: Verlag Wissenschaft und Politik, 1994).

9. "Proposal of the Soviet Delegation," July 20, 1955, *FRUS 1955–1957*, Vol. 5, doc. 251; and Fursenko and Naftali, *Khrushchev's Cold War* 44–45.

10. Marie-Pierre Rey, "L'URSS et la sécurité européenne, 1953–1956," *Communisme* 49–50 (1997) 127–130; Geoffrey Roberts, *Molotov: Stalin's Cold Warrior* (Washington, DC: Potomac, 2012) 142; and Derek Watson, *Molotov: A Biography* (Basingstoke: Palgrave Macmillan, 2005) 248.

11. Brezhnev speech to Central Committee Plenum, Dec. 12, 1966, RGANI, f.2, op.3, d.49, ll. 8–11; and Marie-Pierre Rey, "L'URSS et la sécurité européenne, 1953–1956," 130–134. Khrushchev attempted to force the western powers out of Berlin, of course, but he regarded Molotov's ambition to reunify Germany as a neutral state as too dangerous. He preferred to strengthen communism in East Germany and allow capitalism to survive in the West. See Roberts, *Molotov* 168–172.

12. Memorandum from Abteilung Grundsatzfragen, "Gesprächskonzeption für die Konsultation des Ministers," Dec. 9, 1965, PAAA, Bestand MfAA, A 9742.

13. Crump 142–143; and Mastny, "The Warsaw Pact as History," *A Cardboard Castle?* 28–29.

14. Czechoslovak Foreign Ministry Report, "Zpráva o zasedáni ministrů zahraničních věcí členských států Varšavské smlouvy v Moskvě ve dnech 6.–17. června 1966," June 6, 1966, PHP.

15. Mihail E. Ionescu, "Romania, Ostpolitik and the CSCE, 1967–1975," *Helsinki 1975 and the Transformation of Europe* 130–133.

16. Hungarian Report on the February 1966 Meeting of Warsaw Pact Deputy Foreign

Ministers in Moscow, PHP; Douglas Selvage, "The Warsaw Pact and the European Security Conference, 1964–69: Sovereignty, Hegemony, and the German Question," *Origins of the European Security System* 87; and Mastny, "The Warsaw Pact as History," *A Cardboard Castle?* 30.

17. Wanda Jarząbek, "Hope and Reality: Poland and the Conference on Security and Co-operation in Europe, 1964–1989," CWIHP Working Paper No. 56 (Washington, DC: Woodrow Wilson International Center for Scholars, 2008) 4.

18. "Rede des Genossen Władysław Gomułka, Erster Sekretär des ZK der PVAP," Jan. 19, 1965, PHP. On the Treaty of Rapallo, see Zara Steiner, *The Lights that Failed: European International History, 1919–1933* (New York: Oxford UP, 2005) 166ff.

19. "Rede des Genossen Władysław Gomułka."

20. "Notatka w sprawie propozycji Polski dotyczących bezpieczeństwa europejskiego," Jan. 5, 1967, Wanda Jarząbek, *Polska wobec Konferencji Bezpieczeństwa i Współpracy w Europie: Plany i rzeczywistość 1964–1975* (Warsaw: Instytut Studiów Politycznych Polskiej Akademii Nauk, 2008), doc. 1; and Selvage, "The Warsaw Pact and the European Security Conference" 85–89.

21. Quoted in Selvage, "The Warsaw Pact and the European Security Conference" 87.

22. "Memorandum by Polish Foreign Minister Adam Rapacki," Jan. 21, 1966, *Cold War International History Project Bulletin* 11 (Winter 1998) 239.

23. Wanda Jarząbek, "The Impact of the German Question on Polish Attitudes toward CSCE, 1964–1975," *Journal of Cold War Studies* 18:3 (Summer 2016) 143–144; and Selvage, "The Warsaw Pact and the European Security Conference" 87.

24. Memorandum from Abteilung Grundsatzfragen, "Gesprächskonzeption für die Konsultation des Ministers," Dec. 9, 1965, PAAA, Bestand MfAA, A 9742.

25. MfAA, "Ergänzungen zur Gesprächskonzeption von Genossen Minister Winzer," Dec. 14, 1965, PAAA, Bestand MfAA, A 9742.

26. "Vorschlag der Regierung der DDR an die Regierungen aller europäischen Staaten über die Gewährleistung der europäischen Sicherheit," Jan. 22, 1966, *Sicherheitskonferenz in Europa: Dokumentation 1954–1972*, eds. Friedrich-Karl Schramm, Wolfram-Georg Riggert, and Alois Friedel (Frankfurt a. M.: Alfred Metzner Verlag, 1972) doc. 290a; and "Aktenvermerk über ein Gespräch des Genossen Minister Fischer und des Genossen Botschafter Rittner mit dem Stellvertretenden sowjetischen Außenminister Genossen Semjonow am 17. Januar 1966," Jan. 17, 1966, PAAA, Bestand MfAA C 559/7.

27. Letter from Fischer to Kausch, Jan. 6, 1966, PAAA, Bestand MfAA C 555/73; and Selvage, "The Warsaw Pact and the European Security Conference" 90.

28. Memorandum from Abteilung Grundsatzfragen, "Gesprächskonzeption für die Konsultation des Ministers," Dec. 9, 1965; and Memorandum from Abteilung Westeuropa, "Gegenwärtige Hauptfragen in der Politik der Sowjetunion zur Gewährleistung der europäischen Sicherheit," May 2, 1968, PAAA, Bestand MfAA C 326/77.

29. "Notatka w sprawie propozycji Polski dotyczących bezpieczeństwa europejskiego," Jan. 5, 1967; Selvage, "The Warsaw Pact and the European Security Conference" 86; Selvage, "The Warsaw Pact and Nuclear Non-Proliferation, 1963–1965" 3 and 10–12; Wanda Jarząbek, "Preserving the Status Quo or Promoting Change: The Role of the CSCE in the Perception of Polish Authorities," *Helsinki 1975 and the Transformation of Europe* 145–146; Jarząbek, "Hope and Reality" 4–6; and Zubok, *A Failed Empire* 211.

30. Selvage, "The Warsaw Pact and the European Security Conference" 86; Selvage, "New

Evidence on the Berlin Crisis, 1958–1962" 200; and Mastny, *A Cardboard Castle?* 10. Gomułka claimed that, when his government first advanced the security conference proposal in 1964, it did not consult its allies. Wanda Jarząbek reaches the same conclusion. See Polish Minutes of the PCC Meeting, Warsaw, January 1965, PCC, p. 14; Jarząbek, "Hope and Reality" 6; and Jarząbek, "Preserving the Status Quo or Promoting Change: The Role of the CSCE in the Perception of Polish Authorities," 145–146. By contrast, Douglas Selvage points out that the Poles informed Soviet foreign minister Andrei Gromyko of the proposal, but did not seek his approval. See Selvage, "The Warsaw Pact and the European Security Conference," 86, footnote 3.

31. Selvage, "The Warsaw Pact and the European Security Conference" 86.

32. "Memorandum of the Conference of Foreign Ministers, June 14–15, 1966," *A Cardboard Castle?* doc. 40; Czechoslovak Foreign Ministry Report, "Zpráva o zasedáni ministrů zahraničních věcí členských států Varšavské smlouvy v Moskvě ve dnech 6.–17. června 1966," June 6, 1966; and "Plenum of the Central Committee of the Bulgarian Communist Party," July 12, 1966, PHP.

33. Minutes of Summit of Warsaw Pact Leaders in Bucharest, July 5–7, 1966, *A Cardboard Castle?* doc. 41.

34. "Minutes of the Conversation of the Meeting of the Executive Committee (Politburo) of the Romanian Communist Party (PCR)," July 12, 1966, PHP; "Memorandum by Polish Foreign Minister Adam Rapacki," Jan. 21, 1966; "Statute for the Unified Command of the Armed Forces of the Warsaw Treaty Member-States," July 2, 1966, PHP; and Békés, "The Warsaw Pact, the German Question and the Birth of the CSCE Process, 1961–1970," *Helsinki 1975 and the Transformation of Europe* 114–115; and Crump 154.

35. "Minutes of the Conversation of the Meeting of the Executive Committee (Politburo) of the Romanian Communist Party (PCR)," July 12, 1966, PHP; and Békés, "The Warsaw Pact, the German Question and the Birth of the CSCE Process, 1961–1970" 115.

36. "Extracts from a 'Declaration on Strengthening Peace and Security in Europe,'" July 1966, *Selected Documents Relating to Problems of Security and Cooperation in Europe, 1954–1977* (London: HMSO, 1977), doc. 2; Selvage, "The Warsaw Pact and the European Security Conference" 87–89; and Crump 155–156.

37. "Extracts from a statement on Peace and Security in Europe," April 26, 1969, *Selected Documents*, doc. 4; and "Transcript of Gathering of Warsaw Pact Leaders in Karlovy Vary, April 25, 1967," *A Cardboard Castle?* doc. 42.

38. Vojtech Mastny, "Meeting of the PCC, Budapest, 17 March 1969: Editorial Note," PHP.

39. "Note for HSWP First Secretary János Kádár Regarding the Budapest Meeting of the Warsaw Treaty Political Consultative Committee, March 17, 1969," March 19, 1969, PHP.

40. Cherniaev, *Moia zhizn' i moë vremia* 272; Csaba Békés, "The Warsaw Pact and the CSCE Process from 1965 to 1970," *The Making of Détente: Eastern Europe and Western Europe in the Cold War, 1965–75* 206–207; Békés, "The Warsaw Pact, the German Question and the Birth of the CSCE Process, 1961–1970" 119–120; Selvage, "The Warsaw Pact and the European Security Conference" 93; "Stenographic Transcript of the Meeting of the Executive of the Central Committee of the Romanian Communist Party," March 18, 1969, PHP; Lüthi 340–344; and Christian F. Ostermann, "New Evidence on the Sino-Soviet Border Dispute, 1969–71," *Cold War International History Project Bulletin* 6/7 (Winter 1995) 186–189.

41. "Account of János Kádár at the HSWP Political Committee's session on the WP PCC meeting in Budapest," March 24, 1969, PHP.

42. Telegram from Quai d'Orsay to NATO and Warsaw Pact capitals, April 1, 1969, AMAE,

Affaires Étrangères - Fonds EU - Organismes Internationaux et Grandes Questions Internationales - Sécurité - 1966–70 - 2035; "Stenographic Transcript of the Meeting of the Executive of the Central Committee of the Romanian Communist Party," March 18, 1969, PHP; and Békés, "The Warsaw Pact and the CSCE Process from 1965 to 1970" 208.

43. "Battle for the Backyards," *Time*, April 4, 1969, 38.

44. Frigyes Puja, "On the 15 March Meeting of the Warsaw Treaty Deputy Foreign Ministers," March 16, 1969, PHP; "Stenographic Transcript of the Meeting of the Executive of the Central Committee of the Romanian Communist Party," "Account of János Kádár at the HSWP Political Committee's session on the WP PCC meeting in Budapest," March 24, 1969, PHP; Selvage, "The Warsaw Pact and the European Security Conference" 93; Békés, "The Warsaw Pact, the German Question and the Birth of the CSCE Process, 1961–1970" 120; and Békés, "The Warsaw Pact and the CSCE Process from 1965 to 1970" 208–209.

45. "Appeal to All European Countries, adopted by the Political Consultative Committee of the Warsaw Pact Countries, Budapest," March 17, 1969, *The End of the Post-War Era* doc. 91.

46. Selvage, "The Warsaw Pact and the European Security Conference" 93–94; Federica Caciagli, "The GDR's Targets in the Early CSCE Process: Another Missed Opportunity to Freeze the Division of Germany, 1969–73," *Origins of the European Security System* 109.

47. "Minutes of the Meeting of the Executive Committee of the CC PCR," March 16, 1969, PHP; and Békés, "The Warsaw Pact and the CSCE Process from 1965 to 1970" 206–210.

48. "Report on the Meeting of the Warsaw Treaty Countries' Deputy Foreign Ministers held in Berlin on 21–22 May 1969," May 27, 1969, PHP.

49. Memorandum from Jędrychowski, "Pilna Notatka dotycząca dalszej akcji i konsultacji ze Związkiem Radzieckim sprawie europejskiej konferencji bezpieczeństwa i współpracy," April 4, 1969. Jarząbek, *Polska wobec Konferencji Bezpieczeństwa i Współpracy w Europie*, doc. 2

50. Letter from the SED Politburo to Brezhnev, "Erwägungen zum Problem der europäischen Sicherheit," April 21, 1969, SAPMO, DY 30/3525.

51. Memorandum from Abteilung Grundsatzfragen, "Probleme der Grenzen und der europäischen Sicherheit (Disposition)," June 5, 1969, PAAA, Bestand MfAA C 561/76.

52. "Report on the Meeting of the Warsaw Treaty Countries' Deputy Foreign Ministers Held in Berlin on 21–22 May 1969," May 27, 1969.

53. Memorandum from Titov, Soviet Embassy in Budapest, "Zapis' besedy s zam. ministra inostrannykh del VNR tov. Beloï Siladi," July 26, 1969, RGANI, f.5 op.61 d.399 l.55.

54. Memorandum from Bakin, Soviet Embassy in Warsaw, "O meropriiatiiakh PNR v sviazi s Budapeshtskim obrashcheniem (informatsiia)," Aug. 4, 1969, RGANI f.5 op.61 d.351 ll.93–100; and Memorandum from Jędrychowski, "Dalsza nasza akcja wokół europejskiej konferencji bezpieczeństwa i współpracy," Sept. 13, 1969, Jarząbek, *Polska wobec Konferencji Bezpieczeństwa i Współpracy w Europie*, doc. 4.

55. Memorandum from Gromyko to the Politburo, Aug. 27, 1969; and "Direktivy dlia dvustoronnikh konsul'tatsiï so stranami-ushastnikami Varshavskogo dogovora i dlia soveshchaniia ministrov inostrannykh del etikh stran po voprosam, sviazannym s sozyvom Obshcheevropeïskogo soveshchaniia," Aug. 27, 1969, RGANI f.3 op.72 d.287 ll.16–22 and ll.25–31.

56. Memorandum from Wolniak to Gomułka et al., "Pilna Notatka z rozmowy z v-min. SZ ZSRR tow. Siemionowem," Sept. 26, 1969. Jarząbek, *Polska wobec Konferencji Bezpieczeństwa i Współpracy w Europie*, doc. 5

57. "Foreign Ministry Memorandum to the HSWP Political Committee on Hungarian-Soviet Consultation re: European Security Conference," Oct. 18, 1969, PHP.

58. "Vermerk über ein Gespräch des Ministers für Auswärtige Angelegenheiten der DDR, Genossen Otto Winzer, mit dem stellvertretenden Außenminister der UdSSR, Genossen WS Semjonow, am 25. September 1969," Sept. 25, 1969, SAPMO DY 30/3524.

59. Quoted in Selvage, "The Warsaw Pact and the European Security Conference" 97.

60. Memorandum from Jędrychowski, "Pilna Notatka dotycząca dalszej akcji i konsultacji ze Związkiem Radzieckim sprawie europejskiej konferencji bezpieczeństwa i współpracy," April 4, 1969; and Memorandum from V. Bakin, " O meropriiatiiakh PNR," Aug. 4, 1969; and Jarząbek, "Preserving the Status Quo or Promoting Change: The Role of the CSCE in the Perception of Polish Authorities" 147–148.

61. Memorandum from Wolniak to Gomułka et al., "Pilna Notatka z rozmowy z v-min. SZ ZSRR tow. Siemionowem," Sept. 26, 1969 and Jarząbek, "Preserving the Status Quo or Promoting Change: The Role of the CSCE in the Perception of Polish Authorities" 148.

62. MfAA memorandum, "Information über eine Konsultation des Genossen Staatssekretär Kohrt mit dem Stellvertretenden Außenminister der UdSSR, Genossen Iljitschow, am 26. November 1969 in Moskau," Nov. 27, 1969, SAPMO, DY 30/3525. The GDR Politburo instructed Winzer to make this case directly to Jędrychowski. "Stellungnahme zum polnischen Entwurf über die 'Grundprinzipien eines Vertrages über europäische Sicherheit und Zusammenarbeit,'" Jan. 13, 1970, SAPMO, DY 30/J IV 2/2/1262.

63. Appendix to Memorandum from Winzer to Ulbricht, "Einschätzung der sowjetischen Vorschläge über die Vorbereitung und den Inhalt einer europäischen Sicherheitskonferenz," Sept. 29, 1969, SAPMO DY 30/3524; MfAA memo, "Vorstellungen zur weiteren Diskussion der in den Dokumenten für eine erste europäische Sicherheitskonferenz enthaltenen Gedanken," Nov. 22, 1969, PAAA, Bestand MfAA, C 326/77; and MfAA memo, "Konzeption für die Arbeit in der Kommission I: Die gegenwärtigen territorialen Realitäten in Europa (Grenzen und beide deutsche Staaten)," Nov. 26, 1969, PAAA, Bestand MfAA, C 561/76.

64. "Communiqué of the Conference of Foreign Ministers of the Warsaw Pact Countries, Prague," Oct. 31, 1969, The End of the Post-War Era, doc. 93.

65. "To the Revolutionary Workers and Peasants' Governmenton the 30–31 October 1969 Prague Meeting of the representatives of the Seven Socialist Countries' Foreign Ministries," Nov. 4, 1969, PHP.

66. "The Renouncement of the Use of Force and the Threat to Use Force In the Relationship of the European States(The Draft of the Document's Essential Points)," PHP; and Selvage, "The Warsaw Pact and the European Security Conference" 97–98.

67. Jędrychowski's speech at the Prague Foreign Ministers' Meeting, Oct. 30, 1969, PHP.

68. Memorandum from Bakin, Soviet Embassy in Warsaw, "Informatsiia o konsul'tatsiiakh mezhdu MID VNR i MID PNR po germanskoĭ probleme i voprosam evropeĭskoĭ bezopasnosti," Dec. 2, 1969, RGANI f.5 op.61 d.351 l.179.

69. Memorandum from Tikunov, Soviet Embassy in Bucharest, "Zapis' besedy s pervym zamestitelem ministra inostrannykh del SRR Dzh. Makovesku," Jan. 9, 1970, RGANI, f.5 op.62 d.406 l.23.

70. Selvage, "The Warsaw Pact and the European Security Conference" 96–100.

71. Brezhnev speech to Central Committee Plenum, April 9, 1968, RGANI, f.2, op.3, d.100, l.13; and Brezhnev speech to Central Committee Plenum, June 26, 1969, RGANI, f.2, op.3, d.161, l.7.

72. Memorandum for the MfAA Advisory Board, "Einschätzung des Standes der internationalen Diskussion über die Gewährleistung der Sicherheit in Europa, die Perspektiven für eine europäische Sicherheitskonferenz u.a. Initiativen," n.d. [1968], PAAA, Bestand MfAA C 326/77; and Memorandum from Abteilung Grundsatzfragen, "Die Entwicklungstendenz in den Hauptfragen des Kampfes um ein europäisches Sicherheitssystem," n.d. [1970], PAAA, Bestand MfAA C 561/76.

73. Memorandum from the CPSU Central Committee, Jan. 9, 1969, SAPMO, DY 30/3524; Minutes of the SED Politburo Meeting, Jan. 14, 1969, SAPMO, DY 30/J IV 2/2/1210; SED Politburo memo, "Plan der Aktivitäten und Maßnahmen der DDR für die Vorbereitung einer europäischen Sicherheitskonferenz," Nov. 18, 1969, SAPMO DY 30/J IV 2/2/1253; and Memorandum from Toropov, Soviet Embassy in Oslo, "O sozdanii Norvezhskogo komiteta v podderzhku Venskoĭ konferentsii po voprosam evropeĭskoĭ bezopasnosti," Oct. 13, 1969, RGANI f.5 op.61 d.603 ll.121–122.

74. "Vienna Declaration," Dec. 1, 1969, *Active Coexistence* 22 (October–December 1969) 38.

75. "Report to the Political Committee of the HSWP CC and the Government on the 26–27 January Meeting of the Warsaw Treaty Countries' Deputy Foreign Ministers in Sofia," Feb. 2, 1970.

76. "Draft Speech for Comrade Puja's address to the meeting of deputy foreign ministers of the Warsaw Treaty countries held on 19 June 1970," n.d., PHP.

77. "Minutes of the Meeting of the Deputy Foreign Ministers of the Warsaw Treaty States held on 19 June 1970," June 19, 1970, PHP.

78. Molotov quoted in Roberts, "Moscow's Campaign against the Cold War, 1948–1955" 55. See also Rey, "L'URSS et la sécurité européenne, 1953–1956" 129.

79. "Postanovlenie Politbiuro TsK KPSS 'O meropriiatiiakh v sviazi s Budapeshtskim Obrashcheniem gosudarstv-uchastnikov Varshavskogo Dogovora,'" March 28, 1969, Appendix 2, RGANI f.3 op.72 d.250 ll.13–14 and 34–41; and "Postanovlenie Politbiuro TsK KPSS 'O Meropriiatiiakh v sviazi s itogami Soveshchaniia ministrov inostrannykh del stran-uchastnits Varshavskogo Dogovora v Prage,'" Nov. 13, 1969, Appendix 2, RGANI f.3 op.72 d.300 ll.8–9 and 19–28.

80. "Memorandum from Presidential Assistant Kissinger to President Nixon," April 3, 1969; and "Memorandum of Conversation (USSR)," April 2, 1969, in *Soviet-American Relations*, docs. 15 and 16. Dobrynin met with Undersecretary of State Elliot Richardson on April 4 to present a copy of the Budapest appeal. In response to a question about the scope of the security conference's agenda, Dobrynin said that "any questions could be raised," but that the USSR attached "great importance" to the recognition of current European frontiers. See Richardson-Dobrynin Memcon, April 4, 1969, RMNL, NSC Files, Box 709. See also External Affairs to Canadian Delegation to NATO, April 3, 1969, LAC, RG-25, Vol. 9054, File 20-4-CSCE, Vol. 1; and "Gespräch des Bundesministers Brandt mit dem sowjetischen Botschafter Zarapkin," April 4, 1969, *AAPD 1969* (Munich: R. Oldenbourg Verlag, 2000) doc. 116.

81. "Telegram from Sir Duncan Wilson (Moscow) to Mr. Stewart (London)," March 28, 1969, *DBPO* Series III, Vol. 1 (London: HMSO, 1997) 124–125.

82. "Memorandum from Bakin, Soviet Embassy in Warsaw, "O meropriiatiiakh PNR," Aug. 4, 1969; and Memorandum from Winzer to Ulbricht et al., April 2, 1969, and "Information über eine Mitteilung des Rates der sowjetischen Botschaft, Genossen Grenkow, über diplomatische Schritte der UdSSR zur Vorbereitung einer Konferenz über europäische Sicherheit und Zusammenarbeit," March 31, 1969, SAPMO, DY 30/3524.

83. Macovescu-Bogdan-Hillenbrand Memcon, April 1, 1969, NARA, RG 59, Central Foreign Policy Files, 1967–1969, Box 2081; letter from Olver, UK Embassy in The Hague, to Giffard, FCO, April 11, 1969, UKNA, FCO 41/538; and Telegram from Ignatieff, Canadian Delegation to the Disarmament Conference in Geneva, to External Affairs, Ottawa, April 14, 1969, LAC, RG-25, Vol. 9054, File 20-4-CSCE, Vol. 1.

84. Letter from Ledwidge, UK Embassy in Paris, to Brimelow, FCO, "Finnish Proposal for a European Security Conference," May 28, 1969, UKNA, FCO 41/541; and Thomas Fischer, *Neutral Power in the CSCE: The N+N States and the Making of the Helsinki Accords 1975* (Baden-Baden: Nomos, 2009) 86–89.

85. Thomas Fischer, "'A Mustard Seed Grew into a Bushy Tree': The Finnish CSCE Initiative of 5 May 1969," *Cold War History* 9:2 (May 2009) 182–184; Seppo Hentilä, "Maintaining Neutrality between the Two German States: Finland and Divided Germany until 1973," *Contemporary European History* 15:4 (2006) 484; Thomas Fischer, "Die Sowjetunion, Österreich und die finnische KSZE-Initiative vom 5. Mai 1969," *Osteuropa vom Weltkrieg zum Wende*, eds. Wolfgang Mueller and Michael Portmann (Vienna: Verlag der Österreichischen Akademie der Wissenschaften, 2007); and Petri Hakkarainen, *A State of Peace in Europe: West Germany and the CSCE, 1966–1975* (New York: Berghahn, 2011) 34–35.

86. Seppo Hentilä, *Neutral zwischen den beiden deutschen Staaten. Finnland und Deutschland im Kalten Krieg* (Berlin: Berliner Wissenschafts-Verlag, 2006) 123; and Hentilä, "Maintaining Neutrality between the Two German States" 485.

87. Fischer, "'A Mustard Seed Grew into a Bushy Tree'" 181; and Hentilä, "Maintaining Neutrality between the Two German States" 486.

88. Ibid.

89. Ibid. 478.

90. Diary entry for April 29, 1969, *Urho Kekkosen päiväkirjat*, Vol. 3: 1969–74, ed. Juhani Suomi (Helsinki: Otava, 2003) 44.

91. "Extracts from the Finnish Government Memorandum," May 5, 1969, *Selected Documents* 60–61.

92. "Postanovlenie Politbiuro TsK KPSS 'O nekotorykh meropriiatiiakh v sviazi s obrashcheniem pravitel'stva Finliandii po voprosu podgotovki k sozyvu Obshcheevropeĭskovo soveshchaniia,'" June 6, 1969, RGANI f.3 op.72 d.265 l.31; and d. 266, ll. 34–35.

93. Telegram from External Affairs, Ottawa, to Canadian Delegation to NATO, "European Security: Enckell Visit," May 12, 1970, LAC, RG-25, Vol. 9054, File 20-4-CSCE, Vol. 7; Memorandum from Sous-Direction d'Europe Orientale to Pompidou, "Conférence sur la sécurité européenne," June 15, 1970, AN, 5 AG 2/58; State Department Briefing Paper, "Finnish Views on a Conference on European Security," July 15, 1970, RG 59, Executive Secretariat, Briefing Books 1958–1976, Box 73, The Visit of President Kekkonen of the Republic of Finland, July 1970—Briefing Material; MfAA Memorandum, "Information über den Meinungsaustausch mit dem finnischen Sonderbotschafter, Ralph Enckell, zu Fragen der europäischen Sicherheitskonferenz," Oct. 2, 1970, SAPMO, DY 30/J IV 2/2J/3148; and Interview with Jaakko Iloniemi, *CSCE Testimonies: Causes and Consequences of the Helsinki Final Act, 1972–1989*, ed. Alice Němcová (Prague: Prague Office of the Organization for Security and Co-operation in Europe (OSCE) Secretariat, 2013) 16.

94. Memorandum from Gromyko to the Politburo, Aug. 27, 1969, RGANI f.3 op.72 d.287 l.16; "Ukazaniia dlia besed s Kekkonenom," Aug. 27, 1969, RGANI f.3 op.72 d.287 l. 38–39;

and Politburo Instructions to the Soviet Ambassador to Finland, Dec. 23, 1969, RGANI f.3 op.72 d.310 ll.62–63.

95. Quoted in Hentilä, *Neutral zwischen den beiden deutschen Staaten* 124.

96. US Mission to NATO to the State Department, "NATO Ministerial Meeting—Atmosphere at End of Meeting," June 10, 1966, *FRUS 1964–1968*, Vol. 13: Western Europe Region (Washington, DC: USGPO, 1995) doc. 177. The Danes urged their allies to seize the opportunity to improve East-West relations. See Thomas L. Hughes (INR) to Dean Rusk, "The Possibilities and Limitations of NATO's Role in East-West Relations," Dec. 2, 1966, NARA, RG 59, Executive Secretariat Conference Files, 1966–1972, Box 431, 38th NATO Ministerial Meeting, December 1966, Paris, Vol. II—Memcons; Sub. Misc.; and *Danmark under den kolde krig. Den sikkerhedspolitiske situation 1945–1991*, Vol. 2: 1963–1978 (Copenhagen: Dansk Institut for Internationale Studier, 2005) chapter 37.

97. Summary Record of a Meeting of the North Atlantic Council, July 13, 1966, NATOA, CR(66)32.

98. Memorandum from Diehl, "Dreier-Besprechungen der englischen, amerikanischen und deutschen Planungsstäbe in London vom 10. bis 12. Juli 1967," July 17, 1967, *AAPD 1967* (Munich: R. Oldenbourg Verlag, 1998) doc. 268.

99. Rogers-Debré Memcon, April 9, 1969, AMAE, Secrétariat général - Entretiens et Messages - Vol. 37. See also Memorandum from Sous-Direction d'Europe Orientale, "Réunion du Pacte de Varsovie et déclaration sur la sécurité européenne," March 22, 1969, AMAE, Affaires Étrangères, Fonds EU - Organismes Internationaux et Grandes Questions Internationales - Sécurité - 1966–70 - 2035.

100. William Rogers, "Address Before the North Atlantic Council—The Secretary of State," Dec. 4, 1969, NARA, RG 59, Executive Secretariat Conference Files, 1966–1972, Box 504, NATO Ministerial Meeting December '69 - Vol. 1 - Memcons and Statements. See also Rogers-Pompidou Memcon, Dec. 8, 1969, AMAE, Secrétariat général - Entretiens et Messages - Vol. 40; and Memorandum from Kissinger to Nixon, "Soviet Initiative for a European Security Conference," April 4, 1969, RMNL, NSC Files, Box 709.

101. Telegram from Stewart, FCO, to UK Delegation to NATO, "Warsaw Pact 'Appeal' on European Security," March 18, 1969, UKNA, FCO 41/538; telegram from Wilson, UK Embassy in Moscow, to FCO, "Warsaw Pact Budapest Meeting," March 18, 1969, FCO 41/538; and telegram from French Embassy in London to the Quai d'Orsay, July 21, 1969, AMAE, Affaires Étrangères - Fonds EU - Organismes Internationaux et Grandes Questions Internationales – Sécurité - 1966–70 - 2036.

102. "Gespräch des Bundeskanzlers Kiesinger mit Ministerpräsident Erlander," April 17, 1969, *AAPD 1969*, doc. 128; and Hakkarainen, *A State of Peace in Europe* 25–26.

103. "Summary Record of a Meeting of the Council," April 18, 1969, NATOA, CR(69)15.

104. Memorandum from Rogers to Nixon, "Your Participation in the NATO Ministerial Meeting, April 10–11, 1969," April 7, 1969, NARA, RG 59, Executive Secretariat Conference Files, 1966–1972, Box 488; Telegram from Ruete, "Viereressen am 3.12. in Brüssel," Dec. 4, 1969, *AAPD 1969*, doc. 386; and Paper Prepared for the National Security Council by the Interdepartmental Group for Europe, "East-West Relations," Feb. 18, 1969, *FRUS 1969–1976*, Vol. 12 (Washington, DC: USGPO, 2006) doc. 18.

105. Telegram from US Mission to NATO to State Department, "List of Issues for Possible East-West Negotiations—Senior POLADS September 16," Sept. 17, 1969, NARA, RG 59, Central Foreign Policy Files, 1967–1969, Box 2081, POL 1 Eur E - Eur W 7/1/69; and Floribert

Baudet, " 'It Was Cold War and We Wanted to Win': Human Rights, 'Détente,' and the CSCE," *Origins of the European Security System* 184.

106. Telegram from the State Department to all NATO capitals, "Allied Attitudes toward ESC," Dec. 30, 1969, NARA, RG 59 - Subject Numeric Files, 1970–73, Box 1703.

107. J. L. Granatstein and Robert Bothwell, *Pirouette: Pierre Trudeau and Canadian Foreign Policy* (Toronto: University of Toronto Press, 1991) 3–35.

108. Garthoff, *Détente and Confrontation* 132–133.

109. Connie De Boer, "The Polls: Our Commitment to World War III," *Public Opinion Quarterly* 45:1 (Spring 1981) 126–134.

110. Drew Middleton, "Member Governments Remain Enthusiastic about NATO, but Popular Support Has Declined Sharply," *NYT*, Nov. 30, 1969, 14.

111. "Extracts from the communiqué of the North Atlantic Council Meeting in Paris," Dec. 16, 1966, Selected Documents, doc. 3. Article 13 of the North Atlantic Treaty reads: "After the Treaty has been in force for twenty years, any Party may cease to be a Party one year after its notice of denunciation has been given to the Government of the United States of America, which will inform the Governments of the other Parties of the deposit of each notice of denunciation." Available at: http://www.nato.int/cps/en/natolive/official_texts_17120.htm.

112. Helga Haftendorn, "The Harmel Report and Its Impact on German Ostpolitik," *The Making of Détente* 104–111; Andreas Wenger, "Crisis and Opportunity: NATO's Transformation and the Multilateralization of Détente, 1966–1968," *Journal of Cold War Studies* 6:1 (2004): 59–71; Vincent Dujardin, "Go-Between: Belgium and Détente, 1961–73," *Cold War History* 7:1 (Feb. 2007); and Vincent Dujardin, *Pierre Harmel: Biographie* (Brussels: Le Cri, 2004) 572.

113. Haftendorn, "The Harmel Report and Its Impact on German Ostpolitik" 109.

114. "The Future Tasks of the Alliance," Dec. 14, 1967. Available at: http://www.nato.int/docu/comm/49-95/c671213b.htm.

115. Haftendorn, "The Harmel Report and Its Impact on German Ostpolitik" 109–111.

116. Pompidou-Rogers Memcon, Dec. 8, 1969, AMAE, Secrétariat général - Entretiens et Messages – Vol. 40. See also Memorandum from Sous-Direction d'Europe Orientale to Pompidou, "Conférence sur la sécurité européenne," June 15, 1970, AN, 5 AG 2/58.

117. Brimelow-Beaumarchais Memcon, Nov. 25, 1969, AMAE, Secrétariat général - Entretiens et Messages - Vol. 40; telegram from London to the State Department, Jan. 9, 1970, NARA, RG 59 - Subject Numeric Files, 1970–73, Box 1703; and "Minutes of a National Security Council Meeting," Jan. 28, 1970, *FRUS 1969–1976*, Vol. 39 (Washington, DC: USGPO, 2007) doc. 19.

118. Telegram from US Delegation to NATO to State Department, "European Security Conference," April 2, 1969, NARA, RG 59, Central Foreign Policy Files, 1967–1969, Box 2081; "Current West European Attitudes toward a European Security Conference," April 3, 1969; Briefing Note, "Western European Attitudes toward a European Security Conference," Nov. 22, 1969, NARA, RG 59, Executive Secretariat Conference Files, 1966–1972, Box 506, NATO Ministerial Dec. '69 - Vol. 6 - NATO Briefing Book; Telegram from Ford, Moscow, to External Affairs, "European Security," Nov. 25, 1969, NAC, RG-25 Vol. 9054 File 20-4-CSCE Vol. 4; Telegram from Ruete, Washington, "NATO-Ministerkonferenz Dezember 1969," Dec. 5, 1969, *AAPD 1969*, doc. 388; Telegram from US Embassy in Brussels to the State Department, "Belgian Attitude toward ESC," Jan. 6, 1970, NARA, RG 59, Subject Numeric Files, 1970–73, Box 1703; and Telegram from Oslo to the State Department, Jan. 8, 1970, NARA, RG 59 - Subject Numeric Files, 1970–73, Box 1703, DEF 1 EUR 1/1/70; Telegram from Copenhagen to the

State Department, Jan. 9, 1970, NARA, RG 59, Subject Numeric Files, 1970–73, Box 1703; "Aufzeichnung des Ministerialdirektors Oncken," May 5, 1970, *AAPD 1970*, doc. 197; and Jonathan Søborg Agger, "Striving for Détente: Denmark and NATO, 1966–67," *Transforming NATO in the Cold War* 189–190.

119. Letter from Brimelow, FCO, to Sir Duncan Wilson, Moscow, July 14, 1969, *DBPO* III:I, doc. 35. In a discussion with French officials, Brimelow echoed Stewart's concerns about Western youth. See Brimelow-Beaumarchais Memcon, Nov. 25, 1969, AMAE, Secrétariat général - Entretiens et Messages - Vol. 40.

120. Telegram from Brussels to the State Department, Jan. 6, 1970; Telegram from London to the State Department, Jan. 9, 1970; Telegram from Oslo to the State Department, Jan. 8, 1970; Telegram from Copenhagen to the State Department, Jan. 9, 1970; and Memorandum from Waterfield to Brimelow, "East-West Relations: Procedures for Collective Negotiations," March 24, 1970, UKNA, FCO 41/748.

121. Memorandum from Helmut Sonnenfeldt to Henry Kissinger, Jan. 8, 1970, RMNL, NSC Files, Box 667.

122. See, for example, Nicholas Carroll, "NATO Limbers Up for the Booby-Trap Marathon," *The Sunday Times*, Nov. 30, 1969, 7.

123. Telegram from US Delegation to NATO to State Department, "December Ministerial Mtg: European Security and East-West Issues," Oct. 2, 1969, NARA, RG 59 - Central Foreign Policy Files, 1967–1969 - NATO 3 BEL (BR) 12/13/67 to NATO 3 BEL (BR) 12/1/68, Box 3154; and Memorandum from Referat II A 3, "ESK," March 31, 1970, PAAA, B150, 199.

124. Telegram from Duckwitz, Brussels, "NATO-Ratssitzung mit Außenministerstellvertretern," Nov. 5, 1969, *AAPD 1969*, doc. 349.

125. Speech by Elliot Richardson to the North Atlantic Council, "Opening Remarks by the Under-Secretary: Statement on East West Issues," Nov. 4, 1969, NARA, RG 59, Executive Secretariat, Briefing Books 1958–1976, Box 65.

126. Telegram from Sous-Direction d'Europe Orientale, "Conversations avec les Américains sur la sécurité européenne," April 13, 1970, AMAE, Affaires Étrangères - Fonds EU - Organismes Internationaux et Grandes Questions Internationales - Sécurité – 1966–70 - 2031; telegram from Cadieux, Ottawa, to the Canadian Delegation to NATO, May 13, 1969, LAC, RG-25, Vol. 9054, File 20-4-CSCE, Vol. 1; Memorandum from Cadieux to Sharp, "ESC—Views of Permanent Representative to North Atlantic Council," May 14, 1969, NAC, RG-25 Vol. 9054 File 20-4-CSCE Vol. 1; and "Aufzeichnung des Ministerialdirektors Oncken," May 5, 1970, *AAPD 1970* (Munich: R. Oldenbourg Verlag, 2001) doc. 197.

127. Memorandum from Kissinger to Nixon, "The Recent Warsaw Pact Proposal for a European Security Conference," April 8, 1969, *FRUS 1969–1976*, Vol. 39, doc. 3.

128. Memorandum from Sonnenfeldt to Kissinger, "European Security and Forthcoming NATO Meetings—The Bureaucratic Steamroller Pushes Irresistibly Forward," Oct. 2, 1969, *FRUS 1969–1976*, Vol. 39, doc. 5; and Memorandum from Sonnenfeldt to Kissinger, "State Again Pushes the 'Groundswell' on European Security," Oct. 29, 1969, *FRUS 1969–1976*, Vol. 39, doc. 9. See also Kenneth Weisbrode, *The Atlantic Century: Four Generations of Extraordinary Diplomats Who Forged America's Vital Alliance with Europe* (Cambridge, MA: Da Capo, 2009) 230–235.

129. Kissinger-Pauls Memcon, July 4, 1969, *FRUS 1969–1976*, Vol. 39, doc. 4; Briefing paper by JG MacCracken, "European Security Conference," April 3, 1969, NARA, RG 59, Executive Secretariat Conference Files, 1966–1972, Box 488; and Henry Kissinger, *White House Years* (Boston: Little, Brown, 1979) 414–415.

130. "Summary Record of a Meeting of the Council Held at the NATO Headquarters, Brussels, 39, on Wednesday, 14th May, 1969," June 12, 1969, NATOA, CR(69)22; and "List of Issues for Possible Negotiation with the East," July 14, 1969, NATOA, CM(69)39.

131. Memorandum from Bahr, "Überlegungen zur Außenpolitik einer künftigen Bundes-regierung," Sept. 21, 1969, *AAPD 1969*, doc. 296; and Hakkarainen, *A State of Peace in Europe* 25.

132. Memorandum from Sous-Direction d'Europe Orientale, "Problèmes posés par l'éventuelle convocation d'une Conférence sur la Sécurité Européenne," Nov. 20, 1969, AMAE, Affaires Étrangères - Fonds EU - Organismes Internationaux et Grandes Questions Interna-tionales - Sécurité - 1966–70 - 2032; Rogers-Stewart-Schumann-Scheel Memcon, "Dîner Quad-ripartite du 3 décembre 1969 à l'Ambassade d'Allemagne à Bruxelles," Dec. 3, 1969, AMAE, Secrétariat général - Entretiens et Messages - Vol. 40; Telegram from US Delegation to NATO to the State Department, "Quadripartite Dinner - German Eastern Policy," Dec. 4, 1969, NARA, RG 59, Executive Secretariat Conference Files, 1966–1972, Box 504; and "Declaration of the North Atlantic Council adopted during the Brussels Council meeting," Dec. 5, 1969, *Selected Documents*, doc. 17.

133. Telegram to the Soviet ambassador in Helsinki, Feb. 12, 1970, RGANI, f.3 op.72 d. 319 l.37. See also "Einige Bemerkungen zur gegenwärtigen taktischen Situation," n.d. [Dec. 1969], SAPMO, DY 30/3525; and "Gespräch des Staatssekretärs Bahr, Bundeskanzleramt, mit dem sowjetischen Außenminister Gromyko in Moskau," March 3, 1970, *AAPD 1970*, doc. 87.

134. "Gespräch des Staatssekretärs Bahr, Bundeskanzleramt, mit dem sowjetischen Außen-minister Gromyko in Moskau," Feb. 3, 1970, *AAPD 1970*, doc. 33. See also Pompidou-Brandt Memcon, "Compte Rendu de l'Entretien Élargi entre M Pompidou et M Brandt à Paris, le 26 janvier 1971, 11h," Jan. 26, 1971, AMAE, Secrétariat général - Entretiens et Messages - Vol. 46.

135. Pompidou-Brandt Memcon, "Entretiens en tête à tête entre le Président de la Répub-lique et le Chancelier de la République Fédérale d'Allemagne," Jan. 30, 1970, AMAE, Secré-tariat général - Entretiens et Messages - Vol. 40; and "Gespräch des Bundeskanzlers Brandt mit Staatspräsident Pompidou in Paris," Jan. 30, 1970, *AAPD 1970*, doc. 29.

136. "Extracts from a 'Declaration on Strengthening Peace and Security in Europe,'" July 1966; "Communiqué of the Conference of Foreign Ministers of the Warsaw Pact Countries, Prague," Oct. 31, 1969; and "Appeal to All European Countries, adopted by the Political Consultative Committee of the Warsaw Pact Countries, Budapest," March 17, 1969.

137. "Summary Record of a Meeting of the Council Held at the NATO Headquarters," Nov. 5, 1969, NATOA, CR(69)49; and "Ministerialdirektor Ruete an die Ständige Vertretung bei der NATO in Brüssel," June 24, 1969, *AAPD 1969*, doc. 208.

138. Richardson-Dobrynin Memcon, April 4, 1969, RMNL, NSC Files, Box 709, USSR Vol. 1 (December '68–December '69) (3 of 3).

139. Telegram from External Affairs to the Canadian Mission to NATO, Brussels, April 3, 1969, NAC, RG-25 Vol. 9054 File 20-4-CSCE Vol. 1.

140. Memorandum from Gromyko to the Politburo, Aug. 27, 1969, RGANI, f.3 op.72 d.287 l.18.

141. Telegram to Soviet Ambassadors in Eastern Europe, March 28, 1969, RGANI, f.3 op.72 d.250 l. 32.

142. Memorandum from Winzer to Ulbricht, Honecker, Stoph, and Axen, April 2, 1969, SAPMO, DY 30/3524; and Memorandum from Jędrychowski, "Pilna notatka dotycząca dalszej akcji i konsultacji ze Związkiem Radzieckim sprawie europejskiej konferencji bezpieczeństwa i współpracy," April 4, 1969.

143. Telegram from Beam, Moscow, "Gromyko on ESC," Jan. 7, 1970, RMNL, NSC Files,

Box 667, NSC Files - Europe - European Security Issues (US and Soviet Diplomacy) (February '69–January '70) (2 of 2).

144. Memorandum from UK Mission to NATO, "Preliminary Comments of the UK Authorities on the documents communicated by the Hungarian Ambassador on 26 June," June 29, 1970, AMAE, Affaires Étrangères - Fonds EU - Organismes Internationaux et Grandes Questions Internationales - Sécurité - 1966–70 - 2036.

145. The first products of this exercise were the reports "List of Issues for Possible Negotiation with the East," July 14, 1969, NATOA, CM(69)34; and "List of Issues for Possible Negotiation with the East," Oct. 21, 1969, NATOA, CM(69)46.

146. "Summary Record of a Meeting of the Council Held at NATO Headquarters," May 14, 1969, NATOA, CR(69)22; and Memorandum to Sous-Direction d'Europe Orientale, "Projet de Conférence sur la sécurité européenne," Feb. 2, 1970, AMAE, Affaires Étrangères - Fonds EU - Organismes Internationaux et Grandes Questions Internationales - Sécurité - 1966–70 - 2031.

147. Letter from Brimelow, FCO, to Sir Duncan Wilson, Moscow, July 14, 1969.

148. "Summary Record of a Meeting of the Council Held at the NATO Headquarters," Nov. 5, 1969; and Memorandum from Sous-Direction d'Europe Orientale, "Problèmes posés par l'éventuelle convocation d'une Conférence sur la Sécurité Européenne," Nov. 20, 1969.

149. "Address before the North Atlantic Council—The Secretary of State," Dec. 4, 1969, NARA, RG 59, Executive Secretariat Conference Files, 1966–1972, Box 504. State Department officials had been developing this idea since the spring. See Telegram from Canadian Embassy in Washington to External Affairs, Ottawa, "Budapest Appeal: Views of USA Official," April 24, 1969, NAC, RG-25 Vol. 9054 File 20-4-CSCE Vol. 1.

150. "Summary Record of a Meeting of the Council Held at the NATO Headquarters," Nov. 5, 1969; and "Aufzeichnung des Planungsstabs," Sept. 24, 1969, *AAPD 1969*, doc. 301.

151. Pompidou-Brandt Memcon, Jan. 25, 1971, AN, 5 AG 2/1010.

152. Telegram from Ford, Canadian Embassy in Moscow, to External Affairs, Ottawa, "European Security," Nov. 25, 1969, NAC, RG-25 Vol. 9054 File 20-4-CSCE Vol. 4. Pompidou made a similar point to Manlio Brosio. Pompidou-Brosio Memcon, "Entretien entre le Président de la République et Monsieur Brosio," Nov. 19, 1969, AN, 5 AG 2/257.

153. US Delegation to NATO to the State Department, "NAC Meeting October 1—List of Issues for Possible Negotiation with the East," Oct. 1, 1969, NARA, RG 59, Central Foreign Policy Files, 1967–1969, Box 2081.

154. "Deutsch-britisches Regierungsgespräch in London," March 2, 1970, *AAPD 1970*, doc. 82.

155. "Oral Statements Made by Ambassador Jacob D. Beam to Soviet Premier Alexei Kosygin," April 22, 1969, RMNL, NSC Files, Box 667.

156. Telegram from Quai d'Orsay to Moscow, July 4, 1969, AMAE, Affaires Étrangères - Fonds EU - Organismes Internationaux et Grandes Questions Internationales - Sécurité - 1966–70 - 2036.

157. Pompidou-Brandt Memcon, Jan. 30, 1970, AN, 5 AG 2/1010.

158. Memorandum from the US Delegation to NATO, "Freer Movement of People, Ideas, and Information," April 8, 1971, AMAE, Affaires Étrangères - Organismes Internationaux et Grandes Questions Internationales - Sécurité - 1971–1976 - 2921.

159. De Gaulle-Kiesinger Memcon, March 14, 1969, AMAE, Secrétariat général - Entretiens et Messages - Vol. 36. De Gaulle expressed the same idea to Richard Nixon. See de Gaulle-Nixon Memcon, Feb. 28, 1969, AMAE, Secrétariat général - Entretiens et Messages - Vol. 36.

160. See, for example, US Delegation to NATO to the State Department, "NAC Meeting

October 1—List of Issues for Possible Negotiation with the East"; Memorandum from Sonnenfeldt to Kissinger, Oct. 2, 1969, *FRUS 1969–1976*, Vol. 39, doc. 5; Memorandum from Sous-Direction d'Europe Orientale, "L'URSS et la conférence sur la sécurité européenne," Sept. 8, 1970, AMAE, Affaires Etrangères - Fonds EU - Organismes Internationaux et Grandes Questions Internationales - Sécurité - 1966–70 - 2034; and "Declaration of the North Atlantic Council," Dec. 5, 1969, *Selected Documents*, doc. 17.

161. State Department Briefing Note, "European Security Conference," April 3, 1969, NARA, RG 59, Executive Secretariat Conference Files, 1966–1972, Box 488, NATO Ministerial Meeting - 4/10–11/69 Vol. VII of VII—Briefing Book. Pompidou and Brandt discussed a similar idea. See Pompidou-Brandt Memcon, Jan. 25, 1971, AN, 5 AG 2/1010.

162. "Pamiatnaia zapiska o mnenii ministra inostrannykh del Ianosha Petera otnositel'no evropeĭskoĭ bezopasnosti i Obshcheevropeĭskom soveshchanii, vyrazhennom v khode poseshcheniia im ministra inostrannykh del Armelia vo vremia prebyvaniia v Bel'gii 24–28 fevralia 1970 goda," April 7, 1970, RGANI, f.5 op.62 d.397 l.78.

163. "Declaration on Mutual and Balanced Force Reductions adopted at Reykjavik," June 25, 1968, *Selected Documents*, doc. 9. The December 1969 "Declaration of the North Atlantic Council," for example, used the phrase "mutual and balanced force reductions." See *Selected Documents* 65.

164. "Minutes of a Senior Review Group Meeting," May 14, 1971, *FRUS 1969–1976*, Vol. 39, doc. 48. See also Schumann-Douglas-Home Memcon, July 15, 1970, AMAE, Secrétariat général - Entretiens et Messages - Vol. 44; and US Mission to NATO to the State Department, "UK Views on East-West Relations," Aug. 7, 1970, NARA, RG 59, Central Foreign Policy Files, 1970–1973, Box 2263, POL 1 Eur E-Eur W.

165. See, for instance, "Opening Remarks by the Under-Secretary: Statement on East West Issues," Nov. 4, 1969; Pompidou-Brandt Memcon, Jan. 30, 1970; Schumann-Douglas-Home Memcon, July 15, 1970, AMAE, Secrétariat général - Entretiens et Messages - Vol. 44; and Minutes of a Senior Review Group Meeting, May 14, 1971, *FRUS 1969–1976*, Vol. 39, doc. 48. For a detailed discussion of MBFR's origins, see Helga Haftendorn, "The Link between CSCE and MBFR: Two Sprouts from the Same Bulb," *Origins of the European Security System*, 237–258; Christoph Bluth, "The Origins of MBFR: West German Policy Priorities and Conventional Arms Control," *War in History* 7:2 (2000): 199–224; and Takeshi Yamamoto, "The Road to the Conference on Security and Cooperation in Europe, 1969–1973: Britain, France and West Germany," PhD Dissertation, London School of Economics, 2007, 43–57, 180–197, and 229–243.

166. *The Military Balance 1970–1971* (London: Institute for Strategic Studies, 1970) 92–4; "Minutes of a Combined Senior Review Group and Verification Panel Meeting," Aug. 31, 1970, *FRUS 1969–1976*, Vol. 39, doc. 32; and Letter from Bridges, FCO, to Scott, UK Embassy in Moscow, "East-West Relations and MBFRs," July 23, 1971, UKNA, FCO 41/833.

167. Letter from Bridges, FCO, to Scott, UK Embassy in Moscow, "East-West Relations and MBFRs."

168. "Aufzeichnung des Referats II B 2," April 16, 1970, *AAPD 1970*, doc. 160; and Stephan Kieninger, *Dynamic Détente: The United States and Europe, 1964–1975* (Lanham, MD: Lexington, 2016) 132–136 and 141–143.

169. "Aufzeichnung des Vortragenden Legationsrats Graf zu Rantzau," Jan. 15, 1970, *AAPD 1970*, doc. 9; and Note from Fraser, "Mutual and Balanced Force Reductions: The Situation in NATO," April 21, 1972, DBPO III:III, doc. 1.

170. Memorandum from Kissinger to Nixon, "European Security Conference," Oct. 19,

1970, RMNL, HAK Office Files, Box 71; letter from Bridges, FCO, to Scott, UK Embassy in Moscow, "East-West Relations and MBFRs," July 23, 1971, UKNA, FCO 41/833; and Martin Müller, *Politik und Bürokratie: die MBFR-Politik der Bundesrepublik Deutschland zwischen 1967 und 1973* (Baden-Baden: Nomos, 1988) 63–66.

171. Pompidou-Brandt Memcon, July 3, 1970, AMAE, Secrétariat général - Entretiens et Messages - Vol. 44.

172. Schumann-Gromyko Memcon, Oct. 11, 1969, AMAE, Secrétariat général - Entretiens et Messages - Vol. 39; Schumann-Richardson Memcon, Nov. 12, 1969, AMAE, Secrétariat général - Entretiens et Messages - Vol. 39; and "Audience de Monsieur le Président de la République aux Membres du Conseil de l'Atlantique Nord," May 27, 1971, AN, 5 AG 2/257.

173. Pompidou-Brosio Memcon, Nov. 19, 1969; and Memorandum from Sous-Direction d'Europe Orientale to Pompidou, "Conférence sur la sécurité européenne," June 15, 1970, AN, 5 AG 2/58.

174. Andréani 57; Memorandum from Sous-Direction d'Europe Orientale, "Conférence européenne et réduction équilibrée des forces," July 23, 1970, AMAE, Affaires Étrangères - Fonds EU - Organismes Internationaux et Grandes Questions Internationales - Sécurité – 1966–70 - 2031. France disavowed the section of NATO's Rome communiqué dealing with MBFR. "Declaration on Mutual and Balanced Force Reductions issued by the NATO Council, Rome," May 27, 1970, *The End of the Post-War Era*, doc. 95.

175. Haftendorn, "The Link between CSCE and MBFR," 242.

176. Telegram from US Mission to NATO to State Department, "East-West Negotiations Study: CES Objectives," Feb. 9, 1971, NARA, RG 59, Central Foreign Policy Files, 1970–1973, Box 2264, POL 1 Eur E - Eur W 1/1/71; Minute by Michael Stewart on Memorandum from Waterfield to Brimelow, "NATO: Mutual and Balanced Force Reductions," March 24, 1970, UKNA, FCO 41/682; "Prognosis for MBFR in Light of Rome Communiqué and Declaration Pact Documents," July 24, 1970, NAC, RG-25 Vol. 9054 File 20-4-CSCE Vol. 9; and Briefing Note for Mitchell Sharp, "Negotiations on East-West Problems: Conference on European Security," Nov. 25, 1970, NAC, RG-25 Vol. 9054 File 20-4-CSCE Vol. 10.

177. "Aufzeichnung des Referats II B 2," April 16, 1970; and "Aufzeichnung des Botschafters Roth," March 16, 1971, *AAPD 1971*, doc. 95.

178. "Gespräch des Staatssekretärs Bahr, Bundeskanzleramt, mit dem sowjetischen Außenminister Gromyko in Moskau," Oct. 9, 1972, *AAPD 1972*, doc. 317.

179. Helga Haftendorn, *Sicherheit und Entspannung: Zur Aussenpolitik der Bundesrepublik Deutschland* (Baden-Baden: Nomos, 1983) 523–4; and Hakkarainen, *A State of Peace in Europe* 95–96.

180. Don Oberdorfer, *Senator Mansfield: The Extraordinary Life of a Great American Statesman and Diplomat* (Washington, DC: Smithsonian, 2003) 387–90; and Sargent 58.

181. Minutes of a Senior Review Group Meeting, May 14, 1971; Nixon quoted in Editorial Note, *FRUS 1969–1976*, Vol. 39, doc. 84; Wenger, "Crisis and Opportunity" 59; and Garthoff 114–115.

182. Pompidou-Brandt Memcon, Jan. 25, 1971.

183. Telegram to the Soviet ambassador in Helsinki, Feb. 12, 1970, RGANI, f.3 op.72 d.319 l.36; and Richardson-Dobrynin Memcon, June 10, 1970, RMNL, NSC Files, Box 712, USSR Vol. 8 May 70 - Jul 70.

184. Circular telegram to Soviet ambassadors, Nov. 13, 1969, RGANI, f.3 op.72 d.300 ll.24–25.

185. "Proekt Memoranduma po voprosam, sviazannym s sozyvom obshcheevropeĭskogo

soveshchaniia," June 16, 1970, RGANI, f.3 op.72, d.348, ll.18–19; Soviet memorandum to Warsaw Pact governments on NATO's Rome Communiqué, June 24, 1970, SAPMO, DY 30/3527; and Telegram from Seydoux, Moscow, to the Quai d'Orsay, "Entretien avec M. Gromyko: Sécurité Européenne," June 25, 1970, AMAE, Affaires Étrangères - Fonds EU - Organismes Internationaux et Grandes Questions Internationales - Sécurité - 1966-70 – 2034.

186. "50 Years of Soviet Georgia—Speech by Comrade L. I. Brezhnev," *Current Digest of the Soviet Press*, Vol. 23, No. 20 (June 15, 1971) 5.

187. Memorandum from Kissinger to Nixon, "Brezhnev on Mutual Troop Reductions in Europe," May 15, 1971, *FRUS 1969–1976*, Vol. 39, doc. 49.

188. Memorandum from Sonnenfeldt to Kissinger, "Some Thoughts on Soviet Policy," June 4, 1971, RMNL, NSC Files, Box 715, USSR Vol. 8 June 71–July 71 (2 of 2).

189. Oberdorfer 390–391; and Garthoff, *Détente and Confrontation* 133.

190. "Notes of a National Security Council Meeting," June 17, 1971, *FRUS 1969–1976*, Vol. 39, doc. 63.

191. INR Memorandum, "NATO: East-West Preparatory Talks on MBFR and CES Loom Nearer," June 7, 1971, NARA, RG 59, Central Foreign Policy Files, 1970–1973, Box 2264, POL 1 Eur E - Eur W 5/1/71; Summary Record of a Meeting of the North Atlantic Council, May 7, 1971, NATOA, CR(71)22; and Summary Record of a Meeting of the North Atlantic Council, June 16, 1971, NATOA, CR(71)33.

192. Telegram from de Rose, French Mission to NATO, to Schumann, Paris, "Discussion des aspects militaires de la sécurité à la CSCE," March 23, 1972, AMAE, CSCE 1969-1975, Box 26; and Memorandum from Sous-Direction d'Europe Orientale, "Rencontre au sommet franco-italienne: Conférence sur la Sécurité et la Coopération en Europe," July 1, 1972, AMAE, CSCE 1969-1975, Box 4.

193. Letter from Davidson, UK Delegation to NATO, to Braithwaite, FCO, "SPC Report on MBFR," July 9, 1971, UKNA, FCO 41/832; INR Memorandum, "NATO: Détente in Autumn," Oct. 15, 1971, RMNL, NSC Institutional Files, Box H-187, NSSM 138 (2 of 2); "CSCE Task Force: Second Interim Report," n.d. [April 1972], RMNL, NSC Files, Box 482, MBFR-CSCE Backup Book (Part 3); and Telegram from Rogers, Luxembourg, to State Department, Washington, "Meeting of NAC Council with Secretary Rogers May 5," May 5, 1972, NARA, RG 59, Executive Secretariat Conference Files, 1966–1972, Box 524, Secretary of State's May 1972 Pre-Summit Consultation Follow-Up.

194. Memorandum from Laird to Nixon, "MBFR," Oct.19, 1971, RMNL, NSC Institutional Files, Box H-187, NSSM 138 (1 of 2).

195. "Reply to NSSM 138: A Conference on European Security," Nov. 3, 1971, RMNL, NSC Institutional Files, Box H-187, NSSM 138 (1 of 2). See also National Security Decision Memorandum 108, May 21, 1971, RMNL, NSC Files, Box 482; Memorandum from Kissinger to Nixon, "Gromyko-Beam Conversation on MBFR," May 26, 1971, RMNL, NSC Files, Box 715, USSR Vol. 8 April 71–May 71 (2 of 2); North Atlantic Council Brief, "The Agenda for a Conference on European Security," May 29, 1971, LAC, RG-25 Vol. 9054 File 20-4-CSCE Vol. 14; Telegram from US Embassy in Paris to State Department, "French Attituedes [*sic*] on Berlin, CES, and MBFR," May 31, 1971, NARA, RG 59, Central Foreign Policy Files, 1970–1973, Box 2264; and Memorandum from Sous-Direction d'Europe Orientale, "Conférence de Sécurité Européenne," June 16, 1971, AN, 5 AG 2/91.

196. Memorandum from Sonnenfeldt to Kissinger, "European Question on Soviet-American Principles," July 5, 1972, *FRUS 1969–1976*, Vol. 39, doc. 100.

197. "National Security Decision Memorandum 162," April 5, 1972, RMNL, NSC Files, Box 482, MBFR-CSCE Backup Book (Part 1).

198. Telegram from Rogers, Washington, DC, to US embassies in Europe, "NATOMIN: NATO Ministerial Meeting: Summary Appraisal," June 4, 1971, NARA, RG 59, Executive Secretariat Conference Files, 1966-1972, Box 529, NATO/OECD Mtgs: 6/1-9/71: Memcons and Public Statements Vol. 2 of 3; and "Aufzeichnung des Vortragenden Legationsrat I. Klasse Mertes," Oct. 14, 1971, *AAPD 1971*, doc. 348.

199. INR Memorandum, "NATO and Détente: Facing East at Brussels," Dec. 15, 1971, RMNL, NSC Institutional Files, Box H-187, NSSM 138 (2 of 2); and Rogers-Dobrynin Memcon, Feb. 4, 1972, RMNL, NSC Files, Box 717, USSR Vol. 19 February 72 (1 of 1).

200. Telegram from Alphand, Moscow, to Quai d'Orsay, "Entretiens de M. Alphand à Moscou. Conférence sur la sécurité et coopération en Europe," Feb. 23, 1972, AN, 5 AG 2/1017.

201. Telegram from Rogers, US Mission to the United Nations, to the State Department, "Memoradum of Conversation: FM Gromyko (USSR): Dinner," Sept. 25, 1971, RMNL, NSC Institutional Files, Box H-187, NSSM 138 (2 of 2). See also MfAA Report, "Faktorenanalyse zum Stand der Vorbereitung einer gesamteuropäischen Sicherheitskonferenz," Sept. 25, 1971, PAAA, Bestand MfAA 368/78.

202. "Minutes of a Senior Review Group Meeting," March 29, 1972, *FRUS 1969–1976*, Vol. 39, doc. 87.

203. Memorandum from Sonnenfeldt to Kissinger, "MBFR and CES," Sept. 20, 1971, RMNL, NSC Institutional Files, Box H-187, NSSM 138 (1 of 2).

204. Memorandum from Braithwaite to Bridges, "MBFRs and European Security Conference," July 15, 1971, UKNA, FCO 41/833.

205. Douglas-Home-de Courcel Memcon, June 22, 1971, UKNA FCO 41/833; and telegram from Douglas-Home, FCO, to UK Embassy in Paris, "Conference on European Security," Sept. 27, 1971, UKNA, FCO 41/888.

206. "Minutes of a Senior Review Group Meeting," March 29, 1972.

207. "Memorandum from Secretary of Defense Laird to President Nixon," Nov. 9, 1971, *FRUS 1969–1976*, Vol. 39, doc. 77, footnote 1.

208. Kissinger-Brezhnev Memcon, April 22, 1972, *FRUS 1969–1976*, Vol. 39, doc. 91.

209. Nixon-Brezhnev Memcon, May 24, 1972, *FRUS 1969–1976*, Vol. 39, doc. 95.

210. Minute from Tickell to Wiggin, "Mutual and Balanced Force Reductions (MBFR)," Nov. 30, 1972, *DBPO* III:III, doc. 2.

211. "Summary Record of a Meeting of the Council," April 25, 1972, NATOA, CR(72)20; "Runderlaß des Ministerialdirektors von Staden," June 2, 1972, *AAPD 1972*, doc. 159; "Aufzeichnung des Vortragenden Legationsrats Steger," July 7, 1972, *AAPD 1972*, doc. 199; Paper Prepared in the Department of State, Sept. 18, 1972, *FRUS 1969–1976*, Vol. 39, doc. 113; and Memorandum from Laird to Kissinger, Nov. 1, 1972, Ibid., doc. 118.

212. Hakkarainen, *A State of Peace in Europe* 74; and Sarotte, *Dealing with the Devil* 98.

213. Julia von Dannenberg, *The Foundations of Ostpolitik: The Making of the Moscow Treaty between West Germany and the USSR* (New York: Oxford UP, 2008) 50–66; Egon Bahr, *Zu Meiner Zeit* (Munich: Karl Blessing Verlag, 1996) 284–338; and Hakkarainen, *A State of Peace in Europe* 75–78.

214. Ibid.; and "Leitsätze für einen Vertrag mit der UdSSR," May 20, 1970, *AAPD 1970*, doc. 221.

215. For the texts of the Moscow and Warsaw Treaties, see *The End of the Post-War Era*, doc. 16 and 18.

216. Brandt quoted in Garton Ash 73.

217. Sarotte, *Dealing with the Devil* 98–99.

218. Michael Sodaro, *Moscow, Germany and the West from Khrushchev to Gorbachev* (Ithaca, NY: Cornell, 1991) 185.

219. Randall Newnham, "Economic Linkage and Willy Brandt's Ostpolitik: The Case of the Warsaw Treaty," *German Politics* 16:2 (June 2007): 247–263; Marshall 71–72; and Sarotte, *Dealing with the Devil* 61–63.

220. "Great Fraternity of Peoples, Born of Socialism—Speech by Comrade L. I. Brezhnev," *Current Digest of the Soviet Press*, Vol. 22, No. 35 (Sept. 29, 1970) 6.

221. Ibid. 7.

222. Kovalev, *Iskusstvo vozmozhnogo* 123–125.

223. Rey, "Georges Pompidou, l'Union soviétique et l'Europe," 155–157.

224. Alphand, 538–539; Brezhnev-Pompidou Memcon, Oct. 12, 1970, AN, 5 AG 2/1018; "Protocol on Political Consultations," Oct. 13, 1970, *End of the Post-war Era*, doc. 73; and "Joint Declaration," Oct. 13, 1970, Ibid., doc. 74.

225. Telegram from Beam, Moscow, to State Department, Washington, DC, Sept. 17, 1971, "Brezhnev—Making of a World Statesman," RMNL, NSC Files, Box 716, USSR Vol. XV August–November 1971 (1 of 2); Memorandum to Kissinger, "Brezhnev Visit to France: Preliminary Assessment," Nov. 2, 1971, RMNL, NSC Files, Box 717, USSR Vol. 17 November–December 1971 (2 of 2); Marie-Pierre Rey, *La Tentation du rapprochement: France et l'URSS à l'heure de la détente* (Paris: Publications de la Sorbonne, 1991) 96; and Kovalev, *Iskusstvo vozmozhnogo* 128.

226. "Principles of Cooperation between France and the Soviet Union," Oct. 30, 1971, *The End of the Post-war Era*, doc. 75; and Dubinin, *Diplomaticheskaia byl'* 171–173.

227. Alphand 563; and Rey, "Georges Pompidou, l'Union soviétique et l'Europe," 159–160.

228. Dubinin, *Diplomaticheskaia byl'* 169–170.

229. "Brezhnev's Speech to Polish Congress," *Current Digest of the Soviet Press*, Vol. 23, No. 49 (Jan. 4, 1972) 12.

230. "Soviet-Canadian Protocol on Consultations," May 19, 1971, *Current Digest of the Soviet Press*, Vol. 23, No. 20 (June 15, 1971) 20–30; and "Declaration on the Principles of Good-Neighbor Relations between the Union of Soviet Socialist Republics and the Republic of Turkey," April 17, 1971, Ibid. Vol. 24, No. 16 (May 17, 1972) 8–9. For more on the Canadian-Soviet negotiations, see Circular telegram from Ottawa, "The Kosygin Visit—an Appraisal," Nov. 2, 1971, AMAE, CSCE, 1969–1975, Box 6; Charles A. Ruud, *The Constant Diplomat: Robert Ford in Moscow* (Montreal and Kingston: McGill-Queen's UP, 2009) 109–123; and Granatstein and Bothwell 192–197.

231. "Memorandum of Conversation (USSR)," Feb. 7, 1972, *Soviet-American Relations*, doc. 260; "Memorandum of Conversation (US)," March 9, 1972, Ibid., doc. 268; and "Memorandum of Conversation (US)," March 17, 1972, Ibid., doc. 272.

232. Kissinger-Brezhnev Memcon, April 21, 1972, *FRUS 1969–1976*, Vol. 14, doc. 134; Kissinger-Brezhnev Memcon, April 22, 1972, Ibid., doc. 139; and Georgiĭ Kornienko, *Kholodnaia Voĭna: Svidetel'stvo eë uchastnika* (Moscow: Olma-Press, 2001) 183–184.

233. "Basic Principles of Relations between the United States and the Soviet Union," May 29, 1972, *End of the Post-war Era*, doc. 57.

234. Garthoff, *Détente and Confrontation* 330–331.

235. Kornienko 181; and Aleksandrov-Agentov 226.

236. Brezhnev's speech to Central Committee Plenum, May 19, 1972, RGANI, f.2 op. 3

d.272 ll.25–26; and Nixon-Brezhnev Memcon, May 22, 1972, *FRUS 1969–1976*, Vol. 14, doc. 257. See also Garthoff, *Détente and Confrontation* 333–334.

237. Aleksandrov-Agentov 226–227; and Dobrynin 256–257.

238. Nixon-Kissinger conversation, April 19, 1972, *The Nixon Tapes: 1971–1972*, eds. Douglas Brinkley and Luke A. Nichter (Boston: Houghton Mifflin Harcourt, 2014) 498.

239. Garthoff, *Détente and Confrontation* 330.

240. Kornienko 184.

241. Nixon-Brezhnev Memcon, May 22, 1972; and Kissinger, *White House Years* 1205.

242. "News Conference of Dr. Kissinger, Moscow," May 29, 1972, *Department of State Bulletin* Vol. 66, No. 1722 (June 26, 1972) 885.

243. John Newhouse, *Cold Dawn: The Story of SALT* (New York: Holt, Rinehart and Wilson, 1973) 140–143; and Garthoff, *Détente and Confrontation* 146–150.

244. Minutes of a National Security Council Meeting, June 25, 1969, *FRUS 1969–1976*, Vol. 32, doc. 22.

245. James Cameron, "Moscow, 1972," *Transcending the Cold War: Summits, Statecraft, and the Dissolution of Bipolarity in Europe, 1970–1990*, eds. Kristina Spohr and David Reynolds (New York: Oxford UP, 2016) 82–84; Sargent 62; and Garthoff 152–223.

246. "Gespräch des Bundesministers Scheel mit dem sowjetischen Botschafter Zarapkin," May 23, 1970, *AAPD 1970*, doc. 232.

247. Hakkarainen, *A State of Peace in Europe* 78.

248. Circular telegram from Moscow, March 16, 1971, RGANI, f.3, op.72, d.427, l.33; and Summary Record of a Meeting of the North Atlantic Council, March 3, 1971, NATOA, CR(71)10.

249. Hakkarainen, *A State of Peace in Europe* 83–84.

250. Quoted in Nicolas Badalassi, *En finir avec la guerre froide: La France, l'Europe et le processus d'Helsinki, 1965–1975* (Rennes: Presses universitaires de Rennes, 2014) 129.

251. Hakkarainen, *A State of Peace in Europe* 84–85.

252. Schumann-Gromyko Memcon, May 5, 1971, AMAE, Secrétariat général - Entretiens et Messages - Vol. 48.

253. "Botschafter Ruete, Paris, an das Auswärtige Amt," Jan. 19, 1971, *AAPD 1971*, doc. 21.

254. Memorandum from Sous-Direction d'Europe Orientale, "Échanges de vues sur la conférence de sécurité européenne a la réunion ministérielle de Munich," Nov. 17, 1970, AMAE, CSCE 1969–1975, Box 30; "Record of the Political Consultation of the Ten Held at the Chateau de Val Duchesse," Dec. 3, 1970, UKNA, FCO 41/638; and Telegram from the Canadian Delegation to NATO to External Affairs, Ottawa, "NATO Ministerial Meeting: East-West Relations and ESC," Dec. 4, 1970, LAC, RG-25 Vol. 9054 File 20-4-CSCE Vol. 11. See also Hakkarainen, *A State of Peace in Europe* 111–112; and Badalassi 136–137.

255. Summary Record of a Meeting of the North Atlantic Council, March 3, 1971.

256. National Security Decision Memorandum 91, Nov. 6, 1970, RMNL, NSC Institutional Files, Box H-223; Memorandum from Cable to Bendall, "European Security," Nov. 6, 1970, UKNA, FCO 41/638; telegram from Douglas-Home, FCO, to UK Delegation to NATO, "European Security Problems," Nov. 7, 1970, UKNA, FCO 41/746; "Ministerial Meeting of the North Atlantic Council, Brussels: Draft Main Statement," Dec. 3, 1970, UKNA, FCO 41/638; and Garton Ash 76.

257. See, for instance, Memorandum from the Belgian Foreign Ministry, "Conférence de la sécurité européenne," Nov. 18, 1970, AEU, FMM 36 - Conférence sur la Sécurité et Coopération en Europe (CSCE), 11/11/1970 – 22/12/1972; and telegram from External Affairs, Ottawa,

to Canadian Delegation to NATO, "December Ministerial Meeting—Canadian Approach," Nov. 18, 1970, LAC, RG-25 Vol. 9054 File 20-4-CSCE Vol. 10.

258. Telegram from US Embassy, Bonn, to Department of State, "Lisbon Quadripartite Dinner, June 2, Part V of V," June 4, 1971, NARA, RG 59, Executive Secretariat Conference Files, 1966–1972, Box 529, NATO/OECD Mtgs: 6/1–9/71: Memcons and Public Statements Vol. II of III; and Telegram from Rogers, Lisbon, to Nixon, "Re. NATO Meeting," June 4, 1971, Ibid.

259. "Editorial Note," *FRUS 1969–1976*, Vol. 39, doc. 84.

260. "Extracts from the Communiqué of the North Atlantic Council meeting in Lisbon," June 4, 1971, *Selected Documents*, doc. 34; Hakkarainen, *A State of Peace in Europe* 118–120; and Garton Ash 75–76.

261. Sarotte, *Dealing with the Devil* 113–134.

262. Memorandum from Sous-Direction d'Europe Orientale to Pompidou, "Conférence sur la sécurité et la coopération en Europe (Éléments de discussion)," Sept. 29, 1971, AN, 5 AG 2/678; Circular telegram from Moscow, Oct. 5, 1971, RGANI, f.3 op.72 d.477 ll.77–78; Telegram from the Canadian Mission to the UN to External Affairs, Ottawa, "Conference on European Security," Oct. 13, 1971, LAC, RG-25 Vol. 9054 File 20-4-CSCE Vol. 15 (71-06-01 to 71-10-31); Circular telegram from Bonn, "Sitzung des Politischen Komitees der EG; KSE," Oct. 21, 1971, PAAA, B150, 240; Pompidou-Brezhnev Memcon, Oct. 26, 1971, AN, 5 AG 2/1018; "Botschafter Krapf, Brüssel (NATO), an das Auswärtige Amt," Nov. 17, 1971, *AAPD 1971*, doc. 397; Telegram from French Mission to NATO to Quai d'Orsay, "Dîner quadripartite," Dec. 9, 1971, AMAE, Affaires Étrangères - Organismes Internationaux et Grandes Questions Internationales - Sécurité – 1971–1976 – 2922; Circular telegram from Washington, DC, "NATO Ministerial Meeting: An Overview," Dec. 11, 1971, NARA, RG 59, Executive Secretariat Conference Files, 1966–1972, Box 531, Chiefs of Mission Conference and NATO Ministerial Meeting - Dec. 1971 Vol. I of II; and Memorandum from Rogers to Nixon, "Preparations for Initial Multilateral Talks on Security and Cooperation in Europe," Dec. 22, 1971, RMNL, NSC Institutional Files, Box H-187, NSSM 138 (1 of 2).

263. Neal Ascherson, "Willy Brandt's Ostpolitik: What's at Stake," *New York Review of Books*, April 20, 1972; and Badalassi 151.

264. Aleksandrov-Agentov 224.

265. Brezhnev speech to Central Committee Plenum, May 19, 1972, RGANI, f.2 op.3 d.272 ll.23–24; "Stenogramm des Freundschaftstreffens führender Vertreter der kommunistischen und Arbeiterparteien der sozialistischen Länder," July 31, 1972, PHP; and "Pilna Notatka w sprawach niemieckich na posiedzenie Biura Politycznego w dniu 18 maja 1972," May 18, 1972, *PDD 1972*, doc. 101.

266. Hakkarainen, *A State of Peace in Europe* 155; and Sodaro 216–217.

267. Bonn Communiqué, May 31, 1972, *Selected Documents* 120–122; and "Runderlaß des Ministerialdirektors von Staden," June 2, 1972.

268. John W. Holmes, "The Advantages of Diversity in NATO," *NATO in Quest of Cohesion*, eds. Karl H. Cerny and Henry W. Briefs (New York: Praeger, 1965) 290–295.

Chapter 4: The Meaning of Security

1. Letter from Elliott, UK Embassy in Helsinki, to Douglas-Home, FCO, "CSCE: The First 200 Days," June 13, 1973, UKNA, FCO 28/2166.

2. Testimony of Luigi Vittorio Ferraris at Machiavelli Center oral history conference on the CSCE, Florence, Italy, Sept. 29–30, 2003.

3. Finnish aide mémoire, May 13, 1972, UKNA, FCO 41/1074; memorandum from McLaren to Tickell, "Anglo-Finnish Consultations on the CSCE," Nov. 16, 1972, UKNA, FCO 41/1074; Richard Davy, "34 Nations Begin Preparatory Talks in Helsinki on European Security Conference," *The Times*, Nov. 23, 1972, 7; and "Reima and Raili Pietilä," Randall J. Van Vunckt, ed., *International Dictionary of Architects and Architecture*, Vol. 1 (Detroit: St. James Press, 1993).

4. Albania rejected the Finnish government's invitation to the MPT with characteristic vitriol. "The United States of America and the Soviet Union follow an aggressive policy of hegemony in Europe directed against the independence and sovereignty of the states of this continent," it wrote. Albanian *pour-mémoire*, Nov. 18, 1972, AMAE, CSCE 1969–1975, Box 2. See also memorandum from Podolier to Burns, "Albania and the CSCE," Sept. 18, 1972, UKNA, FCO 28/1693.

5. Memorandum from Referat II A 1, "Bezeichnung und alphabetische Einordnung der beiden Staaten in Deutschland," March 23, 1972, PAAA, B28 109312; telegram from FRG delegation, Helsinki, to Auswärtiges Amt, Bonn, "Delegationsbericht Nr. 2," Nov. 22, 1972, PAAA, B28 109306; "Notes About a Conversation with the USSR's Ambassador Comrade Malzev," Nov. 22, 1972, *Negotiating One's Own Demise? The GDR's Foreign Ministry and the CSCE Negotiations*, ed. Oliver Bange and Stephan Kieninger, CWIHP e-Dossier No. 17 (Washington, DC: Woodrow Wilson International Center for Scholars, 2008); Hakkarainen, *A State of Peace in Europe* 215–218; and Kristina Spohr Readman, "National Interests and the Power of 'Language': West German Diplomacy and the Conference on Security and Cooperation in Europe, 1972–1975," *Journal of Strategic Studies* 29:6 (December 2006) 1082–1091.

6. Telegram from the West German Delegation to the MPT to Bonn, Nov. 22, 1972, PAAA, B28 100001; and James Feron, "European Security Talks on in Finland," *NYT*, Nov. 23, 1972, 16.

7. Telegram from Coté, Helsinki, to External Affairs, "CSCE Helsinki Consultations: Comments on Procedure," Dec. 4, 1972, LAC, RG-25 Vol. 9054 File 20-4-CSCE Vol. 27; circular telegram from Quai d'Orsay, "Préliminaires CSCE," Dec. 7, 1972, AMAE, Affaires Étrangères - Organismes Internationaux et Grandes Questions Internationales - Sécurité – 1971–1976 – 2925; Memorandum from Gromyko to the Politburo, Dec. 27, 1972, RGANI, f.3 op.72 d.539 ll.178–187.

8. John J. Maresca, *To Helsinki: The Conference on Security and Cooperation in Europe 1973–1975*. New ed. (Durham: Duke University Press, 1987) 14–22; Spohr Readman 1091–1098; interview with Édouard Brunner, *CSCE Testimonies* 94–95; Greenhill-Frank Memcon, April 21, 1972, UKNA, FCO 30/1250; and letter from Audland, Bonn, to Tickell, FCO, "CSCE: Official Conference Languages," May 2, 1972, UKNA, FCO 28/1684.

9. Fischer, *Neutral Power in the CSCE* 173–176; Édouard Brunner, *Lambris dorés et coulisses: Souvenirs d'un diplomate* (Geneva: Georg, 2001) 47; and interview with Jacques Andréani, *CSCE Testimonies* 83.

10. Circular memorandum from Halstead, "CSCE: Stage II, Geneva," July 23, 1973, LAC, RG-25 Vol. 9054 File 20-4-CSCE Vol. 37 (73-07-15 to 73-08-10); and telegram from Warburton, Geneva, to FCO, "CSCE: Organisation of Second Stage," Sept. 1, 1973, UKNA, FCO 69/396.

11. Message from Scowcroft to Kissinger, May 6, 1974, *FRUS 1969–1976*, Vol. 39, doc. 202.

12. Hansjörg Renk, *Der Weg der Schweiz nach Helsinki: Der Beitrag der schweizerischen Diplomatie zum Zustandekommen der Konferenz über Sicherheit und Zusammenarbeit in Europa (KSZE), 1972–1975* (Bern: Paul Haupt, 1996) 71 and 175–176; and Peter Steglich and Günter Leuschner, *KSZE—Fossil oder Hoffnung?* (Berlin: Edition Ost, 1996) 44.

13. "Sprawozdanie naczelnika w Departamencie Informacji i Współpracy Kulturalnej z pobytu w ZSRR," April 16, 1974, *PDD 1974*, doc. 100.

14. Sarotte, *Dealing with the Devil* 139–147.

15. Diarmuid Brogan, "Police Throw Security Net around Helsinki," *FT*, Nov. 22, 1972, 7.

16. Brezhnev-Honecker Memcon, June 18, 1974, SAPMO, DY 30/IV 2/2.035/55; Sargent 131–161; and Judt 504–516.

17. Memorandum from Fall to Tickell, "CSCE: Office Meeting at 4.00 pm on 14 December," Dec. 14, 1973, UKNA, FCO 28/2189; Memorandum from Sous-Direction CSCE, "CSCE—Bilan des trois premiers mois de la deuxième phase," Dec. 18, 1973, AMAE, CSCE 1969–1975, Box 28; GDR Politburo Memorandum, "Direktive für das weitere Auftreten der Delegation der DDR während der 2. Phase der Konferenz über Sicherheit und Zusammenarbeit in Europa ab 2.9.1974," Sept. 10, 1974, SAPMO, DY 30/J IV 2/2/1526; "Notatka Informacyjna o rezultatach dotychczasowych prac II fazy KBWE," June 26, 1974, Jarząbek, *Polska wobec Konferencji Bezpieczeństwa i Współpracy w Europie*, doc. 13; "Notatka Informacyjna Obecna rola KBWE w procesie odprężenia," Nov. 13, 1974, ibid., doc. 14; and Siegfried Bock, "Die DDR im KSZE Prozeß," *DDR-Außenpolitik im Rückspiegel. Diplomaten im Gespräch*, eds. Siegfried Bock, Ingrid Muth, and Hermann Schwiesau (Münster: Lit Verlag, 2004) 109. Quotations from telegram from Hildyard, Geneva, to FCO, "CSCE: NATO Council Meeting," Sept. 12, 1974, UKNA, FCO 41/1549; and "Deutsch-französische Direktorenkonsultation am 18.12.1973 in Paris," Dec. 20, 1973, PAAA, B28 111510.

18. Telegram from West German Delegation, Helsinki, to the Auswärtiges Amt, "Delegationsbericht Nr. 1," Nov. 22, 1972, PAAA, B123 100001; memorandum from Walden, UK Embassy in Helsinki, to Fall, FCO, "Despatch on the Conclusion of the CSCE," June 5, 1973, UKNA, FCO 28/2166; "CSCE: Draft Report of the Delegation to the Multilateral Preparatory Talks," June 9, 1973, UKNA, FCO 28/2167; Roger Beetham and Reginald Hibbert, "Observations on British Diplomacy and the CSCE Process," *British Scholar* III:1 (September 2010) 131; "Keep That Light on at Geneva," *The Economist*, Nov. 24, 1973, 16–18; and interview with Jaakko Iloniemi, *CSCE Testimonies* 21. See also, for example, Bernard Margueritte, "Les alliés européens de Moscou redoutent de faire les frais de la détente," *Le Monde*, Jan. 11, 1973, 1; Andreas Kohlschütter, "Kühnes Experiment für den Frieden," *Die Zeit*, July 13, 1973, 3; and Flora Lewis, "Europeans Hopeful on Kissinger's Role," Sept. 5, 1973, *NYT*, 1.

19. See, for example, A. Shitikov, "Obshchee Delo Narodov Evropy," *Pravda*, July 26, 1972, 4; "Dipoli: UdSSR-Initiative brachte neue Fortschritte," *Neues Deutschland*, Jan. 30, 1973, 7; M. Lvov, "The Helsinki Consultations: Some Reflections," *New Times*, March 2, 1973, 14–16; A. Grigor'iants, "Zheneva: Vazhnyĭ Etap," *Izvestiia*, June 4, 1974, 3; and GDR Politburo Memorandum, "Themenplan für die weitere publizistische Behandlung der europäischen Sicherheitskonferen," Aug. 21, 1973, SAPMO, DY 30/J IV 2/2/1464.

20. Letter from Beetham, Helsinki, to Adams, FCO, "CSCE/MPT: Future Soviet Tactics," Feb. 6, 1973, UKNA, FCO 28/2168; Memorandum from Elliott to Maxey, "Discussion with Mr. Mendelevich at Lunch," Nov. 15, 1973, UKNA, FCO 41/1323; Beetham and Hibbert 128; Hakkarainen, *A State of Peace in Europe*, 213–214; Andréani 63–64; Walden, *Lucky George* 150; and Badalassi 200 and 247. For complete lists of participants, see the documents in PAAA, B28 111507; "Liste provisoire des participants," Sept. 20, 1973, UKNA, FCO 41/1322; "Délégations à la Conférence sur la Sécurité et la Coopération en Europe," Feb. 5, 1975, AMAE, CSCE 1969–1975, Box 24; and testimony of Edouard Brunner at Machiavelli Center oral history conference. For examples of the lunches and dinners, see Sherer Diary, YMA, Albert W. Sherer,

Jr. Papers, Box 4. In Geneva, restaurants such as Le Sénat, Au Fin Bec, and the Hotel du Parc des Eaux-Vives were particular favorites.

21. Kovalev, *Iskusstvo vozmozhnogo* 192; Telegram from Shenstone, Geneva, to External Affairs, "CSCE: General Survey," Nov. 13, 1973, LAC, RG-25, Vol. 9054, File 20-4-CSCE, Vol. 41; "Notatka informacyjna o przebiegu i wynikach prac komisji problemowych II fazy Konferencji Bezpieczeństwa i Współpracy w Europie," Dec. 22, 1973, Jarząbek, *Polska wobec Konferencji Bezpieczeństwa i Współpracy w Europie*, doc. 11; Brunner 50–55; and Michael Alexander, *Managing the Cold War: A View from the Front Line* (London: RUSI, 2005) 87.

22. Letter from Walden, FCO, to Fall, Helsinki, "Despatch on the Conclusion of the CSCE," June 5, 1973; Telegram from Lueders, Moscow, to the Auswärtiges Amt, "KSZE, Zweite Phase: Sowjetische Delegation," Aug. 27, 1973, PAAA, B28 111507; Iu. V. Kashlev, *Khel'sinkskiĭ protsess 1975–2005: Svet i teni glazami uchastnika* (Moscow: Izdatel'stvo "Izvestiia", 2005) 41; Kovalev, *Iskusstvo vozmozhnogo* 226–227; Garthoff, *Détente and Confrontation* 331; and Walden, *Lucky George* 149.

23. Letter from Walden, FCO, to Fall, Helsinki, "Despatch on the Conclusion of the CSCE," June 5, 1973; Letter from Hildyard, Geneva, to Callaghan, FCO, "CSCE: The Conclusion of Stage II," July 25, 1975, UKNA, FCO 41/1769; Marie-Pierre Rey, "The *Mejdunarodniki* in the 1960s and First Half of the 1970s: Backgrounds, Connections, and the Agenda of Soviet International Elites," *The Making of Détente*, 51–65; Maresca, *To Helsinki* 124; Alexander 69–71; Badalassi 244; and Interview with Édouard Brunner, *CSCE Testimonies* 97.

24. George Walden, "How They Won the Cold War without Ron and Maggie," *Sunday Times*, Jan. 18, 1998, 8; Testimony of George Walden, *The Helsinki Negotiations: The Accords and Their Impact*, eds. Michael D. Kandiah and Gillian Staerck (London: Institute of Contemporary British History, 2006) 43; and interview with John Maresca, Geneva, Dec. 18, 2005.

25. Alain Frachon, "Jacques Andréani: Diplomate français," *Le Monde*, July 30, 2015, 18; Tam Dalyell, "Obituary: Guido Brunner," *Independent*, Dec. 6, 1997, 22; John Ure, "Hildyard, Sir David Henry Thoroton (1916–1997)," *Oxford Dictionary of National Biography* (Oxford: Oxford UP, 2004); "Sir David Hildyard," *The Times*, April 19, 1997, 23; Maresca, *To Helsinki* 45; and Interview with George S. Vest, July 6, 1990, Foreign Affairs Oral History Collection, Association for Diplomatic Studies and Training.

26. Memorandum by Elliott, "CSCE: Draft Report of the Delegation to the Multilateral Preparatory Talks"; Letter from Hildyard, Geneva, to Callaghan, FCO, "CSCE: The Conclusion of Stage II"; Telegram from Delworth, Geneva, to External Affairs, "CSCE: Briefing for Stage III"; and Fischer, *Neutral Power in the CSCE* 331–340.

27. Letter from Walden, FCO, to Fall, Helsinki, "Despatch on the Conclusion of the CSCE," June 5, 1973, UKNA, FCO 28/2166; and Hakkarainen, *A State of Peace in Europe* 214.

28. Badalassi 237.

29. Testimony of Andrew Burns, *The Helsinki Negotiations*, 39; Letter from Bullard, FCO, to Garvey, Moscow, "Trends in the Soviet Union and Eastern Europe," May 3, 1974, UKNA, FCO 41/1547; and Memorandum from Tickell to Morgan, "CSCE," Nov. 27, 1974, UKNA, FCO 41/1549.

30. Letter from Seydoux, Moscow, to Quai d'Orsay, "Entretien avec M. Doubinine," Sept. 21, 1972, AMAE, Affaires Étrangères - Organismes Internationaux et Grandes Questions Internationales - Sécurité – 1971–1976 - 2924; Letter from Killick, Moscow, to Tickell, FCO, "CSCE," Nov. 9, 1972, UKNA, FCO 28/1695; Letter from Walden, FCO, to Fall, Helsinki, "Despatch on the Conclusion of the CSCE," June 5, 1973; Letter from Elliott, UK Embassy in Helsinki, to Douglas-Home, FCO, "CSCE: The First 200 Days," June 13, 1973; GDR Polit-

buro Memorandum, "Direktive für das Auftreten der Delegation der DDR während der zweiten Phase der Konferenz für Sicherheit und Zusammenarbeit in Europa," Aug. 21, 1973, SAPMO, DY 30/J IV 2/2/1464; Telegram from Politburo to Kovalev, Geneva, Oct. 3, 1973, RGANI, f.3 op.72 d.577 l.216; Memorandum from Winzer to the Politburo, "Zum gegenwärtigen Stand der Arbeit der Sicherheitskonferenz," July 30, 1974, SAPMO, DY 30/J IV 2/2J/5399; GDR Politburo Memorandum, "Direktive für das weitere Auftreten der Delegation der DDR während der 2. Phase der Konferenz über Sicherheit und Zusammenarbeit in Europa ab 2.9.1974," Sept. 10, 1974; Telegram from Hildyard, Geneva, to FCO, "CSCE and the Moscow Visit," Jan. 24, 1975, UKNA, FCO 41/1781; Entry for May 23, 1975, Sherer Diary; Testimony of Keith Bishop, *The Helsinki Negotiations*, 81; Alexander 95; and Maresca, *To Helsinki* 124.

31. Alexander 99.

32. Letter from Ungern-Sternberg, Brussels, to Bonn, "Nichtamtliche Konferenz über europäische Sicherheit und Zusammenarbeit in Brüssel vom 11. - 13.1.72," Jan. 14, 1972, PAAA, B28 109311; "Pilna notatka o naradzie Doradczego Komitetu Politycznego Państw-Stron Ukladu Warszawskiego," Jan. 28, 1972, *PDD 1972*, doc. 19; Letter from Staples, UK Mission to NATO, to Andrews, NATO Political Directorate, "CSCE: Related International Conferences," March 29, 1972, UKNA, FCO 41/1062; Telegram from External Affairs to Canadian Mission to NATO, "CSCE: Related Initiatives: European Youth Security Conference," June 12, 1972, LAC, RG-25 Vol. 9054 File 20-4-CSCE Vol. 20; Letter from Ramsay, FCO, to Smith, UK Mission to NATO, "European Youth Security Conference," July 11, 1972, UKNA, FCO 41/1062; GDR Politburo Memorandum, "Politisch-diplomatische Maßnahmen nach der Ratifizierung der Verträge von Moskau und Warschau," July 25, 1972, SAPMO, DY 30/J IV 2/2/1403; Letter from Beetham, Helsinki, to Ramsay, FCO, "European Youth Security Conference," Aug. 31, 1972, UKNA, FCO 41/1063; Letter from Barder, Moscow, to Reeve, FCO, "Soviet Press on CSCE," Dec. 7, 1972, UKNA, FCO 28/1695; and "Vermerk über das Gespräch beim Kandidaten des Politbüros und Sekretär des ZK der KPdSU, Genossen BN Ponomarjow, am 27. Februar 1973 in Moskau," Feb. 27, 1973, SAPMO, DY 30/IV 2/2.035/55.

33. See, for example, memorandum from the Italian Delegation to the EC's CSCE Sub-Committee, "Étude de la tactique au cours des préliminaires d'Helsinki," Oct. 3, 1972, PAAA, B28 109310; Telegram from Peck, UK Mission to NATO, to FCO, "CSCE," Feb. 23, 1973, UKNA, FCO 41/1282; Memorandum to the Secretary of State for External Affairs, "CSCE: Conclusion of Preparatory Talks," June 6, 1973, LAC, RG-25 Vol. 9054 File 20-4-CSCE Vol. 35; and "Steering Brief for the United Kingdom Delegation," Sept. 13, 1973, UKNA, FCO 41/1310.

34. Telegram from André, Helsinki, to Quai d'Orsay, "Préliminaires CSCE: Attitude de l'Union Soviétique et des Autres Pays de l'Est," Dec. 21, 1972, AMAE, Affaires Étrangères - Organismes Internationaux et Grandes Questions Internationales - Sécurité – 1971–1976 – 2925; letter from Tickell, FCO, to Audland, Bonn, "CSCE/MPT," Feb. 6, 1973, UKNA, FCO 28/2176; memorandum by Elliott, "CSCE: Draft Report of the Delegation to the Multilateral Preparatory Talks," June 9, 1973, UKNA, FCO 28/2167; Letter from Hildyard, Geneva, to Callaghan, FCO, "CSCE: The Conclusion of Stage II"; Telegram from Delworth, Geneva, to External Affairs, "CSCE: Briefing for Stage III," July 23, 1975, LAC, RG-25 Vol. 9054 File 20-4-CSCE Vol. 58; John J. Maresca, "The CSCE at Its Inception: 1975 in Myth and Reality," *OSCE Yearbook 2005* (Baden-Baden: Nomos, 2006) 9–10.

35. Interview with Mario Michese Alessi, *CSCE Testimonies* 145; Kovalev, *Iskusstvo vozmozhnogo* 191–192; Memorandum from Fall to Tickell, "CSCE: Second Stage," Oct. 25, 1973, UKNA,

FCO 28/2189; and Interview with Sir Brian Fall, Feb. 13, 2017, British Diplomatic Oral History Programme (BDOHP).

36. Letter from Elliott, Helsinki, to Tickell, FCO, Jan. 25, 1973, UKNA, FCO 41/1287.

37. Letters from Brezhnev to Nixon, Pompidou, and Heath, Jan. 7, 1974, RGANI, f.3 op.72 d.594 ll. 9–18; Letter from Brezhnev to Nixon, Jan. 9, 1974, RMNL, Nixon Files, HAK Office Files, Box 69, Dobrynin-Kissinger Correspondence Vol. 22 (January–April 1974); Letter from Brezhnev to Ford, March 8, 1975, *FRUS 1969–1976*, Vol. 39, doc. 277; and Letter from Brezhnev to Wilson, March 8, 1975, UKNA, FCO 41/1770.

38. See, for example, Nixon-Kissinger-Gromyko Memcon, Feb. 4, 1974, RMNL, Nixon Files, HAK Office Files, Box 71, Gromyko 1974; and Ford-Kissinger-Gromyko Memcon, Sept. 20, 1974, *FRUS 1969–1976*, Vol. 39, doc. 248. Quotation from Kissinger-Brezhnev Memcon, Oct. 24, 1974, NARA, RG 59, Records of the Office of the Counselor, 1955–1977, Box 8, Soviet Union, Oct. 1974.

39. Telegram from Elliott, Geneva, to FCO, "CSCE: General Situation," May 11, 1974, UKNA, FCO 28/2456; and telegram from Hildyard, Geneva, to FCO, "Committee I: Sub-Committee 1 (Principles)," July 10, 1974, UKNA, FCO 41/1565.

40. Telegram from Elliott, Helsinki, to FCO, "CSCE/MPT," May 19, 1973, UKNA, FCO 41/1292; Telegram from Douglas-Home, FCO, to Cromer, Washington, "CSCE/MBFR," June 7, 1973, UKNA, FCO 41/1226; Letter from Bishop, Geneva, to Burns, FCO, "CSCE: Sub-Committee I: Principles," Oct. 12, 1973, UKNA, FCO 41/1306; and Letter from Elliott, Geneva, to Douglas-Home, FCO, "CSCE: The Second Stage So Far," Dec. 15, 1973, UKNA, FCO 41/1324.

41. Telegram from Shenstone, Geneva, to External Affairs, "CSCE: Timing," Feb. 12, 1974, LAC, RG-25 Vol. 9054 File 20-4-CSCE Vol. 43; Telegram from Elliott, Geneva, to FCO, "General Situation," March 20, 1974, UKNA, FCO 28/2456; and telegram from Elliott, Geneva, to FCO, "General Situation," April 6, 1974, ibid.

42. "Minutes of a Senior Review Group Meeting," May 14, 1971, *FRUS 1969–1976*, Vol. 39, doc. 48; "Minutes of a Senior Review Group Meeting," Nov. 23, 1971, ibid., doc. 78; "Editorial Note," ibid., doc. 84; Kissinger-Thorn Memcon, Feb. 21, 1973, ibid., doc. 129; Kissinger-Pungan Memcon, April 21, 1973, ibid., doc. 142; Letter from Graham, Washington, to Bullard, FCO, March 12, 1973, UKNA, FCO 28/2176; Kissinger-Gromyko Memcon, Feb. 4, 1974, RMNL, Nixon Files, HAK Office Files, Box 71, Gromyko 1974; Ford-Kissinger Memcon, Aug. 15, 1974, GRFL, National Security Adviser Memoranda of Conversations, 1973–1977, Box 5, Aug. 15, 1974 - Ford, Kissinger; Ford-Kissinger Memcon, Sept. 20, 1974; Kissinger-Brezhnev Memcon, Oct. 24, 1974, NARA, RG 59, Records of the Office of the Counselor, 1955-1977, Box 8, Soviet Union, Oct. 1974; and Kissinger-Gromyko Memcon, Feb. 16, 1975, NARA, RG 59, Records of the Office of the Counselor, 1955–1977, Box 8, Soviet Union January–March 1975. Helmut Sonnenfeldt likewise dismissed it as a "ghastly affair," "irrational," and a "feckless exercise." Memorandum from Sonnenfeldt to Kissinger, "SRG Meeting on European Security Conference," Nov. 18, 1971, RMNL, Nixon Files, NSC Institutional Files, Box H-187, NSSM 138 (1 of 2); Memorandum from Sonnenfeldt to Kissinger, "(CSCE) Conference on Security and Cooperation in Europe," n.d. [September 1972], *FRUS 1969–1976*, Vol. 39, doc. 110; and Telegram from Cromer, Washington, to FCO, "US Attitude toward CSCE," Nov. 21, 1972, UKNA, FCO 41/1069.

43. Letter from Heath to Trudeau, Feb. 15, 1973, UKNA, PREM 15/2082; Telegram from Annenberg, London, to State Department, "UK Views on MBFR and CSCE," Feb. 22, 1972,

RMNL, Nixon Files, NSC Institutional Files, Box H-187, NSSM 138 (2 of 2); and Beetham and Hibbert 129–130.

44. Letter from Audland, Bonn, to Tickell, FCO, "Herr Bahr's Views on CSCE," Jan. 31, 1973, UKNA, FCO 41/1340; "Aufzeichnung des Botschafters Roth," May 24, 1973, *AAPD 1973*, doc. 158; Memorandum from Roth, "Sitzung des Bundessicherheitsrats," April 3, 1974, PAAA, B150, 302; and Memorandum from Tickell to Wiggin and Killick, "CSCE," Jan. 17, 1974, UKNA, FCO 41/1550.

45. "Aufzeichnung des Vortragenden Legationsrats Dahlhoff," Nov. 8, 1971, *AAPD 1971*, doc. 386; Hakkarainen, *A State of Peace in Europe* 199.

46. Beetham and Hibbert 128–129.

47. Memorandum from Tickell to Wiggin and Killick, "CSCE," Jan. 17, 1974; and Letter from Seydoux, Moscow, to Schumann, Quai d'Orsay, "Réponse à la demande d'avis du Département sur les aspects culturels de la CSCE," Sept. 7, 1972, AMAE, Affaires Étrangères - Organismes Internationaux et Grandes Questions Internationales - Sécurité - 1971–1976 – 2924.

48. Entry for Feb. 8, 1974, Sherer Diary; and interview with George S. Vest, July 6, 1990.

49. FCO Memorandum, "Meeting of the Foreign Ministers of the Nine," Nov. 20, 1972, UKNA, FCO 30/1253; and Telegram from Canadian Mission to NATO to External Affairs, "MPT Consultations," Nov. 14, 1972, LAC, RG-25 Vol. 9054 File 20-4-CSCE Vol. 25.

50. "Report on European Political Unification, the 'Davignon Report,' " Oct. 27, 1970, *The End of the Post-war Era*, doc. 132 ; "Runderlaß des Ministerialdirektors von Staden," Oct. 28, 1970, *AAPD 1970*, doc. 499; "Runderlaß des Ministerialdirektors von Staden," May 15, 1971, *AAPD 1971*, doc. 174; and Simon J. Nuttall, *European Political Co-operation* (Oxford: Oxford UP, 1992) 49. See also the essays in the *Journal of European Integration History* 9:2 (2003).

51. Daniel Möckli, *European Foreign Policy during the Cold War: Heath, Brandt, Pompidou and the Dream of Political Unity* (London: I.B. Tauris, 2009) 18–57; and "Report of the Political Committee on the Preparation of the CSCE (CP[72]27)," July 28, 1972, UKNA, FCO 41/1060.

52. "Gespräch des Staatssekretärs Frank mit dem Sicherheitsberater des amerikanischen Präsidenten, Kissinger, in Washington," Dec. 1, 1971, *AAPD 1971*, doc. 426; Telegram from Watson, Paris, to State Department, "Differences with French on CSCE," Jan. 24, 1972, RMNL, Nixon Files, NSC Institutional Files, Box H-187, NSSM 138 (2 of 2); Memorandum from Fall to Bullard, "EEC Political Consultations: Ad Hoc Group on the CSCE," May 2, 1972, UKNA, FCO 28/1684; Memorandum from Braithwaite to Tickell, "Ad Hoc Committee on the CSCE Meeting in Luxembourg on 8 May," May 5, 1972, UKNA, FCO 41/1053; Letter from Tickell, FCO, to Peck, UK Mission to NATO, "CSCE: Co-ordination of Discussions in NATO and EEC," May 12, 1972, UKNA, FCO 28/1684; Telegram from Canadian Mission to NATO to External Affairs, "MPT Consultations," Nov. 14, 1972, LAC, RG-25 Vol. 9054 File 20-4-CSCE Vol. 25; Telegram from Canadian Mission to NATO to External Affairs, "Consultations among Alliance Countries during MPT," Nov. 16, 1972, LAC, RG-25 Vol. 9054 File 20-4-CSCE Vol. 26; Telegram from French Mission to NATO to Quai d'Orsay, "CSCE: Consultations entre pays alliés au cours des entretiens préparatoires multilateraux," Nov. 16, 1972, AMAE, Affaires Étrangères - Organismes Internationaux et Grandes Questions Internationales - Sécurité – 1971–1976 – 2925; "Botschafter Krapf, Brüssel (NATO), an das Auswärtige Amt," Nov. 17, 1972, *AAPD 1972*, doc. 378; FCO Memorandum, "Meeting of the Foreign Ministers of the Nine," Nov. 20, 1972; Möckli 63–68; and Hakkarainen, *A State of Peace in Europe* 179–198.

53. Report of the North Atlantic Council, "Conference on Security and Co-operation in Europe," May 16, 1972, NATOA, CM(72)24(Rev.); FCO Memorandum, "Conference on Security and Cooperation in Europe (CSCE): The Work of the Sub-Committee and of the North

Atlantic Alliance," Sept. 14, 1972, UKNA, FCO 30/1254; FCO Memorandum, "Anglo/Finnish Talks 9 and 10 November," Nov. 8, 1972, UKNA, FCO 41/1074; Memorandum from Wiggin to Brimelow, "Impressions of "Davignon Committee" Meeting in Brussels on 25 April," April 26, 1973, UKNA, FCO 41/1296; Letter from Walden, FCO, to Fall, Helsinki, "Despatch on the Conclusion of the CSCE," June 5, 1973; Entry for April 2, 1974, Sherer Diary; and Alexander 36.

54. "Protokol zasedaniia Sekretariata TsK KPSS pod predsedatel'stvom L. I. Brezhneva po mezhdunarodnym problemam," Nov. 20, 1972, National Security Archive, READD-RADD Collection, Reel 16.

55. Gromyko speech to Central Committee Plenum, April 16, 1975, RGANI, f.2, op.3, d.356, l.4; and Kashlev 44.

56. Cherniaev, *Sovmestnyĭ iskhod* 36; Kashlev 39; Robert D. English, *Russia and the Idea of the West: Gorbachev, Intellectuals, and the End of the Cold War* (New York: Columbia UP, 2000) 154–155; Svetlana Savranskaya, "Unintended Consequences: Soviet Interests, Expectations and Reactions to the Helsinki Final Act," *Helsinki 1975, 179–181*; Letter from Adams, Helsinki to Burns, FCO, "CSCE/MPT: Eastern Views," May 10, 1973, UKNA, FCO 28/2176; Alexander 75–76; and Brunner 177.

57. "Stenogramm des Freundschaftstreffens führender Vertreter der kommunistischen und Arbeiterparteien der sozialistischen Länder," July 31, 1972; "Szyfrogram wiceministra Bisztygi (z Moskwy): konsultacje w radzieckim MSZ w sprawie EKBiW oraz rokowań rozbrojeniowych," Jan. 9, 1973, *PDD 1973*, doc. 4; GDR Politburo Memorandum, "Konferenz der Minister für Auswärtige Angelegenheiten der Staaten des Warschauer Vertrages am 15. und 16.1.1973 in Moskau," Jan. 23, 1973, SAPMO, DY 30/J IV 2/2/1431; and "Projekt pilnej notatki w sprawie propozycji radzieckich w związku z II fazą EKBiW," June 8, 1973, *PDD 1973*, doc. 103.

58. MfAA Memorandum, "Zu ersten Runde der multilateralen Konsultation in Helsinki," n.d. [Dec. 1972], PAAA, Bestand MfAA, C 374/78; "Notatka wicepremiera Józefa Tejchmy z rozmowy z sekretarzem generalnym KC RPK," Dec. 2, 1972, *PDD 1972*, doc. 225; Memorandum from Gromyko to the Politburo, Dec. 27, 1972; Memorandum from Drozdenko and Kovalev, Soviet Embassy in Bucharest, "Zapis' besedy s ministrom inostrannykh del SRR Dzh. Makovesku," Feb. 17, 1973, RGANI f.5 op.66, d.625 l. 61; James Feron, "Rumania Protests at Helsinki Talks," *NYT*, Nov. 24, 1972, 11; and James Feron, "Rumania Baffles East Bloc Allies," *NYT*, Nov. 29, 1972, 9.

59. Letter from Hildyard, Geneva, to Tickell, FCO, "CSCE," May 28, 1975, UKNA, FCO 41/1769; and testimony of Sir Crispin Tickell at Machiavelli Center oral history conference.

60. Kovalev, *Iskusstvo vozmozhnogo* 184–189 and 197–199; interview with Yuri Dubinin, *CSCE Testimonies* 197; and Telegram from Shenstone, Geneva, to External Affairs, "CSCE: Soviet Intentions," March 11, 1974, LAC, RG-25 Vol. 9054 File 20-4-CSCE Vol. 44. Within the scope of its instructions, the East German delegation also had latitude to act as it saw fit. See interview with Peter Steglich, *CSCE Testimonies* 124.

61. Brunner 55–56; and Alexander 80–81. On debates within the Soviet government on the formulation of foreign policy, see Dubinin, *Diplomaticheskaia byl'*, 165–166.

62. Interviews with Jacques Andréani and Mario Michese Alessi, *CSCE Testimonies* 74 and 148; Badalassi 235; Alexander 6–7; and interview with Sir Brian Fall, BDOHP.

63. Interview with George S. Vest, July 6, 1990; Interview with Guy E. Coriden, Jr., Nov. 18, 1992, Foreign Affairs Oral History Collection, Association for Diplomatic Studies and Training; Entries for Jan. 11 and 12, 1974, Sherer Diary; and letter from Frowick, State Department, to Maresca, Geneva, May 9, 1975, NARA, RG-59, Conference on Security and Cooperation in Europe, Box 1, CSCE: 1973–75: US Policy.

64. Telegram from Killick, Moscow, to FCO, "CSCE and MBFR," Aug. 10, 1972, UKNA, FCO 41/1070; Brimelow-Lunkov Memcon, Sept. 15, 1972, UKNA, FCO 28/1707; telegram from Quai d'Orsay to French Embassy, Moscow, "Démarche de M. Doubinine au sujet de la CSCE," Dec. 2, 1972, AMAE, Affaires Étrangères - Organismes Internationaux et Grandes Questions Internationales - Sécurité - 1971–1976 – 2925; memorandum from Sous-Direction CSCE, "Conférence sur la Sécurité et Coopération en Europe," Dec. 21, 1972, AMAE, CSCE 1969–1975, Box 6; "Notatka Informacyjna obecna rola KBWE w procesie odprężenia," Nov. 13, 1974; and Dubinin, *Diplomaticheskaia byl'* 171.

65. "Extracts from a 'Declaration on Peace, Security and Cooperation in Europe,'" Jan. 26, 1972, *Selected Documents*, doc. 40.

66. Memorandum to the Politburo from Andrei Gromyko, Aug. 27, 1969. See also "Direktivy dlia dvustoronnikh konsul'tatsiï so stranami-uchastnitsami Varshavskogo dogovora i dlia soveshchaniia ministrov inostrannykh del etikh stran po voprosam, sviazannym s sozyvom Obshcheevropeĭskogo soveshchaniia," appendix to Politburo resolution "O meropriiatiiakh po voprosam podgotovki Obshcheevropeĭskogo soveshchaniia," Sept. 8, 1969, RGANI, f. 3, op. 72, d. 287, ll. 9–10 and 25–31.

67. "Stenogramm des Freundschaftstreffens führender Vertreter der kommunistischen und Arbeiterparteien der sozialistischen Länder," July 31, 1972, PHP; and memorandum from Reeve to Walden, "Soviet Attitudes to CSCE," Aug. 17, 1972, UKNA, FCO 28/1692. Soviet deputy foreign minister Nikolai Rodionov emphasized this point to his Eastern European counterparts the following year. See Frigyes Puja, "Report On the 21–22 May 1973 Meeting of the Warsaw Treaty Countries' Deputy Foreign Ministers," May 28, 1973, PHP.

68. Savranskaya, "Unintended Consequences," 177–178.

69. "Speech by the Head of the Soviet Delegation at the Meeting of the Political Consultative Committee," Jan. 25, 1972, PHP; and "Report of Comrade Leonid Ilych Brezhnev at the Meeting of the Leaders of the Socialist Countries' Communist and Working Parties in Crimea," July 30, 1973.

70. "Pilna notatka z konferencji państw socjalistycznych poświęconej WRP w Helsinkach," May 23, 1973, *PDD 1973*, doc. 93. See also FCO Memorandum, "East European Attitudes to the CSCE," Sept. 29, 1972, UKNA, FCO 28/1694; "Instrukcja ministra spraw zagranicznych dla delegacji polskiej na wiosenną sesję WRP w Helsinkach," April 24, 1973, ibid., doc. 75.

71. "Speech by the Head of the Soviet Delegation at the Meeting of the Political Consultative Committee," Jan. 25, 1972; and "Doklad na drugaria Leonid Ilich Brezhnev na sreshtata na rukovoditelite na komunisticheskite i rabotnicheskite partii na sotsialisticheskite strani v Krim," July 30, 1973, PHP.

72. "Notatka z narady ambasadorów PRL," Dec. 14, 1973, *PDD 1973*, doc. 229.

73. GDR Politburo Memorandum, "Stellungnahme des Politbüros des Zentralkomitees der Sozialistische Einheitspartei Deutschlands und des Ministerrate der Deutschen Demokratischen Republik zur Tagung des Politischen Beratenden Ausschusses des Warschauer Vertrages vom 17. bis 18. April 1974 in Warschau," April 23, 1974, SAPMO, DY 30/J IV 2/2/1501.

74. Pompidou-Brezhnev Memcon, Oct. 27, 1971, AMAE, Secrétariat général - Entretiens et Messages - Vol. 50; Nixon-Brezhnev Memcon, May 22, 1972, *FRUS 1969–1976*, Vol. 14, doc. 257; and "Stenogramm des Freundschaftstreffens führender Vertreter der kommunistischen und Arbeiterparteien der sozialistischen Länder," July 31, 1972, and Nina Tumarkin, *The Living and the Dead: The Rise and Fall of the Cult of World War II in Russia* (New York: Basic Books, 1994) 134.

75. Cherniaev, *Sovmestnyĭ iskhod* 92.

76. Brezhnev-Honecker Memcon, June 18, 1974, SAPMO, DY 30/IV 2/2.035/55. A meeting of Central Committee secretaries emphasized the importance of peace for rebuilding the legitimacy of the socialist cause in the Soviet bloc and beyond. See "Bericht über die Beratung von Sekretären der Zentralkomitees kommunistischer und Arbeiterparteien sozialistischer Länder zu aktuellen Problemen der ideologischen Arbeit und der Auslandspropaganda in Moskau am 18. und 19. Dezember 1973," Jan. 8, 1974, SAPMO, DY 30/J IV 2/2/1484.

77. Memorandum from Drozdenko and Kovalev, Soviet Embassy in Bucharest, "Zapis' besedy s ministrom inostrannykh del SRR Dzh. Makovesku," Feb. 17, 1973; letter from French Embassy, Bucharest, to Quai d'Orsay, "La Roumanie et la CSCE," Nov. 21, 1972, AMAE, CSCE 1969–1975, Box 5; and Amery-Ecobescu Memcon, Jan. 9, 1973, UKNA, FCO 28/2178.

78. "Talks between Comrade Todor Zhivkov and Comrade Leonid Brezhnev at Voden Residence," Sept. 20, 1973, CWIHP. See also MfAA Memorandum, "Zu einigen Fragen der Vorbereitung und Durchführung einer europäischen Sicherheitskonferenz im Kampf um die Schaffung eines europäischen Sicherheitssystems," Oct. 20, 1970, PAAA, Bestand MfAA C 366/78.

79. Cherniaev, *Sovmestnyĭ iskhod* 105.

80. On Alexander's irenic mission, see Adam Zamoyski, *Rites of Peace: The Fall of Napoleon and the Congress of Vienna* (New York: HarperCollins, 2007) 15–34.

81. Memorandum from Kissinger to Nixon, "Conversation with Soviet Ambassador Dobrynin," Dec. 22, 1969.

82. Telegram from State Department to US Mission to NATO, "NATO Discussion of East-West Negotiations: Renunciation of Force and Principles which should Govern Relations between States," Oct. 27, 1970, NARA, RG 59, Central Foreign Policy Files, 1970–1973, Box 2263, POL 1 Eur E - Eur W; and State Department Interagency Task Force Report, "Conference on Security and Cooperation in Europe: Interim Report to the Secretary of State," March 3, 1972, NARA, RG 59, Executive Secretariat, Briefing Books 1958–1976, Box 134; and "The Government of the Federal Republic of Germany to the Government of the Soviet Union," Aug. 12, 1970, *The End of the Post-War Era*, doc. 17.

83. Telegram from von Staden, Bonn, to West German Mission to NATO, "Vorbereitung der KSZE," Aug. 18, 1972, PAAA, B28 109306; memorandum from von Groll, "Berücksichtigung der "Unverletzlichkeit der Grenzen" in einer KSZE-Prinzipienerklärung: Erklärungen der sowjetischen und der polnischen MV-Delegation vom 22.1.1973," Jan. 23, 1973, PAAA, B28 111531; "Runderlaß des Ministerialdirektors von Staden," Jan. 29, 1973, *AAPD 1973*, doc. 28; White House memorandum, "Annotated Version of the General Declaration," n.d. [April 1973], UKNA, FCO 41/1308; and letter from Sykes, UK Embassy in Washington, to Brimelow, FCO, May 22, 1973, UKNA, FCO 41/1303. The Irish remained outside NATO, but strongly backed West Germany because they too had pledged themselves to national reunification. See aide-mémoire from the Irish Embassy in Bonn to the Auswärtiges Amt, April 16, 1973, PAAA, B28 111531.

84. Memorandum from the EC's CSCE Sub-Committee, "Documents explicatifs au sujet des principes du non-recours à la menace ou à l'emploi de la force, de l'inviolabilité des frontières et de l'intégrité territoriale des états," Aug. 22, 1973, AMAE, CSCE 1969–1975, Box 25; Telegram from External Affairs, Ottawa, to Helsinki, "CSCE: Recognition of Post-War Frontiers," March 5, 1973, LAC, RG-25 Vol. 9054 File 20-4-CSCE Vol. 31; and Memorandum from McLaren to Burns, "CSCE: Recognition of Post-War Frontiers," March 9, 1973, UKNA, FCO 41/1302. Baltic lobby groups launched a campaign to influence Western policies on the CSCE

as early as 1973. See memorandum from the Assembly of Captive European Nations, "The European Conference on Security and Cooperation and the Captive European Nations," Sept. 7, 1973, B28 111508.

85. Telegram from Vest, US Mission to NATO to State Department, "East-West Negotiations Study: US Proposed Draft Declaration on Principles Governing Relations between States," Sept. 28, 1971, NARA, RG 59, Central Foreign Policy Files, 1970–1973, Box 2264, POL 1 Eur E - Eur W 5/1/71; Report of the North Atlantic Council, "Conference on Security and Co-operation in Europe," May 16, 1972; "Aufzeichnung des Ministerialdirektors van Well," April 9, 1973, *AAPD 1973*, doc. 101; and Memorandum from Livingston to Hyland, "German Position on Inviolability of Frontiers—Non-Use of Force Linkage," May 3, 1973, RMNL, HAK Office Files, Box 77.

86. Circular letter from Sous-Direction d'Europe Orientale, "Conversations avec les Américains sur la Sécurité européenne," April 13, 1970, AMAE, Affaires Étrangères - Fonds EU - Organismes Internationaux et Grandes Questions Internationales - Sécurité - 1966–70 – 2031; memorandum from de Rose, "Principes régissant les relations entres États," Feb. 23, 1972; FCO memorandum, "Draft Position Paper: The Conference on European Security: The Next Phase," n.d. [March 1972], UKNA, FCO 28/1689; and memorandum from UK Mission to NATO, "Draft Declaration on Guiding Principles for Relations between the States Attending the Conference on Security and Co-operation in Europe," Sept. 13, 1972, UKNA, FCO 41/1065.

87. Telegram from State Department to US Mission to NATO, "East-West Negotiations Study—Principles Governing Relations between States," March 27, 1971, NARA, RG 59, Central Foreign Policy Files, 1970–1973, Box 2264, POL 1 Eur E - Eur W 1/1/71; telegram from US Mission to NATO to State Department, "East-West Negotiations Study: US Proposed Draft Declaration on Principles Governing Relations between States," Sept. 28, 1971; and Memorandum from Braithwaite and Fall, FCO, "The Conference on European Security: The Next Phase: Appendix A," Jan. 20, 1972, UKNA, FCO 28/1688. For the two UN Declarations, see General Assembly Resolution 2625 (XXV), "Declaration on Principles of International Law Concerning Friendly Relations and Co-operation Among States in Accordance with the Charter of the United Nations," Oct. 24, 1970; and General Assembly Resolution 2734 (XXV), "Declaration on the Strengthening of International Security," Dec. 16, 1970. Available at: http://www.un.org/documents/ga/res/25/ares25.htm.

88. Telegram from Seydoux, Moscow, to Quai d'Orsay, "Le projet de conférence européenne et le principe de non ingérence," Feb. 16, 1970, AMAE, CSCE 1969–1975, Box 25; briefing note from the Canadian Mission to NATO, "The Agenda for a Conference on European Security," May 29, 1971, LAC, RG-25 Vol. 9054 File 20-4-CSCE Vol. 14; letter from de Rose, French Mission to NATO, to Quai d'Orsay, "Principes régissant les relations entre États," Feb. 23, 1972, AMAE, CSCE 1969–1975, Box 25.

89. "Speech by Mr. Brezhnev at the Fifth Congress of the Polish United Workers' Party," Nov. 12, 1968, *End of the Post-War Era*, doc. 150; "Soviet-Czechoslovak Treaty," *Survival* 12:7 (1970) 241–243; FCO memorandum, "Draft Position Paper: The Conference on European Security: The Next Phase," n.d. [March 1972]; and telegram from External Affairs to Canadian Mission to NATO, "CES: Principles Governing Relations Between States," April 22, 1971, LAC, RG-25 Vol. 9054 File 20-4-CSCE Vol. 14; and Ouimet 66–69.

90. Quai d'Orsay Memorandum, "Note sur la doctrine Brejnev et la Conférence sur la sécurité européenne," n.d. [December 1969], AMAE, Affaires Étrangères - Fonds EU - Organismes Internationaux et Grandes Questions Internationales – Sécurité - 1966–70 – 2034.

91. Memorandum from von Groll, "Konferenz über die Sicherheit und Zusammenarbeit

in Europa: Politische Aspekte der Sicherheit," Jan. 7, 1971, PAAA, B28 109306; Telegram from State Department to US Mission to NATO, "East-West Negotiations—Principles Governing Relations between States," April 16, 1971, NARA, RG 59, Central Foreign Policy Files, 1970–1973, Box 2264, POL 1 Eur E - Eur W 4/1/71; report of the North Atlantic Council, "Conference on Security and Co-operation in Europe," May 16, 1972; memorandum from the West German Mission to NATO, "Eventual CSCE agenda item on the improvement of interstate relations by adopting a conference document on principles governing relations between states," Aug. 10, 1972, PAAA, B28 109306; and draft memorandum from Sous-direction CSCE, "CSCE Document sur les principes devant régir les relations entre États," n.d. [September 1972], AMAE, CSCE 1969–1975, Box 25.

92. UK Mission to NATO Speaking Note, "Draft Declaration on Guiding Principles for Relations between the States Attending the CSCE," Sept. 22, 1972, UKNA, FCO 41/1065; see also letter from Lever, UK Mission to NATO to Ramsay, FCO, "CSCE: Principles Governing Relations between States," Aug. 22, 1972, UKNA, FCO 41/1065; telegram from Moscow to External Affairs, May 9, 1969, LAC, RG-25 Vol. 9054 File 20-4-CSCE Vol. 1.

93. "Opening Remarks by the Under-Secretary: Statement on East-West Issues," Nov. 4, 1969, NARA, RG 59, Executive Secretariat, Briefing Books 1958-1976, Box 65, Special Session of the North Atlantic Council, Brussels, Nov. 5–6, 1969; and Memorandum from de Rose, "Principes régissant les relations entres États," Feb. 23, 1972, AMAE, CSCE 1969–1975, Box 25.

94. Telegram from Quai d'Orsay to Moscow, "Communication au gouvernement soviétique," July 4, 1969, AMAE, Affaires Étrangères - Fonds EU - Organismes Internationaux et Grandes Questions Internationales – Sécurité - 1966–70 – 2036; Telegram from US Mission to NATO to the State Department, "East-Est [sic] Negotiations Study: Principles Governing Relations between States," Nov. 4, 1971; and Telegram from Boss, FRG Mission to NATO, to Bonn, "Substanz und Verfahren möglicher Ost-West-Verhandlungen: Grundsätze zwischenstaatlicher Beziehungen," Nov. 5, 1971, PAAA, B150, 241. See also Memorandum from the West German Mission to NATO, "Eventual CSCE Agenda Item on the Improvement of Interstate Relations by Adopting a Conference Document on Principles Governing Relations between States," Aug. 10, 1972.

95. "Summary Record of a Meeting of the Council," Nov. 25, 1971, NATOA, CR(71)67.

96. Telegram from US Mission to NATO to State Department, "CSCE: Principles Governing Relations between States"; "Treaty of Economic, Social and Cultural Collaboration and Collective Self-Defense," March 17, 1948, European Foreign Policy: Key Documents, eds. Christopher Hill and Karen E. Smith (New York: Routledge, 2000) doc. 1/1; "Declaration on European Identity," Dec. 14, 1973, ibid., doc. 2/5; "Declaration on Atlantic Relations," June 19, 1974, End of the Post-War Era, doc. 118; and "Report on European Political Unification, the 'Davignon Report,'" Oct. 27, 1970.

97. Michael Cotey Morgan, "The Seventies and the Rebirth of Human Rights," The Shock of the Global: The 1970s in Perspective, eds. Niall Ferguson, Charles S. Maier, Erez Manela, and Daniel J. Sargent (Cambridge, MA: Harvard UP, 2010) 237–250; Sargent chapter 3; and Mark Philip Bradley, The World Reimagined: Americans and Human Rights in the Twentieth Century (New York: Cambridge UP, 2016) chapter 5. Quotation from Brzezinski, Between Two Ages 58.

98. Telegram from US Mission to NATO to State Department, "CSCE: Principles Governing Relations between States," Aug. 24, 1972, RMNL, Nixon Files, NSC Institutional Files, Box H-065, SRG Meeting - CSCE 9/2/72; letter from the Archbishop of Canterbury to Douglas-Home, June 20, 1973, UKNA, FCO 41/1303; and letter from Cassin to Sharp, Oct. 10, 1972,

LAC, RG 25, Vol. 9054, File 20-4-CSCE, Vol. 24. Identical copies are also available in the German and French archives. See PAAA, B28 109298; and AMAE, CSCE 1969–1975, Box 19.

99. Isaiah Berlin, "The Bent Twig: A Note on Nationalism," *Foreign Affairs* 51:1 (October 1972) 26; and Cedric Thornberry, "Worldwide Perspective Unites Teachers of the New Discipline Despite Their Discord," *The Times*, May 21, 1974, XI.

100. See, for example, memorandum to Sharp, "Greece," June 26, 1973, LAC, RG-25 Vol. 9054 File 20-4-CSCE Vol. 36; and telegram from US Mission to UN, Geneva, to State Department, "Human Rights Commission—Alleged Human Rights Violations in Greece," March 30, 1973, AAD.

101. "Proekty zadaniĭ dlia komissiĭ obshcheevropeĭskogo soveshchaniia," Dec. 27, 1972, RGANI, f.3 op.72 d.538 l.188; "General Declaration on Foundations of European Security and Principles of Relations between States in Europe," n.d. [February 1973], UKNA, FCO 41/1302; and FCO Briefing Paper, "European Political Cooperation: Ministerial Meeting," March 16, 1973, UKNA, FCO 41/1295.

102. Telegram from External Affairs to Canadian Delegation to NATO, "CSCE: Principles Guiding Relations between States," March 8, 1973, LAC, RG-25 Vol. 9054 File 20-4-CSCE Vol. 31; memorandum from Walden to Fall, "CSCE: Soviet Draft Declaration," Feb. 13, 1973, UKNA, FCO 28/2168; State Department briefing paper, "Basket I – Security," n.d. [April 1973], RMNL, Nixon Files, HAK Office Files, Box 77, Moscow Trip – CSCE; and "Annotated Version of the General Declaration," n.d. [April 1973], UKNA, FCO 41/1308.

103. "Bundesminister Scheel an Bundeskanzler Brandt," Jan. 31, 1973, *AAPD 1973*, doc. 31; telegram from Elliott, UK Embassy in Helsinki, to Douglas-Home, FCO, "CSCE/MPT," Feb. 10, 1973, UKNA, FCO 41/1288; "Minute from Mr. Brown on CSCE: Principles," March 20, 1973, *DBPO* III:II, doc. 27; and Telegram from the State Department to Moscow, "Inviolability of Borders in Connection with CSCE," May 4, 1973, RMNL, Nixon Papers, NSC Files, Box 722, USSR Vol. 29 May–October 73.

104. "Ministerialdirigent Brunner, z.Z. Helsinki, an das Auswärtige Amt," Jan. 31, 1973, *AAPD 1973*, doc. 32; Memorandum for the Record by Stoessel, "US-Soviet Views on CSCE Preparatory Negotiations," April 19, 1973, RMNL, HAK Office Files, Box 77; Memorandum from Livingston to Hyland, "German Position on Inviolability of Frontiers-Non-Use of Force Linkage," May 3, 1973, RMNL, HAK Office Files, Box 77; and "Pilna notatka z konferencji państw socjalistycznych poświęconej WRP w Helsinkach," May 23, 1973.

105. Telegram from Elliott, Helsinki, to FCO, "CSCE/MPT: Principles," March 30, 1973, UKNA, FCO 41/1303; draft UK Briefing Paper, "CSCE: Tactics for the Fourth Session of Preparatory Talks," April 11, 1973, UKNA, FCO 28/2166; letter from Dain, Bonn, to Adams, FCO, "CSCE: FRG Views," April 11, 1973, UKNA, FCO 41/1340; "CSCE: Draft Report of the Delegation to the Multilateral Preparatory Talks," June 9, 1973; and Fischer, *Neutral Power in the CSCE* 188.

106. "Speech by Edward Gierek at the Prague Meeting of the Warsaw Treaty's Political Consultative Committee," Jan. 25, 1972, PHP; "Aufzeichnung des Ministerialdirektors van Well," April 9, 1973; letter from Dain, Bonn, to Adams, FCO, "CSCE: FRG Views," April 11, 1973, UKNA, FCO 41/3140; Telegram from Elliott, UK Embassy in Helsinki, to Douglas-Home, FCO, "CSCE/MPT: Meeting of Political Directors on 24 and 25 May: Principles," May 23, 1973, UKNA, FCO 41/1303; "CSCE: Draft Report of the Delegation to the Multilateral Preparatory Talks," June 9, 1973; "Pilna Notatka dot. stanu przygotowań i udziału PRL w I fazie Europejskiej Konferencji Bezpieczeństwa i Współpracy," June 25, 1973, Jarząbek, *Polska wobec Konferencji Bezpieczeństwa i Współpracy w Europie*, doc. 10; and MfAA Memorandum, "Argu-

mentationshinweise zu den beiliegenden Schlussempfehlungen der Konsultation über die Vorbereitung der Sicherheitskonferenz in Helsinki," n.d. [June 1973], PAAA, Bestand MfAA, C 374/78. See the Russian and German versions of the MPT's final recommendations: "Zaklyuchitel'nye Rekomendatsii Konsul'tatsii v Khel'sinki" and "Schlussempfehlungen der Helsinki-Konsultationen." Available at http://www.osce.org/item/15723.html.

107. "Generaldeklaration über die Grundlagen der europäischen Sicherheit und die Prinzipien der Beziehungen zwischen den Staaten in Europa," June 25, 1973, SAPMO, DY 30/J IV 2/2J/4754; "Project de Déclaration sur les Principes Gouvernant les Relations entre les États participants à la CSCE," June 28, 1973, PAAA, B28 111509; Auswärtiges Amt Memorandum, "Sprechzettel für die Sitzung des KSZE-Unterausschusses am 17./18.7.73 in Kopenhagen," July 10, 1973, PAAA, B28 111547; Memorandum from Burns, WOD, to Gordon, TRD, "CSCE Principles," Aug. 20, 1973, UKNA, FCO 41/1304; Quai d'Orsay Memorandum, "Documents explicatifs au sujet des principes du non-recours à la menace ou à l'emploi de la force, de l'inviolabilité des frontières et de l'intégrité territoriale des états," Aug. 22, 1973, AMAE, CSCE 1969–1975, Box 25; Memorandum from Fall to Tickell "CSCE: Inviolability of Frontiers," Nov. 16, 1973, UKNA, FCO 41/1306; and "Steering Brief for the Meeting of the CSCE Sub-Committee and Ad Hoc Group of the Nine in Bonn, 7–9 January," Jan. 4, 1974, UKNA, FCO 30/2482.

108. GDR Politburo memorandum, "Schlußfolgerungen für das weitere Auftreten der Delegation der DDR," Jan. 15, 1974, SAPMO, DY 30/J IV 2/2/1486; Kissinger-Gromyko Memcon, Feb. 4, 1974; Telegram from Hildyard, UK Mission in Geneva, to Callaghan, FCO, "MIPT," March 25, 1974, UKNA, FCO 41/1563; letter from Brezhnev to Nixon, Jan. 9, 1974, RMNL, HAK Office Files, Box 69; and Anatoliĭ Kovalev, *Azbuka diplomatii* (Moscow: Interpraks, 1993) 182. The Soviet copies of the Politburo resolution and letters are in RGANI f.3 op.72 d.594 l.4 and ll.9–18.

109. Kissinger-Brezhnev Memcon, March 25, 1974, RMNL, HAK Office Files, Box 76; and Nixon-Genscher Memcon, July 26, 1974, *FRUS 1969–1976*, Vol. 39, doc. 240; Telegram from Casey, State Department, to US Mission in Geneva, "CSCE: Declaration of Principles: Inviolability of Frontiers," March 1, 1974, AAD; and Telegram from Rush, State Department, to US Embassy Moscow, "CSCE: Talks at Geneva—March 18–22," March 26, 1974, ibid. On the Year of Europe, see Jussi Hanhimäki, *The Flawed Architect: Henry Kissinger and American Foreign Policy* (New York: Oxford UP, 2004) 275–277.

110. See Telegram from FRG Mission in Geneva to AA, "Unverletzlichkeit der Grenzen," March 14, 1974, PAAA, B28 100006; memorandum from Tickell to Wiggin and Killick, "CSCE: Inviolability of Frontiers," April 4, 1974, UKNA, FCO 33/2365; and "Gesandter Boss, Brüssel (NATO), an das Auswärtige Amt," Dec. 3, 1974, *AAPD 1974*, doc. 351.

111. Telegram from Miller, Geneva, to State Department, "CSCE: State [*sic*] II Highlights—April 1–5," April 6, 1974, AAD; and Telegram from the French Embassy in Moscow to Paris, "Propos officiels soviétiques sur la CSCE," April 23, 1974, AMAE, CSCE 1969–1975, Box 22.

112. Letter from Brezhnev to Heath, Jan. 7, 1974, RGANI f.3 op.72 d.594 ll.16–18; Kissinger-Brezhnev Memcon, March 25, 1974; letter from Spreckley, Paris, to Bullard, FCO, "Franco/Soviet Relations," Jan. 21, 1974, UKNA, FCO 28/2455; and "Ministerialdirigent Brunner, z.Z. Genf, an das Auswärtige Amt," March 22, 1974, *AAPD 1974*, doc. 102; and Kovalev, *Iskusstvo vozmozhnogo* 193–194.

113. Telegram from Hildyard, UK Mission in Geneva, to Callaghan, FCO, "MIPT," March 25, 1974, UKNA, FCO 41/1563; and Telegram from Hildyard, UK Mission in Geneva, to Callaghan, FCO, "CSCE: Committee I: Principles," March 26, 1974, UKNA, FCO 41/1563. The evidence suggests that the Spanish proposal originated with the Soviets. See telegram from

Dale, Geneva, to State Department, "CSCE: Meeting with Soviet Delegation Head," March 21, 1974, AAD; Kissinger-Brezhnev Memcon, March 25, 1974; and interview with Yuri Dubinin, *CSCE Testimonies* 199–200.

114. Bock et al. 110–111.

115. Kovalev, *Iskusstvo vozmozhnogo* 194–196; Telegram from Dale, Geneva, to State Department, "CSCE: Agreement on Principle of Inviolability," April 5, 1974, RMNL, Nixon Papers, NSC Files, Box 404, Briefing Book for Visit of Soviet Foreign Minister Gromyko April 74; Memorandum from McLaren to Wiggin, "CSCE: Inviolability of Frontiers," April 5, 1974, UKNA, FCO 41/1564; Telegram from Shenstone, Geneva, to External Affairs, "CSCE: Guiding Principles: Inviolability," April 7, 1974, LAC, RG-25 Vol. 9054 File 20-4-CSCE Vol. 44; and Telegram from Hildyard, Geneva, to FCO, "Committee I: Sub-Committee I (Principles)," April 8, 1974, UKNA, FCO 33/2365.

116. "Aufzeichnung des Vortragenden Legationsrats I. Klasse Fleischhauer," May 2, 1974, *AAPD 1974*, doc. 140; and Elliott, Geneva, to James, FCO, "CSCE: German and Berlin Problems," July 18, 1974, UKNA, FCO 33/2365.

117. Memorandum from Sous-Direction CSCE, "RFA et CSCE," May 27, 1974, AMAE, Affaires Étrangères - Europe - République Fédérale d'Allemagne - Politique Extérieure – 1971–1976 – 2982; Kissinger-Callaghan-Sauvagnargues-Genscher Memcon, June 18, 1974, *FRUS 1969–1976*, Vol. 39, doc. 214; and memorandum from Fall to Hildyard, "CSCE: Conversation with the East German Ambassador," Nov. 8, 1974, UKNA, FCO 41/1549.

118. Telegram from Hillenbrand, Bonn, to State Department, "CSCE and German Questions: Bonn Group Study," June 14, 1974, AAD; Nixon-Kissinger-Brezhnev-Gromyko Memcon, June 29, 1974, *FRUS 1969–1976*, Vol. 39, doc. 226; Memorandum from Winzer to the Politburo, "Zum gegenwärtigen Stand der Arbeit der Sicherheitskonferenz," July 30, 1974; Telegram from Shenstone, Geneva, to External Affairs, "CSCE: Peaceful Change of Frontiers," Aug. 1, 1974, LAC, RG-25 Vol. 9054 File 20-4-CSCE Vol. 47; GDR Politburo Memorandum, "Direktive für das weitere Auftreten der Delegation der DDR während der 2. Phase der Konferenz über Sicherheit und Zusammenarbeit in Europa ab 2.9.1974," Sept. 10, 1974; Kissinger-Gromyko Memcon, Sept. 20, 1974; and Ford-Kissinger-Brezhnev-Gromyko Memcon, Nov. 24, 1974, ibid., doc. 261.

119. Memorandum from Sonnenfeldt to Kissinger, Sept. 28, 1974, *FRUS 1969–1976*, Vol. 39, doc. 252; Memorandum from Sonnenfeldt to Kissinger, Oct. 4, 1974, ibid., doc. 254; "Minutes of Secretary of State Kissinger's Staff Meeting," Dec. 5, 1974, ibid., doc. 262; Sonnenfeldt-Van Well Memcon, Dec. 5, 1974, ibid., doc. 264; Ford-Kissinger-Giscard Memcon, Dec. 15, 1974, GRFL, National Security Adviser Memoranda of Conversations, 1973-1977, Box 8; and Telegram from Fernand-Laurent, Geneva, to Quai d'Orsay, "CSCE–Entretien avec M Kovalev," Feb. 11, 1975, AMAE, CSCE 1969–1975, Box 23.

120. Letter from Laver, Geneva, to Fall, FCO, "Peaceful Change of Frontiers (PCF)," Dec. 20, 1974, UKNA, FCO 33/2366; Kissinger-Gromyko Memcon, Feb.17, 1975, *FRUS 1969–1976*, Vol. 39, doc. 272; "Editorial Note," ibid., doc. 273; "Editorial Note," ibid., doc. 275; telegram from State Department to US Embassy in Bonn, "CSCE: Peaceful Change," March 1, 1975, GRFL, National Security Adviser - Presidential Country Files for Europe and Canada, Box 6, Germany - State Department Telegrams From SECSTATE - NODIS (2); memorandum from Tickell to Killick, "CSCE: Talk with Mr. Hartman (State Department): 28 February 1975," March 3, 1975, UKNA, FCO 41/1751; Telegram from Dale, Geneva, to the State Department, "CSCE: Peaceful Change," March 4, 1975, GRFL, National Security Adviser - Presidential

Country Files for Europe and Canada, Box 13; and testimony of John Maresca at Machiavelli Center oral history conference.

121. "Editorial Note," *FRUS 1969–1976*, Vol. 39, doc. 176; Telegram from Hildyard, Geneva, to FCO, "CSCE: Meeting of Foreign Ministers of the Nine," June 6, 1974, UKNA, FCO 41/1543; Davignon Committee paper, "The Position of the Nine at the CSCE," June 10, 1974, UKNA, FCO 30/2486; Letter from Laver, Geneva, to Adams, FCO, "State of Play: Sub-Committee I: Principles," July 30, 1974, ibid.; and Memorandum from Fall to Hildyard, "CSCE: Conversation with the East German Ambassador," Nov. 8, 1974.

122. Memorandum from Gromyko to the Politburo, Aug. 14, 1974, RGANI, f.3 op.72 d.627 ll.98–99; Telegram from Ewart Biggs, Paris, to FCO, "European Political Cooperation: Meeting of CSCE Sub-Committee on 3–4 September," Sept. 4, 1974, UKNA, FCO 41/1543; Kissinger-Gromyko Memcon, Sept. 20, 1974; Kissinger-Brezhnev-Gromyko Memcon, Oct. 24, 1974, *FRUS 1969–1976*, Vol. 39, doc. 258; Ford-Kissinger-Brezhnev-Gromyko Memcon, Nov. 24, 1974; "Minutes of Secretary of State Kissinger's Staff Meeting," Dec. 5, 1974; letter from Laver, Geneva, to Burns, FCO, "Declaration of Principles: State of Play," March 21, 1975, UKNA, FCO 41/1751; and Davignon Committee paper, "Project de rapport à la réunion des Ministres," May 15, 1975, PAAA, B28 111525.

123. "Botschafter Blech, Genf (KSZE-Delegation) an das Auswärtige Amt," March 18, 1975, *AAPD 1975*, doc. 53; letter from Petrie, Bonn, to Hunter, FCO, "Federal German Dogma on Peaceful Change of Frontiers," April 3, 1975, UKNA, FCO 41/1751; "Wyciąg korespondencyjny z szyfrogramu szefa delegacji na II fazę KBWE (z Genewy) o radziecko-amerykańskich uzgodnieniach w sprawie nienaruszalności granic w Europie," March 6, 1975, *PDD 1975*, doc. 77; "Pilna Notatka: uzgodnienia w sprawie granic przed KBWE Warszawa," March 17, 1975, ibid., doc. 86; "Notatka Informacyjna o końcowych wynikach II fazy KBWE," July 24, 1974, Jarząbek, *Polska wobec Konferencji Bezpieczeństwa i Współpracy w Europie*, doc. 15; and GDR Politburo memorandum, "Einschätzung der Schlußdokumente der KSZE," July 28, 1975, SAPMO, DY 30/J IV 2/2/1573.

124. Bock et al., eds. 105–106.

125. See, for instance, James T. Patterson, *Restless Giant: The United States from Watergate to Bush v. Gore* (New York: Oxford UP, 2005) 102; and Judt 501–502.

126. F.H. Hinsley, *Sovereignty*, 2nd ed. (Cambridge: Cambridge UP, 1986) 26.

127. Stephen D. Krasner, *Sovereignty: Organized Hypocrisy* (Princeton: Princeton UP, 1999); and Sargent chapter 4. Commentators in the early 1970s began to consider the ways in which globalization constrained sovereignty. See, for example, Raymond Vernon, *Sovereignty at Bay: The Multinational Spread of US Enterprises* (New York: Basic Books, 1971).

128. Letter from Dodson, Budapest, to Bullard, FCO, "Puja's Article on the CSCE," Sept. 15, 1972, UKNA, FCO 28/1693; "Projekt pilnej notatki o spotkaniu spraw zagranicznych państw członkowskich Układu Warszawskiego," Nov. 16, 1972, *PDD 1972*, doc. 212; GDR Politburo Memorandum, "Direktive für das weitere Auftreten der Delegation der DDR in der multilateralen Konsultation zur Vorbereitung der Sicherheitskonferenz in Helsinki," April 17, 1973, SAPMO, DY 30/J IV 2/2/1444; and MfAA memorandum, "Kurze Problemzusammenstellung zu den Schlußempfehlungen der multilateralen Konsultationen," n.d. [June 1973], PAAA, Bestand MfAA C 374/78.

129. "CSCE: Draft Report of the Delegation to the Multilateral Preparatory Talks," June 9, 1973; and "General Declaration on Foundations of European Security and Principles of Relations between States in Europe," n.d. [Feb. 1973].

130. "CSCE: Draft Report of the Delegation to the Multilateral Preparatory Talks," June

9, 1973; State Department Briefing Note, "Conference on Security and Cooperation in Europe (CSCE): Results of the Multilateral Preparatory Talks," n.d. [June 1973], RMNL, NSC Files, Box 940; and Aryo Makko, *Ambassadors of Realpolitik: Sweden, the CSCE, and the Cold War* (New York: Berghahn, 2016) 173. For further evidence of the Western allies' positive evaluation of the MPT's results on this point, see Briefing Note from Fall, "CSCE/MPT: Principles," May 11, 1973, UKNA, FCO 41/1303; and Elliott, UK Embassy in Helsinki, to Douglas-Home, FCO, "CSCE: The First 200 Days," June 13, 1973.

131. Speech by Andrei Gromyko, *Human Rights, European Politics, and the Helsinki Accord: The Documentary Evolution of the Conference on Security and Cooperation in Europe*, Vol. 1, eds. Igor I. Kavass, Jacqueline Paquin Granier, and Mary Frances Dominick (Buffalo, NY: William S. Hein, 1981) 47; "Vermerk über ein Gespräch mit Vertretern des MID am 27. Juni 1973 über Fragen der 1. Phase der Sicherheitskonferenz in Moskau," June 28, 1973, PAAA, Bestand MfAA, C 388/78.

132. Memorandum by UK Mission in Geneva, "Note for the Record: Sub-Committee I (Principles)," Nov. 26, 1973, UKNA, FCO 41/1307; "Generaldeklaration über die Grundlagen der europäischen Sicherheit und die Prinzipien der Beziehungen zwischen den Staaten in Europa," June 25, 1973, SAPMO, DY 30/J IV 2/2J/4754; and "Generaldeklaration über die Grundlagen der Sicherheit in Europa und die für die Beziehungen zwischen den Staaten in Europa geltenden Prinzipien," Aug. 21, 1973, SAPMO, DY 30/J IV 2/2/1464.

133. Kissinger-Scheel Memcon, July 12, 1973, *FRUS 1969–1976*, Vol. 39, doc. 170; "Projet de déclaration sur les principes gouvernant les relations entre les états participant à la CSCE," Aug. 30, 1973, UKNA, FCO 41/1305; Telegram from Douglas-Home, FCO, to Hildyard, Geneva, "CSCE," Oct. 16, 1973, UKNA, FCO 41/1322; Telegram from Hildyard, Geneva, to FCO, "Committee I: Sub-Committee I (Principles)," Dec. 17, 1973, UKNA, FCO 41/1307; and Davignon Committee paper, "The Position of the Nine at the CSCE," June 10, 1974, UKNA, FCO 30/2486.

134. "Proposal by the Delegations of Austria, Cyprus, Finland, Liechtenstein, Malta, Sweden, Switzerland, and Yugoslavia," July 23, 1974, UKNA, FCO 41/1565; Memorandum from Van Well to Genscher, "KSZE-Prinzipienkatalog: Vorschlag der Neutralen zur Überwindung der Stagnation bei den Verhandlungen zu Korb III," July 19, 1974, PAAA, B28 111532; Telegram from Hildyard, UK Mission in Geneva, to FCO, "CSCE: Neutral Package Deal," July 27, 1974, UKNA, FCO 41/1565; Bock et al., 106; and Badalassi 302–304.

135. Telegram from State Department to US Mission to NATO, "European Borders in CES Declaration on Principles," April 11, 1971, NARA, RG 59, Central Foreign Policy Files, 1970–1973, Box 2264, POL 1 Eur E - Eur W 4/1/71; Telegram from de Rose, French Mission to NATO, to Quai d'Orsay, "Conférence européenne: principes devant régir les relations entre États," April 27, 1971, AMAE, Affaires Étrangères - Organismes Internationaux et Grandes Questions Internationales - Sécurité – 1971–1976 – 2921; telegram from Hildyard, Geneva, to FCO, "Berlin and German Problems in CSCE," July 29, 1974, UKNA, FCO 33/2366; and Badalassi 107.

136. Maresca, *To Helsinki* 82–83.

137. Memorandum from Fall to Tickell, "CSCE: Quadripartite Rights: The Brezhnev Doctrine," July 19, 1974, UKNA, FCO 33/2365; Telegram from Callaghan, FCO, to Hildyard, Geneva, "Berlin and German Problems in CSCE," July 24, 1974, UKNA, FCO 33/2366; and letter from Tickell, FCO, to Hibbert, Bonn, "CSCE and the German Question," Aug. 2, 1974, ibid.

138. EC Memorandum, "Report of the CSCE Sub-Committee and of the CSCE Ad Hoc Group to the Political Committee," Jan. 17, 1975, UKNA, FCO 41/1775.

139. Telegram from Callaghan, FCO, to Hildyard, Geneva, "CSCE: Quadripartite Rights

and Responsibilities," Oct. 8, 1974, UKNA, FCO 41/1566; Memorandum from Burns to Hildyard, "CSCE: Romanian Position," Dec. 20, 1974, UKNA, FCO 41/1561; Telegram from Hildyard, Geneva, to FCO, "CSCE: Quadripartite Rights and Responsibilities," Jan. 31, 1975, UKNA, FCO 41/1750; Telegram from Hildyard, UK Mission in Geneva, to FCO, "CSCE: Quadripartite Rights and Responsibilities (QRR)," Feb. 14, 1975, ibid.; Telegram from Hildyard, UK Mission in Geneva, to Callaghan, FCO, "CSCE: General State of Play," Feb. 28, 1975, *DBPO* III:II, doc. 114; and Interview with Jacques Andréani, *CSCE Testimonies* 77.

140. Memorandum from Burns to Tickell, "CSCE: State of Play," April 29, 1975, *DBPO* III:II, doc. 120; telegram from Hildyard, UK Mission in Geneva, to Callaghan, FCO, "CSCE: QRR," May 14, 1975, UKNA, FCO 41/1752; Memorandum from Tickell to Weston, "CSCE: State of Play," July 3, 1975, *DBPO* III:II, doc. 129; Telegram from Hildyard, UK Mission in Geneva, to Callaghan, FCO, "CSCE: State of Play," July 6, 1975, *DBPO* III:II, doc. 130, footnote 3; and Telegram from Hildyard, UK Mission in Geneva, to FCO, "CSCE: Timing of Stage III and Malta," July 14, 1975, UKNA, FCO 41/1761.

141. Mark B. Smith, "Social Rights in the Soviet Dictatorship: The Constitutional Right to Welfare from Stalin to Brezhnev," *Humanity* 3:3 (Winter 2012): 385–406; and E. Kuz'min, "Bourgeois Democracy: The Deepening Crisis," *Translations from Kommunist* (Nov. 26, 1973) 60. East Germany likewise embraced the rhetoric of human rights—specifically, "socialist human rights"—from the moment of its foundation. See Ned Richardson-Little, "Dictatorship and Dissent: Human Rights in East Germany in the 1970s," *The Breakthrough: Human Rights in the 1970s*, eds. Jan Eckel and Samuel Moyn (Philadelphia: University of Pennsylvania Press, 2014) 49–67.

142. Roger Normand and Sarah Zaidi, *Human Rights at the UN: The Political History of Universal Justice* (Bloomington, IN: Indiana UP, 2008) chapter 7; and Kovalev, *Iskusstvo vozmozhnogo* 184; Telegram from Elliott, UK Embassy in Helsinki, to Douglas-Home, FCO, "CSCE/MPT: Principles," March 22, 1973, UKNA, FCO 41/1302; Telegram from Elliott, UK Embassy in Helsinki, to Douglas-Home, FCO, "CSCE Principles," March 24, 1973, UKNA, FCO 41/1302; and Telegram from Elliott, UK Embassy in Helsinki, to Douglas-Home, FCO, "CSCE/MPT: Principles," March 30, 1973, UKNA, FCO 41/1303. The East German Politburo likewise authorized this compromise if its delegation in Helsinki concluded that it would be impossible to keep human rights out of the declaration. See GDR Politburo Memorandum, "Direktive für das weitere Auftreten der Delegation der DDR in der multilateralen Konsultation zur Vorbereitung der Sicherheitskonferenz in Helsinki," April 17, 1973.

143. Hermann Axen, *Ich war ein Diener der Partei. Autobiographische Gespräche mit Harald Neubert* (Berlin: Edition Ost, 1996) 361–363; Memorandum by UK Mission in Geneva, "Note for the Record: Sub-Committee I (Principles)," Nov. 26, 1973; letter from Bishop, UK Mission in Geneva, to Burns, FCO, "CSCE: Sub-Committee I: Principles," Oct. 12, 1973, UKNA, FCO 41/1306; GDR Politburo memorandum, "Direktive für das Auftreten der Delegation der DDR während der zweiten Phase der Konferenz für Sicherheit und Zusammenarbeit in Europa," Aug. 21, 1973; and GDR Politburo memorandum, "Direktive für das weitere Auftreten der Delegation der DDR," April 23, 1974, SAPMO, DY 30/J IV 2/2/1501.

144. "For a Just, Democratic Peace, for the Security of Peoples and International Cooperation—Speech by Comrade LI Brezhnev," *Current Digest of the Soviet Press*, Vol. 25, No. 43 (Nov. 21, 1973) 6; "In the Interests of Developing Socialism and Strengthening Peace," *Translations from Kommunist* (Sept. 28, 1973) 1–11; O. Khlestov and Y. Reshetov, "The USSR's Vanguard Role in the Struggle for Human Rights," *International Affairs* (December 1973) 58–64; Interview with Peter Steglich, *CSCE Testimonies* 127; Axen 364; and Letter from Vimont,

Moscow, to Quai d'Orsay, "Interprétation soviétique des principes de la coexistence pacifique dans la perspective de la CSCE," Sept. 11, 1973, AMAE, CSCE 1969–1975, Box 29.

145. Memorandum by UK Mission in Geneva, "Note for the Record: Sub-Committee I (Principles)," Dec. 3, 1973, UKNA, FCO 41/1307; and Memorandum by UK Mission in Geneva, "Note for the Record: Sub-Committee I (Principles)," Dec. 4, 1973, ibid.

146. Memorandum from Fall to Adams, "CSCE: Principles: Human Rights," June 19, 1973, UKNA, FCO 28/2173; Letter from Tickell, FCO, to Elliott, Geneva, "CSCE: Committee III," Oct. 14, 1973, UKNA, FCO 41/1328; and Memorandum from Fall to Solesby, "CSCE: Human Rights," Oct. 19, 1973, UKNA, FCO 28/2168. A working group that the British government convened to examine the wisdom of ratifying the UN Covenants worried that doing so would conflict with Britain's immigration policy and handling of the Troubles in Northern Ireland. See the records of the Whitehall Working Group on International Covenants of Human Rights, February–June 1974, UKNA, FCO 41/1570 and FCO 41/1571.

147. GDR Politburo memorandum, "Direktive für das weitere Auftreten der Delegation der DDR," April 23, 1974; Telegram from Hildyard, Geneva, to FCO, "Committee I: Sub-Committee 1 (Principles)," July 10, 1974 ; "Direktive für das weitere Auftreten der Delegation der DDR während der 2. Phase der Konferenz über Sicherheit und Zusammenarbeit in Europa ab 2.9.1974," Sept. 10, 1974; telegram from Dale, Geneva, to State Department, "CSCE Principles: Soviet Approach on Human Rights and Fundamental Freedoms," Sept. 20, 1974, AAD; telegram from Dale, Geneva, to State Department, "CSCE: State [sic] II Highlights - November 11–15," Nov. 16, 1974, AAD; telegram from Kissinger, State Department, to US Mission in Geneva, "Human Rights Commission: Possible Soviet Resolution on Détente and Human Rights," Feb. 20, 1975, NARA, RG-59, Conference on Security and Cooperation in Europe, Box 1, CSCE 1973–75: Human Contacts; and "Final Act of the Conference on Security and Cooperation in Europe," *The End of the Post-War Era* 295–297.

148. Davignon Committee Report, "Rapport oral de la Présidence au Comité politique du 7 novembre," Nov. 6, 1974, PAAA, B28 111524; telegram from Hildyard, Geneva, to FCO, "CSCE: Stage II: September to December Session 1974," Dec. 21, 1974, UKNA, FCO 41/1549; European Commission report, "CSCE 2ème phase: Session de septembre à décembre 1974," n.d. [December 1974], AEU, FD 136; Axen 363–364; and "Notatka informacyjna o końcowych wynikach II fazy KBWE," July 24, 1975, *PDD 1975*, doc. 200.

149. Henry Kissinger, "Moral Purposes and Policy Choices," *Department of State Bulletin* Vol. 69, No. 1792 (Oct. 29, 1973) 529.

150. On the importance of the neutrals, see Maresca, *To Helsinki* 127. Although the Eastern and Western delegations needed the neutrals, each side occasionally doubted their motives. See, for example, Memorandum from Fall to Tickell, "CSCE," June 17, 1974, *DBPO* III:II, doc. 86.

151. Letter from Elliott, Geneva, to James, FCO, "CSCE: German and Berlin Problems," July 18, 1974.

152. Bock et al., eds. 107.

CHAPTER 5: A DECLARATION OF INTERDEPENDENCE?

1. Charles S. Maier, "'Malaise': The Crisis of Capitalism in the 1970s," *The Shock of the Global*, 25–48.

2. Richard Davy, "What Détente Does for the Quality of Life in the Soviet Union," *The

Times, Nov. 22, 1974, 16; Natalya Chernyshova, "Consumers as Citizens: Revisiting the Question of Public Disengagement in the Brezhnev Era," *Reconsidering Stagnation in the Brezhnev Era: Ideology and Exchange*, eds. Dina Fainberg and Artemy M. Kalinovsky (Lanham, MD: Lexington, 2016) 5; William Tompson, *The Soviet Union under Brezhnev* (London: Pearson, 2003) 83–84; Albrecht O. Ritschl, "An Exercise in Futility: East German Economic Growth and Decline, 1945–89," *Economic Growth in Europe since 1945*, eds. Nicholas Crafts and Gianni Toniolo (Cambridge: Cambridge UP, 1996) 520; and Ivan T. Berend, *The Hungarian Economic Reforms, 1953–1988* (Cambridge: Cambridge UP, 1990) 189–193.

3. Stephen Kotkin, *Armageddon Averted: The Soviet Collapse 1970–2000* (New York: Oxford UP, 2001) 15–16.

4. John Van Oudenaren, *Détente in Europe: The Soviet Union and the West since 1953* (Durham: Duke UP, 1991) 261.

5. Angela Stent, *From Embargo to Ostpolitik: The Political Economy of West German-Soviet Relations, 1955–1980* (Cambridge: Cambridge UP, 1981) 165–168.

6. "Zapis' besedy s pervym zamestitelem ministra inostrannykh del SRR Dzhordzhe Makovesku," Jan. 13, 1970, RGANI, f.5 op.62, d.406, ll.6–8; Memorandum from Fielder, Department of Trade and Industry, to Palmer, FCO, "CSCE Applied Science and Technology," Jan. 5, 1973, UKNA, FCO 55/1029; Note from NATO's Economic Directorate, "Industrial Cooperation: List of East-West Agreements," Nov. 19, 1973, PAAA, B28 111537; "East-West Trade: A Special Report," *The Times*, Dec. 17, 1973, I–VIII; Rey, *La tentation du rapprochement* 109–135; and Van Oudenaren 264–265.

7. Georges-Henri Soutou, "Convergence Theories in France during the 1960s and 1970s," *The Making of Détente* 25–48; Zbigniew Brzezinski and Samuel P. Huntington, *Political Power: USA/USSR* (New York: Viking, 1964) 9–14; and Samuel Pisar, *Coexistence and Commerce: Guidelines for Transactions between East and West* (New York: McGraw-Hill 1970) 8.

8. P. Fedoseyev, "The Contemporary Revolutionary Process and Problems of Theory," *Current Digest of the Soviet Press*, Vol. 21, No. 30 (Aug. 20, 1969) 21; and Brzezinski, *Between Two Ages* 144–145.

9. "Prognoza Departamentu Studiów i Programowania: rozwój sytuacji międzynarodowej w latach siedemdziesiątych," April 12, 1972, *PDD 1972*, doc. 71.

10. Chernyshova 5.

11. Garthoff, *Détente and Confrontation*, 343–344; and Memorandum from Marshall to Kissinger, "Exploiting the Soviet Grain Situation," July 13, 1973, RMNL, NSC Files, Box 722, USSR Vol. 29 May–October 73.

12. Report by NATO's Economic Committee, "Recent Economic Trends in the USSR and Eastern Europe," May 19, 1972, PAAA, B28 109290; and Hanson 242–243.

13. Kotkin, *Uncivil Society* 26 and 49.

14. Anthony Kemp-Welch, *Poland under Communism: A Cold War History* (New York: Cambridge UP, 2008) 180–187; Roman Laba, *The Roots of Solidarity: A Political Sociology of Poland's Working-Class Democratization* (Princeton: Princeton UP, 1991) 19–21; and RJ Crampton, *Eastern Europe in the Twentieth Century—and After* (New York: Routledge, 1997) 360.

15. "Stichwortprotokoll der Ausführungen des Kandidaten des Politbüros und Sekretärs des ZK der KPdSU, Genossen Demitschew, am 6.7.1970 mit der Delegation des ZK der SED," July 6, 1970, SAPMO, DY 30/3530; Erik P. Hoffmann and Robbin F. Laird, *"The Scientific-Technological Revolution" and Soviet Foreign Policy* (New York: Pergamon, 1982) chapter 2.

16. Hoffmann and Laird 88–93; and Van Oudenaren 269–270.

17. "Stichwortprotokoll der Ausführungen des Kandidaten des Politbüros und Sekretärs

des ZK der KPdSU, Genossen Demitschew"; and "Prognoza Departamentu Studiów i Programowania."

18. Frank Cain, *Economic Statecraft during the Cold War: European Responses to the US Trade Embargo* (New York: Routledge, 2007) chapters 11 and 12; and Werner D. Lippert, "European Long-Term Investments in Détente: The Implications of East-West Economic Cooperation," *The Long Détente: Changing Concepts of Security and Cooperation in Europe, 1950s–1980s*, eds. Oliver Bange and Poul Villaume (Budapest: Central European University Press, 2017) 82.

19. Fallenbuchl 240–242.

20. Note from NATO's Economic Directorate, "East/West Trade—Situation, Policies, Prospects," Jan. 15, 1973, PAAA, B28 111538.

21. "Projekt pilnej notatki z wizyty ministra spraw zagranicznych w CSRS i NRD," March 27, 1972, *PDD 1972*, doc. 65; Richard Davy, "Pursuing Happiness across Political Boundaries," *The Times*, Jan. 28, 1974, 12; and Kotkin, *Uncivil Society* 45.

22. English 133–145; and Fallenbuchl 237–238. Quotations from English 145.

23. Kotkin, *Uncivil Society* 48–50 and 112–113; and Ritschl 521–522.

24. "For Strengthening the Solidarity of Communists, for a New Upswing in the Anti-Imperialist Struggle—Speech by Comrade L. I. Brezhnev," *Current Digest of the Soviet Press*, Vol. 21, No. 23 (July 2, 1969) 5 and 8.

25. Leonid Brezhnev, "Speech on West German Television," May 21, 1973, *Selected Speeches and Writings on Foreign Affairs* (New York: Pergamon, 1979) 182; and Fallenbuchl 239–241.

26. Cherniaev, *Sovmestnyĭ iskhod* 63.

27. Bucharest Declaration, July 5, 1966, *Selected Documents* 40.

28. Budapest Appeal, March 17, 1969, *The End of the Post-War Era* 257.

29. Victor-Yves Ghébali, *La Diplomatie de la détente: La CSCE, 1973–1989* (Brussels: Bruylant, 1989) 226–227. For contrasting opinions of the ECE's accomplishments, see David Wightman, "East-West Cooperation and the Economic Commission for Europe," *International Organization* 11:1 (Winter 1957): 1–12; Jean Siotis, "The Secretariat of the United Nations Economic Commission for Europe and European Integration: The First Ten Years," *International Organization* 19:2 (Spring 1965): 177–202; and Krishna Ahooja, "Twenty Years of ECE," *Economic and Political Weekly* 2:16 (April 22, 1967) 752–753.

30. Kissinger-Brezhnev Memcon, September 11, 1972, *FRUS 1969–1976*, Vol. 15, doc. 38; Brezhnev speech to Central Committee Plenum, May 19, 1972, RGANI, f.2 op.3 d.272 l.27; "Agreement regarding Trade," Oct. 18, 1972, and "Agreement regarding Settlement of Lend Lease, Reciprocal Aid and Claims," Oct. 18, 1972, *End of the Post-War Era*, docs. 60 and 61.

31. M. A. Lipkin, "Evropeĭskaia integratsiia i sovetskie ekonomicheskie initsiativy (1950-e – pervaia polovina 1970-kh godov)," *Novaia i noveĭshaia istoriia* 3 (2009) 62.

32. "Rede des Leiters der sowjetischen Delegation auf der Tagung des Politischen Beratenden Ausschusses, Genossen L. I. Breshnew, in Prag," Jan. 25, 1972.

33. Edouard Sauvignon, *La Clause de la nation la plus favorisée* (Grenoble: Presses Universitaires de Grenoble, 1972).

34. "Stenogramm des Freundschaftstreffens führender Vertreter der kommunistischen und Arbeiterparteien der sozialistischen Länder," July 31, 1972, PHP.

35. N. Patolichev, "Ekonomicheskim Sviaziam Krepnut,'" *Izvestiia*, Dec. 11, 1969, 2.

36. Frigyes Puja, "Report on the 21–22 May 1973 Meeting of the Warsaw Treaty Countries' Deputy Foreign Ministers," May 28, 1973, PHP.

37. "Sprawozdanie ze spotkania ekspertów KS na temat ekonomicznej problematyki Konferencji Europejskiej (Budapeszt 8–11.IV.70 r.)," April 29, 1970, Jarząbek, *Polska wobec Konfer-*

encji Bezpieczeństwa i Współpracy w Europie, doc. 7; "Zadania i wnioski wynikające z narady ambasadorów PRL przeprowadzonej w dniach 24 i 25 października 1973 r." Dec. 14, 1973, *PDD 1973*, doc. 229; Jarząbek, "Hope and Reality" 31–34; and Csaba Békés, "Hungary, the Soviet Bloc, the German Question, and the CSCE Process, 1965–1975," *Journal of Cold War Studies* 18:3 (Summer 2016) 129–132.

38. Jarząbek, "Hope and Reality" 9–11.

39. "Wytyczne Kolegium Ministerstwa Spraw Zagranicznych do działalności resortu w roku 1973 (fragmenty)," Feb. 21, 1973, *PDD 1973*, doc. 25; "Projekt pilnej notatki w sprawie propozycji radzieckich w związku z II fazą EKBiW," June 8, 1973, ibid., doc. 103; and Note from NATO's Economic Directorate, "Industrial Co-operation: List of East-West Agreements." See also Békés, "Hungary, the Soviet Bloc, the German Question, and the CSCE Process" 97.

40. "Zu einigen Fragen der Vorbereitung und Durchführung einer europäischen Sicherheitskonferenz im Kampf um die Schaffung eines europäischen Sicherheitssystems," Oct. 20, 1970, PAAA, Bestand MfAA, C 366/78.

41. MfAA Memorandum, "Faktorenanalyse zum Stand der Vorbereitung einer gesamteuropäischen Sicherheitskonferenz," Sept. 25, 1971, PAAA, Bestand MfAA, C 368/78.

42. "Sprawozdanie ze spotkania ekspertów KS na temat ekonomicznej problematyki Konferencji Europejskiej (Budapeszt 8-11.IV.70 r.)," April 29, 1970.

43. "Stellungnahme zum Arbeitsmaterial der VR Polen, Abschnitt II: Wissenschaftlich-technische Zusammenarbeit," n.d. [June 1972], PAAA, Bestand MfAA, C 562/76; and Jarząbek, "Hope and Reality" 33.

44. "Proekty zadaniĭ dlia komissiĭ obshcheevropeĭskogo soveshchaniia," n.d. [Dec. 1972], RGANI, f.3 op.72 d.539 ll.188–190; and "Pilna notatka z konferencji państw socjalistycznych poświęconej WRP w Helsinkach," May 23, 1973, *PDD 1973*, doc. 93.

45. Jarząbek, "Hope and Reality" 33–34.

46. "Projekt pilnej notatki o spotkaniu spraw zagranicznych państw członkowskich Układu Warszawskiego," Nov. 16, 1972, *PDD 1972*, doc. 212.

47. "Stenogramm des Freundschaftstreffens führender Vertreter der kommunistischen und Arbeitsparteien der sozialistischen Länder," July 31, 1972, PHP; "Pilna notatka w sprawie radzieckiego projektu deklaracji programowej w związku z II-gim punktem porządku dziennego EKBiW," Nov. 17, 1972, Jarząbek, *Polska wobec Konferencji Bezpieczeństwa i Współpracy w Europie* doc. 9; and Tomas Kolesnichenko, "Mezhdunarodnaia Nedelia," *Pravda*, Sept. 23, 1973, 4.

48. "Pilna notatka na temat udziału Polski w przygotowaniach do EKBiW," June 20, 1972, *PDD 1972*, doc. 127.

49. Puja, "Report on the 21–22 May 1973 Meeting."

50. Quoted in Jarząbek, "Hope and Reality" 34.

51. "Rede des Leiters der sowjetischen Delegation auf der Tagung des Politischen Beratenden Ausschusses, Genossen L. I. Breshnew, in Prag," Jan. 25, 1972, PHP; and Hungarian Politburo Meeting Minutes, "Report on the Meeting of the Warsaw Treaty Political Consultative Committee in Prague, January 25–26 1972," Feb. 1, 1972, PHP.

52. Memorandum from Sous-direction d'Europe Orientale, "Réunion a Budapest des Ministres des Affaires Étrangères du Pacte de Varsovie (21–22 juin 1970)," July 6, 1970, AMAE, Affaires Étrangères - Fonds EU - Organismes Internationaux et Grandes Questions Internationales - Sécurité – 1966–70 – 2036; MfAA Memorandum, "Zu einigen Fragen der Vorbereitung und Durchführung einer europäischen Sicherheitskonferenz im Kampf um die Schaffung eines europäischen Sicherheitssystems," Oct. 20, 1970, PAAA, Bestand MfAA C 366/78;

and "Notatka dyrektora Departamentu Studiów i Programowania w sprawie procesów integracyjnych w Europie Zachodniej," May 3, 1974, *PDD 1974*, doc. 113.

53. Bennett Kovrig, *Of Walls and Bridges: The United States and Eastern Europe* (New York: NYU Press, 1991) 234–249; and Pisar 75–93. Quotation from Pisar 88.

54. Garton Ash 248–249.

55. Memorandum from Sous-direction d'Europe Orientale, "Project de conférence sur la sécurité européenne," Feb. 2, 1970, AMAE, Affaires Étrangères - Fonds EU - Organismes Internationaux et Grandes Questions Internationales – Sécurité - 1966–70 – 2031; and Pompidou-Brandt Memcon, Jan. 25, 1971, AN, 5 AG 2/1010.

56. Paper by the US Delegation to NATO, "ECONAD Contribution to Senior POLADS Report on East West Negotiations," Oct. 30, 1970, UKNA, FCO 41/746.

57. Cain 149–150; and *International Economic Report of the President* (Washington, DC: USGPO, 1973) 50.

58. Letter from Kovner, US Mission to NATO, to Laulan, NATO Economic Directorate, March 15, 1971, UKNA, FCO 69/198; and Memorandum from the West German Mission to NATO, "Preparation of Possible East/West Negotiations," March 17, 1971, ibid.

59. Memorandum to Meyer, "Remarques au sujet du document de la délégation italienne en date du 1e février 1972: Contenu éventuel d'une CSCE," March 1, 1972, AEU, BAC 28/1980/651—1972–73.

60. "East/West Trade—Situation, Policies, Prospects." See also European Commission Memorandum, "La problématique du commerce Est-Ouest," Nov. 16, 1970, AEU, EN 170; Telegram from State Department to US Mission to NATO, "East-West Negotiations Study: Economic Section," April 21, 1971, NARA, RG 59, Central Foreign Policy Files, 1970–1973, Box 2264, POL 1 Eur E - Eur W 4/1/71; and European Commission Memorandum, "Problemi della conferenza sulla sicurezza e la cooperazione in Europa: Iniziative possibili delle comunità europee," July 19, 1971, AEU, EG 208.

61. Memorandum from the Danish Delegation to NATO, "Economic Questions at a Conference on European Security and Cooperation," March 16, 1971, UKNA, FCO 69/198; and Hanson 119–121.

62. "Informal Remarks of US Delegate Experts Meeting," April 13, 1972, UKNA, FCO 28/1684; and "Rapport du Groupe Ad Hoc en exécution du mandat donné par le Comité Politique de rechercher une position harmonisée en vue des travaux de préparation multilatérale de la CSCE," Nov. 23, 1972, AMAE, Affaires Étrangères - Organismes Internationaux et Grandes Questions Internationales -Sécurité – 1971–1976 – 2925.

63. State Department Interagency Task Force, "Conference on Security and Cooperation in Europe: Interim Report to the Secretary of State," March 3, 1972, NARA, RG 59, Executive Secretariat, Briefing Books 1958–1976, Box 134; and "Project de rapport du Groupe Ad Hoc au Comité Politique (IIème partie)," Oct. 24, 1972.

64. "Project de rapport du Groupe Ad Hoc au Comité Politique (IIème partie)," Oct. 24, 1972.

65. Telegram from US Mission to NATO to the State Department, "Summary of Senior POLADS Report on Conference on European Security and Cooperation (CESC)," Nov. 12, 1971, RMNL, NSC Institutional Files, Box H-187, NSSM 138 (2 of 2).

66. NATO Guidelines and Agenda Paper, "Preparation of a CSCE: Economic Cooperation," Nov. 28, 1972, NATOA, CM(72)68(Revised).

67. Memorandum by the Canadian Delegation to NATO, "Preparation of Possible East/West Negotiations of Economic Questions at a Conference on European Security," March 15,

1971, UKNA, FCO 69/198; External Affairs Memorandum, "CSCE: Economic Cooperation," Sept. 15, 1972, LAC, RG-25 Vol. 9054 File 20-4-CSCE Vol. 23 (72-09-01 to 72-09-25).

68. Foreign Office Briefing Note, "NATO Economic Preparations for the CSCE," Nov. 29, 1972, UKNA, FCO 30/1254.

69. "Pour le Ministre de la part de JP Brunet," Oct. 17, 1972, AMAE, CSCE 1969–1975, Box 27.

70. Memorandum from Burns to Kay, "CSCE: Draft Steering Briefs for the Second Committee at the CSCE," Sept. 3, 1973, UKNA, FCO 55/1035.

71. Telegram from the State Department to the US Delegation to NATO, "NATO Discussion of East-West Negotiations: Scientific and Technological Cooperation," Oct. 27, 1970, NARA, RG 59, Central Foreign Policy Files, 1970–1973, Box 2263.

72. Paper by the US Delegation to NATO, "ECONAD Contribution to Senior POLADS Report on East West Negotiations," Oct. 30, 1970; and Paper by the Canadian Delegation to NATO, "Preparation of Possible East/West Negotiations of Economic Questions at a Conference on European Security," n.d. [March 1971], UKNA, FCO 69/198; "Project de rapport du Groupe Ad Hoc au Comité Politique (IIème partie)," Oct. 24, 1972, UKNA, FCO 41/1060; and "Rapport du Groupe Ad Hoc en exécution du mandat donné par le Comité Politique de rechercher une position harmonisée en vue des travaux de préparation multilatérale de la CSCE," Nov. 23, 1972, AMAE, Affaires Étrangères - Organismes Internationaux et Grandes Questions Internationales - Sécurité - 1971–1976 – 2925.

73. "Discours du Président Malfatti," Nov. 19, 1970, AEU, EN 73 1972; Memorandum from Sous-Direction d'Europe Orientale, "Avis de la Commission sur la CSCE," Sept. 16, 1971, AMAE, Affaires Étrangères - Organismes Internationaux et Grandes Questions Internationales - Sécurité – 1971–1976 – 2922; Memorandum from Sous-Direction d'Europe Orientale, "Présence des Communautés Européennes à une CSCE," Feb. 14, 1972, AMAE, CSCE 1969–1975, Box 1; and Telegram from Brimelow, Luxembourg, to the FCO, "CSCE: Report of the Political Ctte: Economic Aspects," May 27, 1972, UKNA, FCO 28/1685.

74. FCO Draft Position Paper, "The Conference on European Security: The Next Phase," February 1972, DBPO III:II, doc. 1; and Badalassi 190–195.

75. "Editorial Note," FRUS 1969–1976, Vol. 15, doc. 22; and "Informal Remarks of US Delegate Experts Meeting," April 13, 1972.

76. Memorandum from Meyer, European Commission, to Herpin, president of the EC's Ad Hoc Group, March 5, 1973, PAAA, B28 111527; see also Memorandum from the Service de Coopération Économique, Quai d'Orsay, "Coopération politique: travaux préparatoires à la CSCE dans le domaine économique," Oct. 9, 1972, AMAE, CSCE 1969–1975, Box 27.

77. Memorandum by the Canadian Delegation to NATO, "Preparation of Possible East/West Negotiations of Economic Questions at a Conference on European Security," March 15, 1971; "Projet de rapport de la présidence sur les travaux du groupe d'étude consacré à la Conférence sur la Sécurité et la Coopération en Europe" n.d. [April 1971], AMAE, Affaires Étrangères - Organismes Internationaux et Grandes Questions Internationales - Sécurité – 1971–1976 - 2921; "Project de rapport du Group Ad Hoc sur la CSCE," Oct. 5, 1971, AEU, EN 86 1971; Memorandum from Braithwaite to Tickell, "Ad Hoc Committee on the CSCE," May 5, 1972, UKNA, FCO 41/1053; "Project de rapport du Groupe Ad Hoc au Comité Politique (IIème partie)," Oct. 24, 1972; NATO Guidelines and Agenda Paper, "Preparation of a CSCE: Economic Cooperation," Nov. 28, 1972; and Foreign Office Briefing Note, "NATO Economic Preparations for the CSCE," Nov. 29, 1972.

78. State Department Interagency Task Force, "Conference on Security and Cooperation in Europe: Interim Report to the Secretary of State," March 3, 1972.

79. Andrei Sakharov, *Progress, Coexistence, and Intellectual Freedom* (New York: Norton, 1968) 67.

80. UK Draft Steering Brief, "CSCE Economic Committee," n.d. [July 1973], UKNA, FCO 55/1034.

81. Paper by the US Delegation to NATO, "ECONAD Contribution to Senior POLADS Report on East West Negotiations," Oct. 30, 1970, UKNA, FCO 41/746; and "Rapport du Groupe Ad Hoc en exécution du mandat donné par le Comité Politique de rechercher une position harmonisée en vue des travaux de préparation multilatérale de la CSCE," Nov. 23, 1972, AMAE, Affaires Étrangères - Organismes Internationaux et Grandes Questions Internationales - Sécurité - 1971–1976 - 2925.

82. Memorandum from Meyer, European Commission, to Herpin, president of the EC's Ad Hoc Group, March 5, 1973; Letter from Brimelow, FCO, to Cromer, Washington, "CSCE: Soviet Draft Declaration," March 8, 1973, UKNA, FCO 41/1302; Greenhill-Puja Memcon, March 16, 1973, UKNA, FCO 28/2176; Telegram from Elliott, Helsinki, to FCO, "CSCE/MPT: Basket II (Economic Questions)," March 23, 1973, UKNA, FCO 41/1290; and Luigi Vittorio Ferraris, *Report on a Negotiation: Helsinki-Geneva-Helsinki 1972–1975*, trans. Marie-Claire Barber (Alphen aan den Rijn: Sijthoff and Noordhoff International Publishers, 1979) 48.

83. Minute from Gordon to Fretwell, "CSCE/MPT: Basket II Discussions," May 24, 1973, *DBPO* III:II, doc. 36; and Telegram from Elliott, Helsinki, to FCO, "CSCE: The First 200 Days," June 13, 1973, ibid., doc. 37.

84. Memorandum from Gordon to Kay, Simmons, and Keeble, "CSCE Economic Aspects (Basket II)," April 17, 1973, UKNA, FCO 55/1031.

85. Ferraris 50; and Minute from Gordon to Fretwell, "CSCE/MPT: Basket II Discussions."

86. Memorandum to Sharp, "CSCE: Conclusion of Preparatory Talks," June 6, 1973, LAC, RG-25 Vol. 9054 File 20-4-CSCE Vol. 35; Telegram from Elliott, Helsinki, to FCO, "CSCE: The First 200 Days"; and "Final Recommendations of the Helsinki Consultations," June 8, 1973, *Selected Documents* 146–149.

87. State Department Briefing Paper, "Results of the Multilateral Preparatory Talks," n.d. [June 1973], RMNL, NSC Files, Box 940, General Secretary Brezhnev Visit to USA June 1973—Background Papers Vol. 1; and Memorandum from Sous-Direction CSCE, "Bilan des 'Recommandations finales' des consultations d'Helsinki," June 19, 1973, AMAE, CSCE 1969–1975, Box 11.

88. Minute from Fall to Tickell, "CSCE," June 17, 1974, *DBPO* III:II, doc. 86.

89. "Projekt pilnej notatki w sprawie propozycji radzieckich w związku z II fazą EKBiW," June 8, 1973; "Notatka informacyjna z konsultacji polsko-radzieckich na tematy ekonomiczne KBWE," March 25, 1974, Jarząbek, *Polska wobec Konferencji Bezpieczeństwa i Współpracy w Europie*, doc. 12; and "Tezy do rozmów ministrów spraw zagranicznych Polski i ZSRR (fragmenty)," Jan. 22, 1975, *PDD 1975*, doc. 22.

90. Memorandum from Sous-Direction CSCE, "Bilan des 'Recommandations finales' des consultations d'Helsinki," June 19, 1973; and Letter from Elliott, Geneva, to Douglas-Home, FCO, "CSCE: The Second Stage So Far," Dec. 15, 1973, *DBPO* III:II, doc. 57.

91. Minute from Cloake to Marshall, "CSCE: Committee II," July 3, 1974, *DBPO* III:II, doc. 88.

92. Noam Kochavi, "Insights Abandoned, Flexibility Lost: Kissinger, Soviet Jewish Emigra-

tion, and the Demise of Détente," *Diplomatic History* 29:3 (June 2005) 503–530; Sargent 211–212.

93. Kissinger-Gromyko Memcon, Sept. 24, 1973, RMNL, HAK Office Files, Box 71; and Kissinger-Gromyko Memcon, Dec. 22, 1973, ibid.

94. Kissinger-Brezhnev Memcon, Oct. 24, 1974, RMNL, National Security Adviser - Kissinger Reports on USSR, China, and Middle East Discussions, Box 1, October 24–27, 1974 - Kissinger/Brezhnev Talks in Moscow (1); and Sargent 213.

95. Briefing Note from Gates to Ford, "Soviet Attitudes at Opening of CSCE Negotiations," Jan. 24, 1975, GRFL, National Security Adviser - NSC Europe, Canada, and Ocean Affairs Staff: Files, Box 44, Conference on Security and Cooperation in Europe, 1975 (1) WH.

96. "Gespräch des Bundesministers Genscher mit dem sowjetischen Außenminister Gromyko auf Schloß Gymnich," Sept. 15, 1974, *AAPD 1974*, doc. 264; Record of Ad Hoc Group Meeting, Bonn, April 17, 1974, UKNA, FCO 30/2484.

97. Minute from Cloake to Marshall, "CSCE: Committee II," July 3, 1974.

98. Memorandum to the Politburo, "Zum gegenwärtigen Stand der Arbeit der Sicherheitskonferenz," July 30, 1974, SAPMO, DY 30/J IV 2/2J/5399; FCO paper for Foreign Secretary Callaghan on the CSCE, Nov. 27, 1974, *DPBO* III:II, doc. 104; Telegram from Hildyard, Geneva, to FCO, "CSCE: Timing of Stage III," July 1, 1975, UKNA, FCO 41/1772; and Letter from Fielder, Geneva, to Popplewell, FCO, "CSCE: Economic Committee," July 4, 1975, UKNA, FCO 41/1760.

99. Minute from Key to Cloake, "CSCE: Commercial Exchanges Sub-Committee: MFN," April 4, 1974, UKNA, FCO 30/2484; and Memorandum from Tickell to Private Secretary, "Prime Minister's Visit to Moscow: CSCE and MBFR," Jan. 27, 1975, UKNA, FCO 41/1781.

100. Letter from Fielder, Geneva, to Alexander, FCO, "CSCE: Economic Committee: The Closing Stages," July 21, 1975, *DBPO* III:II, doc. 135.

101. Ibid.; and Entry for July 16, 1975, Sherer Diary.

102. "Final Act of the Conference on Security and Cooperation in Europe," *The End of the Post-War Era* 304–305.

103. Telegram from Shenstone, Geneva, to External Affairs, "CSCE: General Review," April 6, 1974, LAC, RG-25 Vol. 9054 File 20-4-CSCE Vol. 44; European Commission Memorandum, "Deuxième rapport intérimaire sur la IIème Phase de la CSCE," April 6, 1974, AEU, BAC 28/1980/652 – 1973; Telegram from Delworth, Geneva, to External Affairs, "CSCE: Basket II and III Linkage," Nov. 8, 1974, LAC, RG-25 Vol. 9054 File 20-4-CSCE Vol. 48; and "Botschafter Blech, Genf (KSZE-Delegation), an das Auswärtige Amt," July 22, 1975, *AAPD 1975*, doc. 217.

104. Memorandum from Meyer to Herpin, March 5, 1973, PAAA, B28 111527; and Memorandum from Gordon to Kay, "CSCE Economic Aspects (Basket II)," April 17, 1973, UKNA, FCO 55/1031.

105. Report from Bock to Winzer, "The Course and the Results of the First Phase of the European Security Conference," July 23, 1973, *Negotiating One's Own Demise?*; "Pilna notatka z wizyty ministra spraw zagranicznych Czechosłowacji (fragmenty)," June 8, 1973, *PDD 1973*, doc. 102; and "Notatka Informacyjna o przebiegu i wynikach prac komisji problemowych II fazy Konferencji Bezpieczeństwa i Współpracy w Europie," Dec. 22, 1973, Jarząbek, *Polska wobec Konferencji Bezpieczeństwa i Współpracy w Europie*, doc. 11.

106. MfAA Memorandum, "Bericht über den gegenwärtigen Stand der Ausarbeitung des Abschlußberichtes über die Konsultation in Helsinki," June 2, 1973, PAAA, Bestand MfAA C 374/78; and GDR Politburo Memorandum, "Schlußfolgerungen für das weitere Auftreten der Delegation der DDR," Jan. 15, 1974, SAPMO, DY 30/J IV 2/2/1486.

107. Brezhnev-Honecker Memcon, Oct. 6, 1975, *Risse im Bruderbund: Die Gespräche Honecker-Breshnew*, eds. Hans-Hermann Hertle and Konrad H. Jarausch (Berlin: Ch. Links, 2006) 110.

108. "Vortragender Legationsrat I. Klasse Freiherr von Groll, z. Z. Genf, an das Auswärtige Amt," Oct. 30, 1973, *AAPD 1973*, doc. 347.

109. Department of Trade and Industry Briefing Note, "CSCE Economic Basket," May 15, 1973, UKNA, BT 241/2665; and letter from Gray, Geneva, to Sinclair, FCO, "CSCE: Sub-Committee 5: Science and Technology," Nov. 14, 1973.

110. Letter from Fielder, Geneva, to Popplewell, FCO, "CSCE: Economic Committee: Commercial Exchanges Sub-Committee Paragraph 32 Matters," March 27, 1975, UKNA, FCO 41/1760.

111. Department of Trade and Industry Briefing Note, "CSCE Economic Basket."

112. UK Draft Steering Brief, "CSCE Economic Committee," n.d. [July 1973], UKNA, FCO 55/1034; Letter from Gray, Geneva, to Rothwell, FCO, "CSCE: Sub-Committee V (Science and Technology)," Oct. 15, 1973, UKNA, FCO 41/1326; Letter from Gray, Geneva, to Sinclair, FCO, "CSCE: Sub-Committee 5: Science and Technology," Nov. 14, 1973, UKNA, FCO 55/1037; and Letter from Elliott, Geneva, to Douglas-Home, FCO, "CSCE: The Second Stage So Far," Dec. 15, 1973.

113. Telegram from Delworth, Geneva, to External Affairs, "CSCE: General Assessment," Dec. 21, 1974, LAC, RG-25 Vol. 9054 File 20-4-CSCE Vol. 49; "Final Act of the Conference on Security and Cooperation in Europe," *The End of the Post-War Era* 309–310; Badalassi 396–397; Erez Manela, "A Pox on Your Narrative: Writing Disease Control into Cold War History," *Diplomatic History* 34:2 (April 2010) 299–323; and Memorandum from Kissinger to Nixon, "Moscow Visit—Announcement of Bilateral Agreements," May 15, 1972, *FRUS 1969–1976*, Vol. 14, doc. 227.

114. "Final Act of the Conference on Security and Cooperation in Europe," *The End of the Post-War Era* 306–307; and Telegram from Hillenbrand, Bonn, to State Department, "CSCE: Economic Cooperation Issues," April 24, 1974, AAD; and "Botschafter Blech, Genf (KSZE-Delegation), an das Auswärtige Amt," July 22, 1975.

115. Telegram from Dale, Geneva, to State Department, "CSCE: Stage II Highlights - July 8–12," July 13, 1974, AAD; Telegram from Dale, Geneva, to State Department, "CSCE: Stage II Highlights - September 16–20," Sept. 21, 1974, AAD; and FCO Paper for Foreign Secretary Callaghan on the CSCE, Nov. 27, 1974.

116. Letter from Hildyard, Geneva, to Callaghan, FCO, "CSCE: The Conclusion of Stage II," July 25, 1975, UKNA, FCO 41/1769; Politburo Memorandum, "Einschätzung der Schlußdokumente der KSZE," n.d. [August 1975], SAPMO, DY 30/IV 2/2.035/149; Politburo Memorandum, "Bericht über die Ergebnisse der 2. Phase der europäischen Sicherheitskonferenz," July 28, 1975, SAPMO, DY 30/J IV 2/2/1573; "Notatka Informacyjna o końcowych wynikach II fazy KBWE," July 24, 1975, Jarząbek, *Polska wobec Konferencji Bezpieczeństwa i Współpracy w Europie*, doc. 15.

117. Letter from Elliott, Geneva, to Douglas-Home, FCO, "CSCE: The Second Stage So Far," Dec. 15, 1973.

118. See, for instance, Kotkin, *Armageddon Averted* 18.

119. Eichengreen, *The European Economy* 242–277; and Sargent chapters 4 and 5.

120. Richard Baum, *Burying Mao: Chinese Politics in the Age of Deng Xiaoping* (Princeton, NJ: Princeton UP, 1994) chapter 3; and Ezra F. Vogel, *Deng Xiaoping and the Transformation of China* (Cambridge, MA: Harvard UP, 2011) chapter 14.

121. Hanson 108. On the resistance of these groups to Gorbachev's reforms after 1985, see

Chris Miller, *The Struggle to Save the Soviet Economy: Mikhail Gorbachev and the Collapse of the USSR* (Chapel Hill, NC: UNC Press, 2016) chapter 3.

122. Baum 7–23.

123. Kotkin, *Armageddon Averted* 16.

Chapter 6: The Closed Society and Its Enemies

1. "Conference on Security and Co-Operation in Europe: Background Papers," May 5, 1972, NATOA, CM(72)24 Vol. 3; Brimelow-Kirschläger Memcon, April 27, 1973, UKNA, FCO 41/1344; Hedrick Smith, "The Iron Curtain Is Being Lifted . . . a Little," *NYT*, Oct. 21, 1973, 10; Hedrick Smith, *The Russians* (New York: Quadrangle, 1976) chapter 7; Donald J. Raleigh, *Soviet Baby Boomers: An Oral History of Russia's Cold War Generation* (New York: Oxford UP, 2012) chapters 4–5; Sergei I. Zhuk, *Rock and Roll in the Rocket City: The West, Identity, and Ideology in Soviet Dnepropetrovsk, 1960–1985* (Washington, DC: Woodrow Wilson Center Press, 2010); and Brown, *New Forces in World Politics* 89.

2. Letter from MacDonald, FCO, to Grattan, UK Delegation to NATO, "East/West Negotiations," April 1, 1971, UKNA, FCO 41/896; memorandum from Sedgwick-Jell to Ramsay, "Jamming of BBC Broadcasts," Aug. 27, 1971, ibid.; "Conference on Security and Co-Operation in Europe: Background Papers," May 5, 1972; FCO research memorandum, "Private Travel, Tourism and Labour Mobility in Eastern Europe," March 13, 1973, UKNA, FCO 28/2173; FCO memorandum, "Soviet Impediments to Free Exchanges," July 1973, ibid.; James Feron and Tom Little, "Russian Tourists: And Why They Think the Communist East is the 'Degenerate West,'" *NYT*, Feb. 27, 1972, IR1; Hedrick Smith, "East Bloc Fights West's Ideas, but Flow Goes On," June 13, 1973, *NYT*, 20; Smith, "The Iron Curtain Is Being Lifted . . . a Little"; Smith, *The Russians* 358–361 and 464–473; Timothy Garton Ash, *The Uses of Adversity: Essays on the Fate of Central Europe* (New York: Random House, 1989) 21–22; Anne E. Gorsuch, *All This Is Your World: Soviet Tourism at Home and Abroad after Stalin* (New York: Oxford UP, 2011) chapter 4 and epilogue.

3. Emily S. Rosenberg, *Spreading the American Dream: American Economic and Cultural Expansion, 1890–1945* (New York: Hill and Wang, 1982) 11–37 and 89.

4. *The Geneva Conference of Heads of Government, July 18–23, 1955* (Washington, DC: USGPO, 1955); and editorial, "The Struggle Goes On," *The Times*, Nov. 17, 1955, 11. See also Ghébali 265–272.

5. See, for example, "Russians 'Ready for Talks': Herr Brandt's Hopes of Progress," *The Times*, Nov. 2, 1962, 11; Arthur J. Olsen, "West Approves Brandt's Plan for Contact with East Germans," *NYT*, Jan. 4, 1964, 4; and Peter Grose, "US Plan for Berlin to Propose Tearing Down 8-Year-Old Wall," *NYT*, July 31, 1969, 1.

6. William J. Gibbons, ed., *Pacem in Terris: Encyclical Letter of His Holiness Pope John XXIII* (New York: Paulist Press, 1963) 12.

7. Speech by President Johnson, "Making Europe Whole: An Unfinished Task," *Department of State Bulletin*, Vol. 55, No. 1426 (Oct. 24, 1966) 622.

8. Speech by President Johnson, "Remarks in Cadillac Square, Detroit," Sept. 7, 1964, *Public Papers of the Presidents of the United States: Lyndon B. Johnson, 1963–1964*, Vol. 2 (Washington, DC: USGPO 1965) 1050; Schwartz 20, 48, and 133–134; and Kieninger chapters 2–3.

9. A. Ross Johnson, *Radio Free Europe and Radio Liberty: The CIA Years and Beyond* (Washington, DC: Woodrow Wilson Center Press, 2010) 149–150 and 169–185; Arch Puddington,

Broadcasting Freedom: The Cold War Triumph of Radio Free Europe and Radio Liberty (Lexington: University Press of Kentucky, 2000) chapter 10; Michael Nelson, *War of the Black Heavens: The Battles of Western Broadcasting in the Cold War* (Syracuse, NY: Syracuse UP, 1997) chapters 6–8; Alexei Yurchak, *Everything Was Forever, Until it Was No More: The Last Soviet Generation* (Princeton, NJ: Princeton UP, 2005) 175–190; and Miroslav Vaňek and Pavel Mücke, *Velvet Revolutions: An Oral History of Czech Society* (New York: Oxford UP, 2016) 32–33.

10. Albert Parry, "Samizdat is Russia's Underground Press," *New York Times Magazine*, March 15, 1970, 77.

11. Andrei Sakharov, *Memoirs*, trans. Richard Lourie (London: Hutchison, 1990) 288; Joshua Rubenstein, "Introduction," *The KGB File of Andrei Sakharov*, eds. Joshua Rubenstein and Alexander Gribanov (New Haven: Yale UP, 2005) 20–21; and Margo Picken, ed., *Andrei Sakharov and Human Rights* (Strasbourg: Council of Europe, 2010) 150; Andrei Amalrik, *Will the Soviet Union Survive until 1984?*, rev. ed. (New York: Harper and Row, 1980); and Abraham Rothberg, *The Heirs of Stalin: Dissidence and the Soviet Regime, 1953–1970* (Ithaca: Cornell UP, 1972) 301. On the ideas and the development of the Soviet dissident movement in this period, see Philip Boobbyer, *Conscience, Dissent and Reform in Soviet Russia* (London: Routledge, 2005), especially chapters 5–7.

12. Sakharov, *Memoirs* 314–320; and Andropov to Suslov, Oct. 2, 1971, *The KGB File of Andrei Sakharov*, 129–130.

13. Peter Reddaway, "One of the CIA's Most Zealous Agents," *Uren met Karel van het Reve: Liber Amicorum*, ed. Robert van Amerongen (Amsterdam: Oorschot, 1991) 141–143; and Joshua Rubenstein, *Soviet Dissidents: Their Struggle for Human Rights* (Boston: Beacon Press, 1980) chapter 4.

14. Michael Scammell, "Notebook," *Index on Censorship* 1:1 (March 1972) 6; and Michael Scammell, "How *Index on Censorship* Started," *They Shoot Writers, Don't They?* ed. George Theiner (London: Faber and Faber, 1984) 19–28.

15. "Gespräch des Bundeskanzlers Brandt mit Premierminister Heath in London," April 20, 1972, *AAPD 1972*, doc. 104.

16. Hakkarainen, *A State of Peace in Europe* 183 and 233.

17. Telegram from the US Delegation to NATO to the State Department, "Polads Discussion of Freer Movement," March 1, 1972, NARA, RG 59, Central Foreign Policy Files, 1970–1973, Box 2263.

18. Letter from Scott, Moscow, to Walden, FCO, "Cultural Aspects of the CSCE," Aug. 24, 1972, UKNA, FCO 28/1681; Memorandum from US Delegation to NATO, "Freer Movement of People, Ideas and Information," April 8, 1971, AMAE, Affaires Étrangères - Organismes Internationaux et Grandes Questions Internationales - Sécurité – 1971–1976 – 2921; and Memorandum from the West German Delegation to the EC's CSCE Subcommittee, "Arbeitspapier: Kulturelle Beziehungen," Feb. 25, 1972, PAAA, B28 109310.

19. Robin quoted in Badalassi 204; and Rogers-Stewart-Schumann-Scheel Memcon, "Dîner Quadripartite du 3 décembre 1969 à l'Ambassade d'Allemagne à Bruxelles," Dec. 3, 1969.

20. Telegram from State Department to US Mission to NATO, "NATO Discussion of East-West Negotiations: Freer Movement of People, Ideas and Information," Oct. 27, 1970, NARA, RG 59, Central Foreign Policy Files, 1970–1973, Box 2263, POL 1 Eur E–Eur W; Memorandum from the US Delegation to NATO, "Freer Movement," April 8, 1971; and James Goodby, *Europe Undivided: The New Logic of Peace in US-Russian Relations* (Washington, DC: United States Institute of Peace, 1998) 48–62.

21. Letter from Walden to Staples, "Cultural Aspects of the CSCE," Aug. 4, 1972.

22. Letter from Sous-Direction d'Europe Orientale to Embassies in NATO and Warsaw Pact Capitals, "Conversations avec les Américains sur la Sécurité européenne," April 13, 1970, AMAE, Affaires Étrangères - Fonds EU - Organismes Internationaux et Grandes Questions Internationales - Sécurité - 1966–70 - 2031.

23. Memorandum from Sous-Direction d'Europe Orientale, "Conférence sur la Sécurité européenne et libre circulation des idées et des hommes," March 18, 1971, AMAE, CSCE, 1969–1975, Box 7; Memorandum from the French Delegation to NATO, "Conférence sur la sécurité européenne—Coopération culturelle, libre circulation des hommes, des idées et des informations," April 6, 1971; and FCO paper, "East European Attitudes to the CSCE," March 20, 1972, UKNA, FCO 41/1056.

24. Memorandum from US Delegation to NATO, "Freer Movement of People, Ideas and Information"; Letter from Walden to Staples, "Cultural Aspects of the CSCE," Aug. 4, 1972, UKNA, FCO 28/1680; CSCE Interagency Task Force, "Interim Report to the Secretary of State," March 3, 1972, NARA, RG 59, Executive Secretariat, Briefing Books 1958–1976, Box 134; Letter from Scott, Moscow, to Walden, FCO, "Cultural Aspects of the CSCE"; and Tickell-Sung Memcon, Oct. 11, 1973, UKNA, FCO 41/1339; and Letter from Ramsay, FCO, to Porter, UK Delegation to NATO, "CES: Freer Movement of Peoples etc." Sept. 2, 1971, UKNA, FCO 41/896.

25. Rey, *La Tentation du rapprochement* chapter 6; memorandum from the French Delegation to NATO, "Conférence sur la sécurité européenne—Coopération culturelle, libre circulation des hommes, des idées et des informations," April 6, 1971, UKNA, FCO 41/896; memorandum from the US Delegation to NATO, "Freer Movement of People, Ideas, and Information," April 8, 1971, AMAE, Affaires Étrangères - Organismes Internationaux et Grandes Questions Internationales - Sécurité - 1971–1976 - 2921; "Ministerialdirigent Diesel an die Ständige Vertretung bei der NATO in Brüssel," Sept. 17, 1971, *AAPD 1971*, doc. 313; memorandum from FE Maestrone to NATO's Political Committee, "Questions de fond et procédures pour d'éventuelles négociations Est-Ouest: Libre circulation des personnes des idées et des informations et développement des relations culturelles," April 22, 1971, AMAE, Affaires Étrangères - Organismes Internationaux et Grandes Questions Internationales - Sécurité - 1971–1976 - 2921; telegram from Vest, US Delegation to NATO, to State Department, "Summary of Senior POLADS Report on Conference on European Security and Cooperation (CESC)," Nov. 12, 1971, RMNL, Nixon Files, NSC Institutional Files, Box H-187, NSSM 138 (2 of 2); "Conference on Security and Co-Operation in Europe: Background Papers," May 5, 1972; Auswärtiges Amt memorandum, "Eventual CSCE Agenda Item on the Improvement of Interstate Relations," n.d. [Aug. 1972], PAAA, B28 109306; letter from Brown, FCO, to Staples, UK Delegation to NATO, "CSCE: Cultural Relations," Oct. 20, 1972, UKNA, FCO 28/1682; letter from Walden, FCO, to Staples, UK Delegation to NATO, "CSCE: Cultural Relations," Oct. 30, 1972, ibid; "Conference on Security and Co-Operation in Europe: Cultural Relations," Nov. 13, 1972, NATOA, CM(72)70; and Letter from Ellison, FCO, to Smith, UK Delegation to NATO, "UN Human Rights Commission," Feb. 16, 1973, FCO 41/1282.

26. Telegram from State Department to the US Delegation to NATO, "Proposed Agenda Paper on the Freer Movement of People," Jan. 28, 1972, NARA, RG 59, Central Foreign Policy Files, 1970–1973, Box 2264, POL 1 Eur E–Eur W 1/1/72.

27. Nixon-Kissinger Conversation, April 13, 1971, *The Nixon Tapes, 1971–1972* 64; and letter from Fall to Tickell, March 8, 1973, *DBPO* III:II, doc. 25, footnote 6.

28. Memorandum from Sonnenfeldt to Kissinger, "SRG Meeting on MBFR and CSCE, March 29, 1972," March 24, 1972, RMNL, NSC Institutional Files, Box H-061.

29. "Ministerialdirigent Diesel an die Ständige Vertretung bei der NATO in Brüssel," Sept. 17, 1971; Telegram from Peck, UK Delegation to NATO to Foreign Office, "CES: Freer Movement of Peoples," Sept. 30, 1971, UKNA, FCO 41/897; Auswärtiges Amt memorandum, "Kulturelle Ost-West-Beziehungen und KSE," Dec. 13, 1971, PAAA, B150, 244; Memorandum from Sous-Direction d'Europe Orientale, "Discussions au Conseil Atlantique sur le chapitre de l'ordre du jour de la CSCE consacré à la coopération culturelle et aux contacts entre les hommes," April 10, 1972, AMAE, CSCE, 1969–1975, Box 7; and Memorandum from Seydoux to Schumann, "Réponse à la demande d'avis du Département sur les aspects culturels de la CSCE," Sept. 7, 1972, AMAE, Affaires Étrangères – Organismes Internationaux et Grandes Questions Internationales - Sécurité - 1971–1976 - 2924.

30. FCO briefing note, "CSCE: Cultural Aspects," Sept. 12, 1972, UKNA, FCO 28/1681; telegram from Canadian Delegation to NATO to External Affairs, "CSCE: Draft Agenda: Freer Movement," Dec. 14, 1972, LAC, RG-25 Vol. 9054 File 20-4-CSCE Vol. 27; and telegram from Thomson, UK Delegation to NATO, to FCO, "CSCE Agenda Commissions and Mandates," Dec. 14, 1972, UKNA, FCO 41/1068.

31. Telegram from External Affairs to the Canadian Delegation to NATO, Nov. 21, 1972, LAC, RG-25 Vol. 9089 File 20-4-CSCE Vol. 26; Goodby 58; and Baudet 183–198.

32. Letter from Ramsay, FCO, to Porter, UK Delegation, to NATO, "CES: Freer Movement of Peoples Etc.," Sept. 2, 1971, UKNA, FCO 41/896; and Telegram from State Department to US Mission to NATO, "Statement to NAC on East-West Negotiations Study," May 18, 1971, NARA, RG 59, Central Foreign Policy Files, 1970–1973, Box 2264, POL 1 Eur E–Eur W 5/1/71; and Telegram from US Mission to NATO to State Department, "Secretary Rogers' Statement to NAC on President's Visit to Moscow," May 5, 1972, NARA, RG 59, Executive Secretariat Conference Files, 1966–1972, Box 52, Secretary of State's May 1972 Pre-Summit Consultation Follow-Up.

33. Telegram from French Delegation to NATO to Quai d'Orsay, "CSCE. Discussion des mandats," Dec. 15, 1972, AMAE, Affaires Étrangères – Organismes Internationaux et Grandes Questions Internationales - Sécurité - 1971–1976 - 2925; and Telegram from Canadian Delegation to NATO to External Affairs, Jan. 11, 1973, LAC, RG-25, Vol. 9089, File 20-4-CSCE, Vol. 28.

34. "Speech by the Head of the Soviet Delegation at the Meeting of the Political Consultative Committee," Jan. 25, 1972, PHP.

35. "Informacja o rozmowie Gierek-Breżniew," Dec. 19, 1973, *PDD 1973*, doc. 237.

36. "Comrade Todor Zhivkov's Speech at the Meeting of the Warsaw Treaty's Political Consultative Committee in Prague," Jan. 25, 1972, PHP; and "Speech by Nicolae Ceausescu at the Meeting of the Political Consultative Meeting in Prague," Jan. 25, 1972, PHP. See also the speeches of the other Warsaw Pact leaders at the Prague PCC Meeting, PHP.

37. Rey, "The *Mejdunarodniki* in the 1960s and First Half of the 1970s"; and English chapter 3. Quotation from English 105.

38. Memorandum from Le Gourrierec to Schumann, "La Bulgarie et la Conférence de Sécurité Européenne," Nov. 17, 1972, AMAE, CSCE, 1969–1975, Box 2; MfAA Memorandum, "Zu einigen Fragen der Vorbereitung und Durchführung einer europäischen Sicherheitskonferenz im Kampf um die Schaffung eines europäischen Sicherheitssystems," Oct. 20, 1970; MfAA Memorandum, "Faktorenanalyse zum Stand der Vorbereitung einer gesamteuropäischen Sicherheitskonferenz," Sept. 25, 1971; and Nikolaï Polianskiĭ, *MID: Dvenadtsat' let na sovetskoĭ diplomaticheskoĭ sluzhbe (1969–1981)* (London: Overseas Publications Interchange, 1987) 167.

39. "Prognoza Departamentu Studiów i Programowania: rozwój sytuacji międzynarodowej

w latach siedemdziesiątych," April 12, 1972, *PDD 1972*, doc. 71; Auswärtiges Amt memorandum, "Kritik der WP-Staaten an den Sendungen von RFE und RL sowie der Deutschen Welle und anderen Sendern der westlichen Welt," March 26, 1973, PAAA, B28 111540; Paweł Machchewicz, *Poland's War on Radio Free Europe, 1950–1989*, trans. Maya Latynski (Washington, DC: Woodrow Wilson Center Press, 2014) 185; and Puddington chapters 13–14.

40. Letter from Spence, Moscow, to Wright, FCO, "Free Exchange: A Trojan Horse," Sept. 19, 1973, UKNA, FCO 28/2174.

41. Andropov quoted in Richard Lourie, *Sakharov: A Biography* (Hanover, NH: Brandeis UP, 2002) 226; and Y. V. Andropov, "The Birth of Samizdat," *Index on Censorship* 23:3 (May 1995) 62–3.

42. "Memorandum from the Committee for State Security of the USSR Council of Ministers and the Public Prosecutor's Office," Nov. 20, 1970, Michael Scammell, ed., *The Solzhenitsyn Files: Secret Soviet Documents Reveal One Man's Fight against the Monolith* (Chicago: Edition Q, 1995) doc. 40.

43. Memorandum from Staples, UK Mission to NATO, to Andrews, NATO Political Committee, "Curbing of Soviet Citizens' Contacts with Foreigners," June 25, 1973, PAAA, B28 111541.

44. Savranskaya, "Unintended Consequences" 182–183; and Rothberg 303–304.

45. Ibid. 296–300; and Rubenstein 105–106 and 141–145.

46. "Notatka z rozmów Gierek-Breżniew (fragmenty)," May 15, 1973, *PDD 1973*, doc. 85; and "Speech by the Head of the Soviet Delegation."

47. "Pilna Notatka z rozmowy z tow. W.W. Maszetowem, wicedyrektorem DWKN1 w radzieckim MSZ w dniu 19 stycznia 1972 r.," Jan. 25, 1972, Jarząbek, *Polska wobec Konferencji Bezpieczeństwa i Współpracy w Europie*, doc. 8; "Pilna notatka na temat udziału Polski w przygotowaniach do EKBiW," June 20, 1972, *PDD 1972*, doc. 127; and "Pilna notatka z konferencji państw socjalistycznych poświęconej WRP w Helsinkach," May 23, 1973, *PDD 1973*, doc. 93.

48. Telegram from Douglas-Home, FCO, to UK Embassy, Moscow, "Soviet Views on CSCE and MBFR," March 8, 1972, UKNA, FCO 28/1679; Telegram from Vimont, Moscow, to Quai d'Orsay, "Projet soviétique de déclaration générale sur les bases de la sécurité européenne et les principes régissant les relations entre états en Europe," July 5, 1973, AMAE, CSCE, 1969–1975, Box 25; Hungarian Foreign Ministry Memorandum, "Report on the Consultation of the Warsaw Treaty Countries' Deputy Foreign Ministers Held in Moscow on 15 November 1972," Nov. 17, 1972, PHP; and Mikhail M. Narinski, "L'Union soviétique et le problème des droits de l'homme dans la première moitié des années soixante-dix," *Les droits de l'homme en Europe depuis 1945*, eds. Antoine Fleury, Carole Fink, and Lubor Jílek (Bern: Peter Lang, 2003) 326–327.

49. "Pilna Notatka w sprawie radzieckiego projektu deklaracji programowej w związku z II-gim punktem porządku dziennego EKBiW," Nov. 17, 1972.

50. "Proekty zadaniĭ dlia komissiĭ obshcheevropeĭskogo soveshchaniia," n.d. [Dec. 1972], RGANI, f.3 op.72 d.539 l.189; and GDR Politburo Memorandum, "Direktive für das weitere Auftreten der Delegation der DDR in der multilateralen Konsultation zur Vorbereitung der Sicherheitskonferenz in Helsinki," April 17, 1973, SAPMO, DY 30/J IV 2/2/1444. See also United States Information Agency, *The External Information and Cultural Relations Programs of the Union of Soviet Socialist Republics* (Washington, DC: USGPO, 1973) 59–79; and Charles Andras, "European Cooperation and Ideological Conflict," *East European Perspectives on European Security and Cooperation*, ed. Robert R. King and Robert W. Dean (New York: Praeger, 1974) 19–23.

51. "Stenogramm des Freundschaftstreffens führender Vertreter der kommunistischen und Arbeiterparteien der sozialistischen Länder," July 31, 1972.

52. "Statement by the Representative of the United States of America," n.d. [Nov. 1972], UKNA, FCO 41/1067. The speeches by the French, Dutch, Canadian, West German, and other Western delegations are also in FCO 41/1067.

53. Auswärtiges Amt Memorandum, "Deutsche-polnische Konsultationen über KSZE am 27. August 1973 in Bonn," Aug. 29, 1973, PAAA, B28 111514; Memorandum from Tickell to Wiggin, "CSCE," Jan. 3, 1974, UKNA, FCO 41/1550; and Memorandum from Packenham to Maxey, "Committee III: 22 March," March 22, 1974, UKNA, FCO 28/2458.

54. Douglas-Home-Gromyko Memcon, Sept. 25, 1973, UKNA, FCO 41/1322.

55. GDR Politburo Memorandum, "Direktive für das weitere Auftreten der Delegation der DDR in der multilateralen Konsultation zur Vorbereitung der Sicherheitskonferenz in Helsinki," April 17, 1973. See also MfAA Memorandum, "Zum Verlauf der multilateralen Konsultation in Helsinki," May 8, 1973, PAAA, Bestand MfAA, C 374/78; and "Notatka informacyjna o przebiegu i wynikach prac komisji problemowych II fazy Konferencji Bezpieczeństwa i Współpracy w Europie," Dec. 22, 1973, Jarząbek, *Polska wobec Konferencji Bezpiecze stwa i Współpracy w Europie*, doc. 11. In his December 1972 speech marking the USSR's fiftieth anniversary, Brezhnev made the same points. Letter from Elliott, UK Embassy in Helsinki, to Douglas-Home, FCO, "CSCE: The First Two Hundred Days," June 13, 1973.

56. The Soviet and Eastern European speeches are in ibid.; Telegram from Killick, Moscow, to FCO, "CSCE," Nov. 3, 1972, UKNA, FCO, 28/1694; Letter from du Boulay, Paris, to Tickell, FCO, "CSCE: Soviet Views," Nov. 16, 1972, UKNA, FCO 28/1695; and "CSCE: Draft Report of the Delegation to the Multilateral Preparatory Talks," June 9, 1973, UKNA, FCO 28/2167.

57. Memorandum from Gromyko to the Politburo, Dec. 27, 1972, RGANI, f.3 op.72 d.539 l.182.

58. L. I Brezhnev, "On the 50th Anniversary of the Union of Soviet Socialist Republics," *Current Digest of the Soviet Press*, Vol. 24, No. 51 (Jan. 17, 1973) 13.

59. Memorandum from Brown to Vines, "CSCE: Cultural and Human Relations," Dec. 14, 1972, UKNA, FCO 28/2172; and memorandum from Brown to Walden, "CSCE: Freer Movement," Dec. 15, 1972, UKNA, FCO 28/1683.

60. "Soviet Agenda Put Forward in Helsinki," *The Times*, Jan. 23, 1973, 5; telegram from Shenstone, Helsinki, to External Affairs, "CSCE Consultations: Basket III," April 2, 1973, LAC, RG-25 Vol. 9054 File 20-4-CSCE, Vol. 33; "Instrukcja ministra spraw zagranicznych dla delegacji polskiej na wiosenną sesję WRP w Helsinkach," April 24, 1973, *PDD 1973*, doc. 75; Auswärtiges Amt memorandum, "MV-KSZE, Korb III (menschliche Kontakte, Kulturaustausch, Informationsfluß)," April 25, 1973, PAAA, B28 111543; and MfAA memorandum, "Zum Verlauf der multilateralen Konsultation in Helsinki," May 8, 1973, PAAA, Bestand MfAA C 374/78.

61. Telegram from Elliott, Helsinki, to FCO, "CSCE/MPT," May 5, 1973, UKNA, FCO 41/1291; memorandum from Sous-Direction CSCE, "Consultations politiques franco-allemandes: CSCE," May 9, 1973, AMAE, Affaires Étrangères - Europe - République Fédérale d'Allemagne - Politique Extérieure – 1971–1976 – 2982; telegram from Elliott, Helsinki, to Wiggin, UK Delegation to NATO, May 12, 1973; telegram from Douglas-Home, FCO, to Elliott, Helsinki, "Meeting of Political Directors on 14 May: CSCE: Baskets I, II and III," May 16, 1973, UKNA, FCO 41/1284; telegram from Elliott, Helsinki, to FCO, "CSCE/MPT," May 19, 1973, UKNA, FCO 41/1292; and telegram from the French Embassy in the Hague to the Quai d'Orsay, "Attitude néerlandaise à l'égard de la CSCE," July 5, 1973, AMAE, Affaires

Étrangères - Organismes Internationaux et Grandes Questions Internationales - Sécurité - 1971–1976 - 2926.

62. "Final Recommendations of the Helsinki Consultations," June 8, 1973, *Selected Documents* 149–51.

63. Memorandum from Danish Ministry of Foreign Affairs to Quai d'Orsay, "Development of Human Contacts, Broadening of Cultural and Educational Exchanges and Wider Flow of Information," Feb. 12, 1973, AMAE, Affaires Étrangères - Organismes Internationaux et Grandes Questions Internationales - Sécurité – 1971–1976 – 2926; telegram from Canadian Delegation to NATO to External Affairs, "CSCE: NATO Consultations," Feb. 13, 1973, LAC, RG-25 Vol. 9054 File 20-4-CSCE Vol. 30; and telegram from Canadian Delegation to NATO to External Affairs, "CSCE: NATO Consultations: Human Contacts," March 23, 1973, LAC, RG-25 Vol. 9054 File 20-4-CSCE Vol. 32.

64. Telegram from Elliott, Helsinki, to FCO, "CSCE/MPT," April 10, 1973, UKNA, FCO 41/1291; FCO briefing note, "CSCE: Tactics for the Fourth Session of Preparatory Talks," April 11, 1973, UKNA, FCO 28/2166; and "Instrukcja ministra spraw zagranicznych dla delegacji polskiej na wiosenną sesję WRP w Helsinkach," April 24, 1973.

65. Telegram from Elliott, Helsinki, to FCO, "CSCE/MPT," Feb. 15, 1973, UKNA, FCO 41/1289; memorandum from Burns to Hird, "Anglo-German Information Talks: CSCE/MBFR," March 7, 1973, UKNA, FCO 41/1340; and telegram from External Affairs to Shenstone, Helsinki, "CSCE Consultations: Human Contacts," March 29, 1973, LAC, RG-25 Vol. 9054 File 20-4-CSCE Vol. 32; and letter from Elliott, Helsinki, to Douglas-Home, FCO, "CSCE: The First 200 Days," June 13, 1973.

66. Memorandum by Jürgen Diesel, "Die Vorbereitungsgespräche in Helsinki für eine 'Konferenz über Sicherheit und Zusammenarbeit in Europa,'" May 28, 1973, PAAA, B28 111501; telegram from Elliott, Helsinki, to FCO, "CSCE/MPT: Basket III," May 31, 1973, UKNA, FCO 41/1292; memorandum from Sous-Direction CSCE, "III–Bilan des 'Recommandations finales' des consultations d'Helsinki," June 19, 1973, AMAE, CSCE 1969–1975, Box 11; memorandum to the Secretary of State for External Affairs, "CSCE: Conclusion of Preparatory Talks," June 6, 1973, LAC, RG-25, Vol. 9054, File 20-4-CSCE, Vol. 35; Walden 150; testimony of Brian Fall, *The Helsinki Negotiations* 61.

67. "Pilna Notatka dot. stanu przygotowań i udziału PRL w I fazie Europejskiej Konferencji Bezpieczeństwa i Współpracy," June 25, 1973, Jarząbek, *Polska wobec Konferencji Bezpieczeństwa i Współpracy w Europie*, doc. 10; and MfAA Memorandum, "Kurze Problemzusammenstellung zu den Schlußempfehlungen der multilateralen Konsultationen," n.d. [June 1973], PAAA, Bestand MfAA, C 374/78.

68. Letter from Bullard, Helsinki, to Wiggin, FCO, "CSCE: Soviet Attitude," July 5, 1973, UKNA, FCO 28/2177.

69. Auswärtiges Amt Memorandum, "Sprechzettel für die Sitzung des KSZE-Unterausschusses am 17./18.7.73 in Kopenhagen," July 10, 1973; and Memorandum from Fall to Bullard, "CSCE: Gromyko's Speech and the Soviet Draft Declaration," July 4, 1973, UKNA, FCO 41/1303.

70. Letter from Killick, UK Embassy in Moscow, to Tickell, FCO, "The End of the MPT for the CSCE," June 27, 1973, UKNA, FCO 41/1294.

71. L. I. Brezhnev, "For a Just, Democratic Peace, for the Security of Peoples and International Cooperation," *Current Digest of the Soviet Press*, Vol. 25, No. 43 (Nov. 21, 1973) 6; and External Affairs Memorandum, "Conference on Security and Cooperation in Europe: Soviet Attitudes," Nov. 9, 1973, LAC, RG-25 Vol. 9054 File 20-4-CSCE, Vol. 41.

72. GDR Politburo Memorandum, "Direktive für das Auftreten der Delegation der DDR

während der zweiten Phase der Konferenz für Sicherheit und Zusammenarbeit in Europa," Aug. 21, 1973, SAPMO, DY 30/J IV 2/2/1464; Memorandum from Fall to Tickell, "Secretary of State's Visit to Moscow: CSCE," Nov. 26, 1973; telegram from Ford, Moscow, to External Affairs, "CSCE—Soviet Views," Jan. 9, 1974, LAC, RG-25 Vol. 9054 File 20-4-CSCE, Vol. 42; GDR Politburo Memorandum, "Schlußfolgerungen für das weitere Auftreten der Delegation der DDR," Jan. 15, 1974, SAPMO, DY 30/J IV 2/2/1486; and letter from Spreckley, Paris, to Bullard, FCO, "Franco/Soviet Relations," Jan. 21, 1974, UKNA, FCO 28/2455.

73. Letter from Brezhnev to Nixon, Jan. 9, 1974, NPMP, HAK Office Files, Box 69. For the Soviet copies of the letters, see RGANI f.3 op.72 d.594 ll. 9–18.

74. Kissinger-Gromyko Memcon, Feb. 4, 1974, RMNL, HAK Office Files, Box 71. Gromyko made a similar argument to Walter Scheel. See "Gespräch des Bundesministers Scheel mit dem sowjetischen Außenminister Gromyko in Moskau," Nov. 1, 1973, *AAPD 1973*, doc. 351.

75. S. Mokshin, "Vzaimodeĭstvie kul'tur i bor'ba ideĭ," *Pravda*, Sept. 5, 1973, 4–5.

76. "Memorandum of the Committee for State Security of the USSR Council of Ministers," Aug. 26, 1973, *The Solzhenitsyn Files*, doc. 79; "Memorandum of the Committee for State Security of the USSR Council of Ministers," Aug. 27, 1973, ibid., doc. 80; "From the Minutes of a Politburo Meeting," Jan. 7, 1974, ibid., doc. 99; and Kovalev, *Iskusstvo vozmozhnogo* 200–201. On Solzhenitsyn's arrest and expulsion, see Michael Scammell, *Solzhenitsyn: A Biography* (New York: WW Norton, 1984) chapter 45.

77. Letter from Staples, UK Delegation to NATO, to McLaren, FCO, "The Soviet Union and the CSCE," Feb. 14, 1974, UKNA, FCO 41/1545; telegram from Shenstone, Geneva, to External Affairs, "CSCE and Solzhenitsyn," Feb. 15, 1974, LAC, RG-25, Vol. 9054, File 20-4-CSCE, Vol. 43; telegram from Ford, Canadian Embassy in Moscow, to External Affairs, "CSCE: Soviet Intentions," Feb. 18, 1974, LAC, RG-25, Vol. 9054, File 20-4-CSCE, Vol. 43; telegram from Canadian Delegation to NATO to External Affairs, "CSCE: Impact of Solzhenitsyn Affair," Feb. 21, 1974, LAC, RG-25, Vol. 9054, File 20-4-CSCE, Vol. 43; and letter from Elliott, Geneva, to Bullard, FCO, "Anglo/Polish Relations and the CSCE," Feb. 22, 1974, UKNA, FCO 41/1584. Eastern European governments kept a close eye on international reaction to Solzhenitsyn's expulsion. See, for example, memorandum to the Politburo, "Reaktionen von Bruderparteien auf die Ausweisung Solshenizyns," Feb. 28, 1974, SAPMO, DY 30/J IV 2/2J/5194.

78. Minutes of Kissinger's staff meeting, Oct. 29, 1973, *FRUS 1969–1976*, Vol. 39, doc. 177. Kissinger made the same point in several conversations with Gromyko. See, for example, Kissinger-Gromyko Memcon, Dec. 22, 1973, RMNL, HAK Office Files, Box 71; Kissinger-Gromyko Memcon, Feb. 4, 1974, RMNL, Nixon Files, HAK Office Files, Box 71, Gromyko 1974; and Kissinger-Brezhnev Memcon, March 25, 1974, RMNL, HAK Office Files, Box 76.

79. Kissinger Memcon with Sisco, Sonnenfeldt, et al., March 5, 1974, *FRUS 1969–1976*, Vol. 39, doc. 187.

80. Telegram to Vorontsov, Washington, Feb. 25, 1974, RGANI, f.3 op.72 d.602 ll.109–110.

81. Nixon-Kissinger-Gromyko Memcon, Feb. 4, 1974, RMNL, HAK Office Files, Box 71; memorandum from Hartman to Kissinger, "CSCE: Meeting with Vorontsov on Issue of Respect for National Laws and Customs," Feb. 16, 1974, *FRUS 1969–1976*, Vol. 39, doc. 185; telegram from State Department to Stoessel, Moscow, "CSCE: Soviet Suggestions for Basket III," March 9, 1974, RMNL, NSC Files, Box 723, USSR Vol. 30 Oct. 73–April 74; telegram from State Department to Stoessel, Moscow, "CSCE: Soviet Proposal for Basket III Preamble," April 4, 1974, ibid.; memorandum from Hartman to Kissinger, "Your April 12 Meeting with

Gromyko," April 10, 1974, RMNL, NSC Files, Box 404, Briefing Book for Visit of Soviet Foreign Minister Gromyko April 74.

82. Telegram from Stoessel, Moscow, to State Department, "CSCE: Proposals for Basket III Preamble," April 19, 1974, RMNL, NSC Files, Box 723, USSR Vol. 30 Oct. 73–April 74; "Editorial Note," *FRUS 1969–1976*, Vol. 39, doc. 198; and "Editorial Note," ibid., doc. 200.

83. Memorandum from Sonnenfeldt to Kissinger, April 9, 1974, NARA, RG 59, Records of the Office of the Counselor, 1955–1977, Box 8; and editorial note, *FRUS 1969–1976*, Vol. 39, doc. 200.

84. Kissinger-Brandt Memcon, March 24, 1974, ibid., doc. 193. See also letter from Peck, UK Mission to NATO, to Brimelow, FCO, "Soviet/American Relations," Jan. 26, 1973, UKNA, FCO 28/2168; and memorandum from Tickell to Wiggin, "CSCE," Sept. 18, 1973, UKNA, FCO 41/1321.

85. Telegram from Abrams, Geneva, to State Department, "CSCE: Basket III Preamble," June 5, 1974, AAD; memorandum from Stabler to Kissinger, "CSCE: The 'Laws and Customs' Issue in Basket 3," June 6, 1974, *FRUS 1969–1976*, Vol. 39, doc. 208; telegram from Abrams, Geneva, to State Department, "CSCE: Stage II Highlights—June 3–7," June 8, 1974, AAD; and Markku Reimaa, *Helsinki Catch: European Security Accords 1975*, trans. Mark Waller (Helsinki: Edita, 2008) 86–95.

86. Telegram from Hildyard, UK Mission in Geneva, to Douglas-Home, FCO, "Committee III," Feb. 2, 1974, UKNA, FCO 28/2457; AA Memorandum from Gehl, "KSZE – Sachstand," Feb. 7, 1974, PAAA, B28 111509; telegram from Shenston, Geneva, to External Affairs, "CSCE: Basket III General," Feb. 7, 1974, LAC, RG-25, Vol. 9054, File 20-4-CSCE, Vol. 43; and telegram from Hildyard, UK Mission in Geneva, to Douglas-Home, FCO, "Committee III," Feb. 7, 1974, *DBPO* III:II, doc. 65.

87. Memorandum from Stabler to Kissinger, "CSCE: The 'Laws and Customs' Issue in Basket 3," June 6, 1974; letter from Fall, FCO, to Maxey, Geneva, "CSCE: Non-Internvention: Basket III," June 10, 1974, UKNA, FCO 28/2460; and telegram from US Mission in Geneva to State Department, June 24, 1974, *FRUS 1969–1976*, Vol. 39, doc. 219.

88. Telegram from State Department to US Mission in Geneva, June 8, 1974, ibid., doc. 210; telegram from Hildyard, Geneva, to FCO, "CSCE: Committee III," June 13, 1974, UKNA, FCO 28/2460; telegram from US Mission in Geneva to State Department, June 21, 1974, *FRUS 1969–1976*, Vol. 39, doc. 216; telegram from US Mission in Geneva to State Department, June 22, 1974, ibid., doc. 218; telegram from State Department to US Mission in Geneva, June 25, 1974, ibid., doc. 220; telegram from US Mission in Geneva to State Department, June 27, 1974, ibid., doc. 223; entry for June 27, 1974, Sherer Diary; and "Aufzeichnung des Referats 204," June 14, 1974, *AAPD 1974*, doc. 171.

89. Telegram from US Mission in Geneva to State Department, June 25, 1974, ibid., doc. 221; and telegram from Elliott, Geneva, to FCO, "CSCE: The Long Haul," July 29, 1974, UKNA, FCO 41/1547. Gromyko quoted in Anatoliĭ Kovalev, "Midovtsy i genseki," *Novoe Vremia* 38 (1993) 42–47; Kissinger-Gromyko Memcon, April 28, 1974, RMNL, HAK Office Files, Box 71, Gromyko 1973; and letter from Burns, Geneva, to Fall, FCO, "CSCE: Sauvagnargues' Visit to Moscow," July 16, 1974, UKNA, FCO 41/1547.

90. Brezhnev-Gromyko-Nixon-Kissinger Memcon, June 29, 1974, *FRUS 1969–1976*, Vol. 39, doc. 226.

91. Memorandum from Winzer to the Politburo, "Zum gegenwärtigen Stand der Arbeit der Sicherheitskonferenz," July 30, 1974, SAPMO, DY 30/J IV 2/2J/5399; "Notatka delegacji

na II fazę KBWE w Genewie o opiniach szefa delegacji radzieckiej," June 27, 1975, *PDD 1975*, doc. 173; and Fischer, *Neutral Power in the CSCE* 278–290.

92. Memorandum from Tickell to Wiggin and Goulding, "CSCE: Basket III," March 15, 1974, UKNA, FCO 28/2458.

93. Memorandum from Sous-Direction CSCE, "Note concernant les objectifs et méthodes de travail de la CSCE (Commission III)," Sept. 5, 1973, AMAE, CSCE 1969–1975, Box 21.

94. Telegram from Shenstone, Geneva, to External Affairs, "CSCE: General Review," July 30, 1974, LAC, RG-25, Vol. 9054, File 20-4-CSCE, Vol. 46; and Ferraris 331–32.

95. Telegram from Hildyard, UK Mission in Geneva, to Douglas-Home, FCO, "European Political Cooperation: Ministerial Meeting on 4 March: CSCE," Feb. 28, 1974, UKNA, FCO 41/1541; memorandum from Tickell to Wiggin and Goulding, "CSCE: Basket III," March 15, 1974; telegram from Elliott, UK Mission in Geneva, to Callaghan, FCO, "General Situation," March 20, 1974; telegram from Shenstone, Geneva, to External Affairs, "CSCE: General Review," April 6, 1974, LAC, RG-25, Vol. 9054, File 20-4-CSCE, Vol. 44; and telegram from Elliott, UK Mission in Geneva, to Callaghan, FCO, "General Situation," April 6, 1974, UKNA, FCO 28/2456.

96. Memorandum from Tickell to Wiggin, "CSCE"; "Appeal to the Participants at the Consultative Meeting for the Preparation of the Conference on European Security and Collaboration," Nov. 27, 1972, PAAA, B28 109308.

97. Richard Davy, "Intellectuals Fear Neglect of Freedoms," *The Times*, Oct. 12, 1973, 8; and Richard Davy, "Writers Plead for the Lowering of Barriers," *The Times*, June 14, 1974, 6. The text of the appeal is available in UKNA, FCO 28/2460.

98. Telegram from UK Mission in Geneva to FCO, "Basket III Sub-Committees," July 1, 1974, UKNA, FCO 28/2460; "Pilna notatka z wizyty ministra spraw zagranicznych w Danii (fragmenty)," April 16, 1973, *PDD 1973*, doc. 71; and "Notatka wiceministra Czyrka z polsko-francuskich konsultacji w sprawie stosunków dwustronnych i spraw europejskich," May 16, 1973, ibid., doc. 86.

99. Memorandum from Walden to Tickell, "CSCE: Human Contacts," April 16, 1973, UKNA, FCO 28/2172; telegram from External Affairs to Shenstone, Geneva, "CSCE: Tactics," Oct. 3, 1973, LAC, RG-25 Vol. 9054 File 20-4-CSCE Vol. 40; telegram from FCO to UK Mission in Geneva, "CSCE," Oct. 16, 1973, UKNA, FCO 41/1322.

100. Cherniaev, *Sovmestnyĭ iskhod 69*; "V splochennom stroiu sovetskikh respublik," *Pravda*, Aug. 16, 1973, 2; memorandum from US Mission to NATO, "Brezhnev Adopts 'Victory through Contacts' Line," Aug. 30, 1973, UKNA, FCO 28/2174; and telegram from Ford, Moscow, to External Affairs, "Dissent in USSR," Sept. 17, 1973, LAC, RG-25 Vol. 9054 File 20-4-CSCE Vol. 39.

101. "Pilna notatka w sprawie zniesienia obowiązku wizowego w ruchu osobowym z Finlandią," Nov. 23, 1973, *PDD 1973*, doc. 213; telegram from Hildyard, Geneva, to FCO, "CSCE: Polish Performance," April 6, 1974, UKNA, FCO 41/1584; and Gierek-Olszowski-Kissinger Memcon, Oct. 8, 1974, *FRUS 1969–1976*, Vol. 39, doc. 256.

102. Cherniaev, *Sovmestnyĭ iskhod 62*.

103. Tennent H. Bagley, *Spymaster: Startling Cold War Revelations of a Soviet KGB Chief* (New York: Skyhorse, 2013) 243–245; Kashlev, *Khel'sinkskiĭ protsess* 39; Brunner 51–52; telegram from Dale, Geneva, to State Department, "CSCE: Basket III," July 12, 1974, AAD; and interviews with Jaakko Iloniemi and Édouard Brunner, *CSCE Testimonies* 24 and 111.

104. "Projekt pilnej notatki w sprawie propozycji radzieckich w związku z II fazą EKBiW," June 8, 1973, *PDD 1973*, doc. 103; GDR Politburo Memorandum, "Direktive für das Auftreten

der Delegation der DDR während der zweiten Phase der Konferenz für Sicherheit und Zusammenarbeit in Europa," Aug. 21, 1973; "Vorschlag der Delegationen Bulgariens und Polens die Grundrichtungen der Entwicklung der Kulturellen Zusammenarbeit, der Kontakte und des Austauschs im Bereich der Information," n.d. [August 1973], SAPMO, DY 30/J IV 2/2/1464; "Notatka Informacyjna o rezultatach dotychczasowych prac II fazy KBWE," June 26, 1974, Jarząbek, *Polska wobec Konferencji Bezpieczeństwa i Współpracy w Europie*, doc. 13; and "Information über eine Konsultation des Mitglieds des Politbüros und Sekretär des ZK der SED, Genossen Hermann Axen, im ZK der KPdSU am 18. November 1974," Nov. 18, 1974, SAPMO, DY 30/IV 2/2.035/55.

105. Telegram from Shenstone, Geneva, to External Affairs, "CSCE: Review of Human Contacts," Dec. 17, 1973, LAC, RG-25 Vol. 9054 File 20-4-CSCE Vol. 42; letter from Maxey, Geneva, to Fall, FCO, "CSCE: Sub-Committee on Information," May 21, 1974, UKNA, FCO 26/1652; telegram from Hildyard, Geneva, to FCO, "Basket III Sub-Committees," July 20, 1974, UKNA, FCO 28/2461; telegram from Shenstone, Geneva, to External Affairs, "CSCE: General Review," July 30, 1974; and memorandum from V. Matskevich, Soviet Embassy in Prague, Nov. 26, 1973, RGANI, f.5 op.66 d.583 l.334.

106. "Niepodpisana notatka o naradzie Doradczego Komitetu Politycznego Państw-Stron Układu Warszawskiego," April 20, 1974, *PDD 1974*, doc. 104; letter from Brezhnev to Nixon, June 8, 1974, RMNL, Nixon Files, HAK Office Files, Box 69, Dobrynin-Kissinger Correspondence Vol. 22 (Jan.–April 74); and Wilson-Lunkov Memcon, June 10, 1974, UKNA, PREM 16/391.

107. Kissinger-Brezhnev Memcon, March 25, 1974, RMNL, HAK Office Files, Box 76.

108. Kissinger-Brezhnev Memcon, morning of March 26, 1974, RMNL, HAK Office Files, Box 76.

109. Kissinger-Brezhnev Memcon, evening of March 26, 1974, RMNL, HAK Office Files, Box 76; and Ford-Kissinger Memcon, Aug. 15, 1974, *FRUS 1969–1976*, Vol. 39, doc. 243. Kissinger often invoked the specter of burlesque shows in the USSR to mock Western European ideas on freer movement. See Nixon-Kissinger-Brezhnev Memcon, June 29, 1974, ibid., doc. 226; Kissinger-van Lynden Memcon, Aug. 1, 1974, ibid., doc 241; Kissinger-Pungan Memcon, Aug. 26, 1974, ibid., doc. 244; and Ford-Kissinger-Brezhnev Memcon, Nov. 24, 1974, ibid., doc. 261.

110. Kissinger-Genscher Memcon, July 3, 1974, ibid., doc. 230.

111. "Summary Record of a Meeting of the Council held at the Government Conference Centre, Ottawa," June 19, 1974, NATOA, CR(74)28, Part III; telegram from Johnston, Ottawa, to FCO, "NATO Ministerial Meeting 19 June: CSCE," June 19, 1974, UKNA, PREM 16/391; and Kissinger-Sauvagnargues Memcon, July 4, 1974, ibid., doc. 232.

112. "Extract from Paper Agreed by Political Directors at their Meeting in Bonn on 18 April: Informal Translation," May 31, 1974, UKNA, FCO 28/2460; "Aufzeichnung des Ministerialdirektors van Well, z.Z. München," July 6, 1974, *AAPD 1974*, doc. 202.

113. Memorandum from Tickell to Private Secretary, "CSCE: Review of Objectives," July 5, 1974, UKNA, FCO 41/1547.

114. Telegram from Peck, UK Delegation to NATO, to Callaghan, FCO, "Kissinger Briefing: CSCE," July 4, 1974, UKNA, FCO 41/1547; telegram from External Affairs to Canadian Delegation to NATO, "CSCE: Alliance Consultation: Definition of Suitable Outcome," July 9, 1974, LAC, RG-25, Vol. 9054, File 20-4-CSCE, Vol. 46; Kissinger-Callaghan Memcon, July 7, 1974, *FRUS 1969–1976*, Vol. 39, doc. 234; and "Botschafter Krapf, Brüssel (NATO) an das Auswärtige Amt," Sept. 13, 1974, *AAPD 1974*, doc. 262.

115. Kissinger-van Lynden Memcon, Aug. 1, 1974.

116. "Statement by Ambassador Albert W. Sherer, Jr., to the NATO Delegation Heads' Caucus," July 23, 1974, UKNA, FCO 30/2486; Telegram from Hildyard, UK Mission in Geneva, to Callaghan, FCO, "CSCE: NATO Heads of Delegation Meeting 10 July," July 11, 1974, UKNA, FCO 30/2486; Telegram from Groll, FRG Mission in Geneva, to AA, "KSZE: 1. 'Package Deal,' 2. Amerikanische Initiative (Kissinger-Essentiels)," July 23, 1974, PAAA, B123 100008; and telegram from US Mission in Geneva to State Department, July 23, 1974, *FRUS 1969–1976*, Vol. 39, doc. 238.

117. Telegram from Hildyard, UK Mission in Geneva, to Callaghan, FCO, "US Policy towards CSCE," July 24, 1974, UKNA, FCO 30/2486.

118. Memorandum from Hartman to Sonnenfeldt, "CSCE: Allied Study of Minimum Desired Results," July 19, 1974, NARA, RG 59, Records of the Office of the Counselor, 1955–1977, Box 11.

119. Telegram from Shenstone, Geneva, to External Affairs, "CSCE: General Review," Sept. 27, 1974, LAC, RG-25 Vol. 9054 File 20-4-CSCE Vol. 47; memorandum from Figgis to Tickell, "Talks w Mr. Ellsworth and Admiral Steinhaus," Oct. 4, 1974, UKNA, FCO 41/1558; and memorandum from Tickell to Fall, "CSCE: Talk with Mr. Streator," Oct. 21, 1974, UKNA, FCO 41/1227.

120. Letter from Garvey, UK Embassy in Moscow, to Tickell, FCO, "CSCE," Aug. 20, 1974, UKNA, FCO 41/1549; and memorandum from Fall to Tickell, "CSCE: A View from the Résidence Amat," Nov. 11, 1974, UKNA, FCO 28/2456.

121. Henry Kissinger, *Years of Renewal* (New York: Simon and Schuster, 1999) 305–306.

122. Lou Cannon, "Conservatives Weigh Reagan Strategy," *Washignton Post*, Feb. 16, 1975, 1; Ronald Reagan, "Vladivostok Pact on Missiles Contains Dangerous Inequalities," *Human Events*, March 15, 1975, 15; Roland Evans and Robert Novak, "Two Clues about Reagan," *Washington Post*, May 3, 1975, A19; and Garthoff, *Détente and Confrontation* 493.

123. Editorial Note, *FRUS 1969–1976*, Vol. 39, doc. 279; "Dubcek and European Security," *Washington Post*, April 25, 1975, A26; and "What Price Security?" *NYT*, May 26, 1975, 14.

124. Ford-Kissinger Memcon, May 26, 1975, GRFL, National Security Advisor Memoranda of Conversations, 1973–1977, Box 12.

125. Telegram from Delworth, Geneva, to External Affairs, "CSCE: USA Position," Oct. 4, 1974, LAC, RG-25 Vol. 9054 File 20-4-CSCE Vol. 48; telegram from Blech, Geneva, to Auswärtiges Amt, "3. Kommission: Haltung der amerikanischen Delegation," March 18, 1975, PAAA, B123 100010; memorandum from Clift to Kissinger, "Geneva Trip Report: April 15–17," April 19, 1975, GRFL, National Security Adviser—NSC Europe, Canada, and Ocean Affairs Staff: Files, Box 44, Conference on Security and Cooperation in Europe, 1975 (2) WH; and telegram from Hildyard, Geneva, to FCO, "CSCE: State of Play in Baskets I and III," April 19, 1975, UKNA, FCO 30/3012.

126. "Information über eine Konsultation des Mitglieds des Politbüros und Sekretär des ZK der SED, Genossen Hermann Axen, im ZK der KPdSU," Nov. 18, 1974; and "Direktive für das weitere Auftreten der Delegation der DDR während der 2. Phase der Konferenz über Sicherheit und Zusammenarbeit in Europa ab 2.9.1974," Sept. 10, 1974.

127. Telegram from Hildyard, Geneva, to FCO, "State of Play," Nov. 22, 1974, UKNA, FCO 28/2456; memorandum from Alexander to Hildyard, "Lunch with Members of the Soviet Delegation," Nov. 26, 1974, UKNA, FCO 41/1582; and telegram from Delworth, Geneva, to External Affairs, "CSCE: General Assessment," Dec. 21, 1974, LAC, RG-25 Vol. 9054 File 20-4-CSCE Vol. 49.

128. Letter from Alexander, Geneva, to Burns, FCO, "State of Play," March 26, 1975, UKNA, FCO 28/2671; "Record of Conversation of Cde. L. I. Brezhnev with Leaders of Fraternal Parties of Socialist Countries in Budapest," March 18, 1975, CWIHP Digital Archive. Soviet Deputy Foreign Minister Igor Zemskov made the same claim in a meeting with his Eastern European counterparts. See "Notatka wicedyrektora Departamentu Studiów i Programowania na temat radzieckiej oceny KBWE," March 20, 1975, *PDD 1975*, doc. 90.

129. Telegram from Hildyard, Geneva, to FCO, "Basket III," Feb. 11, 1975, UKNA, FCO 41/1781; memorandum from Tickell to Private Secretary, "CSCE: Easter Break," March 27, 1975, UKNA, FCO 41/1769; memorandum from Helman to Hartman, "Your Meeting with Soviet Ambassador Dobrynin," April 29, 1975, NARA, RG 59, Records of the Office of the Counselor, 1955-1977, Box 7, Soviet Union April-May 1975; and memorandum from Burns to Tickell, "CSCE: State of Play," April 29, 1975, UKNA, FCO 41/1769.

130. Briefing note from Gates to Ford, "EC-9 Representatives at CSCE Weakening on Basket III," Feb. 5, 1975, GRFL, National Security Adviser - NSC Europe, Canada, and Ocean Affairs Staff: Files, Box 44, Conference on Security and Cooperation in Europe, 1975 (1) WH; letter from Brezhnev to Ford, March 8, 1975, GRFL, National Security File, Temporary Parallel File of Documents from Otherwise Unprocessed Parts of the Collection, Box A1; and letter from Brezhnev to Wilson, March 8, 1975, UKNA, FCO 41/1770; memorandum from Tickell to Acland, "CSCE: State of Play," April 18, 1975, UKNA, FCO 41/1769; and telegram from Hildyard, UK Mission to Geneva, to Callaghan, FCO, "CSCE: State of Play," April 19, 1975, UKNA, FCO 41/1769.

131. Letter from Alexander, Geneva, to Burns, FCO, "Basket III: Human Contacts," April 25, 1975, UKNA, FCO 28/2671; memorandum from Burns to Tickell, "CSCE: State of Play," April 29, 1975, UKNA, FCO 41/1769; memorandum from French delegation, "Tactique en Commission III," May 2, 1975, AMAE, CSCE 1969–1975, Box 19; telegram from Abrams, Geneva, to State Department, "CSCE Policy: Global Initiative for Human Contacts," May 8, 1975, NARA, RG-59, Conference on Security and Cooperation in Europe, Box 1, CSCE 1973–75: Culture; telegram from Dale, Geneva, to State Department, "CSCE: Human Contacts—Travel," May 14, 1975, NARA, RG-59, Conference on Security and Cooperation in Europe, Box 1, CSCE–Basket 3–Human Contacts; letter from Alexander, Geneva, to Burns, FCO, "Basket III: Human Contacts and Information," May 16, 1975, UKNA, FCO 28/2671; and telegram from Hildyard, UK Mission in Geneva, to Callaghan, FCO, "CSCE: State of Play," May 16, 1975, UKNA, FCO 41/1769.

132. Kovalev, *Iskusstvo vozmozhnogo* 205–206.

133. Telegram from Hildyard, Geneva, to FCO, "CSCE: State of Play," May 8, 1975, UKNA, FCO 41/1769; and telegram from Hildyard, Geneva, to FCO, "CSCE: State of Play," June 7, 1975, UKNA, FCO 41/1769.

134. Editorial Note, *FRUS 1969–1976*, Vol. 39, doc. 290; Briefing Memorandum for Kissinger, n.d. [June 1975], ibid., doc. 296; letter from Alexander, Geneva, to Burns, FCO, "Basket III: Human Contacts and Information," June 6, 1975, UKNA, FCO 41/1780; telegram from Delworth, Geneva, to External Affairs, "CSCE: Here We Go," June 10, 1975, LAC, RG-25 Vol. 9054 File 20-4-CSCE Vol. 54; letter from Mallaby, UK Embassy in Moscow, to Burns, FCO, "CSCE: Soviet Tactics," June 11, 1975, UKNA, FCO 41/1780; letter from Burns, FCO, to Alexander, Geneva, "CSCE: Soviet Tactics," June 12, 1975, ibid; memorandum from Burns to Tickell, "Basket III: Human Contacts and Information," June 12, 1975, *DBPO* III:II, doc. 125; and Alexander 40–57 and 84.

135. Steglich and Leuschner 42; Bock, "Die DDR im KSZE Prozeß," *DDR-Außenpolitik im*

Rückspiegel, 108; and GDR Politburo Memorandum, "Einschätzung der Schlußdokumente der KSZE," July 28, 1975, SAPMO, DY 30/J IV 2/2/1573.

136. "Notatka delegacji na II fazę KBWE w Genewie o opiniach szefa delegacji radzieckiej," June 27, 1975; "Notatka Departamentu Studiów i Programowania w sprawie trzeciego koszyka KBWE," July 8, 1975, *PDD 1975*, doc. 185; and GDR Politburo Memorandum, "Einschätzung der Schlußdokumente der KSZE," July 28, 1975.

137. Brunner 50–51; and Kovalev, *Iskusstvo vozmozhnogo* 214.

138. Brunner 52; Kovalev, *Iskusstvo vozmozhnogo* 184–185 and 253; Bagley 245; Roĭ Medvedev, *Neizvestnyĭ Andropov: Politicheskaia biografiia Iuriia Andropova* (Moscow: Prava Cheloveka, 1999) 155; and Christopher S. Wren, "K.G.B. Chief Says Foreign Foes Lie," *NYT*, June 10, 1975, 11.

139. "Final Act of the Conference on Security and Cooperation in Europe," *The End of the Post-War Era*, 324–343.

140. NATO Memorandum, "List of Issues for Possible Negotiation with the East," July 14, 1969, NATOA, CM(69)34; memorandum from Hillenbrand to Kissinger, "Issues Related to a Conference on Security and Cooperation in Europe," March 15, 1972, RMNL, Nixon Files, NSC Institutional Files, Box H-061, SRG Meeting—European Security Conference—MBFR 3/29/72 (1 of 2); memorandum from Sonnenfeldt to Kissinger, "SRG Meeting March 29—Our Recommendations on MBFR/CSCE Linkage," March 29, 1972, ibid; and memorandum from Kissinger to Nixon, "MBFR-CSCE," n.d. [April 1972], Nixon Files, HAK Office Files, Box 21, HAK's Secret Moscow Trip, TOHAK/HAKTO File April 1972 (1 of 2).

141. NATO Memorandum "Conference on Security and Co-Operation in Europe," May 16, 1972, NATOA, CM(72)24, Vol. 1 (Revised); memorandum from Sonnenfeldt to Kissinger, "Conference on Security and Cooperation in Europe (Summary)," Sept. 2, 1972, RMNL, Nixon Files, NSC Institutional Files, Box H-065, SRG Meeting - CSCE 9/2/72; "Visit of Mr N M Lunkov to London: Record of Conversation," Sept. 18, 1972, UKNA, FCO 28/1707; Johan Jørgen Holst and Karen Alette Melander, "European Security and Confidence-Building Measures," *Survival* 19:4 (1977) 146–154; and Aurel Braun, "Confidence-Building Measures, Security, and Disarmament," *Canada and the Conference on Security and Co-operation in Europe* 202–227. On the rationale for Eisenhower's Open Skies proposal, see James J. Marquardt, "Transparency and Security Competition: Open Skies and America's Cold War Statecraft, 1948–1960," *Journal of Cold War Studies* 9:1 (Winter 2007) 55–87; and David Tal, "From the Open Skies Proposal of 1955 to the Norstad Plan of 1960: A Plan Too Far," *Journal of Cold War Studies* 10:4 (Fall 2008) 66–93.

142. "CSCE: Brief for the United Kingdom Delegation to the Multilateral Preparatory Talks," n.d. [Nov. 1972], UKNA, FCO 41/1067; "Anglo/French Talks on the CSCE Held at the FCO on 10 November," Nov. 10, 1972, UKNA FCO 30/1253; letter from Staples, UK Mission to NATO, to McLaren, FCO, "CSCE: Confidence Building Measures," June 1, 1973, UKNA, FCO 41/1330; letter from Adams, FCO, to Lever, UK Mission to NATO, "CSCE: Confidence Building Measures," June 25, 1973, ibid.; External Affairs memorandum, "Suslov Visit: CSCE—Military Aspects of Security—Confidence-Building Measures (CBMs)," Sept. 13, 1973, LAC, RG-25 Vol. 9054 File 20-4-CSCE Vol. 39; telegram from Hildyard, Geneva, to FCO, "CSCE: Confidence-Building Measures," Nov. 15, 1973, UKNA, FCO 41/1333; memorandum from Tickell to Wiggin, Killick, and Private Secretary, Dec. 20, 1973, UKNA FCO 41/1324; "Aufzeichnung des Vortragenden Legationsrats I. Klasse Ruth," Jan. 4, 1974, *AAPD 1974*, doc. 2; and "European Political Cooperation: CSCE: Confidence Building Measures; Extract of the Dis-

cussion at the Meeting of Political Directors in Dublin on 23 January," Jan. 23, 1975, UKNA, FCO 41/1755.

143. "Speech by the Head of the Soviet Delegation at the Meeting of the Political Consultative Committee," Jan. 25, 1972, PHP; telegram from Kosciusko-Morizet, Washington, to the Quai d'Orsay, "Conversation avec un diplomate Soviétique: CSCE et MBFR," May 25, 1972, AMAE, Affaires Étrangères - Organismes Internationaux et Grandes Questions Internationales - Sécurité - 1971-1976 – 2923; memorandum from Tickell to Wiggin, "The Lunkov Visit," Sept. 18, 1972, UKNA, FCO 41/1011; memorandum from Pieck, "Deutsch-Sowjetische Konsultationen über KSZE," Oct. 3, 1972, PAAA, BA28 109301; letter from du Boulay, Paris, to Tickell, FCO, "CSCE: Soviet Views," Nov. 16, 1972, UKNA, FCO 28/1695; "Projekt pilnej notatki o spotkaniu spraw zagranicznych państw członkowskich Układu Warszawskiego," Nov. 16, 1972, PDD 1972, doc. 212; and Kovalev, Iskusstvo vozmozhnogo 186.

144. Pavel Auersperg, "Spolupráce v Evropě," Rudé Právo Nov. 15, 1972, 7; "Notatka wicepremiera Józefa Tejchmy z rozmowy z sekretarzem generalnym KC RPK," n.d. [Dec. 1972], PDD 1972, doc. 225; memorandum from Drozdenko and Kovalev, Soviet Embassy in Bucharest, "Zapis' besedy s ministrom inostrannykh del SRR Dzh. Makovesku," Feb. 17, 1973; and "Notatka Wydziału Zagranicznego KC PZPR z wizyty sekretarza ds. zagranicznych KC Rumuńskiej Partii Komunistycznej," Dec. 6, 1973, PDD 1973, doc. 222.

145. Memorandum from Gromyko to the Politburo, Dec. 27, 1972; and Steglich and Leuschner 37.

146. Telegram from Elliott, Helsinki, to FCO, "CSCE Preparatory Talks," Jan. 20, 1973, UKNA, FCO 41/1286; letter from Elliott, Helsinki, to FCO, "CSCE/MPT," Feb. 10, 1973, DBPO III:II, doc. 21; telegram from Elliott, Helsinki, to FCO, "CSCE/MPT," March 31, 1973, UKNA, FCO 41/1290; GDR Politburo Memorandum, "Direktive für das weitere Auftreten der Delegation der DDR in der multilateralen Konsultation zur Vorbereitung der Sicherheitskonferenz in Helsinki," April 17, 1973; memorandum from Burns to McLaren and Tickell, "CSCE Disarmament," May 10, 1973, UKNA, FCO 41/1343; memorandum from Service des Pactes et du Désarmement, "Conférence d'Helsinki: Aspects militaires de la sécurité," May 17, 1973, AMAE, CSCE 1969–1975, Box 26; and "CSCE: Draft Report of the Delegation to the Multilateral Preparatory Talks," June 9, 1973.

147. Telegram from Elliott, Helsinki, to FCO, "CSCE/MPT: Confidence Building Measures and Military Aspects of Security," April 5, 1973, UKNA, FCO 41/1329; telegram from Porter, State Department, to US Mission to NATO, "CSCE: Stoessel-Vorontsov Conversation on MPT Developments," April 18, 1973, RMNL, Nixon Files, HAK Office Files, Box 77, Moscow Trip—CSCE; letter from Adams, Helsinki, to Burns, FCO, "CSCE/MPT: Eastern Views," May 10, 1973, UKNA, FCO 28/2176; memorandum from Burns to Wiggin, "CSCE—Meeting of Political Directors on 14 May," May 11, 1973, UKNA, FCO 41/1296; and "Pilna notatka z konferencji państw socjalistycznych poświęconej WRP w Helsinkach," May 23, 1973.

148. Memorandum from Sonnenfeldt to Kissinger, "Your Discussion with Dobrynin on CSCE," Jan. 13, 1973, FRUS 1969–1976, Vol. 39, doc. 123; and Kissinger-Stoessel Telephone Conversation, April 26, 1973, ibid., doc. 144.

149. Telegram from State Department to Vest, Helsinki, "CSCE: CBM's: Policy on Military 'Movements,'" May 3, 1973, AAD; telegram from White, Helsinki, to State Department, "CSCE: CBM: Policy on Military 'Movements,'" May 3, 1973, ibid.; telegram from Elliott, Helsinki, to FCO, "CSCE/MPT," May 19, 1973, UKNA, FCO 41/1292; telegrma from Elliott, Helsinki, to FCO, "CSCE/MPT: Military Aspects of Security," May 30, 1973, UKNA, FCO 41/1330; memorandum to Sharp, "CSCE: Conclusion of Preparatory Talks," June 6, 1973; "Final Rec-

ommendations of the Helsinki Consultations," June 8, 1973, *Selected Documents* 146; MfAA memorandum, "Kurze Problemzusammenstellung zu den Schlußempfehlungen der multilateralen Konsultationen," n.d. [June 1973]; memorandum from Sous-Direction CSCE, "Bilan des 'Recommandations finales' des consultations d'Helsinki," June 19, 1973; "Pilna Notatka dot. stanu przygotowań i udziału PRL w I fazie Europejskiej Konferencji Bezpieczeństwa i Współpracy," June 25, 1973; and telegram from The Hague to the Quai d'Orsay, "Attitude néerlandaise à l'égard de la CSCE," July 5, 1973, AMAE, Affaires Étrangères - Organismes Internationaux et Grandes Questions Internationales - Sécurité - 1971–1976 – 2926.

150. Cherniaev, *Sovmestnyi iskhod* 106; "Proposal by the United Kingdom Delegation: Agenda Item I: Questions Relating to Security in Europe; Confidence Building Measures," July 5, 1973, UKNA, FCO 41/1330; telegram from Hildyard, Geneva, to FCO, "CSCE: Military Aspects of Security," Nov. 27, 1973, UKNA, FCO 41/1333; letter from Burns, Geneva, to Adams, FCO, "CSCE: CBMs: The Soviet Attitude," Dec. 7, 1973, UKNA, FCO 41/1334; and "Notatka Informacyjna o przebiegu i wynikach prac komisji problemowych II fazy Konferencji Bezpieczeństwa i Współpracy w Europie," Dec. 22, 1973, Jarząbek, *Polska wobec Konfe[rencji Bezpieczeństwa i Współpracy w Europie*, doc. 11.

151. Memorandum from Western Organizations Department, "Brief for Meeting of Senior Political Committee of NATO on 23 November," Nov. 22, 1973, UKNA, FCO 41/1333; GDR Politburo Memorandum, "Schlußfolgerungen für das weitere Auftreten der Delegation der DDR," Jan. 15, 1974; memorandum from Adams to Fall, McLaren, and Tickell, "CSCE: The Russians and Confidence Building Measures," March 20, 1974, UKNA FCO 41/1554; telegram from Garvey, Moscow, to FCO, "CSCE," April 25, 1974, UKNA, FCO 41/1546; telegram from Garvey, Moscow, to FCO, "Call on Gromyko: CSCE," June 7, 1974, UKNA, FCO 41/1547; and "Gespräch des Bundesministers Genscher mit dem sowjetischen Außenminister Gromyko auf Schloß Gymnich," Sept. 15, 1974, *AAPD 1974*, doc. 263.

152. Kissinger-Gromyko Memcon, Feb. 4, 1974, *FRUS 1969–1976*, vol. 39, doc. 183; Kissinger-Brezhnev Memcon, March 26, 1974, ibid., doc. 195; Ford-Gromyko Memcon, Sept. 20, 1974, ibid., doc. 247; Kissinger-Gromyko Memcon, Sept. 20, 1974, ibid., doc. 248; Kissinger-Brezhnev Memcon, Oct. 24, 1974, ibid., doc. 257; and Ford-Brezhnev Memcon, Nov. 24, 1974, ibid., doc. 261.

153. Kissinger-Gromyko Memcon, Feb. 4, 1974.

154. Telegram from Hildyard, Geneva, to FCO, "CSCE: Committee I: Confidence-Building Measures: Future Tactics," Dec. 15, 1973, UKNA, FCO 41/1334; telegram from Kissinger, State Department, to US Embassy in London, "CSCE: Confidence-Building Measures," Jan. 25, 1974, UKNA, FCO 41/1553; telegram from State Department to Kissinger, "CSCE: Confidence-building measures (CBMs)," May 23, 1974, *FRUS 1969–1976*, Vol. 39, doc. 205; telegram from Elliott, Geneva, to FCO, "CSCE: General Situation: Political Directors Meeting in Bonn 27–28 May," May 22, 1974, UKNA, FCO 28/2456; briefing note for Callaghan, "The Secretary of State's Visit to Mr. Schlesinger," May 29, 1974, UKNA, FCO 41/1555.

155. Telegram from Hildyard, Geneva, to FCO, "CSCE: Military Aspects of Security," April 8, 1974, UKNA, FCO 41/1555; memorandum from Tickell to Morgan, "CSCE," Nov. 27, 1974; memorandum from Tickell to Morgan, "CSCE: Confidence-Building Measures," Jan. 24, 1975, UKNA, FCO 41/1755; telegram from Dale, Geneva, to State Department, "CSCE: New Position on Prior Notification of Maneuvers," March 12, 1975, GRFL, National Security Adviser - Presidential Country Files for Europe and Canada, Box 13, Switzerland - State Department Telegrams To SECSTATE - NODIS (3); telegram from Dale, Geneva, to State Department, "CSCE: New Soviet Position on Prior Notification of Maneuvers," March 14, 1975, ibid; tele-

gram from Hildyard, Geneva, to FCO, "CSCE: CBMs," March 19, 1975, UKNA, FCO 41/1756; telegram from Petersen, Bucharest, to FCO, "CSCE: Romanian Views," April 4, 1975, UKNA, FCO 41/1784; and Ford-Ceauşescu Memcon, June 11, 1975, *FRUS 1969–1975*, Vol. 39, doc. 299.

156. Memorandum from Elliott to Maxey, July 7, 1974, UKNA, FCO 41/1547; "Record of conversation of Cde. L. I. Brezhnev with Leaders of Fraternal Parties of Socialist Countries in Budapest," March 18, 1975, CWIHP; Kovalev, *Iskusstvo vozmozhnogo* 186–188 and 198–199.

157. "Ministerialdirektor van Well an die Ständige Vertretung bei der NATO in Brüssel," May 30, 1974, *AAPD 1974*, doc. 156; "Gesandter Freiherr von Groll, z.Z. Genf, an das Auswärtige Amt," July 4, 1974, ibid., doc. 196; "Aufzeichnung des Vortragenden Legationsrats Gehl," Jan. 22, 1975, *AAPD 1975*, doc. 13; and "Botschafter Blech, Genf (KSZE-Delegation) an das Auswärtige Amt," March 18, 1975, ibid., doc. 53.

158. Telegram from Kissinger, State Department, to US Mission in Geneva, "CSCE: CBMs: US Position on Notification of Military Movements," Jan. 15, 1975, GRFL, National Security Adviser - Presidential Country Files for Europe and Canada, Box 13, Switzerland - State Department Telegrams From SECSTATE - NODIS (1); Kissinger-Gromyko Memcon, Feb. 16, 1975, *FRUS 1969–1975*, Vol. 39, doc. 270; memorandum from Clift to Kissinger, May 16, 1975, ibid., doc. 282; Kissinger-Gromyko Memcon, May 19, 1975, ibid., doc. 284; telegram from Ingersoll, State Department, to US Mission in Geneva, May 27, 1975, ibid., doc. 292; memorandum from Sonnenfeldt to Kissinger, June 12, 1975, ibid., doc. 300; and Kovalev, *Iskusstvo vozmozhnogo* 204.

159. Telegram from Dale, Geneva, to State Department, "CSCE: Parameters for Maneuver CBM," June 9, 1975, AAD; telegram from Hildyard, Geneva, to FCO, "CSCE: CBMs," June 9, 1975, UKNA, FCO 41/1757; telegram from Dale, Geneva, to State Department, "CSCE: Parameters for Maneuver CBM," June 11, 1975, AAD; "Ministerialdirektor van Well an Botschafter von Staden, Washington," June 11, 1975, *AAPD 1975*, doc. 154; telegram from Callaghan, FCO, to Washington, June 13, 1975, UKNA, PREM 16/392; telegram from Politburo to Kovalev, Geneva, June 20, 1975, RGANI, f.3 op.72 d.673, ll.66–67; entries for June 9 and 10, 1975, Sherer Diary; and Fischer, *Neutral Power* 298–307.

160. Letter from Burns, Geneva, to Fall, FCO, "CSCE: Confidence-Building Measures: The Longer Term," July 16, 1974, UKNA, FCO 41/1557; telegram from Bruce, US Mission to NATO, to State Department, "CSCE: Annex to Public Opinion Guidance Paper," July 23, 1975, AAD; letter from Hildyard, Geneva, to FCO, "CSCE: The Conclusion of Stage II," July 25, 1975, UKNA, FCO 41/1769; and Robert Cooper, *The Breaking of Nations: Order and Chaos in the Twenty-First Century* (London: Atlantic, 2004) 26–28.

161. "Runderlaß des Staatssekretärs Frank," Oct. 25, 1971, *AAPD 1971*, doc. 366; and "Ministerialdirektor von Staden an die Ständige Vertretung bei der NATO in Brüssel," Nov. 23, 1971, ibid., doc. 412; and "Gesandter Boss, Brüssel (NATO), an das Auswärtige Amt," Feb. 11, 1975, *AAPD 1975*, doc. 24.

162. Letter from Grove, Washington, to Braithwaite, FCO, "CSCE: PGRBS," July 31, 1972, UKNA, 41/1065; letter from de Rose, French delegation to NATO, to Quai d'Orsay, "Principes régissant les relations entre États," Feb. 23, 1972, AMAE, CSCE 1969–1975, Box 25; and testimony of Édouard Brunner at Machiavelli Center conference.

163. Telegram from Killick, Moscow, to FCO, "CSCE and MBFR," Aug. 10, 1972, UKNA, FCO 41/1070; memorandum from Adams to McLaren, "Anglo/Finnish Talks 9 and 10 November," Nov. 8, 1972, UKNA, FCO 41/1074; circular telegram from Callaghan, FCO, "Conference on Security and Co-operation (CSCE)," July 28, 1975, *DBPO* III:II, doc. 137; and interview with Sir Brian Fall, BDOHP.

164. West German Aide-Mémoire, March 23, 1972, AMAE, Affaires Etrangères - Europe - République Fédérale d'Allemagne - Politique Extérieure – 1971–1976 – 2982; and memorandum from Fall to Ramsay, "EEC Political Consultations: Sub-Committee on the CSCE," Oct. 10, 1972, UKNA, FCO 28/1686.

165. "Direktivy dlia dvustoronnikh konsul'tatsiï so stranami-uchastnikami Varshavskogo dogovora," Aug. 27, 1969, RGANI, f.3 op.72 d.287 l.29; "Dalsza nasza akcja wokół europejskiej konferencji bezpieczeństwa i współpracy," Sept. 13, 1969; "Vermerk über ein Gespräch des Ministers für Auswärtige Angelegenheiten der DDR, Genossen Otto Winzer, mit dem stellvertretenden Außenminister der UdSSR, Genossen WS Semjonow," Sept. 25, 1969, SAPMO, DY 30/3524; MfAA memorandum, "Working Material for the Preparation of a European Security Conference," Oct. 10, 1969, CWIHP; and memorandum from US mission to NATO, "US-Romanian Consultations," Oct. 17, 1972, UKNA, FCO 28/1694.

166. Telegram from Killick, Moscow, to FCO, "Call on Gromyko: CSCE," June 30, 1972, UKNA, FCO 28/1685; memorandum from German mission to NATO, "Soviet Views on Principles Governing Relations between States," Nov. 2, 1972, UKNA, FCO 41/1066; and letter from Barder, Moscow, to Fall, FCO, "FRG-Soviet Exchanges on CSCE," Nov. 9, 1972, UKNA, FCO 28/1694.

167. Kovalev, *Iskusstvo vozmozhnogo* 208–209; "Notatka Informacyjna Obecna rola KBWE w procesie odprężenia," Nov. 13, 1974; memorandum from Tickell to Morgan, "CSCE: Structure of the Final Document," Feb. 4, 1975, UKNA, FCO 41/1765; GDR Politburo memorandum, "Schlußfolgerungen für das weitere Auftreten der Delegation der DDR," Jan. 15, 1974; and "Notatka informacyjna w sprawie uchwal KBWE," March 8, 1975, *PDD 1975*, doc. 80.

168. Telegram from Hildyard, Geneva, to FCO, "Dutch Final Act," Feb. 14, 1974, UKNA, FCO 41/1573; telegram from Shenstone, Geneva, to External Affairs, "CSCE: Structure of Final Documents," Feb. 15, 1974, LAC, RG-25 Vol. 9054 File 20-4-CSCE Vol. 43; memorandum from Kissinger to Ford, "Status Report on CSCE," April 30, 1975, *FRUS 1969–1976*, Vol. 39, doc. 280; and Kovalev, *Iskusstvo vozmozhnogo* 209. See also Anthony Aust, *Handbook of International Law*, 2nd ed. (New York: Cambridge UP, 2010) 59.

169. Memorandum from Gromyko to the Politburo, Aug. 27, 1969; "Vermerk über ein Gespräch des Ministers für Auswärtige Angelegenheiten der DDR, Genossen Otto Winzer, mit dem stellvertretenden Außenminister der UdSSR, Genossen WS Semjonow," Sept. 25, 1969; telegram from Gould, Luxembourg, to State Department, "Gromyko on CSCE and MBFR," July 12, 1972, RMNL, NSC Files, Box 720, USSR Vol. 23 June–July 72; "Stenogramm des Freundschaftstreffens führender Vertreter der kommunistischen und Arbeiterparteien der sozialistischen Länder," July 31, 1972; and "Proekty zadaniï dlia komissiï obshcheevropeïskogo soveshchaniia," n.d. [Dec. 1972].

170. Memorandum to Cadieux, "European Security: Possible Canadian Initiative," June 2, 1969, NAC, RG-25 Vol. 9054 File 20-4-CSCE Vol. 1; telegram from FCO to Ottawa, "European Security: Permanent Machinery for East-West Relations," Nov. 4, 1970, UKNA, FCO 41/746; telegram from US mission to NATO to State Department, "East-West Negotiations Study: UK Paper on Permanent Machinery," March 16, 1971, NARA, RG 59, Central Foreign Policy Files, 1970-1973, Box 2264, POL 1 Eur E–Eur W 1/1/71; Pompidou-Brandt Memcon, Jan. 22, 1973, AN, 5 AG 2/1012; and Badalassi 178.

171. Telegram from Seydoux, Moscow, to Quai d'Orsay, "Idées soviétiques au sujet de la CSCE," Sept. 22, 1972, AMAE, Affaires Étrangères - Organismes Internationaux et Grandes Questions Internationales - Sécurité – 1971–1976 - 2924; memorandum from Adams to McLaren, "Anglo/Finnish Talks 9 and 10 November"; "Notatka wiceministra Czyrka z polsko-francuskich

konsultacji w sprawie stosunków dwustronnych i spraw europejskich," May 16, 1973, *PDD 1973*, doc. 86; and memorandum from Hartman and Lord to Kissinger, "CSCE," Feb. 6, 1974, NARA, RG-59, Conference on Security and Cooperation in Europe, Box 1 of 6.

172. Memorandum from Burns to Maxey, "CSCE: The Romanian Point of View," Dec. 5, 1973, UKNA, FCO 41/1337; letter from Burns, Geneva, to Adams, FCO, "CSCE: A Romanian Point of View," May 30, 1974, UKNA, FCO 41/1585; "Notatka dyrektora Departamentu Studiów i Programowania na temat instytucjonalizacji współpracy europejskiej po KBWE," March 13, 1975, *PDD 1975*, doc. 84; and Kashlev, *Khel'sinskii protsess* 38.

173. Telegram to Quai d'Orsay, "Objectifs et stratégie des Neuf à la CSCE: Rapport au Comité Politique," Nov. 7, 1973, AMAE, Affaires Étrangères - Organismes Internationaux et Grandes Questions Internationales - Sécurité – 1971–1976 – 2926; and telegram from Delworth, Geneva, to External Affairs, "CSCE: Questions for Review During Christmas/New Year's Break: II: Follow-Up," Dec. 20, 1974, LAC, RG-25 Vol. 9054 File 20-4-CSCE Vol. 49.

174. GDR Politburo Memorandum, "Schlußfolgerungen für das weitere Auftreten der Delegation der DDR," Jan. 15, 1974; and "Notatka wicedyrektora Departamentu Studiów i Programowania na temat radzieckiej oceny KBWE," March 20, 1975, *PDD 1975*, doc. 90.

175. Memorandum from Tickell to Wiggin, Killick, and Goulding, "CSCE: Follow-up to the Conference," April 23, 1974, UKNA, FCO 41/1574; FCO briefing note, "European Political Cooperation: Political Committee," April 8, 1975, UKNA, FCO 41/1776; and memorandum from Hartman to Kissinger, "CSCE," July 8, 1975, *FRUS 1969–1976*, Vol. 39, doc. 312.

176. Pompidou-Brezhnev Memcon, Oct. 27, 1971, AMAE, Secrétariat général - Entretiens et Messages - Vol. 50; telegram from Seydoux, Moscow, to Quai d'Orsay, "Communication de M. Doubinine au sujet de la CSCE," Sept. 21, 1972, AMAE, Affaires Étrangères - Organismes Internationaux et Grandes Questions Internationales - Sécurité – 1971–1976 - 2924; "Tezy do rozmów ministra spraw zagranicznych z sekretarzem stanu USA," Oct. 8, 1974, *PDD 1974*, doc. 195; and "Stenografische Niederschrift des Berichts des Genossen Erich Honecker über sein freundschaftliches Gespräch mit dem Genossen L. I. Breshnew in der Sitzung des Politbüros," June 18, 1975, SAPMO, DY 30/J IV 2/2/1567.

177. Telegram from Shenstone, Helsinki, to External Affairs, "CSCE/MPT: Canadian Position," Nov. 20, 1972, LAC, RG-25 Vol. 9054 File 20-4-CSCE Vol. 26; Schumann-Gromyko Memcon, Jan. 12, 1973, AMAE, Affaires Étrangères - Organismes Internationaux et Grandes Questions Internationales - Sécurité – 1971–1976 – 2926; "Steering Brief for the United Kingdom Delegation," Sept. 13, 1973; memorandum from Kissinger to Nixon, "Meeting with Foreign Minister Gromyko," Sept. 28, 1973, RMNL, NSC Files, Box 722, USSR Vol. 29 May–Oct. 73; memorandum from Tickell to Wiggin, Killick, and Brimelow, "CSCE," Jan. 3, 1974, UKNA, FCO 41/1550; memorandum from Sous-direction CSCE, "Note complémentaire sur la CSCE en vue des entretiens franco-soviétiques," Feb. 13, 1974, AMAE, CSCE 1969–1975, Box 22; telegram from External Affairs to Canadian Delegation to NATO, "CSCE: Satisfactory Outcome," May 2, 1974, LAC, RG-25 Vol. 9054 File 20-4-CSCE Vol. 45; "Summary Record of the Meeting of the Council," May 17, 1974, NATOA, CR(74)17.

178. Pompidou-Heath Memcon, Nov. 16, 1973, AN, 5 AG 2/1015; letter from Elliott, Helsinki, to Tickell, FCO, March 4, 1974, UKNA, FCO 41/1546; letter from Elliott, Helsinki, to Tickell, FCO, "The Soviet Union and the CSCE," March 5, 1974, ibid.; memorandum from Tickell to Wiggin, "Nixon/Brezhnev Summit Meeting: Communiqué," July 3, 1974, UKNA, FCO 69/515; conclusions of a meeting of the Cabinet, July 4, 1974, UKNA, CAB 128/54; telegram from Rush, Paris, to State Department, "Brezhnev Visit: First Impressions," Dec. 9, 1974, GRFL, National Security Adviser - Presidential Country Files for Europe and Canada, Box

17, USSR (6); and telegram from Peck, UK Delegation to NATO, to FCO, "NATO Ministerial Meeting: CSCE," Dec. 13, 1974, UKNA, FCO 41/1544.

179. Kissinger-Brezhnev Memcon, March 25, 1974; memorandum from Halstead, "Call by the USA Ambassador," March 25, 1975, LAC, RG-25 Vol. 9054 File 20-4-CSCE Vol. 51; FCO briefing note, "European Political Cooperation: Ministerial Meeting Bonn," Feb. 14, 1974, UKNA, FCO 41/1541; telegram from Hibbert, Bonn, to FCO, "Dr. Kissinger's Meeting with Herr Genscher 11 June," June 12, 1974, FCO 69/512; letter from Ford to Brezhnev, n.d. [March 1975], *FRUS 1969–1976*, Vol. 39, doc. 279; memorandum from Fall to Tickell, "CSCE: Meeting of the Political Directors on 28 May," May 27, 1974, UKNA, FCO 41/1542; memorandum from Clift to Kissinger, "Your Meeting with Gromyko: Soviet Impatience at CSCE Growing," May 16, 1975; and Yuri Dubinin, "The Road to Helsinki," *International Affairs* (Moscow) 7 (1994) 81–83.

180. Memorandum from Springsteen to Scowcroft, "Issues Paper on CSCE," Jan. 14, 1975, GRFL, National Security Adviser - NSC Europe, Canada, and Ocean Affairs Staff: Files, Box 44, Conference on Security and Cooperation in Europe, 1975 (1) WH; telegram from Dale, Geneva, to State Department, "CSCE: Stage II Highlights May 26–30," May 31, 1975, AAD; letter from Cleghorn, Geneva, to Figgis, FCO, "CSCE: Mediterranean Declaration," June 3, 1975, UKNA, FCO 41/1761; and briefing note for Hattersley, "Call by Mr. Mintoff on the Minister of State," July 1, 1975, UKNA, FCO 41/1761.

181. Memorandum from Gromyko to the Politburo, Dec. 27, 1972; telegram from Elliott, Helsinki, to FCO, "CSCE/MPT: Malta," June 4, 1973, UKNA, FCO 41/1292; telegram from Elliott, Helsinki, to FCO, "CSCE/MPT: Final Plenary," June 8, 1974, ibid.; telegram from Brunner, Geneva, to Auswärtiges Amt, "Abschluß der MV," June 8, 1973, PAAA, B123 100002; letter from Adams, Geneva, to Burns, FCO, "CSCE: Committee I: Mediterranean Contributions (Algeria and Tunisia)," Oct. 12, 1973, UKNA, FCO 41/1335; letter from Andréani, Geneva, to Jobert, Quai d'Orsay, "Contribution des Pays méditerranéens," April 17, 1974, AMAE, CSCE 1969–1975, Box 14.

182. Memorandum from Sous-direction CSCE, "Vues maltaise: La crise de Chypre et le dialogue euro-arabe," Sept. 13, 1974, AMAE, CSCE 1969–1975, Box 15; memorandum from Tickell to Killick, "Malta and the CSCE," Sept. 19, 1974, UKNA, FCO 41/1577; letter from Figgis, FCO, to Cleghorn, Geneva, "CSCE: Maltese Paper," Dec. 11, 1974, UKNA, FCO 41/1578.

183. Jobert-Gromyko Memcon, June 26, 1973, AMAE, CSCE 1969–1975, Box 29; memorandum from Tickell to Bullard, "Assessment of Soviet and East European Positions at the CSCE," July 9, 1973, UKNA, FCO 28/2186; telegram from Hildyard, Geneva, to FCO, "Timing of Stage III and Malta," July 11, 1975, UKNA, FCO 41/1761; telegram from Delworth, Geneva, to External Affairs, "CSCE: Stage III Timing: Canadian Proposal," July 11, 1975, LAC, RG-25 Vol. 9054 File 20-4-CSCE Vol. 56; telegram from Delworth, Geneva, to External Affairs, "CSCE: Stage III Timing," July 14, 1975, ibid.; telegram from Hildyard, Geneva, to FCO, "CSCE: Timing of Stage III and Malta," July 14, 1975, UKNA, FCO 41/1761; letter from Cleghorn, Geneva, to Figgis, FCO, "CSCE: Mediterranean Declaration," July 18, 1975, ibid.; letter from Shaw, Floriana, to James, FCO, "Malta and the CSCE," July 21, 1975, ibid.; Kissinger-Gromyko Memcon, May 19, 1975, *FRUS 1969–1975*, Vol. 39, doc. 284; Kissinger-Gromyko Memcons, July 10, 1975, ibid., docs. 313 and 314; interview with Sir Michael Alexander, Nov. 25, 1998, BDOHP; and interviews with Jiří Opršal and Jacques Andréani, *CSCE Testimonies* 50 and 80.

184. Telegram from Dale, Geneva, to State Department, "CSCE: CBM'S; Turkish and Soviet Exemptions for Area of Application of Maneuvers Measure," June 10, 1975, AAD; telegram

from Dale, Geneva, to State Department, "CSCE: Turkish Problems," July 12, 1975, ibid.; telegram from Hildyard, Geneva, to State Department, "CSCE: CBMs," July 19, 1975, UKNA, FCO 41/1758; telegram from Hildyard, Geneva, to FCO, "CSCE: Agreement on Outstanding Issues and Confirmation on the Date of 30 July for Stage III," July 19, 1975, UKNA, FCO 41/1769; telegram from Hildyard, Geneva, to FCO, "CSCE: Close of Play," July 21, 1975, ibid; and telegram from Blech, Geneva, to Auswärtiges Amt, "KSZE—letzte Sitzung des Koordinationsausschusses," July 22, 1975, PAAA, B123 100013.

185. Telegram from the Nationalities Council of Michigan to Ford, July 23, 1975, GRFL, America Since Hoover Collection, 1929-80, Box 11, US-Soviet Relations—Conference on Security and Cooperation in Europe (Helsinki); and Ford conversation with Bobelis et al., July 25, 1975, *FRUS 1969–1975*, Vol. 39, doc. 322. See also the letters of protest in GRFL, National Security Adviser - NSC Europe, Canada, and Ocean Affairs Staff: Files, Box 44, Conference on Security and Cooperation in Europe, 1975 (4) WH.

186. "European 'Security' and Real Détente," *NYT*, July 21, 1975, 14; and "Jerry, Don't Go," *Wall Street Journal*, July 23, 1975, 14.

187. James M. Naughton, "Ford Sees 35-Nation Charter as a Gauge on Rights in East Europe," *NYT*, July 26, 1975, 2.

188. Deutscher Bundestag, *Stenographisher Bericht*, 7. Wahlperiod, 183. Sitzung, July 25, 1975, 12865; and Bernd Schaefer, " 'Europe must not become Greater Finland': Opponents of the CSCE–the German CDU/CSU and China," *Origins of the European Security System* 135–136.

189. "Text of Remarks at a Meeting with Representatives of Americans of Eastern European Background Concerning the Conference on Security and Cooperation in Europe," July 25, 1975, *Public Papers of the Presidents: Gerald R. Ford 1975 [PPP:GRF]*, Book II, doc. 430; and Ford-Kissinger Memcon, Aug. 4, 1975, *FRUS 1969–1975*, Vol. 39, doc. 337.

190. Deutscher Bundestag, *Stenographisher Bericht*, 7. Wahlperiod, 183. Sitzung, July 25, 1975, 12797–12803 and 12825–12830. See also "Bundesminister Genscher an Staatssekretär Frank, Bundespräsidialamt," July 7, 1975, *AAPD 1975*, doc. 191.

191. Kovalev, *Iskusstvo vozmozhnogo* 201–202; Cherniaev, *Moia zhizn' i moe vremia* 291–292 and 304; Yuri Kashlev, "The CSCE in the Soviet Union's Politics," *International Affairs* (Moscow) 11–12 (1995) 68; Kashlev, *Khel'sinkskiĭ protsess* 45; A. L. Adamishin, "Zakliuchitel'nyĭ Akt: zanaves opuskaetsia?" *Rossiia v Global'noĭ Politike* 4 (August 2005) 100; and Mark Sandle, "A Triumph of Ideological Hairdressing? Intellectual Life in the Brezhnev Era Reconsidered," *Brezhnev Reconsidered* 145–147.

192. Nixon-Gromyko Memcon, Feb. 4, 1974, *FRUS 1969–1976*, Vol. 39, doc. 184; Kissinger-Brezhnev Memcon, March 26, 1974, ibid., doc. 196; Dobrynin 351; Adamishin 99; Savranskaya, "Unintended Consequences" 180.

193. "Notatka sekretariatu KC PZPR o rozmowie I sekretarza KC PZPR z sekretarzem generalym KC KPZR," June 23, 1975, *PDD 1975*, doc. 170; Kovalev, *Iskusstvo vozmozhnogo* 202; Kashlev, "The CSCE in the Soviet Union's Politics" 68; Deriabin, *Legko li byt' poslom?* 212; Andrei Grachev, *Kremlevskaia khronika* (Moscow: Eksmo, 1994) 64; and Savranskaya, "Unintended Consequences," 180.

194. "Protokol Zasedaniia Politbiuro Tsentral'nogo Komiteta KPSS," July 24, 1975, RGANI, f.3 op.72 d.679 ll.2–3; Kovalev, *Iskusstvo vozmozhnogo* 217–219; Adamishin 99–100; and English 154.

195. Steglich and Leuschner 53; Bock, "Die DDR im KSZE Prozeß," *DDR-Außenpolitik im Rückspiegel* 112; and Hermann Wentker, *Außenpolitik in engen Grenzen: Die DDR im internationalen System 1949–1989* (Munich: Oldenbourg, 2007) 447–448.

196. Telegram from Callaghan, FCO, to Certain Missions, "Conference on Security and Co-operation (CSCE)," July 28, 1975, UKNA, FCO 66/793.

197. Leonov 164; and Iurii Kvitsinskii, *Vremia i sluchai: Zametki professionala* (Moscow: Olma-Press, 1999) 313–314.

198. Leonid Kornilov, "Leonid Il'ich ne znal, chto zipuenaet [*sic*] mekhanizm perestreïki," *Izvestiia*, July 21, 1995, 5.

199. Leonov 164–165.

200. Letter from Brown, FCO, to Timms, Sofia, "CSCE: Freer Movement," Feb. 12, 1973, UKNA, FCO 28/2173; telegram from Delworth, Geneva, to External Affairs, "CSCE: Last Thoughts," Aug. 21, 1975, Personal Papers of W. Thomas Delworth, Ottawa; Bock, "Die DDR im KSZE Prozeß," *DDR-Außenpolitik im Rückspiegel* 109; and Alexander 91.

201. André Glucksmann, *La cuisinière et le mangeur d'hommes: Essai sur les rapports entre l'Etat, le marxisme et les camps de concentration* (Paris: Seuil, 1975); Bernard-Henri Lévy, *La barbarie à visage humain* (Paris: Grasset, 1977); and Tony Judt, *Marxism and the French Left: Studies on Labour and Politics in France, 1830–1981* (New York: NYU Press, 2011) 197–198.

202. Letter from Garvey, Moscow, to Tickell, FCO, "CSCE," Aug. 20, 1974, UKNA, FCO 41/1549. The book was A. V. Kukarkin, *Po tu storonu rastsveta: Burzhuaznoe obshchestvo: kul'tura i ideologiia* (Moscow: Politizdat, 1974).

203. Bock, "Die DDR im KSZE Prozeß," *DDR Aussenpolitik im Rückspiegel* 112; Oliver Bange, *Sicherheit und Staat: Die Bündnis- und Militärpolitik der DDR im internationalen Kontext 1969 bis 1990* (Berlin: Ch. Links, 2017) 256–259; and Jens Gieseke and Doris Hubert, *Die DDR-Staatssicherheit: Schild und Schwert der Partei* (Bonn: Bundeszentrale für politische Bildung, 2001) 86.

204. James J. Sheehan, "The Problem of Sovereignty in European History" *American Historical Review* 111:1 (Feb.. 2006) 1–15; and Brunner 52.

205. Nixon-Kissinger-Brezhnev Memcon, June 29, 1974; Kissinger-Gromyko Memcon, Feb. 4, 1974; letter from Hildyard, Geneva, to Callaghan, FCO, "CSCE: The Conclusion of Stage II," July 25, 1975; and Sheehan, "The Problem of Sovereignty in European History" 6–7.

206. Telegram from Politburo to Kovalev, Geneva, June 20, 1975; GDR Politburo Memorandum, "Bericht über die Ergebnisse der 2. Phase der europäischen Sicherheitskonferenz," July 28, 1975, SAPMO, DY 30/J IV 2/2/1573; GDR Politburo Memorandum, "Einschätzung der Schlußdokumente der KSZE," July 28, 1975, SAPMO, DY 30/J IV 2/2/1573; and Polish Ministry of Foreign Affairs Memorandum, "Notatka Informacyjna o koncowych wynikach II fazy KBWE," July 24, 1975, *Polska Wobec Konferencji Bezpieczenstwa i Współpracy w Europie*, doc. 15.

CHAPTER 7: THE PENS OF AUGUST

1. Kaius Niemi, "When Andrei Gromyko Fell in My Lap," *Helsingin Sanomat* (International Edition) Aug. 2, 2005.

2. Alan Hamilton, "Mr. Wilson has a Busy, Busy Day," *The Times*, July 31, 1975, 14; and Flora Lewis, "Event May Be Historic, But Talk Is Often Small," *New York Times*, Aug. 1, 1975, 2.

3. Jonathan Steele, "Heads Together," *Guardian*, July 31, 1975, 11.

4. Aldo Beckman, "European Supersummit Called Start of New Era," *Chicago Tribune*, July 31, 1975, 2.

5. Steele, "Heads Together."

6. Urho Kekkonen's speech in *Human Rights, European Politics, and the Helsinki Accord*, Vol. 6, 7.

7. Niemi, "When Andrei Gromyko Fell in My Lap."

8. David Spanier, "Helsinki Moves Out its Drunks for Opening of Security Conference," *The Times*, July 30, 1975, 5.

9. Kavass et al., eds., Vol. 6, 16. On Wilson's objectives for the speech, which he drafted himself, see "Prime Minister's Speech at the CSCE Conference in Helsinki: 30 July," July 23, 1975, UKNA, PREM 16/392. Despite warnings from FCO officials, Wilson referred favorably to "peaceful coexistence," presenting it as the only alternative to "co-death." Memorandum from Burns to Tickell, "CSCE: Stage III: Prime Minister's Statement," July 28, 1975, UKNA, FCO 41/1774/2; and Bernard Donoughue, *Downing Street Diary: With Harold Wilson in No. 10* (London: Jonathan Cape, 2005) 482–483.

10. Ibid. 128; Sargent 218–219; and Richard Davy and David Spanier, "Ford Plea for Helsinki Promises to be Kept," *The Times*, Aug. 2, 1975, 1.

11. Kavass et al., eds., Vol. 6, 110.

12. Ibid. 104–105.

13. Ibid. 96.

14. Ibid. 131.

15. Ibid. 65; Renaud Rosset, "Deux discours vedettes," *Le Figaro*, Aug. 1, 1975, 2; Jonathan Steele, "Brezhnev Goes to Defence of Nations' Sovereign Rights," *Guardian*, Aug. 1, 1975, 2; and Kovalev, *Iskusstvo vozmozhnogo* 220–221.

16. Kavass et al., eds., Vol. 6, 64.

17. Ibid. 61.

18. Ibid. 62.

19. Ibid. 30.

20. Ibid. 54.

21. Ibid. 54.

22. Ibid. 150–153. See also Richard Davy, "Differences among Communist Leaders in Translating the Language of Détente," *The Times*, Aug. 12, 1975, 12.

23. Peter Hebblethwaite, "The Vatican's Last Word at Helsinki," *The Times*, Aug. 9, 1975, 14. The CSCE was the first international conference in which the Vatican had participated since the Congress of Vienna.

24. Kavass et al., eds., Vol. 6, 178.

25. Christopher Wren, "Curtain Falls Softly," *NYT*, Aug. 2, 1975, 8; "Et ils s'applaudirent à la russe," *Le Figaro*, Aug. 2–3, 1975, 2; Mikko Pyhälä, "The Signing: Panic, and a Sigh of Relief," *OSCE Magazine*, October 2005, 24; Davy and Spanier, "Ford Plea for Helsinki"; and Maresca 196–197.

26. Kavass et al., eds., Vol. 6, 180.

27. Maresca 197–198.

28. "Ob itogakh Soveshchaniia po bezopasnosti i sotrudnichestvu v Evrope," Aug. 5, 1975, RGANI, f. 3, op. 72, d. 684, ll. 7–11.

29. Steglich and Leuschner 50; "Sprawozdanie z III-ej fazy Konferencji Bezpieczeństwa i Współpracy w Europie," Aug. 2, 1975, *PDD 1975*, doc. 211. See also "Bericht zum Verlauf und zu den Ergebnissen der Konferenz über Sicherheit und Zusammenarbeit in Europa," Aug. 5, 1975, SAPMO, DY 30/J IV 2/2/1575.

30. "Ob itogakh Soveshchaniia po bezopasnosti i sotrudnichestvu v Evrope," Aug. 5, 1975; and "Bericht zum Verlauf und zu den Ergebnissen der Konferenz über Sicherheit und Zusammenarbeit in Europa," Aug. 5, 1975. A few months later, Honecker told Brezhnev, "After Helsinki, a new stage has begun in our struggle for détente in order to guarantee peace." "Stenografische Niederschrift der Verhandlungen der Partei- und Staatsdelegationen der DDR und der UdSSR in Moskau," Oct. 6, 1975, *Risse im Bruderbund* 102.

31. Sh. Sanakoyev, "A New Milestone in European History," *International Affairs* 10 (1975) 1, 13.

32. Yu. Zhukov and Yu. Kuznetsov, "Pobeda razuma," *Pravda*, Aug. 2, 1975, 7.

33. "Repräsentanten von 35 Staaten signierten die Schlußakte der Konferenz von Helsinki," *Neues Deutschland*, Aug. 2–3, 1975, 1.

34. Ryszard Wojna, "Materializacja historycznej idei," *Trybuna Ludu*, July 29, 1975, 2; and Ryszard Wojna, "Nowa jakość sytuacji," *Trybuna Ludu*, Aug. 4, 1975, 2.

35. Malcolm Browne, *NYT*, Aug. 2, 1975; and Karel Outrata, "Nóta konferenci v Helsinkách," *Rudé Pravó*, Aug. 2, 1975, 5.

36. See "Békénkért, biztonságunkért," *Népszabadság*, July 30, 1975, 1; "A harmincöt küldöttség vezetője aláírta a tanácskozás záróokmányát," *Népszabadság*, Aug. 2, 1975, 1; "V interes na vsichki narodi," *Rabotnichesko Delo*, July 29, 1975, 1; "V imeto na mira, signurnostta i sŭtrudnichestvoto v Evropa i sveta," *Rabotnichesko Delo*, Aug. 2, 1975, 1; "Un eveniment istoric în viată continentului," *Scînteia*, July 30, 1975, 1.

37. Yu. Zhukov and Yu. Kuznetsov, "Pered zavershayushchim etapom," *Pravda*, July 29, 1975, 4. The Chekhov story is "Man in a Case." See Anton Chekhov, *The Lady with the Little Dog and Other Stories*, trans. Ronald Wilks (London: Penguin, 2002) 61–73.

38. "West Accused by Soviet on Helsinki Security Text," *NYT*, Nov. 19, 1975, 8. Another source puts the papers' combined circulation at 18.5 million. See Matthias Peter, *Die Bundesrepublik im KSZE-Prozess* (Berlin: De Gruyter Oldenbourg, 2015) 556. For the full text, see "Zakliuchitel'nyi Akt," *Pravda*, Aug. 2, 1975, 2–6; and "Zakliuchitel'nyi Akt," *Izvestiia*, Aug. 2, 1975, 2–6.

39. "Schlußakte der Konferenz über Sicherheit und Zusammenarbeit in Europa," *Neues Deutschland*, Aug. 2–3, 1975, 5–10; Snyder, *Human Rights Activism and the End of the Cold War* 71. Three other East German periodicals also printed the Final Act in full, raising its total circulation to two million copies.

40. "Závěrečný Akt," *Rudé Právo*, Aug. 6, 1975, 3–6.

41. "Dokument końcowy Konferencji Bezpieczeństwa i Współpracy w Europie," *Trybuna Ludu*, Aug. 2–3, 1975, 3; "Charta mírové spolupráce Evropy," *Rudé Právo*, Aug. 2, 1975, 3; "Az európai biztonsági és együttműködési értekezlet Helsinkiben aláírt záróokmánya," *Népszabadság*, Aug. 3, 1975, 3; and "Zakliuchitelen akt na Obshtoevropeiskoto sŭveshtanie," *Rabotnichesko Delo*, Aug. 2, 1975, 1, 6; and "Un succes important, o etapă nouă care impune eforturi și mai intense pentru edificarea securităţii europene," *Scînteia*, Aug. 3, 1975, 6.

42. Memorandum from V. Pavlov, Budapest, "O reaktsii v VNR na itogi Obshcheevropeĭskogo Soveshchaniia v Khel'sinki (Informatsiia)," Sept. 12, 1975, RGANI, f. 5, op. 68, d. 1493, ll. 93–99. The Polish government published the Final Act in a policy journal, bookended by interpretive commentary and Edward Gierek's summit speech. See *Sprawy Międzynarodowe* 28:10 (October 1975). Combined with the Final Act's widespread circulation in the USSR and East Germany, this fact seems to contradict Romuald Spasowski's claim that the Soviets ordered

the Poles to embargo the text of the agreement. See Romuald Spasowski, *The Liberation of One* (New York: Harcourt Brace Jovanovich, 1986) 548–549.

43. Auswärtiges Amt Memorandum, "Nach der KSZE," Aug. 1, 1975, PAAA B28 111546; and Auswärtiges Amt Memorandum, July 27, 1975, PAAA, B28 111548.

44. Telegram from Callaghan, FCO, "Conference on Security and Co-operation (CSCE)," July 29, 1975, UKNA, FCO 66/793; telegram from Callaghan, FCO, "Conference on Security and Co-operation (CSCE)," July 28, 1975, UKNA, FCO 66/793; and telegram from Delworth, Geneva, to External Affairs, "CSCE: Last Thoughts."

45. Kissinger-Thorn Memcon, Aug. 1, 1975, *FRUS 1969–1976*, Vol. 39, doc. 333; see also "Talking Points on European Trip," Aug. 9, 1975, GRFL, National Security Adviser, Staff Assistant Peter Rodman: Files (1970) 1974–77 Box 2, Chronological File, July–October 1975.

46. Cabinet Meeting, Aug. 8, 1975, *FRUS 1969–1976*, Vol. 39 doc. 339, footnote 9; see also Cabinet Meeting Memorandum of Conversation, Aug. 8, 1975, GRFL, National Security Adviser Memoranda of Conversations, 1973–1977, Box 14, Aug. 8, 1975 - Cabinet Meeting.

47. "Interview with Paul Duke and Martin Agronsky of the Public Broadcasting Service," Aug. 7, 1975, *PPP:GRF 1975: Book II*, doc. 479; telegram from Callaghan, FCO, "Conference on Security and Co-operation (CSCE)," July 28, 1975; memorandum from Killick to Cartledge, "Conclusion of CSCE," Aug. 4, 1975, UKNA, FCO 41/1769; and memorandum from Allen MacEachen to Cabinet, "Conference on Security and Cooperation in Europe," July 21, 1975, NAC, RG-25, Vol. 9054, File 20-4-CSCE, Vol. 58.

48. Memorandum from Elliott, Helsinki, to Callaghan, FCO, "The CSCE Summit: Finland's Place in the Sun," Aug. 12, 1975, UKNA, FCO 41/1774/3; memorandum from Killick to Cartledge, "Conclusion of CSCE," Aug. 4, 1975, UKNA, FCO 41/1769; and telegram from Callaghan, FCO, "Conference on Security and Co-operation (CSCE)," July 29, 1975.

49. Don Cook, "Reds Facing Adjustments on People's Rights," *Los Angeles Times*, Aug. 2, 1975, A14.

50. Jonathan Steele, "A Fire under the Cold War," *Guardian*, July 30, 1975, 3. See also "The Congress of Helsinki," *The Times*, Aug. 2, 1975, 13.

51. Andreas Kohlschütter, "Nüchtern zum Gipfel," *Die Zeit*, Aug. 1, 1975, 1.

52. Raymond Aron, "La Foire aux diplomates," *Le Figaro*, July 30, 1975, 1–2; and Raymond Aron, "Le Congrès parle," *Le Figaro*, Aug. 2–3, 1975, 1–2.

53. André Fontaine, "Les mots et les choses," *Le Monde*, July 29, 1975.

54. Matthias Walden, "Der finnische Zauberberg," *Die Welt*, Aug. 2–3, 1975, 1; and Axel Springer, "Von Jalta bis Helsinki—immer gibt der Westen nach," *Die Welt*, Aug. 7, 1975, 2.

55. "Speech to Chelsea Conservative Association," July 26, 1975, Margaret Thatcher Foundation. Available at: www.margaretthatcher.org.

56. "Solzhenitsyn Warns Congress of Pacts," *Los Angeles Times*, July 16, 1975, B11; letter from George Kennan to Patricia Davies, Aug. 9, 1975, George Kennan Papers, Mudd Library, Princeton University, Box 10, Folder 12; George Urban, "A Conversation with George F. Kennan," *Encounter* (September 1976) 42; and Robert Conquest, "Proverbs of Détente," *National Review*, Jan. 23, 1976, 31. I am grateful to John Gaddis for sharing Kennan's letter with me.

57. Telegram from Callaghan, FCO, "Conference on Security and Co-operation (CSCE)," July 29, 1975, UKNA, FCO 66/793; and George W. Ball, "Capitulation at Helsinki," *Newsweek*, Aug. 4, 1975, 13.

58. "Verbatim Record of the Talks between the Prime Minister and M. Deng Xiaoping," May 12, 1975, CWIHP.

59. Tickell, FCO, to Youde, Peking, "Briefing of the Chinese on NATO Summit and East/West Negotiations," June 5, 1975, UKNA, FCO 41/1769.

60. Quoted in David Bonavia, "China Sees Helsinki as Another Munich," *The Times*, Aug. 1, 1975, 6.

61. "Pilna Notatka, Narada ministrów spraw zagranicznych krajów wspólnoty socjalistycznej w Moskwie (15–16.XII.1975)," Dec. 31, 1975, *PDD 1975*, doc. 351. See also "Zapis z posiedzenia Kierownictwa MSZ w dniu 8.IX.1975 r.," Sept. 8, 1975, *PDD 1975*, doc. 233; "Okólnik wiceministra Kułagi: instrukcja w sprawie interpretacji Aktu końcowego KBWE," Sept. 23, 1975, *PDD 1975*, doc. 243; "Kierunki Działania PRL w Związku z Realizacją Uchwał Konferencji Bezpieczeństwa i Współpracy w Europie," Dec. 1, 1975, *PDD 1975*, doc. 320; and "Zapis' besedy s zamestitelem ministra inostrannykh del PNR Eugeniushem Kulagoï," Oct. 16, 1975, RGANI f.5, op.68, d.1816, ll. 117–119.

62. CPSU Central Committee Memorandum, "Meropriiatiia sviazannye s realizatsieï nekotorykh polozheniï i dogovorennosteï, zafiksirovannykh v Zakliuchitel'nom akte Obshcheevropeïskogo soveshchaniia, po voprosam sotrudnichestva v gumanitarnykh i drugikh oblastiakh (informatsiia, kul'tura, obrazovanie)," Dec. 11, 1975, RGANI f.3, op.72, d.703, ll.75–81; SED Politburo Memoranda, "Bericht über die Ergebnisse der 2. Phase der europäischen Sicherheitskonferenz," "Einschätzung der Schlußdokumente der KSZE," and "Vorschlag für die Berichterstattung von der 3. Phase der Konferenz über Sicherheit und Zusammenarbeit in Europa in Presse, Rundfunk und Fernsehen," July 28, 1975, SAPMO, DY 30/J IV 2/2/1573; Honecker's Report to the SED Politburo, "Bericht zum Verlauf und zu den Ergebnissen der Konferenz über Sicherheit und Zusammenarbeit in Europa," Aug. 5, 1975, SAPMO DY 30/J IV 2/2/1575.

63. CPSU CC Memorandum, "Meropriiatiia sviazannye s realizatsieï nekotorykh polozheniï i dogovorennosteï, zafiksirovannykh v Zakliuchitel'nom akte Obshcheevropeïskogo soveshchaniia, po voprosam sotrudnichestva v gumanitarnykh i drugikh oblastiakh (informatsiia, kul'tura, obrazovanie)," Dec. 11, 1975.

64. "Okólnik wiceministra Kułagi: instrukcja w sprawie interpretacji Aktu końcowego KBWE," Sept. 23, 1975.

65. Ibid.

66. Memorandum from V. Pavlov, Budapest, "O reaktsii v VNR na itogi Obshcheevropeïskogo Soveshchaniia v Khel'sinki (Informatsiia)," Sept. 12, 1975.

67. Memorandum from Oskar Fischer, Dec. 5, 1975, PAAA, Bestand MfAA C 3785. See also Memorandum from V. Pavlov, Budapest, "O reaktsii v VNR na itogi Obshcheevropeïskogo Soveshchaniia v Khel'sinki (Informatsiia)," Sept. 12, 1975.

68. CPSU CC Memorandum, "Meropriiatiia sviazannye s realizatsieï nekotorykh polozheniï i dogovorennosteï, zafiksirovannykh v Zakliuchitel'nom akte Obshcheevropeïskogo soveshchaniia, po voprosam sotrudnichestva v gumanitarnykh i drugikh oblastiakh (informatsiia, kul'tura, obrazovanie)," Dec. 11, 1975.

69. "Sprawozdanie z III-ej fazy Konferencji Bezpieczeństwa i Współpracy w Europie," Aug. 2, 1975, *PDD 1975*, doc. 211.

70. CPSU CC Memorandum, "O meropriiatiiakh, sviazannykh s realizatsieï nekotorykh polozheniï I dogovorennosteï Zakliuchitel'nogo akta Obshcheevropeïskogo soveshchaniia," Dec. 11, 1975, RGANI f.3, op.72, d.703, ll.72–74; CPSU CC Memorandum, "Meropriiatiia sviazannye s realizatsieï nekotorykh polozheniï i dogovorennosteï, zafiksirovannykh v Zakliuchitel'nom akte Obshcheevropeïskogo soveshchaniia, po voprosam sotrudnichestva v gumanitarnykh i drugikh oblastiakh (informatsiia, kul'tura, obrazovanie)," Dec. 11, 1975;

"Kierunki Działania PRL w Związku z Realizacją Uchwał Konferencji Bezpieczeństwa i Współpracy w Europie," Dec. 1, 1975; "Notatka informacyjna o polsko-czechosłowackich negocjacjach umowy o współpracy kulturalnej i naukowej (fragmenty)," Dec. 10, 1975, *PDD 1975*, doc. 327; "Zapis' besedy s zamestitelem ministra inostrannykh del PNR Eugeniushem Kulagoï," Oct. 16, 1975; Memorandum from V. Pavlov, Budapest, "O reaktsii v VNR na itogi Obshcheevropeïskogo Soveshchaniia v Khel'sinki (Informatsiia)," Sept. 12, 1975; Memorandum from V. Ia. Pavlov, Budapest, "Zapis' besedy s chlenom TsK VSPR, ministrom inostrannykh del VNR tov. Frid'eshem Puïeï," Aug. 26, 1975, RGANI, f.5, op.68, d.1517, ll.183–189; memorandum from G.I. Ragulin, Warsaw, "Zapis' besedy s zam. ministra inostrannykh del PNR Iuzefom Chirekom," Oct. 15, 1975, RGANI, f.5, op.68, d.1816, ll.110–113; and "Evaluation of the Helsinki Final Act by the Czechoslovak Party Presidium," April 28, 1976, *A Cardboard Castle?* doc. 78.

71. CPSU CC Memorandum, "Meropriiatiia sviazannye s realizatsieï nekotorykh polozheniï i dogovorennosteï, zafiksirovannykh v Zakliuchitel'nom akte Obshcheevropeïskogo soveshchaniia, po voprosam sotrudnichestva v gumanitarnykh i drugikh oblastiakh (informatsiia, kul'tura, obrazovanie)," Dec. 11, 1975.

72. Ibid. and "Evaluation of the Helsinki Final Act by the Czechoslovak Party Presidium," April 28, 1976.

73. Ibid.

74. CPSU CC Memorandum, "Meropriiatiia sviazannye s realizatsieï nekotorykh polozheniï i dogovorennosteï, zafiksirovannykh v Zakliuchitel'nom akte Obshcheevropeïskogo soveshchaniia, po voprosam sotrudnichestva v gumanitarnykh i drugikh oblastiakh (informatsiia, kul'tura, obrazovanie)," Dec. 11, 1975.

75. "Okólnik wiceministra Kułagi: instrukcja w sprawie interpretacji Aktu końcowego KBWE," Sept. 23, 1975; Memorandum from V. Pavlov, Budapest, "O reaktsii v VNR na itogi Obshcheevropeïskogo Soveshchaniia v Khel'sinki (Informatsiia)," Sept. 12, 1975; "Zapis z posiedzenia Kierownictwa MSZ w dniu 8.IX.1975 r.," Sept. 8, 1975; "Notatka Informacyjna o wizycie w Polsce ministra SZ Kanady, Allana J. MacEachena (29 września - 4 października 1975)," October 1975, *PDD 1975*, doc. 266; "Szyfrogram ambasadora w Waszyngtonie o amerykańskich interwencjach w sprawie łączenia rodzin," Oct. 17, 1975, *PDD 1975*, doc. 272; "Problematyka Łączenia Rodzin w Świetle 'Trzeciego Koszyka' KBWE i Zadania Praktyczne," Dec. 5, 1975, *PDD 1975*, doc. 325.

76. "Kierunki Działania PRL w Związku z Realizacją Uchwał Konferencji Bezpieczeństwa i Współpracy w Europie," Dec. 1, 1975.

77. "Kierunki Działania PRL w Związku z Realizacją Uchwał Konferencji Bezpieczeństwa i Współpracy w Europie," Dec. 1, 1975; CPSU Central Committee Memorandum, "Meropriiatiia sviazannye s realizatsieï nekotorykh polozheniï i dogovorennosteï, zafiksirovannykh v Zakliuchitel'nom akte Obshcheevropeïskogo soveshchaniia, po voprosam sotrudnichestva v gumanitarnykh i drugikh oblastiakh (informatsiia, kul'tura, obrazovanie)," Dec. 11, 1975; "Zapis' besedy s zamestitelem ministra inostrannykh del PNR Eugeniushem Kulagoï," Oct. 16, 1975; Svetlana Savranskaya, "Unintended Consequences: Soviet Interests, Expectations and Reactions to the Helsinki Final Act," *Helsinki 1975* 184; and "Evaluation of the Helsinki Final Act by the Czechoslovak Party Presidium," April 28, 1976.

78. "Kierunki Działania PRL w Związku z Realizacją Uchwał Konferencji Bezpieczeństwa i Współpracy w Europie," Dec. 1, 1975.

79. Cherniaev, *Sovmestnyï iskhod* 212.

80. "Szyfrogram ministra spraw zagranicznych (z Nowego Jorku) o rozmowie z ministrem

spraw zagranicznych RFN," Sept. 22, 1975, *PDD 1975*, doc. 242; and "Kierunki Działania PRL w Związku z Realizacją Uchwał Konferencji Bezpieczeństwa i Współpracy w Europie," Dec. 1, 1975; "Bericht zum Verlauf und zu den Ergebnissen der Konferenz über Sicherheit und Zusammenarbeit in Europa," Aug. 5, 1975; and "Brezhnev stands by Helsinki pledge," *Guardian*, Aug. 16, 1975, 2.

81. CPSU CC Memorandum, "Meropriiatiia sviazannye s realizatsieĭ nekotorykh polozheniĭ i dogovorennosteĭ, zafiksirovannykh v Zakliuchitel'nom akte Obshcheevropeĭskogo soveshchaniia, po voprosam sotrudnichestva v gumanitarnykh i drugikh oblastiakh (informatsiia, kul'tura, obrazovanie)," Dec. 11, 1975; CPSU CC Memorandum, Dec. 15, 1975, RGANI, f.3, op.72, d.705, ll.212–214; and F. Stephen Larrabee, "Soviet Attitudes and Policy toward Basket Three," *Radio Liberty Research*, March 15, 1976, in Vojtech Mastny, *Helsinki, Human Rights, and European Security: Analysis and Documentation* [hereafter *HHRES*] (Durham, NC: Duke UP, 1986) doc. 22.

82. "Okólnik wiceministra Kułagi: instrukcja w sprawie interpretacji Aktu końcowego KBWE," Sept. 23, 1975; "Kierunki Działania PRL w Związku z Realizacją Uchwał Konferencji Bezpieczeństwa i Współpracy w Europie," Dec. 1, 1975; Memorandum from V. Ia. Pavlov, Budapest, "Zapis' besedy s chlenom TsK VSPR, ministrom inostrannykh del VNR tov. Frid'eshem Puĭeĭ," Aug. 26, 1975; "Zapis' besedy s zamestitelem ministra inostrannykh del PNR Eugeniushem Kulagoĭ," Oct. 16, 1975; CPSU Politburo Memorandum from Grechko, Gromyko, and Andropov, "O poriadke osushchestvleniia mer doveriia, predusmotrennykh Zakliuchitel'nym aktom Soveshchaniia po bezopasnosti i sotrudnichestvu v Evrope," Dec. 10, 1975, RGANI, f.3, op.72, d.705, ll.143–145; "Pilna Notatka, Narada ministrów spraw zagranicznych krajów wspólnoty socjalistycznej w Moskwie (15–16.XII.1975)," Dec. 31, 1975; and "Evaluation of the Helsinki Final Act by the Czechoslovak Party Presidium," April 28, 1976. For statistics on the participants' fulfilment of their CBM obligations, see Marie-France Desjardins, "Origins, Negotiations, and Implementation of the Confidence-Building Measures of the Conference on Security and Co-operation in Europe," PhD Dissertation, King's College London, 2001, 281–286.

83. Ibid.

84. "Ob itogakh Soveshchaniia po bezopasnosti i sotrudnichestvu v Evrope," Aug. 5, 1975; "Zapis z posiedzenia Kierownictwa MSZ w dniu 8.IX.1975 r.," Sept. 8, 1975; "Kierunki Działania PRL w Związku z Realizacją Uchwał Konferencji Bezpieczeństwa i Współpracy w Europie," Dec. 1, 1975; "Evaluation of the Helsinki Final Act by the Czechoslovak Party Presidium," April 28, 1976; O. Melikian, "Mezhdunarodnaia Razriadka, Obshcheevropeĭskoe Soveshchanie i 'Tretiĭ Mir,'" *Aziia i Afrika Segodnia* 11 (Oct. 23, 1975) 5–7; and Georgi Arbatov, *The System: An Insider's Life in Soviet Politics* (New York: Times Books, 1992) 195.

85. FCO Note for Cabinet, "CSCE," July 23, 1975, UKNA, FCO 41/1769.

86. Memorandum to the Cabinet, "Conference on Security and Cooperation in Europe," July 21, 1975, LAC, RG-25, Vol. 9054, File 20-4-CSCE, Vol. 58.

87. NATO Senior Political Committee Report, "Public Information Aspects of a Possible CSCE Agreement," June 26, 1975, NATOA, CM(75)41.

88. Ford-Kissinger Memcon, Aug. 4, 1975, *FRUS 1969–1976*, Vol. 39, doc. 337; and Ford-Miki Memcon, Aug. 5, 1975, GRFL, National Security Adviser Memoranda of Conversations, 1973–1977, Box 14, Aug. 5, 1975 - Ford, Japanese Prime Minister Takeo Miki.

89. Cabinet Meeting, Aug. 8, 1975.

90. Kissinger-Rabin Memcon, Aug. 23, 1975, GRFL, National Security Adviser - Kissinger Reports on USSR, China, and Middle East Discussions, Box 4, Aug. 21–Sept. 1, 1975 - Sinai

Disengagement Agreement - Vol. I (4). See also Kissinger-Ch'iao Memcon, Sept. 29, 1975, GRFL, National Security Adviser - Kissinger Reports on USSR, China, and Middle East Discussions, Box 2, Sept. 28, 1975 - Kissinger's Meeting with PRC Officials in New York.

91. See, for example, Henry Kissinger's speech in Detroit, "Building an Enduring Foreign Policy," Dec. 15, 1975, *Department of State Bulletin*, Vol. 73, No. 1903 (Dec. 15, 1975) 849. On Kissinger's "heartland speeches," see Hanhimäki, *The Flawed Architect*, 434–436; and Jeremi Suri, *Henry Kissinger and the American Century* (Cambridge, MA: Harvard UP, 2007) 244–246.

92. Auswärtiges Amt memorandum, "Nach der KSZE," Aug. 1, 1975, PAAA, B28 111546; and Auswärtiges Amt memorandum, "KSZE," Sept. 15, 1975, PAAA, B28 111520.

93. Telegram from US embassy in Moscow to State Department, "CSCE and Eastern Europe: Some Random Thoughts," July 24, 1975, GRFL, National Security Adviser - Presidential Country Files for Europe and Canada, Box 20, USSR - State Department Telegrams To SEC-STATE - EXDIS (7).

94. Memorandum from Clift to Kissinger, "Monitoring Implementation of the CSCE Final Act," Aug. 27, 1975, GRFL, National Security Adviser - NSC Europe, Canada, and Ocean Affairs Staff: Files, Box 44, Conference on Security and Cooperation in Europe, 1975 (4) WH; and John J. Maresca, *Helsinki Revisited: A Key US Negotiator's Memoirs on the Development of the CSCE into the OSCE* (Stuttgart: Ibidem-Verlag, 2016) 71–79.

95. "Botschafter Krapf, Brüssel (NATO), an das Auswärtige Amt," Sept. 19, 1975, *AAPD 1975*, doc. 275; Summary record of NATO Council meeting, Oct. 1, 1975, PAAA B28 111554; and NATO draft report on "The Information and Human Aspects of the Conference on Security and Cooperation in Europe," September 1975, PAAA, B28 111522.

96. Auswärtiges Amt memorandum, "Bericht der Arbeitsgruppe über Fragen in Zusammenhang mit der Durchführung der Schlussakte der KSZE," Oct. 30, 1975, PAAA, B28 111525.

97. Auswärtiges Amt memorandum, "Nach der KSZE," Aug. 1, 1975, PAAA, B28 111546.

98. FCO memorandum, "CSCE: Stage III: Steering Brief," July 23, 1975, UKNA, FCO 41/1774/5.

99. Memorandum from Hildyard, Geneva, to Callaghan, FCO, "CSCE: The Conclusion of Stage II," July 25, 1975, UKNA, FCO 41/1769; and Auswärtiges Amt memorandum, "Nach der KSZE."

100. FCO memorandum, "CSCE: Stage III: Steering Brief"; and memorandum from Burns to Alexander, "CSCE: Follow-up," Aug. 12, 1975, UKNA, FCO 66/793.

101. Auswärtiges Amt memorandum, "Stand der Ost-West-Beziehungen nach Helsinki," Sept. 15, 1975, PAAA, B28 111520.

102. Vladimir V. Kusin, "Challenge to Normalcy: Political Opposition in Czechoslovakia, 1968–77," *Opposition in Eastern Europe* 47–48; and Rubenstein 211.

103. Paul Goldberg, *The Final Act: The Dramatic, Revealing Story of the Moscow Helsinki Watch Group* (New York: William Morrow, 1988) 18.

104. Commission on Security and Cooperation in Europe, *Implementation of the Helsinki Accords: Hearings before the Commission on Security and Cooperation in Europe*, Vol. 1, Feb. 23, 1977 (Washington, DC: USGPO, 1977) 54.

105. Bukovsky 437.

106. Testimony of Richard Davy, *The Helsinki Negotiations* 48–49; and Craig R. Whitney, "East Germans with Kin in West Await Proof of Helsinki Accord," *NYT*, Aug. 4, 1975, 2.

107. Bondy quoted in Jonathan Bolton, *Worlds of Dissent: Charter 77, the Plastic People of the Universe, and Czech Culture under Communism* (Cambridge, MA: Harvard UP, 2008) 25.

108. Malcolm Browne, "No Excitement in Prague," *NYT*, Aug. 2, 1975, 8; Kusin 47–48; Thomas 96.

109. Interview with Geremek quoted in Patrick G. Vaughan, "Zbigniew Brzezinski and the Helsinki Final Act," *The Crisis of Détente in Europe* 13–14. On Polish dissidents' initial pessimism, see also Władysław Bartoszewski, "Flying through the Fear Barrier," *Index on Censorship* 14:2 (1985) 22.

110. Thomas 99–100.

111. James F. Clarity, "A Freed Writer Defying Moscow," *NYT*, July 23, 1975, 9.

112. Robert F. Drinan, *The Mobilization of Shame: A World View of Human Rights* (New Haven, CT: Yale UP, 2001) 73; Liudmila Alekseeva, *Soviet Dissent: Contemporary Movements for National, Religious, and Human Rights* (Middletown, CT: Wesleyan UP, 1985) 336; and Goldberg 33–48; Gal Beckerman, *When They Come for Us We'll Be Gone: The Epic Struggle to Save Soviet Jewry* (Boston: Houghton Mifflin Harcourt, 2010) 328–335; *A Chronicle of Human Rights in the USSR* 20–21 (April–June 1976) 5–8; Andrei Amalrik, *Notes of a Revolutionary* (New York: Knopf, 1982) 310–313; Yuri Orlov, *Dangerous Thoughts: Memoirs of a Russian Life* (New York: William Morrow, 1991) 188–192. Orlov's toast is quoted in James Baker's speech to the 1990 Copenhagen Conference, in Samuel F. Wells, Jr., ed., *The Helsinki Process and the Future of Europe* (Washington, DC: Wilson Center Press, 1990) 186.

113. *Dissent in Poland: Reports and Documents in Translation* (London: Association of Polish Students and Graduates in Exile, 1977) 12–18; and "Explanatory Statement by the Secretariat of the Polish Episcopate regarding the Proposed Changes to the Constitution," in *Political Opposition in Poland, 1954–1977*, 224–228.

114. Michael H. Bernhard, *The Origins of Democratization in Poland: Workers, Intellectuals, and Oppositional Politics, 1976–1980* (New York: Columbia UP, 1993) 87; and Jacques Rupnik, "Dissent in Poland, 1968–78: The End of Revisionism and the Rebirth of Civil Society," *Opposition in Eastern Europe* 84–85.

115. Rupnik 90–91; Bernhard 119–124 and 140; Kotkin, *Uncivil Society* 101.

116. Adam Michnik, "A New Evolutionism," *Letters from Prison and Other Essays*, trans. Maya Latynski (Berkeley: University of California Press, 1985) 142–143.

117. Hajek and Mlynar interview quoted in Kusin 48–49; H. Gordon Skilling, *Charter 77 and Human Rights in Czechoslovakia* (London: Allen and Unwin, 1981) 27 and 159; and Jiří Hájek, *Dix ans après: Prague 1968–1978* (Paris: Éditions du Seuil, 1978) 177–187.

118. Skilling, *Charter 77* 14; Bolton 115ff. and 147–151. One Plastic People lyric mocked official slogans about the virtues of communist foreign policy: "Peace, peace, peace / Is like toilet paper." Bolton 138.

119. Bolton 24–29 and 140; Tom Stoppard, "Prague: The Story of the Chartists," *New York Review of Books*, Aug. 4, 1977; and Kusin 51.

120. Bolton 153.

121. Skilling, *Charter 77* 217–222. Quotation from 217–219.

122. "Ostpolitik—aber mit Würde," *Die Zeit*, March 25, 1977, 9.

123. Skilling, *Charter 77* 221–222; and Kusin 52.

124. Leslie Colitt, "E. Germans Act to Stem Flow of Would-be Emigrants," *Financial Times*, Jan. 12, 1977, 4; and "Helsinki Accord's Echo in East Europe," *Financial Times*, Jan. 12, 1977, 4; Werner Volkmer, "East Germany: Dissenting Views during the Last Decade," *Opposition in Eastern Europe* 121.

125. "Gütlich trennen," *Der Spiegel*, Nov. 3, 1975, 44–49; "Als ihre Kritik zu laut wurde,

mußten die Dissidenten in Haft," *Die Welt*, Aug. 29, 1977, 3; Hanisch 130–144; Rubenstein 237; and Volkmer 123.

126. Klaus Ehring and Martin Dallwitz, *Schwerter zu Pflugscharen: Friedensbewegung in der DDR* (Reinbek bei Hamburg: Rowohlt, 1982) 39.

127. Skilling, *Charter 77* 153; Kotkin, *Uncivil Society* 113–114; David Ost, *Solidarity and the Politics of Anti-Politics: Opposition and Reform in Poland since 1968* (Philadelphia: Temple UP, 1990) 64–73; and Garton Ash, *The Uses of Adversity* 115–116.

128. Václav Havel, "The Power of the Powerless," *Open Letters: Selected Writings 1965–1990*, ed. Paul Wilson (New York: Vintage, 1992) 146ff.

129. Stoppard, "Prague: The Story of the Chartists."

130. Thomas 107; and Jan Józef Lipski, *KOR: A History of the Workers' Defense Committee in Poland, 1976–1981* (Berkeley: University of California Press, 1985) 279–280.

131. Lipski 281–283; and Jiří Dienstbier's remarks at conference "From *Solidarność* to Freedom," Warsaw, Aug. 29–31, 2005. http://www.girodivite.it/IMG/pdf/raport_25-en.pdf.

132. George Schöpflin, "Opposition and Para-Opposition: Critical Currents in Hungary, 1968–78," *Opposition in Eastern Europe* 160–161; and Rubenstein 236.

133. *Dissent in Poland*, 72–78.

134. "Auch Bürger in der Tschechoslowakei wollen ihre Rechte verteidigen," *Frankfurter Allgemeine Zeitung*, Jan. 7, 1977, 5. See also "Charter 77 and Article 19(2)," *The Times*, Feb. 10, 1977, 17; and Skilling, *Charter 77* 151.

135. Heinrich Böll, "Helsinki war keine Falle," *Die Zeit*, May 20, 1977, 33; and Kusin 47. See also Benjamin Gutmann, "Relais et réseaux de la Charte 77 en France, entre 1977 et 1989," *Bulletin de l'Institut Pierre Renouvin* 33 (2011), 49–64.

136. Savranskaya, "Unintended Conseqeunces" 26.

137. Snyder, *Human Rights Activism* 40–41.

138. Memorandum from Clift to Scowcroft, "HR 10193 (Establishment of a Congressional Commission on Security and Cooperation in Europe)," Oct. 28, 1975, GRFL, White House Central Files Subject File - FG 431: Commission on Security and Cooperation in Europe, Box 216, FG 431 Commission on Security and Cooperation in Europe, 8/9/74–6/30/76; Memorandum from Scowcroft to Friedersdorf, "Signing Ceremony for the Case-Fenwick CSCE Commission Bill," May 26, 1976, GRFL, White House Central Files Subject File - FG 431: Commission on Security and Cooperation in Europe, Box 216, FG 431 Commission on Security and Cooperation in Europe, 8/9/74–6/30/76; memorandum from Scowcroft to Ford, "Signing Ceremony for S. 2679 Establishing a Commission on Security and Cooperation in Europe," June 3, 1976, GRFL, National Security Adviser - NSC Press and Congressional Liaison Staff: Files, 1973–1976, Box 8, June 3, 1976 - Signing Ceremony for S. 2679 (Commission on Security and Cooperation in Europe).

139. Mastny, *HHRES* 11; and Snyder, *Human Rights Activism* 45–46.

140. Commission on Security and Cooperation in Europe, *Report of the Study Mission to Europe to the Commission on Security and Cooperation in Europe* (Washington, DC: USGPO, 1977); and Commission on Security and Cooperation in Europe, *Implementation of the Final Act of the Conference on Security and Cooperation in Europe: Findings and Recommendations Two Years after Helsinki* (Washington, DC: USGPO, 1977).

141. See, for example, "Don't Forget Helsinki," *The Economist*, July 31, 1976, 10–11; Anthony Lewis, "Echoes of Helsinki," *NYT*, Aug. 2, 1976, 23; and "The Belgrade Watch," *Wall Street*

Journal, June 15, 1977, 24. This editorial recanted the *WSJ*'s criticism of the Final Act two years earlier. "We were wrong," it said.

142. Snyder, *Human Rights Activism* 49–51; and Mastny, *HHRES* 12.

143. Sargent 224–227; Sarah B. Snyder, "Through the Looking Glass: The Helsinki Final Act and the 1976 Election for President," *Diplomacy and Statecraft* 21:1 (March 2010): 87-106; and Leo P. Ribuffo, "Is Poland a Soviet Satellite? Gerald Ford, the Sonnenfeldt Doctrine, and the Election of 1976," *Diplomatic History* 14:3 (Summer 1990): 385-403; and transcript of Ford-Carter Debate, Oct. 6, 1976, Commission on Presidential Debates, http://www.debates.org /index.php?page=october-6-1976-debate-transcript.

144. Zbigniew Brzezinski, "The Deceptive Structure of Peace," *Foreign Policy* 14 (Spring 1974) 55.

145. Sargent 229–230.

146. Vaughan 14–16; and Snyder, *Human Rights Activism* 92–93.

147. "Department Comments on Subject of Human Rights in Czechoslovakia," *Department of State Bulletin*, Feb. 21, 1977, 154.

148. Mastny, *HHRES*, 14–15; and Rudolf L. Tőkés, "Human Rights in Eastern Europe," ibid., doc. 38.

149. Vaughan 17–18.

150. Savranskaya, "Unintended Consequences," 185; and Cherniaev, *Sovmestnyĭ iskhod*, 202–203.

151. Chazov 86–87; David K. Shipler, "Soviet Calls Sakharov a Judas, Nobel Prize '30 Pieces of Silver,'" *NYT*, Oct. 29, 1975, 4; and Andrei Sakharov, "Peace, Progress, and Human Rights," *Andrei Sakharov and Human Rights* 53.

152. Joachim Scholtyseck, "GDR Dissidents and Human Rights Issues," *From Helsinki to Belgrade: The First CSCE Follow-up Meeting and the Crisis of Détente*, eds. Vladimir Bilandžić, Dittmar Dahlmann, and Milan Kosanović (Bonn: Bonn UP, 2012) 295–296; and Hanisch 144–177.

153. Bolton 172–178; Skilling, *Charter 77* 213; and Kusin 54.

154. Brezhnev quoted in *A Cardboard Castle?* 45.

155. Memorandum from G. M. Kornienko, "Record of Conversation with U.S. Attaché in the USSR Jack Matlock," Nov. 12, 1975, CWIHP.

156. G. Shakhnazarov, "Mirnoe Sosushchestvovanie i Sotsial'nyi Progress," *Pravda*, Dec. 27, 1976, 4–5; I. Aleksandrov, "O Svobodakh Podlinnykh i Mnimykh," *Pravda*, Feb. 20, 1976, 3–5; memorandum from S. V. Chervonenko, "Zapis' besedy s prezidentom Frantsii V. Zhiskar d'Estenom," Oct. 9, 1975, RGANI, f.5, op.68, d.2031, ll.195–200; and G. Arbatov, "Manevry Protivnikov Razriadki," *Izvestiia*, Sept. 3, 1975, 3–4. A version of the article appeared a month later in the *New York Times*: Georgi A. Arbatov, "Reciprocity after Helsinki," Oct. 8, 1975, 41.

157. Memorandum from G.M. Kornienko, "Record of Conversation with U.S. Attaché in the USSR Jack Matlock," Nov. 12, 1975; Arbatov, "Manevry Protivnikov Razriadki"; and Kovalev, *Azbuka diplomatii* 198.

158. "Brezhnev's Report to the Congress," *Current Digest of the Soviet Press*, Vol. 28, No. 8 (March 24, 1976) 8–9; Leonov 166; "Dobrye plody razriadki," *Izvestiia*, July 31, 1976, 1; "V interesakh mira i progressa," *Pravda*, Aug. 1, 1976, 1; and "Taking the Measure of Helsinki," *Time*, Aug. 9, 1976, 28.

159. Articles 47, 50, and 51, *Constitution (Fundamental Law) of the Union of Soviet Socialist Republics* (Moscow: Novosti Press Agency, 1977); and Jacques Amalric, "Quatre conditions de la détente présentées par M. Giscard d'Estaing à M. Brejnev," *Le Monde*, June 22, 1977, 1,

8. See also Martin Nicholson, "The New Soviet Constitution: A Political Analysis," *The World Today* 34:1 (January 1978) 14–20.

160. "Pilna Notatka, Narada ministrów spraw zagranicznych krajów wspólnoty socjalistycznej w Moskwie (15–16.XII.1975)," Dec. 31, 1975; and Douglas Selvage, "The Superpowers and the Conference on Security and Cooperation in Europe, 1977–1983," *Die KSZE im Ost-West Konflikt: Internationale Politik und gesellschaftliche Transformation 1975–1990*, ed. Matthias Peter and Hermann Wentker (Munich: Oldenbourg, 2012) 21.

161. Hanisch 188–197; Savranskaya, "Unintended Consequences" 187; William Korey, *The Promises We Keep: Human Rights, the Helsinki Process, and American Foreign Policy* (New York: St. Martin's Press, 1993) 63–64; Vaughan 20; Skilling, *Charter 77* 140; and Williamsburg Conference, "From Helsinki to Belgrade," *HHRES*, doc. 40.

162. Ibid.; and Vaughan 18–20.

163. Breck Walker, " 'Neither Shy nor Demagogic'—The Carter Administration Goes to Belgrade," *From Helsinki to Belgrade*, 188–189; and telegram from Toon, US Embassy Moscow, to State Department, "Human Rights in the Soviet Union: Where Do We Go from Here?" Feb. 14, 1977, AAD.

164. Walker 190.

165. Korey 69 and 94.

166. Ibid. 95–97.

167. Ibid. 78–83.

168. Carroll Sherer, "Breakdown at Belgrade," *HHRES*, doc. 49; and Albert W. Sherer, Jr., "Goldberg's Variation," *Foreign Policy* 39 (Summer 1980): 154–159.

169. David A. Andelman, "A Series of Caucuses and Conflicts," *HHRES*, doc. 50; and Korey 88–89. Quotation from 89.

170. Telegram from Goldberg, Belgrade, to State Department, "Belgrade CSCE—Soviet Warning in Basket One Human Rights Debate," Oct. 31, 1977, AAD; and Korey 84–87 and 90–91.

171. Korey, *The Promises We Keep* 92–93; Ian MacDonald, "A Small Harvest," *HHRES*, doc. 53; Hanisch 197–207; and Steglich and Leuschner 80–81.

172. Ian MacDonald, "The Weary Consensus," *HHRES*, doc. 54.

173. Hanisch 207–213; "Speech by Brezhnev at the Political Consultative Committee Meeting in Moscow," Nov. 22, 1978, *A Cardboard Castle?* doc. 84; Kashlev, "The CSCE in the Soviet Union's Politics," 69; and testimony of Sergei Kondrashev, *SALT II and the Growth of Mistrust: Transcript of the Proceedings of the Musgrove Conference of the Carter-Brezhnev Project*, ed. Svetlana Savranskaya and David Welch (Washington, DC: National Security Archive, 1995) 17.

174. Korey 98–100.

175. Snyder, *Human Rights Activism* 111–113.

176. Ibid. 115–125; and Robert L. Bernstein, *Speaking Freely: My Life in Publishing and Human Rights* (New York: New Press, 2016) 149.

177. Ibid. 127–129.

178. Oliver Bange, "SS-20 and Pershing II: Weapon Systems and the Dynamization of East-West Relations," *The Nuclear Crisis: The Arms Race, Cold War Anxiety, and the German Peace Movement of the 1980s*, eds. Christoph Becker-Schaum et al. (New York: Berghahn, 2016) 70–86; Westad chapters 6–8; and Zubok, *A Failed Empire* 251–253.

179. Savranskaya, "Unintended Consequences," 187; Rubenstein 241–251; Korey 97; Jimmy Carter, "Soviet Implementation of Basket One," *HHRES*, doc. 65; and memorandum to the

Politburo from Andropov, Gromyko, and Zimianin, "O lishenii Rostropovicha i Vishnevskoĭ sovetskogo grazhdanstva," *Istoricheskiĭ Arkhiv* 5 (1993) 177–179.

180. "The Szczecin Agreement," Aug. 30, 1980, *From Solidarity to Martial Law: The Polish Crisis of 1980–1981: A Documentary History*, eds. Andrzej Paczkowski and Malcolm Byrne (Budapest: Central European University Press, 2007) doc. 6; and Max Kampelman, "Poland and the CSCE," Nov. 16, 1982, in Max M. Kampelman, *Three Years at the East-West Divide: The Words of U.S. Ambassador Max M. Kampelman at the Madrid Conference on Security and Human Rights*, ed. Leonard R. Sussman (New York: Freedom House, 1983) 93.

181. Bogdan Borusewicz's remarks at conference "From *Solidarność* to Freedom," Warsaw, Aug. 29–31, 2005.

182. Ouimet 150–151; Zubok, *A Failed Empire* 266; and Archie Brown, *The Gorbachev Factor* (New York: Oxford UP, 1996) 222, footnote 53.

183. Ouimet 164–166.

184. Ibid. 167–204; and Zubok, *A Failed Empire* 269–270. Suslov quotation from Ouimet 202.

185. Kashlev, "The CSCE in the Soviet Union's Politics," 69; Mastny, *HHRES* 20; and interview with Peter Steglich, *CSCE Testimonies* 129.

186. Korey 123–124 and 142–144; Snyder, *Human Rights Activism* 151–154; "Letter to the Madrid Conference from Mírov Prisoners," *HHRES*, doc. 68; and Susan Ovadia, "French Activists Demand Firmness in Madrid," ibid., doc. 70. Sakharov quoted in Rubenstein 290.

187. Snyder, *Human Rights Activism* 145–149; Mastny, *HHRES* 23–24; and Brunner 43.

188. Korey 132; and Snyder, *Human Rights Activism* 148.

189. Max M. Kampelman and George Urban, "Can We Negotiate with the Russians? (and if so, how?)" *Encounter* (February 1985) 10–13.

190. Quoted in Skilling, *Charter 77* 323.

191. Vladimir Lomeiko, "Realities and Prospects of Détente as Seen in Moscow after the Belgrade Experience," *The Belgrade Conference: Progress or Regression*, eds. Cornelis C. van den Heuvel and Rio D. Praaning (Leiden: New Rhine, 1978) 33–34; "Summary of the Deputy Foreign Ministers' Preparatory Meeting for the CSCE Madrid Conference," July 8–9, 1980, *A Cardboard Castle?* doc. 88; Clive Rose, *Campaigns against Western Defence: NATO's Adversaries and Critics*, 2nd ed. (Houndmills, Basingstoke: Macmillan, 1986) chapter 7; Selvage, "The Superpowers and the Conference on Security and Cooperation in Europe, 1977–1983," 28–30; Steglich and Leuschner 91–92; and Mastny, *HHRES* 21.

192. James M. Markham, "US Delegate Cites Soviet Rights Cases," *NYT*, Nov. 25, 1980, A7.

193. Arie Bloed, ed. *The Conference on Security and Co-operation in Europe: Analysis and Basic Documents, 1972–1993* (Dordrecht: Kluwer Academic Publishers, 1993) 52–53; and Mastny, *HHRES* 25.

194. Gregory F. Domber, *Empowering Revolution: America, Poland, and the End of the Cold War* (Chapel Hill, NC: UNC Press, 2014) 29–41; Hans-Dietrich Genscher, *Rebuilding a House Divided: A Memoir by the Architect of Germany's Reunification*, trans. Thomas Thornton (New York: Broadway, 1998) 81; Sandra Cavallucci and Nino De Amicis, "Italy: Diversity within United Solidarity," *Solidarity with Solidarity: Western European Trade Unions and the Polish Crisis, 1980–1982*, ed. Idesbald Goddeeris (Lanham, MD: Lexington, 2010) 79; Spasowski 661; Snyder, *Human Rights Activism* 139–142; and Korey 155.

195. Douglas Selvage, "The Politics of the Lesser Evil: The West, the Polish Crisis, and the CSCE Review Conference in Madrid, 1981–1983," *The Crisis of Détente in Europe* 41–47; and Genscher 104.

196. Anatoly Adamishin and Richard Schifter, *Human Rights, Perestroika, and the End of the Cold War* (Washington, DC: US Institute of Peace, 2009) 98–100; and Selvage, "The Superpowers and the Conference on Security and Cooperation in Europe, 1977–1983," 53–54.

197. Selvage, "The Politics of the Lesser Evil" 50–51; *HHRES*, docs. 109–118; Hanisch 271–286 and 326–364; Genscher 105; Steglich and Leuschner 109–110; and Bloed 54.

198. Domberg 81; and "Summary of the Committee of Ministers of Foreign Affairs Meeting in Sofia," Oct. 20, 1983, *A Cardboard Castle?* doc. 101.

199. Vojtech Mastny, *The Helsinki Process and the Reintegration of Europe, 1986–1991: Analysis and Documentation* (New York: NYU Press, 1992) [hereafter *HPRE*] 5; Don Oberdorfer, *From the Cold War to a New Era: The United States and the Soviet Union, 1983–1991*, updated ed. (Baltimore: Johns Hopkins UP, 1998) 65–68; and Robert Service, *The End of the Cold War 1985–1991* (New York: Public Affairs, 2015) 50–51.

200. Christian Peterson, *Globalizing Human Rights: Private Citizens, the Soviet Union, and the West* (New York: Routledge, 2012) 118; and Korey 160.

201. Snyder, *Human Rights Activism* 156–157; Scholtyseck 296–297; and Hanisch 351–352.

202. Interview with Édouard Brunner, *CSCE Testimonies* 110.

203. Selvage, "The Superpowers and the Conference on Security and Cooperation in Europe, 1977–1983," 30 and 40–44; and Cherniaev, *Sovmestnyĭ iskhod* 70.

EPILOGUE: REUNIFICATIONS

1. Leon Aron, *Roads to the Temple: Truth, Memory, Ideas, and Ideals in the Making of the Russian Revolution, 1987–1991* (New Haven, CT: Yale UP, 2012) 11–16; and Kotkin, *Armageddon Averted* 66–67.

2. Zubok, *A Failed Empire* 279 and 310; and Svetlana Savranskaya, "The Logic of 1989: The Soviet Peaceful Withdrawal from Eastern Europe," *Masterpieces of History: The Peaceful End of the Cold War in Europe, 1989*, eds. Svetlana Savranskaya, Thomas Blanton, and Vladislav Zubok [hereafter *MoH*] (Budapest: Central European UP, 2010) 11–13.

3. Brown, *Gorbachev Factor*, 89–129; Mikhail Gorbachev and Zdeněk Mlynář, *Conversations with Gorbachev: On Perestroika, the Prague Spring, and the Crossroads of Socialism* (New York: Columbia UP, 2002) 49–50; Marie-Pierre Rey, " 'Europe Is Our Common Home': A Study of Gorbachev's Diplomatic Concept," *Cold War History* 4:2 (2004) 42–46; and Zubok, *A Failed Empire* 280–282.

4. Arbatov, *The System* 308–312. Quotation on 311.

5. Savranskaya, "Unintended Consequences" 188; English 193–228; and Archie Brown, *Seven Years That Changed the World: Perestroika in Perspective* (New York: Oxford UP, 2007) 157–189.

6. Zubok, *A Failed Empire* 282.

7. Mikhail Gorbachev, "Dialogue with Participants of the Issyk-Kul Forum," Oct. 20, 1986, *Mikhail Gorbachev: Prophet of Change: From the Cold War to a Sustainable World* (Forest Row, East Sussex: Clairview, 2011) 6.

8. Zubok, *A Failed Empire* 282–283; and Archie Brown, "The Gorbachev Revolution and the End of the Cold War," *Cambridge History of the Cold War*, Vol. 3, 257–258.

9. Quoted in Zubok, *A Failed Empire* 317.

10. Quoted in English 220.

11. "Notes of a Meeting between Mikhail Gorbachev and Foreign Policy Advisers," Oct. 31, 1988, *MoH*, doc. 31.

12. "Gorbachev CPSU Central Committee Political Report," *FBIS*, Feb. 26, 1986, O33.

13. "Diary of Anatoly Chernyaev regarding a Meeting between Mikhail Gorbachev and Helmut Kohl," Oct. 28, 1988, *MoH*, doc. 30.

14. "Soviet Transcript of the Malta Summit," Dec. 2–3, 1989, *MoH*, doc. 110.

15. Rey, " 'Europe Is Our Common Home' " 39; Savranskaya, "The Logic of 1989" 46; and Zubok, *A Failed Empire* 330.

16. Quoted in Anatoly Chernyaev, *My Six Years with Gorbachev*, trans. and eds. Robert D. English and Elizabeth Tucker (University Park, PA: Pennsylvania State UP, 2000) 56.

17. Eduard Shevardnadze, "No One Can Isolate Us, Save Ourselves. Self-Isolation Is the Ultimate Danger," trans. Vitaly Chernetsky, *Slavic Review* 51:1 (Spring 1992) 119.

18. Quoted in Rey, " 'Europe Is Our Common Home' " 41.

19. "The Political Report of the CPSU Central Committee to the 27th Congress of the Communist Party of the Soviet Union," *Current Digest of the Soviet Press*, Vol. 38 No. 8 (March 26, 1986) 31–32; and Kovalev, *Iskusstvo vozmozhnogo* 383–384.

20. "Speech by Mikhail Gorbachev at a Dinner with Wojciech Jaruzelski," July 11, 1988, *MoH*, doc. 27.

21. "Speech by Gorbachev at the Political Consultative Committee Meeting in Warsaw," July 15, 1988, *A Cardboard Castle?* doc. 135. See also Chernyaev, *My Six Years with Gorbachev* 105.

22. "Address by Mikhail Gorbachev to the Council of Europe in Strasbourg," July 6, 1989, *MoH*, doc. 73.

23. Cherniaev's comments at 1998 Musgrove Conference, *MoH* 135.

24. Quoted in Zubok, *A Failed Empire* 319.

25. Savranskaya, "The Logic of 1989" 14–18.

26. Shakhnazarov comments at 1998 Musgrove Conference, *MoH* 124; and Zubok, *A Failed Empire* 315.

27. Compare Savranskaya, "The Logic of 1989" 3–11, and English 200, with Mark Kramer, "The Collapse of East European Communism and the Repercussions within the Soviet Union (Part 1)," *Journal of Cold War Studies* 5:4 (Fall 2003) 178–256.

28. "Record of Conversation between Mikhail Gorbachev and Lazar Moisov," March 14, 1988, *MoH*, doc. 20; and Kramer, "The Collapse of East European Communism" 185–186.

29. "Record of Conversation between Mikhail Gorbachev and Helmut Kohl," *MoH*, doc. 63.

30. Andrei Grachev, *Gorbachev's Gamble: Soviet Foreign Policy and the End of the Cold War* (Cambridge: Polity, 2008) 58–60 and 70–77; Arkady N. Shevchenko, *Breaking with Moscow* (New York: Knopf, 1985) 265-66; and Kashlev, *Khel'sinkskii protsess* 45.

31. Mastny, *HHRES* 304–311.

32. Ibid. 279–282.

33. Ibid. 31–32; and Garton Ash, *The Uses of Adversity* 150–156.

34. Snyder, *Human Rights Activism* 159–160.

35. Grachev, *Gorbachev's Gamble* 75–76.

36. Yakovlev Memorandum to Gorbachev, "The Priority of Political Development," Dec. 25, 1985, in *To the Geneva Summit: Perestroika and the Transformation of U.S.-Soviet Relations*, National Security Archive Briefing Book No. 172, doc. 30. Available at: http://nsarchive.gwu.edu/NSAEBB/NSAEBB172/.

37. Minutes of Politburo Meeting, Aug. 29, 1985, in *To the Geneva Summit: Perestroika and the Transformation of U.S.-Soviet Relations*, National Security Archive Briefing Book No. 172, doc. 12. Available at: http://nsarchive.gwu.edu/NSAEBB/NSAEBB172/.

38. Notes on Politburo Meeting, Nov. 13, 1986, *V Politbiuro TsK KPSS: Po zapisiam Anatoliia Cherniaeva, Vadima Medvedeva, Georgiia Shakhnazarova (1985–1991)*, ed. Anatoly Cherniaev et al. (Moscow: Al'pina Biznes Buks, 2006) 111–112.

39. Yuliya von Saal, *KSZE-Prozess und Perestroika in der Sowjetunion: Demokratisierung, Werteumbruch und Auflösung 1985–1991* (Munich: Oldenbourg, 2014) 79–150.

40. Snyder, *Human Rights Activism* 171–172. Quotation from 172.

41. Ibid. 161; von Saal 83–84; and Rubenstein and Gribanov, eds. 323–328.

42. Service 237.

43. Mastny, *HPRE* 8; and Service 236–237.

44. Quoted in Chernyaev, *My Six Years with Gorbachev* 39. See also Zubok, *A Failed Empire* 316.

45. Jack F. Matlock, Jr., *Autopsy on an Empire: The American Ambassador's Account of the Collapse of the Soviet Union* (New York: Random House, 1995) 106; and von Saal 122.

46. Quoted in Chernyaev, *My Six Years with Gorbachev* 71.

47. "Summary of the Meeting of Ministers of Foreign Affairs in Warsaw," March 19–20, 1986, *A Cardboard Castle?* doc. 111.

48. Eduard A. Shevardnadze's speech to CSCE Review Meeting, Nov. 5, 1986, *HPRE*, doc. 13; and Snyder, *Human Rights Activism* 177–178.

49. Genscher 107.

50. English 216–217; speech by Marshal Sergei Akhromeev, Aug. 29, 1986, *HPRE*, doc. 9; Yuri Fokine et al., "Helsinki 30 Years Later," *International Affairs* (Moscow) 51:5 (Oct. 2005) 189–190; Service 204; and Mastny, *HPRE* 19–20.

51. Richard Rhodes, *Arsenals of Folly: The Making of the Nuclear Arms Race* (New York: Knopf, 2007) 219.

52. Lynn E. Davis, "Lessons of the INF Treaty," *Foreign Affairs* 66:4 (Spring 1988) 728–729.

53. *A Cardboard Castle?* 62. Gorbachev quoted in Zubok, *A Failed Empire* 300.

54. Miller, chapters 3, 4, and 6; Nove 394–407; and Eichengreen, *The European Economy since 1945* 296–303.

55. Kovalev, *Iskusstvo vozmozhnogo* 384–386; and Bloed 55–56.

56. Interview with Jiří Opršal, CSCE *Testimonies* 57–58; Kornilov, "Leonid Il'ich ne znal, chto zipuenaet [sic] mekhanizm perestreĭki"; and Kashlev, "The CSCE in the Soviet Union's Politics" 71.

57. Roland Eggleston, report for RFE/RL, Dec. 2, 1988, *HPRE*, doc. 28; Andrei A. Kovalev, *Russia's Dead End: An Insider's Testimony from Gorbachev to Putin*, trans. Steven I. Levine (Lincoln, NE: Potomac, 2017) 45–48; Snyder, *Human Rights Activism* 195–202; Service 272; and von Saal 250–252.

58. Mastny *HPRE* 17–18; and Bloed 58–59.

59. "Report on the Committee of Ministers of Foreign Affairs Meeting in Moscow," March 24–25, 1987, *A Cardboard Castle?* doc. 121; and "Records of the Political Consultative Committee Meeting in Berlin," May 27–29, 1987, ibid., doc. 123.

60. "Speeches at the Foreign Ministers' Meeting in Sofia," March 29–30, 1988, *A Cardboard Castle?* doc. 128; and "Report by the Bulgarian Foreign Minister at the Unofficial Meeting of Foreign Ministers at Niederschönhausen near Berlin," April 10, 1989, ibid., doc. 141;

Walter Süß, "Die Wiener KSZE-Folgekonferenz und der Handlungsspielraum des DDR-Sicherheitsapparates 1989," *Die KSZE im Ost-West Konflikt* 219–231; and Mastny, *HPRE* 18.

61. Mastny, *HPRE* 16.

62. "Records of the Foreign Ministers' Meeting in Warsaw," Oct. 26–27, 1989, *A Cardboard Castle?* doc 147.

63. Quoted in Zubok, *A Failed Empire* 323.

64. Mastny, *HPRE* 23; and Maresca, "The CSCE at Its Inception" 4.

65. Von Saal 150–171. Shevardnadze quoted in Zubok, *A Failed Empire* 325.

66. Mary Elise Sarotte, *1989: The Struggle to Create Post-Cold War Europe* (Princeton, NJ: Princeton UP, 2009) 29–47.

67. Snyder, *Human Rights Activism* 228.

68. Philip Zelikow and Condoleezza Rice, *Germany Unified and Europe Transformed: A Study in Statecraft* (Cambridge, MA: Harvard UP, 1995) 31.

69. Mastny, *HPRE* 22.

70. "Memorandum of Eppelman-Iazov Conversation," April 29, 1990, *A Cardboard Castle?* doc. 152.

71. See, for example, Genscher 296 and 302; and letter from Sir C. Mallaby (Bonn) to Sir J Fretwell, "The German Question," Nov. 8, 1989, *DBPO* III:VII, doc. 34.

72. Charles S. Maier, *Dissolution: The Crisis of Communism and the End of East Germany* (Princeton, NJ: Princeton UP, 1999) 127; and Mary Sarotte, *The Collapse: The Accidental Opening of the Berlin Wall* (New York: Basic, 2014) 18.

73. Ibid. 65 and 80.

74. Jacques Lévesque, *The Enigma of 1989: The USSR and the Liberation of Eastern Europe*, trans. Keith Martin (University of California Press, 1997) 162; Rey, " 'Europe Is Our Common Home' " 56; Chernyaev, *My Six Years* 115; and "Records of the Political Consultative Committee Meeting in Moscow," June 7, 1990, *A Cardboard Castle?* doc 153. Gorbachev quoted in Alexander von Plato, *Die Vereinigung Deutschlands—ein weltpolitisches Machtspiel: Bush, Kohl, Gorbatschow und die internen Gesprächsprotokolle*, 3rd ed. (Berlin: Ch. Links, 2009) 128.

75. Quoted in Chernyaev, *My Six Years* 237. See also Rey, " 'Europe Is Our Common Home' " 56.

76. Quoted in Sarotte, *1989* 73.

77. Thomas Blanton, "US Policy and the Revolutions of 1989," *MoH* 89–90; "Soviet Transcript of the Malta Summit"; and "Memorandum of Conversation of George H. W. Bush, John Sununu, Brent Scowcroft, and Helmut Kohl," Dec. 3, 1989, *MoH*, doc. 111.

78. Rey, " 'Europe Is Our Common Home' " 57–58; and Speech by François Mitterand, Dec. 31, 1989, *HPRE*, doc. 61.

79. Sarotte, *1989* 175 and 225.

80. Speech by James A. Baker, Dec. 12, 1989, *HPRE*, doc. 59.

81. Sarotte, *1989* 64; and Frédéric Bozo, *Mitterand, the End of the Cold War and German Unification*, trans. Susan Emanuel (New York: Berghahn, 2009) 131–132.

82. Sarotte, *1989* 162–165.

83. Ibid. 167 and 176–183; Zelikow and Rice 278 and 341; Genscher 370–371; telegram from Hurd, FCO, to Mallaby, Bonn, "Secretary of State's Meeting with Genscher: 28 May," May 29, 1990, *DBPO* III:VII, doc. 205; and NATO's London Declaration on a Transformed North Atlantic Alliance, July 5–6, 1990. Available at: http://www.nato.int/docu/comm/49-95/c900706a.htm.

84. Sarotte, *1989* 127; and Bozo, *Mitterand* 145–147 and 297–300.

85. Zelikow and Rice 187.

86. "Record of Conversation between Mikhail Gorbachev and James Baker," Feb. 9, 1990, *MoH*, doc. 119; "Letter from James Baker to Helmut Kohl," Feb. 10, 1990, *MoH*, doc. 120; minute from Hurd to Thatcher, "The German Question," Jan. 16, 1990, *DBPO* III:VII, doc. 99; letter from Powell to Wall, "Prime Minister's Talk with President Bush," Feb. 24, 1990, ibid., doc. 155; "Sowjetische Befürchtungen vor einem 'revanchistischen Deutschland' nach Helmut Kohl," *Die Kreml und die deutsche Wiedervereinigung 1990*, ed. Stefan Karner et al. (Berlin: Metropol, 2015) doc. 8; and Sarotte, *1989* 122, 144–45, 197.

87. Michael Evans and Michael Binyon, "'Cheerful' Start to Security Summit," *The Times*, Nov. 19, 1990, 1; R.W. Apple, Jr., "34 Leaders Adopt Pact Proclaiming a United Europe," *NYT*, Nov. 22, 1990, A1; Alan Riding, "The Question That Lingers on Europe: How Will the Goals Be Achieved?" *NYT*, Nov. 22, 1990, A17; and "The Thrill of Europe's Rebirth," *Economist*, Nov. 24, 1990, 63.

88. "Charter of Paris for a New Europe," in Bloed 537–566.

89. "OOVer and Out," *Economist*, Nov. 24, 1990, 64; and Ernest Beck, "1992 End for Eastern Alliance," *The Times*, Nov. 21, 1990, 10.

90. Quoted in R.W. Apple, Jr., "34 Leaders Adopt Pact Proclaiming a United Europe."

91. Quoted in R.W. Apple, Jr., "For 2 Blocs, Old Enemies, an Era Ends," *NYT*, Nov. 20, 1990, A1, A14.

92. "Address by Mikhail Gorbachev to the Council of Europe in Strasbourg."

93. Anatoly S. Chernyaev, "Foreword," *MoH*, xxii.

94. Savranskaya, "The Logic of 1989" 35–36; and Sarotte, *1989* 105–106.

95. Letter from Powell to Wall, "Prime Minister's Meeting with the German Foreign Minister," Feb. 14, 1990, *DBPO* III:VII, doc. 147; and Zelikow and Rice 173–174.

96. Ibid. 139.

97. Ibid. 173–174. Baker quoted on 187.

98. Quoted in ibid. 244. See also Mastny, *HPRE* 27–28.

99. Maresca, *Helsinki Revisited* 122.

100. Ibid. 125.

101. Ibid. 122.

102. Ibid. 126–128; Mastny, *HPRE* 35–37 and docs. 91–92 and 98–99; and Bloed 60.

103. "Charter of Paris for a New Europe"; and Bobbitt 637.

104. Ibid. 637–638; and Andrew McEwen, "East-West Pact on Human Rights," *The Times*, Nov. 16, 1990, 1.

105. George Bush, "Remarks to the Conference on Security and Cooperation in Europe in Paris, France," Nov. 19, 1990, *Public Papers of the Presidents of the United States: George Bush, 1990*, Book II (Washington, DC: USGPO, 1991) 1643.

106. "Charter of Paris for a New Europe."

107. Philip Zelikow, "The New Concert of Europe," *Survival* 34:2 (Summer 1992) 12.

108. Michael Binyon and Michael Evans, "Paris Summit Gives Belated Welcome to Post–Cold War Era," *The Times*, Nov. 17, 1990, 9.

109. Kissinger, *Years of Renewal* 635. On Kissinger's claim that he understood the value of the Final Act while still in office, see Robert Kagan, "The Revisionist: How Henry Kissinger Won the Cold War, or so He Thinks," *The New Republic*, June 21, 1999: 38–48.

110. Michael Binyon, "Japan the Only Absent Friend," *The Times*, Nov. 22, 1990, 8.

111. Jeffrey Mankoff, *Russian Foreign Policy: The Return of Great Power Politics*, 2nd ed. (Lanham, MD: Rowman and Littlefield, 2012); and Sergei Karaganov, "Ending the Cold War," *Current Digest of the Russian Press*, Vol. 66 No. 15 (April 7, 2014) 15–16.

112. See, for example, Chen Kane and Egle Murauskaite, eds., *Regional Security Dialogue in the Middle East: Changes, Challenges and Opportunities* (New York: Routledge, 2014); Jay Lefkowitz, "Let's Confront North Korea on Human Rights," *Wall Street Journal*, Dec. 23, 2008, A11; and Ray Takeyh, "Beware of Iranians Bearing Talks," *Washington Post*, Sept. 27, 2009, B2.

113. Carl von Clausewitz, *On War*, eds. and trans. Michael Howard and Peter Paret (Princeton, NJ: Princeton UP, 1976) 80.

BIBLIOGRAPHY

ARCHIVES

Archives du Ministère des Affaires Étrangères, La Courneuve, France

Archives Nationales, Pierrefitte-sur-Seine, France

Archives of the European Union, Florence, Italy

Gerald R. Ford Presidential Library, Ann Arbor, Michigan

Library and Archives Canada, Ottawa, Canada

Manuscripts and Archives, Sterling Memorial Library, Yale University, New Haven, Connecticut

National Archives and Records Administration, College Park, Maryland

National Archives, Kew, London, United Kingdom

National Security Archive, Washington, DC

NATO Archives, Brussels, Belgium

Politisches Archiv des Auswärtigen Amts, Berlin, Germany

Richard M. Nixon Presidential Library, Yorba Linda, California

Rossiĭskiĭ Gosudarstvennyĭ Arkhiv Noveĭsheĭ Istorii, Moscow, Russia

Stiftung Archiv der Parteien und Massenorganisationen der DDR im Bundesarchiv, Berlin, Germany

PUBLISHED DOCUMENTS

Akten zur Auswärtigen Politik der Bundesrepublik Deutschland. Munich: R. Oldenbourg, 1998–2006.

Albert, Judith Clavir, and Stewart Edward Albert, eds. *The Sixties Papers: Documents of a Rebellious Decade.* New York: Praeger, 1984.

Andropov, Y. V. "The Birth of Samizdat." *Index on Censorship* 23:3 (May 1995): 62–3.

Bloed, Arie, ed. *The Conference on Security and Co-operation in Europe: Analysis and Basic Documents, 1972–1993.* Dordrecht: Kluwer Academic Publishers, 1993.

Brinkley, Douglas, and Luke A. Nichter, eds. *The Nixon Tapes: 1971–1972.* Boston: Houghton Mifflin Harcourt, 2014.

Cherniaev, Anatoliĭ et al., eds. *V Politbiuro TsK KPSS: Po zapisiam Anatoliia Cherniaeva, Vadima Medvedeva, Georgiia Shakhnazarova (1985–1991).* Moscow: Al'pina Biznes Buks, 2006.

Commission on Security and Cooperation in Europe. *Implementation of the Final Act of the Conference on Security and Cooperation in Europe: Findings and Recommendations Two Years after Helsinki.* Washington, DC: USGPO, 1977.

Commission on Security and Cooperation in Europe. *Implementation of the Helsinki Accords: Hearings before the Commission on Security and Cooperation in Europe*, Vol. 1, Feb. 23, 1977. Washington, DC: USGPO, 1977.

―――. *Report of the Study Mission to Europe to the Commission on Security and Cooperation in Europe*. Washington, DC: USGPO, 1977.

Constitution (Fundamental Law) of the Union of Soviet Socialist Republics. Moscow: Novosti Press Agency, 1977.

Deutscher Bundestag, Stenographischer Bericht. 7. Wahlperiod, 183. Sitzung, July 25, 1975. Bonn: Deutscher Bundestag, 1975.

Documents de la Conférence des quatre ministres des affaires étrangères de France, des États-Unis d'Amérique, du Royaume-Uni et de l'Union des républiques soviétiques socialistes, tenue à Berlin du 25 janvier au 18 février 1954. Paris: Documentation Française, 1954.

Documents on British Policy Overseas. London: The Stationery Office, 1997–2009.

Documents Relating to the Meeting of Foreign Ministers of France, the United Kingdom, the Soviet Union and the United States of America, Berlin, 25 January–18 February 1954. London: Her Majesty's Stationery Office, 1954.

Foreign Relations of the United States. Washington, DC: USGPO, 1961–2006.

The Geneva Conference of Heads of Government, July 18–23, 1955. Washington, DC: USGPO, 1955.

Hertle, Hans-Hermann, and Konrad H. Jarausch, eds. *Risse im Bruderbund: Die Gespräche Honecker-Breshnew*. Berlin: Ch. Links, 2006.

International Economic Report of the President. Washington, DC: USGPO, 1973.

Kampelman, Max M. *Three Years at the East-West Divide: The Words of U.S. Ambassador Max M. Kampelman at the Madrid Conference on Security and Human Rights*. Ed. Leonard R. Sussman. New York: Freedom House, 1983.

Kavass, Igor I., Jacqueline Paquin Granier, and Mary Frances Dominick, eds. *Human Rights, European Politics, and the Helsinki Accord: The Documentary Evolution of the Conference on Security and Co-operation in Europe, 1973–1975*, Vols. 1–6. Buffalo, NY: W. S. Hein, 1981.

Kudriashov, Sergeĭ, ed. *General'nyĭ sekretar' L. I. Brezhnev 1964–1982*. Moscow: Arkhiv Prezidenta Rossiĭskoĭ Federatsii, 2006.

Mastny, Vojtech, and Malcolm Byrne, eds. *A Cardboard Castle? The Inside History of the Warsaw Pact, 1955–1991*. Budapest: Central European University Press, 2005.

Mayall, James, and Cornelia Navari, eds. *The End of the Post-War Era: Documents on Great-Power Relations, 1968–1975*. Cambridge: Cambridge UP, 1980.

Navrátil, Jaromír, ed. *The Prague Spring 1968: A National Security Archive Documents Reader*. Budapest: Central European University Press, 1998.

Němcová, Alice, ed. *CSCE Testimonies: Causes and Consequences of the Helsinki Final Act, 1972–1989*. Prague: Prague Office of the OSCE Secretariat, 2013.

Paczkowski, Andrzej, and Malcolm Byrne, eds. *From Solidarity to Martial Law: The Polish Crisis of 1980–1981: A Documentary History*. Budapest: Central European University Press, 2007.

Polskie Dokumenty Dyplomatyczne. Warsaw: Polski Instytut Spraw Międzynarodowych, 2005–2010.

Public Papers of the Presidents of the United States. Washington, DC: USGPO, 1964–1991.

Report of the CPSU Central Committee to the 24th Congress of the Communist Party of the Soviet Union. Moscow: Novosti, 1971.

Rubenstein, Joshua, and Alexander Gribanov, eds. *The KGB File of Andrei Sakharov*. New Haven: Yale UP, 2005.

Savranskaya, Svetlana, Thomas Blanton, and Vladislav Zubok, eds. *Masterpieces of History: The Peaceful End of the Cold War in Europe, 1989.* Budapest: Central European University Press, 2010.

Scammell, Michael ed. *The Solzhenitsyn Files: Secret Soviet Documents Reveal One Man's Fight against the Monolith.* Chicago: Edition Q, 1995.

Schramm, Friedrich-Karl, Wolfram-Georg Riggert, and Alois Friedel, eds. *Sicherheitskonferenz in Europa: Dokumentation 1954–1972.* Frankfurt a. M.: Alfred Metzner, 1972.

Selected Documents Relating to Problems of Security and Cooperation in Europe, 1954–77. Cmnd. 6932. London: Her Majesty's Stationery Office, 1977.

Soviet-American Relations: The Détente Years, 1969–1972. Washington, DC: USGPO, 2007.

Statement on the Stand of the Rumanian Workers' Party Concerning the Problems of the World Communist and Working-Class Movement, Endorsed by the Enlarged Plenum of the CC of the RWP Held in April 1964. Bucharest: Agerpres, 1964.

Suomi, Juhani, ed. *Urho Kekkosen päiväkirjat*, Vol. 3: 1969–74. Helsinki: Otava, 2003.

23rd Congress of the Communist Party of the Soviet Union. Moscow: Novosti, 1966.

US House of Representatives Committee on Foreign Affairs. *Report of the Subcommittee for Review of the Mutual Security Programs on Military Aid to Western Europe.* Washington, DC: USGPO, 1963.

Online Documents

Bange, Oliver, and Stephan Kieninger, eds. *Negotiating One's Own Demise? The GDR's Foreign Ministry and the CSCE Negotiations.* CWIHP e-Dossier No. 17. Washington, DC: Woodrow Wilson International Center for Scholars, 2008. https://www.wilsoncenter.org/publication /negotiating-ones-own-demise-the-gdrs-foreign-ministry-and-the-csce-negotiations.

British Diplomatic Oral History Programme, Churchill College, Cambridge. https://www .chu.cam.ac.uk/archives/collections/bdohp.

Central Foreign Policy Files, Access to Archival Databases, US National Archives and Records Administration. https://aad.archives.gov/aad/.

Cold War International History Project Digital Archive. http://digitalarchive.wilsoncenter .org/.

Foreign Affairs Oral History Collection, Association for Diplomatic Studies and Training, Arlington, VA. http://www.adst.org.

Machiavelli Center Oral History Conference on the CSCE, Florence, Italy, Sept. 29–30, 2003. http://win.machiavellicenter.net/csce.

Parallel History Project on Cooperative Security. http://www.php.isn.ethz.ch/lory1.ethz.ch /index.html.

Pedlow, Gregory W., ed. *NATO Strategy Documents, 1949–1969.* http://www.nato.int/archives /strategy.htm.

To the Geneva Summit: Perestroika and the Transformation of U.S.-Soviet Relations. National Security Archive Briefing Book No. 172. Washington, DC: National Security Archive, 2005. http://nsarchive.gwu.edu/NSAEBB/NSAEBB172/.

Watts, Larry, ed. "Divided Loyalties Within the Bloc: Romanian Objection to Soviet Informal Controls, 1963–1964." CWIHP e-Dossier No. 42. Washington, DC: Woodrow Wilson International Center for Scholars, 2013. https://www.wilsoncenter.org/publication/divided -loyalties-within-the-bloc-romanian-objection-to-soviet-informal-controls-1963.

Watts, Larry, ed. "Romania Security Policy and the Cuban Missile Crisis," CWIHP e-Dossier No. 38. Washington, DC: Woodrow Wilson International Center for Scholars, 2013. https://www.wilsoncenter.org/publication/romania-security-policy-and-the-cuban-missile-crisis.

INTERVIEWS AND ORAL HISTORIES

Author's interview with John Campbell, by telephone, April 11, 2008
Author's interview with Richard Davy, Oxford, June 8, 2016
Author's interview with Thomas Delworth, Ottawa, July 25, 2003
Author's interview with Brian Fall, London, June 9, 2016
Author's interview with John J. Maresca, Geneva, Dec. 18, 2005

PERIODICALS

Aziia i Afrika Segodnia
The Baltimore Sun
Chicago Tribune
A Chronicle of Human Rights in the USSR
Cold War International History Project Bulletin
Current Digest of the Soviet Press
Department of State Bulletin
The Economist
Encounter
Le Figaro
Financial Times
Foreign Affairs
Foreign Broadcast Information Service Daily Reports
Foreign Policy
Frankfurter Allgemeine Zeitung
The Guardian
Harper's
Helsingin Sanomat
International Affairs (Moscow)
Istoricheskii Arkhiv
Izvestiia
The Los Angeles Times
Le Monde
National Review
Népszabadság
Neues Deutschland
The New Republic
New York Review of Books
The New York Times
Newsweek

Pravda
Rabotnichesko Delo
Rudé Právo
Scînteia
Der Spiegel
Sprawy Międzynarodowe
Time
The Times
Translations from Kommunist
Trybuna Ludu
The Wall Street Journal
The Washington Post
Die Welt
Die Zeit

BOOKS AND ARTICLES

Abadie, Frédéric, and Jean-Pierre Corcelette. *Georges Pompidou: Le désir et le destin*. Paris: Balland, 2004.

Adamishin, A. L. "Zakliuchitel'nyĭ Akt: Zanaves opuskaetsia?" *Rossiia v Global'noĭ Politike* 4 (August 2005): 94–110.

Adamishin, Anatoly, and Richard Schifter. *Human Rights, Perestroika, and the End of the Cold War*. Washington, DC: US Institute of Peace, 2009.

Ahooja, Krishna. "Twenty Years of ECE," *Economic and Political Weekly* 2:16 (April 22, 1967).

Aitken, Jonathan. *Nixon: A Life*. London: Weidenfeld and Nicolson, 1993.

Aleksandrov-Agentov, A. M. *Ot Kollontaĭ do Gorbacheva: vospominaniia diplomata, sovetnika A.A. Gromyko, pomoshchnika L.I. Brezhneva, Iu.V. Andropova, K.U. Chernenko i M.S. Gorbacheva*. Moscow: Mezhdunarodnye Otnosheniia, 1994.

Alekseeva, Liudmila. *Soviet Dissent: Contemporary Movements for National, Religious, and Human Rights*. Middletown, CT: Wesleyan UP, 1985.

Alexander, Michael. *Managing the Cold War: A View from the Front Line*. London: RUSI, 2005.

Allain, Jean-Claude, et al. *Histoire de la Diplomatie Française*. Paris: Perrin, 2005.

Alphand, Hervé. *L'Étonnement d'être: Journal (1939–1973)*. Paris: Fayard, 1977.

Amalrik, Andrei. *Notes of a Revolutionary*. New York: Knopf, 1982.

———. *Will the Soviet Union Survive until 1984?* Rev. ed. New York: Harper and Row, 1980.

Ambrose, Stephen E. *Nixon: The Education of a Politician, 1913–1962*. New York: Simon and Schuster, 1987.

Andréani, Jacques. *Le Piège: Helsinki et la chute du communisme*. Paris: Odile Jacob, 2005.

Applebaum, Anne. *Iron Curtain: The Crushing of Eastern Europe, 1944–1956*. New York: Doubleday, 2012.

Arbatov, Georgi. *The System: An Insider's Life in Soviet Politics*. New York: Times Books, 1992.

Aron, Leon. *Roads to the Temple: Truth, Memory, Ideas, and Ideals in the Making of the Russian Revolution, 1987–1991*. New Haven, CT: Yale UP, 2012.

Aron, Raymond. *The Great Debate: Theories of Nuclear Strategy*. Trans. Ernst Pawel. Garden City, NY: Doubleday, 1965.

Association Georges Pompidou. *Georges Pompidou et l'Europe*. Paris: Complexe, 1993.

Aust, Anthony. *Handbook of International Law*, 2nd ed. New York: Cambridge UP, 2010.

Axen, Hermann. *Ich war ein Diener der Partei. Autobiographische Gespräche mit Harald Neubert*. Berlin: Edition Ost, 1996.

Bacon, Edwin, and Mark Sandle, eds. *Brezhnev Reconsidered*. New York: Palgrave Macmillan, 2002.

Badalassi, Nicolas. *En finir avec la guerre froide: La France, l'Europe et le processus d'Helsinki, 1965-1975*. Rennes: Presses universitaires de Rennes, 2014.

Bagley, Tennent H. *Spymaster: Startling Cold War Revelations of a Soviet KGB Chief*. New York: Skyhorse, 2013.

Bahr, Egon. *Zu Meiner Zeit*. Munich: Karl Blessing, 1996.

Bange, Oliver. *Sicherheit und Staat: Die Bündnis- und Militärpolitik der DDR im internationalen Kontext 1969 bis 1990*. Berlin: Ch. Links, 2017.

Bange, Oliver, and Gottfried Niedhart, eds. *Helsinki 1975 and the Transformation of Europe*. New York: Berghahn, 2008.

Bange, Oliver, and Poul Villaume, eds. *The Long Détente: Changing Concepts of Security and Cooperation in Europe, 1950s–1980s*. Budapest: Central European University Press, 2017.

Baron, Samuel H. *Bloody Saturday in the Soviet Union: Novocherkassk, 1962*. Stanford, CA: Stanford UP, 2001.

Bartoszewski, Władysław. "Flying through the Fear Barrier." *Index on Censorship* 14:2 (1985).

Baum, Richard. *Burying Mao: Chinese Politics in the Age of Deng Xiaoping*. Princeton, NJ: Princeton UP, 1994.

Beckerman, Gal. *When They Come for Us We'll Be Gone: The Epic Struggle to Save Soviet Jewry*. Boston: Houghton Mifflin Harcourt, 2010.

Becker-Schaum, Christoph, et al., eds. *The Nuclear Crisis: The Arms Race, Cold War Anxiety, and the German Peace Movement of the 1980s*. New York: Berghahn, 2016.

Beetham, Roger, and Reginald Hibbert. "Observations on British Diplomacy and the CSCE Process." *British Scholar* III:1 (September 2010): 127–138.

Békés, Csaba. "Hungary, the Soviet Bloc, the German Question, and the CSCE Process, 1965–1975." *Journal of Cold War Studies* 18:3 (Summer 2016): 95–138.

Bell, Daniel. *The End of Ideology: On the Exhaustion of Political Ideas in the Fifties*. New York: Free Press, 2000.

Berend, Ivan T. *An Economic History of Twentieth-Century Europe: Economic Regimes from Laissez-Faire to Globalization*. New York: Cambridge UP, 2006.

———. *The Hungarian Economic Reforms, 1953–1988*. Cambridge: Cambridge UP, 1990.

Bernhard, Michael H. *The Origins of Democratization in Poland: Workers, Intellectuals, and Oppositional Politics, 1976–1980*. New York: Columbia UP, 1993.

Bernstein, Robert L. *Speaking Freely: My Life in Publishing and Human Rights*. New York: New Press, 2016.

Berstein, Serge, and Jean-Pierre Rioux. *The Pompidou Years, 1969–1974*. Trans. Christopher Woodall. New York: Cambridge UP, 2000.

Bilandžić, Vladimir, Dittmar Dahlmann, and Milan Kosanović, eds. *From Helsinki to Belgrade: The First CSCE Follow-up Meeting and the Crisis of Détente*. Bonn: Bonn UP, 2012.

Binder, David. *The Other German: Willy Brandt's Life and Times*. Washington, DC: New Republic, 1975.

Black, Conrad. *The Invincible Quest: The Life of Richard Milhous Nixon*. Toronto: McClelland and Stewart, 2007.

Bluth, Christoph. "The Origins of MBFR: West German Policy Priorities and Conventional Arms Control." *War in History* 7:2 (2000): 199–224.

Bobbitt, Philip. *The Shield of Achilles: War, Peace, and the Course of History*. New York: Knopf, 2002.

Bock, Siegfried, Ingrid Muth, and Hermann Schwiesau, eds. *DDR-Außenpolitik im Rückspiegel. Diplomaten im Gespräch*. Münster: Lit Verlag, 2004.

Bolton, Jonathan. *Worlds of Dissent: Charter 77, the Plastic People of the Universe, and Czech Culture under Communism*. Cambridge, MA: Harvard UP, 2008.

Boobbyer, Philip. *Conscience, Dissent and Reform in Soviet Russia*. London: Routledge, 2005.

Bourges, Hervé, ed. *The French Student Revolt: The Leaders Speak*. Trans. B. R. Brewster. New York: Hill and Wang, 1968.

Bowker, Mike, and Phil Williams. *Superpower Détente: A Reappraisal*. London: Sage, 1988.

Bozo, Frédéric. *Deux stratégies pour l'Europe: de Gaulle, les États-Unis et l'Alliance atlantique: 1958–1969*. Paris: Plon, 1998.

———. *Mitterand, the End of the Cold War and German Unification*. Trans. Susan Emanuel. New York: Berghahn, 2009.

Bozo, Frédéric, Marie-Pierre Rey, N. Piers Ludlow, and Bernd Rother, eds. *Visions of the End of the Cold War in Europe*. New York: Berghahn, 2012.

Bracke, Maud. *Which Socialism, Whose Détente? West European Communism and the Czechoslovak Crisis, 1968*. Budapest: Central European University Press, 2007.

Bradley, Mark Philip. *The World Reimagined: Americans and Human Rights in the Twentieth Century*. New York: Cambridge UP, 2016.

Brandt, Willy. *Berliner Ausgabe*. Eds. Helga Grebing, Gregor Schöllgen, and Heinrich August Winkler. Vol. 6. Bonn: J.H.W. Dietz, 2005.

———. *In Exile: Essays, Reflections, and Letters 1933–1974*. Trans. R. W. Last. London: Oswald Wolff, 1971.

———. *My Life in Politics*. Trans. Anthea Bell. London: Hamish Hamilton, 1992.

———. *A Peace Policy for Europe*. Trans. Joel Carmichael. New York: Holt, Rinehart, and Winston, 1969.

———. *People and Politics: The Years 1960–1975*. Trans. J. Maxwell Brownjohn. Boston: Little, Brown, 1978.

Breslauer, George W. *Khrushchev and Brezhnev as Leaders: Building Authority in Soviet Politics*. London: George Allen and Unwin, 1982.

Brezhnev, Leonid. *Selected Speeches and Writings on Foreign Affairs*. New York: Pergamon, 1979.

Brezhneva, Luba. *The World I Left Behind: Pieces of a Past*. Trans. Geoffrey Polk. New York: Random House, 1995.

Brown, Archie. *The Gorbachev Factor*. New York: Oxford UP, 1996.

———. *The Rise and Fall of Communism*. New York: HarperCollins, 2009.

———. *Seven Years that Changed the World: Perestroika in Perspective*. New York: Oxford UP, 2007.

Brown, Seyom. *New Forces in World Politics*. Washington, DC: Brookings, 1974.

Brunner, Édouard. *Lambris dorés et coulisses: Souvenirs d'un diplomate*. Geneva: Georg, 2001.

Brzezinski, Zbigniew. *Between Two Ages: America's Role in the Technetronic Era*. New York: Viking, 1970.

Brzezinski, Zbigniew, and Samuel P. Huntington. *Political Power: USA/USSR*. New York: Viking, 1964.

Buchan, Alastair. *The End of the Postwar Era: A New Balance of World Power*. London: Weidenfeld and Nicolson, 1974.

Buchan, Alastair, ed. *Europe's Future, Europe's Choices*. New York: Columbia UP, 1969.

Buchan, Alastair, and Philip Windsor. *Arms and Stability in Europe: A British-French-German Enquiry*. London: Chatto and Windus, 1963.

Bukovansky, Mlada. *Legitimacy and Power Politics: The American and French Revolutions in International Political Culture*. Princeton, NJ: Princeton UP, 2002.

Bukovsky, Vladimir. *To Build a Castle: My Life as a Dissenter*. New York: Viking, 1978.

Bull, Hedley. *The Anarchical Society: A Study of Order in World Politics*. New York: Columbia UP, 1977.

Cain, Frank. *Economic Statecraft during the Cold War: European Responses to the US Trade Embargo*. New York: Routledge, 2007.

Calleo, David. *The Atlantic Fantasy: The US, NATO, and Europe*. Baltimore: Johns Hopkins UP, 1970.

Cerny, Karl H., and Henry W. Briefs, eds. *NATO in Quest of Cohesion*. New York: Praeger, 1965.

Chazov, Evgeniĭ. *Zdorov'e i vlast': Vospominaniia "kremlevskogo vracha."* Moscow: Novosti, 1992.

Chekhov, Anton. *The Lady with the Little Dog and Other Stories*. Trans. Ronald Wilks. London: Penguin, 2002.

Chen Jian. *Mao's China and the Cold War*. Chapel Hill, NC: UNC Press, 2001.

Cherniaev, Anatoliĭ. *Moia zhizn' i moë vremia*. Moscow: Mezhdunarodnye Otnosheniia, 1995.

———. *My Six Years with Gorbachev*. Trans. and eds. Robert D. English and Elizabeth Tucker. University Park, PA: Pennsylvania State UP, 2000.

———. *Sovmestnyĭ iskhod: Dnevnik dvukh epokh, 1972–1991 gody*. Moscow: Rosspen, 2010.

Clark, Ian. *International Legitimacy and World Society*. New York: Oxford UP, 2007.

———. *Legitimacy in International Society*. New York: Oxford UP, 2005.

Cleveland, Harold van B. *The Atlantic Idea and Its European Rivals*. New York: McGraw-Hill, 1966.

Cocks, Paul, Robert V. Daniels, and Nancy Whittier Heer, eds. *The Dynamics of Soviet Politics*. Cambridge, MA: Harvard UP, 1976.

Cohen, Warren I., and Nancy Bernkopf Tucker, eds. *Lyndon Johnson Confronts the World: American Foreign Policy 1963–1968*. New York: Cambridge UP, 1994.

Cointet, Jean-Paul et al., eds. *Un politique: Georges Pompidou*. Paris: Presses universitaires de France, 2001.

Collins, Robert M. "The Economic Crisis of 1968 and the Waning of the 'American Century,'" *American Historical Review*, 101:2 (April 1996): 396–422.

Cooper, Robert. *The Breaking of Nations: Order and Chaos in the Twenty-First Century*. London: Atlantic, 2004.

Crafts, Nicholas, and Gianni Toniolo, eds. *Economic Growth in Europe since 1945*. Cambridge: Cambridge UP, 1996.

Craig, Gordon A., and Francis L. Loewenheim, eds. *The Diplomats 1939–1979*. Princeton, NJ: Princeton UP, 1994.

Crampton, R. J. *Eastern Europe in the Twentieth Century—and After*. New York: Routledge, 1997.

Crump, Laurien. *The Warsaw Pact Reconsidered: International Relations in Eastern Europe, 1955–1969*. New York: Routledge, 2015.

Daalder, Ivo H., and I. M. Destler. *In the Shadow of the Oval Office: Profiles of the National Secu-*

rity Advisers and the Presidents They Served—from JFK to George W. Bush. New York: Scribner, 2009.

Dallek, Robert. *Nixon and Kissinger: Partners in Power*. New York: Random House, 2007.

Danmark under den kolde krig. Den sikkerhedspolitiske situation 1945–1991, Vol. 2: 1963–1978. Copenhagen: Dansk Institut for Internationale Studier, 2005.

Daum, Andreas W., Lloyd C. Gardner, and Wilfried Mausbach, eds. *America, the Vietnam War, and the World: Comparative and International Perspectives*. New York: Cambridge UP, 2003.

Davy, Richard. "Helsinki Myths: Setting the Record Straight on the Final Act of the CSCE, 1975." *Cold War History* 9:1 (Feb. 2009): 1–22.

de Boer, Connie. "The Polls: Our Commitment to World War III," *Public Opinion Quarterly* 45:1 (Spring 1981): 126–134.

de Gaulle, Charles. *Discours et messages*, Vols. 4 and 5. Paris: Plon, 1970.

———. *Mémoires d'espoir, Tome 1: Le renouveau (1958–1962)*. Paris: Plon, 1970.

Deletant, Dennis, and Mihail Ionescu, "Romania and the Warsaw Pact: 1955–1989," CWIHP Working Paper No. 43. Washington, DC: Woodrow Wilson International Center for Scholars, 2004.

Deriabin, Iurii. *Legko li byt' poslom? Zapiski o zhizni i kar'ere diplomata*. Moscow: Ves' Mir, 2010.

DiNunzio, Mario R., ed. *Woodrow Wilson: Essential Writings and Speeches of the Scholar-President*. New York: NYU Press, 2006.

Dissent in Poland: Reports and Documents in Translation. London: Association of Polish Students and Graduates in Exile, 1977.

Dobrynin, Anatoly. *In Confidence: Moscow's Ambassador to Six Cold War Presidents*. New York: Times Books, 1995.

Domber, Gregory F. *Empowering Revolution: America, Poland, and the End of the Cold War*. Chapel Hill, NC: UNC Press, 2014.

Donoughue, Bernard. *Downing Street Diary: With Harold Wilson in No. 10*. London: Jonathan Cape, 2005.

Drinan, Robert F. *The Mobilization of Shame: A World View of Human Rights*. New Haven, CT: Yale UP, 2001.

Dubinin, Yuri. *Diplomaticheskaya byl': Zapiski posla vo Frantsii*. Moscow: Rosspen, 1997.

———. "The Road to Helsinki," *International Affairs* (Moscow) 7 (1994): 76–94.

Dujardin, Vincent. "Go-Between: Belgium and Détente, 1961–73," *Cold War History* 7:1 (Feb. 2007): 95–116.

———. *Pierre Harmel: Biographie*. Brussels: Le Cri, 2004.

du Réau, Elisabeth and Christine Manigand, eds. *Vers la réunification de l'Europe: Apports et limites du processus d'Helsinki de 1975 à nos jours*. Paris: L'Harmattan, 2005.

Eckel, Jan, and Samuel Moyn, eds. *The Breakthrough: Human Rights in the 1970s*. Philadelphia: University of Pennsylvania Press, 2014.

Edmonds, Robin. *Soviet Foreign Policy: The Brezhnev Years*. New York: Oxford UP, 1983.

Ehring, Klaus, and Martin Dallwitz. *Schwerter zu Pflugscharen: Friedensbewegung in der DDR*. Reinbek bei Hamburg: Rowohlt, 1982.

Eichengreen, Barry. *The European Economy since 1945: Coordinated Capitalism and Beyond*. Princeton, NJ: Princeton UP, 2007.

———. *Globalizing Capital: A History of the International Monetary System*. Princeton, NJ: Princeton UP, 1996.

Eley, Geoff, and Jan Palmowski, eds. *Citizenship and National Identity in Twentieth-Century Germany*. Stanford, CA: Stanford UP, 2008.

English, Robert D. *Russia and the Idea of the West: Gorbachev, Intellectuals, and the End of the Cold War*. New York: Columbia, 2000.

Fainberg, Dina, and Artemy M. Kalinovsky, eds. *Reconsidering Stagnation in the Brezhnev Era: Ideology and Exchange*. Lanham, MD: Lexington, 2016.

Feenberg, Andrew, and Jim Freedman. *When Poetry Ruled the Streets: The French May Events of 1968*. Albany, NY: SUNY Press, 2001.

Ferguson, Niall. *The House of Rothschild*, Vol. 2. New York: Penguin, 2000.

Ferguson, Niall, Charles S. Maier, Erez Manela, and Daniel J. Sargent, eds. *The Shock of the Global: The 1970s in Perspective*. Cambridge, MA: Harvard UP, 2010.

Féron, Bernard, and Michel Tatu. *Au Kremlin comme si vous y étiez: Khrouchtchev, Brejnev, Gorbatchev et les autres sous les feux de la Glasnost*. Paris: Le Monde, 1991.

Ferraris, Luigi Vittorio. *Report on a Negotiation: Helsinki-Geneva-Helsinki 1972–1975*. Trans. Marie-Claire Barber. Alphen aan den Rijn: Sijthoff and Noordhoff International Publishers, 1979.

Fink, Carole, Philipp Gassert, and Detlef Junker, eds. *1968: The World Transformed*. New York: Cambridge UP, 1998.

Fischer, Thomas. "'A Mustard Seed Grew into a Bushy Tree': The Finnish CSCE initiative of 5 May 1969," *Cold War History* 9:2 (May 2009): 177–201.

———. *Neutral Power in the CSCE: The N+N States and the Making of the Helsinki Accords 1975*. Baden-Baden: Nomos, 2009.

Fitzpatrick, Sheila. *The Cultural Front: Power and Culture in Revolutionary Russia*. Ithaca, NY: Cornell UP, 1992.

———. *Education and Social Mobility in the Soviet Union, 1921–1934*. Cambridge: Cambridge UP, 1979.

Fleury, Antoine, Carole Fink, and Lubor Jílek, eds. *Les droits de l'homme en Europe depuis 1945*. Bern: Peter Lang, 2003.

Fogelsong, David. *American Mission and the "Evil Empire": The Crusade for a "Free Russia" since 1881*. New York: Cambridge UP, 2007.

Fokine, Yuri, et al. "Helsinki 30 Years Later," *International Affairs* (Moscow) 51:5 (October 2005): 184–200.

Frieden, Jeffry A. *Global Capitalism: Its Fall and Rise in the Twentieth Century*. New York: W. W. Norton, 2006.

Friedman, Jeremy. *Shadow Cold War: The Sino-Soviet Competition for the Third World*. Chapel Hill, NC: UNC Press, 2015.

Fursenko, Aleksandr, and Timothy Naftali. *Khrushchev's Cold War: The Inside Story of an American Adversary*. New York: Norton, 2006.

———. *"One Hell of a Gamble": Khrushchev, Castro, and Kennedy, 1958–1964*. New York: Norton, 1997.

Fürst, Juliane. *Stalin's Last Generation: Soviet Post-war Youth and the Emergence of Mature Socialism*. New York: Oxford UP, 2010.

Gaddis, John Lewis. *We Now Know: Rethinking Cold War History*. New York: Oxford UP, 1997.

Garthoff, Raymond. *Détente and Confrontation: American-Soviet Relations from Nixon to Reagan*. Rev. ed. Washington, DC: Brookings, 1994.

Garton Ash, Timothy. *In Europe's Name: Germany and the Divided Continent*. New York: Vintage, 1993.

———. *The Uses of Adversity: Essays on the Fate of Central Europe*. New York: Random House, 1989.

Gavin, Francis J. *Gold, Dollars, and Power: The Politics of International Monetary Relations, 1958–1971*. Chapel Hill, NC: UNC Press, 2004.

———. *Nuclear Statecraft: History and Strategy in America's Atomic Age*. Ithaca, NY: Cornell UP, 2012.

Genscher, Hans-Dietrich. *Rebuilding a House Divided: A Memoir by the Architect of Germany's Reunification*. Trans. Thomas Thornton. New York: Broadway, 1998.

Ghébali, Victor-Yves. *La Diplomatie de la détente: La CSCE, 1973–1989*. Brussels: Bruylant, 1989.

Gibbons, William J., ed. *Pacem in Terris: Encyclical Letter of His Holiness Pope John XXIII*. New York: Paulist Press, 1963.

Gill, Graeme. *Symbols and Legitimacy in Soviet Politics*. New York: Cambridge UP, 2011.

Gitlin, Todd. *The Sixties: Years of Hope, Days of Rage*. New York: Bantam, 1987.

Glucksmann, André. *La cuisinière et le mangeur d'hommes: Essai sur les rapports entre l'Etat, le marxisme et les camps de concentration*. Paris: Seuil, 1975.

Goddeeris, Idesbald, ed. *Solidarity with Solidarity: Western European Trade Unions and the Polish Crisis, 1980-1982*. Lanham, MD: Lexington, 2010.

Goldberg, Paul. *The Final Act: The Dramatic, Revealing Story of the Moscow Helsinki Watch Group*. New York: William Morrow, 1988.

Goodby, James. *Europe Undivided: The New Logic of Peace in US-Russian Relations*. Washington, DC: United States Institute of Peace, 1998.

Gorbachev, Mikhail. *Mikhail Gorbachev: Prophet of Change: From the Cold War to a Sustainable World*. Forest Row, East Sussex: Clairview, 2011.

Gorbachev, Mikhail, and Zdeněk Mlynář. *Conversations with Gorbachev: On Perestroika, the Prague Spring, and the Crossroads of Socialism*. New York: Columbia UP, 2002.

Gorsuch, Anne E. *All This Is Your World: Soviet Tourism at Home and Abroad after Stalin*. New York: Oxford UP, 2011.

Granatstein, J. L., and Robert Bothwell. *Pirouette: Pierre Trudeau and Canadian Foreign Policy*. Toronto: University of Toronto Press, 1991.

Grachev, Andreĭ. *Gorbachev's Gamble: Soviet Foreign Policy and the End of the Cold War*. Cambridge: Polity, 2008.

———. *Kremlevskaia khronika*. Moscow: Eksmo, 1994.

Gray, William Glenn. *Germany's Cold War: The Global Campaign to Isolate East Germany, 1949–1969*. Chapel Hill, NC: UNC Press, 2003.

Gregory, Paul R., and Robert C. Stuart. *Soviet Economic Structure and Performance*. 4th ed. New York: Harper and Row, 1990.

Gutmann, Benjamin. "Relais et réseaux de la Charte 77 en France, entre 1977 et 1989." *Bulletin de l'Institut Pierre Renouvin* 33 (2011): 49–64.

Habermas, Jürgen. *Legitimation Crisis*. Trans. Thomas McCarthy. Boston: Beacon Press, 1975.

———. *Toward a Rational Society: Student Protest, Science, and Politics*. Trans. Jeremy J. Shapiro. Boston: Beacon Press, 1970.

Haftendorn, Helga. *Coming of Age: German Foreign Policy since 1945*. Lanham, MD: Rowman and Littlefield, 2006.

———. *Sicherheit und Entspannung: Zur Aussenpolitik der Bundesrepublik Deutschland*. Baden-Baden: Nomos, 1983.

Hájek, Jiří. *Dix ans après: Prague 1968–1978*. Paris: Éditions du Seuil, 1978.

Hakkarainen, Petri. *A State of Peace in Europe: West Germany and the CSCE, 1966–1975*. New York: Berghahn, 2011.

Hanhimäki, Jussi. *The Flawed Architect: Henry Kissinger and American Foreign Policy*. New York: Oxford UP, 2004.

Hanisch, Anja. *Die DDR im KSZE-Prozess 1972–1985*. Munich: Oldenbourg, 2012.

Hanson, Philip. *The Rise and Fall of the Soviet Economy: An Economic History of the USSR from 1945*. London: Pearson, 2003.

Harrison, Hope M. *Driving the Soviets Up the Wall: Soviet-East German Relations, 1953–1961*. Princeton, NJ: Princeton UP, 2003.

Hassner, Pierre. "Change and Security in Europe Part I: The Background," *Adelphi Papers* 8:45 (Feb. 1968).

Havel, Václav. *Open Letters: Selected Writings 1965–1990*. Ed. Paul Wilson. New York: Vintage, 1992.

Heiss, Mary Ann, and S. Victor Papacosma, eds. *NATO and the Warsaw Pact: Intrabloc Conflicts*. Kent, OH: Kent State UP, 2008.

Held, Joseph. "Hungary: Iron out of Wood," *Problems of Communism* (November–December 1966).

Helleiner, Eric. *Forgotten Foundations of Bretton Woods: International Development and the Making of the Postwar Order*. Ithaca, NY: Cornell UP, 2014.

Hentilä, Seppo. "Maintaining Neutrality between the Two German States: Finland and Divided Germany until 1973," *Contemporary European History* 15:4 (2006): 473–493.

———. *Neutral zwischen den beiden deutschen Staaten. Finnland und Deutschland im Kalten Krieg*. Berlin: Berliner Wissenschafts-Verlag, 2006.

Herring, George C. *America's Longest War: The United States and Vietnam, 1950–1975*, 3rd ed. New York: McGraw-Hill, 1996.

Hildebrand, Klaus. *Von Erhard zur Großen Koalition 1963–1969*. Stuttgart and Wiesbaden: Deutsche Verlags-Anstalt and F.A. Brockhaus, 1984.

Hinsley, F. H. *Sovereignty*, 2nd ed. Cambridge: Cambridge UP, 1986.

Hoffmann, Erik P., and Robbin F. Laird. *"The Scientific-Technological Revolution" and Soviet Foreign Policy*. New York: Pergamon, 1982.

Hoffmann, Stanley. *Primacy or World Order: American Foreign Policy since the Cold War*. New York: McGraw-Hill, 1978.

———. "Restraints and Choices in American Foreign Policy," *Daedalus* 91:4 (Fall 1962): 668–704.

Holst, Johan Jørgen, and Karen Alette Melander. "European Security and Confidence-Building Measures." *Survival* 19:4 (1977): 146–154.

Holsti, K. J. "Bargaining Theory and Diplomatic Reality: The CSCE Negotiations." *Review of International Studies* 8:3 (July 1982): 159–170.

Howard, Michael. *The Invention of Peace: Reflections on War and International Order*. New Haven, CT: Yale UP, 2001.

Hunt, Michael H. *The American Ascendancy: How the United States Gained and Wielded Global Dominance*. Chapel Hill, NC: UNC Press, 2007.

Ikenberry, G. John. *After Victory: Institutions, Strategic Restraint, and the Rebuilding of Order after Major Wars*. Princeton, NJ: Princeton UP, 2001.

Isaacson, Walter. *Kissinger: A Biography*. New York: Touchstone, 1996.

Isserman, Maurice, and Michael Kazin. *America Divided: The Civil War of the 1960s*. New York: Oxford UP, 1999.

Jarząbek, Wanda. "Hope and Reality: Poland and the Conference on Security and Cooperation in Europe, 1964–1989." CWIHP Working Paper No. 56. Washington, DC: Woodrow Wilson International Center for Scholars, 2008.

———. "The Impact of the German Question on Polish Attitudes toward CSCE, 1964–1975." *Journal of Cold War Studies* 18:3 (Summer 2016): 139–157.

———. *Polska wobec Konferencji Bezpieczenstwa i Wspolpracy w Europie*. Warsaw: Instytut Studiow Politycznych Polskiej Akademii Nauk, 2008.

Jebb, Gladwyn. *Halfway to 1984*. New York: Columbia UP, 1966.

Jersild, Austin. *The Sino-Soviet Alliance: An International History*. Chapel Hill, NC: UNC Press, 2014.

Johnson, A. Ross. *Radio Free Europe and Radio Liberty: The CIA Years and Beyond*. Washington, DC: Woodrow Wilson Center Press, 2010.

Johnston, Andrew M. *Hegemony and Culture in the Origins of NATO Nuclear First Use, 1945–1955*. New York: Palgrave Macmillan, 2005.

Judt, Tony. *Marxism and the French Left: Studies on Labour and Politics in France, 1830–1981*. New York: NYU Press, 2011.

———. *Postwar: A History of Europe since 1945*. New York: Penguin, 2008.

Junes, Tom. *Student Politics in Communist Poland: Generations of Consent and Dissent*. Lanham, MD: Lexington Books, 2015.

Kandiah, Michael D., and Gillian Staerck, eds. *The Helsinki Negotiations: The Accords and Their Impact*. London: Institute of Contemporary British History, 2006.

Kane, Chen, and Egle Murauskaite, eds. *Regional Security Dialogue in the Middle East: Changes, Challenges and Opportunities*. New York: Routledge, 2014.

Kaplan, Lawrence S. *NATO Divided, NATO United: The Evolution of an Alliance*. Westport, CT: Praeger, 2004.

Karner, Stefan, et al., eds. *Die Kreml und die deutsche Wiedervereinigung 1990*. Berlin: Metropol, 2015.

Kaser, M. C., ed. *The Economic History of Eastern Europe, 1919–1975*. Oxford: Oxford UP, 1986.

Kashlev, Iurii. *Khel'sinkskii protsess 1975–2005: Svet i teni glazami uchastnika*. Moscow: Izdatel'stvo "Izvestiia," 2005.

———. "The CSCE in the Soviet Union's Politics," *International Affairs* (Moscow) 11–12 (1995): 66–72.

Katzer, Nikolaus. *"Eine Übung im Kalten Krieg." Die Berliner Außenministerkonferenz von 1954*. Cologne: Verlag Wissenschaft und Politik, 1994.

Kemp, Walter A. *Nationalism and Communism in Eastern Europe and the Soviet Union: A Basic Contradiction?* Houndmills, Basingstoke: Macmillan, 1999.

Kemp-Welch, Anthony. *Poland under Communism: A Cold War History*. New York: Cambridge UP, 2008.

Keys, Barbara J. *Reclaiming American Virtue: The Human Rights Revolution of the 1970s*. Cambridge, MA: Harvard UP, 2014.

Kieninger, Stephan. *Dynamic Détente: The United States and Europe, 1964-1975*. Lanham, MD: Lexington, 2016.

Kilian, Werner. *Die Hallstein-Doktrin: Der Diplomatische Krieg zwischen der BRD und der DDR 1955–1973*. Berlin: Duncker und Humblot, 2001.

King, Robert R., and Robert W. Dean, eds. *East European Perspectives on European Security and Cooperation*. New York: Praeger, 1974.

Kissinger, Henry A. *The Necessity for Choice: Prospects of American Foreign Policy*. New York: Harper, 1961.

Kissinger, Henry A. *White House Years*. Boston: Little, Brown, 1979.

———. *A World Restored: Metternich, Castlereagh, and the Problems of Peace, 1812–1822*. Boston: Houghton Mifflin, 1957.

———. *Years of Renewal*. New York: Simon and Schuster, 1999.

Klimke, Martin, and Joachim Scharloth, eds. *1968 in Europe: A History of Protest and Activism, 1956–1977*. New York: Palgrave Macmillan, 2008.

Klimke, Martin, Jacco Pekelder, and Joachim Scharloth, eds. *Between Prague Spring and French May: Opposition and Revolt in Europe, 1960–1980*. New York: Berghahn, 2011.

Kochavi, Noam. "Insights Abandoned, Flexibility Lost: Kissinger, Soviet Jewish Emigration, and the Demise of Détente," *Diplomatic History* 29:3 (June 2005): 503–530.

Korey, William. *The Promises We Keep: Human Rights, the Helsinki Process, and American Foreign Policy*. New York: St. Martin's Press, 1993.

Kornienko, Georgiĭ. *Kholodnaia voĭna: Svidetel'stvo eë uchastnika*. Moscow: Olma-Press, 2001.

Kotkin, Stephen. *Armageddon Averted: The Soviet Collapse 1970–2000*. New York: Oxford UP, 2001.

———. *Uncivil Society: 1989 and the Implosion of the Communist Establishment*. New York: Modern Library, 2009.

Kovalev, Anatoliĭ. *Azbuka diplomatii*. Moscow: Interpraks, 1993.

———. *Iskusstvo vozmozhnogo: Vospominaniia*. Moscow: Novyĭ Khronograf, 2016.

———. "Midovtsy i genseki." *Novoe Vremia* 38 (1993): 42–47.

———. "Na beregakh Zhenevskogo ozera: Liricheskii reportazh," *Druzhba Narodov* 1978 (4): 113–123.

Kovalev, Andrei A. *Russia's Dead End: An Insider's Testimony from Gorbachev to Putin*. Trans. Steven I. Levine. Lincoln, NE: Potomac, 2017.

Kovrig, Bennett. *Of Walls and Bridges: The United States and Eastern Europe*. New York: NYU Press, 1991.

Kozlov, Denis. *The Readers of* Novyi Mir: *Coming to Terms with the Stalinist Past*. Cambridge, MA: Harvard UP, 2013.

Kozlov, Denis, and Eleonory Gilburd, eds. *The Thaw: Soviet Society and Culture during the 1950s and 1960s*. Toronto: University of Toronto Press, 2013.

Kramer, Mark. "The Collapse of East European Communism and the Repercussions within the Soviet Union (Part 1)," *Journal of Cold War Studies* 5:4 (Fall 2003): 178–256.

———. "The Soviet Union and the 1956 Crises in Hungary and Poland: Reassessments and New Findings," *Journal of Contemporary History* 33:2 (April 1998): 163–214.

Krasner, Stephen D. *Sovereignty: Organized Hypocrisy*. Princeton, NJ: Princeton UP, 1999.

Kvitsinskiĭ, Iuriĭ. *Vremia i sluchaĭ: Zametki professionala*. Moscow: Olma-Press, 1999.

Laba, Roman. *The Roots of Solidarity: A Political Sociology of Poland's Working-Class Democratization*. Princeton, NJ: Princeton UP, 1991.

Lacouture, Jean. *De Gaulle*, Vol. 3. Paris: Éditions du Seuil, 1986.

Lauren, Paul Gordon. *The Evolution of International Human Rights: Visions Seen*. Philadelphia: University of Pennsylvania Press, 2003.

Lawrence, Mark Atwood. *The Vietnam War: A Concise International History*. New York: Oxford UP, 2008.

Leffler, Melvyn P. *For the Soul of Mankind: The United States, the Soviet Union, and the Cold War*. New York: Hill and Wang, 2007.

Leffler, Melvyn P., and Odd Arne Westad, eds. *The Cambridge History of the Cold War*. New York: Cambridge UP, 2010.

Leonov, Nikolaĭ. *Likholet'e*. Moscow: Mezhdunarodnye Otnosheniia, 1995.

Lévesque, Jacques. *The Enigma of 1989: The USSR and the Liberation of Eastern Europe*. Trans. Keith Martin. Berkeley: University of California Press, 1997.

Lévy, Bernard-Henri. *La barbarie à visage humain*. Paris: Grasset, 1977.

Lipkin, M. A. "Evropeĭskaia Integratsiia i Sovetskie Ekonomicheskie Initsiativy (1950-e – pervaia polovina 1970-kh godov)," *Novaia i Noveĭshaia Istoriia* 3 (2009): 47–64.

Lipski, Jan Józef. *KOR: A History of the Workers' Defense Committee in Poland, 1976–1981*. Berkeley: University of California Press, 1985.

Little, Richard, and Steve Smith, eds. *Belief Systems and International Relations*. New York: Basil Blackwell, 1988.

Litwak, Robert. *Détente and the Nixon Doctrine: American Foreign Policy and the Pursuit of Stability, 1969–1976*. New York: Cambridge UP, 1984.

Logevall, Fredrik, and Andrew Preston, eds. *Nixon in the World: American Foreign Relations, 1969–1977*. New York: Oxford UP, 2008.

Loth, Wilfried, and Georges-Henri Soutou, eds. *The Making of Détente: Eastern and Western Europe in the Cold War, 1965–75*. New York: Routledge, 2008.

Lourie, Richard. *Sakharov: A Biography*. Hanover, NH: Brandeis UP, 2002.

Löwenthal, Richard. "Changing Soviet Policies and Interests," *Adelphi Papers* 10:66 (1970).

Ludlow, N. Piers, ed. *European Integration and the Cold War: Ostpolitik-Westpolitik*. New York: Routledge, 2007.

Lundestad, Geir. *"Empire" by Integration: The United States and European Integration, 1945–1997*. New York: Oxford UP, 1998.

Lüthi, Lorenz M. *The Sino-Soviet Split: Cold War in the Communist World*. Princeton, NJ: Princeton UP, 2008.

Machchewicz, Paweł. *Poland's War on Radio Free Europe, 1950–1989*. Trans. Maya Latynski. Washington, DC: Woodrow Wilson Center Press, 2014.

MacMillan, Margaret. *Nixon in China: The Week That Changed the World*. Toronto: Viking, 2006.

Maddison, Angus. *The World Economy: Historical Statistics*. Paris: Development Centre of the Organisation for Economic Co-operation and Development (OECD), 2006.

Maier, Charles S. *Dissolution: The Crisis of Communism and the End of East Germany*. Princeton, NJ: Princeton UP, 1997.

Makko, Aryo. *Ambassadors of Realpolitik: Sweden, the CSCE, and the Cold War*. New York: Berghahn, 2016.

Manela, Erez. "A Pox on Your Narrative: Writing Disease Control into Cold War History," *Diplomatic History* 34:2 (April 2010): 299–323.

Mankoff, Jeffrey. *Russian Foreign Policy: The Return of Great Power Politics*, 2nd ed. Lanham, MD: Rowman and Littlefield, 2012.

Maresca, John J. "The CSCE at Its Inception: 1975 in Myth and Reality," *OSCE Yearbook 2005*. Baden-Baden: Nomos, 2006.

———. *Helsinki Revisited: A Key US Negotiator's Memoirs on the Development of the CSCE into the OSCE*. Stuttgart: Ibidem-Verlag, 2016.

———. *To Helsinki: The Conference on Security and Cooperation in Europe 1973–1975*. New ed. Durham, NC: Duke UP, 1987.

Marquardt, James J. "Transparency and Security Competition: Open Skies and America's Cold War Statecraft, 1948–1960," *Journal of Cold War Studies* 9:1 (Winter 2007): 55–87.

Marshall, Barbara. *Willy Brandt: A Political Biography*. Basingstoke: Macmillan, 1997.

Martin, Garret Joseph. *General de Gaulle's Cold War: Challenging American Hegemony, 1963–1968*. New York: Berghahn, 2013.

Mastny, Vojtech. *Helsinki, Human Rights, and European Security: Analysis and Documentation*. Durham, NC: Duke UP, 1986.

——. *The Helsinki Process and the Reintegration of Europe, 1986–1991: Analysis and Documentation*. New York: NYU Press, 1992.

Mastny, Vojtech, Sven G. Holtsmark, and Andreas Wenger, eds. *War Plans and Alliances in the Cold War: Threat Perceptions in the East and West*. London: Routledge, 2006.

Matlock, Jr., Jack F. *Autopsy on an Empire: The American Ambassador's Account of the Collapse of the Soviet Union*. New York: Random House, 1995.

Mazower, Mark. *Governing the World: The History of an Idea*. New York: Penguin, 2012.

Medvedev, Roĭ. *Neizvestnyĭ Andropov: Politicheskaia biografiia Iuriia Andropova*. Moscow: Prava Cheloveka, 1999.

Meneguzzi Rostagni, Carla, ed. *The Helsinki Process: A Historical Reappraisal*. Padua: CEDAM, 2005.

Merseburger, Peter. *Willy Brandt, 1913–1992: Visionär und Realist*. Stuttgart: Deutsche Verlags-Anstalt, 2002.

Messmer, Pierre, ed. *Georges Pompidou hier et aujourd'hui: Témoignages*. Paris: Breet, 1990.

Michnik, Adam. *Letters from Prison and Other Essays*. Trans. Maya Latynski. Berkeley: University of California Press, 1985.

The Military Balance 1970–1971. London: Institute for Strategic Studies, 1970.

Miller, Chris. *The Struggle to Save the Soviet Economy: Mikhail Gorbachev and the Collapse of the USSR*. Chapel Hill, NC: UNC Press, 2016.

Mlynář, Zdeněk. *Nightfrost in Prague: The End of Humane Socialism*. Trans. Paul Wilson. New York: Karz, 1980.

Möckli, Daniel. *European Foreign Policy During the Cold War: Heath, Brandt, Pompidou and the Dream of Political Unity*. London: I.B. Tauris, 2009.

Morgenthau, Hans J. "Arguing about the Cold War," *Encounter* (May 1967): 37–41.

Moyn, Samuel. *The Last Utopia: Human Rights in History*. Cambridge, MA: Harvard UP, 2010.

Mueller, Wolfgang, and Michael Portmann. *Osteuropa vom Weltkrieg zum Wende*. Vienna: Verlag der Österreichischen Akademie der Wissenschaften, 2007.

Müller, Martin. *Politik und Bürokratie: die MBFR-Politik der Bundesrepublik Deutschland zwischen 1967 und 1973*. Baden-Baden: Nomos, 1988.

Munting, Roger. *The Economic Development of the USSR*. London: Croon Helm, 1982.

Murray, Williamson, and Jim Lacey, eds. *The Making of Peace: Rulers, States, and the Aftermath of War*. New York: Cambridge UP, 2009.

Nathans, Benjamin. "The Dictatorship of Reason: Aleksandr Vol'pin and the Idea of Rights under 'Developed Socialism,'" *Slavic Review* 66:4 (Winter 2007): 630–663.

Neer, Robert M. *Napalm: An American Biography*. Cambridge, MA: Harvard UP, 2013.

Nelson, Michael. *War of the Black Heavens: The Battles of Western Broadcasting in the Cold War*. Syracuse, NY: Syracuse UP, 1997.

Newhouse, John. *Cold Dawn: The Story of SALT*. New York: Holt, Rinehart and Wilson, 1973.

Newnham, Randall. "Economic Linkage and Willy Brandt's Ostpolitik: The Case of the Warsaw Treaty," *German Politics* 16:2 (June 2007): 247–263.

Nicholson, Martin. "The New Soviet Constitution: A Political Analysis." *The World Today* 34:1 (January 1978).

Nixon, Richard M. "Asia after Viet Nam," *Foreign Affairs* 46:1 (October 1967): 111–125.

————. *RN: The Memoirs of Richard Nixon*, Vol. 1. New York: Warner Books, 1979.

————. *Six Crises*. Garden City, NY: Doubleday, 1962.

Normand, Roger, and Sarah Zaidi. *Human Rights at the UN: The Political History of Universal Justice*. Bloomington, IN: Indiana UP, 2008.

Nove, Alec. *An Economic History of the USSR, 1917–1991*. 3rd ed. New York: Penguin, 1992.

Nuti, Leopoldo, ed. *The Crisis of Détente in Europe: From Helsinki to Gorbachev, 1975–1985*. New York: Routledge, 2009.

Nuttall, Simon J. *European Political Co-operation*. New York: Oxford UP, 1992.

Oberdorfer, Don. *From the Cold War to a New Era: The United States and the Soviet Union, 1983–1991*. Updated ed. Baltimore: Johns Hopkins UP, 1998.

————. *Senator Mansfield: The Extraordinary Life of a Great American Statesman and Diplomat*. Washington, DC: Smithsonian, 2003.

Orlov, Yuri. *Dangerous Thoughts: Memoirs of a Russian Life*. New York: William Morrow, 1991.

Osiander, Andreas. *The States System of Europe, 1640–1990: Peacemaking and the Conditions of International Stability*. New York: Oxford UP, 1994.

Ost, David. *Solidarity and the Politics of Anti-Politics: Opposition and Reform in Poland since 1968*. Philadelphia: Temple UP, 1990.

Ostermann, Christian F. "New Evidence on the Sino-Soviet Border Dispute, 1969–71," *Cold War International History Project Bulletin* 6/7 (Winter 1995).

Ouimet, Matthew J. *The Rise and Fall of the Brezhnev Doctrine in Soviet Foreign Policy*. Chapel Hill, NC: UNC Press, 2003.

Patterson, James T. *Restless Giant: The United States from Watergate to Bush v. Gore*. New York: Oxford UP, 2005.

Perlmutter, David D. "Photojournalism and Foreign Affairs," *Orbis* 49:1 (Winter 2005): 109–122.

Peter, Matthias. *Die Bundesrepublik im KSZE-Prozess: Die Umkehrung der Diplomatie*. Berlin: De Gruyter Oldenbourg, 2015.

Peter, Matthias, and Hermann Wentker, eds. *Die KSZE im Ost-West Konflikt: Internationale Politik und gesellschaftliche Transformation 1975–1990*. Munich: Oldenbourg, 2012.

Peterson, Christian. *Globalizing Human Rights: Private Citizens, the Soviet Union, and the West*. New York: Routledge, 2012.

Peyrefitte, Alain. *C'était de Gaulle*, Vol. 2. Paris: Fayard, 1997.

Phillips, Andrew. *War, Religion and Empire: The Transformation of International Orders*. New York: Cambridge UP, 2011.

Picken, Margo, ed. *Andrei Sakharov and Human Rights*. Strasbourg: Council of Europe, 2010.

Pisar, Samuel. *Coexistence and Commerce: Guidelines for Transactions between East and West*. New York: McGraw-Hill 1970.

Polianskiĭ, Nikolaĭ. *MID: Dvenadtsat' let na sovetskoĭ diplomaticheskoĭ sluzhbe (1969–1981)*. London: Overseas Publications Interchange, 1987.

Pompidou, Alain, and Éric Roussel, eds. *Georges Pompidou: Lettres, notes et portraits, 1928–1974*. Paris: Robert Laffont, 2012.

Pompidou, Georges. *Entretiens et Discours, 1968–1974*, Vol. 2. Paris: Plon, 1975.

————. *Le Noeud gordien*. Paris: Plon, 1974.

Ponomaryov, B., A. Gromyko, and V. Khvostov, eds. *History of Soviet Foreign Policy*. Trans. David Skvirsky, Vol. 2. Moscow: Progress Publishers, 1973.

Pons, Silvio. *The Global Revolution: A History of International Communism, 1917–1991*. Trans. Allan Cameron. New York: Oxford UP, 2014.

Prazmowska, Anita. *Wladyslaw Gomulka: A Biography*. London: I. B. Tauris, 2016.

Puddington, Arch. *Broadcasting Freedom: The Cold War Triumph of Radio Free Europe and Radio Liberty*. Lexington: University Press of Kentucky, 2000.

Pyhälä, Mikko. "The Signing: Panic, and a Sigh of Relief." *OSCE Magazine*, October 2005.

Radchenko, Sergey. *Two Suns in the Heavens: The Sino-Soviet Struggle for Supremacy, 1962–1967*. Palo Alto, CA: Stanford UP, 2009.

Raina, Peter. *Political Opposition in Poland*. London: Poets and Painters Press, 1978.

Raleigh, Donald J. *Soviet Baby Boomers: An Oral History of Russia's Cold War Generation*. New York: Oxford UP, 2012.

———. "'Soviet' Man of Peace: Leonid Il'ich Brezhnev and His Diaries." *Kritika* 17:4 (Fall 2016): 837–868.

Reimaa, Markku. *Helsinki Catch: European Security Accords 1975*. Trans. Mark Waller. Helsinki: Edita, 2008.

Renk, Hansjörg. *Der Weg der Schweiz nach Helsinki: Der Beitrag der schweizerischen Diplomatie zum Zustandekommen der Konferenz über Sicherheit und Zusammenarbeit in Europa (KSZE), 1972–1975*. Bern: Paul Haupt, 1996.

Retegan, Mihai. *In the Shadow of the Prague Spring: Romanian Foreign Policy and the Crisis in Czechoslovakia, 1968*. Iasi: Center for Romanian Studies, 2000.

Rey, Marie-Pierre. "'Europe Is Our Common Home: A Study of Gorbachev's Diplomatic Concept." *Cold War History* 4:2 (2004): 33–65.

———. "L'URSS et la sécurité européenne, 1953–1956," *Communisme* 49–50 (1997): 121–135.

———. *La Tentation du rapprochement: France et l'URSS à l'heure de la détente*. Paris: Publications de la Sorbonne, 1991.

Reynolds, David. *Summits: Six Meetings That Shaped the Twentieth Century*. New York: Basic Books, 2007.

Rhodes, Richard. *Arsenals of Folly: The Making of the Nuclear Arms Race*. New York: Knopf, 2007.

Rials, Stéphane. *Idées politiques du président Georges Pompidou*. Paris: Presses universitaires de France, 1977.

Ribuffo, Leo P. "Is Poland a Soviet Satellite? Gerald Ford, the Sonnenfeldt Doctrine, and the Election of 1976," *Diplomatic History* 14:3 (Summer 1990): 385-403.

Rigby, T. H., and Ferenc Fehér, eds. *Political Legitimation in Communist States*. New York: St. Martin's Press, 1982.

Roberts, Geoffrey. *Molotov: Stalin's Cold Warrior*. Washington, DC: Potomac, 2012.

Rose, Clive. *Campaigns against Western Defence: NATO's Adversaries and Critics*, 2nd ed. Houndmills, Basingstoke: Macmillan, 1986.

Rosenberg, Emily S. *Spreading the American Dream: American Economic and Cultural Expansion, 1890–1945*. New York: Hill and Wang, 1982.

Rothberg, Abraham. *The Heirs of Stalin: Dissidence and the Soviet Regime, 1953–1970*. Ithaca, NY: Cornell UP, 1972.

Rothschild, Joseph, and Nancy M. Wingfield. *Return to Diversity: A Political History of East Central Europe since World War II*. New York: Oxford UP, 2008.

Roussel, Eric. *Georges Pompidou, 1911–1974*. Paris: Perrin, 2004.

Rubenstein, Joshua. *Soviet Dissidents: Their Struggle for Human Rights*. Boston: Beacon Press, 1980.

Ruud, Charles A. *The Constant Diplomat: Robert Ford in Moscow*. Montreal and Kingston: McGill-Queen's UP, 2009.

Sakharov, Andrei. *Memoirs.* Trans. Richard Lourie. London: Hutchison, 1990.

———. *Progress, Coexistence, and Intellectual Freedom.* New York: Norton, 1968.

Sargent, Daniel J. *A Superpower Transformed: The Remaking of American Foreign Relations in the 1970s.* New York: Oxford UP, 2015.

Sarotte, Mary Elise. *The Collapse: The Accidental Opening of the Berlin Wall.* New York: Basic, 2014.

———. *Dealing with the Devil: East Germany, Détente, and Ostpolitik, 1969–1973.* Chapel Hill, NC: UNC Press, 2001.

———. *1989: The Struggle to Create Post-Cold War Europe.* Princeton, NJ: Princeton UP, 2009.

Sauvignon, Edouard. *La Clause de la nation la plus favorisée.* Grenoble: Presses universitaires de Grenoble, 1972.

Savranskaya, Svetlana, and David Welch, eds. *SALT II and the Growth of Mistrust: Transcript of the Proceedings of the Musgrove Conference of the Carter-Brezhnev Project.* Washington, DC: National Security Archive, 1995.

Scammell, Michael. *Solzhenitsyn: A Biography.* New York: W. W. Norton, 1984.

Schmidt, Gustav, ed. *A History of NATO: The First Fifty Years.* Basingstoke: Palgrave, 2001.

Schwartz, Thomas Alan. *Lyndon Johnson and Europe: In the Shadow of Vietnam.* Cambridge, MA: Harvard UP, 2003.

Schwarz, Hans-Peter. *Adenauer. Der Staatsmann: 1952–1967.* Stuttgart: Deutsche Verlags-Anstalt, 1991.

Seabury, Paul. *The Rise and Decline of the Cold War.* New York: Basic Books, 1967.

Selvage, Douglas. "The Warsaw Pact and Nuclear Nonproliferation, 1963–1965," CWIHP Working Paper No. 32. Washington: Woodrow Wilson International Center for Scholars, 2001.

Servan-Schreiber, Jean-Jacques. *Le Défi américain.* Paris: Denoël, 1967.

Service, Robert. *The End of the Cold War 1985–1991.* New York: Public Affairs, 2015.

Sheehan, James J. "The Problem of Sovereignty in European History." *American Historical Review* 111:1 (February 2006): 1–15.

———. *Where Have All the Soldiers Gone? The Transformation of Modern Europe.* Boston: Houghton Mifflin, 2008.

Shevardnadze, Eduard. "No One Can Isolate Us, Save Ourselves. Self-Isolation Is the Ultimate Danger." Trans. Vitaly Chernetsky. *Slavic Review* 51:1 (Spring 1992): 117–121.

Shevchenko, Arkady N. *Breaking with Moscow.* New York: Knopf, 1985.

Shub, Anatole. *An Empire Loses Hope: The Return of Stalin's Ghost.* New York: W. W. Norton, 1970.

Shulman, Marshall D. *Beyond the Cold War.* New Haven: Yale UP, 1966.

Siotis, Jean. "The Secretariat of the United Nations Economic Commission for Europe and European Integration: The First Ten Years," *International Organization* 19:2 (Spring 1965): 177–202.

Skilling, H. Gordon. *Charter 77 and Human Rights in Czechoslovakia.* London: Allen and Unwin, 1981.

———. *Czechoslovakia's Interrupted Revolution.* Princeton, NJ: Princeton UP, 1976.

Smith, Hedrick. *The Russians.* New York: Quadrangle, 1976.

Smith, Mark B. "Social Rights in the Soviet Dictatorship: The Constitutional Right to Welfare from Stalin to Brezhnev." *Humanity* 3:3 (Winter 2012): 385–406.

Smith, Martin A. *NATO in the First Decade after the Cold War.* Dordrecht: Kluwer, 2000.

Snyder, Sarah B. *Human Rights Activism and the End of the Cold War: A Transnational History of the Helsinki Network*. New York: Cambridge UP, 2011.

———. "Through the Looking Glass: The Helsinki Final Act and the 1976 Election for President," *Diplomacy and Statecraft* 21:1 (March 2010): 87–106.

Sodaro, Michael. *Moscow, Germany and the West from Khrushchev to Gorbachev*. Ithaca, NY: Cornell UP, 1991.

Solzhenitsyn, Alexander. *One Day in the Life of Ivan Denisovich*. New York: Signet, 1998.

Sonnenfeldt, Helmut. "Linkage: A Strategy for Tempering Soviet Antagonism," *NATO Review*, no. 1 (February 1979).

Spasowski, Romuald. *The Liberation of One*. New York: Harcourt Brace Jovanovich, 1986.

Spencer, Robert, ed. *Canada and the Conference on Security and Cooperation in Europe*. Toronto: University of Toronto Centre for International Studies, 1984.

Spohr, Kristina, and David Reynolds, eds. *Transcending the Cold War: Summits, Statecraft, and the Dissolution of Bipolarity in Europe, 1970–1990*. New York: Oxford UP, 2016.

Spohr Readman, Kristina. "National Interests and the Power of 'Language': West German Diplomacy and the Conference on Security and Cooperation in Europe, 1972–1975," *Journal of Strategic Studies* 29:6 (December 2006): 1077–1120.

Steel, Ronald. *The End of Alliance: America and the Future of Europe*. New York: Viking, 1964.

———. *Pax Americana*. New York: Viking, 1967.

Steglich, Peter and Günter Leuschner. *KSZE—Fossil oder Hoffnung?* Berlin: Edition Ost, 1996.

Steiner, Zara. *The Lights That Failed: European International History, 1919–1933*. New York: Oxford UP, 2005.

Stent, Angela. *From Embargo to Ostpolitik: The Political Economy of West German–Soviet Relations, 1955–1980*. Cambridge: Cambridge UP, 1981.

Stone, Randall W. *Satellites and Commissars: Strategy and Conflict in the Politics of Soviet-Bloc Trade*. Princeton, NJ: Princeton UP, 1996.

Suri, Jeremi. *Henry Kissinger and the American Century*. Cambridge, MA: Harvard UP, 2007.

———. *Power and Protest: Global Revolution and the Rise of Détente*. Cambridge, MA: Harvard UP, 2003.

———. "The Promise and Failure of 'Developed Socialism': The Soviet 'Thaw' and the Crucible of the Prague Spring, 1964–1972," *Contemporary European History* 15:2 (2006): 133–158.

Swain, Geoffrey, and Nigel Swain, *Eastern Europe since 1945*. 4th ed. New York: Palgrave Macmillan, 2009.

Tal, David. "From the Open Skies Proposal of 1955 to the Norstad Plan of 1960: A Plan Too Far." *Journal of Cold War Studies* 10:4 (Fall 2008): 66–93.

Taubman, William. *Khrushchev: The Man and His Era*. New York: W. W. Norton, 2003.

Theiner, George, ed. *They Shoot Writers, Don't They?* London: Faber and Faber, 1984.

Theoharis, Athan G. *The Yalta Myths: An Issue in US Politics, 1945–1955*. Columbia, MO: University of Missouri Press, 1970.

Thomas, Daniel C. *The Helsinki Effect: International Norms, Human Rights, and the Demise of Communism*. Princeton, NJ: Princeton UP, 2001.

Tismaneanu, Vladimir. "Gheorghiu-Dej and the Romanian Workers' Party: From De-Sovietization to the Emergence of National Communism," CWIHP Working Paper No. 37. Washington, DC: Woodrow Wilson International Center for Scholars, 2002.

Tismaneanu, Vladimir, ed. *Promises of 1968: Crisis, Illusion, and Utopia*. Budapest: Central European University Press, 2010.

Tőkés, Rudolf L. *Opposition in Eastern Europe*. London: Macmillan, 1979.

Tompson, William. *The Soviet Union under Brezhnev*. London: Pearson, 2003.

Trachtenberg, *A Constructed Peace: The Making of the European Settlement, 1945–1963*. Princeton, NJ: Princeton UP, 1999.

Triffin, Robert. *Gold and the Dollar Crisis: The Future of Convertibility*. Rev. ed. New Haven, CT: Yale UP, 1961.

Tumarkin, Nina. *The Living and the Dead: The Rise and Fall of the Cult of World War II in Russia*. New York: Basic Books, 1994.

UNESCO. *Statistics on Radio and Television, 1950–1960*. Paris: UNESCO, 1963.

———. *Statistics on Radio and Television, 1960–1976*. Paris: UNESCO, 1979.

United States Information Agency. *The External Information and Cultural Relations Programs of the Union of Soviet Socialist Republics*. Washington, DC: USGPO, 1973.

Vaïsse, Maurice. *La Grandeur: politique étrangère du général de Gaulle, 1958–1969*. Paris: Fayard, 1998.

van Amerongen, Robert, ed. *Uren met Karel van het Reve: Liber Amicorum*. Amsterdam: Oorschot, 1991.

van den Heuvel, Cornelis C., and Rio D. Praaning, eds. *The Belgrade Conference: Progress or Regression*. Leiden: New Rhine, 1978.

Van Oudenaren, John. *Détente in Europe: The Soviet Union and the West since 1953*. Durham, NC: Duke UP, 1991.

Van Vunckt, Randall J., ed. *International Dictionary of Architects and Architecture*. Vol. 1. Detroit: St. James Press, 1993.

Vaněk, Miroslav, and Pavel Mücke. *Velvet Revolutions: An Oral History of Czech Society*. New York: Oxford UP, 2016.

Vernon, Raymond. *Sovereignty at Bay: The Multinational Spread of US Enterprises*. New York: Basic Books, 1971.

Vick, Brian. *The Congress of Vienna: Power and Politics after Napoleon*. Cambridge, MA: Harvard UP, 2014.

Vogel, Ezra F. *Deng Xiaoping and the Transformation of China*. Cambridge, MA: Harvard UP, 2011.

Volkogonov, Dmitri. *Autopsy for an Empire: The Seven Leaders Who Built the Soviet Regime*. Ed. and trans. Harold Shukman. New York: Simon and Schuster, 1999.

von Clausewitz, Carl. *On War*. Ed. and trans. Michael Howard and Peter Paret. Princeton, NJ: Princeton UP, 1976.

von Dannenberg, Julia. *The Foundations of Ostpolitik: The Making of the Moscow Treaty between West Germany and the USSR*. New York: Oxford UP, 2008.

von Plato, Alexander. *Die Vereinigung Deutschlands—ein weltpolitisches Machtspiel: Bush, Kohl, Gorbatschow und die internen Gesprächsprotokolle*, 3rd ed. Berlin: Ch. Links, 2009.

von Saal, Yulia. *KSZE-Prozess und Perestroika in der Sowjetunion: Demokratisierung, Werteumbruch und Auflösung 1985–1991*. Munich: Oldenbourg, 2014.

Walden, George. *Lucky George: Memoirs of an Anti-Politician*. London: Allen Lane, 1999.

Waltz, Kenneth N. "The Politics of Peace," *International Studies Quarterly* 11:3 (September 1967): 199–211.

Watson, Derek. *Molotov: A Biography*. Houndmills, Basingstoke: Palgrave Macmillan, 2005.

Weisbrode, Kenneth. *The Atlantic Century: Four Generations of Extraordinary Diplomats Who Forged America's Vital Alliance with Europe*. Cambridge, MA: Da Capo, 2009.

Wells, Jr., Samuel F., ed. *The Helsinki Process and the Future of Europe*. Washington, DC: Wilson Center Press, 1990.

Wenger, Andreas. "Crisis and Opportunity: NATO's Transformation and the Multilateralization of Détente, 1966–1968," *Journal of Cold War Studies* 6:1 (2004): 22–74.

———. *Living with Peril: Eisenhower, Kennedy, and Nuclear Weapons*. Lanham, MD: Rowman and Littlefield, 1997.

Wenger, Andreas, Christian Nuenlist, and Anna Locher, eds. *Transforming NATO in the Cold War: Challenges beyond Deterrence in the 1960s*. New York: Routledge, 2007.

Wenger, Andreas, Vojtech Mastny, and Christian Nuenlist, eds. *Origins of the European Security System: The Helsinki Process Revisited, 1965–75*. New York: Routledge, 2008.

Wentker, Hermann. *Außenpolitik in engen Grenzen: Die DDR im internationalen System 1949-1989*. Munich: Oldenbourg, 2007.

Westad, Odd Arne. *The Global Cold War: Third World Interventions and the Making of Our Times*. New York: Cambridge UP, 2005.

White, Theodore H. *The Making of the President 1968*. New York: Atheneum, 1969.

Wicker, Tom. *One of Us: Richard Nixon and the American Dream*. New York: Random House, 1995.

Wightman, David. "East-West Cooperation and the Economic Commission for Europe," *International Organization* 11:1 (Winter 1957): 1–12.

Wilczynski, J. *Socialist Economic Development and Reforms: From Extensive to Intensive Growth under Central Planning in the USSR, Eastern Europe and Yugoslavia*. London: Palgrave Macmillan, 1972.

Williams, Kieran. *The Prague Spring and Its Aftermath*. Cambridge: Cambridge UP, 1997.

Wills, Garry. *Nixon Agonistes: The Crisis of the Self-Made Man*. Boston: Houghton Mifflin, 2002.

Wohlforth, William Curti. *The Elusive Balance: Power and Perceptions during the Cold War*. Ithaca, NY: Cornell UP, 1993.

Yurchak, Alexei. *Everything Was Forever, Until It Was No More: The Last Soviet Generation*. Princeton, NJ: Princeton UP, 2005.

Zamoyski, Adam. *Rites of Peace: The Fall of Napoleon and the Congress of Vienna*. New York: HarperCollins, 2007.

Zeiler, Thomas W. *American Trade and Power in the 1960s*. New York: Columbia UP, 1992.

———. *Free Trade, Free World: The Advent of GATT*. Chapel Hill, NC: UNC Press, 1999.

Zelikow, Philip. "The New Concert of Europe." *Survival* 34:2 (Summer 1992).

Zelikow, Philip, and Condoleezza Rice. *Germany Unified and Europe Transformed: A Study in Statecraft*. Cambridge, MA: Harvard UP, 1995.

Zelizer, Julian E. "Détente and Domestic Politics," *Diplomatic History* 33:4 (September 2009): 653–670.

Zhuk, Sergei I. *Rock and Roll in the Rocket City: The West, Identity, and Ideology in Soviet Dnepropetrovsk, 1960–1985*. Washington, DC: Woodrow Wilson Center Press, 2010.

Zimmerman, William. *Soviet Perspectives on International Relations, 1956–1967*. Princeton, NJ: Princeton UP, 1969.

Zubok, Vladislav. *A Failed Empire: The Soviet Union in the Cold War from Stalin to Gorbachev*. Chapel Hill, NC: UNC Press, 2007.

———. "The Soviet Union and Détente of the 1970s," *Cold War History* 8:4 (November 2008): 427–447.

———. *Zhivago's Children: The Last Soviet Intelligentsia*. Cambridge, MA: Harvard UP, 2009.

Zubok, Vladislav, and Constantine Pleshakov. *Inside the Kremlin's Cold War: From Stalin to Khrushchev.* Cambridge, MA: Harvard UP, 1996.

Zwass, Adam. *The Council for Mutual Economic Assistance: The Thorny Path from Political to Economic Integration.* Armonk, NY: ME Sharpe, 1989.

Doctoral Dissertations

Desjardins, Marie-France. "Origins, Negotiations, and Implementation of the Confidence-Building Measures of the Conference on Security and Co-operation in Europe." PhD Dissertation, King's College London, 2001.

Yamamoto, Takeshi. "The Road to the Conference on Security and Cooperation in Europe, 1969–1973: Britain, France and West Germany." PhD Dissertation, London School of Economics, 2007.

INDEX